SYMLOG

SYMLOG

A System for the Multiple Level Observation of Groups

Robert F. Bales and Stephen P. Cohen
with the assistance of Stephen A. Williamson

THE FREE PRESS
A Division of Macmillan Publishing Co., Inc.
NEW YORK

Collier Macmillan Publishers
LONDON

Copyright © 1979 by The Free Press
                    A Division of Macmillan Publishing Co., Inc.

The Free Press
A Division of Macmillan Publishing Co., Inc.
866 Third Avenue, New York, N. Y. 10022

Collier Macmillan Canada, Ltd.

Library of Congress Catalog Card Number: 79-7480

Printed in the United States of America

printing number

1   2   3   4   5   6   7   8   9   10

Library of Congress Cataloging in Publication Data

Bales, Robert Freed
    SYMLOG: a system for the multiple level observation of
groups.

    Bibliography: p.
    Includes indexes.
    1. SYMLOG System. 2. Small groups. I. Cohen,
Stephen P.   joint author. II. Williamson.
Stephen A., joint author. III. Title.
HM133.B343   1979   301.18'5   79-7480
ISBN 0-02-901300-3

Contents

List of Figures

List of Tables

Preface

This book is the work of many people, as in fact most books are. But in the case of SYMLOG, a complex system for the study of groups, the necessary pieces of the system are so diverse that it is doubtful whether any single person could have produced it all—the theory, the measuring instruments, the mathematical parts, the computer programs, the graphic displays, the methodological studies of validity and reliability, to say nothing of the testing of the method in several different kinds of live groups to provide feedback to leaders and members for their use in personal and group self-study.

The SYMLOG System is the cumulative result of the study of many academic self-analytic groups in the Social Interaction Laboratory of the Department of Psychology and Social Relations at Harvard University and, before that, in the Department and Laboratory of Social Relations. The senior author has been engaged in teaching the course in group psychology for which the SYMLOG System was designed since 1954. Most of the people who have helped to produce SYMLOG have been connected with that course in one way or another.

Stephen P. Cohen, the co-author, taught in the Group Psychology course for a number of years, as did the assisting author, Stephen A. Williamson. The three of us, Bales, Cohen, and Williamson, have worked on SYMLOG both from behind and in front of the one-way mirror. Many of the theoretical insights and developmental changes in the system have had their inception in the analysis of our observations made from behind the one-way mirror, or in discussing feedback with the group after the group sessions. Teaching fellows in the course, who have shared these experiences with us at various times, include Joanne Martin, Phyllis Burrows, Jeff Howard, and Richard Polley. Edward L. Pattullo, Associate Chairman of the Department of Psychology and Social Relations, has helped in the support of the Social Interaction Laboratory and the Group Psychology course in many ways and has also taken his turns in front of and behind the one-way mirror. Daniel Perschonok, a lecturer in the Department, has taught the summer school session of the course for many years and has contributed many insights. Students in the course have often become involved and have continued to help with the research operations in subsequent terms. Three in particular come to mind: Susan Fiske, who was our first really expert scorer; Virginia Bales; and Eliot Freeman, who first struggled with the problems of putting the data into the computer. More recently, Susan Borkum took up this task and presided over the computer input during the term when we first achieved regular and effective computer analysis of observations for feedback to the group.

The SYMLOG project as such really started with the vision of rapid computer-produced feedback to the group. When the first remote input console arrived on the thirteenth floor of William James Hall, next door to the Social Interaction Laboratory, Philip Stone, who had earlier designed a computerized content analysis system for use in the Group Psychology course (see Stone et al., 1966, and Dunphy, 1968) offered to help the authors "get on the air" with an observational system for real-time feedback. Phil Stone wrote the first programs for input of observational data to the computer. In keeping with our vision of real-time feedback, we installed the remote console directly in the observation room, complete with an operator. Thinking we might actually be able to process the observations of the first part of a session and receive feedback in the observation room in time to help us monitor the latter part of the same session (an ambition still not achieved), we worked up a simple format and had observers write their observations on three-by-five cards. The cards were collected every five minutes and given to the operator of the computer console, who worked away busily to input the data. Those cards gradually developed into the present SYMLOG Interaction Scoring Form.

The first try fell far short of our hopes, but it started us on the way. The input process turned out to be more time-consuming and error-prone than we had anticipated. It was in fact the end of the first term (or was it the second?) before we had usable feedback. We marveled at the volume of the computer print-outs, but they fell short of giving us marvelous insights, and it took so long to get them that they were not helpful in the guidance of the group. We entered a period of slow progress.

Prior to the beginning of the SYMLOG project, the senior author had completed *Personality and Interpersonal Behavior* (Bales, 1970), which brought an interaction scoring method for observers (Bales, 1950), and a rating method for the use of group members into the same frame of reference—the three-dimensional factor analytic space which is central to the SYMLOG System. At the time the computer console arrived in our observation room, Bales was busy writing a book for the use of the participant-observer in making studies of natural groups in the field. The theoretical backbone of the projected book was a debriefing questionnaire for the investigator to fill out after he had gone home, and the questions were generated by the insight that the three-dimensional space seemed appropriate not only to the description of the behavior of participants but also to the description of their "definition of the situation" in content terms—the situation or task with which the group was immediately dealing, and also their views of the larger society and various images that were the focal points of their attitudes and values. The participant-observer's debriefing questionnaire, formulated in terms of a series of "levels" very similar to those of the present SYMLOG System, was reformulated to meet the needs of a real-time observational system and became the present SYMLOG Directional Definitions (see Appendix A).

The observation manual for SYMLOG Interaction Scoring was written, passed back and forth between Bales and Cohen, and rewritten and revised six or seven times. The Directional Definitions were also revised each time. Changes were made in response to experience in teaching the method, in which all three authors were engaged, and in response to theoretical considerations, convenience, and also what seemed to be a natural order of syntax in the formation of the "message." We soon realized that the SYMLOG "message"—a single observation—is in fact a simple sentence in a simple language. Meanwhile we kept trying to explain to our colleagues and to each other what we were doing, and found it quite hard. It seemed to be a strange set of ideas, at first, that both behavior and content can be described in terms of the same three-dimensional space, that one needs to deal with multiple levels of behavior and content, and that one needs to describe the view of each participant separately as well as the views of each observer. Somewhere along the way, in response to the need to refer to the whole set of ideas and procedures simply, Steve Cohen came up with the acronym "SYMLOG"—to stand for *SY*stematic *M*ultiple *L*evel *O*bservation of *G*roups. Once we got it all in one word, the name stuck. Originally the term SYMLOG referred to the observation method alone, but then, by extension, it came to refer to the whole SYMLOG System.

Meanwhile, thanks to a grant from the Milton Fund, we were able to keep storing our observations on computer and preparing for the later analysis. Steve Cohen took the leadership in this, assisted by Steve Williamson, who was ultimately able to untangle several years of observations, in spite of numerous changes in format, and wrote a thesis on developmental patterns in the groups we had observed (Williamson, 1977). Many of our impressions of normal frequencies of variables and how these frequencies change over time or in response to special conditions came from his many tabulations and analyses of these observations. Some of the findings are given briefly in Part IV of this book, but the main presentation will come in later publication.

The Field Diagram, showing the location of group members in one particular two-dimensional plane of the three-dimensional space, preceded the main development of what is called "multiple level field theory" in this book. In working to find a way to study whether there is any uniformity in the way in which individuals in a given part of the space react to individuals in each other part of the space, Bales constructed the Field Diagrams for each individual member, based on member ratings. In the studying of these diagrams in relation to each other and in relation to actual events in another group being currently observed, the ideas of the dynamic structure of the field represented in the "Polarization-Unification Overlay" (see Appendixes P, Q, R) suddenly came together and took shape. The concepts were consistent with earlier findings of Cohen (see Cohen, 1972) regarding the relationships of individuals to each other according to location in the space, which had brought into question a still earlier hypothesis concerning coalitions in the space (see Bales, 1970). The new concepts centering on the ideas of polarization and unification of images in the field were developed by Bales in the writing of a "Manual for the Case Study of Groups" for use by members of the Group Psychology course, to help them apply what they learned in the self-analytic group to a case study of a natural group outside of the laboratory. The rating forms then in use were further simplified to make the application of the method more practical for the case study. The results of these theoretical efforts and of the case studies that students and others made using the case study manual are represented in Part I of the present book, which is a revision of the case study manual.

Bonny K. Parke, a postdoctoral fellow associated with the project, has adapted the adjective rating form to children's vocabulary and styles of behavior and has made a long series of case studies of classroom groups and of the families of selected children from the classroom. She has made factor analytic studies of the ratings, revised the set of adjectives repeatedly, and has helped teachers to interpret relationships of children in the classroom using teacher ratings. These studies have helped greatly in strengthening the intuitive validity and practical utility of the rating methods, and the multiple level field theory centering on the Field Diagram (see Parke, 1977).

Martha Stark, a psychiatrist at the Harvard University Health Services, has made a case study that indicates the usefulness of the methods in helping a therapist to conceptualize problems of the individual patients in group therapy. In addition to making her own ratings of the behavior of members in each group session, about a third of the way through the series of sessions she asked members (as an outside procedure ancillary to the therapy) to rate themselves and members of their family, as well as the two or three persons with whom they were currently associated in any emotional way. She held separate interviews with patients outside the regular sessions to discuss the diagrams made from their individual ratings. The conferences seemed to have beneficial effects, not only in raising questions and promoting insight of individual members about the developmental sources of their problems in relation to family members but also in deepening the content of the group therapy sessions.

From the work of both Bonny Parke with teachers and Martha Stark with group therapy patients, it appears to be quite easy to explain the meaning of the dimensions represented on the Field Diagram to people who have no background or interest in the theory or methods as such and to elicit further insights about relationships in the group by discussion of the constellation of images on the Field Diagram.

Shortly after the adaptation of previous rating forms into the adjective list for use in case studies, Stephen Cohen joined forces with Myron Wish, Head of the Interpersonal Communication Research Department at the Bell Laboratories, to make a careful study of the adjective rating items and their relationship to SYMLOG Interaction Scores. Myron Wish and his colleagues, including Peter Bricker, were engaged in studies of interpersonal relationships through the use of observer ratings (see Wish, 1975; Wish, Deutsch, and Kaplan, 1976). Since Stephen Cohen was able to obtain the help of students who had been trained to do SYMLOG Interaction Scoring in the Group Psychology course, it was possible to compare the Rating method with the Interaction Scoring method, as well as to compare Wish's rating adjectives with ours, and with Osgood's (see Osgood, Suci, and Tannenbaum, 1957), whose factor space seemed to be similar to ours and to that of Wish. The results of this study are given in Part III of this book and are embodied in the most recent revision of the simplified Adjective Rating Form (see Appendixes C and D). The study was financed by the Bell Laboratories, to whom we are grateful. Special thanks are also due to Chen Sun for his help in managing details of the study.

Just in the nick of time, it seemed, Howard Swann, a mathematician interested in social interaction, arrived at the Social Interaction Laboratory for a year's sabbatical. During his year's visit he made critical contributions in the development of the mathematical rationale for the transformation of SYMLOG Interaction Scores for plotting on the Field Diagram, where they may be compared directly with the retrospective Ratings of group members. He found a congenial reception from Scott Bradner, the manager of the Computer-Based Laboratory of the Department of Psychology and Social Relations. We are greatly indebted to Scott Bradner for his help and to the Department for many hours of computer time. In the course of the year, Howard Swann developed the mathematical formulations and the computer programs for the major kinds of analysis and preparation of feedback that we had wished for at the beginning of the SYMLOG project. Along the way he involved Richard Polley, at that time a teaching fellow in the Group Psychology course, in the process of the programming. Since then Richard Polley has developed additional programs and has trained the rotating observer teams to prepare and present the feedback with great effectiveness. We are most grateful to Howard Swann and Richard Polley as contributors to the present book (see Appendixes S, T, and U).

Gary Alan Fine deserves the credit for the first use of the method in a regular well-designed experimental study (see Fine, 1976). He tested the hypothesis that the introduction of a new person into a group, with a very salient and well-defined location in the space, would set up a pattern of polarization–unification in the group which would result in the movement of the images group members have of each other in a direction predictable from the pattern of polarization–unification. It is worth noting that significant results were obtained with the use of only two moderately well-trained SYMLOG Interaction Scorers, although we know from Stephen Cohen's study that it is preferable to have a team of about five. Although the SYMLOG System has not yet been used extensively in experimental studies, it appears to be as well adapted to experimental work as to work in the classroom and to the study of groups in the field.

During the course of the project we have benefited greatly from intellectual interchange with several postdoctoral fellows and visiting scholars, who have spent a term or more with us observing and discussing the groups and methods. These include Robert Rossel, Robert Koenigs, William F. Hill, Johann Schneider, and Manson Solomon. We are grateful to these colleagues for their insights and for the stimulation they have provided.

Parts of the book have gone through many revisions and duplications for classroom use, as well as for the final manuscript. We are most grateful to Hilary Bencini-Tibó for the final and major part of this work and, for work in the earlier stages, to Susan Smith and Pamela Pattison.

Part I

Systematic Multiple Level Field Theory

Robert F. Bales

Chapter 1

A Practical Approach to the Study of Groups

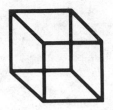

The term SYMLOG, taken as the title of this book, is an acronym for something hard to describe: "A *SY*stem for the *M*ultiple *L*evel *O*bservation of *G*roups." It is not easy to describe SYMLOG simply, because it is in fact something new in the world. It is easier to describe what it is for. It is a set of methods for the study of groups—groups of many kinds, but basically small natural groups, such as families, teams, or classroom groups, where the personalities of the specific persons involved and their relationships with each other are the focus of interest.

SYMLOG is a "system" for the study of groups in the sense that it consists of a number of different parts, integrated to serve the purpose of making a particular group easier to understand and work with. Although it is a large and complex system in its entirety, it has the great virtue of being very flexible in its application and can be made very simple. One may use only a small part of it for a given study and still have the advantages of being able to relate the findings to a working body of theory and methods that have been used in other similar studies.

The SYMLOG System is designed so that in its most compact reduction it can be applied by a single person in the study of a single group in any setting, without the use of any special apparatus. This may be done through the use of what is called the SYMLOG Adjective Rating Form (see Appendix C), which may be used to help recall and describe, retrospectively, the characteristic behavior of any group of individuals one has seen in interaction with each other. The ratings may easily be tabulated and analyzed without the benefit of any complicated mathematics or statistics—and without any computer programs. This means that a practicing group therapist, a classroom teacher, an administrator, or in fact any interested group member, a parent or other member of a family for example, can use the basic methods and theory of the SYMLOG System.

The general theory and methods of SYMLOG provide a way to do something useful and to gain in understanding of a particular group, even though the opportunities of making technical observations in the group are very limited. A teacher, a psychologist leading a therapy group, or a sociologist studying some natural group may not be able, or may not wish, to introduce sound recording,

3

questionnaires, special interviews, or the like. The SYMLOG Rating method provides a systematic way of recapturing from one's own memory a sufficiently good picture of individuals and their relationships in the group to raise many important questions and perhaps to provoke new insights. The *Rating* method, along with some of the main features of the basic theory, is described in detail in Part I of this book. We shall use it to make a demonstration of the case study of a single group.

The Rating methods (and there are actually several of these) constitute one set of parts of the SYMLOG System, concerned with the initial gathering of information about the group. Another set of parts concerned with the initial gathering of information about the group is an act-by-act observational method called SYMLOG *Interaction Scoring.* "Scoring" is distinguished from "Rating" in that it is a method for making detailed observations and descriptions of acts one by one, in the course of the actual interaction, at the time each act occurs. Ratings may be used for retrospective descriptions; Scoring requires that one be able to write down observations currently while watching and listening to the interaction of group members. It is thus to some degree obtrusive, whereas retrospective ratings made by a participant-observer may be completely unobtrusive and hence are practical across a broader range of groups and situations. SYMLOG Interaction Scoring usually requires a special arrangement with the group members, either to make observations currently or to make a sound or video recording, which may then be used later for the actual scoring. The SYMLOG Interaction Scoring method is described in detail in Part II of this book. The Scoring Form is shown in Appendix F.

Although SYMLOG Interaction Scoring requires some training to do and takes longer than the Rating method, it has the advantage of richness of detail and particularly tends to give insight into the way in which different kinds of topics the persons in the group talk about affect relationships in the group. SYMLOG Scoring captures information not only about the behavior of individuals but also about the *content* of what they say and the *attitudes* they express. This is the meaning of the term *"Multiple Level Observation"* as included in the acronym "SYMLOG." Learning how to do SYMLOG Interaction Scoring is a way of improving one's ability to observe and is also the basis of a detailed kind of feedback to group members that may be more helpful to them in pinpointing specific aspects of their behavior, content, preoccupations, and attitudes than the more global SYMLOG Adjective Ratings.

The two approaches to gathering information about personalities and relationships in groups, Rating and Scoring, are discussed in detail in Part III of this book by Stephen P. Cohen. The two procedures give overlapping and related, but not identical, information and ideally are used to supplement each other. Part III of the book presents a careful and substantial study of the reliability of the two methods, based on videotaped extracts of the interaction of a family. The observations are also used to demonstrate some of the kinds of clinically oriented information that may be obtained about the specific family.

SYMLOG Interaction Scoring of a video tape, as contrasted with retrospective Rating, probably tends to reduce to some extent the effects of the researcher's particular biases and selective memory, particularly if there is much lapse of time between the actual observation and the retrospective rating. Video and sound recordings have the disadvantage, however, of requiring considerable time to analyze. The number of sessions recorded may be so great that it is impractical to analyze all of them, and a representative selection must be made. In some cases it may be more practical to review the sound or video recordings, or other notes, and then apply the Rating procedure, which depends upon memory. The Rating procedure may also have the advantage of greater representativeness if one happens to have had long and varied experience of the interaction of group members, as compared to a small and perhaps unrepresentative sample of the interaction in the form of one or a few sound or video recordings.

In some cases the group members can be asked, and are willing or even eager, to make SYMLOG Adjective Ratings of each other. This method has great advantages. It supplies a large amount of information that would otherwise be inaccessible even by extended observation. The picture of the group provided by each person can be compared directly with the picture provided by each other person and with the picture provided by the researcher's own ratings. This is demonstrated in Part I of this book by the case study of an "academic self-analytic group"—a group organized for the purpose of learning methods of observation and theory about groups in an academic setting. The SYMLOG System was developed in an undergraduate college course called "Group Psychology"—a setting that is optimum for the simultaneous learning of participants and the development of theory and methods by researchers.

In the academic self-analytic group all methods may be employed: Ratings by group members of each other, Ratings of group members by Research Observers, SYMLOG Interaction Scoring of act-by-act behavior, as well as extensive discussion of all these results in the group itself. Part IV of this book is devoted to a discussion of the use of the SYMLOG System for training in observation and feedback to group members in an academic self-analytic group.

At the end of a period of such self-analytic work it is also advantageous to employ a retrospective questionnaire asking about the Significant Relationships that have developed in the course of their interaction (see Appendix V by Stephen P. Cohen). These free-form retrospective analyses are a valuable supplement to the more systematic instruments in helping the researcher to understand how each individual group member feels and what the ratings mean. The use of this questionnaire is demonstrated in Chapter 12 of Part I of this book.

If it is not practical or desirable in the particular group to obtain ratings from all group members, the ratings of some of them may still be helpful. If no ratings from group members are available, the researcher may still elicit some surprising insights by making a rating as he or she *imagines* it would be made from the point of view of *each other member* of the group. Experience with this procedure suggests that one can remember a good deal more using this imaginary "role taking" procedure than by making ratings from one's "own point of view" only. Attributing certain perceptions in imagination to various *other* members of the group (even though it is all in one's own imagination) seems to enable one to separate the perceptions from one's own imagined self to some extent, and permits one to remember and recognize things that may otherwise be suppressed. This procedure is a practical application of the insights of the very early social psychologists Charles Horton Cooley (1926) and George Herbert Mead (1934), among others, as to the significance of the ability to "take the role of the other" in the development of the personality of the individual, as well as in the evolution of human mentality and society in a more general sense. Cooley's article is entitled, appropriately for the present context, "The Roots of Social Knowledge." Students in the course in Group Psychology have made it clear that the role taking method can be a significant help to greater understanding of a group in case studies they have made of their families using this method. A case study of the self in the family by a student using the Rating method is included in Part I of this book, pp. 142–149. A study of this kind is perhaps the most accessible and the most likely to be rewarding of all the introductory case studies one might make and is ideal as an exercise in a group psychology course.

Perhaps more often than not people are somewhat reluctant to study themselves or to be studied. Even when they are motivated, as in self-analytic groups and in therapy groups, there is a good deal of ambivalence and legitimate resistance. All methods of study affect the behavior of individuals and change the relationships of the persons engaged in the study to some extent. They may not want this to happen. Thus, there are ethical questions to be considered.

It is hoped that users of the present methods will realize that they will have to undertake ethical responsibilities to some degree, no matter which particular methods they may apply, and that they may not see very well in advance what problems may appear. Students in courses should ask for advice or supervision as they sense they need it. Students on their own who are not yet professionally mature should try to find competent professional guidance.

Everything that one may do in the study of a group may have some potential effects on group members. Talking with them, asking questions, writing down notes, making sound recordings, making video tapes, all affect to some extent the behavior and attitudes one may want to study. Bringing out information about behavior, attitudes, or perceptions through attempts to measure them often tends to change them. Of course, this may be what is desired, but not necessarily.

When a person's perception is changed by the process of measurement, the behavior tendency perceived may be increased or exaggerated, or may be suppressed. Or also, the person may resolve to change and may begin to do so. In various ways, then, whoever is making the study may become responsible, in part, for behavior, its continuation, or its change. It is especially perplexing if one is in a position of trying to test a particular hypothesis and it turns out that, in order to make the test, it seems to be necessary to elicit or amplify objectionable behavior or to stand by and fail to help.

At least some of the potential ethical problems in the development of basic theory in social psychology are reduced by taking a case study approach rather than an experimental approach. The acceptance of responsibility to try to help also reduces ethical problems. This approach has the great advantage of realism in the acceptance of one's own involvement in any behavior one tries to study. It avoids excessive separation of "theory" and "practice." Knowledge gained through the case study of natural groups, in which the researcher takes his or her own behavior into account as among the causes to be studied, is already knowledge at the applied level. And it is by no means certain that this approach to developing basic theory is slower or less effective than an experimental approach.

Although the perspective of this book is one of practical application, the development of basic theory is of equal importance to the authors; it is their hope, justified by experience so far, that case studies will serve theoretical as well as practical aims. The theory of the SYMLOG System is another set of parts, integrated with the methods of measurement—both the rating methods and the scoring methods. It is a theory of the basic dynamics of groups of interacting persons that is uniquely broad and integrative. Its main outlines will be given in Part I of this book and further articulated in Part II. It may be called "Systematic Multiple Level Field Theory." It will be characterized in broad outlines in the next chapter and then articulated in a series of chapters following that, each based on a "heuristic hypothesis" and illustrated with the case study that forms the narrative backbone of Part I.

The theory is implemented by numerical and statistical methods of analysis, and the results are summarized in graphic diagram form for further intuitive use in analysis, illustration, and feedback to group members. The numerical and graphic methods are described in detail in Part V of the book, which is a set of technical appendixes. The casual user of the book may not need to go far in the technical direction, but the details are all included for the use of teachers, researchers, and theorists who may want to put the full system in operation. The rating and scoring methods are not only designed for theoretical clarity and usefulness in teaching but also designed to produce recorded information that can be used in computer analysis of the data without intermediate coding. The computer programs that are available and a part of the system, though not necessary to many of its uses, are described in Appendixes S, T, and U by Howard Swann and Richard Polley.

The SYMLOG System, then, is a "system" in the sense that it consists of a number of different methods of measurement, integrated with a broad and consistent social psychological theory on the one hand and with practical procedures on the other, for the processing and analyzing of data, including computer programs. It is adapted for use in natural groups as well as for use in laboratory training and experimental groups. It is especially appropriate for group self-studies. Its use in academic self-analytic groups has been mentioned. However, it is also appropriate for nonacademic group self-studies, in which the members want to initiate a discussion of their relationships and modes of operation with a view toward improvement.

If a group so desires, a self-study may be started by a simple procedure in which the members describe each other's behavior using the simplified SYMLOG Adjective Rating Form (see Appendix C). The leader or consulting researcher may then add up the ratings and prepare a set of diagrams that may be used for discussion by the group members. Although both the initial rating procedure and the resulting diagrams are simple and easy to understand, they summarize a large amount of important information. Discussion of the information in itself may initiate appropriate trends toward improvement in the group or may provide insight into specific steps that might be taken by the group leader or others to stimulate improvement. The procedure may be repeated at intervals as a means of guiding development of the group according to group goals.

A SYMLOG group self-study is a democratic procedure carried on mainly through the participation and insight of group members. In some groups a self-study of this kind may fit very naturally with the existing goals of the group, for example, in therapy groups of various kinds, in family therapy, in academic self-analytic groups, and in various kinds of reeducative and training groups. Individuals in groups of these kinds are usually prepared to discuss interpersonal relationships within the group, and they may welcome a SYMLOG group self-study as directly in line with their goals.

The situation may be different in other kinds of groups. Members of a residential organization, for example, or a group of roommates or of friends, a family, or a team of some kind, in which members spend a good deal of time with each other, may want to make a group self-study because their interpersonal relations are very important to them. However, they may also have reservations for fear that some delicate relationships will be made worse, or some individuals may be put in a difficult position. A SYMLOG group self-study probably should not be undertaken if some members of the group have serious reservations about it. In such a case a study may be undertaken by the leader or another interested member, based on his or her own observations and ratings alone. The insights so obtained may be used simply to improve that member's own participation or leadership in the group. Another alternative is for the members to agree to make the ratings but to specify in advance some limitations on the amount and kind of information to be presented to them in a "feedback" session.

A group case study made by a single interested individual may be preferred in impersonally oriented groups, where a group self-study does not fit into the definition most members have of the group goals, though their interpersonal relationships may, in fact, have an important bearing on the realization of the purposes of the group. Many work groups would probably fall into this category, as well as many committees, boards of trustees, administrative groups, and other formally organized, task-oriented groups. Some groups are organized or even legally constituted to represent conflicting constituencies. In these cases effective leadership may require considerable skill in containment or resolution of conflict. A group self-study may not fit well with the degree of formality, competition, or conflict in such a group. Nevertheless, a case study of the group by a leader or any participant, or by a nonparticipant observer of the group, may be feasible and potentially helpful to the group.

It is quite feasible for a classroom teacher to make a case study of the classroom group as an aid to better teaching. A study may be especially helpful where some of the students have problems in adjusting to others, including problems of status, or ethnic or religious differences. Some teachers will be able to employ the method with no more help than this manual. Teachers or other leaders who wish to make a case study may be able to find help through a social or clinical psychologist who can guide them through the study and help them work out the implications.

In the SYMLOG System, all behavior and content in the interaction of a group is described (whether by Rating or by Scoring) by reference to a concept of a three-dimensional space (see p. 23). The three dimensions describe the quality of behavior of members or the images suggested in the content of what they say. The dimensions, described in terms of behavior adjectives are: (1) Dominant vs. Submissive, (2) Friendly vs. Unfriendly, and (3) Instrumentally Controlled vs. Emotionally Expressive. Appendix A gives extended definitions of these dimensions. The three dimensions constitute a descriptive system in a theoretical sense, hence the relevance of the term "Systematic" in the name for the body of theory "Systematic Multiple Level Field Theory."

The "M" and the "L" in the acronym "SYMLOG" stand for the terms *Multiple Level*. In SYMLOG Interaction Scoring each act is regarded as having several levels or aspects of meaning. Each aspect of the meaning, or each level, is coded separately. The system distinguishes between *nonverbal* aspects of behavior, and the more overt *intended acts* directed to other persons. These are referred to as different "levels." Both levels refer to the "behavior" of the individual in the sense that they describe what the individual *does* as contrasted with the content of what he *says*.

What the person says may be called the "content" of his communication. SYMLOG Interaction Scoring recognizes and keeps separate several different *classes of content*. They are, briefly: (1) references to (or descriptions of) the *self*, (2) references to the *other* (a specific other group member), (3) references to the group as a whole, (4) references to the immediate external *situation* in which the group interaction takes place, (5) references to general features of the environing *society*, and (6) references to any kind of thing, real or imaginary, which the observer judges to be informative about the imagination and feeling of the person speaking, a class of content called *fantasy* images. The way in which these kinds of content are coded into the three dimensions may be seen in Appendix A. These classes of content are also referred to loosely as "levels."

Finally, SYMLOG Interaction Scoring recognizes the expression of *attitudes* or *value judgments* in favor of, or against, any kind of *image* mentioned in one of the above classes of content. Value judgments are said to be *pro*, or *con*. The expression of these value judgments is regarded as still another "level." Appendix A again offers illustrations of these descriptive categories.

Each act of communicating is thus regarded as having "multiple levels" of meaning, and the three-dimensional system allows one to sort out the meaning on each of the levels separately. The term "level" is used loosely. For summary purposes it is convenient to collapse several "levels" into a more general "level." In this more general sense, one can say that SYMLOG Interaction Scoring recognizes three general levels of interaction, each made up of sublevels: (1) a *Behavioral* level, including both nonverbal behavior and intended acts, (2) a level of *Content Images*, including images of self, other, group, situation, society, and fantasy, and (3) a level of *Value Judgment* about the content image, including pro and con directions. These distinctions are illustrated at length in Appendix A.

The SYMLOG Interaction Scoring procedure is based directly upon the descriptions given in Appendix A. The SYMLOG Adjective Rating procedure works with an abbreviated set of adjectives, which approximate a description of the Behavioral level. The levels are not clearly distinguished in the Rating procedure, which makes the Rating procedure much simpler than the Scoring, though inherently more ambiguous. In practical use, however, the Ratings seem to tap very well in most cases the intuitive global perceptions that group members have of each other.

The SYMLOG Adjective Rating System, then, provides a simplified way for a participant-observer to make a study of a group in a completely unobtrusive way or to help the members of the group to make a self-study from their own ratings, if they wish to do so. The SYMLOG Interaction Scoring System provides a way for more highly trained observers to make fine-grained qualitative studies of the behavior, content images, and value judgments of group members in live interaction. Both the Rating and Scoring methods can be used in a laboratory setting for experimental studies and to provide multiple perspectives on the group interaction which may be useful to group members for education, therapy, or training. The SYMLOG Rating and Interaction Scoring methods taken together constitute a uniquely comprehensive and highly integrated system for the study of the behavior of individuals in groups. The system is practical, but it is also strongly theoretical in its origins and implications. In the next chapter we shall set it briefly against its theoretical background.

Chapter 2

Theoretical Background

The present book is confined mostly to an exposition of the SYMLOG System and its practical use. Unfortunately, most of the analysis of its theoretical connections with other points of view, as well as much of its empirical grounding, must be left to future publications. It is essential to future publications that the connected and detailed descriptions contained in the present book be available for reference, and the size and complexity of the system simply do not leave room in a single book for much else.

Although the connections cannot be analyzed in detail, some of the more closely related theories can at least be mentioned. The system is an immediate outgrowth of the senior author's earlier work, *Personality and Interpersonal Behavior* (Bales, 1970), which in turn is a continuation of the effort begun in the observation method titled *Interaction Process Analysis* (Bales, 1950). Those works and the present one contain elements from a considerable number of theories in psychology, sociology, and related fields.

The assumptions made in the present work about motivation, the general nature of personality, the powers of the ego, and the importance of the various mechanisms of ego defense, as well as many of the concepts of the nature of interpretation and its place in therapy come from psychoanalytic theory (S. Freud, 1900, 1933; A. Freud, 1936).

The concepts of the nature of the individual perceptual evaluative field have their source partly in gestalt psychology, as represented in both Lewinian field theory and the group dynamics school (Lewin, 1951; Cartwright and Zander, 1968). The theory of polarization and unification is closely related to various theories of social cognition: balance theory (Newcomb, 1953; Heider, 1958), congruity theory (Osgood and Tannenbaum, 1955), dissonance theory (Festinger, 1957), consistency theory (Abelson et al., 1968), and attribution theory (Kelley, 1971), although the relationships to these various cognitively oriented theories are complex and far from adequately worked out.

On the more sociological side the present theory has much in common with symbolic interaction theory (Mead, 1934; Blumer, 1969; Goffman, 1959) in the emphasis given to the importance of the self-image and the individual definition of the situation, and in the stress on the communication of "meaning" in the manner and content of social interaction, rather than on the physical substrate of behavior.

Small group interaction theory as it has grown out of the laboratory tradition has been important in providing many of the concepts of role differentiation, leadership, and small group structure in other respects, as well as groundwork in the actual observation and classification of social interaction (Hare, Borgatta, and Bales, 1965; Hare, 1976; Shaw, 1971).

Social exchange theory (Thibaut and Kelley, 1959; Homans, 1961; Blau, 1964, 1968) is represented at the small group level in the concepts that the behavior and content presented to each other by the participants in interaction constitute rewards and punishments or have both benefits and costs, which the participants over time attempt to adjust into a mutually rewarding exchange, though the theory does not assume that the efforts will reach a stable equilibrium or that a stable state, if found, will be one of unification rather than one of polarization or dissolution of the group. The *relativistic* nature of the costs and benefits individuals perceive by comparing their lot with that of others in the same social interaction field, is also assumed, as emphasized in reference group theory (Merton and Kitt, 1950) and in social evaluation theory (Pettigrew, 1967).

In general sociology there is a theoretical conflict as to how much emphasis should be given to the influence of common values and norms of participants in a social interaction field and how much to the conflicts of interest between the various participants and to differences in their relative power. This problem, often represented as a conflict between adherence to structural–functional theory (Parsons, 1951) and adherence to conflict theory (Dahrendorf, 1959), receives a kind of answer, perhaps, in the present approach, where both unification and polarization are recognized, but the relative preponderance of the two is determined empirically and may be different for each social interaction field.

The elements of the SYMLOG System, both in theory and methods, from the general fields of personality study, clinical psychology, and individual and group psychotherapy, as well as the fields of group training, organization development, social group work, and family therapy, are too numerous even for specific mention. Perhaps it will be useful to recognize, however, that one of these fields, the field of family therapy, is only beginning to make its impact felt on existing theory and methods in psychology and sociology. In the opinion of the present author, the work of family therapy is full of important potentials. The works of Bowen (1971) and Minuchin (1974) have been of particular interest to the present author, especially with regard to the concepts of "triangles" of interpersonal relationships within families and how they may be dealt with, which are closely related to the concepts of polarization and unification in the present work, and the various ways in which polarizations may be neutralized (see Chapter 11).

Systematic multiple level field theory (the name offered for the basic theory of the SYMLOG System) is not an eclectic assembly of elements from these many sources, however, but a newly developed and integrated whole based on new methods of observation and expressed in a new language and set of concepts. It was not in fact developed by a careful fitting together of deductions from these various sources but grew inductively from a long continued effort to understand social interaction from observation, to construct measuring instruments for recording and analyzing the dynamics of small groups and for feedback of useful information to participants. It has been a "grounded theory" (see Glaser and

Strauss, 1967) from the first. The theory of the SYMLOG System can be understood and used appropriately without knowledge of its many connections with other theories. Potential users of the methods described in this book need not be intimidated by the fact that they know little, perhaps, of the long list of theories and fields mentioned.

The theory of SYMLOG gives emphasis equally to the dynamics of groups and to the dynamics of individual personalities of group members. It gives an articulate way to get back and forth from a consideration of each individual personality to a consideration of the dynamic field properties of the total group-and-situation constellation.

Getting back and forth from a view of each individual separately to a view of the inclusive group constellation of individuals is made possible in the present theory by the fact that, according to the theory, the *same dimensional system* (see Figure 3, p. 23) is appropriate for both levels. The theory provides the means for the observation and measurement, the conceptualization and representation, of *each individual perceptual field* (see Chapter 12, p. 109), as well as the *inclusive social interaction field* (see Figure 10, p. 54) constituted by the behavior and interaction of the individuals. The same kind of dimensional representation, a *Field Diagram,* is used for both types of fields. A "social interaction field" includes all the individual perceptual fields that in various ways mirror it and help to make it up.

The orientation of multiple level field theory is psychoanalytic in many respects, but psychoanalytic theory does not provide the conceptual means for representing adequately the interpersonal and total inclusive group levels of social processes or a way of getting from a view of the individual level of psychological processes to a view of the pairs of individuals and on to a view of the total inclusive social interaction field.

The term "multiple levels" in the context of "multiple level field theory" refers partly to the fact that the psychological processes of each individual exist "in depth." Psychoanalytic theory, as a "depth" psychology, strongly emphasizes the importance of recognizing multiple levels, and in this emphasis the two theories are in agreement. But SYMLOG theory tries to formulate, in addition, what happens when two or more individuals interact together in relation to objects of common orientation ("images"). It is held that the social interaction process *adds new levels* of complication of meaning and that these new levels of complication, as individuals perceive and act in the more complicated field, are folded back into their individual psychological processes. To understand the individual processes once this has happened, one has to be able to understand the social interaction field. Psychoanalytic theory gives no good way to describe the structure and dynamics of the social interaction field. In SYMLOG theory there is a way. Figure 10 (p. 54) is a Field Diagram based upon the average of all individual members' subjective perceptions (and evaluations) of the field. It contains a set of *inscriptions* (such as a tracing of the "reference circle" and the "opposite circle," the "line of balance," and others) representing the SYMLOG theory of the structure and dynamics of that particular social interaction field, from which new inferences can be made, as we shall later see.

In the SYMLOG System, the measurements for the construction of both the individual perceptual fields and the inclusive social interaction field are based on the observation of individual acts of social interaction, whether the observations are made by members or nonmembers; whether the observations are made in a time-ordered series, act by act, as in SYMLOG Interaction Scoring, or by global retrospective recall, as in SYMLOG Ratings.

The social interaction field is an inclusive representation of the data of all individual fields. It is derived from a combination of all subjectives views, including that of the researcher. When one wishes to look at the summary result of the ways in which the subjective views tend to converge, one may make a diagram of the *group average field,* as shown in Figure 10. One does not depend upon an average, however, since each individual field is unique and diverges from the others in important respects. In order to take this into account one looks at individual perceptual fields in *alternation.* In the "alternation" mode of analysis, the subjective meaning of an act to the member who performs the act is translated by the researcher-theorist into the subjective meaning it probably has for each of the other participants taken separately. The meanings of their reactions, in turn, are translated back into the subjective view of the first. The members' ratings of each other give the means of making these translations.

Multiple level field theory is closely related to gestalt field theory, realizing in many respects, I believe, the aspirations of Kurt Lewin and his school, but it differs from Lewin's field theory (see Lewin, 1939, 1947, 1951) in several important ways. Multiple level field theory is based on the observation of specific acts of social interaction as its primary grounding in empirical reality. Hence, the social interaction field is "operationally defined" from the beginning, whereas the gestalt field theriests have tended to begin with an abstract concept of the individual psychological field or "life space" apart from any means of measurement. For experiments, they have selected plausible operational definitions for the measurement of the variables they feel they need to represent for a particular experiment. They have not as a rule proceeded inductively to build general purpose measuring instruments based upon observation that can be applied in any situation of social interaction.

Because multiple level field theory is based on the observation of specific acts of social interaction, the measurement of its variables is anchored in time. In SYMLOG Interaction Scoring, every bit of evidence about the state of a variable or the structure of a dynamic field is obtained from some act of recording some piece of behavior that was observed to occur at some particular identifiable time (see Part II of this book). It is true that in retrospective Rating there is a collapsing of time, and one may lose track of just when some act observed occurred. But even so, the rating is based upon actual observation. It takes a lot of observation and a long time to get the amount of information necessary to construct the representation of a "field," either an individual perceptual field or an inclusive social interaction field. Lewin aspired to an a-historical theory dealing with the dynamics of the present field (for which physics was his model), and implicitly made the unfortunate assumption that one could obtain measurements of all the variables in the "present" field without paying enough attention, perhaps, to the fact that measurement of many variables takes a long time and can be defined only by time-anchored or historical events. Lewin did not want to get bogged down in a historical definition of variables. And he wanted to escape the concrete "phenotypical" conception of variables. Without formulation of the "phenotypical" component, however, one cannot make empirical measurements.

SYMLOG field theory is also different from gestalt field theory in that it takes account of *multiple fields*. SYMLOG field theory keeps in perspective (1) *each individual perceptual field* at a given time, (2) the *multiple level behavior* of each separate individual at a given time, (3) the *process of interaction* between individuals *over time,* (4) the developing relationship of *each individual* to *each other individual* in the group, (5) the overall pattern of the inclusive group constellation or *social interaction field* during a given time period, and (6) the dynamic *changes over time of the social interaction field*. This can be done because of the explicit methods of measurement and representation.

Lewin's theory, like Freud's, was constructed from the perspective of the single individual. The concept for this perspective in Lewin's theory is the "life space"; in Freud's theory it is the personality consisting of the interaction of its major parts, "Ego, Super-Ego, and Id." The extension of the individual perspective to *each of many individuals in social interaction with each other* was never accomplished, in either case.

Lewin's concept of the "life space" was extended without any essential modification to serve as a kind of "*group* life space." The group was treated as a *point* in the space, and the group was said to "locomote" as a point through the space toward a single goal. The extension of the individual life space to the group was mostly metaphorical and introduced a host of logical and conceptual problems.

Freud's concept of "Ego, Super-Ego, and Id" was also metaphorically extended (informally by others) to serve as a classification of the kinds of roles individuals play in a group. The results, while provocative and not entirely without value, remained unfortunately metaphorical and vague.

Neither Freud nor Lewin started from a concept of social interaction as a primary reality, and neither developed general methods of measuring it. As a result, in both cases the empirical grounding of the variables remained ambiguous, and the multiple-individual, multiple-level combination of perspectives was never clearly achieved. There were no suitable general measurements upon which the necessary concepts could be based.

Perhaps it needs to be said that, although SYMLOG field theory is based upon observations of "behavior" in the broad sense (including the content of things said), it is not a variety of "behavioristic" theory, if by "behavioristic" one means a theory that rules out of consideration the subjective views of the persons interacting. On the contrary, social interaction field theory is strongly phenomenological in taking into account the subjective view of the actor (each of them), in paying attention to many subjective elements of behavior and regarding them as real determinants, in emphasizing the actor's unique "definition of the situation," and in emphasizing the prominent role of the levels of meaning and symbols. In these respects SYMLOG field theory is very similar to "symbolic interactionism." The present approach departs from the more extreme phenomenology of some symbolic interactionists, however, who tend to emphasize the subjectivity, uniqueness, and variability of meaning in the perception and behavior of each individual to such an extent that it seems hopeless to try to use any kind of systematic method, any standardized approach, or to look for any general tendencies.

SYMLOG field theory is case-oriented and naturalistic (in that sense, "clinical") in spite of the considerable use of measurement, statistics, and geometry. The Field Diagrams look clean, cool, and precise, but they represent evanescent and uncertain subjective views of behavior and meaning, the real stuff with which one deals in working practically with people. The SYMLOG System provides extensive means for recognizing and conceptualizing individual differences between persons, general characteristics of the individual personality, and inconsistencies of direction of motivation, values, and behavior within the same personality, as well as consistencies. In using the system, one recognizes and characterizes unique properties of each group of individuals in interaction. In making SYMLOG interaction observations and in analyzing Field Diagrams, one pays attention to all the pair relationships in the group, as well as to the overall pattern characteristics of the group as a whole. In making observations at the image level and the value judgment level, and in making the Field Diagrams appropriate to these levels, one recognizes and portrays the relationships of persons to psychologically significant symbols and objects of common orientation. The SYMLOG System allows the tracing of changes through time of all the variables it measures.

Such a degree of inclusiveness is possible because of the complex of elements recognized in the original observation and description of the smallest unit observed in SYMLOG Interaction Scoring—the single act of the single individual. The observation of the single act of a single individual is the building block of all the more complex ways of analyzing patterns of behavior, whether patterns characterizing the individual personality or patterns characterizing the inclusive social interaction field. Acts are observed, recorded, sorted, counted, and aggregated in different ways to detect complicated patterns.

But the idea of an atomistic building block is only half of what is required. The other necessary conception is that the single act of the single individual is a complex, multiple-level entity in itself, compounded of many causal determinants, mirroring in microcosm the social interaction field in which it occurs. The description of the single act, using the SYMLOG Scoring format, calls for the description on different levels of a number of different characteristics of the same act. The levels include the "behavioral" elements, the "image content" presented in communication, and the evaluative attitude of the actor about the image, or the "value judgment."

For certain purposes, then, the researcher-theorist regards the single act as a unit—each act counts as one unit. Single acts are added together with other single acts to get larger aggregates and to describe larger patterns. For other purposes, however, the researcher-theorist regards the single act itself as a multiple level pattern of subunits or characteristics, which can be examined one by one in fine detail.

The way in which *each act* may be observed and assessed in terms of the multiple levels of behavior it contains is described in the SYMLOG Interaction Scoring Manual, Part II of this book. SYMLOG *Rating* may best be understood as a simplified global version of the operations performed in SYMLOG *Scoring*. The theoretical heart of SYMLOG is evident only in the Scoring method, not in the Rating.

The act of Rating (or Scoring) of the behavior of another person or of the self is best regarded as *still another level* of behavior of the rater. This seems especially clear when the information is to be returned to the group for their discussion. As a group member, one performs the Rating (or Scoring) in the expectation that each person rated will know how one describes him or her, and one expects that person will react in some way. This makes a difference in the way one rates or scores. The same pressures come to bear on Rating behavior as on other interactive behavior, only with some modifications in the strength of some of the pressures. The behavior of the person rated is measured by the behavior of the person rating. "Measuring" is also behavior. Consequently, one does not expect anybody's ratings or scores to be independent of his or her personality or location in the social interaction field. The observer, whether Scoring or later Rating, is a part of the total field. A group member's ratings of the other members' behavior is a part of his or her own behavior, and the Ratings give information about the rater as well as about other members and about the social interaction field as a whole. The ratings of each person must be analyzed. Every person's ratings are "subjective." (Appendix T deals with ways of exposing and utilizing differences between raters or scorers.)

There is no "objective" view of the total field. One approaches what is ordinarily meant by "objectivity" by putting together and averaging or in some other way combining the "subjective" views of as many persons as one can.

The case study we are about to begin is based entirely on Ratings. This perspective is chosen, with special emphasis on the ratings of the single researcher-rater, because this is the approach that can be applied to more groups and situations than any other. In the course of this case study various hypotheses are offered that may be helpful in anticipating what may happen in a group—or understanding what is currently happening—on the basis of a SYMLOG analysis.

These hypotheses are presented in a very tentative way. They are tentative in at least two respects. First, they have not been very extensively tested, even as such hypotheses *can* be tested. They are at the growing edge of the body of theory. More important, they are tentative in that the theory leads one to believe that even at best they can never be very certain in a particular case. In fact, one may be glad that the events they predict are not certain, for one would like to be able to intervene helpfully in some cases before the predicted events happen.

The tentative hypotheses are presented as "heuristic hypotheses." Their purpose is to promote the learning of the researcher and the group members engaged in the self-study. This is a different purpose from trying to show a hypothesis is right. The single case study is never adequate, of course, to show that, nor for that matter is a great number of studies. But a single case may be enough to show that something important has been forgotten in the formulation of the hypothesis. This in itself may often result in basic advances in theory.

The researcher making case studies discovers with monotonous regularity that "circumstances alter cases." The circumstances affecting human behavior are very complex and often unpredictable. As a result the researcher comes to expect that nearly any general hypothesis, no matter how reasonable it seems, is apt not to hold in a given case or, at best, to explain only a little. One can do something to improve his understanding by measuring many factors and using constructs that take many things into account, as the present methods try to do, but effective prediction is still tenuous.

When a heuristic hypothesis fails, the researcher may receive, in compensation, as it were, a feeling of sudden insight—one may realize that there is something very important in the present case that has been overlooked before. Such an insight (though sometimes wrong) may indeed be accurate for the given case and may help the researcher to do a better job in that group or situation as an adviser, leader, therapist, or educator, or even to improve basic theory. If any of these is an outcome, then we may say that the hypothesis was "heuristic," though perhaps wrong in part, in that it promoted discovery and useful learning.

In the case study we shall use as an illustration for Part I of this book, it will be necessary for the author of this part to speak somewhat personally on occasion, since he was a member of the group studied and was, of course, responsible in some ways for the behavior he studied and its interpretation. He also tried to help individuals in various ways and tried to improve the operation of the group for its given purposes, as well as to improve basic theory. One can hardly try to help or improve matters in a group without making value judgments. I shall try to explain my own value positions on the various issues raised by the heuristic hypotheses and to offer such advice as I can. The advice should also be taken as tentative and as heuristic in intention.

Chapter 3

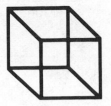

How to Start
with Your Own
Ratings of a Group

Figure 1 shows a Field Diagram for one of the groups in the Group Psychology course. The members of the group have given permission for the use of their group for this illustrative case study. The names and nicknames, however, have been changed. If one wishes to become acquainted with the people immediately, a short tour through Chapter 12 may help.

The Field Diagram shown as Figure 1 is constructed from ratings made by the author. I was the instructor in the group and am shown on the Field Diagram as a member of the group, designated RFB. Thus, the rating shown for RFB is a self-rating. The instructor is not a typical member of an academic group, of course. One might expect his ratings to carry special weight in the feedback. For years I avoided making the ratings in order to avoid undue influence on the perception of other group members. The ratings for the diagram in this particular case were made after the ending of the group. I no longer avoid making the ratings, because I have settled it in my mind that influence is inevitable and that the thing to do is to exercise it in the best way I can. I make the ratings along with all other group members, and I take the flak for my ratings, as they do. I think the moment of truth is as good for me as for them.

In most situations of application a rating can be made early in the history of the group if the researcher has a reasonable number of impressions. A rating may be made in advance of the composition of the group if the researcher has some useful amount of information about each of the prospective participants. Such a rating may help to decide some questions as to whom to include in a given group in order that the group as a whole may function most effectively for the given purposes. Ratings can be repeated at intervals over time, as a guide to progress, although it is probably rather difficult to avoid considerable influence of the earlier ratings on the later ones.

In the SYMLOG rating procedure each individual member of the group is rated separately, ordinarily on the basis of observations of his or her interactive behavior or image content. (For instructions, see Appendix B). The ratings

FIGURE 1 Individual Field Diagram: RFB's Ratings (Raw Totals)

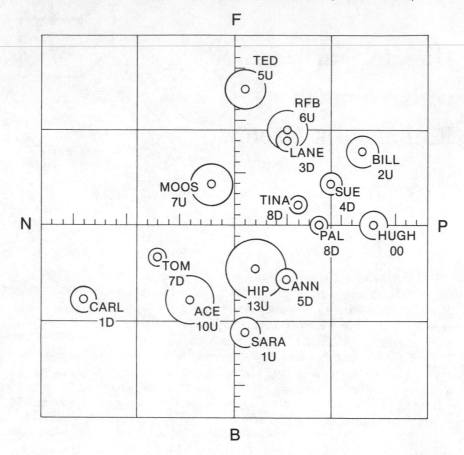

describe each individual as he or she *has been,* in *that* group, over the *specific time period* decided upon in advance of the rating, as seen and evaluated by the *particular rater*. Each member, as a rater, rates each other member, and the self, as the rater EXPECTS the others on the average will rate him or her, and finally as the rater WISHES that others might rate him or her. In my ratings, diagrammed in Figure 1, I omitted my WISHED FOR rating (possibly because the group was actually over). Hence, it is not shown on the diagram. No doubt it would have been quite close to my EXPECTED rating, but somewhat more positive.

The *level* of the behavior or content to be rated must be decided upon in advance and specified. In the present case the rating was done by reading the descriptions of each direction of the behavior at the ACT level, as described in Appendix A. Since that time Stephen P. Cohen and I have prepared a simpler adjective rating form designed for practical use in case studies of natural groups where the Appendix A descriptions are too unwieldy. This simplified SYMLOG Adjective Rating form is shown as Figure 2 (see also Appendix C). If one

FIGURE 2 The SYMLOG Adjective Rating Form

Your Name_____ Group _____

Name of person described _____ Circle the best choice for each item:

		(0)	(1)	(2)	(3)	(4)
U	. . . . active, dominant, talks a lot	never	. . rarely	. . sometimes	. . often	. . always
UP	. . . extroverted, outgoing, positive	never	. . rarely	. . sometimes	. . often	. . always
UPF	. . . a purposeful democratic task leader	never	. . rarely	. . sometimes	. . often	. . always
UF	. . . an assertive business-like manager	never	. . rarely	. . sometimes	. . often	. . always
UNF	. . authoritarian, controlling, disapproving	never	. . rarely	. . sometimes	. . often	. . always
UN	. . . domineering, tough-minded, powerful	never	. . rarely	. . sometimes	. . often	. . always
UNB	. . provocative, egocentric, shows off	never	. . rarely	. . sometimes	. . often	. . always
UB	. . . jokes around, expressive, dramatic	never	. . rarely	. . sometimes	. . often	. . always
UPB	. . entertaining, sociable, smiling, warm	never	. . rarely	. . sometimes	. . often	. . always
P	. . . . friendly, equalitarian	never	. . rarely	. . sometimes	. . often	. . always
PF	. . . . works cooperatively with others	never	. . rarely	. . sometimes	. . often	. . always
F	. . . . analytical, task-oriented, problem-solving	never	. . rarely	. . sometimes	. . often	. . always
NF	. . . legalistic, has to be right	never	. . rarely	. . sometimes	. . often	. . always
N	. . . . unfriendly, negativistic	never	. . rarely	. . sometimes	. . often	. . always
NB	. . . irritable, cynical, won't cooperate	never	. . rarely	. . sometimes	. . often	. . always
B	. . . . shows feelings and emotions	never	. . rarely	. . sometimes	. . often	. . always
PB	. . . affectionate, likeable, fun to be with	never	. . rarely	. . sometimes	. . often	. . always
DP	. . . looks up to others, appreciative, trustful	never	. . rarely	. . sometimes	. . often	. . always
DPF	. . . gentle, willing to accept responsibility	never	. . rarely	. . sometimes	. . often	. . always
DF	. . . obedient, works submissively	never	. . rarely	. . sometimes	. . often	. . always
DNF	. . self-punishing, works too hard	never	. . rarely	. . sometimes	. . often	. . always
DN	. . . depressed, sad, resentful, rejecting	never	. . rarely	. . sometimes	. . often	. . always
DNB	. . alienated, quits, withdraws	never	. . rarely	. . sometimes	. . often	. . always
DB	. . . afraid to try, doubts own ability	never	. . rarely	. . sometimes	. . often	. . always
DPB	. . . quietly happy just to be with others	never	. . rarely	. . sometimes	. . often	. . always
D	. . . . passive, introverted, says little	never	. . rarely	. . sometimes	. . often	. . always

compares it with the longer descriptions of Appendix A, it will be seen to combine, to some extent, the ACT level and the NON (nonverbal) level and to depend to some extent also on the other levels. It is, however, centered on the ACT level.

For a general purpose preliminary assessment, if the simplified adjective rating form is not used, the ACT level as described in Appendix A or the ACT level plus the NON level are the ones ordinarily used. Additional levels may be rated separately and compared with each other and with the ACT level in order to throw light on problems of special interest.

In order to understand the Field Diagram and the meaning of the location of the member "images" plotted upon it as shown in Figure 1, it is necessary to take a short detour to grasp the meaning of the three dimensions of the SYMLOG theory and the way in which they may be used to constitute a three-dimensional "space," as shown in Figure 3. It is possible to describe the quality of behavior—more specifically, of any act of interpersonal behavior—by reference to three dimensions. The dimensions, described in adjectives that apply to behavior, are: (1) Dominant vs. Submissive, (2) Friendly vs. Unfriendly, and (3) Instrumentally Controlled vs. Emotionally Expressive. Each "dimension" has two ends, qualitatively the opposite of each other. Each dimension may also be thought of as having a zero point in the center, at the origin of the two opposite directions.

For the sake of more easily grasping the logical relationships of the "directions" we want to visualize, we may think of the three dimensions in relation to each other as if they were the dimensions of an actual physical space. Figure 3 is a perspective drawing of a three-dimensional cube, which may be thought of as enclosing the three-dimensional space we want to visualize. The labels on the directions indicate how the behavioral descriptive names are translated into names descriptive of directions in the physical space model, U, D, P, N, F, and B. The spatial names of the dimensions are U–D (for Upward–Downward), P–N (for Positive–Negative), and F–B (for Forward–Backward). The letters on the smaller cubes, made up of various combinations of the directional names, U, D, P, N, F, and B, give the names of directions in between the main ones. There are twenty-six directional names in all. These twenty-six directions are taken as the basis for the more fine-grained definitions of the variables of the SYMLOG system, as shown in Appendix A, and in more compact form in Figure 2.

Each of the adjective rating items shown in Figure 2 is labeled with a combination of letters, e.g. "U," "UP," "UPF," which indicates the direction in the three-dimensional space the item is designed to measure. A comparison of each adjective rating item with its corresponding direction (or vector) in the three-dimensional space as shown in Figure 3 will give a rapid intuitive understanding of the heart of the SYMLOG System.

Once the SYMLOG three-dimensional space is understood, the Field Diagram in Figure 1 is easily understood. The Field Diagram shows a *two*-dimensional plane is it would be seen if one were looking into the cube from the top. The Field Diagram is also calibrated with a numerical scale on each direction and is divided at the zero point—and again halfway out along each direction for more

FIGURE 3 The SYMLOG Three-Dimensional Space

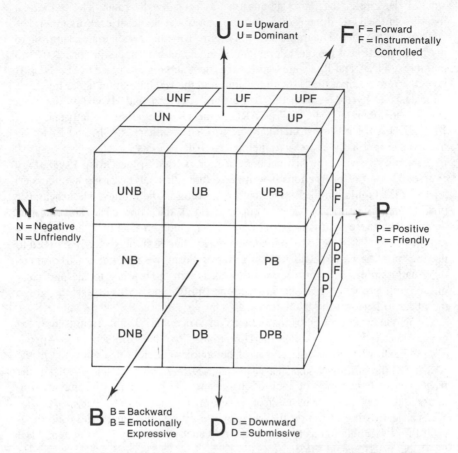

The SYMLOG Three-Dimensional Space, Showing Classes of Directions, or Locations, Defined by Logical Combinations of the Six Named Reference Directions. (The cube is seen from an outside point. The Directions are named from a reference point at the intersection of the three dimensions, looking Forward.)

convenient measurement—but the *logic* of the space is given by the cube model of Figure 3.

The location of each individual in the two dimensions P–N and F–B is derived from the ratings and is shown as a point on the Field Diagram, as in Figure 1. The point proper is enclosed with a very small circle (called the core circle), to make it more easily visible. The summary ratings of the individual's behavior on the two dimensions P–N and F–B are thus shown by the location of the point in the plane of the diagram. The summary rating of the individual's behavior on the U–D dimension is shown by the relative size of the outer circle inscribed around the point. The larger the outside circle, the more dominant the behavior; the smaller the circle, the more submissive, as seen by the rater. The numerical location in the U–D dimension is written below the name of each member.

Thus, on the Field Diagram shown in Figure 1 it can be seen that, according to my ratings, HIP was the most dominant member, with a final rating of 13U. Two members, TINA and PAL, are tied for the most submissive place at 8D. HUGH is on the zero point of the U–D dimension, and the small notation under his name indicates this by the symbol 00. It may also be seen that HUGH is the most friendly member, at 13P, while CARL is the most negative, or unfriendly, at 14N. TED is the most instrumentally controlled member, at 13F, and SARA is the most emotionally expressive member at 10B.

Appendix B shows the instructions for ratings used in the Group Psychology course. This set of instructions is written so that self-analytic group members do a part of the tabulation themselves before handing in the ratings. The researcher making ratings of a nonacademic group follows the same basic procedure as described in these instructions and may also include an EXPECT and a WISH rating, if relevant. When group members unfamiliar with the system are asked to use the simplified SYMLOG Adjective Rating Form, the researcher will ordinarily greatly simplify the instructions to make them appropriate to the particular group, will probably give the instructions orally, and will not ask the group members to perform the tabulations.

Using the more complex instructions in Appendix B, the ratings may be made directly on a form called the *Directional Profile* Form shown in Appendix G. Each of the twenty-six types of behavior separately distinguished in the SYMLOG three-dimensional space is called a *Direction* of behavior. A list of the frequency of occurrence of each of the twenty-six directions of behavior (obtained either by rating or by interaction scoring) is called a *Directional Profile*. The vertical listing of the profile, as shown on the Directional Profile Form, is useful for the tabulation as to how frequently each directional "component" (U, D, P, N, F, B) is said to occur.

Appendix H contains a *Key*, which fits against the Directional Profile of a given individual and makes it easy to locate and add together the component numbers for the summary at the bottom of the Directional Profile Form. The summary represents the conversion of the twenty-six ratings actually made into a location of the person rated in each of the three *dimensions*.

Appendix G contains RFB's ratings of the members of our illustrative group. A little study of the profiles as I have filled them out for the description of each member, along with the instructions and the use of the key, will make clear how the summary totals are obtained for each individual, representing his or her location in the three-dimensional space. These numbers may then be used directly for the plotting of the points on the Field Diagram, as in Figure 1.

A series of Appendixes (H through O) deals with the details of just how the Field Diagram is constructed and how the plots are made. The details of these procedures have been worked out and are described in full in order to obtain sufficient uniformity and exactness for the analysis of the *constellation* of images. The application of a transparent overlay with a graphic inscription, the

Polarization-Unification Overlay, to the Field Diagram is the means of applying the main SYMLOG theory to the particular group (see Appendixes P, Q, and R). The Field Diagram and the Overlay, in conjunction, constitute an easily understood graphic computer.

In our illustrative group we are lucky enough to have member ratings of each other. Figure 4 shows the average ratings received by each member from all other members and is called a "Group Average Field Diagram," as distinguished from an "Individual Field Diagram." The Field Diagram of Figure 1 may be compared with that of Figure 4 to form some idea of how close an individual researcher, using the rating method, may come to the result of all group member ratings added together and averaged.

In comparing Figure 1 with Figure 4, the viewer's first reaction may be one of dismay! The points in Figure 4, the Group Average Ratings, are certainly much closer together, indeed, RFB seems to have exaggerated everything. There is some resemblance in the places where individual images are found in the cluster (for example, CARL is off in the NB corner of each of the two diagrams), but the scale seems to be quite different in the two diagrams.

At this point we have to recognize that in the averaging together of many individuals' diagrams to obtain the Group Average Diagram, a lot of cancellation has gone on. Insofar as individuals differ from each other in their placement of given images, the average location of the points will tend to regress toward the zero point of each of the two dimensions. If we want the Group Average Diagram to be more comparable in absolute scale to an Individual Diagram, we have to compensate in some way for the tendency of the average ratings to regress toward the zero point of the diagram. How shall we do this?

We shall simply *expand* each diagram we want to make comparable to another for our purposes of analysis, and we shall expand it by just the amount necessary to bring the most "far out" image to the edge of the diagram. Figure 5 shows this expansion accomplished. Appendix K explains in detail how it is done. We may note that the diagram of Figure 5 seems more clear than that of Figure 4 and note especially that it is easier to see the smaller clusters. Notice also that the circles have been left the same size and the scale numbers for the U–D locations have not been expanded. There are two reasons for this. One is that it is not necessary, since we are primarily interested in the relative positions of the images in the P–N, F–B plane, specifically the angles of the vectors by which they depart from the zero point (and our expansion has not changed these angles at all). The second reason is that the diagram is clearer when the image circles do not become too large. We take it as a rule that, when an image field or constellation is expanded, the expansion is made in the P–N and F–B dimensions only, leaving the U–D locations unexpanded.

If one is expanding the diagram of a single individual rater, one may feel an objection that the original scale has been lost and that we no longer have the sense of the relative constriction or expansiveness in the way the rater used the scale ("not often, sometimes, often"); or, indeed, one may lose the sense that the people in the group actually did form a very tight cluster. Actually, the information about the relative constriction has not been lost—it is preserved in

FIGURE 4   Group Average Diagram: All Members' Ratings (Raw Averages)

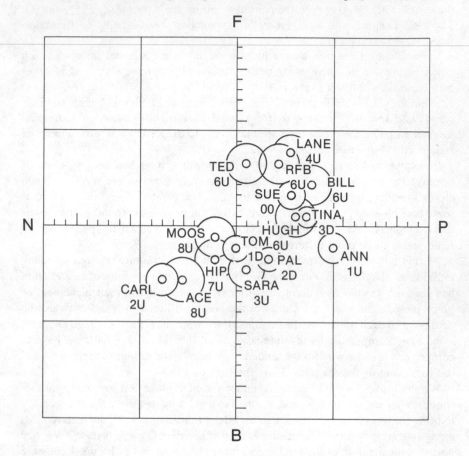

the "Expansion Multiplier" which is put at the top of the diagram (see Figure 5). If there is no expansion, this index is 1. The higher it is above 1, the more the diagram has been expanded, hence the smaller the original constellation.

A second point is quite important: If the original constellation consists of points that are close together but all on one side of the zero point, let us say in an area about the size of a quarter of the diagram, they will still appear to be clustered after the expansion. (See, for example, the cluster of images TED, LAIN, RFB, BILL, SUE, HUGH, and TINA in Figures 4 and 5). The sense of the cluster has not been lost in the expansion. If the points are contained within a given angle, say 90 degrees, before expansion, as these points are, they will still be contained within that angle after expansion. Expansion does not change the angular scatter. On the other hand, if the points are clustered, but on both sides of the zero point, they will be expanded away from each other and will appear more polarized in the expanded diagram than in the original. This is a desirable feature of the expansion. Our theory says that the angular scatter of images is an appropriate measure of unification versus polarization (two key concepts of our theory,

FIGURE 5 Group Average Diagram, Expanded (Expansion Multiplier = 1.843)

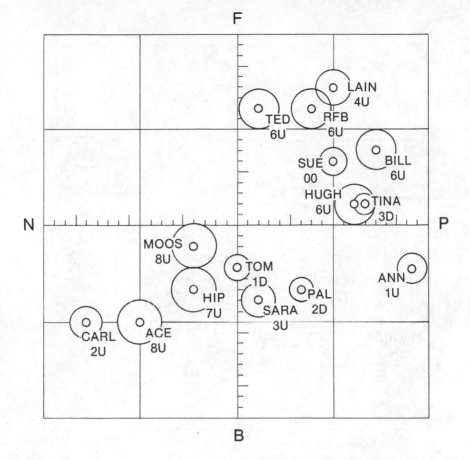

as we shall see). A small angular scatter makes for relative unification, a large angular scatter makes for polarization.

My individual rating of the group, shown in Figure 1 in its original form, fills quite a large part of the total field of the diagram, but in order to make it a little more comparable to our expansion of the Group Average Diagram, as shown in Figure 5, we may expand it. The procedure described in Appendix K is followed. The result is shown in Figure 6. It turns out that the Expansion Multiplier needed is only 1.199, whereas the Multiplier needed to expand the Group Average Diagram was 1.843. (The larger the Multiplier, the smaller we know the original constellation was.) My expanded diagram is shown as Figure 6. It differs only slightly from the original in Figure 1, of course. We may now compare my diagram, in Figure 6, with the Group Average Diagram in Figure 5. The agreement looks considerably better now, although there are various differences, which we shall analyze in detail as we proceed. But first we need to apply the polarization–unification overlay and to add several inscriptions to help in the analysis.

FIGURE 6 Individual Field Diagram: RFB's Ratings, Expanded (Expansion Multiplier = 1.199)

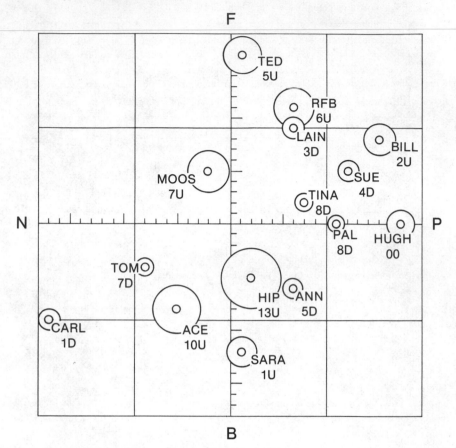

If one has to depend upon his own ratings alone to make a Field Diagram for further analysis, one is under a considerable handicap, of course. It is not nearly as reliable as having the members' Interpersonal Ratings of each other. But, for that matter, one would be better off still to have, in addition, the observations of non–group-member observers represented in their SYMLOG Interaction Scorings and, ideally, observers' SYMLOG Ratings, too. It is very plain from experience that each individual in the group, including, of course, yourself as an observer, whether or not an active participant, and each individual non–group-member observer, sees the group in his or her own way. The variety within our illustrative group may be sampled by looking through Chapter 12, which shows the Field Diagram for each member separately. These differences will be examined in detail later. For the moment, we may note that they are considerably different from each other, though not absolutely so. One may intuitively feel that it is best to study each individual's perception of the field separately but that there is, after all, considerable convergence, so that it makes sense to add them together to make a Group Average Field Diagram. Actually, we do both.

Are there some raters who can do a consistently better job, over many groups, of approximating the group average than other raters? There may be some relevant special abilities in the perception and understanding of behavior and image content—abilities that have some generality in the sense that they help the rater do a representative job in the rating of many different kinds of other persons. It seems reasonable to suppose that experience with people may help, especially if it is with many kinds of people. It also seems probable that *trying hard* to understand other people as *individuals* can help. It is an implicit assumption of the use of the SYMLOG System in observer training that learning to make fine discriminations as to the directions and levels of behavior—conceptualization, in brief—can help (see Parts III and IV of this book). Probably, also, self-analysis, aided by seeing the results of other persons' observations and ratings, can help. One can certainly recognize at least some characteristic biases in one's perception and evaluation of others and perhaps can learn, to a certain extent, to make corrections for these by taking special pains to do so.

In any case, in participating in most groups the best one can do, practically, is to make the most of one's own perceptions. Much more, probably, can be done with the many impressions that one has stocked in memory than the rating at the ACT level, which we have been using so far. One procedure is to continue the rating for other levels, to make Field Diagrams for each, and to compare them with each other.

Another procedure for eliciting more of the impressions you already have stocked in memory about a group in which you have participated is to "identify" yourself with each of the group members in turn and try to fill out hypothetically their ratings of themselves and each of the other members. This procedure, though it may be somewhat long and painstaking, seems to be effective in exposing biases in the researcher's own perception that are not noticed when one rates only from one's own point of view. I have the impression from experience that many memories otherwise lost are retrieved when one applies this procedure and compares the field diagrams. This implies that a very perceptive and empathic researcher will be able to approximate not only the Group Average Field Diagram but also the Individual Field Diagram of each member taken separately. Whether this is indeed the case remains to be seen.

It is surely possible, to some degree, to "take the role of the other," to "put one's self in the other's shoes," and "to see the self as others see us." Often we do not try hard to do any of these things. The SYMLOG Rating procedure, applied at the different levels and from the point of view of each person in the group vis-à-vis each other person, gives a practical and systematic way in which the researcher can in fact try *very* hard! And along the way a number of intriguing questions, and sometimes real insights, are likely to occur.

Using one's own ratings alone, it is possible to treat them as if they were acceptably accurate and as if they did represent, tolerably well, the Group Average Field Diagram. One will be more ready to do this, of course, if one has made ratings in one or two groups and has had them well corroborated by actual member ratings or by observers' SYMLOG Interaction Scores. In any case, given the assumption of reasonable representativeness, it is possible to go ahead and apply certain heuristic hypotheses to the data shown in one's own Field Diagram. These hypotheses are spelled out in detail in Chapters 6–12. They may have some practical value in that they call attention to certain possibilities of concrete events in the particular group to which they apply, events that have not yet, perhaps, occurred but on the basis of past experience with other groups seem probable enough to be worth anticipating.

Before coming to the heuristic hypotheses one by one, however, it will be helpful to consider a little further the nature of the "fields" represented in various kinds of Field Diagrams.

Chapter 4

The Concept of a Field:
Two Types of Fields

The Field Diagram functions as a graphic summary of information about the members of the group and their locations, as seen from the point of view of some individual rater or, alternatively, some number of raters added together and averaged. When a Field Diagram has been constructed from the ratings, a graphic representation of the general theory of individual and social interaction fields is applied to the constellation of images in the Field Diagram by the use of the Polarization–Unification Overlay (see Appendixes P, Q, and R). From this graphic procedure it is possible to derive a number of heuristic hypotheses about individual members and about the probable operation of the group.

The set of images in the mind of any given individual member is hypothesized to constitute a "field"—it may be called the *individual perceptual field*. When the term "perceptual field" is used, it should always be understood to include the "evaluative reactions" or attitudes of the rater, as well as his or her "percep-tions" in the more restricted sense. The individual perceptual-evaluative field is sometimes called simply the "individual field," meaning the social interaction field as seen by a particular individual. The individual perceptual field is only a part of the more inclusive social interaction field.

The *social interaction field* is hypothesized to be a dynamic entity that in-cludes all of the individual perceptual fields, plus the overt behavior by means of which individuals attempt to communicate to each other the contents of their individual perceptual-evaluative fields. The overt behavior and meaningful con-tent of the communication interact with and change the individual perceptual fields, which in turn affect the overt behavior in a circular process. A social interaction field consists, theoretically, of all the individual perceptual fields and all the communicative acts of members in interaction with each other, through some period of real time, at multiple levels of perception, evaluation, behavior, and content. The individual member's *psychological process of constructing* his or her own perceptual-evaluative picture of the field may be thought of as one more level of behavior of the individual. Only a small part of any individual field can be communicated in overt interaction. A social interaction field theoretically includes all the individual perceptual fields and all the images in the individual perceptual fields, although the actual total of all these elements is never known by any one person or observer. Thus a social interaction field includes more, theoretically, than can be observed or communicated, even through exhaustive discussions and ratings. In its entirety it is, and must remain, a hypothetical entity for this reason. It can be described in enough detail, however, to serve many practical purposes.

What *can* often be observed at a given time in a social interaction field is the focusing of attention of some number of members on one set of words or some physical object or event, which the observer conceptualizes as an "image" to which the members are co-oriented. For example, one may see members of a group grow excited at, and discuss with a strong focus of attention, a set of images such as the "proper attitude to take toward authority." Of course, we assume that there are differences in the way different members view whatever is at the focus of their attention, and the observer probably has a still somewhat different view. The question can be raised, theoretically, as to whether the observer is ever justified in assuming that these views are nearly enough the same to permit one to say there is *an* image, that is, a single image or set of images, at the center of the attention of each member. Still, the observer can detect many signs of a common focus of attention, and the observer simply calls that focus "an image" for heuristic purposes and then asks what different "images" different individuals have of that "image" or focus.

A social interaction field, at least that part of it we can observe, often tends to develop toward a clearer pattern over some period of time. A *focal image,* presented in communication, may change as group members communicate about it. As the group members talk about the image, their pictures of each other also tend to change to some extent. There often seems to be a patterning of the whole constellation of communicated images, including sometimes the members' images of each other, which can be described as tending toward *unification* or *polarization*.

We are talking for the moment about attitudes toward the *images talked about*. It is important to note that the concepts of unification and polarization are clear only when one specifies a given *level* of behavior or content. A group may polarize or disagree in their attitudes about a given image (their attitudes pro and con the image of "authority," for example, may be at polar extremes), but they may in fact grow more similar in their overt behavior toward each other at the ACT level—they may all move in a more negative direction, for example. At the image level they are polarized; at the ACT level they are unified, or convergent, in a negative direction.

Many of the heuristic hypotheses, to be described later, concerning an individual rater's field involve the concepts of *unification* and *polarization* of the images in the individual's perception. When a field of images is "unified" the images tend to be perceived as similar in important respects (above all, in terms of the evaluation the rater gives them), and their differences may be minimized. When a field of images is "polarized" the images tend to be divided into two (sometimes more) subgroups in the individual's perception and evaluation, very different from each other—in fact opposed to each other—and the differences between the two subgroups may be exaggerated. Under some conditions there may be a tendency to unify the images within each of the two (or more) polarized subgroups. Thus, both tendencies, unification and polarization, may be working within the same individual field in relation to different sets of images.

The similarities and differences in images we are concerned with are those of the perceived location of the images in each of the three dimensions of the SYMLOG space (U–D, P–N, and F–B). As noted above, similarities and differences must be examined separately for each of the levels. For example, two individuals may behave similarly toward each other (both may be negative at the ACT level as seen by an observer) but may see some external image (say the image of "authority") in conflicting ways. One may see "authority" as good (perhaps U*P*F), and the other may see it as bad (perhaps U*N*F). So far as the images that the two group members have of each other are concerned, each may see the other as negative, as a result of the argument, and the self as positive.

According to the general theory, individuals are believed to react to each other in terms of the similarities and differences they see between themselves, between themselves and third persons, and between themselves and images of third objects to which they are co-oriented (see Newcomb, 1953). Each individual as an actor is visualized as subjectively tending to "move" the self-image and also to "move" the images of others in response to the actor's perception of the total pattern, or "gestalt," of the images in the field. The "total pattern" for the individual actor, of course, includes images of persons and the things talked about in the present group. But the total pattern for the individual actor also includes images from his or her *past experience* and other images aroused by the things talked about in the group, things in the environment of the group, and so on. On a given Field Diagram for a given individual, we never have a representation of *all* the images we suppose may actually be present and interacting in the person's mind. On the Field Diagrams we have looked at so far, only the images the members have of themselves and other members have been included.

But we often know a good deal about how the actor views the self and other members of the group. And in situations where we participate or observe, we usually know a good deal about the images presented by each individual in his or her verbal content and how the actor feels about them, that is, whether he or she tends to accept given images or to reject them. We often, then, have enough images located on an Individual Field Diagram for us to surmise the general location in the space of the set of images the individual tends to associate with each other as similar (that is, to unify), and to surmise whether the actor tends to polarize the distribution of images into two or more subgroups. In case the individual tends to polarize the images, we also can form a general idea of the location in the space of the set of images the individual will tend to reject.

The polarization–unification pattern of a *social interaction field,* as distinct from that of an individual perceptual field, is maintained only by the immediate overt and communicative interaction of persons. To the extent that the interaction is *intermittent,* with *long time lapses* between actions and reactions, the particular polarization–unification pattern will tend to *collapse.* The common attentional focus will be broken. When a field pattern collapses, the images cease to exert unifying and polarizing influences on each other. As other images begin to command the attention of individuals, another pattern may form, or the group may discontinue interaction.

On the other hand, to the extent that the overt communication in a social interaction field is *immediate* and *face-to-face* (or visually carried), and *involves large numbers* of persons, the tendencies toward unification and polarization of individual image fields become stronger and more overpowering to each or most of the individuals—as in a crowd or a mob. For the field pattern to form, it is usually necessary that some dramatic event, image, or set of images get into the focus of attention of a sufficient number of interacting individuals. At that point others are led to pay attention by seeing that many are already paying attention. As events involving the images of common attention transpire, the reactions of others are seen, and seeing others reveal their attitudes in turn tends to strengthen the images and to sharpen the evaluative reaction of the observing individual. A circular reaction sets in—a runaway amplification of the evaluative reactions, the images, and the overt interactive behavior of the self and others. What happens in a crowd or mob, of course, is unusual in the numbers of persons involved and in the dramatic extremes of the images and the interaction, but crowd behavior seems to throw into high relief certain features that are found in less extreme form in many social interaction fields. The movement may be toward either unification or polarization of the images, or toward a combination of the two. The buildup may continue to some high point and hold for some time, but not indefinitely. When the focus on the central dramatic images is lost, the behavior of individuals becomes uncoordinated, and they cease to affect each other in an amplifying fashion.

The polarization–unification pattern of a social interaction field is inherently unstable and transient. It is maintained by attention. All the factors that influence and regulate attention are important to its character. The principal images involved in a polarization of a social interaction field stand out in the perception of individuals (to varying degrees, of course) as a "figure" against a "ground," to use terms from gestalt psychology. To the degree that the unification or polarization of the field builds and amplifies, and so long as it holds, the "background" is held in abeyance while the "figure" commands attention. A particular field pattern, however, is sustained by overt behavior and communication, that is, by overt social interaction—in real time, against real interferences with communication, and at real costs of time, energy, and emotional investment to each individual. A given field pattern of attention is in competition with many other elements in the minds of the individuals, who are holding those elements in the background while the "figure" (the focal images and their effects on the group) commands their attention.

Some patterns of polarization–unification are fleeting, some last a few minutes, some last a whole meeting of an hour or more, and some recur again and again in a given group until they can be called chronic. It seems to be characteristic, however, that in a given instance a polarization or unification has a noticeable onset in some identifiable event, object, set of words, or the like, which functions as a "focal image." The pattern of polarization and unification among the associated images then amplifies in intensity and propagates over more individuals in the group in a rapidly rising growth curve. The attention given to the particular constellation of images and related intermember behavior for a period becomes preemptive of attention to anything else. Underneath the socially apparent surface, however, individuals are still subjectively dealing with a multiplicity of images, feelings, and concerns, which are only temporarily held in the background. Without warning, some of these images, feelings, and concerns may break through into communication, and the existing polarization–unification pattern may collapse.

The term "collapse" is used with the implication that the time required for a pattern to break up and disappear seems often to be less than that of its appearance, growth, and holding period. The imagery and pattern of polarization–unification in a group may change markedly within a few moments or less than a minute. Thus field patterns often tend to appear suddenly, mount in clarity and intensity, and hold more or less steady in a pattern of polarization or unification for a period, and then collapse.

Some collapses are only temporary, however. A given pattern may be reinstated again and again if there are conditions that renew attention to the same or related imagery. There may be a particular problem in the environment of the group, for example, that demands renewed attention. Or the group may have some persistent problem of its organization or mode of functioning that will give rise to a chronic series of similar polarization–unification patterns. Particular personality characteristics of individual members may repeatedly force their way to attention, or particularly difficult or harmonious relationships between individuals in pairs or subgroups may become chronic concerns of the group.

The Field Diagram of the present method can be used to represent either an individual perceptual-evaluative field of images or an inclusive social interaction field. The *dimensions* required to describe these two types of fields are believed to be comparable, and many of the basic assumptions concerning polarization, unification, the nature of images, the nature of attention, and so on are very similar or the same. So, within limits, the two types of fields are comparable, and gains in understanding one may help in understanding the other.

But the two types of field are also different in important respects, and we need to take great care not to confuse them or unwittingly to substitute one for the other in our theorizing. The social interaction field is inclusive of all the individual perceptual-evaluative fields and includes still more. To understand the real processes of interactive behavior, we need to be able to visualize each type of field clearly and then to work back and forth from the one to the other.

In order to think clearly about both types of fields, we also need to be sharply aware of the measurements on which any given Diagram is based and to realize that no single set of measurements adequately represents the total field—either the Individual Field or the total Social Interaction Field. Different kinds of measurement get at different kinds of things, and they should not be expected to agree in all respects. Retrospective Ratings of behavior are not the same as time-ordered Interaction Scorings. The Ratings of behavior by group members are not the same as the Ratings by nonmember observers. My Ratings are not the same as your Ratings. My Ratings are not the same as my own SYMLOG Interaction Scorings. My Ratings are not the same as the aggregated and averaged Ratings by group members. The average group Ratings toward the beginning of the group are not the same as the average group Ratings toward the end of the group. And so on. These points are all painfully obvious, but they would be much less obvious if we did not have specific measuring procedures. When one attempts to theorize about personalities and groups without specific measuring procedures, the mind simply refuses (or is unable), after a certain point, to make the necessary distinctions, and confusion finally wins.

As a lone researcher one is particularly interested in one's own Ratings, and these are always retrospective. For practical purposes, one studies a summary of the past in order to anticipate things that may happen in the future. One wants a way to get from the information he has now to a conceptualization that will help anticipate events that may occur in the group, that will help one take action to avoid undesirable events, to recognize current problems and deal currently with them or help bring about desirable events. This is a very big order, and one should not expect too much. Even if one's theory were very good indeed, this is trying to make very little information go a very long way.

The information portrayed in any Field Diagram has always been captured, in fact, by observations taken *one at a time* and then aggregated in some way over some period of time. This is true not only of observations taken down currently in real time, as in SYMLOG Interaction Scoring, but also of retrospective Ratings made by group members or observers. Ratings can be made only on the basis of some period of experience or observation, the separate events of which are aggregated in some intuitive way, with a certain amount of distortion, when the person makes the Rating.

Thus, any field pattern represented on a Field Diagram is a selection and an abstraction from behavior that has already occurred. The behavior may not continue. In fact, if we believe, more or less, the theory that has been briefly foreshadowed above, we will realize that any actual field pattern we see portrayed on a Field Diagram has in the literal sense collapsed long since. Whether it will recur is never certain. Experience shows, however, that there is a considerable stability in the way members view themselves and each other, and there is thus a kind of average or chronic pattern that helps to understand the past, and to some extent to anticipate the future. Transient patterns related to transient images occur as modifications or departures from a chronic pattern which tends to reassert itself.

One does not know, when one stops aggregating observations at some point and makes a Field Diagram, whether any pattern one may see is unusual or very characteristic. To a certain extent we deal with this problem just by waiting long enough so that we have what seems like a lot of information and feel that we are now getting repetitious information. We wait until things have "settled down," in other words. The problem with this solution is that, if we wait too long, the exercise of making and studying a Field Diagram comes too late to do any good.

On the other hand, the theory also leads one to believe that, once a field pattern forms in a particular meeting and starts to become preemptive, a certain short-time predictability also sets in. Once the circular reinforcement and amplification set in, a field pattern tends to develop in ways we can anticipate to some extent until the given pattern is overcome by another pattern. Hence a knowledge of certain kinds of characteristic patterns can be put to use in the midst of the process in real time, if one can read sufficiently well the premonitory signs and has a knowledge of the chronic patterns of the group. Some of the characteristics, perhaps most of them, have already come into being and are the signs by which we recognize the pattern. Some of the others, which theoretically would fit with the pattern and are believed to be probable, have not yet appeared and may still be developing. A good leader, teacher, or therapist can think faster than the polarization or unification of the social interaction field develops, sometimes, and can intervene effectively.

It is in the hope of catching and better understanding some of these developments in a social interaction field that one wishes to build up the necessary background of analysis of the particular group in which one works or participates. A pattern of unification or polarization in any group under given circumstances will have certain strong tendencies, which may be hard to counter head on. On the other hand, some of the conditions helping to give rise to the pattern may be very susceptible to change with a little additional effort. Small changes, if strategically introduced, may sometimes make critically large differences in the outcome. Hence it is of value to the practical participant or group leader to be able to make a careful assessment of the chronic pattern of the group and to have a good sense of what may be changed, and what may not, when a transient pattern of polarization or unification sets in.

Chapter 5

Analyzing a Field for Polarization–Unification

Figure 7 shows the Field Diagram of RFB's Ratings, as shown earlier in Figure 6, but now with an added inscription to represent an analysis of the location and direction of polarization of the chronic field one would infer to exist in the group, on the basis of the pattern of distribution of image points.

For practical purposes one hopes that his own Diagram represents tolerably well the group Average Field Diagram, since the group members may not actually be rating, and one wants to make the best analysis he can using his own ratings *as if* they were representative. In the present case we do have the members' ratings of each other and can check immediately to see how the two diagrams compare. The Group Average Field for our group with the polarization–unification inscription is shown as Figure 8. In due time we shall pursue the comparison of the two diagrams in detail. First, however, it is necessary to explain the inscriptions on the diagrams.

The inscriptions represent the application of the general theory of individual and social interaction fields to each of the diagrams. The location of the inscription is found by the application of what is called the *Polarization–Unification Overlay* (see Appendix P).

The Overlay is a transparent plastic sheet on which is laid out the particular geometric configuration shown, which represents certain features of the general theory. The transparent Overlay can be moved around over the Field Diagram in search of the best fit between the lines and areas on the Overlay and the particular pattern of images found on the Field Diagram. When the desired fit is found, the configuration of lines and areas of the Overlay is inscribed upon the Field Diagram, as shown in Figure 7 and, as separately determined, in Figure 8. The method of fitting the Overlay to an Individual Field Diagram is described in Appendix Q, and for a Group Average Field Diagram in Appendix R.

The details of the Overlay are given in Appendix P, "How to Construct the Polarization–Unification Overlay." The names of the lines and areas, which represent various aspects of the theory, are as follows.

The *Line of Polarization* (the solid line tipped with arrowheads at either end) passes across the Field Diagram in a given direction, located by a procedure to be

FIGURE 7   RFB's Field Diagram, with Overlay Inscription (Expansion
Multiplier = 1.199)

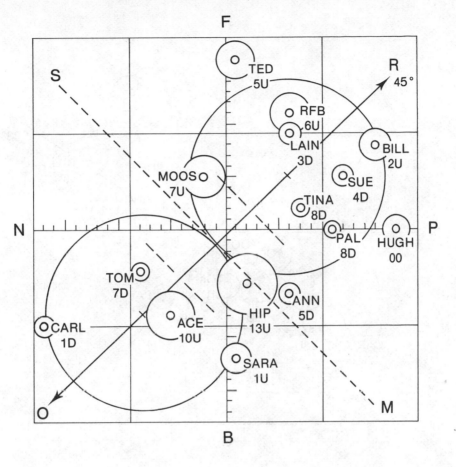

described later. One end of the Line of Polarization is marked with an "R,"
which stands for *Reference Direction.* The other end of the Line of Polarization is marked with an "O," which stands for *Opposite Direction.*

A dashed line called the *Line of Balance* intersects the Line of Polarization at
the mid-point at an angle of exactly 90 degrees, and so passes across the Overlay
at right angles to the Line of Polarization. One end of the Line of Balance is
marked with an "M," which stands for *Mediator Direction.* The other end is
marked with an "S," which stands for *Scapegoat Direction.* These terms
have reference to the possible social-psychological significance to the rater of
any image found far out in one direction or the other.

There are two large circles on the Overlay, one on either side of the Line of
Balance, each centered on the Line of Polarization. These represent the two polar
fields of the polarization. The circle nearest the "R" is called the *Reference
Circle.* The one nearest the "O" is called the *Opposite Circle.*

The total area of the Field Diagram left outside the two circles, when the

FIGURE 8 Group Average Field Diagram, with Overlay Inscription (Expansion Multiplier = 1.843)

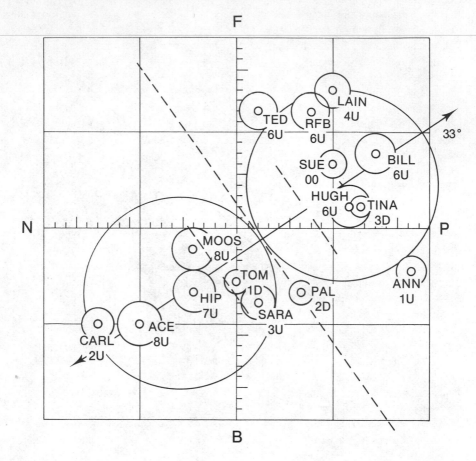

Overlay is placed in any given position on the Field Diagram, is called the *Residual Area*. That area, however, is divided by the Line of Balance into two areas, one called the *Residual Area on the Reference Side,* and the other called the *Residual Area on the Opposite Side*.

An area running along the Line of Balance on both sides of it is represented on the Overlay by two short dashed lines, one on either side of the Line of Balance and parallel to it. Each line is placed just halfway between the Line of Balance and the center of the Reference or Opposite Circle. The area on either side of the Line of Balance extending to the dashed line is called a *Swing Area*. One is called the *Swing Area on the Reference Side,* the other the *Swing Area on the Opposite Side*. Both sides together are called the *Swing Area*.

In the general theory, the swing area represents a set of locations between the two opposite poles, within which it may be difficult or impossible to determine whether the image is clearly identified by the rater with one pole or the other. When the image represents an individual, one heuristic hypothesis is that the rater thinks the individual may be in some conflict as to which side to take in the polarization or perhaps is forced to a middle position by rejection of both poles. Or the rater may see the person as "undecided" but amenable to persuasion either way, in which case the person is seen as exercising something like a "swing vote" in a political polarization. Hence the term "Swing Area."

In Figure 7 it will be seen that the images are not all within the Polarization–Unification pattern. TED, HUGH, and ANN are isolated in the Residual Area, and several other images overhang the two Overlay Circles. Since RFB was the rater, and his EXPECTED self-image location is within the PF circle, that one is taken as his Reference Circle and is labeled with an "R." ACE is shown quite near the center of RFB's Opposite Circle. The outer circle of HIP's image has a large "overhang" in the Residual Area, and he also overlaps both Overlay Circles. HIP is in the Swing Area on the Opposite Side, and MOOSE (designated MOOS on diagrams, in deference to a four-letter limit) is in the Swing Area on the Reference Side. ANN is very near the Line of Balance. HUGH is in the Residual Area. He is far over on the Reference Side but seems isolated, not within the Reference Circle, as seen by RFB, the rater. (It was my intuitive perception during the course of the group that HUGH was in the Swing Area and that he functioned as a Mediator. In retrospect, it is also clear that my intuitive concept of Mediation was associated with the direction P, as well as with nearness to the Line of Balance. It is not clear just why, in my actual rating, HUGH did not end up where I had more intuitively placed him.)

As we see, then, for any placement of the Overlay on the Field Diagram, the images portrayed on the Field Diagram may be assigned to a given *topological area* (a general name for the areas described above). The topological areas *of the Overlay* represent certain general theoretical concepts as to the properties of polarized fields. The topological areas as located *on the Field Diagram* by the placement of the Overlay represent the heuristic hypotheses as to how the general theory applies to this particular group. Finally, then, the location of an individual, both in relation to the dimensions P–N and F–B on the Diagram and in relation to the topological areas determined by the placement of the Overlay, suggests the kind of social psychological "role" the individual may play in the group.

In Figure 7, where we are dealing with a diagram constructed from the perceptions of a single rater, we should properly say that the locations of the images of group members in the various respects just mentioned suggest the kinds of roles the *rater* sees those group members as playing. The way the particular rater sees the group members is influenced by their overt behavior and the content of what they may have said, but the rater always perceives according to his or her own particular perceptual-evaluative framework. An "unbiased" perception would simply be one that accurately *represents* the average perception-evaluation of some large population of raters. Such a population, however, may in turn be "biased" in relation to some still larger population. The "unbiased perception," then, is simply one with the "average bias" of whatever is taken as the reference population.

There is a similar relativity with regard to the naming of the directions as indicated by the placement of the Overlay. What is the "Reference Direction" for me (and by implication the direction of my preferred movement) may well be the "Opposite Direction" for ACE. If one can speak of the Reference Direction for *the group* (something like a "group goal"), one can do it only by an arbitrary decision to take, as the criterion, the *average* Reference Directions of all individuals, or of the most dominant ones, or of the subgroup containing the most individuals. Whichever decision one may make, if there is an individual or subgroup in the opposite circle, one ignores the fact that the direction of what one has arbitrarily called the "group goal" is the direction opposite to that in which members of the opposite subgroup would like to move. It is a very common mistake in theorizing about groups to suppose that, without actually testing the consensus in a given group, one can speak unambiguously about "*the* group goal," "*the* leader of the group," "*the* norms of the group," and so on. This is the mistake of so-called consensus-oriented sociology, as criticized by the so-called conflict-oriented sociologists (see Dahrendorf, 1959).

The opposed directions of the arrowheads at either end of the Line of Polarization represent a theoretically assumed general tendency on the part of raters to separate images into two groups, one of which is associated with the self-image, the other tending to be dissociated from the self-image. It is quite true that some persons seem to try to include all members of the interacting group within their Reference Circle, along with their self-image, and so may be said to have a "unifying tendency" in their perception. But the general assumption of the present theory is that in such a case there is an opposite area in the perceptual-evaluative field of the individual, within which some important images of persons or things *outside* of the present interacting group fall, perhaps generally held in the "background" of perception, but ready on appropriate occasions to assume the position of "figure" and focus of attention. These images may presumably be suppressed or repressed images of feared or rejected persons or influences from earlier experience.

When other members of the interacting group talk of images that are similar enough to the repressed images of feared or rejected persons or influences from the past, or when some group member acts in a way that suggests the past images, the reference person harboring the repressed images may "transfer" them to the present image or person, and so actively "polarize" his or her previously "unified" field. This is the hypothesis of "transference" in psychoanalytic theory (Freud, 1933; Fairbairn, 1954; Foulkes and Anthony, 1957). Transference of positive feelings from past loved persons or influences is also likely, given the right conditions. It is appropriate to speak of both "positive" and "negative" transference.

The ubiquitous tendency of individuals to polarize image fields in their minds is rooted, one may suppose, in the fundamental nature of "evaluation," which is present to some degree in all perception (see Pettigrew, 1967). To evaluate is to place a value on an image in relation to other images. When large numbers of images are evaluated in the course of development of the individual, it is likely not only that some will be considered better than others but also that some will be considered actively bad. The dimensions of the SYMLOG space are simply what seem to be the main dimensions along which people most frequently tend to polarize images of persons, what they do, and what they say (see Bales, 1970).

The SYMLOG dimensions are dimensions of "evaluation"; they tend to be bipolar, hence it is appropriate to say that they are dimensions of probable "polarization."

The general-purpose Polarization–Unification Overlay illustrates and embodies the assumptions that, in an individual perceptual evaluative field, so far as the total potential field of images is concerned, polarization is likely and unification is typically a matter of unification of images at one pole or the other, or both. Thus, polarization of the *total* field (figure and ground) into two clusters of images and unification of images within each polar cluster is the most general expected pattern. The two polar circles of the Overlay represent this assumption. An opposite polar cluster of images may appear to be missing in the "figure" of the gestalt prominent in the mind of an individual for a given time, but images clustered around the opposite pole are assumed to be held in the "background."

In the Overlay, representing the general theory, the Reference Circle represents the presumed tendency of the individual to cluster images around the self-image or to move the self-image toward association with some subgroup of images as relatively accepted or acceptable. The Opposite Circle represents the presumed tendency to cluster images around other images dissociated from the self-image as relatively unacceptable, or rejected. In the Overlay the two circles are the same size. The size of the circles is chosen, more or less as a guess, to be just the maximum size that will fit within one quadrant of the Field Diagram. The idea is that, from the point of view of the perceiving and evaluating rater, two images, for example, located within the same quadrant of the space will be at the same end of each of the two dimensions, P–N and F–B, and hence the rater will not tend to polarize them with relation to each other but rather will tend to cluster them within the same subgroup, particularly when they are opposed by another cluster of rejected images. The center point of each circle is located at a distance half as far out from the center of the diagram as the measurement procedure allows. This is also an arbitrary guess, but seems good enough for the present. Any *fixed* center point (which really means any fixed design on the Overlay) will work only in a rough average way at best.

The idea of a circular periphery around the center of a cluster, beyond which a given image will tend not to be assimilated to the cluster, seems consistent with several basic concepts. One is that from any point, representing an image to which a person may be attracted, the strength of attraction is likely to fall off with increasing distance in any direction, somewhat in the manner of mutual gravitational attraction. Or, to state the same idea from the viewpoint of the rater within his or her own cluster of Reference images: As any given image departs farther and farther from the center of the cluster, the feeling of similarity of that image to others in the cluster would be expected to fall off and eventually turn to a perception of opposition and perhaps rejection.

Another basic concept consistent with the idea of a circular periphery, or at least a gradual falling off in the probability that a given image will be assimilated to a cluster, according to increasing distance, is the concept of increasing "cost." When a person as rater subjectively "moves" an image in order to make it fit within a cluster, this movement must involve some kind of "psychological work" or "cost." If so, the cost involved is likely to increase as the distance between the images increases, so that at some point a slowly increasing benefit curve will be overtaken and crossed by a more rapidly increasing cost curve. At this point the reader will note the entry of economic concepts, which I take to be an integral part of the general theory.

Another general idea relevant to the *size* of the reference circle, if not to the idea of a circular periphery, is that important properties of the location of an image are its direction and degree of departure from the center of the Diagram, which find their formal representation as a "vector." The graphic representation is a line drawn outward from the center of the Diagram to the location of the point, perhaps with an arrow at the end to indicate the direction in which the vectoral force is operating. In this conceptualization, the relationship between two points can be expressed in terms of the *angle* separating the two vectors. If the vectors are thought of as two directed forces that interact with each other (in the mind of the individual), vector theory, as well as intuition, tells us that the two forces will add together and so reinforce each other to some degree when the directions of the vectors fall within an angle of 90 degrees; but beyond 90 degrees, the forces will begin to oppose and cancel each other. If the angles are thought of as expressing correlations of direction, then within an angle of 90 degrees the correlation between the two directions will be positive; at exactly 90 degrees, the correlation will be zero; and at an angle of more than 90 degrees, the correlation will be negative. (See Appendix D for a discussion of the ideal angles of the vectors in the SYMLOG space.)

For the size of the reference and opposite circles chosen and represented on the Overlay, points within a given circle will lie within an angle of 90 degrees as long as the center of the circle is at least halfway out in one of the directions. For many fields, then, the images within a given circle may be thought of as "pulling more or less in the same direction from the neutral point" and thus "adding their forces," as being "somewhat similar in their behavior," and as being "correlated with each other" in the mind of the rater.

While none of these general ideas is conclusive, they tend to suggest that the size of the circles chosen and the idea of a circular periphery may not be a bad general approximation. One may add, however, that this conception suggests that a point directly on the line of polarization but at the extreme may fall outside the circle, being, as it were, "in the right direction but too far out." This may not seem too convincing intuitively, although it does suggest the commonsense idea that sometimes a leader may get "too far ahead" of his followers.

The foregoing arguments have been made with reference to the perceptual evaluative field of the individual rater. When we contemplate a total social interaction field, we have to think about the perceptual fields of each of the individuals involved as they affect each other. We have to think about the probability that some particular individuals may communicate their attitudes more readily than others, that they will communicate particular images rather than possible others, and that the proportion of all the images active in individual perceptual fields that are actually communicated may be very small. Social interaction fields may not be very well predicted by simply adding together the contents of all individual perceptual evaluative fields, even if we had the information, since what gets into the overt behavior and communication is a small subset of the contents of all the individual fields, highly selected, and then elaborated in the social process in new ways.

In addition, when we are considering the total social interaction field rather than an individual perceptual field, we have to think about the probability that pairs or larger subsets of individuals will form alliances within a cluster, vis-à-vis other subsets of individuals or vis-à-vis images of third objects on other levels (images from the situation, from fantasy, and so on) (see Gamson, 1964; Bowen, 1971; Minuchin, 1974). We have to think about the probability that when individuals work together in an alliance they may develop more mutuality of perception, and they may come to perceive greater similarity among the individuals in a given cluster (see Deutsch, 1949; Campbell, 1958). Subsets of individuals may experience reward in working together, increasing, perhaps, the liking of persons within the subgroup for each other and increasing their dislike of persons in the other subgroup. We have to consider also that "everything has its limits" (see Sorokin, 1957), that runaway feedbacks may not continue to amplify forever, that new unifications and polarizations are constantly forming in the perceptual evaluative fields of individuals, and that one of these individual patterns may reach sufficient strength to break through into the overt social interaction field at any time.

Our ability to trace out the circular reactions, amplifications, limits of amplification in a given direction, tendencies toward reversal of direction, and so on, in social interaction fields, is quite limited so far. The present general theory (represented by the Overlay, for example) does not yet go far in taking these complications into account, although it provides a definite place for their recognition and formulation, since it clearly distinguishes the individual perceptual evaluative field from the social interaction field and yet allows for the description of the two in comparable terms.

The present general theory, so far as it is represented by the Polarization–Unification Overlay applied to the Group Average Field Diagram, hypothesizes that the operation of all the many factors I have just mentioned tends, on the average, toward the formation of subgroups of individuals in a long-continuing social interaction field, and that the polarization of those subgroups on many issues tends to build up or amplify, up to some point, and then to hold in a more or less chronic pattern with various transient departures. The conditions under which these assumptions may or may not be justified are not at present completely clear, and I shall make no attempt to specify at this point even those things that might be said.

In spite of many reservations, then, we use the same Polarization–Unification Overlay for the examination of both the perceptual evaluative fields of single individuals and the group average field, which represents more nearly the total social interaction field. We use the basic concepts of polarization and unification for thinking about both individual perceptual fields of images and social interaction fields, although we emphasize that the social interaction field is, theoretically, vastly more inclusive and complicated. The Polarization–Unification Overlay, used with either type of field, should be recognized as a *conventional device,* only symbolic of our hoped-for general theory, rather than a strict implementation of a clear existing theory. Perhaps we should say that it is an "icon"—a kind of conventional picture of the thing desired. It is not really the exact computer it might appear to be. But perhaps it can be improved, and perhaps for many purposes it is an improvement over what we can do without it. At least it seems to give the cognitive leverage to consider some problems that are almost too complicated to think through intuitively, and I believe it helps practically in considering the characteristics of individuals and groups.

A different placement of the Overlay on the Group Average Field Diagram, given the same constellation of image points, represents a different hypothesis as to the way average tendencies are operating in the social interaction field. One adjusts the Overlay this way and that as a convenient way of intuitively searching for the placement that seems to fit best the existing constellation—that is, for the hypothesis as to what kind of dynamic field of interacting forces, if it did actually exist, through the interaction of all its parts, would best account for the existing location of the points. If there is a good hypothesis, it yields predictions as to which existing locations of images may tend to be stable, which may tend to change, and in what direction, given time and opportunity. A good hypothesis helps to visualize special strains that may exist for given persons at given points in the social interaction field. A good conception of the chronic polarization of the group, for example, may help to anticipate the way in which the injection of new images, through new members, new tasks, or simply new conversational content, may change the dynamic structure of the field and hence the character of the group.

The procedure of searching for the best fit of the Overlay on the Field Diagram is described in detail in two Appendixes—Q, "How to Use the Overlay with the Individual's Field Diagram" and R, "How to Use the Overlay with a Group Average Field Diagram." In general, the basic procedure is the same, but the interpretation for the two types of fields differs. When the best fit is found, the field may be classified into one of several general types of pattern. Three general types may be distinguished: (1) *Unified Fields,* in which all of the images shown cluster in one circle; (2) *Polarized Fields,* in which all or most of the images shown appear to fall into two polarized circles, with the possible exception of several in the Residual Area; and (3) *No Clear Field Pattern,* in which the images shown appear to fall either into two alternative polarizations or into no clear pattern. Figure 8 shows the location of the Overlay on the Group Average Field Diagram of our illustrative group. This is a Polarized Field, with one image, that of PAL, clearly outside the polarization, and three others, ANN, TED, and LAIN, mostly in the Residual Area.

If there are images outside the polarization, they may be scattered here and there in the Residual Area, not sufficiently close to the Line of Balance to suggest that the persons they represent may play roles as Mediator or Scapegoat; on the other hand, one or more images may be sufficiently close to the Line of Balance to suggest that the persons they represent may play, or could potentially play, one of these two roles. In Figure 8 PAL is very close to the Line of Balance, but she is not far out on the line. ANN is far out on the Positive Side of the Residual Area but is not close to the Line of Balance. If ANN were close enough to be in one Swing Area or the other, alongside the Line of Balance, then we might have a higher expectation that she might function as a Mediator. The placement of the

Overlay and the theory that goes with it raise these kinds of questions, which might not otherwise occur to one.

Once a formal fit of the Overlay to an Individual Field Diagram has been made, using the procedure described in Appendix Q, one proceeds to consider a series of more detailed heuristic hypotheses about the possible significance to the individual of the location of particular images in particular areas of the dynamic field. The Field Diagram of each member of our case study group is discussed in detail in Chapter 12. For the moment, one may mention briefly some of the interesting questions one may raise.

First, one may be interested in where the individual's EXPECTED self-image falls in the supposed dynamic pattern. In some Individual Fields, the rater seems to take the self-image as the central point of reference and apparently tends to range the other images in the Reference Circle around the EXPECTED self-image in such a way that the self-image is at the center of the circle. In other cases the self-image is not at the center of the circle and may be said to be "displaced." In my rating of the illustrative group, shown in Figure 7, the pattern may be described as a Polarized Field, with the self-image of the rater (RFB) displaced, and with scattered images in the Residual Area. Whether the self-image is centered (approximately) in the Reference Circle or is displaced may have some significance for the way the individual sees his or her position in the Reference subgroup. In some cases, the rater's EXPECTED image is outside of what appears to be the reference subgroup, and this raises questions as to the individual's possibly disappointed aspirations to belong.

Second, the WISHED FOR location of the self-image in relation to the dynamic pattern would seem to have important implications. Often the WISHED FOR location is in the same direction away from the zero point of the pattern as the EXPECTED image, only farther out, as one might well expect wishes to be. Sometimes, however, it is on or near the Line of Balance, approaching the Mediator or Scapegoat location, and occasionally it is even in the Opposite Circle, which raises important questions about the present state of conflict of the individual.

Third, in looking at the pattern of ratings an individual has made in relation to the placement of the Overlay, one immediately notices whether the total pattern (whatever it is) approaches a unified cluster or a bipolar pair of clusters. One wonders how much actual rejection the individual may feel in relation to persons whose images are in the Opposite Circle, and why they are placed there.

Not infrequently, one or more individuals may be placed in the Swing Area, close to the Line of Balance, and with regard to these one wonders whether they are viewed with ambivalence by the rater or whether perhaps the person rated has given a good reason for the rating by showing ambivalence in behavior and attitudes.

Fourth, since the two ends of the Line of Balance are marked with an M and an S, one notices the close approach of any image to this line, especially if the image is far out, and wonders whether the person so indicated does indeed play the role of Mediator or Scapegoat in the group, or whether he or she is earmarked by the rater for such a role, though the person may not yet have been singled out for actual performance of the role in the overt interaction of the group.

There are a considerable number of interesting questions raised when one views the constellation of images as rated by a given individual in relation to the general theory of polarization–unification, and additional questions and hypotheses when one compares the individual's ratings to the group average constellation. Some of the more general questions can be approached statistically by looking at the ratings of many individuals in many groups (see Appendix T). Others, more particular ones, lead into problems of the organization of the particular personality and can be approached only by study of the individual (see Chapter 12, particularly the case of TOM).

In the series of questions that occur as one analyzes a Diagram, one may sense the possibility that there may be an order of increasing complexity of organization of a perceptual field of images, from a kind of simple pattern of organization of the field to more and more complex forms, finally ending in one so complex that no order can readily be perceived. It may be that on the average (apart from particular personality characteristics of the rater) it is simpler or more satisfying for the rater to take the self as the central point of reference and to range all other images around that point than to accept a displacement of the self-image away from the center of the rated universe. Whether or not the self-image is displaced, it may be simpler for the rater to perceive or accept a unified pattern than a polarized pattern. If a polarization must be accepted, it may be easier to perceive or accept a completely polarized pattern than one in which some images fall outside the polarization. If some images must fall outside, it may be easier to perceive or accept a polarized pattern with one or more active agents in the orthogonal directions (a mediator or scapegoat) than a pattern in which images outside the major polarization are simply scattered around with no apparent relation to the polarization. And finally, it may be easier to perceive or accept a doubly polarized pattern, with the possibility of fluctuation back and forth from one polarized pattern to another, than it is to perceive and accept a random scattering of images with no clear pattern at all. (The diagram of TOM, Figure 28, p. 143 illustrates a doubly polarized pattern.) As one searches for the reasons why an individual organizes an image field in a certain way, one goes through a kind of hypothetical simulation of the psychological processes that a group member is imagined to go through as he tries to form a picture of the group and his relationships to other members.

We assume that the processes leading to the formation of a pattern of polarization or unification of the *inclusive social interaction field* are somewhat similar to the subjective processes individuals go through, and that they in fact include the subjective processes of each. But the processes of social interaction also involve some kind of negotiation or adjustment back and forth between individuals, as each attempts to persuade or influence the others to organize the field as he or she does subjectively. An individual will say in effect, "I see such and such a thing [an image] as Negative, don't you?" And the person addressed may answer something like, "Yes, but it also seems to me not to be very Dominant, so maybe we can ignore it for a while." The first may reply, "I don't think we can ignore it. It also seems to be making some kind of threatening gestures which indicate that it is emotionally working itself up to something." The other may say, "Yes, I see what you mean. I don't like it." And so on.

When we simply *average* the locations of an image that is actually seen in different locations by each group member, we are making the assumption that the simple arithmetical process of averaging is an acceptable representation of what the outcome of overt negotiation of the kind just illustrated will be. We know from experience that sometimes it will and sometimes not. It probably depends on many things, such as the relative dominance of the members, and it seems a good guess that a model for combining the fields of individuals that differentially weights the ratings of members according to their degree of dominance may be better than one that simply averages the ratings of everybody as if they exercised equal influence. But to decide whether a more complex model would be better is a refined job of model building for the future. As a first approximation, simple averaging is adopted as the model.

The averaging of locations which is used to arrive at the Group Average Field, then, is a kind of crude imitation of *some* of the effects of actual overt social interaction, given the variety of individual perceptual fields of members. But the application of the Overlay helps the researcher-theorist to carry the process of speculation a few steps farther.

If one finds a group average pattern like that of Figure 8, for example, consisting of a constellation of images that looks like two subgroups and two or three images in the residual area, questions such as the following begin to come to mind: Are the persons represented as two clusters of images, which suggest two opposed subgroups, actually operating as subgroups? If the two subgroups actually operate overtly as such, do they actually often oppose each other, and are they likely to continue to do so? Does the pattern we see represent a stable state, or are the locations of persons in each others' eyes still changing, moving perhaps toward a more extreme polarization of the two subgroups and a more extreme clustering of the persons within each subgroup? Or are there limits to the degree of exaggeration of this pattern, so that it is likely to collapse, reverse, or form in some other way? And what about the persons in the Residual Area? In the present case, does either PAL or ANN actually function as a mediator, or could one or the other or both do so if the possibility were pointed out to them? Does TED actually function as a scapegoat, or narrowly escape doing so? And so on.

The general theory does not go far enough to answer these questions for a particular group or even, as yet, for groups on the average. But it does help one to formulate such questions. And since the questions are asked about particular persons and particular relationships, one gets ideas as to what additional information from particular persons might lead to a better understanding, or how one might tentatively try to interpret the positions of various members to them either within or outside regular sessions and perhaps suggest that they try to bring about certain changes that appear to be possible and desirable.

If group members who have rated each other receive back from the researcher a summary diagram like that of Figure 8, will they recognize it as representing fairly well the preponderant tendencies operating in their relationships? Will they "see the handwriting on the wall," as it were, or see it more clearly than they have previously, and begin to act either to reinforce it or to change it? Will the members of a subgroup such as the one in the PF quarter of the field in Figure 8, for example, begin to make their behavior and attitudes toward important images still more similar, with the result that the images on the Diagram representing them will cluster even more closely together? Will they more clearly recognize one of the members as a leader of the subgroup or some combination of two or three working cooperatively as leaders in the PF direction? Will members of the subgroup more generally begin to see how they can cooperate more closely to realize their similar objectives? These things, or some of them, may or may not happen, depending on many conditions that are not taken into account. But at least the appearance of a cluster on a Diagram, or a near-cluster, may raise a series of more pointed questions about the actual degree of explicit subgroup formation—whether the clustering represents a stable state, whether the cluster is still in the process of forming, whether it has proceeded about to its natural limit and is on the verge of "reversing" in some way that will make some other polarization likely, and so on.

We have theoretical reasons to suppose, and also experience suggests, that for many, if not most, subgroups there is a limit to the trend of movement toward greater closeness, at which the ambivalence of some members toward each other reaches a critical point and their negative reactions toward each other reach a critical point. At that point the negative reactions of some members to each other will begin to outweigh the positive. The negative reactions of these members toward each other may then come into a mutually aggravating and amplifying phase, thus tending to disperse the cluster and setting the stage for a polarization between formerly united members. There is some reason to expect, perhaps, that a polarization more or less at right angles to the former direction of unification is the most likely, on the average, but it would interrupt us too much to try to explain, for the moment, why this seems most likely. Let us illustrate instead.

In our illustrative group, I think it is true that the members of the subgroup of which I was a part (within the PF Circle in Figure 8), generally worked together in a very cooperative way for group analysis and were indeed often opposed to, or opposed by, members in the NB Circle. LAIN, who was seen as very close to me, RFB, on the Diagram, apparently identified with me through most of the course, but toward the end apparently experienced a reversal in her attitude toward me when she recognized that members of the opposite subgroup were attributing too much task concern to her and not enough friendliness. At the time of the ratings she placed me, and TED also, outside her reference circle and over the line into the Negative side of the space (see Figure 23, p. 127). At the same time she placed herself farther over on the Positive side of the space and not as far Forward, that is, less far in the direction of behavior that seems highly instrumentally controlled or task-oriented. She polarized what I think was formerly a unified relationship.

As another example of polarization within a cluster that appears only partly unified, we may mention the relationship between TED, near the NF periphery of the PF subgroup circle (Figure 8), and two of the women members, SUE and TINA, close to the center of the subgroup circle. This relationship appeared to be cyclical and unstable. TED wanted very much to gain the approval of these two women, partly just because they were women, as he indicated, and he more or less explicitly asked for their support in the group sessions. But their attitudes toward him appeared to be ambivalent and perhaps to fluctuate. They gave him some mild overt support in the group sessions, but in their ratings toward the end of the group both of them placed him on the negative side of the space, in their opposite circle, not in the same reference group with themselves (see Figures 27 and 30, pp. 139 and 155).

The placement of the Overlay on the Group Average Field Diagram (Figure 8), indicates a polarized relationship between the subgroup in the PF quarter and the subgroup in the NB quarter. Intuitively, to me, there seemed to be two subgroups also (see my Diagram in Figure 7), although the polarization in my Diagram is not so marked, nor is the clustering within each subgroup quite so close, as on the Group Average Diagram. I would say, also, that my intuitive division of the group into two subgroups during its sessions was not so clear as it turns out to be in my Diagram made after the group ended. And the Group Average Field Diagram (Figure 8) shows the clustering around the two poles as more marked or exaggerated than does mine. One *might* infer from it that both subgroups were internally fairly well organized and stable. We have just seen that this is not quite the case, for the PF subgroup. And the NB subgroup seems, upon close scrutiny, to be even more shaky and subject to internal polarizations.

All or nearly all of the relationships between the members of the NB subgroup seemed very ambivalent and likely to switch suddenly into conflict. CARL and ACE usually stuck together, for example, in their attacks on TED and LAIN, but their relationship with each other seemed forced, full of hostile joking, and volatile. On one occasion CARL jokingly grabbed ACE by the neck in a gesture meant to tell him to quiet down on a particular issue, but ACE mistook the gesture for a more serious attack and reacted with a panic-stricken defense. HIP and MOOSE periodically broke out into quarrels. SARA, a black woman some-what older than HIP, a black male, identified with him as a member of a minority group and as a friend outside the self-analytic group and took a proprietary interest in him, but she "gave him the business" on various occasions for making himself (and her) too conspicuous. TOM, who appears on the Group Average Diagram (Figure 8) to be a marginal member of the NB subgroup, was, by his own definition, really very ambivalent about nearly everybody in the group, as well as in his family situation and life outside the group (see TOM's case, pp. 142–149). If he "cooperated" with other members in the NB sub-group, it was only in the passive sense of dragging his heels in relation to efforts of the PF subgroup.

In the NB subgroup, then, as well as in the PF subgroup, there were internal strains in the relations of subgroup members to each other, which led to periodic outbreaks of negative feeling. Both groups were subject to internal polarization, in spite of appearing on the Diagram to be unified. Intuitively it seemed to me, however, that the internal solidarity of the NB subgroup was much more precari-ous than that of the PF subgroup. It seems likely to me that individuals shown in some kind of cluster on the Negative side of any given Group Average Diagram are less likely to be Positive in their attitudes toward each other than are those on the Positive side. A subgroup on the Negative side is not necessarily the same kind of thing as a subgroup on the Positive side, and we probably need to take this into account in our expectations.

Now let us add two final inscriptions. The first is called the "Dominant

Triangle.'' It is made by connecting the center points of the images of the three most dominant members with a solid line, as shown in Figures 9 and 10. On my diagram, Figure 9, the most dominant members (indicated by the three largest image circles) are HIP, ACE, and MOOSE. These three image center points are connected by the inscription of solid lines, to make a triangle. The Group Average Diagram, Figure 10, shows the same three members as most dominant, though in somewhat different locations and not in the same rank order.

Empirically we know that there is a high correlation between how dominant a member is according to ratings received (how far upward he or she is in the U direction). and how much he or she talks, though the amount of talking is not the only determinant (see Bales, 1970). We also know, from empirical experience, that the persons who talk the most in face-to-face groups also typically get talked to the most, and, not unexpectedly, they talk with each other for the most part (see Bales et al., 1951). The two or three most dominant members may not think of themselves as a ''subgroup,'' since they may well be in polarized conflict with each other and may differ considerably in their location in the P–N, F–B plane of the field. In the particular sense of exercising brute influence, however, at the ACT level of overt interaction they may form a ''dominant subgroup'' through their closure of conversation opportunities to others. This may polarize the group in the Upward–Downward dimension.

Earlier we have seen that a ''subgroup'' on the Negative side of the space may not be the same kind of thing as a ''subgroup'' on the Positive side of the space. Now it becomes apparent that a ''subgroup'' in the Upward part of the space may be quite different from either of the other two types of ''subgroups.'' By now we may also expect that a ''subgroup'' in the Downward part of the space is likely to be still something else.

The Downward ''subgroup,'' if any, is not marked by any special inscription. Usually the most Downward members are scattered around in the P–N, F–B plane and do not view themselves as belonging to a ''subgroup.'' They hardly ever act in concert, in my experience, except perhaps in the sense that they stay silent in concert, but this is not very salient, and if they have a ''message'' for the dominant subgroup, it usually takes a long time for the message to penetrate the consciousness of the more dominant members. Visually on the Diagram, the most Downward members appear as points enclosed by the smallest image circles.

The inscription of the Dominant Triangle thus highlights the location of a possibly overactive dominant subgroup, defined by their high interaction with each other and the resulting factual closure of conversation opportunities to others (see Bales, 1956). The choice of the top *three* members is arbitrary. (It does not make sense, of course, if there are only two or three members in the group.) But the inclusion of three persons in the inscription allows for the possibility that one person may be representing one polar subgroup, another the opposite polar subgroup, and a third may be playing a major mediating or scapegoat role. This is plainly not the case in the present group.

If it were the case in fact that the three most dominant members were taking those three roles, the triangle would probably cover a fairly large area, and the

FIGURE 9 RFB's Field Diagram, with Dominant Triangle and Perimeter
(Expansion Multiplier = 1.199)

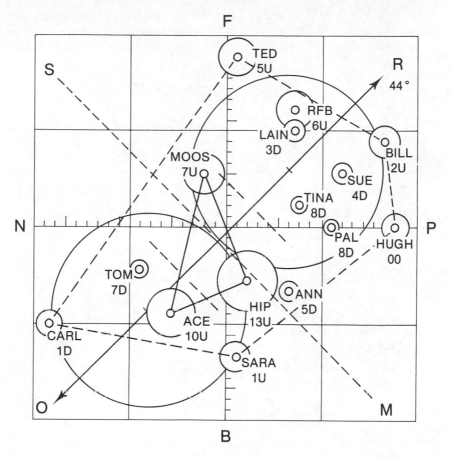

images of many other group members would fall within it. This large coverage, in turn, would tend to suggest a certain representativeness of the dominant subgroup, as the leaders of the other important subgroups, even though they were badly divided among themselves and took up a good deal of time. On the other hand, if the inscribed triangle covers only a small area, including no other members, the pattern would tend to suggest that the most dominant members are not in the same sense representing the positions of members in all parts of the space, and hence their domination would be likely to be felt as more onerous. ACE, HIP, and MOOSE in the present group are located fairly close to each other on both diagrams. The triangles in both diagrams are small, and in neither one do they enclose the location of any other member.

For practical purposes, one needs a rule of thumb as to what to do if there is a tie between number three and number four in rank. The rule suggested is to include as many as are tied with number three. The inscription may thus be a

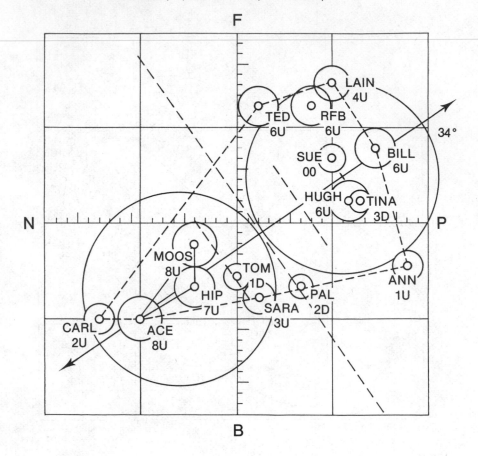

FIGURE 10   Group Average Field Diagram, with Dominant Triangle and Perimeter (Expansion Multiplier = 1.843)

four- or five-sided polygon, in which case it is probably better to drop the geometrical terminology and speak of the Dominant subgroup, the "four most dominant members," or the like.

The final inscription is called the *Perimeter*. It is a lightly dotted line which highlights the location of the members who are most distant from the center of the total constellation of image points. The Perimeter is the shortest set of lines that will include or enclose all point locations in the two-dimensional plane of the diagram. If one imagines the points as pegs standing up on a peg board (the plane of the Diagram), and imagines stretching a rubber band to enclose all pegs around the outside, the rubber band will then trace the Perimeter as it contracts against all outstanding pegs (see Figures 9 and 10).

The Perimeter is an irregular polygon which shows its main extensions in the directions of the members who are in the most extreme positions with regard to the dimensions P–N and F–B, regardless of their positions in the Upward–Downward dimension. The Perimeter is a useful inscription in that it may call attention to some moderate or low participators who are nevertheless salient because they are "far-out" in their given direction. In Figure 10, CARL, SARA, and ANN are examples. The Perimeter may also intersect, or fall close to, still other members who, although they may not be far out in an absolute sense from the center of the diagram, are nevertheless the farthest out in their given direction.

On Figure 10, for example, PAL falls close to the Perimeter in the Mediator direction located by the Overlay. There are no extreme exemplars of persons in this position on the Diagram. If there is some need on the part of some members to have an exemplar of a PB image in the group, then we would suppose that PAL might become salient in their perception, even though she is not far out in this direction in an absolute sense.

On the Group Average Diagram, Figure 10, it should be noted, I have omitted any distinction between a "Reference Direction" and an "Opposite Direction." (The ends of the line of polarization are not labeled R and O, as in Figure 9.) This reflects the fact that in the Group Average Diagram, as contrasted with the individual diagram, one has no predetermined point of reference, unless one takes it arbitrarily to be the same as one's own preference, the preference of the majority, or the like. Such a choice, if the group is polarized, will not command consensus. This, as I have mentioned above, is essentially the point the so-called conflict theorists in sociology have been trying to make vis-à-vis the consensus theorists. The consensus theorists tend to view society with assumed consensual norms or values of some kind as their theoretical point of reference. Whatever kind of behavior or value position does not conform to those assumed norms or values is thought of as "deviant." The conflict theorists, on the other hand, tend to view society as a constant power struggle between individuals and subgroups with different sorts of values, and the amount of genuine consensus underlying the working of the society is thought to be minor in significance for understanding what goes on. The conflict theorists emphasize differential power (more or less in the sense of dominance), rather than value consensus, as their point of reference.

The present theory, though it deals explicitly only with small groups, requires a resolution of this dilemma. The present theory treats the degree of consensus and the degree of conflict, as well as the importance of sheer power, as possibly different according to the particular group and social interaction field. The theory provides the means for describing most, if not all, of the major types of values and behavior one is likely to observe or imagine (see Appendix A), and it does not beg the question as to whether a given group or social interaction field will be primarily unified or primarily polarized.

Although the general tendency to polarize a field of images sufficiently different from each other is thought to be present in the perceptual and evaluative processes of all individuals, it is not maintained that the images at the opposite pole from the individual's preferred reference direction must be the images of other persons in the particular group studied. The tendency to unify images that are sufficiently similar is thought to be general (as well as the tendency to polarize images that are sufficiently different). The *Directions* of the system (U, D, P, N, F, B) give the means of defining what one means by "sufficiently similar'' and ''sufficiently different.'' (Images within a vector angle of 90 degrees from the origin are thought to be sufficiently similar, those separated by an angle of more than 90 degrees are thought to be sufficiently different.) Many kinds of configuration are possible within a given image field or social interaction field.

In the case of our illustrative group, both diagrams indicate that there tend to be two polarized subgroups but also indicate that not all members fall within one or the other of the two polarized groups. There are important differences as to who is shown outside the polarization, however. For example, RFB's diagram (Figure 9) shows HUGH to be outside the PF subgroup, though not far outside. However, he is the member most far out in the P direction, and he is also relatively salient, since he is on the Perimeter.

By way of contrast, the Group Average Diagram (Figure 10) shows HUGH to be a member of the PF subgroup and shows ANN (instead of HUGH) to be the most extreme member in the P direction. The Group Average Diagram shows PAL to be salient with regard to the Line of Balance, whereas RFB's diagram shows her to be a member, though close to the periphery, of the PF subgroup. ANN, in RFB's diagram, is near the line of balance and on the Positive side. Whether either of these members tended to act as Mediators, as one might wonder, will be discussed later.

Both diagrams show SARA and TED to be salient, being on the Perimeter, and on opposite sides of the space. Both diagrams show CARL and BILL to be salient because on the Perimeter, and opposite sides of the space. Both diagrams show the midpoint of the Dominant Triangle to be on the NB side of the Line of Balance, but the two diagrams are different in that RFB shows MOOSE as a member, though on the periphery, of the PF subgroup, while the Group Average Diagram shows him to be a member of the NB subgroup. This is an important difference. How did it come about?

It is likely that I was influenced by the fact that I perceived MOOSE's behavior as strongly F in his tendency to intellectualize, to follow out implications rationally, and so on. He often looked to me for approval of these tendencies, which for the most part I gave, but in a particular context outside the group. MOOSE often came to see me for the discussion of scoring problems after a period of observation (members of our illustrative group also acted as a team of observers of another similar group). These discussions were not very salient to the rest of the members of the group, probably, although they could have been observed. My ratings of MOOSE were probably different from those of other group members because I observed different behavior.

The discussion of the group, organized in terms of a series of heuristic hypotheses, will now be continued in the next six chapters. The discussion will be based on the Group Average Diagram. Chapter 12 will discuss some hypotheses about the significance of the different ways in which individual members may see the field. It will analyze the diagram of each member separately and will give a more concrete picture of each member as a particular person. It may be that some readers will prefer to continue by reading Chapter 12.

In the practical sense we are interested in the possibility of using the diagrams to crystallize the expectations of the researcher, and perhaps the members of the group, as to probable future events and to help the participants and/or the leader of the group to guide the future processes in a more desirable way. It has to be recognized, of course, that different individuals have different concepts of the desirable. If knowledge is sound, it may be used in different ways for different purposes. If the present concepts can help a UPF leader, they may also help a UNB leader. As one who identifies with the UPF type of leader, however, I tend to the optimistic view that better understanding of value positions and value conflicts, which can be obtained through group self-study, discussion, analysis, negotiation, mediation, and the like, may give a group the cognitive intellectual means of resolving value conflicts on a higher level of value judgment.

I think one need have little fear that knowledge of the weak points in the integration of a group will work to the ultimate disadvantage of the group, provided the knowledge is obtained as part of a voluntary group self-study. The heuristic hypotheses that follow in the next few chapters are designed to raise a series of questions as to what may be critical weak points in the group or strategic opportunities for change. Let us now take up the hypotheses one by one.

Chapter 6

Dominant Members May Clash Early in the Group

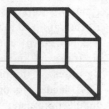

The heuristic hypothesis that dominant members may clash early in the group is meant to apply to the early part of the history of the group—within the first third of its total history—and it may apply even so early as the beginning of the first meeting. The conflict of dominant members with each other, if it exists in the group, is likely to be chronic. Many transient polarizations of the group are also likely to involve a clash of the dominant members or their early participation, even if the polarization is set off by less dominant members.

The earlier period of a group's history (if it is a group comparable to the self-analytic groups I know best) is often marked by struggles among the most dominant members, particularly if they are found at widely separated points in the space or in separate quadrants. MOOSE, ACE, and HIP are located by the inscription of the Dominant Triangle in our illustrative group (see Figure 10, p. 54). By the end of the first session, I had the impression that all three were extremely verbal, imaginative, intelligent, picturesque in their speech, impulsive, and fast in their reaction times. MOOSE (a mathematician) was more square in his habits of thought (farther F at the ACT level) than ACE and HIP, but he consciously aspired to be an outlaw type and made many value statements in favor of the UN and UNB directions. ACE and HIP were more dramatic and exhibitionistic than MOOSE. HIP chose his nickname for use in this group because he liked its connotations of super-awareness and higher status.

The interaction of MOOSE, HIP, and ACE was not a conflict in the P–N, F–B dimensions; indeed, they seemed to cooperate to keep things in an uproar a good deal of the time. There was a lot of joking conflict among them, but the more serious conflict was between the three of them on one side, representing a kind of anti-authoritarian outlaw coalition, and TED, on the far Forward Perimeter of the group. The Position of TED was UNF—dominant, disapproving, and authoritarian—early in the history of the group. As a result of the conflicts in which he found himself, not only vis-à-vis the NB subgroup but also vis-à-vis the P members of the group, he made a determined effort to moderate the amount of his participation, to become less disapproving, to behave in a more friendly manner, and to form alliances with members on the P side, particularly with the women, whose approval he sought. That he succeeded to some degree is seen by the fact that in the end-of-term rating (which is shown on our Group Average Diagram) he received a rating on the positive side, although still quite far forward.

Thus the most vocal conflict in the group was established early in the group's history and was moderated only with difficulty, and never completely, during the rest of the group's history. In the early period TED was, I would say, among the most dominant members, though he later held the lid on, except for periodic explosions. During the early period of the group's history, I had the impression that the line of polarization ran from the NF quadrant to the NB quadrant, along the negative side of the space. It later shifted to the PF versus NB directions, as it appears in our Diagrams, but there was a persistent tendency for it to shift back to the NF versus NB quadrants. In the individual field diagrams of HIP (Figure 19, p. 118) MOOSE (Figure 17, p. 111), and ACE (Figure 18, p. 114), it may be noted that they continued to place TED in the NF quadrant.

It is not the case in this particular group that the members located by the inscription of the Dominant Triangle clashed ideologically with each other, or at least they appeared to have a good time competing with each other. In many groups, however, I would expect the major ideological conflict within the group to be located by the Dominant Triangle, and often the triangle will be elongated and lie along the line of chronic polarization.

The conflict between dominant members is likely to appear early in the history of the group because the personality characteristics that make for a high rating on dominance are likely to include fast reaction times, verbal facility, impulsiveness, and hence the tendency to preempt the time of the group. People who talk easily also tend to talk a lot and tend to start talking without waiting for others to pause and let them in. Less dominant people who wait for a pause or a logical place to come in tend to lose out in the competition for talking time, if the competition is severe.

The imagery that many dominant and talkative persons present in their content is likely to be in favor of dominant behavior, the pursuit of power, the joy of action, and so on. Both in their behavior and in the content of their presented imagery, they tend to constitute a competitive challenge to each other, and an early clash or fireworks display of some kind is likely. By the same line of theorizing one would be led to expect that early meetings may give a relatively good prediction of the long-term order of dominance of persons in the group. Very broadly speaking, I would say that this is true in my experience.

It is not necessary that two highly dominant members be far apart in the P–N or F–B dimensions in order to clash. If both are high in the U direction, that may be enough to arouse the competitive struggle between them. Thus it sometimes happens, as in this case, that the early struggles between the most dominant members may as easily occur within a given quadrant as across quadrants. The interpretation is often made by other group members that a "struggle for leadership" is going on, but I have gained the impression from many such experiences that "leadership" of the rest of the group is often not a conscious motive of the persons involved in a struggle for dominance. Their preoccupation with each other is often more direct and personal—impulsive and competitive. They give little thought to the problems of "leading" other persons in the group, persuading or representing the majority of members, or the like.

As a rule, it is quite difficult to moderate the tendencies of very dominant members to overtalk. There is often not much choice but for the rest of the group to combine in complaint and slowly to work out norms of greater restraint on the part of more dominant members. It takes some time for enough other members to recognize what is going on and to combine, in spite of their other differences, to bring pressure to bear on the more dominant members. It is all the more difficult when those who would prefer a more equal gradient of participation have to increase their participation above their preferred level in order to compete with the more dominant persons. It is often true also that, in spite of some felt dissatisfaction, the more submissive members in fact help to create, by their lack of efforts to participate, the vacuum so willingly filled by the more dominant members.

Is it not the responsibility of the designated leader to take a more active role in such a case and try to prevent domination of the rest of the group by a Dominant member or subgroup, if it occurs? It is my inclination to do so, but in the self-analytic group I usually try to delay direct intervention for a period during which I work by trying to make it clear what is happening, in the hope that other members, spread more widely through the group, will become sufficiently aware of the problem to take the initiative in dealing with it. This delay is part of the educational intention of the Group Psychology course to help people become aware of what is going on, to help them verbalize their understanding of it, and to leave the initiative open for them to do something about it themselves, instead of depending upon the person in authority to do it. This indirect approach tends to be more successful in activating the next most dominant persons down the rank order than persons farther on down, and in fact may never activate the most submissive. There is no advantage in prolonging the delay past the point where one sees fairly clearly that the indirect approach is not going to activate the persons next lower down. The approach needs to change according to the personalities of group members and the time in the group's history.

It is a serious challenge to the designated leader of a group if there is a dominant subgroup with aims and values considerably different from his or her own. Faced with this challenge in a group other than a self-analytic group I might do things differently. I might try to compose the group by selecting members in the first place so as to have a more moderate gradient of participation, if I had an opportunity to do so. If I had to include a strongly dominant member with values counter to my own, I would try to include one or two other quite dominant members who had values consistent with my own, so I might have some help. And I would try to avoid giving too much help to a dominant member with goals different from my own by not including too many other persons who would support him or her.

If I were confronted by seriously dominant opposition in a group already formed, I might increase my own dominance and simply compete by reacting more quickly, by trying to inject more interesting content, or by offering better solutions for group problems, if I were able. I would certainly look for allies, and I would look closely at the members in the swing area on both sides of the Line of

Balance to see who might be persuaded to add support to my subgroup. I might try to provoke and lead a revolution of the equalitarians against the more dominant. I might assert my authority, if I had any, although it is my impression that when you are down to that you are down to the last straw.

All of this is the exercise of "power politics," of course, but one does not avoid power politics in a group simply by trying to stay out of the way. Not all groups have serious power problems, but when they do, one must attempt to deal with them by countervailing power, in my opinion, or be prepared to have one's values defeated. This is as true in "tender-minded" groups, such as therapy groups, educational groups, and groups with altruistic purposes, as in "tough-minded" groups. It is a disconcerting thought for example, that many therapy groups as well as some classrooms may fail to help most of the individuals in them very much simply because the group is stuffed too full of members with problems too serious to be contained by the rest of the group.

One needs to recognize that domination of the group by a dominant individual or subgroup is more than a denial of participation time to others. It is also a preemption of the attention of the whole group to the kind of images that happen to be the preoccupation of the dominating persons and the value conflicts they happen to have among themselves. This may or may not be optimum for other persons in the group. A polarization or unification about certain images in a social interaction field tends to be preemptive. The actual time for communication in many groups is often painfully short, compared with the time required for discussion of all the matters that really need attention. It is all too easy to jam the time available with a kind of content that fails to meet the needs of many in the group.

It seems to make good practical sense to try to find an optimum gradient of participation in a particular group, appropriate to its given purposes and to the needs of the persons in the group. The achievement of the common purposes of the group may not necessarily call for the same gradient as the needs of the persons as individuals, of course, and one may have to make some kind of compromise in defining an optimum that will take both criteria into account. Also, the optimum gradient will surely differ somewhat from group to group and from task to task.

What can be said about the optimum gradient in the self-analytic group? My feeling is that since it is meant to give an opportunity for each person to consider, in discussion with others, his or her own social interaction patterns, personality, and self-picture, each person should have an adequate amount of talking time, exposure and practice time distributed through the total series of sessions. This does not necessarily mean strictly equal time. A major problem of some persons is that they talk too much or too little, and they need time to display this problem too.

I have never seen a group in which there was no significant gradient of participation, although value statements in favor of equality are very common. (In SYMLOG language these would be classified as images PRO P in GRP.) The tendencies of individuals each to seek his or her own characteristic rate of participation, high, middling, or low, are quite persistent (Borgatta and Bales, 1953). I think actually to try to obtain strictly equal participation is unrealistic. It would take more energy and investment of time in the group to bring this about in fact than it would be worth. Group members sometimes employ mechanical means to bring this about (e.g. some kind of "round robin"), but these mechanical constraints seldom work well or for long, and if one tried very hard to enforce them, the mechanical means would become aversive. On the other hand, as I have implied above, the gradient due to the natural accidents of group formation and operation may be too steep.

What then is a realistic goal? Let us ask the question with regard to our illustrative group. Figure 11 shows the gradient of participation as perceived by RFB and the gradient as determined by the group average perceptions.

There is a considerable difference. RFB saw the general level of dominance as lower but the gradient as somewhat steeper than the members did, particularly at the top. Why the difference? We have to remember that averages of many judgments tend to cancel out the more extreme judgments. No doubt that is happening here. There is, however, an additional plausible explanation. For this particular group an "outside social phase" was scheduled after the regular meeting, during which the members were free to sort themselves out as they wished, talk in smaller subgroups in the lounge, and go to the cafeteria or wherever they wished, within the limits of the building. Meanwhile, I remained in the group meeting room for another session with observers of the group. Thus, the members' ratings were made on the basis of more extensive observation than mine, including the outside social phase in particular. There is little doubt, from many comments by the members, that many or most of the low participators considerably increased their participation in the outside social phase, where it was possible to talk with chosen others without the competition of the most dominant members.

I instituted the outside social phase, in fact, with the intention of increasing the participation opportunities and a hope of increasing the satisfaction of persons who would otherwise be low participators in the self-analytic session. Perhaps we are seeing evidence that the attempt worked, so far as the students were concerned, even though it may not have equalized the participation gradient of the self-analytic session very much. There were no complaints from the low participators in this group, as there have sometimes been at the end of other groups. There was concern, as usual, about the low participation of certain members in the self-analytic sessions, but more than once TINA and PAL, as well as others who were near the bottom, avowed they were perfectly well satisfied.

The self-analytic session is the prototype of the group meeting of strictly limited time in which it is very difficult to get around to everybody. Any polarization or unification that may occur is likely to lock certain members into the participation interchange and to lock certain other members out. If a particular polarization or unification hangs on for a whole session, as it sometimes does, the participation gradient is apt to be too steep. In the present case the outside social session immediately afterward apparently permitted a considerable recovery. Participation withheld during the more formal meeting apparently tended to rebound toward a greater equality in the more informal decentralized sessions,

FIGURE 11 Participation Gradients

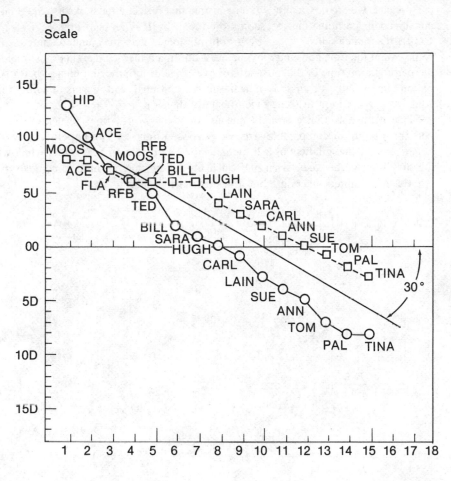

but in fact the gradient did not reach literal equality, or even approach it, in the overall perception of members.

The gradient shown by the average of group members' ratings in the present case is closer to what I would regard as optimum than the gradient shown by my ratings. Both gradients curve away from a straight line, but in opposite directions. So far as I can see, there is no reason why, on the average, a straight-line gradient could not be achieved.

In studies I have made previously of raw participation in small problem-solving groups, it is true, the gradient is hardly ever a straight line. In groups of more than four, one or more dominant members tend to take the lion's share of the time (Bales, Strodtbeck, Mills and Roseborough, 1951). However, in the present case we are not dealing with measures that reflect almost exactly the time consumed in participation (as scores produced by IPA tend to do; see Bales, 1950), but rather with *ratings* by group members, who may underestimate to some extent the time consumed by the most dominant members and overestimate the participation time of the most submissive. In addition, the amounts of participation are usually discussed in self-analytic groups, and norms tending to equalize participation to some extent usually develop.

Since it appears that a straight-line gradient of *ratings* may be achievable, perhaps a group of comparable size and purpose might set as a hopeful or ideal goal a straight-line gradient of a 20-degree slope with no members actually below the dividing line between U and D. Such a gradient may be hard to achieve in strictly time-limited meetings, but it seems worth trying for.

Chapter 7

Far-out Members May
Clash Sooner or Later

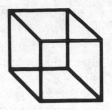

The heuristic hypothesis that far-out members may clash sooner or later is meant to apply to the chronic polarization of the group. "Far-out" members means the members on or near the Perimeter. "Sooner or later" means after the beginning period, in the middle period or even close to the ending of the group's history.

Since this hypothesis and the one covering Downward members in the next chapter attempt to give some expectations as to when various kinds of events may occur, it is desirable to make a short digression here to comment on the way in which members of groups conceive of and measure time, as it relates to the total life span of the group (see Williamson, 1977, for a study of time trends in our self-analytic groups). For groups that will meet over a limited time span known to the members in advance, it is my impression that the total visualized span tends to be divided into parts that are quite vague in the beginning but are brought into conceptual life for the group by crucial polarizations or unifications around specific dramatic events, which thereafter serve as time markers.

If there is no strict agenda, the total vague visualized time of the life of the group tends to be divided up into smaller parts, marked by specific events in the group's history, as the group goes along. Some kind of simple division into Beginning, Middle, and End tends to appear in the consciousness of members, sequentially, no matter how long or short in chronological or calendar time the visualized life span of the group may be. For self-analytic groups, and perhaps many others, two additional time periods are often imagined, which may be called "Before the Beginning" and "After the End." If these titles seem to have mythological or even religious overtones, that is not inappropriate, at least in self-analytic groups. For groups like self-analytic groups that have the time and the motivation to create and analyze imagery, these imagined periods may well be the focus of religious and philosophical concerns.

During the actual Beginning of a group's history, the imagined period Before the Beginning may be salient as a domain of content and imagery, with a focus on such questions as "Who are we?" "Where did we come from?" "What are we here for?'' ''How did the group come together?'' ''Who or what brought us together?'' ''Why were we brought together?'' ''What is our goal?'' and the like.

After a certain amount of interaction some particularly salient event, often a polarization or perhaps a striking unification, tends to be seen as a marker event. The marker event tends to move the group members, in their own perception, out of the Beginning and into a Middle period, during which they may focus on how they were in the Beginning and how they emerged from the prior state. In therapy groups or self-analytic groups the marker event may be one in which the group as a whole has managed to combine in a polarization against some person or object outside the group, as in a revolt against some external authority, or it may be a revolt against the leader, or it may be an episode in which a less dominant subgroup has managed to exert some effective control over the more dominant subgroup, and a new more democratic leader has appeared. After some such marker event, the Beginning is brought to a close in the perception of members. The Beginning now appears as the period in which the group was formed, or formed itself, and somehow assumed an effective life of its own, able to act in an independent way. The marker event is sometimes known as ''the time we became a group.''

The Middle period is regarded as a normal period of normal activity. It is the time of efforts to realize the purposes of the group, as visualized by the members. Not infrequently in self-analytic groups some group members visualize their real purpose as becoming a friendly solidary group. (The value statements they make may be scored in SYMLOG language, PRO P in GROUP.) Other members visualize the purpose of the group as analytic work (expressed as PRO F in GROUP). There is often a fluctuating struggle around those two goal directions, with a kind of ''pulsation'' from a polarization along the P–N dimension to a polarization along the F–B dimension. The Middle period is indefinite in length and may be the longest period in chronological time.

The Ending period sets in, often rather suddenly, when some event or image makes it evident that the remaining time is finite and short. The period of the Ending is often devoted to a consideration of what will happen, or should happen, After the End.

The time ''eras'' of a group's history are defined by the perceptions of the members, not automatically by the calendar or by the clock (see Schutz, 1962; Berger and Luckman, 1966). Periods in the life of the group are in themselves ''images,'' and may be the focus of unifications, polarizations, events of group formation, and dissolution.

Chronological time within a single meeting or calendar time over a series of meetings is always a scarce resource, and of course always, by definition, dwindling. The pressure on individuals to get done whatever they want to get done grows as the time becomes more limited. Toward the end of the meeting, or the end of the group life span, the limitation of time may become quite oppressive, anxiety-provoking for many, and urgent. As the time still available diminishes, the pressure increases.

The image of time as a dwindling resource may not be at all salient in the Beginning period (either of a series of meetings or the beginning of any particular meeting). In the Beginning, the persons who most want to talk and make the most strenuous efforts to obtain time compete most strongly with each other; since the image of dwindling time is not a very salient countervailing force, they often obtain a good deal of time without too much opposition from less dominant members.

As the more dominant members exceed some ill-defined appropriate share, however, the other members tend to feel increasingly that the large participators should cease dominating so much. The pressure grows—a partly consensual pressure—to give others a chance. Perhaps the issue comes to a dramatic confrontation of some kind, which provides a marker event. Or perhaps some of the struggles for dominance among the top members are settled with bargain-like arrangements—one agrees, in effect, to give the other top place, if the other will pay sufficient attention and cooperate with the first. The pair relations of the most dominant members may turn from competition to quasi-cooperation. The act or content of the settlement may not be seen—it may occur outside the group. A dominant pair may begin by competing with each other, and continue by implicitly agreeing to cooperate in dominating the others, or they may simply stop competing so strongly with each other.

At some point a set of persons next down the rank order of dominance is apt to become more active and begin to bargain, as it were, for the acceptance of images and group norms that better satisfy their values. Often these values may be characterized as more PRO P in GROUP, and less PRO U in SELF, that is, more friendly and equalitarian, less power-oriented and individualistic. There is a tendency, I have the impression, at least in some groups, for this process to continue down the hierarchy of participation in a kind of "continuous revolution."

Those lowest in the tendency to participate are apt not to be brought into overt participation until quite close to the end of the existence of the group. Pressures mount, but sometimes not until desperately close to the end, to have the low participators participate. Their nonparticipation, now so salient, seems to arouse guilt in some of those who have taken more time. The low participators are urged to speak, are questioned, and so on, often without much success. Remaining quiet is the submissive members' weapon of retaliation in some cases, at least until they have made their passive disapproval felt. The approaching end may make it easier to reveal some matters of content, because there is not enough time to deal with the issues raised. Since these problems and issues often involve negative attitudes toward the self and toward the group, the content may be revealed only when the probable consequences of revealing it becomes less threatening.

One may see the same set of changing pressures on participation operate within the time span of a single meeting. Quite frequently a negative low participator, or one with fears, will introduce his or her problem and come into the discussion for the first time very close to the end of the meeting, with only a few minutes, or even no time, left.

The following heuristic hypothesis is suggested, then: During any time period of group existence that has a definite anticipated end (whether a single meeting or the total life of the group) but no definite agenda, the high participators will tend to participate proportionately more at the beginning and decrease somewhat in the middle or toward the end. Vice versa, the low participators will tend to participate proportionately less at the beginning, and increase toward the end, often only quite close to the end. The middle participators will tend to increase their participation from the beginning to the middle, and to hold, or decrease, toward the end. An effective leader can moderate these tendencies to some extent.

Now to come back to the heuristic hypothesis with which we started this chapter: Far-out members may clash "sooner or later." Some members on the Perimeter of the group may be high participators and so may clash sooner rather than later, but the Perimeter is very likely to include some who are not high participators but are nevertheless likely to become salient in the middle or ending portion of the meeting or life of the group because they espouse and symbolize relatively extreme value positions, as compared to other members. Their overt or nonverbal interaction in itself may constitute the controversial image (for example, a member may put his feet up on the table, push his chair back, and look discontented), but in the usual case their content images and value judgments also play a part.

Sometimes the salience of a given member may be due not so much to the extremeness of his or her position as to the accident that he or she epitomizes or symbolizes some general problem of the group or some hoped-for solution. In our illustrative group, ANN is on the Perimeter, far out in the P direction in the Group Average Diagram (see Figure 10). It will be noted that, in RFB's diagram (Figure 9), she is not nearly so far out—not on the Perimeter, in fact, though close to it. The reasons for this discrepancy are not entirely clear—I was surprised to see that my summary rating of ANN was not more Positive—but several reasons occur to me. The first is that ANN's participation in the outside social phase may have been under less strain and more positive than in the self-analytic session. Another possibility is that the group members in their rating were more influenced by ANN's value statements and that I was more influenced by her ACT level and NONverbal behavior. (It probably goes without saying that even though one tries to make the rating on the basis of the ACT level, as I did, it is likely that impressions from behavior and content on other levels may influence the rater.)

In the self-analytic sessions ANN was often almost desperately anxious that the members of the group should be "nice to each other" and that they should declare their obligations to be friendly. She made many value statements PRO P in GROUP, or PRO PB in GROUP. On the other hand, her tone of voice was often anxious, strained, desperate, and somewhat negative and complaining. At the ACT level, in my perception, she was not notable for warm, outgoing, spontaneous friendly behavior. In the social session outside she may have been. I did not observe this period, since I remained in the regular group meeting room working with the observer group. On the other hand, group members who also very much wanted the group to be more friendly may have fastened on her value statements and wishfully rated her as quite positive at the ACT level.

To digress for a moment on the problems of the lone researcher in trying to approximate the group average rating: Perhaps my rating would have been closer to the group average if I had made ratings on all levels and added them together.

Or perhaps it would be better to compare all levels and take the rating in a given direction that would be the most extreme, with the thought that one might stand a better chance in that way of picking up the most salient thing about the person, no matter on what level—the thing that might become a controversial or wished-for image to others. As it stands, the theory is that all levels tend to be picked up to some extent when one makes the ratings on the ACT level. A rating of the ACT level may work poorly when there are considerable discrepancies of direction in the person's behavior or content on different levels. If there is a discrepancy, one may tend to select one level rather than the other as the basis for one's global impression. Not infrequently in the process of rating one becomes conscious of dilemmas because of discrepancies between levels. Perhaps the most economical procedure would be to try to stick to the ACT level when rating on that level but to make a note of all points at which discrepancies are sensed. Special ratings can then be made with regard to these points and later can be taken into account.

At any rate, in this case ANN's desire to have people declare themselves to be in favor of warm, friendly behavior turned out to be exactly what MOOSE could not stand. MOOSE was in favor of extreme individualism and did not want to feel obligated to anybody. (For more about MOOSE, see the discussion of his field diagram, Figure 17, p. 111). MOOSE declared that he would not be bound to be friendly, and ANN started to cry. The group was immediately polarized along the line connecting the location of the two, P versus N. It later appeared that ANN's appeal may have served, unwittingly, as a protest on behalf of the women in the group against the all-male dominant subgroup (MOOSE, ACE, and HIP), which up to that point had been conducting something like a bullfight, plowing up the earth with their hoofs and filling the air with horrid sound. All of the women, ANN, TINA, SUE, LAIN, PAL, and SARA, are found on the Positive side of the space.

One memorable image ANN had presented prior to the onset of the polarization with MOOSE was the image of the disadvantages suffered by "dwarfs." After a considerable complaint about man's inhumanity to circus dwarfs, she said, "Dwarfs are people, too." (In SYMLOG language this would be PRO P in SOC, or perhaps one might better score it, PRO P in FAN.) It later appeared that there had been a particularly threatening person in ANN's past (her father, who had a psychotic episode) who was the original source of the unfeeling treatment that ANN feared, and in that relationship ANN herself was the person in the helpless position. The image of her father, negative and threatening during the psychotic episode, apparently transferred to MOOSE in the present situation.

In retrospect it seems to me that it was this incident, a kind of revolt of the women against the male chauvinists, or of the suppressed against the oppressors, or of the dwarfs against the monsters, or of the Positives against the Negatives, that marked the end of the first era of the group in the classical manner—by a revolt against tyrants. In the expectation of many group leaders, this classical marker event is expected to be a revolt against the leader and symbol of authority (see Slater, 1966). I suspect that this is a special case, common though it may be, and whether or not there is a revolt against the leader depends upon the leader to a considerable extent and particularly upon the mode of leadership. It is more likely to happen, in my experience, if the leader's behavior lacks friendliness and veers toward extreme F, in the instrumentally controlled direction, with a little negative component. It is my impression from experience over the years with many self-analytic groups, during which I have changed from a location almost directly F to one that is quite strongly P and moderately F, that by more friendly behavior the leader can considerably reduce the probability that a negative transference will polarize the group against him. On the other hand, if the leader believes that such an event is inevitable, or even desirable, he may be motivated to give ample cause for a revolt against him.

MOOSE's reaction to ANN seemed obviously tied to formative events in his own past. I say this partly because of the marked emotional quality of his value statements in this pattern of polarization on several occurrences. At other times, however, when the polarization was not activated, he told of a situation in his family that might have played a part in his present feelings. He was the oldest of a very large family of children and not only was responsible for herding his little brothers and sisters around and keeping them out of trouble but often had to share and give up what he would rather have kept for himself. On one occasion, toward the end of the group, he brought bubble gum for all of the members—and threw the pieces around the table!

Although MOOSE was not on the Perimeter and so does not technically qualify as a "far-out" member defined in this mechanical way, he was in fact far enough out and more or less directly across the space from ANN. It is with each other, across the space, that far-out members are in theory most likely to clash. The far-out person in one direction may be subjectively trying to dissociate his or her self-image from an image on the opposite side of the space, an image retained from the past. The person so motivated is psychologically prepared to "mistake" any present persons who come close to the threatening location for the original threat. This "mistake" in perception and feeling and the subsequent acting upon it is called "transference" when it occurs in the situation of psychoanalytic treatment and the analyst is taken as the threat. But it happens very commonly in everyday life, in my experience, and certainly in therapy and self-analytic groups.

In the case of MOOSE and ANN, both persons were involved in a parallel and interlocked way. Apparently MOOSE saw ANN as a pesky little sister who wanted him to take care of her (see his comments, p. 112), and ANN saw MOOSE as an unfeeling monster who had once had her in his power. Each apparently epitomized for the other a threatening image; each recoiled from the threatening image and attempted to defend the self by seeking a position at the opposite side of the space. MOOSE declared his independence and proclaimed his right to feel and do as he pleased. ANN pleaded for a pact of friendliness, which only threatened MOOSE the more. Each constituted a rejected and threatening image to the other. They both continued to recoil further, and the polarization amplified. (The field diagrams for MOOSE, Figure 17, and ANN, Figure 26, indicate that MOOSE is in the direction of rejected images for ANN, and that ANN is near the Scapegoat location for MOOSE.)

In this case, the polarization is complex. Each member of the pair transfers an image or images from the past onto the other. In addition, each reacts to the transference of the other by exaggeration of his or her defensive behavior (called "counter-transference" in psychoanalysis), which in turn, amplifies the original transference.

Probably not all cases of polarization are so complex. There are instances in which only *one* member of the pair seems to be making a highly specific transference from the past to the other. There are still other instances where one gets no evidence of specific images from the past on *either* side, but rather a clash of generalized values or ideology, or simply of behavior and manner. It may be that generalized value positions often have their origin in specific family situations or specific formative events in the person's life history, but often it is not possible to do more as an observer than become alert to such a possibility, since no evidence is available at the time.

Our theoretical position assumes, however, that the reasons for polarization are general to all evaluative perception of social images. The case of the "double-headed amplifying transference" (MOOSE and ANN) is a complex case of polarization, although it may not actually be rare. However, if polarization in perception were not very general, the dimensions of the evaluative space (U–D, P–N, F–B) would not appear so generally in broad-scale empirical studies of interpersonal ratings and personality descriptions as they do (see Bales, 1970). The heuristic hypothesis that persons far out on the Perimeter of the space in a given group are likely to clash sooner or later is an inference that follows more or less directly from the theory that the space is constituted in the first place by polarizing tendencies in perception and evaluation. All the hypothesis does is alert the researcher as to who in the group is perhaps most exposed or likely to be involved and give some idea as to when the polarization is likely to occur at the overt level in group participation.

What about the part of the leader of the group in all this? Can or should he or she try to prevent it? What can be done about it, if anything?

It seems to me that there is not much prospect of averting polarizations centering on far-out members in groups where members have any significant freedom of self-expression. Nor is it desirable, presumably, in groups with an educational or therapeutic purpose that involves learning to deal with interpersonal conflicts. It is important, it seems to me, for a leader, a therapist, or a mediator in such groups to help see that nobody gets hurt, to see that the polarization does not amplify too far or hold on too long. There is often a point at which it will seem to the alert and well-prepared leader that the polarization is sufficiently clear to most members of the group for the work of interpretation to be effective, with sufficient evidence in view and sufficient emotional involvement in the issues for learning to result. The leader, mediator, or therapist, should be ready for that moment and should arrest the amplifying pattern at that point, if possible, by accurate interpretation—deep enough to collapse the polarization, but not so deep as to seem obscure or to arouse unnecessary resistance.

The optimum depth of interpretation is often, it seems to me, quite close to the commonsense level. It is often effective simply to take the role of each of the contending persons or subgroups in turn, to call attention to the nonverbal behavior of each, to call to mind the various things they have said that help to understand how they may be seeing and feeling the situation at present and trying to arouse an empathic understanding in the persons on each side as to how the persons on the other side are perceiving them.

In a therapy group one may go on, perhaps, to transference interpretations specific to the individuals involved. In a self-analytic educational group one is likely to pay more attention to the motivational factors that are more general to other members of the group and that help explain why people other than the principals have been drawn into the polarization. In a self-analytic educational group one is not likely to have much information about the life history or current outside life situations of the individuals in any case, nor is one in a good position, ordinarily, to assume the amount of responsibility necessary for continuing with the individual on progressively deeper levels, as in therapy.

Perhaps it goes without saying that the leader, educator, or therapist should try to be prepared, so far as possible, for polarizations that have a high probability of occurring. I believe it is possible to form, from the early interaction of individuals in a group, some rather reasonable expectations as to what issues and what persons may become salient later. An early rating and the construction of a field diagram enable the leader to develop a ''theory'' of the specific group, which can then be revised and strengthened as new information comes along. The attempt to do this is likely to sensitize the leader to aspects of the behavior and image content communicated by individuals in their natural interaction with each other, which will permit a better estimate of the optimum time for interpretation and will give more accuracy and substance to the interpretation. The lines dividing the intentions of therapy, the intentions of mediation, and leadership may be very thin at the crucial moment. Quite apart from any therapeutic effects, accurate interpretation of the proper depth is very possibly the most effective means of collapsing many polarizations. Humor, the great collapser of polarizations in everyday life, is a form of accurate interpretation of just the proper depth, when it works, but of course humor is not always appropriate.

It would take too long to detail all of the encounters of persons on opposite sides of the Perimeter in our illustrative group. There was a series of attacks by CARL on TED. They were serious and emotional. CARL saw TED as much more to the negative side than the group on the average did, but he was joined in this by ACE, another member of the NB subgroup. CARL and ACE cooperated in the self-analytic sessions, although in many ways ACE and CARL were different and even at polar extremes. CARL was a serious and devoted ideological ''revolutionary'' who talked little, but in very strong terms. So far as real dedication was concerned, he was as ''square'' a revolutionary as you are likely to find. ACE was anything but ''square.'' He was for frivolity on all possible occasions and expected to ''rip off the capitalist system by joining it.''

For CARL, TED was a symbol of some kind of square paternalistic conservatism (see p. 134). Possibly TED represented a specific self-image CARL was attempting to escape, although this never did become clear in the group. The PF subgroup in general, but particularly those to the F side, were regarded very negatively by CARL and ACE as symbols of conservative values and attitudes. On the field diagrams of both CARL (Figure 25, p. 135) and ACE (Figure 18, p. 114) it can be seen that they have ''moved'' the more forward members into the negative forward area. ACE has made a clean break in his perception between the more F members of the PF subgroup, whom he has moved into the NF quadrant, and those less far forward, whom he has moved *en masse* to the B quadrant, leaving not a single image in the PF quadrant!

There were other encounters between members on opposite sides of the Perimeter. There was no overt encounter between SARA and TED, so far as I know, although there were evidences of conflict of feeling toward TED on SARA's part. LAIN was attacked by CARL and by ACE. BILL rose rather slowly into prominence, toward the latter part of the middle period, but at that time he took both ACE and CARL to task, rather gently but effectively, without losing the support of most members of the group. During the ending period, I believe, BILL was regarded as the leader. He had moved from a more downward and positive position at the time of the first rating to a position quite characteristic of the person in the group who is likely to be regarded by the members as "the leader."

Although many persons may be active and dominant, the term "leader," in popular connotation, tends to attach to a member in the UPF location, not too far Upward, and perhaps just a little to one side or the other of the 45-degree vector. BILL is a good example. TED is a good example of an aspirant for leadership who was too far forward and not far enough P for this particular group constellation. It is necessary for a successful leader to have adequate concern for both the task accomplishment of the group and the maintenance of group solidarity through the encouragement of positive relationships among the members. Sometimes this requires a partnership of two persons, one of whom specializes somewhat on the task-oriented side, and the other on the side of maintaining group solidarity (Bales, 1958). But in any case, the most strategic location for the successful exercise of leadership is interdependent with the constellation formed by the location of the other members, particularly the relative need they feel for friendliness (P), or task accomplishment (F).

In the next chapter we shall maintain that the successful leader should also pay close attention—and perhaps give differential encouragement—to the most submissive members.

Chapter 8

Downward Members May Come in Last

Leo Durocher's epigram, "Nice guys come in last," does not quite express the point I want to make, but it comes uncomfortably close. My own generalization pales and stumbles beside it: Downward members in the chronic polarization of the group tend to come into more active participation, if at all, during the Ending period of the group history.

The general reasons for this expectation have been discussed above in reference to the way pressures toward participation change over time. In spite of the seemingly self-evident quality of the hypothesis, it is not a very strong one, and many things can happen that may tend to prevent its realization.

In our illustrative group, SUE, PAL, TINA, and TOM come out at zero U–D or below on the Group Average Diagram. For each of these persons the case was, of course, different. Perhaps only SUE is a very good example of the hypothesis. She was a very sensible, calm, and empathic person, a little older than the undergraduates in the course. Most of the storms blew over her or past her, and although she was a solid member of the PF subgroup and it was clear where her sympathies lay, she was not attacked, nor did she attack others. Toward the ending, however, as Bill rose to a more salient position, so did she. It was as if she had slowly and carefully been taking the measure of the situation and, as the time shortened, began to deliver her opinions with more frequency and more quiet force.

It will be noticed in examining the field diagrams of individual members, that SARA (Figure 24, p. 132), another woman member, moves SUE to the negative side. SUE (Figure 27, p. 139) moves SARA even more dramatically to the negative side. The reasons for this mutual dislike are not clear, although it is my impression that it is quite common for negative feeling to build as some person in the general neighborhood of a leadership position begins to move upward and forward. Perhaps SARA, as another woman but not at all near a leadership position, felt a twinge of disapproval or even envy as she saw SUE rise, even though mildly, toward a leadership position. SARA may have given signs of this, and SUE may have retaliated. On the other hand, it is not uncommon for persons in or near leadership positions to "back off" in response to negative reactions from others and to move downward, backward, and more toward the positive direction as they sense disapproval or a lack of support. LAIN, as we have noted earlier, apparently reflected this tendency in her self-ratings, in response to criticism.

The women in this group, SUE, PAL, TINA, ANN, SARA, and LAIN, tended on the average to be somewhat low in participation, which is not unusual in my experience. I ascribe it to the effect of the traditional feminine role vis-à-vis males. This group, however, more than any other I can remember, suffered in the self-analytic sessions from an all-male dominant subgroup. The women did not, however, form a very coherent subgroup, so far as I could tell, either in the self-analytic sessions or in the outside social sessions. What happened, rather, is that they took full advantage as individuals of the outside social sessions and perhaps obtained their main satisfaction in participation there. TINA, LAIN, and SUE, I understand from what group members said, generally talked with members of the PF subgroup, while ANN, PAL, and SARA often talked with members of the NB subgroup. The two subgroups of the chronic polarization apparently tended to remain segregated to some extent in the outside social sessions. Indeed, the subgrouping may have been more clear there than in the self-analytic sessions.

PAL, a very attractive and vivacious girl, explained early, and more than once in the group, that she did not feel she had much to say but was not unhappy with a low participation rate. She was apparently quite active in the outside social session and to a certain extent went back and forth between the two subgroups, welcome in both. She was also a very good student and presented to me a strong academic interest, which she tended to conceal, I think, from group members. This may explain why my diagram (Figure 9) puts her much farther forward than does the Group Average Diagram (Figure 10). Mine shows her, in fact, as a member of the PF subgroup. MOOSE, incidentally, is a parallel case in this respect. On my diagram he is shown as a peripheral member of the PF subgroup, because I placed him considerably farther forward and not so far negative as did the Group Average Diagram. MOOSE, as I have mentioned, often sought me out, apart from other group members, in order to talk about problems of scoring and points of theoretical interest.

Although TINA was a low participator in the self-analytic sessions, she explained early, as did PAL, that she did not want to participate much, that she did not feel embarrassed and had no trouble speaking when she had something to say. The issue came up periodically in the group, but always with the same result. She did not increase her participation during the Ending period, or if so, only a little. She was a special student from another university, and that may have persuaded her that she should not become a prominent member of this group. But on the other hand, I believe she was very active in the outside social sessions, and in fact was well satisfied with her participation opportunities there. It is also the case that she had strong academic and applied interests in the course and found these interests satisfied very adequately without much participation in the self-analytic sessions.

TOM, although generally a low participator, does not fit the generalization well. TOM was not in fact diffident, and occasionally he came in with explosive force. He did so early in the group history. But he appeared to be very much in conflict about many things and said that he was (see his case study, pp. 142–151). He seems not to have been able to identify with either subgroup and put his wished-for self-image on the Line of Balance of his diagram, closer to ANN than to anyone else. He was not really a member of the NB subgroup, from his own point of view, although the Group Average Diagram makes him appear to be. It is true, however, that from the point of view of the PF subgroup members, he was less than no help in moving the group in their preferred direction.

It appears to me that TOM probably rejected both polar subgroups and felt what is called an "avoidance-avoidance" conflict between the two, that is, his reaction to each was avoidance. In such a case we may find that the person not only stays near the Line of Balance but also reduces participation to a low level, as TOM did. Nor did TOM particularly increase his participation toward the end. At that time he felt under some pressure to participate more, and he apologized, saying that his difficulties outside the group had preoccupied him all term.

It may appear by now that the heuristic hypothesis is not worth much. It is, in fact, a good example of an expectation one would like to see defeated. I am pleased that I have not felt obliged to set up an experiment in order to "prove" the hypothesis, since I believe that the *persistence* of the effect in a natural group (if not its initial appearance), may be the result in some cases of the failure of the leader to do something that might moderate or prevent the effect. Once having made a "prophecy" there is a temptation to fulfill it, using means that conceal the subtle operation of one's own hand.

From experience in the Group Psychology course, I feel reasonably convinced that there are likely to be some members in any given group in the course who will not respond or will not be able to respond to the situation, the rest of the group, and the indirect teaching method with the initiative that is optimum. Some individuals will tend to remain too inactive unless special attention is given to them. In the course format under which our illustrative group was formed, the outside social session was included in an attempt to provide special opportunities, and I am pleased with the results. It is true that the attempt to provide outside social opportunities may not have led to greater analytic efforts—this is difficult to tell. The average academic performance of this group was very good indeed, but of course the teaching of observational methods and other features of the course were all geared to improving cognitive understanding as well as providing experience. The introduction of the manual for case studies, of which the present part of this book is a later development, and the course requirement of a case study of an outside group appear to have led to another strong cognitive gain.

The problem of making special efforts to elicit more participation from the low participators is present within a given session, as well as over the life span of the group. I try to bring in the low participators earlier in the session than their natural tendency prompts them to enter, once I come to suspect they may not participate otherwise. I sometimes comment on their nonverbal behavior as possibly indicating their reactions to what is going on or take a little time out to relate events of the session or its content to things they may have said in previous sessions. I also try to bring the discussion toward a close with a little time left and ask those who have not participated what their reactions are.

I realize that this approach of paying special attention is likely to create and preserve a special role and status for the low participators, perhaps an undesirable kind of dependence, but I think a certain level of participation is a precondition to the success of the delayed action interpretive approach on the part of a teacher, leader, or therapist. If the participation of a group member is too low, the delayed action interpretive approach fails. A first step in remedying the situation is to establish participation, almost no matter how. If participation can be established by a more direct approach, the delayed action approach can then be employed tentatively, with high attention always given, to encourage still more participation. But optimum balance of direct encouragement and more indirect waiting and encouragement through attention is always a delicate problem in relation to persons who tend toward low participation.

Chapter 9

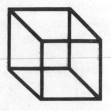

Salient Images May Polarize or Unify the Group

So far we have been concentrating on the images that group members have of *each other*. The general theory of polarization–unification has been applied to the images of different specific group members in the minds of other members.

In many groups, however, members talk mostly about images of persons, things, and events not in the group and apparently not closely associated with themselves. Even in self-analytic groups, a large number of the topics revolve around images of elements of the external SITUATION, elements of the general SOCIETY, or elements from FANTASY. A considerable part of the analysis in self-analytic groups consists in discovering ways in which images of these more distant persons and objects may also be serving as indirect ways of talking about the present SELF, OTHER, or GROUP (see Slater, 1966; Dunphy, 1968). It is true in all kinds of groups, presumably, that to some extent images of more distant persons and objects serve as indirect ways of talking about the present self, other, or group, but this is not always recognized and is generally not stated. The indirect, unstated meanings may become the basis, however, of polarizations or unifications in the group.

Anything an individual says, any kind of content issue or image, may become salient if it is has meanings or associations that are very important to some or most of the members. Changes in the situation or environment of the group, changes in the customary arrangement of objects (even, in self-analytic groups, an accidental isolation of one of the chairs), various kinds of accidents, the presence in the group of persons who are not members—anything may become a general focus of attention, develop into a salient image, and become the focus of a polarization or unification, if the meanings, either direct or indirect, are important to the members.

Here is an example from our illustrative group of a salient image of something located *outside* the group. Our group was one of two similar groups meeting at the same time, each of which observed the other in turnabout fashion. Our group was called Group B, and for the first session it did not participate as a self-analytic group but observed. The other group, Group A, met in self-analytic session, observed by our Group B from the observation room. When Group B came in from the observation room for its first self-analytic session, it had Group A to talk about. Not surprisingly, the members found it easier to talk about Group A than the members of Group A had found it to talk about themselves.

The members of Group B began to build an image in discussion of their own group as much more talkative, extroverted, and fun to be with than Group A. Group A was perceived as rather inhibited and introverted; the general feeling was that it would not be much fun to be a member of Group A. The image of Group A developed by this discussion was located in the Downward, perhaps in the Downward Negative direction. The members of Group B, by way of contrast, felt considerably unified by the development of flattering self-images and images of each other clustered happily in the Upward Positive direction. Perhaps as a partial consequence, however, the members of Group B developed a norm (also a type of image; see Sherif, 1936) that may be described in SYMLOG language as PRO UP in GROUP. That is, they developed an expectation based on experience that members of the group would in the future approve of outgoing, open, sociable behavior (see Direction UP in Appendix A). In the eyes of the dominant subgroup, MOOSE, HIP, and ACE, these norms may have been preceived as something closer to PRO U in GROUP (the expectation that others would approve of active, talkative, dominant behavior in the group), or even PRO UNB in GROUP (the expectation that the group would approve of exhibitionistic, narcissistic, conspicuous behavior). Whether or not a group norm was formed, the UNB values of the dominant subgroup thereafter gave the rest of the group a good deal of trouble.

Perhaps it is worth mentioning that I have given up the format in which two regular full-sized groups observe each other in turnabout fashion, because I became convinced that in our conditions it tended to result in intergroup competition and conflict (see Sherif et. al., 1961). The format of the Group Psychology course at present calls for a small observer group, a subset of five or six regular members drawn from a single regular full size group, a different subset each week. This procedure has the advantage of giving an opportunity to teach observation to members while they are on the observer team in order to provide feedback to the regular group, without the disadvantage of creating rejection of the regular group by the observers or rejection of the observers by the regular group. This format also seems to permit the acceptance of an additional research observer group, which joins the full group only during the feedback sessions on Fridays.

Another example of a salient image located "outside the group" was ANN's image of dwarfs, who, she said, tend to be derogated in the public mind. She felt they "should be treated as people, too". The statement on the face of it was a value judgment PRO P in SOC, but it referred to an image that coincided in location with the more downward and positive members (including the women) of the group, and so, in latent content, was PRO P in GROUP, and CON UN in GROUP. The fantasy image of dwarfs served as an indirect image of the disadvantaged part of the present group, according to the group's later analysis of the episode.

A salient image at the opposite end of the same polarization was provided by MOOSE, who introduced a discussion of "monsters" in movies (King Kong, Frankenstein's monster, Dracula, etc.). For some reason, he mused in a puzzled way, "these monsters have a tendency to strangle their love objects." This image was located presumably somewhere in the UN direction of the level FAN (see Appendix A), as a SYMLOG observer would score it, but it presumably had latent reference, for some members of the group, to UN in GROUP, or perhaps even to UN in MOOSE. Combined with ANN's image, MOOSE's image formed a polarization that might be called "The Monsters and the Dwarfs." (In another group, a similar set of polar images was called "Beauty and the Beast.")

Another illustration of polarization–unification in the group was one that might be called "The Capitalistic System and the Unemployed Girls." In this case the image of the Capitalistic System was located somewhere in the far UNF direction. That location seemed to be sufficiently far removed from the self-images of group members so that the group was relatively unified in opposition to the image.

The concrete events of the episode were these: LAIN had been telling of a trip on which she had been a passenger in a car with other students. The driver of the car picked up two girl hitchhikers. The two girls were unemployed and were headed south. The girls talked of the pleasure of doing just what they wanted to do, traveling where they pleased, while remaining on unemployment benefits. In telling of the incident, LAIN expressed her ambivalence about the rightness of the girls' attitudes. CARL and ACE took up the girls' side. CARL blamed their unemployment on the inevitable incidence of unemployment in a capitalistic system. ACE defended the right of anybody and everybody to have a good time. TED, who was often in a polarized conflict with ACE and CARL, in this case agreed as to the undesirability of the Capitalistic System, and in effect the group was more or less unified: opposed to the image of a bad Capitalistic System and unified to some degree on the side of the Unemployed Girls. The discussion continued a short while on the evils of the Capitalistic System, and then the topic lapsed. This was a transient unification of the self-images of the members of the group and was not characteristic.

However, while the polarization was in effect, during what we might call the particular "dynamic episode," the impression upon an observer of the discussion and how he imagined the members might perceive the group in relation to the CON Image and the PRO Image can be represented as in Figure 12. Actual methods by which one may detect such episodes and track their development through time, including measures that might be employed at the end of such an episode, are presented in Appendix S.

We have made a number of assumptions in order to produce the representation shown in Figure 12. Briefly, they are as follows:

1. In placing the image of the Capitalistic System on the diagram, we assume that it has connotations to the members of great power and externality, as well as threat. Hence we make the image large, indicating dominance. We arbitrarily make it as dominant as it can be made, 18U.

2. We assume that evaluative attitudes toward the image are negative and of considerable intensity. Hence we locate the image far out on the negative side of

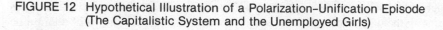

FIGURE 12 Hypothetical Illustration of a Polarization–Unification Episode (The Capitalistic System and the Unemployed Girls)

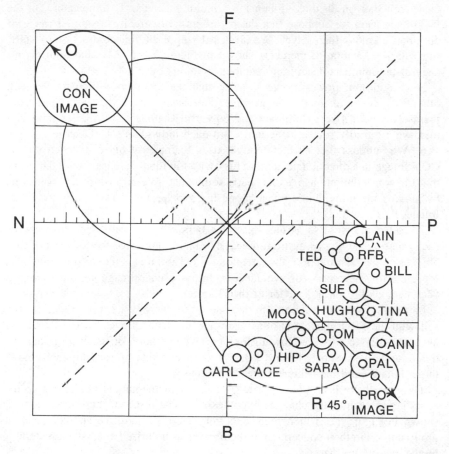

the space. We arbitrarily put it as far out as possible, and still keep the image in the space (see Appendix K).

3. We assume that the members identify the image with the authoritarian work demands of the larger society, and hence it is located as far forward as it can be in the space (see Appendix K). The combination of assumptions 1, 2, and 3 may be summarized by saying that we assume that the members view the CON Image as extremely UNF. Observers of the actual session, using SYMLOG Interaction Scoring, would produce a record of their understanding of the attitudes of the group members toward the jointly determined image, and we are making the assumption that it would turn out, on tabulation of their scores, that group members are expressing attitudes CON UNF in SOC. (See the manual for SYMLOG Interaction Scoring, Part II, and the discussion of the Image Formation Diagram in Appendix S.)

4. We assume that, relative to the focus of attention on the threatening UNF Image, the attention members give to their individual differences, and indeed to the group as a whole, is reduced. The group occupies a smaller part of the

perceptual fields of the members, which means that the perceived differences among them are reduced. Relatively speaking, we suppose they will seem to be closer together on all three dimensions, including the U–D dimension. On the U–D dimension we suppose that the members will perceive a smaller range of dominance among themselves. We arbitrarily represent this contraction by starting with the location of members shown in Figure 10 (p. 54), and multiplying each of the numbers describing member locations by .50.

5. In addition, however, we suppose that the members will perceive each other as less dominant on the average than usual, since they are comparing themselves with a very dominant and powerful U image. In order to represent this, we arbitrarily subtract one unit from each individual's U–D score.

6. We suppose that each individual tries to increase his distance from the CON Image in a direction peculiar to his own individual defenses, with the result that the constellation changes its shape somewhat. We arbitrarily represent this by moving the individual's image along his own vector in relation to the CON Image, by three units.

7. However, we also assume that members will generally tend to perceive each other as moving away from the CON object, and since the location of that object is in the NF direction, the direction away from it is in the PB direction. We represent this perception of avoidance by moving each image six units along a vector parallel to the PB vector of the Diagram.

8. Finally, we may suppose, to the extent that there is a desire to identify the self with the PRO image—in our illustration the Unemployed Girls—there will be a tendency to converge toward the perceived location of the PRO image, in this case as we assume, toward PB. We represent this by moving each image three units toward the center of the PRO image.

Thus, we have been able to specify a set of mathematical operations corresponding to each of the changes hypothesized. The result of these operations is shown in Figure 12, which represents very well the intuitive conception of a group unified in their conception of themselves as polarized against a threatening image external to the group.

We are not able to justify all of the component hypotheses of the theory of what happens during a polarization like that described above, and of course the mathematical operations are quite arbitrary. However, we are approaching the point of being able to bring empirical data from naturally operating groups to bear upon the study of the processes of polarization and unification. The observational methods of SYMLOG Scoring and retrospective rating, plus the computerized analytical methods described in Appendix S, seem to provide the necessary tools. For the present discussion, however, it will be useful for us to consider the general assumptions and the rationale for supposing that changes something like those portrayed in Figure 12 may occur.

First off, it can be seen that we assume that each ACTOR has the power to "move," in a perceptual-evaluative sense, the location of the SELF image, the images of OTHERS, the PRO and CON images, the Line of Polarization and the Line of Balance, and can increase or decrease the extent of the field by focusing attention on new objects or dropping the focus of attention on some. We suppose that this regularly happens under various conditions of emotional arousal and changes in focus of attention. We attribute extensive mental powers to the ACTOR, although we assume that the general constellation of the Group Average Field as others see it and communicate about it also has various facilitating and constraining effects.

One may suppose that all movements of images in the field take place by alterations of subjective and/or objective behavior of the ACTOR at any of the multiple levels we have talked about. The subjective behavior may include various kinds of imaginative and rational thinking. Sometimes, we suppose, the ACTOR makes some kind of rationalistic calculation of the "costs" and "benefits" of moving this way or that, but in many cases the ACTOR simply imagines the self or other image to be in a desired location by "sheer fantasy."

The self-image for most people surely seems to have some kind of continuity, some hard core of identity that remains the same from moment to moment and act to act. But the self-image also has many shifting aspects that come into prominence or fall out of the focus of attention of the ACTOR according to motivational needs and the constellation of the total field of images (see Allport, 1955). On some occasions the ACTOR will pay primary attention to the way the ACTOR's representation of the SELF has acted overtly (at the ACT level) and will tend to locate or describe the ACTOR's SELF in a way that will approximate fairly well the ratings others would give the ACTOR. The ACTOR may change the location of the ACTOR's SELF-image by changing his overt behavior, which, by degrees, changes the perceptions that others have of him. And so, by degrees, he receives a kind of confirmation from others of the changes he has tried to bring about. But this is a rather slow method and may cost a lot of effort. More subjectivistic ways may be much quicker, cheaper, and even, for some purposes, more successful.

On some occasions the ACTOR may feel obliged to ACT in a way that is far removed from the ideal, or WISHED-FOR, location of the SELF-image. This might be the case, for example, if one preferred a location for the SELF on the Positive side of the space but were confronted with an active threat from some person on the Negative side of the space and felt obliged to ACT in a Negative way to deal with the active threat. In such a case, the ACTOR may disengage his representation of his self-image from the overt Negative behavior itself and pay primary attention instead to the PRO Image that he or she is trying to defend. The ACTOR "identifies" the SELF with the PRO Image instead of with the behavior; that is, the ACTOR in fantasy moves the SELF-image (by shifting of attention and imaginal transformation) toward the location of the PRO Image. The undesirable overt Negative behavior is "rationalized away" (see A. Freud, 1936) by treating it as a temporarily necessary means to protect the valued PRO Image. The Negative behavior, which the ACTOR regards as "forced," is attributed to the threatening CON Image and is not regarded as characteristic of the SELF. If the threat is removed so that the ACT level behavior can again become positive, then the ACTOR may restore an emphasis on present overt ACT level behavior as a representative component of the SELF.

One whole branch of contemporary social psychological theory is devoted to the study of the processes by which the ACTOR tends to protect the SELF-image and generally to build a personal theory as to the causes of his own and others' behavior through the attribution of the causal cores of particular kinds or acts of behavior to the SELF, the OTHER, the GROUP, the SITUATION, and the other levels of images (see Heider, 1958; Festinger, 1957; Kelley, 1972; Abelson et al., 1968).

Presumably there are considerable differences between persons in the emphasis they ordinarily give to the different levels of their behavior, image contents, and value judgments as the basis for the SELF-concept. Some people seem to be more "realistic" or "objective" (pay more attention to their ACT level behavior) than others. Some people seem to be "idealistic" or "value-oriented" and pay more attention to the values (PRO images) that they try to promote or realize. Still other people pay much attention to their fantasies or other image content. At the fantasy level it is possible to express tendencies that can hardly be recognized by the ACTOR as associated with the SELF-image at all (see Freud, 1900, 1901). Presumably all of the levels of behavior, content, and value judgment ordinarily contribute to some extent to the individual's conception of his or her SELF-image, and the ACTOR, according to the present constellation of needs and possibilities, shifts the degree of attention given to these various components and in some cases ignores, suppresses, or represses the associations of some of them to the SELF-image. This is essentially the psychoanalytic view of "the Ego and the mechanisms of defense." The ACTOR in our theory is a concept for essentially the same mental functions said to be performed by the ego in psychoanalytic theory (see S. Freud, 1933; A. Freud, 1936). Social psychologists generally use the term "cognitive processes" to mean about the same thing.

In trying to reconcile various theoretical approaches to the understanding of behavior, it is important to recognize that the functioning of the ACTOR is complex. "Reward" and "Punishment," for example, are important in changing behavior, as learning theory maintains (see Skinner, 1953, 1957), and so, presumably, are "Costs" and "Benefits," as theories of economic rationality assume (see Homans, 1961), but what constitutes reward or benefit, cost or punishment, is presumably determined by the interpretive behavior called the ACTOR. It makes a difference what the ACTOR is paying attention to, how long the person works at interpretation and rational calculation, what he tends to overlook or suppress, and so on. It also makes a difference what kinds of general values the ACTOR prefers to try to maximize.

The ACTOR, we suppose, in the normal case *interprets what aspect* of behavior or intention is being rewarded or punished by the others and also what the intentions of the OTHER are in rewarding or punishing. In natural human interaction, if one wishes to reinforce some aspect of behavior by reward, one must have a reasonably good understanding of how the attempt to reward will be interpreted and how it will relate to the OTHER's values, or the attempt may backfire. If reward and punishment are not seen by the ACTOR as part of a natural process of cooperation and collaboration between ACTOR and OTHER, they may well be perceived as selfishly and manipulatively applied by the OTHER, and hence they may not produce the effect the OTHER expects.

In natural human interaction, if the OTHER in fact intends unilateral control over the ACTOR, the probability is high that the intention will be perceived as such before long, even if the OTHER is attempting to "give rewards." In our group, for example, TED was eager to move his image in the eyes of others into a more Positive location, and as a part of his effort he appealed for the support of "the women" in the group with some attempts at flattery. However, both TINA and SUE interpreted his lumping together of all "the women" as a kind of illegitimate appeal to their presumed favorability to women's liberation and reacted negatively rather than positively. What TED apparently intended as a reward or an inducement to feel positively about him turned out to be an alienating factor in their feeling about him.

We are now in a position to try to visualize a little more exactly how, and by what steps in time, an ACTOR may move the SELF-image and other elements of the constellation of images in his or her perceptual-evaluative field. It is important to realize at the outset that the mode of action and reaction in relation to PRO images—those which the ACTOR regards with a positive value judgment—is probably significantly different from the mode of action and reaction in relation to CON images. Let us consider these one at a time.

Figure 13 represents a hypothetical case showing *one* way in which the *benefits* and *costs* of moving the SELF-image closer to or farther away from a PRO image may change according to how close together the two images are at a given time. The ACTOR in our example is not presumed necessarily to know the shape of these two curves in advance of any movement and may have to discover what they are by a series of moves with tests of costs and benefits after each move.

It is supposed that there are *both* costs and benefits in the location of the SELF-image at any given distance from the location of the PRO image. (This is distinctly different, one should note, from the assumption that PRO images promise only benefits and CON images promise only costs.) The distance separating the two images at any given time represents the ACTOR's degree of "identification" of the SELF-image with the PRO image. Relative nearness represents a perceived similarity of the SELF-image to the PRO image. Relatively great distance separating the two images in the ACTOR's perceptual field represents perceived dissimilarity. However, insofar as the PRO image is regarded very positively, we suppose it to result in a motivational need in the ACTOR to decrease the distance (increase the similarity) by some means or other.

In the hypothetical case shown in Figure 13, the *Benefits* are assumed to increase in an accelerating upward curve as the ACTOR is able to visualize (or actually realize) a closer and closer identification of the SELF-image with the PRO image. However, it is *also* supposed that the *Costs* of such movement toward identification increase as the perceived similarity increases. In this particular case, at a certain point the curve of costs begins to rise faster than the curve of benefits, and at a certain point still closer to the PRO image, the costs of a closer identification become higher than the benefits.

We make the assumption that, if the ACTOR has sufficient knowledge of the shape of the two curves as they later turn out to be in fact or a sufficiently clear idea of them (whether correct or not) in advance of actual overt behavior, he or she tends to locate the WISHED-FOR image of the SELF at the point beyond which the costs become higher than the benefits, that is, at the crossover point of the two curves.

FIGURE 13 Hypothetical Curves of Benefits and Costs to an Individual in Moving SELF-IMAGE toward and away from a PRO IMAGE

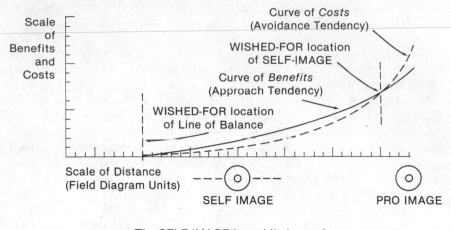

(The SELF IMAGE is mobile in moving toward and away from the PRO IMAGE.)

The actual EXPECTED location of the SELF-image may be considerably short of that point in a given case, since it depends upon the way the ACTOR supposes others perceive the ACTOR's SELF, and this in turn is supposed to rest, at least in part, upon the ACTOR's behavior, and the ACT level behavior, of course, may lag considerably behind the wishes. The discrepancy between the EXPECTED location of the SELF-image, and the WISHED-FOR location of the SELF-image is supposed to result ordinarily in a motivation to behave in such a way at the ACT level as to approximate more closely the WISHED-FOR location. However, even though the motivation may be present, it is not assumed that the behavior at the ACT level does in fact approximate the WISHED-FOR location much more closely. The individual may try to change behavior at the ACT level in the direction of the PRO image but encounter costs he did not anticipate, and then back off (Festinger, 1942; Lewin et al., 1944).

There are presumably quite a number of separable components of both benefit and cost, and I shall not attempt to make a working breakdown of these components at this point, although it must be done if the theory is to have any real substance. It is not necessary to assume, however, that the ACTOR must be capable of infinite economic calculations. As Figure 13 implies, the "rationalistic" term "*costs*" is regarded as measurable (in approximation) by the observation of the onset of an "avoidance tendency." Similarly, the rationalistic concept "*benefits*" is measurable (again, only approximately) by the observation in behavior of the onset of an "approach tendency."

One does not need to assume that persons always act highly rationally in their approach and avoidance tendencies, or indeed that rationality beyond a certain point in many problems is practical or even possible. In order to be highly "rational," the ACTOR has to know quite exactly, and in advance of behavior at the ACT level, what the shapes of the curves of cost and benefit will later prove to be. The degree of rationality possible depends upon how much the ACTOR knows (or thinks he knows) about the costs and benefits to be encountered and how far in advance the ACTOR has the knowledge.

In real behavior a highly rational computation of costs and benefits in advance of action is often replaced by a seesawing back and forth between approach and avoidance. With regard to an image perceived as generally PRO, for example, trying a closer approach, then sensing error by an excess of costs over benefits, then reversing direction by beginning to avoid, then sensing error again by sensing an unnecessary loss of benefits, then switching back to approach, and so on—this kind of seesawing, given enough time, will often accomplish something approximating a rational solution, though not always.

In some cases the ACTOR seems not to "zero in" on the best point but continues to oscillate back and forth, and in some cases the oscillation is wide and erratic. In some cases also, the ambivalence felt toward the image may be so great that, if the costs exceed the benefits in moving toward it or if "oscillation" does not solve the problem, the ACTOR makes an extreme reclassification of the PRO image into a CON image and makes a "catastrophic" avoidance move (see Zeeman, 1976). (I shall not try at this point in this rather abstract theory to specify when these various kinds of outcome will tend to appear.)

Ordinarily we may suppose that, when first beginning to pay attention to a given focal object or image, the ACTOR makes an initial classification of it as either PRO or CON on the basis of an initial comparison of its apparent costs and benefits. In other words, we assume that the ACTOR has at least a rudimentary "theory" about the nature the object and a preexisting attitude of some kind about it, PRO or CON. In addition to just moving toward it or away from it from moment to moment, and comparing costs and benefits each time, the ACTOR presumably also tries to "confirm" or "disprove" the general theory that the object is, after all, mostly PRO or mostly CON. While the ACTOR has in mind the theory that the image is PRO, we suppose that the tendency is to approach more closely, with a mental set something like that shown in Figure 13. If approach continues as long as the benefits exceed the costs, under the general theory of the object as PRO, the ACTOR may reach a point where, for the moment, costs exceed benefits. As a rule, however, the general theory that the image is PRO is not given up, but a minor seesawing will set in, as the ACTOR searches for the best location with regard to it.

By way of contrast, we suppose, if the ACTOR has a general theory that the image is CON and this theory is guiding behavior, the tendency is to avoid, and keep on avoiding, in the effort to minimize costs, with a mental set something like that represented in Figure 14. In this particular hypothetical illustration, the costs to the ACTOR of having the SELF-image located anywhere near the CON image are shown as very high, and it is assumed that the ACTOR will start moving the SELF-image away, increasing the distance, or decreasing the perceived similarity, between the SELF-image and the CON image. After some degree of separation is achieved, in our particular illustration, some benefits begin to appear, and for some distance, as the ACTOR moves the SELF-image farther from the CON image, the costs continue to decrease and the benefits to increase.

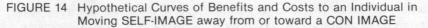

FIGURE 14   Hypothetical Curves of Benefits and Costs to an Individual in Moving SELF-IMAGE away from or toward a CON IMAGE

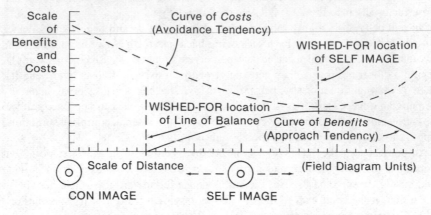

(The SELF-IMAGE is mobile in moving away from and toward the CON IMAGE)

For this particular illustration we have made an assumption that the benefits do not increase to a point above the costs. Indeed, a point is reached where the benefits begin to fall off again. At this point on our diagram, the costs also begin to rise again. (For example, in cases where the CON image is that of another group member, the benefits of further separation may come to a point of no further rise, so long as the ACTOR feels some need to remain in the same group with the OTHER. In such cases the ACTOR would tend to adjust the SELF-image to the location most nearly approximating a crossing of the two curves (see Thibaut and Kelley, 1959).

In other cases, we may suppose, a point may be found in the process of moving farther away where the benefits surpass the costs, and it may be that in such a case the ACTOR may "break away" from the fixation of attention on the CON image and start movement in some other direction of increasing benefits. Perhaps in some such cases the ACTOR starts a search for a PRO image or may "imagine" an appropriate PRO image as a theory to justify continued movement along a path that seems to be leading to increasing benefits.

It is important to emphasize that our theory assumes that each individual may have different cost and benefit curves (or may experience costs and benefits differently in the course of movement) and may regard the same object or person differently. This assumption of individual differences makes the theory more complex but seems necessary in order to be realistic. Empirical measurement of individual cost and benefit curves with regard to each major dimension of movement seems difficult but not entirely out of reach. If we can recognize the important types of dynamic episodes using the methods described in Appendix S, statistics applied to many similar episodes involving the same individual will yield something approximating the desired cost and benefit curves.

Figures 13 and 14 also show a representation of the WISHED-FOR location of the Line of Balance. In Figure 13 (for the PRO image) the WISHED-FOR location of the Line of Balance is placed as far as possible from the WISHED-FOR location of the SELF-image and in a direction that leaves the SELF-image on the same side of the Line of Balance as the PRO image. We assume that the intercept of the Line of Balance on the Curve of Benefits locates a base line level of benefits from which subjective increases in benefits may take place as the SELF-image is moved toward the PRO image. To set the Line of Balance farther away, then, has the retrospective effect of making the benefits seem greater ("You've come a long way, Baby!").

We suppose then, that in the ACTOR's attempt to visualize the benefits of moving the SELF-image closer to the PRO image, the ACTOR tends to place as great a distance as possible between the WISHED-FOR location of the SELF-image and the WISHED-FOR location of the Line of Balance, in order to visualize the benefits to be as great as possible. This tendency may be thought of as a kind of wishful suppression of attention to other costs and other benefits associated with the relation of the SELF to other images (or an ignorance of them). The ACTOR may tend, for the time being, to shut out consideration of other images in order to maximize the benefits related only to the single image. Insofar as there is some actual shutting out (and not just ignorance of costs and benefits that have never yet been experienced), the process we visualize is similar to that called "suppression" in psychoanalytic theory and may also be similar, when relatively complete and prolonged, to "repression" (see S. Freud, 1933; A. Freud, 1936).

In Figure 14 also, in relation to a CON image, the ACTOR is presumed to place as great a distance as possible between the WISHED-FOR location of the SELF-image and the WISHED-FOR location of the Line of Balance, consistent with minimal costs. The Line of Balance in this case is similar to a fortified line holding back the CON image from association with the SELF-image. The CON image may also be further accentuated and pushed still farther out toward the other side of the space from the location of the SELF-image. The concept of this psychological process is similar to the concepts of "dissociation" (of the SELF-image from the CON image) and "projection" (of unwanted aspects of the SELF-image onto the CON image) in psychoanalytic theory (see A. Freud, 1936; Klein, 1957).

If we now broaden our attention (as the ACTOR must also do, sooner or later) to consider the dynamics of the case where the ACTOR is oriented to both a PRO image and a CON image (still a very simplified case), perhaps we can imagine from our own experience something of what tends to happen (see Figure 15). The WISHED-FOR SELF-image, we may suppose, tends to be moved closer to the PRO image up to some point where the costs of further movement are too great. The PRO image itself may then be moved toward the WISHED-FOR SELF-image some distance. Provided the CON image is located far enough away from the PRO image and the EXPECTED SELF-image is between the two (not always the case), there is no conflict in direction of movement introduced by considering both the PRO and the CON images, since the WISHED-FOR SELF-image may be moved toward the PRO image and away from the CON image at the same time. The configuration in such a case is that shown in Figure 15, which also

FIGURE 15   Hypothetical Relative Locations of the PRO Image, the CON
Image, the WISHED-FOR Self-Image, the EXPECTED Self-Image,
and the Line of Balance

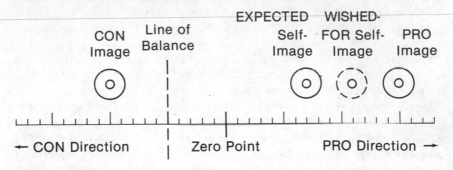

shows the EXPECTED SELF-image approaching the WISHED-FOR location
but falling somewhat short of it. Similarly in this case, there is no problem in the
location of the Line of Balance, except for minor adjustments, since in moving it
in such a way as to increase its distance from the WISHED-FOR SELF-image, it
is also pushed closer as a fortified line against the CON image, with the
WISHED-FOR SELF-image and the PRO image close together on the same side
of the PRO–CON dimension.

In the configuration of Figure 15, the problems for the ACTOR are those not
of major conflict but of making finer adjustments of costs and benefits by moving
the location of the various elements: the PRO image, the WISHED-FOR SELF-
image, the EXPECTED SELF-image, the Line of Balance, and the CON image.
The psychological processes called "identification" (of the WISHED-FOR
SELF-image with the PRO image), "focusing of attention" on the present
polarization, "suppression" and "repression" (of the costs and benefits in relation to still other images), "dissociation" (of the WISHED-FOR and EXPECTED
SELF-images from the CON image), "projection" (of disowned elements
of the SELF, whether WISHED-FOR or EXPECTED, upon the CON image)—
presumably can all operate without interference with each other, and indeed
in such a way as to reinforce each other. It is something like this set of
psychological processes operating in a circular and amplifying fashion in feedback upon each other that I suppose contributes to the outcome we see as the
tendency toward "polarization" with the CON image on one side of the Line of
Balance and the WISHED-FOR and EXPECTED SELF-images, with the PRO
image, on the other (see A. Freud, 1936; Klein, 1957; Heider, 1958).

In view of the assumptions we have made concerning the tendency of individuals, if they can do so without conflict, to move the WISHED-FOR and the
EXPECTED SELF-images in the direction that seems PRO to the ACTOR, it is
of interest to examine the locations of these images for the members of our case
study group. These locations are plotted in Figure 16, which also shows the
rating actually RECEIVED.

As one may see on Figure 16, there is a general tendency for the WISHED-
FOR location to be the farthest out in the P direction, with the EXPECTED

FIGURE 16 Comparison of Locations WISHED FOR, EXPECTED, and actually RECEIVED (Expansion Multiplier = 1.36)

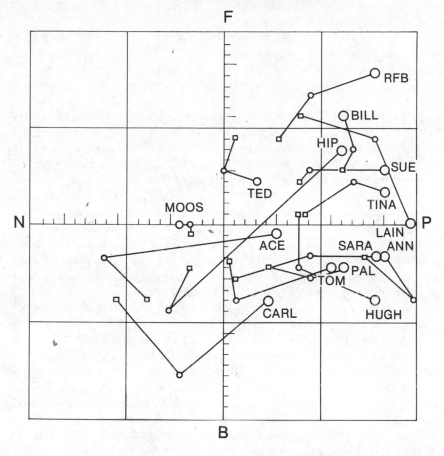

ratings falling short of that, and for the ratings RECEIVED to fall shorter still. The average rating WISHED FOR (before the Expansion Multiplier was applied) was 7.4P, the average EXPECTED was 3.4P, and the average RECEIVED was 2.4P. There are important exceptions to the general tendency, however, particularly for the members who were rated on the Negative side. Both HIP and ACE seem to have overestimated the Negative ratings they might receive, that is, they EXPECTED more Negative ratings than they actually RECEIVED. Perhaps they wished to avoid the disappointment of being informed by the ratings that they were not only on the Negative side but were not even aware of how Negative they were. On the reasoning that it is important to avoid disappointment, one might suppose that individuals who EXPECT their rating to be Negative, and who are in fact rated on the Negative side by others, might also tend to say they WISH for a Negative rating. This seemed to be the case for MOOSE, who says he WISHES for a Negative rating. Although this may happen in some cases, it is probably rare. It is not true for CARL, ACE, and HIP. Like MOOSE, they received ratings on the Negative side, as they EXPECTED to, but nevertheless all three of them WISHED FOR a Positive location.

In some groups (not the present one) I have collected ratings from individuals prior to the beginning of the group as to how they think they would have been rated in the groups around college in which they had participated during the preceding term. These kinds of self-ratings show a configuration very similar to that of Figure 16—a rather tight cluster on the Positive side, extending neither very far Forward nor Backward. It may be that self-ratings made with this kind of nonspecific context tend to be wishful. Individuals may also have tended to pick friendship groups as the reference groups for their ratings, and perhaps it may be true that their participation in friendship groups may be more Positive on the average than in the self-analytic group. Both of these explanations, however, tend to imply that it is very common for the WISHED-FOR location of the SELF-image to be on the Positive side of the space. This is useful to know, if true, partly because it gives us some general expectations as to most people's motivation, but also because it tends to imply that self-ratings made without any reality check are probably not usually much good as predictors of behavior of the individual if the individual is placed in a new group with a particular constellation of other persons and possibilities of behavior.

Transient polarizations or unifications of the group that catch on and amplify rapidly up to some preemptive level of attention are supposed generally to involve focal images that have some characteristics in common with suppressed and repressed images of a considerable number of group members (that is, they may involve multiple transferences). When the image is suitably provocative and at the same time open to varied projection, when the similarities of the suppressed and repressed images in the minds of various members are great enough, and when the number of persons having some kind of emotionally important reaction PRO or CON is great enough, the emotional charges invested in the repressed images of the various members tend to be transferred to the present image. The present image is then treated according to the suppressed or repressed feelings attached to the previous images. The present image becomes a surrogate of emotionally important images already present in the minds of individuals. For those acquainted with psychoanalytic theory, these ideas will be perfectly familiar (see S. Freud, 1900, 1928; A. Freud, 1936; Fairbairn, 1954; Ezriel, 1957).

It is not necessary to have much information about the life history of individuals in order to see these psychological processes at work. The suppressed images in self-analytic groups often have their immediate focus in some ignored but easily recognized feature of the group or situation. Present objects or images may arouse anxiety states, incipient anger, depression, or affection. In the groups I have studied, for example, the mirror of the observation room and the group of observers behind the mirror usually arouse some anxiety. In an early meeting of a recent group, one of the members of the group began to take notes as one might in a college class. This unfortunate member became the focus of attention and was the subject of a prolonged emotional discussion as to whether one should take notes during the group sessions. The member who had tried to take notes was required to explain repeatedly why she had done it. The polarized concentration of attention on this member, in which she was disapproved as a deviant, collapsed when the interpretation was made that perhaps there were some unexpressed feelings about the observers writing down things behind the mirror that were being displaced upon the present group member. In order for the phenomena of transient polarization or unification to manifest themselves, it is not necessary for the suppressed images to have their sources in the specific developmental histories of individuals, although these images also occasionally come to the surface in self-analytic groups.

In a group interaction field, during a polarization, the sheer volume of acts expressing PRO and CON attitudes toward a set of images and the interactive repercussions of these acts tend to preempt the attention of all or most of the individuals in the group, to absorb all the attention they can pay, as it were (see F. Allport, 1924), and to draw their attention away from other images that might ordinarily compete for attention and introduce considerations of other costs and benefits. The result, for the short term, is a lowering of the degree of rationality, an exaggerated focus of attention on one or a few images, an escalation of the attribution of Negative and/or Positive traits to the image(s), a selective suppression or repression of mitigating or normalizing traits attributed to the image (see Allport and Postman, 1947), and a "movement" of the location of the image in the discussion content, by new attributions, to a location where it comes near to unifying the group of participants or to separating the group into two conflicting subgroups (see the Image Formation Diagram, Appendix S).

All of these characteristics of transient polarizations or unifications in groups help to explain why they are transient. They are too exaggerated to last. While they last, however, they tend to be preemptive—more powerful in their demand for attention and more "far-out" in their imagery than the mean locations of members' images of each other in the Group Average Space.

In the case of a transient appearance of a very salient image that *all* members for any reason tend to regard as Positive, all members will be motivated to increase their identification with the image, and the Line of Balance will become something like the "boundary" of the group—it will be set in such a way that all members place their self-images on the Positive side of it. The group members will tend to "unify" their self-images around the focal image.

In the case of a very salient image that all members regard as Negative, all members will be motivated to dissociate the SELF-picture from the location of the image and to increase their distance from it. The Line of Balance will be pushed toward the location of the Negative image, as a kind of fortified line, and the image itself may be moved to a more extreme location in order to make this possible or to increase the distance.

In the case of a very salient Positive image, the Line of Balance is like a protective outer boundary which keeps the self-images of group members enclosed in the same location as the Positive image. And in the case of a chronic polarization of members vis-à-vis each other, the Line of Balance is a kind of compromise boundary spread over a vaguely defined area, comparable to a "no-man's-land," which for each subgroup represents a fortified boundary vis-à-vis the other subgroup and a protective enclosure for the self-images of the same subgroup. With all of the underlying complications, it can easily be seen that the location of the Line of Balance as shown on the Polarization-Unification overlay can hardly be exact and in fact is simply a conventional representation. Nevertheless, it is a highly useful one, since it raises the question as to whether the total group may be divided into subgroups and, if so, who may be in a marginal position between two or more subgroups. In the next chapter we shall explore in further detail the way in which repeated processes of polarization in the minds of members may result in the formation of subgroups with recognized leaders and followers.

Chapter 10

Polarization May Tend to Create Leaders and Subgroups

When a polarization of attitudes about some image is chronic in a group, particular members tend to take the leading roles in expressing the PRO and CON attitudes about the image. Over time, others may come to depend upon such leading members to represent them, and the group members may tend to gravitate into two (or more) subgroups. The PRO content images presented by members of a given subgroup tend to be found in a cluster in a given quarter of the space. Members who find themselves on the same side of an issue may then tend to seek each other out and associate with each other outside the sessions of the group as a whole.

Transient polarizations show the same tendencies in miniature or abbreviated form. A pattern of polarization may first form in the mind of one individual before it appears in overt interaction and communication. The act of communicating first about an image of potential importance to other members is *an act of leadership*. The value judgment of the acting individual PRO or CON the focal image is usually clear in the act of communication. Other members, in focusing attention on the image, also focus attention on the person who communicated it. The first communicator is thus put in the position of a potential leader.

Whoever *responds* to the initial communicator tends to convey his or her own attitude, PRO or CON the focal image, and also an attitude, Friendly or Unfriendly, toward the initial communicator. The initial communicator and the other members now know whether the responder is on the same side of the issue as the initial communicator. If the responder is on the same side, a subgroup has begun to form—initial communicator and positive responder. If the responder is on the other side, he or she is put in the position of the prospective leader of a polar subgroup.

As each additional member enters the field of participation with regard to the same image, there is some degree of pressure to join one side or the other. The choice is not absolute—it is possible to become the potential leader of some kind of third party, a party with a middle compromise position, or perhaps a completely different alternative position. One may also, of course, abstain. Persons who do not join one of the two polar subgroups may later be seen to have the power of exercising a "swing vote" that may help one side or the other.

It may take some time for the full constellation to develop, but at a minimum two or three beginning acts may be enough to precipitate the essential features of the polarization around the focal image and to move the potential leaders of the polarized subgroups into prominence. The important point is that the polarization of attitudes about an image and the appearance of potential leaders and subgroups are almost always linked.

Of course, an event outside the group may suddenly capture the attention of all members, and a similar pattern of polarization may appear in the minds of all the members even prior to any communication between them. But as soon as verbal communication concerning the focal image begins, it is necessarily the communication of a particular individual, and that particular individual is apt to be put in a position of prominence as a potential leader, or at least as a focus of attitudes. This is probably true even if the communication is not verbal but nonverbal expressive behavior.

It is not always the case that an opposition subgroup appears. The group may be essentially unified either by strong acceptance of an image all members regard as Positive or by strong rejection of an image all members regard as Negative. In such cases of unification the group may have only one leader, and perhaps not even a single one who is preeminently visible. Polarized, rather than unified, patterns, however, are very common, and in this case the two subgroup leaders tend to be visible by their greater participation, by their conflict with each other, and by the centering of attention on them and their communication. Many polarized patterns do not have any visible third party leader. Potential mediators or scapegoats may remain invisible through a lack of participation.

The probability that a group will develop a chronic pattern of unification is surely much lower than the probability that it will experience transient patterns of unification. I would expect that the chronic pattern in many groups is some pattern of at least mild polarization and that most groups of three or more either have some individuals in a third-party position, or that one or some of the individuals act as mediators or scapegoats at particular times, even though they are usually members of one of the polar subgroups. There is no law of nature or behavior that says a given individual cannot act in various ways, flexibly, according to felt need, or even that an individual will have one and only one unambiguous and consensual image in the minds of other members. Our location of an individual's image at one average point on the Group Average Field Diagram is a convention, obviously, and it rests on the arbitrary averaging out, or canceling out, of whatever flexibility of behavior and variety of image the individual may show. We should always be prepared in our thinking to back away from the results obtained by arbitrary averaging and to look at the underlying variety, flexibility, and conflict whenever it appears that we are losing crucial information by the aggregation and averaging.

The actual development of leaders and subgroups from the kind of slight beginnings in a single transient pattern described above depends on the interaction of the members of the subgroup with each other. In the course of time, many transient episodes result in the gradual definition of general-purpose positions of members. Usually there is some interaction among the members of a given subgroup outside, as they discuss what has happened in the group, and sometimes they develop plans to cooperate when the group meets again as a whole. This need not be a highly self-conscious or intentional process. (In the case of the political caucus, of course, it is, but that is a large-scale, fully developed, and extreme case, as compared to what happens in most small informal groups.) The case of purely cold-blooded, consciously planned combination for the sake of defeating an opposite side is perhaps common in politics on the large scale, but I would suppose it to be rarer in informal groups.

In the less self-conscious process of subgroup formation in small groups, members who have taken the same or similar positions in a polarization seek each other out to discuss their position further. They find other similarities among themselves and begin to develop a subgroup solidarity, to some extent, in the ordinary case.

However, we have to recognize that, even though the process of subgroup formation may not be highly self-conscious or calculated, the individuals of a pair (each pair) opposite an image that both reject are also then located in relation to each other so that their cooperation is advantageous in furthering the rejection of the image. The combination encourages a coalition, even though the individuals are not self-conscious in their intention to form an active coalition.

In the Group Average Field Diagram of our illustrative group, Figure 10, CARL and ACE, for example, are in a position that tends to "add their forces" to each other in relation to the avoidance of TED. One vector of avoidance proceeds from CARL to TED, the other from ACE to TED, let us say. The angle separating these two vectors is small—less than 10 degrees. Vectors that close to each other are acting in very nearly the same direction, and in vector theory they are assumed to add together in a direction which splits the difference between the two according to their force. The possibility of adding their separate forces in rejection of TED creates a situation where CARL and ACE are likely to feel rewarded by cooperating with each other in this rejection.

When the vectors of rejection or acceptance of some image proceeding from the locations of two members toward the location of the reference image form an angle of less than 90 degrees, we take this formal property of the locations to indicate the possibility of advantage to be gained from cooperation with respect to the reference image or object. We then make the further assumption that if the situation and the possible advantage continue over a long period, there will be some tendency for an actual combination (alliance, coalition, cooperation) to appear among the individuals so located with regard to a scapegoat or a mediating image, even though the individuals in question may be considerably separated in the space and even opposed to each other in other respects, provided those other respects are for the time being less important.

Thus we would expect that over time the emerging leaders of polar subgroups would tend to seek recruits, not only among those who may be far out in the leader's own polar direction (these may not need to be recruited) but also among those in the marginal zone on either side of the Line of Balance, or perhaps even beyond. Conversely, we would expect that, over time, the more submissive members who are close around the polar area will tend to seek leadership from among the more dominant members in that area.

The potential polarization between dominant and submissive members in a given reference subgroup may be neutralized to a considerable degree by the advantage of alliance with each other vis-à-vis a polar opposition subgroup. The relationship between leader and led in a reference subgroup may thus be viewed as one more kind of coalition. It is of considerable importance to realize that the more submissive, and often rather silent, members (at least those on the Positive side of the group field) will ordinarily tend to be drawn toward acceptance of the more dominant leadership that is provided in their reference subgroup as shown on the Field Diagram. The Field Diagram shows dominant and submissive members close together if they are similar in location on the P–N, F–B dimensions (though they may be far apart in the U–D dimension). It is this property which makes the Field Diagram so useful. Members (on the Positive side at least) who appear close to each other on the Group Average Diagram are likely, over time, to form alliances with each other to some degree and to become a recognizable subgroup with one or more leaders.

It seems probable that persons on the Positive side of the Field Diagram are more likely to form such a subgroup than persons on the Negative side. CARL and ACE, in our illustrative group did cooperate in the sessions to attack TED (joined sometimes by MOOSE and HIP), but their own relationship with each other seemed full of barely suppressed negative feelings. The same is true of the relations between all the members (CARL, ACE, MOOSE, HIP, TOM, and SARA) who are shown on the Group Average Diagram within the NB reference circle. These members hardly formed a cohesive subgroup. TOM drifted into the area because of multiple conflicts and did not identify himself with the NB reference group, while SARA (an ambivalent acquaintance of HIP on the outside) more often than not gave HIP a joking hard time on the few occasions when she entered into overt interaction in the group.

The many generalizations in the literature concerning the probability of ''similarity'' leading to ''liking'' may well apply more strongly on the Positive side of the Field or may not hold at all on the Negative side. It seems more likely that those on the Negative side tend to be drawn together in temporary coalitions for temporary advantages in opposition to some third person or subgroup, but that little liking or lasting solidarity may result.

The standard Overlay is presumably defective in several important respects with regard to locating subgroups. First, the centers of the reference and opposite circles are separated by *one* general-purpose interval. In fact, probably one should be able to adjust this interval to fit the specific case. Sometimes the separation will be large, sometimes small. Second, on the standard Overlay the circles are of the *same* general-purpose size. In fact, probably the size should depend to some extent upon the number of images within the circles, on the assumption that the images (and the persons or entities they stand for) exert an interactive multiplying and clustering influence on each other. It may well be that a circle with many images in it should be larger than a circle with only one or two images in it. Third, the multiplying and clustering influence may work mostly on the Positive side of the field, and less strongly, if at all, on the negative side. Fourth, on the standard Overlay the Line of Balance is located *equidistant* from the two circle centers. In fact, the line may be placed differently by each individual in the group, depending on the total constellation as he sees it, and it may hardly ever be placed equidistant from the two circle centers, either by individuals or as an average of all individuals. Fifth, on the standard Overlay, the swing area is indicated with two arbitrary boundaries, each *exactly halfway* between the line of balance and the center of the relevant circle. In fact, the uncertainty in the measurement of this area may always be so great that no reliable predictions may be made.

The design of the standard Polarization–Unification Overlay is *not,* in other words, the theoretically most general formulation of the nature of image fields or social interaction fields. The standard Overlay is simply a set of practical (hypothetical) estimates that may be used as a first approximation. The fitting of the Overlay to an image field is a hypothetical theoretical operation, and it may be very difficult to make exact.

In spite of its probable inexactness, the fitting of the overlay to an image field is a highly useful heuristic procedure, since it raises a whole set of strategic questions about the possible dynamic relationships among the images, from subparts of the constellation as a whole down to the pair relationships, and these questions may then be used as a means of eliciting further information of a confirming or disconfirming nature. This is the kind of guidance needed for effective leadership.

In the next chapter we shall see how an accurate analysis of the dynamic constellation of the group may yield strategic heuristic hypotheses as to how the existing constellation may be changed, particularly means by which polarizations may be neutralized.

Chapter 11

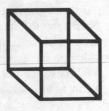

Polarization May Be Neutralized by Mediation, Scapegoating, or Domination

A sufficiently dominant far-our Positive member on or near the Line of Balance may be in a position to act as a Mediator and may neutralize a polarization or even unify the group. The other end of the Line of Balance may be called the "Scapegoat Location," and a person or an image near that location in a given polarization may become the focus of displaced hostility from members in both subgroups of the polarization. This deflection of hostility may tend to neutralize the polarization or even to unify the two subgroups. To call attention to these two locations in relation to any given polarization, the Polarization–Unification Overlay shows an "M" on one end of the Line of Balance, standing for "Mediator Location," and an "S" on the other end of the line, standing for "Scapegoat Location."

These hypotheses as to how a polarization may be neutralized apply to the chronic polarization of the group over the entire span of its existence, but they may also have a relevant meaning within the span of a single meeting or for the duration of a single polarization.

In our illustrative Group Average Diagram, Figure 10 (p. 54), ANN is a far-out Positive member but not near the Line of Balance. PAL is very near the Line of Balance but is not very far out. Neither is very dominant. PAL acted as a mediator in the outside social phase but hardly at all in the self-analytic phase. She apparently liked and felt close to HUGH. In the outside social phase she stuck with him a good deal of the time and moved back and forth from the PF to the NB subgroup for conversation. Incidentally, it was not the case that the two subgroups were always segregated on the outside, though there was a tendency toward segregation. PAL was animated and friendly in relation to essentially all members, so far as I could tell. On her Field Diagram (Figure 29, p. 152) it will be noted that she sees herself as not too far from the Line of Balance. Her

WISHED-FOR location is very close to the Line of Balance. She rates nearly all members of the group on the Positive side. CARL is the only member left isolated on the Negative side. Probably PAL's low participation in the self-analytic session was partly a result of not wanting to take sides in the polarization, but not feeling sufficient confidence to undertake mediation in the public context. It was through her behavior outside that PAL accomplished whatever she did toward mediation, not through her behavior or content imagery in the main sessions.

Although ANN was a little more dominant, as shown on the Group Average Diagram, and very far out on the Positive side, her image is not near the Line of Balance, and she did not visibly act as a Mediator. Her Field Diagram (Figure 26) shows the images rather closely brought together but apparently polarized in the PB versus the NF direction—exactly at right angles to the main polarization of the group. Her self-image, both expected and wished-for, was on the PB end, far out toward P. Her value statements in favor of a friendly group were more salient as an image in the PB direction than her behavior, perhaps. In the outside social phase, she apparently talked mostly with the NB subgroup and, in fact, made good friends with CARL. It may also be seen in her Field Diagram that she moves CARL considerably in the Positive direction very near to the Line of Balance. One hypothesis as to how it came about that ANN, on the far Positive side, and CARL, on the far Negative side, came together (instead of clashing as one might expect from their positions on the Group Average Diagram), is that both she and CARL formed an alliance vis-à-vis rejected NF images, with which they were both concerned (see CARL's diagram, Figure 25, p. 135).

For whatever reasons, it is not uncommon in my experience, for a woman in ANN's position—far out Positive and strongly unifying in her values—to form a special relationship outside the group with a man on the far out Negative perimeter of the group. Sometimes "opposites attract," as the saying goes. Opposites may sometimes attract in the F–B dimension as well, but the three or four most salient instances of "opposites attracting" I remember have all been located far Positive and far Negative. In each case, it seemed as if the woman felt compelled in some way to bring the negative male back into the group. In the clinical literature similar instances have sometimes been called "the Rescue fantasy."

On my diagram (Figure 9, p. 53), HUGH appears on the far Positive side, although he is a long distance from the Line of Balance. In fact, I perceived him as a Mediator throughout the group, not from an inference based on his location in the field but through a direct impression of his intentions. He nearly always appealed to both sides when he intervened in any conflict, was very ingratiating, and spoke well of everybody. It was usually difficult to tell which side he was on. My impression was that he usually started with a statement of agreement with one side and ended with an agreement with the other side. The main clue as to which side he favored was the one with which he ended. HUGH was interested in politics and believed in friendliness and compromise. He was extroverted, often anecdotal and entertaining. It is true, however, that many of his fantasy images were of carefree dominant Negative behavior—he remembered many barroom fights with enthusiasm. He was certainly regarded by ACE and HIP as "one of the boys." He talked mostly with the NB subgroup in the outside social phase, I believe, although he may have cruised from group to group a good deal, with PAL. All in all, perhaps HUGH did as well in a Mediator's role as anyone in the group could have done, but it was not in fact notably effective, and he seemed to fade somewhat as the group neared its ending phase. I am unable to account for the fact that he appears so far forward in both my diagram and the Group Average Diagrams (Figures 9 and 10); indeed, he appears in the latter as a part of the PF subgroup.

The heuristic hypothesis about Mediators does not state that there *will* be an effective Mediator. It should be understood as a theoretical statement about possibilities and opportunities. For every polarization there is, theoretically, a middle position along the Line of Balance, between the two polar positions, and a person (or a salient image other than a member of the group) far out along the Line of Balance theoretically may have a certain strategic power vis-à-vis the polarization. If the image of the person or the values he or she favors is far out along the Line of Balance, the value position may have an appeal to persons in both subgroups as an alternative position to their own.

In the case of our illustrative group, with a chronic PF versus NB polarization, a person far out in the PB direction (on the Line of Balance) might have had some appeal to the PF subgroup because of the P element. At the same time, the PB person or image might have had some appeal to the NB subgroup because of the B element. HUGH appealed to the PF subgroup because he was so obviously a person of good will and friendliness. He also appealed to the NB subgroup because he was a jolly entertainer with lots of fantasies about fighting. Of course, in some cases the PF subgroup may not like the B element, and the NB subgroup might not like the P element. But it is still true that the attitude at each pole toward the PB image is less decidedly rejecting than toward the images at the directly opposite pole. The person on the Line of Balance is something like a "compromise candidate."

In addition, it may be that the person or subgroup on the Line of Balance actually offers a substantive position in terms of values and behavior, group norms and group goals, that is an active *alternative* to the two poles of an existing conflict. Not every "compromise candidate" offers an active alternative—a creative synthesis—but some do. For example, imagine the following polarized conflict. One leader and subgroup define the situation as calling for PF behavior, for example: "We will have to cooperate closely, but I think we can succeed. Let's try hard together" (PRO PF in GRP). The opposition leader and subgroup define the situation as calling for NB behavior, for example: "The more we succeed the higher they will place the standard. Let's tell them we refuse to go along with the game" (PRO NB in GRP). The orthogonal mediating position to these two opposed directions, PF and NB, is PB. A mediator might define the situation as one calling for PB behavior, for example: "All they want is for us to have a good time. We brought along this keg of beer, let's drink it" (PRO PB in GRP). Perhaps this is not a very "creative" synthesis, but it does combine the desire of the PRO PF group for friendly behavior in the group (P) with the desire of the PRO NB behavior for evasion of authoritative standards (B). One can imagine the suggestion of such an alternative direction of behavior succeeding in neutralizing the polarization. One can also imagine that a convergence of negative attitudes on a scapegoat outside the group, for example, "Let's go get the timekeeper" (CON NF in SIT), might also neutralize the polarization within the group.

The hypothesis is that the two directions of the Line of Balance (M versus S) indicate an alternative polarization of the total field of possibilities of behavior, images, and values. It is a polarization exactly at right angles to that indicated by the actual position of the Line of Polarization. According to the theoretical hypothesis, such a polarization, if actualized, will tend to exert a contracting and collapsing effect upon the first. It will tend to do this, presumably, if the persons who are interacting are unable to sustain two polarizations in their perception and evaluation at once and the new polarization is very strong. To sustain two polarizations at once as the going norms or ruling values in a live ongoing process of interaction, one would suppose that the resources of attention devoted to the pattern would have to be something like twice as large as for a single polarization, there would have to be something like twice the volume of communication, and so on. I tend to believe that there is a persistent tendency for image fields in actual social interaction, and for the perceptual-evaluative fields of the individual in isolation, for that matter, to polarize along one axis at a time and to unify at each pole, or at least the Positive pole. It may even be the case (I think it is) that it is hard to concentrate with equal attention and fervor on both the process of unification at a given pole and the process of polarization between the two poles. A unification tendency, say in the Positive direction, may be preemptive and draw attention away from the latent P-N polarization that may also be there in secondary strength. By the same token, one might suppose that the rejection of a Negative image can also be preemptive; that, insofar as the polarization is strongly salient, the unification of the group will be a secondary factor in the background.

To some extent, then, although polarization and unification often go together as two processes operating at the same time, they are in competition for the same resources of attention, and when one process is in the figural position, the other is likely to drop somewhat into the background.

Thus, a sufficiently dominant person who represents or presents images far out on the Line of Balance is in a position to command attention and to present an alternative direction that may have appeal to persons on both sides of a polarization. Insofar as attention is fastened on such an alternative, the salience of the original polarization drops, the persons who were maintaining it by their attention and opposition are drawn into an alternative focus of attention, and the polarization tends to collapse (see Sherif, 1958).

There is an interesting question as to whether any person who is rejected by the rest of the group or who perhaps takes a deviant position in the opposite direction from that of the major part of the group is properly called a "Scapegoat." The Polarization-Unification Overlay makes a distinction between the Opposition Direction and the Scapegoat Direction. Is this a worthwhile distinction? In the Opposition Direction one may find an opposition leader of an opposition subgroup, and it does not seem accurate in such a case to speak of the opposition leader as a "Scapegoat." And in the case where a single individual takes a deviant position without any followers (see Schachter, 1951) and so draws a stream of persuasive communication designed to make him give up the deviant position, it seems not to be quite accurate to call such a person a "Scapegoat."

What all three of these cases have in common is that a given person becomes the target of negative attitudes and acts from all or many others in the group. But "the scapegoat" in antique custom was an actual goat or other animal, chosen to bear the bad luck or sins of the community. The scapegoat was symbolically loaded with sins on an occasion of atonement, and driven out or led out into the wilderness. It was not really the goat's fault. The goat was the innocent victim of "displacement"—the guilt for sins he did not really commit were placed upon him. In the cases where we now say that a person is made a "scapegoat" perhaps the innocence of the goat is not always so complete—in many instances, no doubt, there is some symbolic appropriateness, perhaps some behavior or expressions of attitude that provide the excuse. What is really closer to the heart of the meaning, perhaps, is that the Negative behavior toward the Scapegoat is excessive and "displaced" from its original target; it is taking the place of Negative behavior that would otherwise be directed against the self or some other person or subgroup. The displacement of the Negative behavior from its original target makes it possible to overcome a previous polarization, that between the self-image as seen in action and the wished-for self-image, or between the self and fellow group members, or between polarized subgroups. This overcoming of a polarization effects a unification or an "atonement," a reconciliation so that the two are now "as one." This is the meaning of the "Scapegoat Direction" on the Polarization-Unification Overlay. The Scapegoat Direction is the orthogonal direction along the Line of Balance between the Reference Circle or subgroup, and the Opposite Circle or subgroup. An image close to that line, especially if far out, may be symbolically appropriate as a target for the displacement of Negative feelings that the persons in the two polarized subgroups feel for each other. A person who serves as a target for displaced Negative feelings and so tends to neutralize a polarization is thus properly called a "Scapegoat."

To try to build group unity by repeatedly provoking rejection of some Scapegoat image seems questionable ethically, but that it very often happens spontaneously can hardly be doubted. A leader whose own image is quite far out in the UNF direction can sometimes divert Negative reactions that arise from his or her own behavior and displace the Negative feelings upon a Scapegoat image in the NB direction by building up the presumed threat from that quarter, offering to defend the group, and asking the group to combine against the threat. In this way, a UNF leader or other group member in danger of rejection may neutralize the polarization between himself and other group members by switching the line of polarization to the orthogonal direction, thereby placing himself and the other group members on the Positive side of the Line of Balance vis-à-vis the Scapegoat image. Fiedler (1964) has found that there are certain unfavorable situations in which leaders who presumably tend toward the UNF type do paradoxically well. Perhaps this is the explanation, but it would require more careful analysis of his findings and probably new data to tell whether this is the case.

Sometimes individuals are rejected and avoided or attacked by other group members who have moved their images of the individual to the Negative side of the Line of Balance (see Schachter, 1951). Sometimes marginal or isolated individuals are subjected to a build-up of rejection until they are motivated to redefine their self-image and move it over to the other side of the line, in identification with the majority of group members. It appears that this punishing mode of forcing redefinition of the self-image may be facilitated by removing as many supporting elements from the self-image as possible (perhaps by isolation, perhaps by removal of customary clothing, cutting the hair, or provoking of anxiety and fatigue, as in "brainwashing"; see Schein, 1957) and by verbal attempts to make the existing self-image of the attacked person look as bad as possible to him. Some kinds of therapy—or at least intended therapy—proceed by this strategy. Synanon is perhaps the most dramatic example (see Yablonsky, 1965). The "new self-image" of the individual is established on the "Positive" or Reference side of the Line of Balance from the point of view of the unanimous group, while the image of the "former unreconstructed self" of the individual is established on the "Negative" or Opposite side.

Even in unifications of the group by acceptance of a positive image, there may be a Negative contrast image in the background. It is quite possible, and perhaps it is even the most common case, for both PRO and CON images to be represented in the polarization. This was the case, in fact, in our earlier example of "The Capitalistic System and the Unemployed Girls," although the build-up of imagery on the Positive side was not very marked.

It is not the case that simply being on the Line of Balance is enough to give one an alternative to the opposing pulls of a polarization. If one is simply in the middle of the polarization, and neither very dominant nor far out on the Line of Balance, he or she may be in "no man's land." Some persons tend to end there and subside into submissive inaction, I think, because of conflict. In our illustrative group, TOM seemed to react in this fashion. Graphically, the image of such a person would appear as a small circle located near the intersection of the lines of polarization and balance, in the "swing area" (see Figure 10, p. 54). To be equally attracted in both directions or to reject both directions equally without an alternative might put one in the middle. Or, at worst, one might have both conflicts at once and feel an "approach–avoidance" conflict, or ambivalence, toward both poles (see Miller, 1944; Lewin, 1951).

One logical alternative remains as a direction in the space orthogonal to either of the two polarizations mentioned thus far (the Reference Direction versus the Opposite Direction, and the Mediator Direction versus the Scapegoat Direction). The remaining alternative direction is the Dominant Direction—the direction straight upward from the P–N, F–B plane, upon which the other polarizations are located. Graphically the image of a person in this location would appear as a large circle located in the swing area near the intersection of the lines of polarization and balance. The person who comes closest to this position in our illustrative group (on the Group Average Diagram, Figure 10) is MOOSE, and indeed his approach was qualitatively close to straight domination. He was very able, intellectually and verbally, and talked rapidly in a rather loud voice. It was hard to interrupt him, and although HIP and ACE were quite capable of doing so, they did not usually try to talk him down in a mode of straight domination. And yet MOOSE was not conspicuously Negative or disliked. Indeed, some of the members of the PF subgroup put him on the Positive side of the field and identified him as a member of the PF subgroup. (see LAIN, Figure 23, and SUE, Figure 27). The use of straight domination as a mode of neutralizing polarization is akin to the use of force for "pacification" of warring subgroups. One perhaps does not see it very often in polite small groups, probably less often than some form of mediation or scapegoating, but it remains a possibility so long as there are individuals in the group who have the physical strength or personality to intimidate the others. It probably is of major importance in groups somewhat outside the control of the larger-scale social structure, such as boy's gangs, but even in polite self-analytic groups I have been surprised at how often some male in the group will express the fear of physical attack from some larger male.

Of the various modes of neutralizing a polarization, mediation in some form seems to be ethically the least problematic and to offer the most opportunities for developmental or therapeutic change of individuals and improvement in group operation. Interpretation of the existing conflicts can be a natural part of the mediating approach, and this offers the hope of constructive change rather than just temporary relief. In the larger context of group dynamics and individual needs, however, there may be cases where some resort to scapegoating or domination, or some combination of these, may be justified as a temporary expedient or as a means of bringing effective mediation to bear. In particular, both normal leadership and mediation often require some degree of dominance. And it is also true that a too literal-minded devotion to mediation, which does not take into account the essential underlying dynamics of the polarization, may quickly become monotonous, discredited, and ineffective. To a considerable degree this is what happened to HUGH's attempts at mediation, and it happened even more clearly in the case of ANN, who desperately but ineffectively insisted on the values of group unity.

In some groups it is very hard to fill the requirements for unification of the group around a mediating image, but it seems probable that optimal socialization, learning, therapy, and group recovery from task efforts all require periodic unification of the self-images of group members around some Emotionally Expressive Positive Image or set of such images, and perhaps require ACT level behavior of one or more actual group members or the leader in this direction. In other words, in order to do the best job as a parent, a teacher, a therapist, a group leader, or an ordinary participant in a group, one should be able to respond to the periodic need for Dominant, Friendly, and Emotionally Expressive Behavior (UPB).

From my own experience and efforts to theorize about these problems, I feel it is not helpful, in general, for a parent, teacher, therapist, or group leader to have an extreme or a fixed image of the self, or a one-directional conception of the proper behavior for the role. Unhappily, most of the recognized methods and ideals of therapy, in particular, are marked by a single-minded concentration on behavior and content (of the therapist) in one direction. Basically the same thing may be said of conceptions of good parenthood, good teaching, and good group leadership, however. There are conflicting conceptions, and they change and fluctuate in time, from Freud (1933) to Rogers (1970), from Ellis (1962) to Perls (1969), from Theory X to Theory Y (McGregor, 1960). As popular conceptions or theories they tend to be simplified and exaggerated, and in practice to represent polarizations much like those we study in small self-analytic groups.

Different individuals at different times—and the group as a whole at some times—require positive support for the expression of Unfriendly and Emotional behavior, or the presentation of such images, and from this expression of Negative feelings the member or members may be led in a more Friendly, and later, more Instrumentally Controlled direction. I tend to conceive of this sequence as a kind of orbital movement of the average imagery of the group around the space in a counter-clockwise direction.

In the normal case of problem-solving, decision-making groups, after some period of concentration on Instrumentally Controlled behavior—task performance—people tend to "run out of gas," that is, they begin to experience too high a ratio of costs to benefits and thereupon tend to turn in the Unfriendly (N), and then Emotionally Expressive (B) directions (see Bales and Strodtbeck, 1951). From this point it is desirable (in my opinion) for the leader to help pick up the orbital movement, after a suitable period of expression, and bring the group behavior and imagery around to the Positive or Friendly direction again. After some period of reintegration of the Positive feelings of members toward each other and the group, another period of Instrumentally Controlled behavior (toward the F direction) may begin again. This is a kind of optimum phase movement (not always realized) in task-oriented groups. It is optimum, in my opinion, for the leader and members to accept the idea that effective work may reach a peak only periodically and will probably be overcome occasionally by fatigue and conflict. One needs to provide and reinforce some periods of recess, play, recovery, and some periods of Positive behavior and reidentification of members with each other and with the leader.

In self-analytic groups and therapy groups, in contrast to groups that are task-oriented in relation to situational requirements, the optimum movement during a session may be different. After a period of social amenities and assertion of solidarity (ACT level P behavior), the main activity and imagery may perhaps best proceed to the expression of individual experiences and fantasy (ACT level B behavior). The imagery of the fantasy sooner or later tends to provoke polarization of some kind on the Image level (often accompanied by a rise of ACT level N behavior), or a unification of the group around some P image (often with a rise of ACT level P behavior). At some point, perhaps with the help of the leader (or in a therapy group, the therapist), the group may begin a process of more rational analysis of the imagery and events just past (ACT F). There may be several episodes of this kind in a given session. At the very end, the behavior may well turn to the Friendly (P) and Emotionally Expressive (B) directions again, as the solidarity of the group is reasserted by resumption of normal social contact, joking, laughter, recovery, and goodbys. It is probably optimum, as well as very usual, for both task-oriented and therapy groups to begin with a social phase of Positive behavior of short duration at least, and to end with such a phase.

These kinds of phase movement do not happen uniformly or automatically. The optimum phase movements are extremely vulnerable to all kinds of reversals, distractions, fadeouts, confusions, and catastrophes (see Williamson, 1977). A conception of optimal movements needs rather to be formulated as a set of values or group norms and will hardly be realized with much dependability in most groups without the understanding efforts of the leader and group members. It is well to try to formulate conceptions that have proved useful in a given group into articulate group norms or expectations, which group members consciously try to realize, and not to suppose that there is some "law of group development" or "law of inevitable phase movement" that will automatically operate with optimum results (see Bennis and Shepard, 1956; Slater, 1966; Tuckman, 1965; Williamson, 1977).

There are a number of ways of anticipating, as a leader or therapist, the kinds of imagery that may be presented in a group and the effects that given kinds of images may have. The most systematic way is to recall, or to tabulate from SYMLOG records, the value statements PRO and CON that members have made. We can thus discover, for each person as actor, what directions are most likely to be reacted to, PRO and CON. This will ordinarily be a part of the conceptualization of the personality of the individual and will give a generalized picture of the kinds of images that threaten or reassure that particular person. In a therapy group, where much information about life history is presented, the therapist will often be able to surmise why these images are salient to the person.

In the midst of interaction in the group, however, one must depend upon whatever comes to mind as to what individuals have said and done previously and how the images mentioned previously compare with the present image. Much of the skill of mediation and interpretation in a self-analytic training group or a therapy group depends upon having paid close attention to the images different persons have presented and upon deliberate attempts to make comparisons and form conceptualizations of the common features of images. Individuals form and change their conceptualization of themselves by recall and consolidation of the imagery they have presented in their behavior and expressions of attitude. And groups form norms and reach solidarity and definitions of their common purposes by the same means—recall and consolidation of imagery.

Chapter 12

Each Individual Field Is Unique

In the preceding chapters we have examined the dynamics of our case study group in terms of a number of heuristic hypotheses applied to the Group Average Field Diagram. We recognize, however, that the group average is in many ways a crude summary, and that in fact each individual perceives and experiences the members and their processes of interaction in a unique way—not entirely differently, but in some ways significantly so. If we want to understand better why individuals act and react as they do, we need to know how each individual sees the field.

We have at our disposal the ratings made by each individual and also the comments each has made on a questionnaire given at the very end of the group— the "Significant Relationships" questionnaire (see Appendix V, by Stephen P. Cohen). The questionnaire asks each group member to comment on the relationships that have been most significant to him or her personally and to comment separately on those that seem to have been most significant to the group as a whole. The term "significant" is defined in the broadest possible way, so as to include all varieties of relationship by quality and emotional tone, that is, Negative as well as Positive, fantasied as well as real, outside the group as well as inside the regular sessions. Since there are hardly any bounds on the comments that may be elicited by this free-form questionnaire, it is difficult to give any summary treatment, but taken in conjunction with the individual's ratings they often provide valuable qualifications, revisions, and additions, as well as confirmations, of the inferences that may be made from the ratings alone.

We shall take up the ratings and comments of each member of the group in turn, starting with the member who was regarded as most dominant in the Group Average Ratings, and proceeding down in the order of dominance. This order has the advantage of presenting the views of each member in something like the degree of salience of these views to other group members. The members who were most dominant, by and large, talked early and had a large impact upon the group. The content they offered and the personal image they presented in their behavior were necessarily of concern to the group. Implicit in these ideas is another heuristic hypothesis that might be worth examining in individual case studies, namely: The Group Average Field Diagram will provide better inferences about the roles of individuals in the group if the individual members' ratings are weighted according to their degree of dominance before adding them together. With this hypothesis in mind, then, let us begin with the ratings of MOOSE, who was the most dominant member.

MOOSE

MOOSE's ratings of the group members are shown as Figure 17. In comparing his diagram with the Group Average Diagram, Figure 10, one may note a good deal of similarity. He divides the group into two subgroups, separated along a line of polarization fairly similar in angle, and with the same persons in each subgroup, with one exception, that of PAL. He rates PAL more negatively, for some reason that is not clear, but from MOOSE's point of view, Negative is not necessarily bad. He rates himself somewhat on the Negative side and, even more surprisingly, indicates that is where he WISHES to be rated.

MOOSE expressed a good deal of anxiety in the group that he would become obligated in some way to other members by giving or receiving Positive behavior. He felt that an obligation to be Positive would suppress his individuality; he reserved the right to do exactly what he thought best for himself, which included the right to be Negative if that was the way he felt. Actually, MOOSE's appearance was not often Negative. He was large, his movements were gentle and a little awkward, and he often had a smile on his face and a twinkle in his eye.

It never did become completely clear in the group what had happened to MOOSE to make him so distrust persons who were seen as (too) Positive, but the emotional character of the rejection was marked on occasion in his tone of voice and particularly in the polarization involving ANN and himself. The reasons given by MOOSE were mostly at the level of value judgments (CON P in SEL, CON P in GROUP, CON P in SOC) and at the level of self-description (PRO UN in SEL). There were also some fantasies about monsters and stranglers (UN in FAN), which were somewhat loosely associated with the self. On the other hand, there was much that was attractive about MOOSE, and his behavior was less negative than his value statements, though it was certainly very dominant.

MOOSE's EXPECTED rating is very accurate in the P–N/F–B dimensions, although he overestimates the degree to which he will be seen as dominant and makes himself more singular in this respect than the group average perception makes him. The kind of group MOOSE wanted was not necessarily one that was Negative, but one in which everyone was unfettered and dominant like himself, or as he wished to be. According to his theory of society and of groups, self-restraint was unnecessary (CON D in SOC, CON D in GRP, CON D in SEL), and normative restraint was also unnecessary (CON F in SOC, CON F in GRP).

On the other hand, it is clear that he is ambivalent on these issues, and when confronted with a living exemplar of his theories, HIP, he finds himself on the side of law and order. He mentions his relationship with HIP as the one most significant to him and comments, "HIP arouses in me anger and resentment.

FIGURE 17   MOOSE's Diagram (Expansion Multiplier = 2.086)

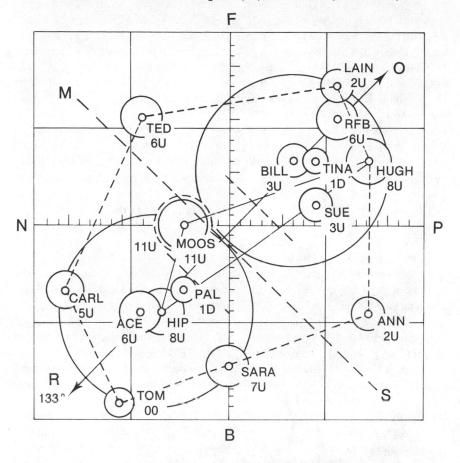

This relationship was developed in the group because he constantly blocks discussion, changes subjects, and cuts off possibilities for openness.'' Actually MOOSE was a concentrator in mathematics and philosophy—hardly subjects characterized by a lack of restraint. If MOOSE was an anarchist, he was a philosophical anarchist, not one in practice. He does not react well to ACE either, the most vocal champion of individualistic anarchism in the group. MOOSE says of his relationship with ACE that it was "negative. Mainly I wish he would go away. ACE is fine by himself, but I find him really obnoxious in the group.''

   The second most significant relationship MOOSE mentions is that with RFB, far out on the opposite pole from ACE in MOOSE's diagram. The relationship with RFB is described as one of "admiration, intellectual interest, developed both in and out of the group. I am interested in SYMLOG, and RFB knows more about it than anyone else. So he received a constant stream of questions concerning scoring and analysis of various actions. I admire him because I think he didn't miss much at all. I think he always knew what was going on.''

MOOSE perceives ANN as far out on the perimeter in the PB direction, and not far from the Line of Balance. She is a good deal more salient in his diagram than in the Group Average Diagram. Her location, as identified from the placement of the Overlay in MOOSE's case, is in the Scapegoat direction, and it is clear that they did clash early in the group. Of his relationship with her, however, MOOSE says it was "friendly, developed both in and out of the group. ANN is my polar opposite in the group. Thus it became very important to me to come to understand how and what she was thinking. She also reminds me of my sister." We see some evidence here that MOOSE's early experience in taking care of his smaller brothers and sisters had some importance in shaping his attitudes and values, and it seems probable that he is making a transference to ANN of some earlier feelings toward his sister. He felt obligated to take care of his smaller brothers and sisters but resented the way in which their dependent needs tied him down.

The relationship MOOSE indicated as most important to the group as a whole was that of TED versus ACE and CARL. This relationship he described as "violent (verbally)." The relationship developed in the group rather than outside, and it "generated lots of talk." The talk was "centered around the question, 'Is it nice to be nasty?' " Ted thought it was not nice to be nasty but in the process of the argument succeeded in putting himself quite far out on the Negative side in MOOSE's perception, as shown on the diagram.

MOOSE also saw TED as polarized, unwillingly, versus the women in the group, particularly TINA, ANN, and SUE. This relationship was characterized by MOOSE as one of "benign goodwill" on TED's side but "annoyance" on the women's side. "TED was insistent on protecting the women, who were equally insistent that they had no need or desire for his protection." The relationship "developed outside the group, but showed itself in the group." This relationship must have had undertones of meaning for MOOSE, since it was parallel to his own relationship to his sisters in that TED was showing the kind of protectiveness that MOOSE was trying to repudiate.

TED, in MOOSE's diagram, seems to be in the perfect position to serve as the Scapegoat for both subgroups, and perhaps he did serve this function for MOOSE. We should note, however, that the placement of the Overlay must be at least partly wrong in MOOSE's case since it indicates TED in the direction for mediator rather than in the S direction. MOOSE's location within the circle of the NB subgroup (though barely within it) led to the assumption in the placement of the Overlay, that NB was MOOSE's reference direction, and hence that PB was the Scapegoat direction. It is true that ANN is located in the PB direction, and the relationship was indeed ambivalent, with ANN apparently serving as the rejected dependent sister for MOOSE. However, TED also seems to be serving as a Scapegoat in the sense of being rejected, as MOOSE describes it, by both subgroups. The error in the labeling of the Overlay directions is perhaps that in most respects MOOSE seems to have identified himself with the PF subgroup rather than with the NB subgroup, contrary to what the location of his image in the field seems to suggest. If PF is taken as MOOSE's Reference Direction, then TED's location in the NF direction becomes the Scapegoat location. Perhaps the theoretical lesson of this is that one should not take too seriously the labeling of the directions R and O and the directions M and S when the perceiving person is himself too close to the Line of Balance, hence probably in conflict. MOOSE seems in fact to have had an approach–avoidance conflict in each of the two dimensions.

MOOSE is very close to the Line of Balance in his own diagram, and although he was classed with ACE and HIP in the Group Average Diagram, by his statements on the questionnaire he put himself in the same subgroup with LAIN, BILL, and others in a polarization versus HIP and ACE. Of the relationship between these two subgroups he says that it was "ambivalent." The relationship developed in the group and "generated lots of discussion. It was a fight over how F (analytic) the group should be." In the end, it was impossible for MOOSE to take an anti-analytic, anti-intellectual stand.

In addition to that, HIP was a competitor for the attention and approval of RFB. MOOSE resented the fact that HIP constantly interfered with intellectual analysis, as indicated above, but he adds, "I also resented the fact that he seemed much more interested in what RFB was doing and thinking than in what we were doing and thinking as a group." MOOSE felt that the relationship between HIP and RFB was important to the group as a whole. He says, "I couldn't tell where it was generated, or how either side felt. It was just obvious that HIP was watching RFB very closely all the time."

Finally, we should not overlook the fact that MOOSE's ratings were actually very constricted, as indicated by the size of the Expansion Multiplier required to bring them out to the edge of the diagram: 2.086. MOOSE's ratings, in other words, were multiplied by slightly more than two. In their raw form the numbers were less than half as large, $1/2.086 = 48\%$. MOOSE's ratings, in fact, were the most constricted in the P–N/F–B dimensions of any member of the group (although TED was a close second). The significance of this, in view of MOOSE's generally expansive personality, is not clear. Perhaps his ratings were constrained by his conflicts in each of the two dimensions. Perhaps he saw himself as more or less in the center of the group and leading by straight dominance, the one direction in which he felt free to go. As we have earlier seen, domination is one means by which polarizations in the dimensions P–N/F–B can be neutralized.

ACE

ACE has the most wildly unusual diagram in the group (see Figure 18). He sees the polarization of the group as extending from NF toward B, almost 90 degrees different from the group average perception. In order to obtain the NF subgroup, ACE has moved BILL, LAIN, TED, and RFB all in the negative direction, most markedly BILL. From ACE's point of view, BILL was probably seen as the emergent leader of the subgroup, although TED is seen as most dominant. This subgroup constitutes the objectionably authoritarian element in the group, from ACE's point of view.

In order to obtain the members for the opposing subgroup, ACE has moved all of the remaining members found in the PF area of the Group Average Diagram, SUE, HUGH, and TINA, out of that area and into the B subgroup. PAL and

FIGURE 18 ACE's Diagram (Expansion Multiplier = 1.185)

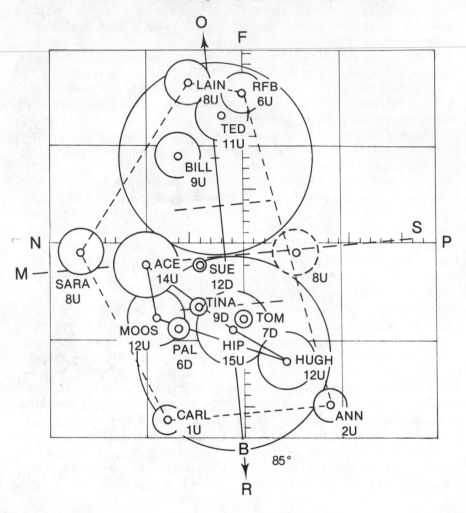

SARA are also moved to the NB quadrant. HUGH and ANN are moved considerably Backward and more Negative, although they remain in the PB quadrant. After ACE's onslaught, not a single member of the group remains in the PF quarter of the field!

ACE's diagram is also unusual in that he perceives a higher average level of dominance than any of the other members. He sees HIP at an all-time high level of 15U, followed by himself at 14U. HUGH and MOOSE are also members of the dominant subgroup, with 12U each. In spite of his close partnership with CARL, ACE does not exaggerate CARL's dominance and places him much farther Backward than himself.

ACE sees himself on the Line of Balance, curiously enough, not within the subgroup circle that one would tend to infer is his Reference Circle. He

EXPECTS to be seen on the Negative side of the line of balance, however, and, except for SARA, he expects to be seen as the most Negative member of the group.

The significance of ACE's placement of himself on the Line of Balance and on the Negative side (in spite of a WISH to be seen on the Line of Balance on the Positive side) is not clear. It is, however, similar in its placement to MOOSE's placement of himself—that is, in a very dominant position very near the middle of the group. It may be that this is a characteristic picture for the person who decides to "divide and conquer"—to identify with neither subgroup, but to neutralize the conflict by domination and to accept the perception that others will have of him as Negative as well as dominant. It is curious that ACE places SARA near the Line of Balance but even farther toward the Negative side than himself. There was no indication that ACE did not like SARA; on the contrary, he openly complimented her in the group quite early—he said he "liked her style." Perhaps he viewed it as a style of nonidentification with others, which, like his own style, was likely to give rise to Negative perceptions but nevertheless had its advantages. On the other hand, SARA's comment (see p. 133) indicates that she may have resented ACE's superior attitude toward less mature members of the group, and he may have picked this up and retaliated.

One may wonder if ACE's placement of his EXPECTED image on the Line of Balance may be an indication that he tended to some extent to reject both poles of the polarization. From many encounters in the group it was clear that he rejected the cluster LAIN, BILL, TED, and RFB. He mentions his conflict with LAIN as important to the group. It was not clear that ACE rejected the cluster at the B pole—but if he did not, in some sense, why did he move himself Forward at the same time he moved them Backward? Was he subjectively gathering a group of followers and placing himself at the Forward periphery of that subgroup? Or was he placing himself in a mediating position between them and the Forward cluster, and to some extent accepting as well as rejecting both subgroups? It is not clear. Perhaps he was doing both.

ACE associated himself closely with CARL, though with some fear and ambivalence, apparently. On one occasion CARL jokingly grabbed ACE by the neck as if to choke him to keep him quiet, and ACE mistook the move as a serious attack. Perhaps CARL was rougher than he had intended to be. It appeared that the relationship between the two was complicated and contained some strains, but they generally stuck together and supported each other in the self-analytic sessions. ACE had a joking relationship with HIP and often talked "man-to-man" with HUGH. So it is difficult to believe that he actively rejected the people he moved into the B cluster, but it is not so difficult to believe that he was somewhat ambivalent. He may also have been ambivalent and not simply Negative about at least some of the persons in the NF cluster. Although ACE took mostly a counter-instrumental role in the group, it seemed clear that he was capable of highly directed instrumental behavior on occasion, particularly with regard to his visualized role in the business world.

It is of interest that ACE also placed his WISHED-FOR image on the Line of Balance, and on the Positive rather than on the Negative side of the field. ACE expected that group members would see him as Negative but wished that they would see him as positive. We have almost no information about his family background that might help us understand why he did not seem to mind being seen on the Negative side of the space, but we do know that his family was broken in some way and he was cared for part time by a maternal grandmother. He indicated that he developed a pattern of deception of both mother and grandmother as he shuttled back and forth between them.

There is not much evidence that he saw himself as a Positive Mediator, but that he had some kind of mediating role in mind—perhaps with himself as a kind of Dominator-Scapegoat-Mediator—is suggested by the fact that he put both his EXPECTED and his WISHED-FOR image on the Line of Balance and moved a considerable number of image points Backward in the space in order to do so.

On the Significant Relationships questionnaire ACE indicated that the relationship between himself and TED was the most significant to him personally. "I had a great deal of trouble standing him. He is anathema to some of the things I believe in, both in terms of values, and in ways of interacting." Of the relationship between himself and CARL on the one side and TED on the other, which ACE thought most important to the group as a whole, ACE says, "Neither CARL nor I could stand TED, and this was the basis for the most acrimonious polarization in the group." With regard to CARL, ACE says, "I like CARL— and I am gratified that despite vast differences in values we get along. I feel there is mutual respect and support." He also says, "CARL was always a great exponent of rationalism, and certainly of nonviolence, but his tendency to look angry made the 'strangulation scene' with yours truly actually frightening to people—including yours truly."

On his diagram ACE placed ANN in a far PB direction, and he says of her, "There is a mutual liking, and mild sexual attraction and flirtation." In another context, in illustrating the discrepancies that sometimes appear between the nonverbal and other aspects of behavior, he said, "ANN would quite often disagree with others and actually launched some fairly heavy attacks. However, her soft-spokeness, and the fact that her voice quavered, and her very friendly demeanor muted these signs of negativity, she was rated almost universally positive."

Regarding HUGH, whom ACE rated less positively and much farther Backward than the group average, well within his Reference Circle, ACE says, "HUGH usually allied himself very strongly with the UNB group. However, his friendly voice and physiognomy seemed to belie such an orientation so he was rated P. . . . I admire many aspects of HUGH's ways of dealing with people and situations—especially his control and deliberateness. I think I've learned from him." ACE indicated that the relationship between himself and HUGH and MOOSE was important to the group. It was, he says, "a strong coalition on the value level that would come to my support at times." It is not exactly clear what values ACE has in mind, since HUGH did not seem to share the strong value on individualism which ACE and MOOSE seemed to have in common. However, HUGH did have in common with ACE and MOOSE a certain liking for male dominance and carefree expression of aggression, at least on the fantasy level.

ACE also mentions the relationship between himself, CARL, and HIP. The three of them, he says, constituted "the strongest B coalition—it really dominated the group."

HIP

The most unusual thing about HIP's ratings (see Figure 19) is that he places his WISHED-FOR image toward the far extreme of the Positive subgroup, very close, indeed, to the image of RFB; but on the other hand, EXPECTS that he will be seen as a member of the NB subgroup.

That the relationship of HIP and RFB was unusual in some way was apparent to everybody in the group. HIP kept his eyes on me almost constantly, and almost always during his participation and immediately afterward he looked at me as if for approval (NON DPF). This was often observed by others and commented upon in the group. HIP gave many indications that he wanted to act as a kind of helper or lieutenant to me, but on the other hand he kept up a joking conflict with me. He seemed to take great pleasure in trying to anticipate what I was going to do or say, in "beating me to the punch," and in jokingly analyzing my behavior. He was helped in this effort by the fact that he had taken the course the term before and so understood some things that were going on better than some others. (It was possible to repeat the course at that time, and both HIP and SARA had taken the course the previous term.)

For my part, I liked HIP very much and enjoyed the joking conflict, although I found his "flashy footwork" a little wearing at times and endorsed the complaint of other members that he prevented any serious analysis of his role, as well as any serious involvement in the group by his evasive tactics. I often encountered HIP at lunch, and we often sat and talked. He dropped most of his evasive manner at those time. It seems clear to me that HIP did indeed identify with me and that in his own way he took the course very seriously, liked it, and got a lot out of it. At the end of his final examination he wrote: "UNB (HIP) to UPF (FREED) Have a Good Summer & Thanx for I learned a lot about *myself* & people who are interacting within my environment!"

There is some indication that the observation by the other group (Groups A and B observed each other) may have been particularly anxiety-provoking for HIP. On his examination HIP wrote about the hostility between the two groups, which he believed was caused by their observation of each other. During a vacation in the middle of the term two of the four microphones were stolen from the ceiling, and HIP felt it must have been done by somebody uncomfortable about the observation. He suggested that "the microphone theft was another act of discontent with being observed (such as putting a coat over a camera, et al.). The fact that only two mikes were taken tells me that the person wanted to show displeasure but was still guarded at displaying total hostility. Because the majority of electronic observation (including the oscilloscope) was done by tape recorder & microphones—two mikes were taken. This would allow the continuation of the sessions (especially interactive) but would show displeasure." It is true that one of the advanced students who had taken the course before was engaged in monitoring voice quality by using an oscilloscope, but this was not mentioned by

FIGURE 19 HIP's Diagram (Expansion Multiplier = 1.291)

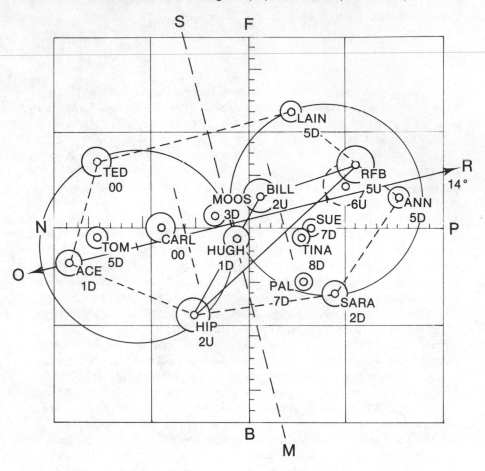

any other member of either of the two groups. I think it possible not only that HIP was made unusually anxious by the observation but also that his very close observation of me was a defense against being observed, and perhaps also a kind of retaliation. On one occasion HIP engaged in a "staring match" with me, which he won.

I think it likely that HIP felt considerable conflict about power, as well as about authority—that he both identified strongly with persons in positions of power and potential authority over him and also mistrusted and rejected such persons. His role as a joker in the group was a kind of compromise expression of both of these tendencies and also served to mediate, to his mind, the conflict between the two subgroups.

It will be noted, however, that HIP did not see the group polarized for and against a negative authority image (as ACE did), but much more nearly Positive versus Negative. And with the exception of his own WISHED-FOR image and the image of RFB, HIP tended to put the women on the Positive side, and the men on the Negative side. Both BILL and HUGH are moved from their Positive location in the Group Average Diagram into the neutral part of the space. There is some suggestion, perhaps, that the conflict between Positive and Negative felt by HIP had some relation to earlier attitudes toward women (as Positive) and men (as Negative). On the questionnaire, HIP mentioned only the relationship between himself and SARA, whom he had known before in the group they had attended and on the outside. This relationship, he says, was the "only one I feel was extremely significant." The relationship was one of "good friends—she really helped (protected?) me in a lot of situations within the group." The term "(protected?)," interpolated by HIP himself, suggests he made a transference to SARA as a mother figure. He indicated that this relationship was also important to the group as a whole: "She helped HIP out of some situations which she (and probably he) felt were threatening."

Another feature of HIP's ratings is unusual and perhaps related to his feelings about dominance or power. His ratings are exceptionally flat along the U–D gradient. He places himself at only 2U, and also BILL at only 2U. Only one person, RFB, is placed higher than that, at 5U. HIP's own WISHED-FOR rating, however, is at 6U. It is astonishing that he places MOOSE at 3D, and ACE at 1D! It is debatable whether these ratings reflect his perceptions in fact or an attempt to compensate for his scoring difficulties. In the SYMLOG Scoring HIP more than once complained that all he could see was U, and that nearly every act he recorded was scored U.

There were several hostile encounters in the group between HIP and TED, but HIP does not mention his relationship with TED. He does, however, indicate that the relationship of ANN and TED was important to the group. He says "they always ended up arguing between each other (if ANN spoke). I believe there may be some *denied* mutual attraction."

HIP mentions only one more relationship in his questionnaire, that between himself and CARL, but phrased in the third person and presented as important to the group as a whole. He says, "Really think HIP liked CARL and his style." As for the rest, HIP says, "within our group—that's about all that I saw." There is no mention of ACE, who received HIP's most Negative ratings, and no discussion of any of the women except SARA and ANN, although he placed all of the women on the Positive pole of his ratings.

RFB

My own ratings are shown as Figure 9 and have been sufficiently discussed. They are mentioned here only because we are taking up the views of group members in order of their rated dominance, and I was fourth on the gradient.

TED

TED's ratings (Figure 20) were quite constricted and required a multiplier of more than 2. It is not clear whether he was trying to obtain a relative unification

FIGURE 20 TED's Diagram (Expansion Multiplier = 2.004)

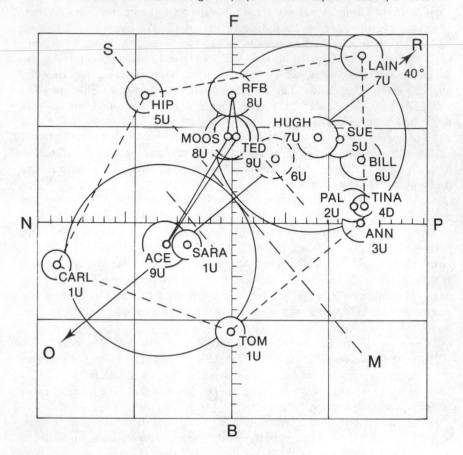

of the group by constricting his ratings, but it is possible. During the first part of the term, TED was located farther out in the NF region of the space and made strong efforts throughout the term to escape the perception others had of him as too authoritarian and tried hard to be accepted as a part of the PF subgroup. One of the notable features of TED's ratings is that he moves HIP out of the NB quadrant and far into the NF quadrant, the location TED himself was trying to escape. We may remember, from HIP's diagram (Figure 19), that HIP placed TED in the NF quadrant, not too far from the location in which TED placed him. It appears, in other words, that each perceived the other as authoritarian and disapproving, and this did indeed appear to characterize their attitudes toward each other. Each seems to have tried, in his own perception, to make the other the authoritarian Scapegoat. In TED's diagram, HIP is found directly on the Line of Balance in the S direction. Curiously enough, however, neither mentions the relationship with the other as significant.

TED mentions his relationship with BILL as the most significant to him personally, "both inside, when we frequently signalled each other and encouraged or discouraged various behavior, and outside. We actually went some other place 'alone twice and a third time in the same group—we communicated a great deal. I trust him and respect him, and he supported me—all three reciprocated, I believe.'' BILL is placed much farther out in the Positive direction than Forward in TED's diagram, and three persons are placed farther Forward than TED's placement of himself, LAIN, RFB, and HIP. In the placement of his WISHED-FOR location, TED indicates that he wished to become, or to be seen, as less far Forward and more Positive than he earlier was in the group. The location is still a little farther Forward than Positive, however.

TED identifies the second most important relationship as that between himself and CARL. This relationship was characterized, he says by ''very intense negativity and distrust inside the sessions (though we generally avoided each other outside) which made the group uncomfortable and polarized it around crystallized issues.''

TED identifies his relationship with RFB as the third most important to him-self. ''Though there has been virtually no explicit interaction, and few clear signals from him, I sense that I too hold his sense of values regarding life and relationships, and this vicarious support has considerably strengthened my self-concept—much as my relationship with BILL has done—in this dimension.'' The relationship of RFB to the group as a whole was mentioned as most impor-tant to the group. TED described it as ''essentially trusting (on the part of group members) but wary. Essentially respectful, but at times doubtful. [There was] some aloofness [in RFB's manner?] consequent of his vague disapproval and explicit condemnation of various values.'' The relationship was, TED thought, ''generally [similar to that of] parent-child.''

TED certainly perceived polarization in the group, not only between himself and CARL, as mentioned above, but between ACE on the one side, and RFB and himself on the other. ''Within the group,'' he says, ''the central values were challenged and clarified by these actors. The resultant friendliness or lack thereof of these struggles also keyed the mood of the discussions.'' TED also saw ACE as reinforced by HIP, MOOSE, and HUGH. ''At various times, his values received support from these adherents, in ascending order. This was the B pole, often negative toward the rest of the group.'' This last remark is a little paradoxi-cal since in the actual rating TED places all three, HIP, MOOSE, and HUGH, on the Forward side. It is possible that TED made the ratings primarily in terms of behavior and not of values. The ratings are defined with terms that are mostly behavioral in their direct meanings, but of course the distinctions between values and behavior are not always clear, and it does appear that in most persons' ratings (perhaps not those of TED) the value position taken by the actor tends to influ-ence the others' perception of his behavior.

TED mentions his relationship with MOOSE as personally important to him, and in terms that suggest some positive feelings. ''Especially outside of class, discussions we frequently have, have served to clarify my own self image through his reflection, and to help me appreciate the complexity of other per-sonalities. Our friendship is relatively positive but essentially intended to be productive.'' It will be noted that TED rates MOOSE in the exact location of his own EXPECTED rating; both are on the neutral line, in the P–N dimension, and out on the Forward side, along with RFB nearby. The importance to TED of the value-controlled direction, F, is indicated by the final set of relationships he mentions as important to the group, his own relationships to BILL, SUE, and LAIN. He saw these persons as the core of the subgroup with which he identified himself: "the positions of these three actors frequently coincided with the focus of an F pole, often positive, which was—per value statements—generally advanced by TED."

It is of interest that TED places PAL, TINA, and ANN very close together and in a primarily Positive location, but he does not mention them as involved in the relationships important to him or to the group. It may be remembered that he tried, in various contexts, to obtain some kind of acceptance from these women, as well as from SUE, and perhaps, as ACE indicated, offered them some kind of protection—a protection they did not want. They did not respond positively to him, and in the end he does not mention them.

BILL

BILL's diagram is shown as Figure 21. The diagram shows a strong polarization between a PF subgroup, with which BILL identifies himself, and an NB subgroup. However, BILL appears to see a third small subgroup in the swing area in the mediating direction, consisting of HUGH, PAL, and possibly SARA. MOOSE also has a position somewhat removed from the main NB subgroup, not within the Swing Area but at least distinguished considerably from the NB subgroup in that he is on the Forward side.

The PF subgroup in BILL's diagram is quite closely clustered, all falling easily within his reference circle and all, in fact, in the polar half of the circle. BILL was six or seven years older than the rest of the group, of foreign origin, and had mild language difficulties. However, he also had a considerable amount of experience as a group therapist. He was a postdoctoral special student in Psychology studying with RFB. In the early part of the group BILL was not very active and probably was concerned lest he might be rejected. His comments nearly always had a Positive tone, and it is notable that even in the final questionnaire every one of the relationships he mentions as important to him or to the group were Positive relationships. Although the polarization of the group shows clearly on his diagram, he does not mention it at all in his questionnaire answers.

Toward the end of the group BILL began to be more active and was generally strong and Positive in his behavior. It will be noted that his WISHED-FOR location, unlike that of most of the members, is less Positive than his EXPECTED location, and more Forward. BILL was explicitly trying in his participation, meanwhile, to move more definitely into a position of analytic task leadership and not to be so constrained by a desire to be seen positively.

All of the relationships BILL mentions as important to him were with members of the PF subgroup. He mentions first the relationship with RFB, which he says was "friendly and cooperative, in and outside the group." The relationship was marked by "trust, affection, and respect." RFB and BILL had separate contact outside the group as a part of BILL's postdoctoral program and talked frankly

FIGURE 21 BILL's Diagram (Expansion Multiplier = 1.406)

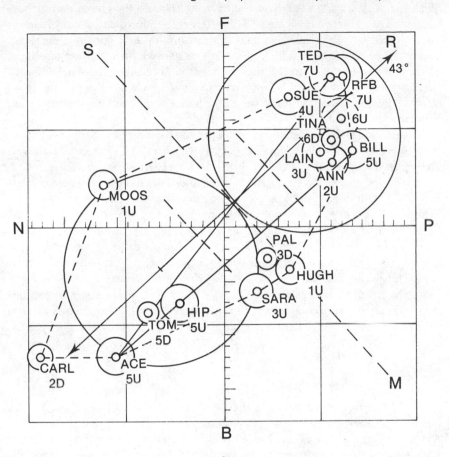

about all aspects of the group. They formed, in fact, an alliance. The relationship between them was similar in quality to that which often pertains between a task-oriented leader in a group, who has a more Forward and less Positive position (RFB), and a social-emotional leader, who has a less Forward and more Positive position (BILL) (see Bales, 1958). Cooperation between such a pair is not infrequently the core leader relationship in task-oriented groups. In the present instance the distance separating the two was perhaps less than it often is, and perhaps less than optimum. It would have helped, for example, if I had had a closer relationship with HUGH, who perhaps came closer to functioning as a social-emotional leader than BILL and had more influence with the members of the NB subgroup.

BILL mentions next the relationship to LAIN, which was marked by "some kind of affection, having some things in common intellectually and emotionally." BILL mentions his relationship with LAIN as important to the group as a whole, and there he says the relationship was "friendly, forward, positive, and human."

It will be noted that BILL rates TED much more positively than the group does on the average, and he also mentions his relationship with TED as important to him. It was, he says, "a very friendly exchange outside the group, and supportive in the group sessions. We are very different, but this didn't do any harm to our relationship." BILL also mentions this relationship as important to the group as a whole and recognized a kind of complementarity in their desired directions of movement. The relationship was a "positive exchange, supportive, [with] BILL moving slowly toward N [and] TED moving toward positive." Here, then, is an interesting instance fitting the concepts of social exchange theory (see Homans, 1961; Blau, 1968; Thibaut and Kelley, 1959).

Of his relationship with another member of the PF subgroup, SUE, BILL says there was "not very much going on, but I felt her [to be] more mature and flexible in the dimensions F–B and P–N." The relationship was "friendly."

Toward the end of the group BILL more and more directly confronted ACE and CARL with regard to behavior and attitudes of theirs that he felt were not helpful to the group, but in his questionnaire answers the only references he makes to members of the NB subgroup are made in a context of help they were receiving from other members. BILL felt that the relationship between ANN and CARL was important to the group. He says they were "friends in the outside phase, CARL feeling less and less comfortable in the negative position, ANN becoming much more organized." Of SARA and HIP, BILL says the relationship was one of "protection, simplicity, and friendliness." These terms seem to me to be descriptive of BILL's relationship to the group as well.

HUGH

HUGH's ratings are shown as Figure 22. The most striking thing about them is that he has taken apart the two opposing subgroups as they appear in the Group Average Diagram, in the directions PF and NB, and has moved the members in such a way as to show the group as perhaps even polarized in the direction PB versus NF. It is true that the NF area is not heavily populated, in fact only TED and HIP appear to be surely there, but LAIN and MOOSE are close to the periphery of HUGH's opposite circle. Most of the rest of the members have been brought into the PB circle, or nearly so, ranged around HUGH himself near the center. The constriction of ratings is considerable, requiring an expansion multiplier of 1.885, and the conformation of the perimeter is not much elongated, which may indicate a desire for the group to be unified. There are, in fact, a number of evidences that HUGH is strongly motivated to avoid polarization and to neutralize existing polarizations by mediation. By professed ambition, HUGH wanted to work in politics or perhaps in international affairs. His WISHED-FOR image is far out in the PB direction, indeed, off the diagram.

The most important relationship to himself, HUGH indicates, is with PAL. As we know, PAL was a kind of companion in mediation with him outside the group. HUGH says, "I suspect this relationship was a bit obvious, as we usually sat together. But, our relationship of affectionate friendship was developed *outside* the group, though simultaneously [within the group?]."

Next in importance, however, HUGH mentions his relationship with TED.

FIGURE 22 HUGH's Diagram (Expansion Multiplier = 1.885)

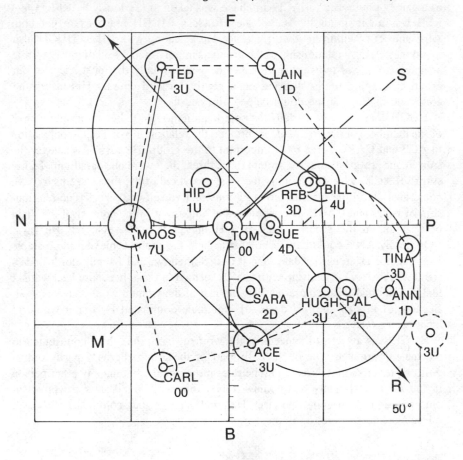

TED, as we can see from HUGH's diagram, is at the extreme opposite pole along HUGH's line of polarization, and he has been moved considerably in a Negative direction. HUGH's smoothing over of the potential conflict is evident in what he says: "While I can't say TED is a close friend, I do value his opinions. At times he infuriates me, mainly because I don't understand his moral righteousness, but he is a warm and friendly guy, which I like in people." HUGH then adds a parenthetical characterization: "(Present Conflict, with a potential for cooperation)." This is a very characteristic example of HUGH's tendency to voice both sides of a conflict and then attempt to smooth over or soften the difference.

With regard to CARL and ACE, however, with whom HUGH is really in tune, he speaks with enthusiasm: "I just flat out like these dudes. I like their directness and no bullshit attitudes. Both CARL and ACE remind me of some of my co-workers in the summer. While both may be a bit rude, I admire their honesty, which I often lack." It is notable that on his diagram HUGH moves ACE to the Positive side, not far from his own location, and also moves CARL in the Positive direction, though he does not get him over the line. HUGH mentions the relationship of ACE and RFB as important to the group and says, "What started as a game of authority for ACE, I believe was taken too seriously by RFB. I feel RFB was a bit unfair to ACE." Nevertheless, HUGH manages to get both ACE and RFB within his own reference circle, along with BILL. HUGH also mentioned BILL's relationship to the group as important and said of him, "While at times BILL was too forward for me, he was certainly the most adept in our group at keeping things directed on a gently forward course. His increasing command of English, no doubt helped him and us."

HUGH does not entirely deny the polarization thought to be important by most of the members of the group. He mentioned the relationship of TED in opposition to ACE and CARL as the most important to the group. He says, "Whatever the split in our group, it centered around these three; they were our paradigm. To my surprise, ACE, who was initially the least analytical of the three, seems to have come away with the most in terms of constructive self-analysis." The relationship of ANN and CARL was mentioned as important in the context of the main polarization in the group, which HUGH interprets as F versus B. He says, "Originally ANN could have been able to help the group achieve a more stable F–B balance at an earlier date than it did. Somehow, and I really don't understand why, ANN's friendship with CARL seemed to make her more backward. I feel if ANN had talked more, earlier, the rest of the women would have as well. Because of this [if she had done so], our male-dominated F–B split wouldn't have been as severe."

HUGH was aware of the needs of the women, then, though he contributed to the male-dominated tone of the early part of the group. Perhaps partly out of guilt, he remarks of TINA, whom he rates more positively than any other person in the group, "I really don't know TINA that well, but she is a woman of presence and great self-assurance. Her well thought-out comments, however infrequent, never failed to impress me."

LAIN

LAIN's diagram is shown as Figure 23. It shows the polarization of the group roughly along the same angle as the Group Average Diagram, but there are several interesting differences. Many more members are directly along the straight P vector, for one thing. And for another, RFB and TED are isolated in a subgroup by themselves out in the Scapegoat direction. In addition, LAIN's EXPECTED self-image is located considerably less far forward than the rating she actually RECEIVED, and her WISHED-FOR location is directly on the P vector, and quite far out. None of these unique features is recognized by LAIN in her comments, which seem to be oriented rather to the Group Average Diagram, but, as we shall later see, there may be an explanation.

LAIN indicates that the most important relationship to her was with BILL. This relationship was one of "friendship, cooperation, support. I felt close to BILL and often talked with him outside the group. I felt that he was an effective group leader and I watched how he worked, trying to learn from him. In the self-analytic phase we often supported each other's forward moves. Our close-

FIGURE 23 LAIN's Diagram (Expansion Multiplier = 1.222)

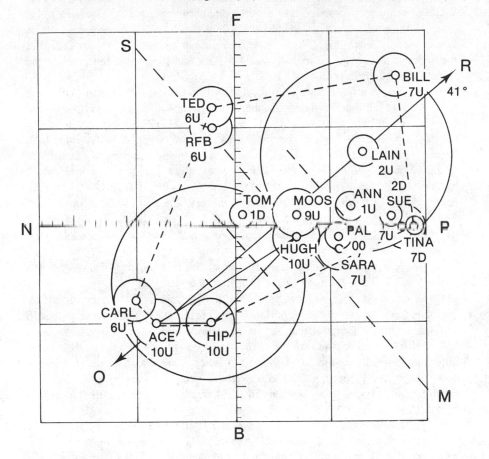

ness on the graph reflects our intentional alliance.'' LAIN and BILL are indeed close on both the Group Average Diagram and her own, but it is perhaps a little inconsistent that her WISHED-FOR location is not on the PF vector, where BILL and her EXPECTED images are found, but directly on the P vector and far out, along with SUE and TINA.

The polarization in the group focused partly upon LAIN, and she mentions her relationship with ACE as second most important. The relationship was one of ''conflict, curiosity, distrust. This relationship developed mostly inside the group, where we often were on opposite sides of a polarization and sometimes expressed hostility towards each other. I spoke with ACE a few times in the outside phase, but usually felt frustrated or rebuffed. ACE aroused many negative feelings in me, including a certain haughtiness or disdain. However, this conflict was personally valuable and I feel that I learned a lot about myself and about people who are very different from me. At times ACE made clear statements of his values, feelings, and position that caused me much thought and questioning.'' No doubt the feelings of ''haughtiness or disdain'' that LAIN felt were picked up by ACE and felt as authoritarian disapproval. Conversely, LAIN's feelings were the focus of his own disapproval, as we have seen from his diagram (Figure 18), where he moved LAIN and all the other ringleaders of the PF subgroup over to the Negative side of the diagram. Very probably the other members of this subgroup, namely TED, BILL, and RFB, also felt some of the same authoritarian disapproval of ACE that LAIN felt.

Within her own reference subgroup, LAIN felt that the relationship with SUE and TINA was important. These are the two persons whom she placed far on the Positive side of her diagram, along with her own WISHED-FOR location. Her relationship with these two, she says, was one of "friendship, warmth, tacit support and cooperation. The relationship was developed mostly outside the group, although within the in-group phase we usually supported each other, often by non-verbal signs—smiles, eye contact. I shared with SUE and TINA deeply personal problems which I did not share with very many other people until later. The comfort and support from them extended beyond the class situation, although I did not see them outside of class. At times I felt I was their spokesman within the group, the contact point in the group for those two downward members. ANN, within the group, was also part of this relationship. But outside the group [she] was not as much [a part] of the relationship."

However, all of these persons, plus PAL, SARA, and TOM, are mentioned by LAIN as forming a subgroup important to the group as a whole. The relationship of these members she describes as one of "cooperation, friendship, alliance." "This is really a subgroup of the women and downward people. It was more important toward the middle of the group when there was a lot of discussion about the rights of the upward and downward people. Discussion of this issue continued for two or three sessions in and outside the group until the current polarization between NB and PF broke and scattered the subgroup." However, these are the persons (along with MOOSE and HUGH) who seem to form a tight subgroup along the P vector in LAIN's diagram. We may not be far wrong if we suppose that these members remained important to LAIN, particularly the women, as a support group to which she wished in fact to retire from her actual position farther Forward, where she was more exposed to the attacks of ACE and CARL.

Although HIP is placed near CARL and ACE on LAIN's diagram, her feelings about him were different, very possibly because HIP's attitudes toward authority were different from those of CARL and ACE. HIP's attitudes toward RFB, for example, contained a large component of positive feeling, although mixed with distrust and competitiveness. LAIN mentions the relationship between HIP and RFB as important to her personally. She says, "I felt a great deal of curiosity towards HIP, especially in his relationship to RFB, but also in general, about how he operated in the group. I felt friendly toward HIP, saw him outside of class and talked with him about what was happening in the group. But the importance of the relationship to me was the interest I had in watching HIP react, dodge, and parry the thrusts of the group and in trying to understand his concern with RFB's authority." As we may guess from the isolated position in which LAIN places RFB and TED, on the Scapegoat line, LAIN probably had ambivalent attitudes about authority herself, and more specifically about task-oriented leadership.

This may account, in part, for her feeling of curiosity about HIP, which one may suppose is an interest that may be based upon an attraction to some person, object, or event that stirs repressed or suppressed feelings.

Certainly in a part of her consciousness LAIN thought of herself as in a relationship of "cooperation, forward movement" with RFB and BILL. Of this group, which she thought was important to the group as a whole, she said, "This block of people pushed the group forward and was responsible for initiating much of the forward activity. All three were close together on the chart, showing that the group recognized the alliance." However, it is on the Group Average Diagram (Figure 10) that these three are close together, and in LAIN's own ratings they are quite widely separated, with RFB placed a little on the Negative side of the field, in LAIN's Scapegoat direction, alongside of TED.

LAIN thought the relationship of TED with ACE and CARL was important to the group. It was a relationship of "conflict, hostility, polarization. There was conflict on the value, norm, and act level. The group talked about it a lot. There was overt hostility both in and outside the group." Countering this relationship of polarization, however, was the relationship between TED and BILL, which was one of "friendship, cooperation. This was an important relationship both in and out of the group. TED and BILL supported each other in the group and often talked together outside. They were important allies—TED often supported BILL by clarifying and stressing the importance of what BILL said. BILL protected TED by being a friendly attacker and exposing TED's shortcomings so that TED's opponents, ACE and CARL, would not have the chance."

Finally, LAIN mentions the relationship of CARL, MOOSE, and HUGH as important to the group. It was a relationship, she says, of "cooperation [and] unification, but ambivalence. They formed a network across the space which tended to moderate conflict and pull together opposing sides. Inside the group, in both the self-analytic and the theoretical phase, they provided a lot of material for the group to process. They exchanged ideas a lot on the outside and provided a cooler forum for airing value and norm conflicts." LAIN recognizes, then, that MOOSE and HUGH performed mediating functions for the group as a whole and were not simply full-time members of the NB subgroup.

What further can be said about the peculiarities of LAIN's diagram? It seems likely to me that LAIN wished to overcome the implication that she was too instrumentally oriented and not Positive enough. She was attacked by CARL and ACE on various occasions for trying too hard to be a task leader. It is my impression from talking with LAIN that she wished to be a successful leader and was rather dismayed at the Negative reactions she got from CARL and ACE, in particular, but also she was disappointed at the reactions to her from the rest of the group. Her interventions often tended to result in silence. When she talked to me about this I suggested that part of the reason might be that she did not often enough provide the actual content required to answer the task needs, but rather asked others to provide it. She often made leader-like motions but did not really take the lead in a substantive sense by providing content in the form of either analysis or other matter for discussion. LAIN may have felt that the far-out Forward direction she tended to take at the ACT level was too exposed to criticism and wished for a more Positive reaction.

LAIN places both TED and RFB in an isolated subgroup on the Line of Balance in the Scapegoat direction, in her ratings. At the same time she moved herself and other members of the PF subgroup in the Positive direction. In many respects it appeared to me that LAIN was quite closely identified with me and regarded me positively, hence her rating is something of a puzzle to me. What happened?

On one occasion quite far along in the middle period of the group, the group had been discussing a member of the *other* group (remember, our group was one of two, who observed each other). Somebody said of a girl in the other group, "She talks too much and never says anything." An objection was made that this was an unkind remark. Whereupon ACE replied, "We can say anything we like about the members of the other group. We don't have to pay any attention to whether they like it or not." I responded with disapproval of ACE's view, saying that I would not permit this attitude to become a group norm; that we were obliged by our original agreement and by the real nature of the situation to show consideration for each other and to protect each other.

My remarks, while advocating a norm of PRO P in GROUP, and also PRO P in SIT, vis-à-vis the other group, were, at the ACT level, certainly UNF— moralistic and disapproving of ACE. (It turned out that possibly ACE had not read the relevant part of the syllabus, containing the basic agreement, since he entered the course a little late, so perhaps his remark was not intentionally a breach of the agreement, as it seemed to me.) Whether or not I had justification, there was no doubt that on this occasion I departed from my usual mildly Positive analytic approach during the self-analytic session.

I used this incident later in the group to illustrate the way in which a leader may err, by moving too strongly in the UNF direction: I said that if one does this often, he or she may become viewed as a Negative threat against which the group may unify. I said that I expected my image had been moved during this incident to a UNF location and hoped that it would not stay there. My guess, however, is that in this encounter with ACE I stepped into the role of authoritarian disapproval LAIN felt she had been occupying vis-à-vis him, and that she became somewhat frightened of what might happen if she continued to show her disapproval of ACE. This perhaps was added to the criticism I had made of her leadership concerning not enough content, and this perhaps was added to the image of the criticism that had been made of the girl in the other group who "talked too much and never says anything." Perhaps for these reasons, LAIN subjectively withdrew from her far-Forward role and gave it to me. She moved her WISHED-FOR image away from the exposed Forward position and to a far-Positive location, following it with her EXPECTED image as far as she could without being too unrealistic. And at the same time she took me at my word that I had veered in the UNF direction and told no less than the truth in answering on the ratings that I behaved in a UNF way "sometimes."

If something like this actually happened, it is consistent with the general heuristic hypothesis that when images are placed outside the polarization (contrary to the Group Average Rating) and on or near the Line of Balance, the person so rating may wish, in some partial sense at least, to be there and to exercise some influence, or to have some other person exercise influence, or to receive or escape the reactions of others to the image placed in that location. This hypothesis applies to my own attitudes vis-à-vis HUGH and ANN, in that I wished that they would act as a pair to mediate, from the Positive side, between the polar subgroups. LAIN in the present instance, wished, perhaps, that TED and RFB would act as a Scapegoat pair to act out her disapproval of ACE, to take the flak from ACE and CARL, and to maintain the polarization from the NF quarter, thus taking the heat off her and the rest of the PF subgroup, leaving them in a position to mediate.

SARA

SARA's diagram is shown as Figure 24. SARA shows a polarized pattern with a more or less clear interval between two subgroups, but it differs from the Group Average Diagram in that all the members of the NB subgroup are moved in the Positive direction right up to the border of the Positive side, and the PF subgroup is moved Backward. Thus, even though the pattern is still polarized, the polarization is minimized. SARA has moved both herself and PAL in the PF direction so as to become members of the PF, or P, reference group. She has also taken TOM along. In the Group Average Diagram both SARA and TOM are in the NB subgroup, and PAL is on the Line of Balance. It is clear that SARA does not want to be identified as a member of the NB subgroup, although her conflicted and mostly silent behavior has put her there in the eyes of others. SARA has located her WISHED-FOR image even farther Positive, so it seems fairly clear that she identified herself with the P direction, if not with the whole PF subgroup.

That SARA was seen within the periphery of the NB subgroup was also due in part, perhaps, to her friendship on the outside with HIP, which was known to the group. But it was also due in part, I think, to SARA's ambivalence about participation. She was quiet most of the time but came in strongly on occasion. She was very expressive and dramatic when she did talk, and she talked almost exclusively about events outside of the group, usually about her participation in a drama group and about the characters in plays. Most of the time, however, she appeared to be inhibited and a little Negative. She often came in late and often assumed a posture that made it seem she would rather disappear than participate. Her only safe communications with the group, it appeared, were her occasional animated and entertaining accounts of affairs in the drama group. She talked only once, near the end, about her attitudes toward other group members, when the group was in the process of a "round robin" trying to get a little more specific about their feelings for each other. At that time she said other members seemed "sort of blurred" to her. She did not talk about herself in an analytic way at any time. It seems probable that she feared rejection and counteracted this fear only periodically by short periods of very active and dramatic participation.

One further notable feature of SARA's diagram is the fact that she moved SUE a considerable distance in the Negative direction and into the Negative side, very near the Line of Balance in the Scapegoat direction. Sara felt some special Negative feeling, apparently, which may have been connected with the fact that SUE was a female, that she was quiet most of the time, and so was like SARA in

FIGURE 24   SARA's Diagram (Expansion Multiplier = 1.359)

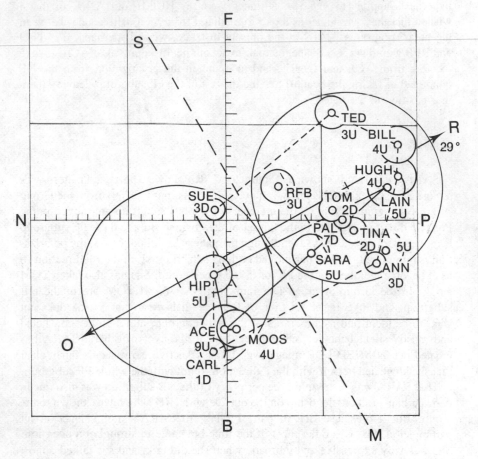

these respects, but unlike SARA she was quite controlled and effective in the instrumental direction. This may have been bothersome to SARA, since she moved LAIN, RFB, and BILL also away from the F direction toward B. SUE is the only member whom SARA moved in the Negative direction. However, as we will see later from SUE's diagram (Figure 27, p. 139), SUE moved SARA even more markedly in the N direction and so may have given SARA cause.

On her questionnaire, SARA seems to have avoided comments on relationships that may have been of special significance to her, with the exception of her relationship with TINA and TOM, both very quiet like herself, and both near her on her diagram. She says, "I feel particularly comfortable next to these people as they are thoughtful and listen."

SARA comments on the relationship between MOOSE and ACE, curiously enough, because the relationship she would have expected between them seemed not to be overt. MOOSE and ACE are placed almost identically on her diagram. She says, "These two individuals seemed to have a silent merger behind them—not necessarily consciously felt by either of them, as it may go against their highly individualistic characters. I'm surprised that they did not become friendlier." Of CARL and HIP, also in the NB or B subgroup in SARA's diagram, she says, "Both of them have their own defense systems that seem to make them negative. Taken out of the confines of the group they are highly sensitive and witty."

On the other side of the polarization, SARA comments on the relationship between TED and BILL. "It first seemed that TED wanted a reciprocal admiration of intellectual pursuits and felt he could get it from BILL. TED frequently sat by BILL, as he felt BILL would not clash with the intellectual direction in which TED wanted the course to go." The relationship of TED with ANN, SUE, and TINA was important to TED for his own protection, SARA thought. She said, "TED tried to be very protective of these women and wanted a reciprocal relationship should CARL or ACE attack him, or, as a matter of fact, if he felt as if he were being attacked by any member of the group. This is to say that TED likes positive vibrations and his level of tolerance for handling negative statements aimed at him is low." SARA apparently tended to see the polarization in the group as focused mainly on TED, and in her diagram it is TED that she has left out in the most Forward location. Of TED and ACE she says, "These two clashed from the beginning, thereby setting a norm wherein the group would have an abhorrence of someone who wanted to be 'the leader.'"

SARA seems to have been intimidated by the NB subgroup. Of the relationship between ACE and the group she says, "ACE tended to treat whatever personal experiences that were related by the younger group members from 'a superior position of a worldly adult who recognizes the naïve escapades of these babes in the woods.'" SARA, it will be remembered, along with HIP, was taking the course a second time and probably hoped that her difficulties in participation, which were very similar the first time around, would yield to another try. It may be that she was intimidated both by the superior attitude of ACE and by the gung-ho task-orientation of TED. Neither pole of the major polarization in the group provided the kind of group atmosphere in which SARA could blossom—namely the atmosphere of a friendly, expressive group, oriented to light social conversation.

SARA probably welcomed the relationship of ANN to ACE, which bridges the polarization in her diagram. She says, "ANN, by becoming friends with ACE, is not so placating to him and knows how to handle his outbursts. Hence, ACE is not seen as an ogre." SARA has moved ACE, along with all the other members of the NB subgroup, up to the border of the Positive side in her diagram, in the effort, apparently, to make them less threatening and perhaps in order not to have to acknowledge that she sees them negatively, but apparently she is not quite able to get them across the border.

Although SARA does not mention her relationship with HIP, except for the remark that both HIP and CARL have defense systems that make them Negative in the group though "taken out of the confines of the group they are highly sensitive and witty," HIP's own statement that his relationship to SARA was the only one he felt was extremely significant and that she helped him out of threatening situations in the group and protected him lead one to suppose that her relationship with HIP was significant also to SARA. Her relationship to him seemed to me to be a maternal one, the relationship of a "mother hen to her chick" (see p. 136), and similar in many respects to the relationship ANN established with CARL (see p. 138).

CARL

CARL's diagram is shown as Figure 25. In raw form, his ratings were quite constricted, as we see from the size of the expansion multiplier required, 1.79. His polarization of the group is more nearly along the F–B dimension than the P–N, and NB appears to be his reference direction. TED is very far out in the Negative field, in the Scapegoat direction. ANN and HUGH also appear as prominent members on the Line of Balance and out in the Mediating direction, though not very far out. However, nobody receives very Positive ratings from CARL. Most of the members of the PF subgroup (all except RFB) have been moved in a Negative direction. CARL has moved his EXPECTED rating in a Positive direction, compared to the location he RECEIVED on the Group Average Diagram. His WISHED-FOR image is on the Positive side, though rather far Backward.

From the location of his WISHED-FOR image and the fact that no other members are near it, one might suppose that CARL feels in some respects that other members of the group do not do as well in the PB direction as they should. CARL expressed a pervasive sense of dissatisfaction and rejection of SOCIETAL images of many kinds, but particularly those of the economic system, which he viewed mostly as UNF. He was indignant over the plight of the poor. He seemed to imply that he wanted some kind of care to be taken of the poor (PRO UPB in SOCIETY), but he did not enlarge on this much, and the image did not become clearly articulated in group interaction. He does appear to be in agreement with ANN that "dwarfs should be treated like people too," and this may be a part of the basis of his friendship with her, along with their mutual rejection of images in the UNF direction. CARL's values were probably PRO UPB in SOC, as well as CON UNF in SOC, but unfortunately his interaction with group members appeared to most as ACT NB. CARL wished in some abstract sense to be nurturant apparently, but in his behavior and also in some of his other values he appeared to others to be alienated and rejecting.

The relationship CARL mentioned as most important to him personally was that with TED. He says, "This relationship was hostile and developed inside the group. Since TED spoke a lot, my attitude toward him greatly affected my performance in the group. The N ratings that I received may be a result of my Negative interactions with TED." The relationship CARL mentioned as most important to the group as a whole was that between TED and ACE, however. He says, "This relationship was openly hostile and was important because their hostility was often the topic of discussion. Further, TED's actions were often tailored relative to what he thought ACE's reactions would be." The relationship between TED and the women in the group was also mentioned prominently: "TED has adopted a paternalistic, protective 'chivalrous' attitude toward the women in the group, particularly the quieter women. His actions in this regard and the resulting discussion was a major part of the self-analytic phase." It is

FIGURE 25 CARL's Diagram (Expansion Multiplier = 1.790)

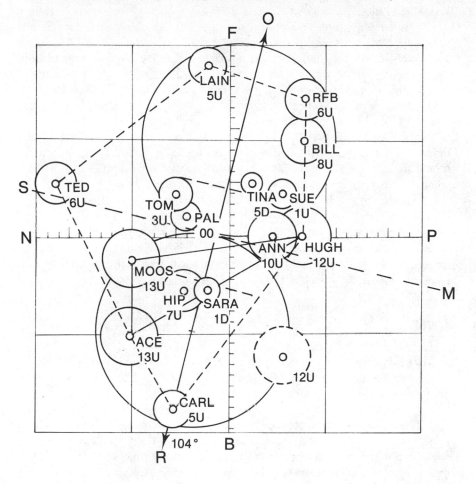

safe to assume that CARL had Negative feelings about "paternalism" generally, explicitly in an economic context. Although CARL had a major concern for the plight of the poor, he probably did not believe it could be improved by some kind of paternal or maternal care within the existing economic system. On an ideological level, at least, he was probably convinced that the poor would have to fight for their rights and did not want them to be "co-opted" by some kind of superficial paternalism.

CARL mentioned his relationship with ANN as important to him personally. "The relationship is friendly, and developed mostly outside the self-analytic phase. It was important because the fact that ANN and I were friends and had spoken outside class was often referred to, and was important to me because all friendships are important to me." In view of the somewhat enigmatic nature of the basis of this relationship it would be of great interest if CARL had given more information, but this is all he offers. CARL mentions one other of the women: "TINA talks very little. Therefore, when she speaks people in the group are surprised, pay extremely careful attention, and, I suspect, give her words more weight than they normally would.''

CARL's other comments are all concerned with relationships within the NB subgroup. ''My relationship with ACE,'' he says, ''is friendly and developed completely inside the group. It was significant because it evoked a conflict within me. I dislike what ACE stands for (business school) but I like ACE personally.'' These remarks raise some question however, as to whether CARL and ACE would have developed any relationship if they had met in some other group, where they might not have had a common focus of dislike, as they had in TED. Of himself and HIP, CARL says, ''This relationship is a friendly one that developed inside the group. HIP was always a good audience for statements of mine I thought were funny or clever. There were also times that I defended him when the group was attacking him.'' Finally, of the relationship of HIP and ACE, CARL says, ''These two guys receive a lot of negative 'flak' from some members of the group, and they often defend each other. This 'alliance' is an important element of the group.'' This remark again raises the question as to the degree to which subgroup relationships between members on the Negative side of the space may be determined by common circumstances or instrumental advantages rather than by attractive elements in each other's personalities.

ANN

ANN's diagram is shown as Figure 26. The constellation of ANN's diagram is unusual in that there are very few members of the group within what appears to be her Reference Circle, at least when the overlay is fitted in the standard way. She appears to see the group as polarized, in that the perimeter is elongated, but there is no clear separation between two subgroups. ANN appears to have moved herself and two other very quiet members, TINA and TOM, into the PB corner, which is also the location of her WISHED-FOR image. This little subgrouping is reminiscent of a pattern that I have seen in other groups and have called the ''mother hen and her chicks.'' ANN mentions TOM in her questionnaire. She says, ''From the beginning TOM made efforts to be warm and friendly towards me, and I've appreciated it. We see each other outside class time and we've established a warm friendship.'' ANN does not mention TINA specifically, but she does comment on a subgroup of all of the women with one exception: ''(except perhaps SUE)'' ''Due to the men's incredible overt activity, the women as a whole seemed to have had a very submissive role.''

It is not clear whether ANN tended to ''mother'' TOM and TINA in the outside phase or whether she tended to seek support, or perhaps both. I have seen several instances of a female member on the far Positive side, not active in the self-analytic sessions of the group, who formed a protective and nurturant relationship on the outside with one or two quiet members, usually in the PB quarter and nearby. These little subgroups seem to be a carryover of a commonly wished-for family relationship pattern (loving mother and loving child). These subgroups are of a different kind from the two main subgroups we see on the Group Average Diagram. They differ from the major polar contending subgroups in that the

FIGURE 26 ANN's Diagram (Expansion Multiplier = 1.276)

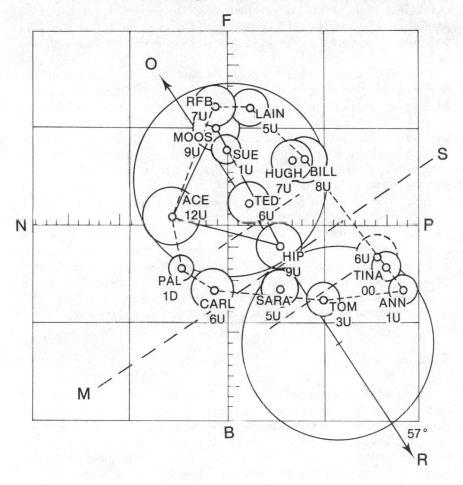

leader is not very active within the main group, though perhaps more active than the followers, and also in that they are often a third-party subgroup, located on or near the Line of Balance of the main group. (The relationship between HUGH and PAL seems to have been somewhat similar, although in this case I gather that it was the male who took the more protective and nurturant role—this too is not unusual in my experience.)

ANN moved SARA in a Positive direction and into her Reference Circle. She moved HIP and CARL in a Positive direction, though not into her Reference Circle. She also moved TED closer to her, though he is still in the opposite circle. She says of TED, "At first TED aroused in me the urge to help, too cooperate, and trust. He appealed to me several times for these things. But my relationships with him have mostly showed me how I used to be in a few ways—and to extremes, as he is, or says he is. I've really realized quite a few things listening and talking to him." ANN mentions her relationship with CARL as one that was personally important to her. "Outside the group, especially,

CARL has always been wonderful to me. He has always been worthy of my trust and respect. Seeing his obvious negativity inside the group however, has been a great experience. I've learned it is possible to like someone but sometimes not what he says, and also, how to argue with what someone says—not with who he is.''

All of the members of the PF subgroup on the Group Average Diagram have been moved negatively by ANN, except for TED. Nevertheless she mentions BILL first on her list of significant relationships. She says, ''Although I'd always felt positively towards BILL, I couldn't relate well to him. Now I can. It tells me I've changed. Lately, our relating has been extremely understanding and helpful. Because I have so much respect for BILL, this pleases me a lot.'' RFB, however, along with LAIN and MOOSE has been relegated to the polar extreme of ANN's diagram. Perhaps these persons, and SUE as well, seemed foreign to ANN because of their relatively high degree of emotional control and apparent self-sufficiency. ANN seemed rather attracted to persons who may have appeared to need help in some way, who were in some way different from the majority of other members or isolated. She is the only person in the group, for example, who mentioned the fact that HIP and SARA were black. She says, ''I'm not sure of the effect it had on the group, but their being black and the only two to repeat the course seemed to make some difference.'' In her diagram she places both SARA and HIP closer to her than any of the other members except TOM and TINA.

SUE

SUE's diagram is shown as Figure 27. It shows a clear polarization with all of the members contained in or overlapping one or the other of the two polar circles. Nevertheless there seem to be several still smaller subgroups and more or less isolated individuals, especially on the Negative side. The subgroup of CARL, ACE, and SARA is quite far separated from HIP, and also from TED. SUE makes no remarks about SARA in her questionnaire, but it is clear that she perceived SARA as quite Negative and has moved her very far from the group average location. As we may recall, SARA had also moved SUE into the Negative side, (pp. 131–132) but not nearly so far as SUE has moved her. We may infer that there was a mutually reinforcing dislike between the two, though it never surfaced for discussion, and the fact that SUE moved SARA much farther in the Negative direction than SARA moved SUE raises a question as to whether or not the initial impetus toward a relationship of mutual dislike may have been given by SUE.

SUE's answers on the questionnaire are somewhat puzzling, in view of the ratings she gave people. She first mentions a long list of persons—MOOSE, ACE, TED, TOM, TINA, HIP, LAIN, BILL, ANN, PAL—and then says, ''I have very positive feelings for all the people mentioned above except for ACE.'' Both TED and HIP, however, are far removed from her Reference Circle; indeed, they are peripheral to her opposite circle. We must remember that the ratings ask for descriptions of behavior, not for liking or disliking as such. We have many indications that feelings of liking or disliking influence the ratings one

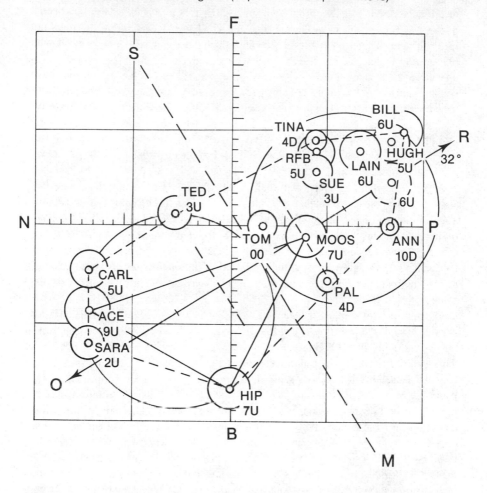

FIGURE 27 SUE's Diagram (Expansion Multiplier = 1.343)

person gives to another, but we have also seen that sometimes persons like others who receive ratings that put them on opposite sides of the space (e.g. ANN and CARL), so we should not consider the ratings given as identical with likes or dislikes. It is perhaps true, however, that a relationship of liking between persons who consider themselves very different, or who are rated by others as very different, presents something of a puzzle. Liking of persons for others who are similar to them seems easier to understand. When dissimilar persons like each other or seek each others' company and continue to interact, we are tempted to suppose that there is some underlying exchange of satisfactions of repressed or suppressed needs, involving multiple levels of motivation within each personality, and these relationships are a challenge to understanding.

Of the long list, SUE then chooses the four most important for discussion, in rank order of their importance to her. She first mentions MOOSE and says the relationship was "friendly, supportive, trusting—it was talked about in private conversation with MOOSE. Of all the group members, I feel closest to

MOOSE.'' This is not exactly a transparent relationship, considering the great dominance of MOOSE within the group and the fact that he was considered to be in the NB subgroup in the Group Average Diagram, but SUE moves him definitely into her PF Circle of Reference and quite close to herself. Perhaps she was responding in part to MOOSE's Positive attitude toward her. Perhaps SUE was attractive as a woman to MOOSE, but especially so because she was very self-contained and made no demands for protective care. As we know, demands for protective emotional care were the kind MOOSE felt as most threatening. It is not unlikely that one of the topics SUE and MOOSE discussed was TED's attempt to give protective care to SUE and the other women, so it could have become quite clear to MOOSE that SUE did not want this sort of thing, and it may have attracted him.

Next, SUE mentions her relationship with ACE: ''He frequently aroused my anger in group sessions, especially when he would express values directly opposite to mine. —[The conflict was] not directly confronted, either within the group or in the outside phase. However, I talked about my feelings about ACE with others in the outside phase. In the group I indirectly expressed my anger by frequently challenging his statements.'' This relationship seems to be what we may usually expect between persons on the two extremes of a chronic group polarization.

Of her relationship to TED, SUE says, ''I liked TED, but had difficulty unconditionally supporting everything he said. I felt when I disagreed he took it more personally than I had intended in that he expected me to behave differently. This problem was discussed once within the group and several times in the outside phase, but it basically remains unresolved. My relationship with TED is probably best described as ambivalent.'' As we see on SUE's diagram, TED is placed in the Negative side of the space and not within SUE's reference group. She saw him more negatively and much less far Forward than did the Group Average Diagram. Perhaps we may infer from this, and from what SUE says, that it was TED's offer to protect her, which really also involved an appeal to be protected, that aroused SUE's ambivalence most. It was not TED's task-orientation that put her off—she herself had that. But she also seemed to have a strong self-sufficiency and a value on independence, and in this respect she was similar to MOOSE.

SUE also mentions BILL as personally significant to her. She says, ''I trust BILL and admire his ability to get along with so many people. I don't think I ever expressed this either in the group or in the outside phase.'' This relationship seems to be about what we may expect of a leader–follower relation between two persons in the same Reference Circle on the P to PF vector. It is expressed in the ratings and seems transparent, and from BILL's ratings and comment (pp. 123, 124), the relationship seems to have been mutual and symmetrical, though perhaps not very intense.

It is notable that none of the relationships on which SUE comments in detail involves reference to any of the other women in the group. Apparently SUE felt little solidarity with the women's group as such, and we may remember that when ANN grouped all the women together she made an exception of SUE. The exact significance of this is not clear. Perhaps it was partly a matter of greater maturity on SUE's part—she was in a postgraduate course in one of the professional schools of the university, and she was several years older than any of the other women. It may also have been related to her self-sufficient resolution of the dependence-independence problem that was still unresolved in some of the other women. And, of course, it may also have been related to an unconflicted heterosexual orientation—an interest in men rather than women.

The relationship SUE mentioned as most important to the group as a whole was that of RFB and ACE. She says, "I think that ACE dominated the group until those sessions in which he began to perceive negative feedback from RFB. After that, ACE's position seemed less dominant." It was quite true that, after some time during which I tried not to influence the dominance order developing in the group (except, of course, for the inescapable influence of failing to do some of the things expected of a leader), I concluded that it would be best for me to try to moderate the dominance of the most active individual members. And it is also true (see p. 130) that I was unwilling to see some of the value positions expressed by ACE become group norms and reacted to him with disapproval.

The next most important relationship SUE mentions is that of CARL and TED: "I think their conflict was a recurring theme involving self-righteousness on the part of each. It was highlighted in the last session." This comment of SUE's touches on one point seldom made in the group, but I think a true and important one. That is, it was not only TED who acted in a way one tends to attribute to the authoritarian personality (see Adorno et al., 1950), but CARL as well. In CARL's case, however, the disapproval that seemed authoritarian in quality at the ACT level was expressed in the making of anti-authoritarian statements at the value statement level. On the ACT level, in other words, he often seemed UNF, while on the value statement content level his attitudes were CON UNF. It was also true, to make matters more complicated, that TED quite often expressed attitudes CON UNF. But for some variety of reasons, though both TED and CARL behaved in a UNF way and expressed attitudes CON UNF, TED was perceived as located mostly in the UNF direction, and CARL was perceived as mostly located in the NB direction. Perhaps it was the amount of talk. TED was very voluble. CARL was not. In TED's case the UNF behavior resulted in a UNF group average perception of him, at least toward the beginning of the group. In CARL's case the DNB nonverbal behavior and the CON UNF value statements resulted in an NB perception of him, on the average.

SUE next mentions the relationship of BILL to the group: "I think BILL's relationship with the entire group was a very great influence in moving the group in a positive and forward direction. I found this to be a consistent relationship in all group meetings." BILL, then, from SUE's point of view, was the leader of her reference subgroup, the PF subgroup, and moved the group in the direction she wanted it to go.

HIP and TOM are mentioned finally. SUE says, "I think their conflict began in the session on homosexuality and for the most part remained unresolved on TOM's part and not acknowledged on HIP's part. It surfaced occasionally throughout the course. I feel that had it been resolved it might have altered TOM's participation in the meetings." This also may be a true perception on SUE's part, not mentioned by any of the other group members in the questionnaire comments. In the discussion HIP made a rather exaggerated display of male heterosexual dominance, which offended TOM and tended to put him in the position of a submissive loser. It is probable that he never forgave HIP for this injury and withdrew from participation partly as a matter of passive retaliation. But we shall see when we read TOM's case study in the next section that there is more to it than that.

TOM

TOM's diagram is shown as Figure 28. TOM's diagram is unique in that there is evidence of a double polarization. Most of the members are clustered in one or the other of the two polarized subgroups, but the perimeter of his constellation is elongated not in the direction of this polarization but in the orthogonal direction. On one end of this second polarization is ANN, probably in the Mediator's direction, and on the other end are HIP and CARL, close to the Scapegoat direction. TOM's EXPECTED image is in the Swing Area on the side of what is probably the rejected subgroup for him, and his WISHED-FOR location is in the residual area, very close to the Line of Balance and out on the Mediator's side, approaching the image of ANN.

It will be recalled that TOM was one of the persons (TINA was the other) whom ANN moved into the same subgroup with herself in the ratings. There is, in fact, a close correspondence between ANN's placement of TOM and herself, and TOM's placement of his WISHED-FOR image and his image of ANN. It seems plausible that TOM wished ANN would take the lead in Positive mediation and wished to follow her. It happens that TOM's case study of his family, written as a part of the course, throws some light on the problem. TOM has read what follows and has kindly given permission for the use of what he has written. His name, of course, like the others in the group, is fictitious.

TOM was a freshman at the time of participation in the group, and his parents had been divorced two years before. "For the preceding two years, before this," TOM says, "there had been continual fighting between my father and my mother, between my father and myself, and to a lesser extent, between my father and my sister." TOM presents two diagrams of his family based on ratings at the ACT level and on ratings at the PRO value statement level. It was his concern to determine through the study what had happened in the family and, more exactly, what had changed at the time the major conflict set in. "Before this point, my parents had been relatively happy; the change occurred because of a change in my father."

TOM's diagram based on PRO value statements (not shown here), indicates that the members of the family were all on the Positive side and remained so throughout the conflict. The father has a position slightly to the PF side, while TOM, his sister, and his mother all have positions out moderately in the PB direction.

During the period of the conflict, however, the ACT level locations of the family members changed drastically. When they all interacted together, their

FIGURE 28   TOM's Diagram (Expansion Multiplier = 1.262)

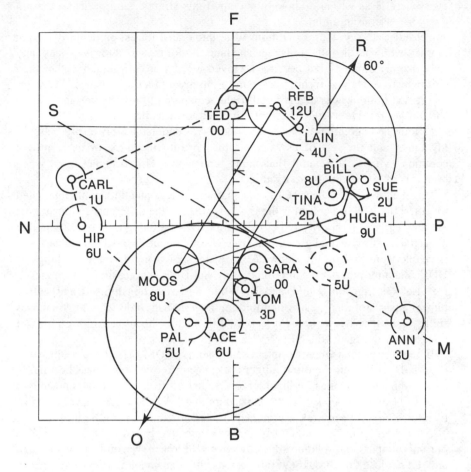

behavior was all on the Negative side, with the father out in an extreme Negative location, close to the position of HIP on TOM's self-analytic group diagram. TOM and his mother were both out about midway in the N direction, and both somewhat on the B side. TOM, however, was more Negative than his mother. The sister was out slightly in the NF direction. However, when TOM and his mother and sister interacted together in the absence of the father, the behavior of his mother and sister changed, but TOM's did not. TOM remained at about 4D, 9N, and 4B. His mother, however, moved upward from 1D to 7U, and into the PF quadrant at 7P,2F. And his sister moved upward also, from 1U to 7U, and into the PB quadrant at 4P, 4B. It appears that in this combination TOM and his mother were in conflict, with his sister in the mediating position.

What happened? TOM says, "The change that took place in my father was from a rational person into a paranoiac. He saw everyone around him as 'sick,' as out to sabotage and destroy his work (he is a doctor, and had been investigating some new disease, which he subsequently believed everyone had.) Everyone was out to get him, particularly my mother; he saw himself as always right and everyone else as wrong, although he denied this attitude, and projected it onto everyone else around him.

"Needless to say, these conditions were intolerable for us, particularly for my mother, who was the butt of his rage and hate. As for myself, I too was 'sick' and 'just like my mother,' but because he loved me, I was 'misguided' rather than evil by nature. He was trying to save me from my mother's influence. My sister he seemed to think was relatively all right, compared to my mother and me, so she did not receive as much hostility directed towards her as we did.

"From the beginning of this period, there was understandably a split between my father and the rest of us. Against his hostility the three of us formed a coalition, which had several fluctuating tendencies. This becomes clear when both sets of ACT ratings are examined.

"In the first set [when TOM, his mother, sister, and father all interacted together] the P-N dimension is the most significant; the differences in the others are not nearly as large. My father is 3U (and 16N), although it would seem that his active hostility would give him a large U component, he also felt and acted as if people were pushing him down. Hence, he scored highly on such things as DNF (shaming others by acting martyred) and DNB (expressing unhappiness). He also was high on both F and B. While disassociating himself and setting himself apart from us . . . he often told me how he had to do what he knew was right, no matter what we thought (e.g. B, NB)." But "he also set himself high *in relation to us* (e.g. UNF, NF):"

In these situations where all interacted together, TOM says, "My mother was slightly D. Although she often fought back, she also often felt it was best not to say anything to provoke him, in order to save herself from lectures and invectives (e.g. D). Her 2B reflects this too; she had more of an inclination to avoid contact than to get involved in useless arguments. The situation was similar for me, for I also had 2B. Yet I was more D. My mother is a relatively self-confident person in normal interpersonal relationships (she was UPF on the second set of ratings), and did not lose this throughout this period, although she did often submit to my father. I, on the other hand, already had a lot of problems, and it made me even more unsure of myself to be constantly criticized for whatever I did wrong. I felt more suppressed than my mother, who somehow was strong enough to retain her sense of self. My sister was slightly more U and F. Not being as much in the thick of things, she was likely to start conversations with my father, as she was the only one who had his respect to any degree. Because of this, she was also more able to resort to reason and logic in dealing with him; he listened to her, whereas with my mother and me, he twisted and distorted what we said, resulting in more emotional displays of anger on our part."

Still commenting on the ratings of the situation where all members of the family interacted together, TOM says: "Although these ratings can thus be interpreted, the differences are clearer on the P-N dimension. In relation to my father, all four of us are N. My father is the most, being 16N. He instigated the hostility and, for the most part, started the fights. My sister is the least, at 2N. Because his behavior towards her was considerably less antagonistic, she had no need to be so towards him. My mother and I fall in between them, with my being a little bit more N. This was because I was less able to control my rage, and even got some pleasure out of antagonizing my father, as a way to release my pent-up anger.

"Because my mother and I were close in the global space, with respect to my father, we formed a close coalition against him." We may pause at this point to take note of the implication of TOM's remark for our system of locating sub-groups through the use of the overlay. Since all of the members of the family in this case were on the Negative side (at least in the ACT level ratings during that period) the images all fall within one circle on the Negative side, and even with expansion the overlay would not locate the polarization. Again we are reminded that the kinds of inferences that seem often justified on the Positive side of the space, to the effect that nearness in the space tends to predict subgrouping, are often not justified on the Negative side of the space. Although polarization in the F–B dimension on the Negative side may be detected with the overlay, the images may all be within one Circle of Reference, and polarization between the members may still be the reality.

The polarization of himself and his mother vis-à-vis his father, says TOM, "explains the fact that not infrequently, my father would tell me that I was just like my mother, and thus beyond hope—there was nothing else he could do for me. I often felt as if I were 'conspiring' with my mother against my father, and this made me feel quite guilty. Yet for me this coalition served an important function—it helped me confirm that my father was 'sick,' and my mother was not. When my father would tell me stories about my mother to prove his point about how awful she was, I would turn to her and she would explain the way things had really happened. At the same time, my mother sometimes complained to me about the way he treated her, something which she did against her better judgment. She realized that I was being used in the situation, particularly by my father, and often, when I would express anger at him to her, she would try to explain to me that he really did love me, and was different before this had happened.

"My sister was only a peripheral member of this coalition. This, of course, was because she got along relatively well with my father, and so the polarization between them wasn't as great. However, she was much closer to us in that she recognized his behavior as paranoid and irrational. The only difference was that she was more able to contain her anger and distance herself, as she was already away at college. Furthermore, her anger was not as personal; she was angry not at how he treated her, which was relatively all right, but at how he treated my mother and me.

"From the way the space looks, it would seem that the greatest polarization would be between my father and sister, the most and least Negative." The father, we may recall, was at 3U, 16N, and the sister at 1U, 2N, 2F; TOM and his mother were in between. "But this is misleading. If I were to rate my father vis-à-vis his relationship with my sister, he would be much less than 16N. That figure applies basically for his relationship with my mother and myself. Instead of seeing my sister at the polar end, it would be better to see the polarization with my mother and myself at one end, my sister in a swing zone on one side, and my father on the other end. If anyone were to mediate between the two extremes, then, it would be my sister. She was, in fact, the closest link between the two [sides], close to both of us, yet able to get along bearably with my father about my mother, trying to lessen his anger against her. She [sister] often tried to reason with my father.

"Seeing as how we were all on the N side, it might not be clear why there was such a large polarization. This is more easily understood by taking into account the second set of ratings on the ACT level. The first set, except in the case of my father, is not a fair example of the normal interpersonal behavior of my mother, my sister, and myself, for it reflects their behavior only as regards my father. The second set, although it is basically how we interacted with each other, is a better sample of our day-to-day interaction, particularly for my mother and sister."

In the second set of ratings, "the coalition seems somewhat shifted. My mother (UPF) and my sister (UPB) are in clear and direct opposition to the UN behavior of my father. I, on the other hand, remain in pretty much the same area of the space. From this second set, my place in the coalition is seen as more tenuous. In direct opposition to my father, I was able to stay close to my mother. However, this did not hold true out of that context. Particularly towards my mother, I was very hostile. This was usually unreasonable and unfair, and although I knew it, I continued. A large part of the reason was that it was easier to take out my hostility towards my father on my mother. My father was very fragile and easily hurt; I often felt like I was acting the role of father and he that of the son. Therefore, I couldn't get angry at him too often, and compensated for this by releasing my pent-up anger against my mother.

"Yet this was not the only reason. When my father is placed on the same global space as this set of ratings, my tenuous position between the two is evident." (TOM is visualizing father at 3U, 16N; mother at 7U, 7P, 2F; and himself at 4D, 9N, 4B.) "My father was very convincing; although on a rational level, I knew what he was saying about my mother and about other things as well, was distorted, I still found it hard to block it all out. I often doubted my mother, inside, and against what I knew was right, and this came out in the form of anger against her. These ratings, then, emphasize my position as an intermediary, caught in the middle, with my father attacking my mother to me, and my mother trying to reassure me that she was not the way he said she was.

"In this aspect of the coalition, my sister was close to my mother, as the ratings show" (the sister was at 7U, 4P, 3B); "they got along quite well. I needed a black and white dichotomy between my mother and father; that she was always 'right' and he was always 'wrong,' in order both to keep myself from being torn between the two of them, and to be able to believe that what he said about me was 'wrong' too. My sister, being more secure, was able to get along with my father, and listen to what he said, without having an identity crisis. She accepted the fact that my mother wasn't perfect, but that basically, she was a great person, and was able to keep what my father said in the context of his paranoid reactions. It was thus to her that I turned when I was upset, and, as the rating shows, she was UPB towards me, being protective and consoling me. Again, she was in a position of mediation, only in this function she mediated more between my mother and me than between my father and me. Whereas in the first set of ratings her position is such that she could possibly bring the two polar extremes together, in this set she is in a position to unify the weakening coalition against the other extreme.'' That is, the sister was able to reunify TOM and his mother, whose coalition was weakened by TOM's ambivalent feelings toward his mother and his reluctance to reject his father totally, into a coalition with herself (the sister), and at the same time partially to neutralize the polarization of TOM, mother, and sister, on the one side, versus father on the other. The sister, in other words, tended to neutralize both polarizations. ''She is, in this way'', TOM says, ''a sort of social-emotional leader.'' And in this perception, TOM provides a perfect illustration of many of the main points of the general theory of polarization, unification, mediation, scapegoating, and neutralization. It also becomes clear that he transferred this set of hopes and expectation onto ANN, who has the place of his sister on his diagram of the self-analytic group, both out on the PB vector and on the Line of Balance, in the Mediator's location. ANN, however, is even farther out on this vector in his diagram of the group than was TOM's sister

TOM continues: ''These two sets of ratings, then, emphasize two different aspects of the 3-person coalition. In the explicit context of opposition to my father, my mother and I were a close coalition, with my sister joining in times of extreme necessity, but otherwise relatively uninvolved. Outside that explicit context, the coalition between my mother and sister was close, with my sister keeping me in it by her UPB behavior. Although my mother also served this function at times, it was often hard for her because of my hostile behavior towards her.

''It is now interesting to compare these ACT ratings with the VAL ratings.'' TOM is referring to what we would now call ratings of the PRO value statements the individual tends to favor (see Appendix W). ''The question I posed in the beginning,'' TOM continues, ''was on what level my father had changed primarily. From these ratings, it appears that it was more his outward behavior than his values that changed.

''For all practical purposes, the direction of my mother's, my sister's, and my values are the same, basically PB. For all of us, this differs from ACT level behavior. For myself, I think this is more my ideal value system than the one I really act on. But for my mother and sister, I feel this reflects not an inconsistency in their personalities, but simply a sign of the different meanings of the dimensions on different levels. While both are U on the ACT level, because both are self-confident, they are high on both U and D on social values, so that the two directions cancel each other out. A lot of the D values deal with feeling that life and people are basically good, and this is something they both believe.

''Although my father's values are different, they are not nearly as divergent from us as his ACT behavior. He is, as might be expected, not as P as we are in regard to values, and is also more F. These are easy to understand. He is not particularly F, except in relation to the rest of us. In a normal state of mind, as he is these days, he is still a bit more conservative than the rest of us, and this alone could account for the difference. Yet, in that period, when he didn't understand what was going on around him, his tendency to stick to traditional beliefs about work and behavior was increased. As for his being less P, he understandably moved more towards pessimistic cynicism and away from the optimistic idealism that he's had before. Whereas now he would definitely agree with a value such as PF, it was not possible at a time when he was full of distrust for everyone. Thus, although his values became more rigid and negative, this seems to have been more a result than a cause. His changed behavior on the ACT level, he perceived as a change in everyone else, and this led to a tightening of his values to a dogmatic (for him) degree. Even so, he retained enough of his basic values so that the discrepancy on the VAL level between him and the coalition of my mother, sister, and I is not so great as on the ACT level. In other words, it was basically his behavior that became exceedingly negative and cause the split, not his values.

"That this is true is clear to me intuitively. Were I to rate my father the way he is today, now that he is pretty much better, he would be on the P side, like my mother on the ACT level. He would score high, for example, on PF and UPF, and low on things like UN and UNF. The change in that rating would be much larger than the change in his VAL rating. This, as I've said, would be somewhat more B and P, but because he was not as N on that level when he wasn't well, he didn't have as far to change back to be as P as my mother. Thus, primarily a behavior change, not a value change, occurred.

"It is undoubtedly no coincidence that I had the same group type role in my family as I have in our group, DNB. Having learned that role, I have applied it to other situations. However, the transference is not quite that simple. In the beginning of this group, I was in fact rated slightly DP, and it wasn't until later that I became more DNB. The difference between this group and my family was that in my family I knew that no matter how much hostility I expressed, I would remain a member of it, and would still be loved. In other groups, however, this was not so, and so I had to cover it up to a large extent, which is why I was rated DP. Later on in the semester, however, I began to feel that how I was rated was less important than saying how I felt, so I did that more, and the result was a DNB rating.

"The description of the DNB role type, toward failure and withdrawal is somewhat accurate." TOM is referring here to the role type descriptions in *Personality and Interpersonal Behavior* (Bales, 1970). Students are required to read this book for general background and familiarization with the space, although it plays less of a role in the groups now than earlier, since the SYMLOG feedback provides constant current characterizations of group members' behavior of a more specific and concrete kind, with less inference required. In this respect, SYMLOG feedback resembles the general approach of self-monitored behavior modification as compared to the global role-type descriptions, which involve more inference and have more the character of clinical interpretations, and like clinical interpretations may sometimes overshoot the mark, miss it wildly, or strike at a level that is too deep, though accurate, for easy acceptance by the recipient.

In this case, TOM felt that the DNB description was "somewhat accurate." He says, "I do feel alienated from other people to a large extent, and am often discouraged and dejected. Part of this undoubtedly comes from the depression and ambivalence about, and desire to withdraw from, my family. I felt oppressed by my father, encouraging a movement in a D direction, and he was quite high on pessimistic cynicism, at least for him, feeling himself a martyr in a hostile world. It is also true, as with most people on the N side of the space, that at this period particularly, there was a great discrepancy between my parents. My confusion is clear from the hostile ACT behavior towards both. Finally, my father was indeed very high on moralistic (not necessarily inhibiting) demands, and low on emotional warmth. He was not flexible in this regard, and this made it harder for me, in terms of the model, to return to the positive side of the space after the demands he made.

"However," TOM concludes, "I do not see my DNB position as a static state, in which I will remain forever. I am not satisfied with the way I am; I am trying to change myself through understanding things better, and I can see changes occurring. I would like eventually to be slightly U, and alternating between the PF and PB spaces, but I suppose before I achieve this I have to go through a long period of acting 'toward failure and withdrawal.'"

Against this background, TOM's relationships in the group become more understandable, and he describes them with equal clarity. He mentions his relationship with ANN as the most important to him personally: "ANN is the only person in my group I've really gotten friendly with outside. During a period in which I felt uncomfortable with people I didn't know, I did feel very comfortable with her from the beginning, because I sensed her warmth for people in general, and me in particular. The only problem is that at times I am quite sexually attracted to her, and some of her actions seem somewhat seductive, but she is involved with someone else right now. In a way this is also a relief, because I don't really want to get involved deeply with anyone right now—I have too many other things to deal with first." All of this is quite consistent with the hypothesis (not explicitly stated by him however) that TOM transferred his feelings toward his sister to ANN, regarded her as a helpful Mediator in his doubly polarized conflict, and moved psychologically toward her, as symbolized in the location he gave her on his field diagram and the direction in which he moved his WISHED-FOR image.

It is equally plausible that TOM transferred his Negative feelings toward his father to HIP, whom he puts in almost exactly the same position (far-out N) as he put his father in his family. That this was not simply a gratuitous placement of a Negative transference on HIP, however, is clear from SUE's account of HIP's contemptuous treatment of TOM (see pp. 141–142). TOM mentions his relationship with HIP as the second most important to him and says, "I had very strong negative feelings for HIP. I often felt furious at him for his attempts to convey his powerful, 'together,' 'hip' image of himself. I felt contemptuous of him. I also got angry at his attempts to distance himself by his elusiveness, his one-line jokes which I didn't find funny, etc., in order to keep in a dominant position. Also, his continual obsession with power (references to 'who's controlling the traffic,' the sarcastic comments he directed at RFB, etc.). Because of this anger, it was hard for me to feel positively towards him. I recognize this anger as largely the result of my own insecurities about being weak—if I had a better feeling about myself, there would be no need to act so violently."

TOM mentions his relationship with ACE as the next most significant relationship. TOM does not place ACE far in the Negative direction; indeed, ACE is quite close to TOM's EXPECTED location, though at 6U, whereas TOM expected 3D. He says, "The feelings I have for ACE are ambivalent. On a surface level, intellectually, I reject the idea of approaching relationships 'penis-first,' and of his whole attitude and value system." TOM is referring here to a remark ACE made in characterizing his approach to women. Apart from the rather flamboyant and exhibitionistic implications of the metaphor, ACE meant in substance that he placed satisfactory sexual relationships with a woman above all other characteristics of the relationship, and if the sexual relationship did not turn out to be satisfactory, he broke the relationship.

TOM continues: "But on a deeper level, because of my feelings of insecurity, I envy that he can sleep around while I don't, and this makes me feel sort of DPB towards him. [Perhaps TOM means DNB here.] In other words, if he liked me, I would have some sort of masculinity by association. But this makes me feel hypocritical, because I don't want to feel this way, and am trying to work it out."

Next, TOM mentions his relationship with BILL. He says, "I felt very warmly towards BILL. I felt a lot of respect for him: he was older, like ACE, and was also very U, but was more positive in his orientation to people, and generally more secure. I got support from him—he was UPB and understood what I was feeling when I expressed it. Because he tended to deal with people generally more as equals than ACE, I wasn't so D in my attitude toward him." Although TOM characterizes BILL in this remark as UPB, on his diagram BILL is placed in a location just a little more U than the location in which TOM placed his mother (BILL 8U; mother 7U), and more positively (BILL 12P; mother 7P), and a little more Forward (BILL 4F; mother 2F). There is, after all, a very substantial similarity in the two locations, and it is possible that BILL was the person in the self-analytic group to whom TOM transferred his Positive attitudes toward his mother, as well as those toward his sister. No such interpretations were made in the group, however.

TOM mentions the relations between BILL and the group as important to the group as a whole. He says, "BILL served two important functions in the group. He was UPF in that he was consciously analytical, continually attempting to understand the group process, and asking other people how they understood it. He was also UPB, being very protective of many of the members. He encouraged them to express what they felt and was reassuring as well."

TOM places HIP in direct contrast to BILL. He says, "This relationship (HIP to the group) was more significant in the beginning, and then resurfaced at the last meeting. The aspect that was most important for the group as a whole was his obsession with taking control of the group. This was strongest at the beginning, when HIP attempted to distance himself and approach RFB in his very F orientation. This was also B in that he effectively cut himself off. After a while, he was attacked for this, and he stopped to a large extent, trying to take control, although he did keep up his distancing tactics. At the last meeting, he was again extremely F, as in the beginning, and his elusiveness also reached a new peak. Throughout, he was defensive about his attempts to take over, denying them, and consequently was somewhat hostile. He also blocked F movement in his exhortations to drop the subject if it got tense or uncomfortable."

TOM's description is accurate, as other members also saw HIP, but it is also possible to see, perhaps, some additional reasons for the probable transference TOM made to HIP of attitudes toward his father. There is a resemblance between HIP and TOM's father in their tactics: a certain irrational concern with control, a tendency to be excessive, a tendency to deny what seemed to others to be facts, an erratic switch from F to B in approach, a tendency to cut himself off from others, a tendency to be hostile, and perhaps other resemblances.

But the most significant relationship to the group as a whole, as seen by TOM, was the relationship of TED versus ACE and MOOSE. "This was the main polarizing relationship of the group. Even when these three were not in direct opposition, the ideas that created that opposition were present. TED was UNF on the ACT level (actually I rated him F, because of mixed messages he gave, but in his conflict with them he was UNF). He had set ideas for what the group should be and do—he invaded their space by saying everyone should share and be interdependent. This threatened ACE and MOOSE, because of their fear of commitments, and this caused a lot of hostility on their part. TED's reaction to this was in a DNF fashion."

Finally, TOM mentions the relationship of HUGH to the group as important and compares him to BILL. He says, "Hugh also served two different functions. He also travelled up and down the F–B dimension with ease. He was always relieving tension by telling jokes and dramatizing, making expansive bodily movements and facial expressions. He was also UPF—he mediated between the different factions and was friendly with those on both sides. This, of course, is related to his interest in politics. Yet he never fully exploited his potential position to become the group leader. If anyone was (the group leader) by the end, besides RFB, it was BILL. LAIN attempted, but failed—for some reason, she didn't command the respect BILL did, although she is very close to him on the global ratings."

After TOM's analysis of his own situation in the family and in the self-analytic group, we perhaps have more insight into the conflicts that beset him in the group and that appeared to keep him in the middle of two fluctuating polarizations.

In the family, TOM's mother represented the UPF pole, and TOM represented the DNB pole. In the self-analytic group, apparently BILL took TOM's mother's place at the UPF pole, and TOM was in the same role as in the family—DNB. In the family, TOM's sister represented the UPB direction, and TOM's father represented the N direction. In the self-analytic group, apparently ANN took his sister's place, and HIP took his father's place. TOM's role and conflicts in the family seem to have been reproduced in his perceptions of persons and his reactions in the self-analytic group.

PAL

PAL's diagram is shown as Figure 29. The most striking feature of it, perhaps, is the way in which she seems to have moved all images, with the sole exception of CARL, over on the Positive side, as if there were some very threatening image

FIGURE 29   PAL's Diagram (Expansion Multiplier = 1.993)

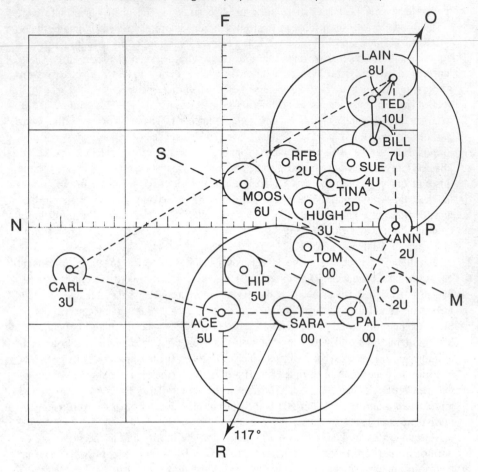

in the NF location, from which she wished to remove everyone as far as possible. A polarization Forward and Backward is shown, nevertheless, with the members in more or less the usual relative locations.

PAL herself is shown with a B subgroup, but toward the Positive side of it, and close to the Swing Area. Her WISHED-FOR image is more Positive and outside the subgroup, very near the Line of Balance, in the mediating direction. MOOSE is shown as her polar opposite, very near the Line of Balance in the Scapegoat direction. CARL seems to be completely isolated, very far out in the residual area on the Negative side of the space. Whatever perceptual and evaluative transformations PAL used to move others to the Positive side of the space apparently failed to work for CARL.

TED is moved to a more Positive location in PAL's diagram than in almost any other, and he, LAIN, and BILL are shown as the dominant triangle. The more dominant members of the NB subgroup as shown on the Group Average Diagram all appear to have been held Downward in PAL's perception, and she has emphasized instead the leadership coalition as she sees it. Thus, she has emphasized the Positive and deemphasized the Dominant.

On her application for the course, PAL gives some indications of her feelings about herself and the general atmosphere of Harvard. She says, ''I think that this course sounds very exciting, for several reasons. I would be very interested in learning more about my own personality, as I feel that being at Harvard for 5 months [she was a freshman] has put me in a state of flux, coming from a high school 'golden girl' past i.e., varsity cheerleader, guitar teacher, class secretary) to Harvard has changed me quite a bit, and I am a lot less sure of my own personality now. I was a leader, but am now growing shy in groups. I've found myself in here. I think a course like this, being with other people in a personal atmosphere, will teach me a lot about myself and where I am. I am very interested in people—more than anything else—and I know I'd really enjoy this study. Another reason I'd like the course is because after a semester of huge lecture courses at Harvard I feel like a teeny number—this would be a very nice change.''

The most important relationship PAL developed was a friendship with HUGH. She says the relationship was ''very friendly. It began in the group and developed outside of it. He was the first to give me confidence and encourage me to speak. He is sure to remain a good friend, even after the end of the group.'' It was fortunate for PAL, probably, that she found a good friend in HUGH, in view of the rather intimidating nature of some of the more dominant males.

The next most important relationship PAL mentions as that between CARL and TED. The relationship, she says, ''made me very angry. I felt an urge to stick up for TED, but lacked the nerve to attack CARL. [Their relationship] made the group edgy. It made me a little scared to show all of my feelings. It dominated many meetings.'' She also says that this relationship was the most important to the group as a whole. It ''caused most hostility within the group. It often made people angry. It seemed to show how vulnerable we are as a group. It brought out strong feelings from almost everyone.'' CARL, however, seems to have been the one most feared and blamed, since he is placed in the far Negative side of PAL's diagram, while TED is moved over to the far Positive side.

ACE is an exception. All members except CARL and ACE are put on the Positive side of the diagram. ACE is put exactly on the line. The relationship with him is mentioned by PAL as the next most important to her and to the women in the group generally. She says he was ''interesting to me due to change in my view of him. ACE and I are friendly, yet I felt threatened by his statements about women at first. Later I came to accept them and I like him more now.'' But she also mentions ACE in relation to ''CARL, or HUGH, or HIP, or sometimes MOOSE'' and says that ACE ''confuses me. ACE seems always to support these, though is often not supported by them.'' In this ''he shows us another side of his personality. I tend to see it as insecurity, but maybe I'm wrong. He seems to favor a 'one of the guys' image.'' PAL here makes an interpretation that has often been made of one of the motivations for exaggerated male dominance and show of virility, namely insecurity—the fear of not being regarded as grown up and fully male (see Adorno et al., 1950).

The next important relationship PAL mentions is her own with TINA. The relationship, she says, is "supportive. I feel a bond with her that has been discussed only in the outside phase. It's nice for me to know she is there, interested in what I say, and generally in agreement." It is of some interest that PAL looks for support from TINA, who, along with herself, is at the bottom of the order of dominance, rather than from one of the more dominant women. However, her need for support in the more dominant direction is apparently met by her relationship with HUGH.

PAL mentions the relationship of HIP to RFB as of some importance to the group. She says that the relationship "puzzles me. HIP defers to RFB yet makes fun of him and his authority. He places RFB on a 'professor' level and keeps him there, while otherwise he may have been more a part of the group if he had wanted to be." It appears, however, that HIP is much less threatening to PAL than ACE. Perhaps ACE was more threatening because he paid particular attention to women in a sexually aggressive way, whereas the main objects of HIP's attention were persons in positions of power and authority.

Finally, PAL mentions the relations of "BILL (LAIN to the group)." There is some confusion in PAL's mention, since she places her reference to LAIN and the group in parentheses, after the mention of BILL. It is not clear to whom precisely she refers when she says, "Keeps us on the group task. Shows interesting insights into our experiences. Has often kept the group from total B behavior. We often rebel against their F-ness." In her comment, she appears to be talking about one of them, probably BILL, in the singular, but then, without transition, she passes to a reference to both of them. One has the impression that they are like rather distant father and mother figures who have some difficulty in keeping their children on the track but are always there trying, with some success.

TINA

TINA's diagram of the group is shown as Figure 30. It is notable as an illustration of an unusually clear and neat polarization, with both subgroups drawn quite closely together, and a very clear interval separating the "good guys" from the "bad guys". The "bad guys" include the very high participators in the group, and TINA locates the dominant triangle in the core of her Opposition subgroup. Clearly, TED is one of them. The Line of Polarization is mostly P versus N, with an angle of only 19 degrees off P toward F. TINA's EXPECTED location is very near the center of her Reference subgroup, and her WISHED-FOR image is very close to the rating she RECEIVED. She does appear, however, to have minimized the spread of members in the F–B dimension, both in her Reference subgroup and in her Opposition subgroup. There is nobody very close to the Line of Balance, though SARA is near the Swing Area in TINA's Reference Circle and somewhat isolated from the others, who appear in a tight knot, all in the most Positive half of the Positive space. The appearance of polarization is not a result of the expansion of the points—the expansion multiplier is only slightly more than 1, and the images on both sides of the polarization come quite close to the edge.

TINA was a sophomore at the time of participation in the group and was a

FIGURE 30 TINA's Diagram (Expansion Multiplier = 1.185)

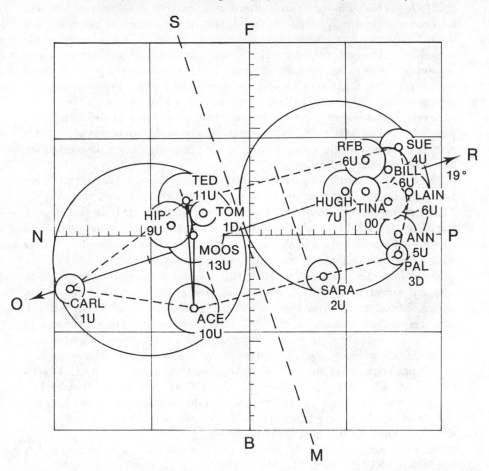

special undergraduate student from another university—two facts concerning her status that might have tended to produce some inhibition in her participation. She was not, however, in any way timid in her appearance or behavior—she was rather quite self-contained, confident, and determined. She appeared to have no difficulty in participating when she wished to and seemed to remain silent most of the time as a matter of choice, perhaps feeling that it was the best way for her to learn. As is quite often the case with low participators, her written work was very articulate and of high academic quality.

TINA mentions her relationship with TED as the most important to her personally. The "nature of the relationship" she says, was "conflict; basically the relationship was discussed between TED and me in the outside phase, although it was discussed once in the group and TED made his feelings known to me a few times by his comments to me in the group." As we have seen from her diagram, TINA saw TED as a member of the negative subgroup in her field, and moved his image considerably in the Negative direction from its group average location.

TED, as we have mentioned some number of times, was highly motivated to change his behavior in the Positive direction, to make it less dominant, and less far Forward. He openly asked for the support of the women in the group and wanted particularly to improve his image in their eyes. TINA was one of the women he addressed most particularly, and apparently in the outside social session as well as in the self-analytic group. TINA did not show a warm response to him personally, although she did not reject him openly. In her perceptual-evaluative field, however, TED apparently remained unreconstructed. He is seen as not only quite Negative but also as quite Dominant. He is carried along, as it were, by the general polarizing current which seems to permeate TINA's perceptual-evaluative field and to produce the unusually clear separation of the Negative from the Positive subgroups.

The next three relationships TINA mentions as important to her personally are all relationships with the women in the group. The first mentioned is with PAL. The nature of this relationship, TINA says, was "identification, support, friend-ship. Both PAL and I had similar feelings about participating in the group, and our levels of participation in the self-analytic phase were comparable. [There was] a lot of non-verbal communication [between us] in the group."

Next TINA mentions a subgroup consisting of all of the women in the group with the exception of SARA, who, as we see in the diagram, is somewhat separated from the other members in TINA's Reference subgroup. The relation-ship among these women (SUE, PAL, LAIN, ANN, and TINA) was one of "mutual understanding; we often exchanged glances in the group, as we often re-acted similarly to what was going on in the group. A bond was formed between us."

One other special relationship is picked out from these, however, TINA's relationship with SUE. This relationship, says TINA, was one of "friendship, understanding. I frequently talked with SUE in the outside phase, and I liked her and found her to be very supportive and understanding. We often had similar feelings about what had gone on in the group."

The most important relationship to the group as a whole, as TINA saw it, was that between HIP and RFB. This was a relationship of "conflict. HIP often tried to defy RFB's authority, to undermine what he regarded as RFB's power. It was talked about in the group, and conflicts arose between them in the group."

Next most important was the relationship between ACE and "ANN (as spokesman for women's feelings in the group.)" "At first, ANN seemed to mistrust ACE and dislike him, yet she gradually learned to accept him, and helped to re-interpret his actions to the group so that he could be more accepted and be seen in a more positive light."

The relationship between ANN and CARL was also important and somewhat similar, in that it was a relationship between a woman far out on the Positive side and a man far on the Negative side, but the quality was somewhat different. The relationship, says TINA, was one of "cooperation. Their comments and attitudes toward each other were manifested in the group. ANN helped to draw CARL closer to the group, and helped to decrease the negativity of his remarks."

Finally, TINA mentions the relationship between TED and CARL, which she says was one of "conflict. There was a struggle between these two moralists with different sets of values. Arguments between these two often occurred in the group setting.'' TINA is surely right about the conflict between TED and CARL as one between ''two moralists with different sets of values''. However far in the B direction CARL may have been, his opposition to the F direction as it appeared in the group was not at all the kind of opposition that SARA, for example, apparently felt. Hers was a preference for emotionally expressive behavior. CARL's was a principled conviction that conventional values in the economic sphere were wrong, an attitude which he maintained in a rather surly emotional way. In his rejection of them, however, he did not give up the moralism that often tends to go along with a strong acceptance of authority. In order to understand CARL better, it seems clear, we would have to know more about his earlier relationships to authority and its ties to political and economic ideology.

Concluding Remarks

We have now completed our introduction to the multiple level field theory underlying the SYMLOG System and have shown in detail how the Adjective Rating procedure may be used as an entry to the general theory. We have seen that the Rating procedure may be used in a completely unobtrusive way for the study of a group by a leader or other participant, or that it may be employed by all members of the group rating each other to produce a powerful increase in their knowledge of their own relationships and perceptions of each other.

I hope the case study has made it easier to gain an appreciation of some of the most important concepts of the general theory—the concepts of the individual perceptual field, the group average field, the inclusive social interaction field, and the ways in which the field may be structured dynamically as a unified or polarized constellation of images in the minds of individual members, more or less similar in their perceptions. We have seen how the location of given members' images in the group average field may affect the group as a whole, and how members in different locations may affect each other. We have seen the way in which knowledge of the constellation may help participants to define desirable changes and at times to exert strategic influence. It is apparent that different individuals may have markedly different perceptions of the constellation and that one can understand their behavior more easily, and perhaps help to change it, by understanding these individual differences.

Up to this point in our introduction to the general theory (multiple level field theory), we have depended primarily upon the SYMLOG Adjective Rating procedure, which taps retrospective perceptions. It has been an advantage to be able to approach the general theory through the perceptions of individual members, because the measurements are easy to make, are easy to understand when summarized, and may be represented easily in field diagrams. But the SYMLOG System includes also a method for describing the overt acts of individuals as they occur in real time, as well as their nonverbal behavior and the content of what they say. The observation system for describing the behavior as it occurs, act by act, is called SYMLOG Interaction Scoring, as distinguished from SYMLOG Adjective Rating. The two methods describe the behavior from complementary perspectives and serve to validate and enrich each other. The general theory of multiple level fields integrates the two approaches as two interdependent levels, and the same kinds of diagrams are used to portray both levels, the overt act level and the retrospective perception level.

The next part of the book is devoted to a detailed description of the SYMLOG Interaction Scoring procedure. In Part III, the Adjective Rating and the Interaction Scoring methods are compared as to their relative advantages, their respective reliabilities, and the ways in which they tend to validate and complement each other.

Part II

The SYMLOG Interaction Scoring Manual

Robert F. Bales
and Stephen P. Cohen

Chapter 13

Introduction to SYMLOG Language

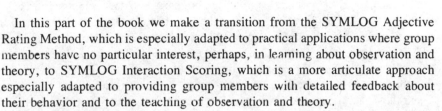

In this part of the book we make a transition from the SYMLOG Adjective Rating Method, which is especially adapted to practical applications where group members have no particular interest, perhaps, in learning about observation and theory, to SYMLOG Interaction Scoring, which is a more articulate approach especially adapted to providing group members with detailed feedback about their behavior and to the teaching of observation and theory.

Since SYMLOG Interaction Scoring is a method of producing a record of behavior and content in real time, that is, during the actual interaction, it involves coding a large volume of information into more compact form and turns out to be a kind of miniature language, with special abbreviations and conventions. The present part of the book is devoted to the presentation of the SYMLOG language, the basic concepts, and the conventions of scoring. A Glossary of the Language is given in Appendix A.

Part III deals with the ways in which the two methods (Rating, and Interaction Scoring) are complementary to each other, with their correlations, and with the reliability of observations one can hope to obtain using either or both of the methods. Part IV gives some norms for the kinds of observations one can make using the Interaction Scoring method and suggests ways in which one may improve the training of scorers and present useful feedback to group members. Part V contains various technical appendixes, which help in the processing and presentation of the observations either for feedback to group members or for research.

The SYMLOG Interaction Scoring method is designed especially for use in a setting where a self-analytic group and observer group cooperate in a learning process. With various adaptations the method may be used, or approximated, in many other kinds of situations. In the context of the kind of course for which it is especially designed, SYMLOG yields personally focused information for individual participants in the self-analytic group and allows them to monitor stabilities or change in their behavior over time. Observers obtain information on their own individual perceptions and biases and trace improvements in their observation.

SYMLOG Interaction Scoring is not necessarily confined to a special academic situation. Some natural situations will permit the current recording of observations, and nearly all will permit reconstruction from memory of the investigator. Sometimes a tape recorder may be used, which will permit an approximate SYMLOG reconstruction. It is quite clear that the single observer is often considerably biased. But, on the other hand, natural interaction in the field offers many opportunities for learning by observation that simply cannot be duplicated in the laboratory or academic setting. The present method, it is believed, offers considerable help to the observer in coverage, scope, and systematic arrangement of variables and in the breadth and consistency of its general theory.

The acronym SYMLOG may suggest a language associated in some way with a computer. Programs are available, which permit the observations, with no intermediate recoding, to be entered into computer storage and then to be analyzed and displayed in field diagrams and time plots as well as subjected to statistical analysis. Observations may be entered into the computer directly, without intermediate recoding, because they are taken in a standard format. But the standard format also makes it possible for any reader of a SYMLOG record to classify and tabulate observations by hand easily and to locate specific instances of anything of interest. The most important tabulations for training in observation and the preparation of feedback can be prepared by hand by individual observers, using the original observation sheets. The feedback of results to group members and observers needs to be accomplished with little time lag. The attempt to use the computer for this purpose may hinder rather than help, because the input of the data to the computer and the trouble-shooting of the programs may be time consuming as well as expensive. On the other hand, the research possibilities of the method are greatly expanded by computer handling of the data.

The kinds of information provided by SYMLOG for feedback to group members represent important departures from the kinds of feedback available in leader-centered therapy groups, intensive encounter groups, human relations training groups, or classrooms. In the self-analytic group provided with observer feedback, for which SYMLOG was originally designed, a great volume of highly differentiated information is provided. There is strong encouragement toward self-analysis and development of perception and understanding. Voluntary choice of the participant in the selection and evaluation of the information is maximized. The number of persons who communicate their evaluations either directly or in feedback messages is made as large as possible. The "power of the majority" within the group is broken by what amounts to an individual secret ballot of each observer. The procedure is very democratic in terms of who has the power to influence whom. The means of influence are primarily intellectual or informational. The division of the total group into a participation group and a rotating observer group tends to prevent the "tyranny of conformity" that sometimes develops in self-enclosed small groups. In this respect, the groups in the procedure using SYMLOG differ from all types of groups that depend on an emotional build-up of some kind in a self-enclosed group. SYMLOG, of course, could be used to observe such self-enclosed groups. However, the introduction of SYMLOG *feedback* would greatly alter the situation, moving it away from strong emotionality and toward diversity of social influence processes.

Group members sometimes wonder about differences in the way other group members perceive them or why they are perceived as they are by intimate others outside the group. The individualized log of behavior may afford some insight into varying interpretations of one's own behavior. One might understand better why some people see hostility where others see objectivity and rationality, for example, by noticing that some observers attend to nonverbal behavior, while others focus on the content of values expressed. The differentiated data obtainable in SYMLOG may make others' perception of one more understandable and may help focus on what specifically can be altered to produce change in their perception, if change is desired. In the self-analytic and observer group setting for which SYMLOG was originally designed, no assumption one way or the other is made about whether the individual participant may want to try to change his behavior. The goal is understanding, not necessarily change. However, some members do want to modify their behavior in some way and are able to receive help.

SYMLOG provides feedback of a kind that is democratic, systematic, and detailed. Its virtues and limitations are clearly laid out, the specific references of each observation are available for comment, disagreement, or new understanding. As such, it is an important alternative or supplement to the forms of feedback provided by friends, by fellow group members, and by therapists and teachers.

Chapter 14

The Format of the
SYMLOG Message

The observer, sitting and watching the group, (optimally, but not necessarily, from an observation room) has a supply of observation sheets, as shown in Figure 31. On the back of the first page the observer draws a large diagram of the table with members' names written in at the proper places. (If members' names are not yet known, they may be designated temporarily by number of by some other temporary sign.) Sometimes it is necessary to revise the space diagram, if people change their positions. In many meetings, however, a single diagram will do well enough for the whole meeting. The main purpose of the diagram is to fix the names of the group members in the mind of the observer, so that group members can be identified quickly.

The name of the observer is written at the top of each page. The designation of the group, the date, and the page number are also written at the top of each page.

The observer writes a series of "messages" on the form. A single sheet has space for twenty messages. Since messages are usually written at a rate of about one per minute, and by good scorers considerably faster, four or five pages will usually be necessary for a single hour's meeting.

A "message" is written as a communication between the observer and the group member designated in the message as the ACTOR. It is assumed that the message will later be read by the appropriate group member. It is assumed that other group members and observers will also read the message. Like a telegram, the message is short, but it must be understandable to the persons who will read it.

The SYMLOG message constitutes the formulation of the observer's judgment that an event significant to the group process has just taken place. The observer wishes to record this significant occurrence for the log of the group and for feedback to the member of the group who initiated the interaction event. Each message may be said to have the unwritten preamble, "The following significant event (or series of behaviors constituting a significant interaction event) has just taken place in the group."

Suppose at the first meeting of the group, only a minute or two after the beginning of the meeting, one of the members of the group, TOM, makes a

FIGURE 31 The SYMLOG Interaction Scoring Form

Observer _____ Group_____ Date_____ Page_____

Draw a diagram of the physical location of group members on back of page 1

Time	Who Acts	Toward Whom	Act/ Non	Direc- tion	Ordinary Description of Behavior or Image	Pro/ Con	Direc- tion	Image Level

pleasant social remark to break the ice. The message written by an observer in the SYMLOG format might read something like this:

10 TOM GRP ACT UP a really friendly group PRO UP (in) GRP

Each part of the message is put in its appropriate column on the form. The first column is headed TIME. The "10" in our illustrative message is written in the TIME column and indicates that the act took place at ten minutes after the hour. The word TOM is the abbreviation for the group member's name and it is written under the heading WHO ACTS. The word GRP is the abbreviation for the group as a whole as the addressee of the communication, and it is written under the heading TOWARD WHOM. The two columns are thought of as grouped together, and specify the ACTOR and the RECEIVER of the ACT. The headings may be read together: WHO ACTS TOWARD WHOM.

The next element of the message is the technical word ACT written under the heading ACT or NON. It means in this instance just about what it seems to mean, namely that TOM acts or behaves overtly in a way apparently intended to communicate with others. The technical word NON stands for nonverbal behavior. If the behavior appears to the observer as not necessarily intended to communicate but nevertheless gives signs of the ACTOR's attitudes and feeling, then the behavior is classified as NON.

All communications are conveyed through behavior in the broad sense, and all behavior is classified as either ACT or NON. The term ACT refers to acts of intended communication. Behavior at the ACT level also has nonverbal components and accompaniments, which help the RECEIVER and the observer to understand the meaning of the communication. Unless the nonverbal components give a different (and perhaps unconscious or unintended meaning), the ACT classification is enough. So ACT means intended overt acts of communication toward the other, *including their nonverbal components,* so long as the nonverbal components do not give a different or contrary meaning.

The nonverbal behavior of the ACTOR at any time may be regarded as important and, if so, should be scored. When there are nonverbal signs that contradict the intended meaning of an ACT, then it is especially important to write an additional message that gives the NON meaning. If there is not sufficient time, it is more important to write the message giving the NON meaning than the ACT meaning. There are many instances when the ACTOR gives nonverbal signs without intending to communicate, and the observer should constantly remain alert to the nonverbal behavior, since it may be unobtrusive but nevertheless very important.

The next element of the message is written under the heading DIRECTION, which means the DIRECTION of ACT or NON, and in our illustrative message the code written there is "UP." This code term in this case actually consists of the two subelements, "U" and "P". The first element, U, stands for the term "Upward," which means "Ascendant or Dominant." The second element of the code, P, stands for the term "Positive," which means "Friendly." The code term UP combines these two meanings and uses them as a qualitative description of the behavior. Thus the message says that TOM acted toward the group as a whole in a way the observer judged to be more or less ascendant or dominant, but at the same time friendly. The reader might like to get a better idea of what is implied by these adjectives and can do so by looking into Appendix A under the direction UP.

The final three elements of the message format are concerned with what kind of IMAGE is presented in the *content* of what the ACTOR says (as distinguished from the direction of his *behavior,* with which we have been dealing so far.) Suppose TOM had said, "You know, this seems like a really friendly group." In these words he presents an *image* of what "the group" is, or might be. He almost makes a suggestion that if other people in the group agree with him, as he senses they will, then they might try to make it even more friendly. The words "a really friendly group" carry some impression of genuine feeling and seem to coalesce into something we might call an "image," a kind of compact picture of an emotionally toned "thing," to which a name has been given, so that it can now be discussed and reacted to by all members. This is (approximately) what an IMAGE is.

An IMAGE is *a picture of an emotionally loaded focus of attention.* Sometimes attention may focus on a tangible physical object brought into the group, or some object in the immediate environment, but more often a set of words or a name of some kind is used as the means of focusing attention. More exactly speaking, an "image" is something that exists in the mind of an individual. It is a "picture" in the mind of the individual that comes from some "perception" of some outside "object" or from some set of memories and feelings that are aroused by a set of words. The observer cannot see the psychological entity inside the ACTOR, of course, but one can usually locate the set of words around which the attention seems to focus or the physical objects or events to which the ACTOR and the RECEIVERS are paying attention.

The description under the title ORDINARY DESCRIPTION OF BEHAVIOR OR IMAGE is a few words in uncoded language, preferably some of the words used by the ACTOR. The number of words used must be few, however, as in our example, "a really friendly group," since the remaining spaces of the message format are used to classify the IMAGE and the actor's attitude toward it. In rare cases the actor may act out the image in mimicry, without words. In this case, the observer describes the imitative behavior. Sometimes the observer records a nonverbal or other act with no IMAGE, for example, a sigh or a smile. In this case, the behavior is described under the heading ORDINARY DESCRIPTION OF BEHAVIOR OR IMAGE.

The column of the observation sheet immediately following the description of the BEHAVIOR OR IMAGE is headed PRO or CON. This is a judgment by the observer as to whether the IMAGE is something the ACTOR is *in favor* of (PRO), or *against* (CONTRA, or CON). In our example, the word "really" preceding the word "friendly" seems to imply a favorable feeling. The classification of the ACTOR's attitude toward the IMAGE is thus PRO. If the observer cannot make out what the attitude of the ACTOR is toward the Image, a question mark is put in the column. It is quite common for a person to act in a friendly way toward the other person to whom he is talking while both refer to an image of some third person or object about which they both feel negatively. The ACT or NON classification refers to the attitude of the ACTOR toward the

RECEIVER, whereas the PRO or CON classification refers to the attitude of the ACTOR toward the *IMAGE* (or some element or aspect of the IMAGE).

The IMAGE in a given case may be an image of the self. When a person talks about SELF, for example, either PRO or CON attitudes may be expressed about those images. The term ACTOR does not mean the same thing as the term SELF. The term ACTOR refers to the person in the capacity of acting, behaving (including thinking and feeling), as seen from the perspective of the *observer*. The observer attributes the act to "the ACTOR." The ACTOR is the observer's name for the mental processes within the acting person's mind that are supposed to be psychologically *acting upon the images in that same person's mind*. On the other hand, the term SELF is the observer's name for the IMAGE the ACTOR may have of self. Thus, in SYMLOG language, it makes perfectly good sense to write that the ACTOR expresses a PRO or CON attitude about the SELF.

SYMLOG language implies that an Image or a field of images is only a *part* of the mental process of the person, and that there is another part that is *acting upon the IMAGES* in the person's mind. The name for that part is the ACTOR. The term ACTOR is a term for something we do not really understand. It is what is sometimes called a "primitive," or an "undefined" term. Although we cannot define it except as a kind of unknown part of the mental process, there is no difficulty for the observer in writing down the *name* of the person WHO ACTS. All the observer supplies is the name of the person perceived as acting.

In our example, TOM's attitude toward the image is rendered: PRO UP (in) GRP. This means that he is in favor of some UP *element in* the group. When the message is written on the observation form, the word "in" is omitted, as indicated by the parentheses, but it is understood to be there, and in reading the message it is included, since it is needed to complete the meaning. In this case, we translate TOM as saying that he is in favor of *ascendant friendly behavior* on the part of everybody in the group. He is not presumably in favor of *everything* that the GRP could be or could mean. For example, he is probably *not* in favor of the negative behavior that may also appear as an element of the group. He is, in effect, saying, "I propose that we adopt a *norm* of friendly behavior in this group." The particular *element in* the general image of the group that he is in favor of is just one of the many possible elements that could be a part of the general concept or image of "the group." Somebody else may be CON UN in GRP, that is, against dominant unfriendly behavior. Somebody else may recommend instead, PRO F in GRP—i.e., serious problem solving (see Appendix A, Direction F). TOM is in favor of (PRO) the *UP* element in the GRP.

The SYMLOG language, by use of the terms PRO and CON, permits the observer to record the kinds of *Value Judgments* individuals make and recommend to each other. Hence, the language gives the means of recording and describing the development of "group norms," since essentially what we mean by a "group norm" is a PRO or CON value judgment about an element in some general image upon which members seem to agree.

At this point we may begin to see more clearly what is meant by the "Multiple Level" observation of behavior. It means the observation and recording of both the simple and the more complex levels of behavior in the *same message* about the *same act or piece of behavior*. The method assumes behavior to be multiple leveled and provides a way to record each of several levels. What are these levels, so far?

The simplest two levels, ACT and NON, we have grouped together and called the *Behavioral Level,* or simply *Behavior* (see Appendix A, the description of each direction). Sometimes it is convenient to speak of interpersonal behavior on these two levels as "interaction," "social interaction," or "the social interaction level."

The next level recognized by the SYMLOG terminology is a global level of content presented in communication called the *Image Presented* (see Appendix A). As we shall see, there are several major classes of images, classified in a rough sort of way in terms of decreasing degrees of association with the self-image. These global types of IMAGES, which we also call "levels" are: images of SELF, images of the OTHER, images of the GROUP, images of the SITUATION, images of SOCIETY, and images from FANTASY. Any image presented by the ACTOR is classified by the observer into one of these six global types, and this, of course, is the meaning of the final column on the observation form, headed IMAGE LEVEL. In our example, there is no difficulty in seeing that TOM's IMAGE of a "really friendly group" is an image of the GROUP. The technical term GROUP means simply the present interacting group of persons, or sometimes more specifically the membership group, if some person present is regarded as not a member.

But a SYMLOG description of an *Image Presented* is never left as just a global classification of the IMAGE LEVEL, as SELF, OTHER, GRP, etc. The global Image is always supplied with a qualifying adjective, which points to the specific *element in* the global IMAGE on which the actor is focusing attention. Thus, it is the UP *element in* the group, and not simply "the group" that TOM is recommending in his PRO statement. One of the major assumptions and simplifications of the SYMLOG language is that an important meaningful aspect of any IMAGE may be grasped and expressed by focusing attention on the way it "acts," as if it were a kind of behavior entity in its own right. Since in this metaphorical sense it "acts," the directional classification appropriate for the "acts" of persons can be used to describe this action element. An IMAGE is thus a cognitive representation in the mind. An important emotional potential of it can be understood by determining for what kind of "act" it stands. The way it "acts" is the ELEMENT we choose for further specifying the IMAGE. The UP ELEMENT in GRP is the friendly ascendant behavior that is one of the ways in which the group (or its members) can act.

The DIRECTION of the ELEMENT is always combined with the classification of the global IMAGE in order to give the classification of the specific ELEMENT of the IMAGE. Thus, the ACTOR may refer to U in SEL (ascendance or dominance in the self) or UP in GRP (some element in the present group that acts in an ascendant or dominant and friendly way) and so on. The DIRECTION OF ELEMENT column on the message format is used for one of the twenty-six directional designations (see Appendix A, Directions). The final column, headed IMAGE LEVEL, is used for the global image designation.

The class or level of IMAGE called OTHER, abbreviated OTH, is always converted into the name of the specific other meant. The image class OTHER refers *only to persons in the present participating group,* and these persons always have code names. In recording the message, the *code name of the particular person* is always supplied instead of the general term OTH. (This need not be done in the case of a reference to an image of the SELF, since the reader of the record knows that the name of the person referred to as SEL is always the same as the name of the person given as the ACTOR. But since there are often a number of OTHERs in the group, the name of a given OTHER must be specified to make it clear who is meant.) The combination of the specific *name* of the OTHER referred to with the *element* of that person's behavior given by the DIREC-TIONAL qualifier thus gives the observer the power to be quite specific in reporting the attitudes and feelings that group members have about themselves and about each other. This is very relevant, of course, in a self-analytic group, where a great deal of the content is of just this kind.

The level of *Image Presented* is thus a very large set of possible sublevels and specific images. The presentation of an image by the ACTOR may be regarded as an aspect of behavior on a higher or more complex level than the "behavioral" level, because it is a content reference that *stands for* other acts of behavior, both past and expected to come. We may say that the image communicates "meaning" and "feeling" from the ACTOR to the RECEIVER (and to the observer), about some entity that is not simply the ACT of the ACTOR. The ACT may be said to "carry" the IMAGE, and the image "carries" a meaning (the specific element of the image).

And now we may observe that a still higher level of behavior is assumed to exist in the distinction of PRO or CON. This level may be called the level of *Value Judgment* (see Appendix A, each Direction). It is not only the case that the ACTOR constitutes IMAGES and their ELEMENTS in his mind and communicates them to the RECEIVER. The ACTOR also makes value judgments about the ELEMENTS of the IMAGES and tries to change images so that they mean something different both for the ACTOR and for the RECEIVERS. The ACTOR may make a value judgment that puts a negative value on an IMAGE that a moment earlier was regarded as positive. The ACTOR may decide and say that the self as ACTOR does not like ascendant behavior in the SELF as a person (CON U in SEL). The ACTOR may decide and say that the self as ACTOR does not like friendly behavior in the OTHER (CON P in JOHN). This kind of value judgment may supersede the more spontaneous liking or disliking of the element of the image. The ability to make such value judgments is the level referred to in psychoanalytic theory of personality as the "superego." SYMLOG language permits the observer to record the highest-level value judgments that the ACTOR makes of the ELEMENTS in the IMAGE, as well as the lower-level semantic meaning (the DIRECTION) of the ELEMENT.

We may summarize by saying that SYMLOG recognizes three *major sets* of levels of behavior. These are (1) *The Behavioral Levels;* (2) *The Levels of Image Presented;* and (3) *The Levels of Value Judgment.*

The *Behavioral Levels* include two sublevels, ACT and NON. The *Levels of Image Presented* include six sublevels, SEL, OTH, GRP, SIT, SOC, and FAN, each of which is combined with a set of twenty-six directional specifiers, and two of which (SELF and OTHER) are subdivided into the names of each of the persons in the group. The *Levels of Value Judgment* are subdivided into PRO or CON (or "?") and the PRO or CON judgments are applied to each Element of an Image. In the SYMLOG message each piece of communication is described at all three major sets of levels if they appear. This is the meaning of the name, Systematic Multiple Level Observation of Groups. The person may ACT toward an OTHER without presenting an IMAGE. Or the person may ACT and present an IMAGE without communicating a value judgment PRO or CON. Or the person may ACT and communicate a value judgment, PRO or CON, about an ELEMENT in a IMAGE.

A concise summary of the elements of the message format and some scoring hints follow. Strictly speaking, each message is considered to include the name of the observer, the designation of the group, and the date in addition to the elements of the message we have just described. For convenience, this general heading is recorded only once, at the top of the first observation sheet. The elements of the message may be defined more exactly as follows:

> *Observer:*   A short code, usually not over four letters representing the observer's name, e.g., John Doe may be represented as JD, or JOHN. Each observer indicates the abbreviation he or she wants to use, the instructor or investigator then compiles the list, checks to eliminate any duplications, and issues the standard list of abbreviations with names attached for use by observers and group members.

> *Group:*   A short code to represent the group being observed. It might be Group A or B, Red or Blue—whatever the group is called.

> *Date:*   The date on which the session observed is occurring, represented by numbers for the Month, Day, and Year in that order, e.g., 9/26/78. Slashes are used to separate the numbers.

The rest of the message, following the above three elements, may be called the "body" of the message. The elements of the body of the message may be defined as follows:

> *Time:*   A two-digit number representing the minute from the beginning of the hour period in which the session occurs. For example, if a session is scheduled at 9:00 A.M., the time 9:10 A.M. is designated by the two-digit number, 10. If the scheduled time of the beginning of the meeting is 9:00 A.M., then the time 10:01 A.M. is designated by the number 61, and so on consecutively for succeeding minutes. A digital clock is necessary to obtain sufficient accuracy to coordinate the observations of more than one observer. (Without a digital clock observers tend to round to the nearest five-mintue mark.) Accuracy by minute, and proper sequence within the minute, are important in comparing the observations of different observers, and for proper recall of actual events.

> *Who Acts* (Actor):   A short code name representing the name of the group member who is making the communication and whose behavior is being observed. The same names are used as the names for the persons as observers. (Each group member indicates the abbreviation he or she would like to use; the instructor checks for duplications and issues the list of standard

abbreviations, with full names attached.) It is necessary to avoid use of the same code name for two different persons, of course.

Toward Whom (Receiver):   The other person (or the group as a whole) to whom the actor is talking or toward whom the actor is acting. The group as a whole may be indicated as the Receiver with the use of the abbreviation GRP, if this seems most appropriate. The name of the specific person, as designated by the code name (see above) is ordinarily used. If the communication is addressed to some person outside the group (rare) the abbreviation OTH may be used.

ACT or NON: The classification of the communication at the Behavioral Level, either as ACT (an overt act toward the other intended to carry a communicated content) or as NON (an unintended nonverbal sign of emotion, feeling, or attitude, given off previous to or during the actor's overt intended communication, or instead of overt communication, as shown in facial expression, tone of voice, bodily movement, position, or posture). The same piece of behavior may be described by two messages, one at the ACT level and one at the NON level, if the directions are different. If the directions are the same, the message at the ACT level suffices.

Direction of Act or Non: The directional classification of either Act or Non, (whichever has been specified), in terms of twenty-six directions (or twenty-seven if "Ave" is counted). The direction describes the behavior qualitatively, according to the definitions given in Appendix A. The direction of the behavior at the ACT or NON level is *independent* of the direction of any element contained in an IMAGE. The direction of ACT or NON describes the ACTOR's attitude toward the RECEIVER (as seen by the Receiver). (The direction of an ELEMENT in an IMAGE describes the way the IMAGE is imagined to act toward the ACTOR.)

Ordinary Description of Behavior or Image: A few words in ordinary English, the actor's words if feasible or a paraphrase, to tell the reader the content the observer is selecting as an IMAGE. (The *global* classification of the image selected is given in the last column, and the direction of the specific element in the image is given in the next to last column.) If the behavior classified at the ACT or NON level carries no IMAGE byond itself, the space headed ORDINARY DESCRIPTION OF BEHAVIOR OR IMAGE is used to describe in ordinary language what the ACT or the Nonverbal Behavior sign was. The ordinary language description of the behavior or image is critically important in feedback, since members always want to be able to recognize what it was that the observer was scoring, and they cannot tell otherwise.

Pro or Con: One of these two codes, or a question mark, is written to indicate whether actor appears to be in favor of (PRO) or against (CON) the directional element of the IMAGE selected for attention. Value judgments PRO or CON are treated as independent of the direction of the element of the image. They are "higher-order" positive or negative judgments of the directional elements. Thus, the actor may express a PRO value judgment about an element that may be ACT N or, vice versa, the actor may express a CON value judgment about an ACT P element. (See Appendix A, each direction, for illustrations). A PRO or CON statement is usually more or less equivalent to a proposal for a group norm—a suggestion as to what value judgments others should also make.

Direction of the Element of the Image: An element selected from a global image is described by the directional term that seems best to express the meaning it has for the actor. Sometimes this is apparent from context, tone of voice, etc., sometimes not. Often the meaning is similar for the actor and for the other group members. If one supposes the actor gives an image a particular meaning not the same as other group members give it, the meaning for the actor is the one chosen. The DIRECTION OF THE ELEMENT, in other words, is the direction ACTOR seems to assign to the element.

Image Level: The observer may well have a list of the six levels as a reminder of the various classes of IMAGES: SEL, OTH, GRP, SIT, SOC, and FAN. Images are assumed to have different psychological qualities according to these general classes. Brief definitions are given below.

SEL: Images of the SELF, that is, the self of the actor, as visualized by the actor. The term SEL is written in the message, and the reader determines who is meant by looking to see who is given as ACTOR. An image of the self is given by a remark that indicates a characterization of the self or some element of it by references to own behavior, thoughts, feelings, or by the use of adjectives or trait names. When a situational, societal, or fantasy image is presented that the actor seems to accept, or claim, as a part of the self-image, the IMAGE is classed as SEL. Thus, "I come from an upper-class family," would probably be scored PRO U in SEL.

OTH: Images of particular members of the immediately interacting group, *other* than the actor. The term OTH is *not* written in the message. Rather, *the abbreviated name of the group member meant is given.* The OTH in question may be same as the RECEIVER of the ACT or it may not. An image of an OTHER is given by a remark that indicates a characterization of that other person, or some aspect or element of the person; by references to behavior, thoughts, or feelings of the other; or by the use of adjectives or trait names. Images of non-group members are classified as either in the SITUATION, in SOCIETY, or in FANTASY. However, when the actor uses images from the situation, society, or fantasy in order indirectly to characterize some person in the group, the IMAGE is classified as OTHER and the name of the person is given. Thus, "John says he comes from an upper class family," would probably be scored (PRO or CON) ? U in JOHN.

GRP: Images of the present interacting GROUP, considered as a collectivity, that is, as constituting a higher-order entity. The GROUP in this sense can be described in somewhat the same terms as a person, that is, by references to characteristic or normative behavior, thoughts, feelings, or by the use of adjectives or trait names describing some particular aspect of or element in the GROUP. Note that "GROUP" is an IMAGE and that images exist in the minds of the individual actors. When the actor uses images from the situation, society, or fantasy in order indirectly to characterize the GROUP, the IMAGE is classified as GRP. Thus, "We may as well give up. We don't have any power in this situation," would probably be scored PRO D in GRP.

SIT: Images of objects or aspects of the SITUATION immediately external to the interacting membership group and constituting its immediate environment. Includes the task or tasks, if any, but also all of the freedoms, possibilities, and psychologically significant features of the immediate environment for provoking or supporting any kind of behavior, thoughts, or feelings. The situation, the immediate environment, is described in terms of these meanings it has for the members—the images they construct of it, rather than in the observer's terms. References to persons outside the membership group, but who interact to some degree with it (for example the observers), may be classified as images of the SITUATION. For example, "Those observers, sitting in judgment, make me nervous," would probably be scored CON UNF in SIT.

SOC: Images of the SOCIETY within which the group and its immediate situation exist. Elements of the society in this global sense may be publicly known persons, groups, occupations, social classes, institutions, or any element of the society as defined and referred to by the actor. The directional description of an element is often that meaning which it has for the majority portion of society, but if the actor's definition of it seems to be different, the actor's meaning is taken. Images of elements in SOCIETY are often vague, abstract, stereotyped, ideological, and prejudicial, and the direction assigned depends upon the actor's attitude. Images of other societies and international relations are included in SOC. Thus, "The international situation is a mess" might be scored CON UNB in SOC.

FAN: Images that seem to arise in the imaginal processes or the FANTASY of the actor, or seem to have a strong emotional meaning for the actor though based upon actual experience. Classification of an image as FAN does not imply it has no factual basis—it means that its present significance for the actor is given by its fantasy-arousing potential. The actor may not think of the image as one from fantasy; the actor may think of it as purely factual (see Appendix A for examples). In case of conflict as to whether to classify an IMAGE in FAN or in some other class, the FAN classification is preferred. The use of the term FANTASY in SYMLOG is much broader than in ordinary defintion. Any report of doings of the ACTOR in contexts other than the group are scored as FAN, because they are assumed to function as arousers of fantasy in other group members, who have no direct access to the outside life of the ACTOR.

As a final comment on the set of components contained in the message format, we may note that all of them, with the exception of the natural language description of the BEHAVIOR or the IMAGE, are written in code words of three or four letters and in a standard order. This, of course, is needed for further operations of sorting, counting, and preparation of various statistics.

Although the message of the individual observer is made available to the individual group member, and as such may give an important insight, much of the power of the method depends upon the aggregation of the observations over time and over all members of the observation team. In this adding together, the peculiarities and biases of individual observers tend to cancel each other out, and their similarities and common perceptions tend to emerge. These common perceptions and interpretations are perhaps more convincing to the group members than single messages. This statistical approach provides an important element of "objectivity" in a process that begins with individual "subjective" judgments.

It is often true in psychology and sociology that in providing for a statistical approach one may lose the possibility of a "naturalistic" approach—that is, the possibility of looking at the individual act in its full context and in relation to many levels of determinants. In SYMLOG, however, the naturalistic approach is preserved. One can recapture the memory of the individual act, locate it on the sound record, compare the observations of different observers, and examine it at its various levels of meaning. One can analyze it "in depth" as usual in the "clinical" approach. But, in addition, one may obtain statistical information about the frequency with which observers have picked up similar aspects of behavior. The present method thus integrates a "statistical" with a "naturalistic" approach, and its use may be turned in either direction, as needed.

Chapter 15

The Spatial Model of the Directions

The observer's perceptions of some multiple level piece of behavior are formulated into a "message." When this message is transmitted back to the group member it may be called an "interpretation." That is to say, the message contains a characterization of the actor's behavior. In the example given, the behavior of TOM is characterized as both somewhat dominant and somewhat friendly. This is recorded in the message by a Directional Code of two letters, "UP."

Figure 32 shows the SYMLOG three-dimensional space (also shown earlier as Figure 3.) In the language of SYMLOG the dimension from dominant acts to submissive acts is said to range from "Upward" to "Downward," as if the dimension were the vertical dimension of an ordinary physical space. From the center point of such a spatial model the dimension ranges Upward, in the direction called U, and Downward in the opposite direction, called D. U as a location is at the top of the space, D is at the bottom. The dimension is designated U–D.

Figure 32 also shows the dimension from friendly to unfriendly. The dimension is said to range from "Positive" (friendly) to "Negative" (unfriendly). From the center point the dimension is visualized as extending horizontally toward the right side of the space in the direction called Positive, and toward the left side of the space in the direction called Negative. P is the Positive terminus, N is the Negative terminus. The dimension is designated as P–N. The dimension P–N is defined as theoretically independent in relation to the dimension U–D. Location of a point in relation to one dimension thus gives no information about (is independent of) the location of that point in relation to the other dimension. The two dimensions are represented as at right angles to each other.

The directions shown by arrows on Figure 32 may also be thought of as representing vectors or directional forces proceeding from the central point of the space outward toward the points of termination. Attitudes and motives of various kinds in the individual personality are thought of as having the property of vectors, that is, as forces tending in a given direction with a certain strength toward a given kind of overt behavior. The space encompasses the locations of the various possible kinds of behavior. The observer does not actually observe the

FIGURE 32 The SYMLOG Three-Dimensional Space

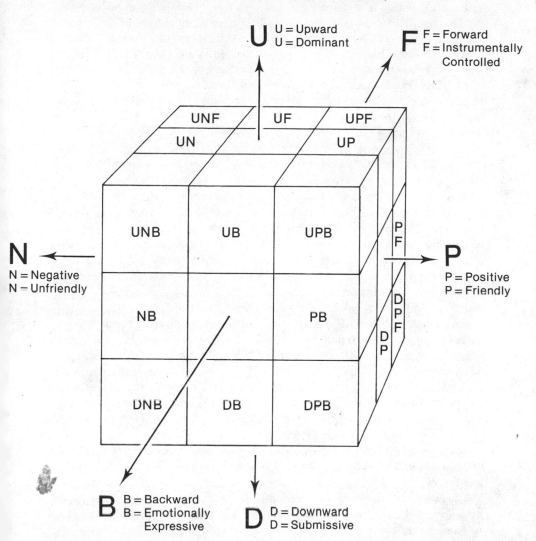

attitude or motivational element, of course. For any given act of overt behavior the observer only names the behavior from which the underlying vector is inferred. In our example, TOM's ice-breaking friendly ACT is said to be at location UP. This implies that the observer perceived it to contain discernable components of both dominance and friendliness simultaneously. What are sometimes perceived to be component attitudes or motivational elements of the actor's behavior are attributions by the observer. The observer, of course, has no special "inside access" to the attitudes and motivational forces of the personality of the actor. The observer, in fact, is reporting what effect the actor's behavior is having upon the observer himself (or herself). The observer's perception, however, even though subjective, is often very similar to that of the receiver of the act, and the actor's perception is not necessarily very different. SYMLOG does not assume similarity but rather provides a way to discover the similarities as well as differences among actor, receiver, and observer. This is done by obtaining observations from group members as well as nonparticipant observers.

Figure 32 also shows the dimension from "Backward to Forward" as independent of the other two dimensions. Behavior in the "Forward" direction includes such acts as careful analyzing and reasoning. Behavior in the "Backward" direction includes such acts as joking, laughing, and doodling. It will be helpful to read the definitions of the various directions in Appendix A containing the component F or B, since the concepts involved are more complex than those necessary to form a good idea of U–D and P–N.

In terms of interpersonal behavior (rather than just the abstract spatial model), "Forward" means "instrumentally controlled." An equally good description is "work-oriented or value-controlled." To say that behavior appears to be "value-controlled" means that the actor seems to use considerable higher-order intellectual control in the guidance of the behavior, that is, the actor thinks, reconsiders, makes value judgments about complex choices, makes decisions, and attempts to implement them and follow their implications. In order to do this, or as a result of doing this, or both, the actor tends to moderate or tone down spontaneous feelings and emotions and waits or works instrumentally for later gratification. The behavior is "controlled" or guided by certain values or previsualized end states, which the actor is working to realize.

In contrast, "Backward" means "emotionally expressive or counteractive to value-control." "Emotionally expressive" often means the *absence* of higher-order intellectual control. On the other hand, the phrase "counteractive to value-control" means, not the *absence* of higher order intellectual control, but the attempt to *circumvent* or *overcome* a previously established control. In the present set of dimensions, the direction "Backward" means *either* absence *or* counteraction of higher-order control. The direction "Backward" is thus a complex concept involving two components (absence of control and counteraction of control) that do not necessarily move together, and are sometimes alternative to each other. The two components are alike, however, in their tendency to interfere with a particular level of value control.

The concept of the Forward direction is the primary point of reference for the dimension F–B. The core meaning of Forward is "behavior carefully controlled by some higher-order mental process." The higher-order control may be only the perceived necessities of work or instrumental action, or it may be some set of value-judgments and decisions—both components are alike in that they can be used to exert or exercise control over one's instrumental behavior. The meaning of Backward is then defined secondarily and residually as *that which tends to contravene Forward movement*. Utter innocent lack of control may do it, or sophisticated counteraction of control may do it. The concept of the Backward direction combines these two disparate components.

Since these long terms and definitions are a little hard to remember, one may say more briefly that "Forward" means "instrumental" and "Backward" means "expressive," if one remembers that the term "expressive" has a special meaning within the system of concepts. The terms "task-oriented, nonemotional" versus "emotional, non–task-oriented" are also sometimes appropriate.

Spontaneous behaviors that seem to show little conflict in the actor between Backward and Forward movement are placed at the zero point of the F–B dimension. Simple Positive behavior, for example a smile at the time of meeting, would be classified neither Forward nor Backward, but as simply "Positive." (See definitions of ACT P, ACT N, ACT U, and ACT D, for examples of behavior placed at the zero point on the F–B dimension.)

Behaviors that show considerable components of both Backward and Forward movement, but with the two vectoral forces about evenly balanced, are also placed at the zero point on the F–B dimension, that is, at the middle, neither F nor B. Thus, when an act is described as neither F nor B, it may be that *neither* component is present to any degree, or it may be that *both* are present, but approximately *balanced*. (This possible double meaning of the zero point is also present on the dimensions U–D and P–N.)

In behavior that is described as Forward (work-oriented or value-controlled), the actor may attempt either to control only his own behavior or may also attempt to control the behavior of others, or to set up mutual controls if none exist. Thus Forward behavior often involves appeal to existing social norms and established concepts or their implicit use. Social norms or rules if accepted may help to emphasize continuity and focus of attention, concentration on a specific task or method of operation, and the application of order and rationality in thinking. In order to reinforce work-orientation and value-control the actor may try to get the group to accept certain social norms. These attempts themselves, moreover, often have a feeling of work-orientation or value-control about them.

It should be noted, however, that movement toward higher-order value controls is distinguished in the present system from raw dominance or ascendance. The dimension F–B is logically independent of the dimension U–D. "Higher-order value controls" involve *self-control* according to some rule or normative pattern. "Raw dominance" or "ascendance" need not involve establishment of self-control and is unrelated to rule-derived consistency. The distinction between the direction U and the direction F should be explored by reading all of the definitions involving either or both components in Appendix A. Briefly, one may say that U is the direction of "power," while F is the direction of "authority," if it is understood that one is referring to legitimately established authority binding upon the actor as well as the other.

In behavior that is described as Backward (emotionally expressive or counteractive to value-control) the actor may show either an *absence* of intellectual or normative control or *resistance* to it. The control that is resisted may be either self-control or control by the other who is attempting to set up or enforce a social norm or value. The behavior often seems strongly motivated by emotion or feeling, and when it is oriented to counteract some particular type of value-control, the actor may propose counter-values to justify the resistance. (Thus it cannot be said that Backward behavior is simply behavior without reference to *any* value controls. But Backward behavior is justified by values of freedom from certain other value controls, while Forward behavior is justified by a positive evaluation of the value controls on impulse.)

Backward behavior is often "expressive" in the sense that it emphasizes or depends upon imagination and fantasy as "guides" to behavior. The interaction tends to be unfocused on a specific topic or task, to show sharp breaks and shifts in attention rather than continuity, and to appear disorderly in the looseness of meanings of words and acts. The actor may engage in side talk or side activity in preference to the communication with others necessary to work through to a conclusion in spite of difficulties. The actor may show either an antipathy or indifference to the smooth workings of normative control of the behavior of self or others, especially in regard to emotions and feelings. The actor may demonstrate an orientation counter to such control by intentional resistance or may simply seem to have failed to internalize the controlling norms or concepts to which the other or others in the group make reference. The person acting counter to value-control may urge this approach upon others, perhaps attempting to create a group subculture with counteractive norms, or the behavior may be simply an individual expression.

In our example, TOM's act of breaking the ice with a socially positive remark may seem neither very strongly "controlled" (intellectual control over feeling) nor very strongly "counter-to-control" (resistant to intellectual control). In the description of the act given in the observer's message, the direction was given as UP. Neither F nor B is mentioned, and this omission is meant to indicate that on the F–B dimension the act was around the zero point (or balance point) of the forces pulling in the two directions. If the observer had felt that the act was very strongly "controlled," he would have added an F, and the directional code would have read UPF. If he had felt that the act was strongly "counter-to-control," he would have added a B, and the code would have read UPB.

The combination of one, two, or three letters standing for the direction of the act is called the Directional Code or simply the Direction. The directional code of the act names its location in the three-dimensional logical model shown in Figure 32. The observer decides which directional code seems most appropriate. Detailed verbal descriptions of the kinds of acts having the quality of each direction at each level are found in Appendix A. The observer studies these detailed descriptions and uses them to build up a general idea of the dimensions and levels. The general idea of the levels and dimensions is then used to characterize the act at the time the observation is actually made.

In practical terms, then, in deciding upon the proper scoring of the direction for TOM's ice-breaking friendly act, the observer went through a three-step process. *First,* thinking of the act and its context, the observer asked: *"Does it seem noticeably Upward (dominant) or noticeably Downward (submissive), or not noticeably either?"* In this case the act was the first of its kind, it also seemed to reflect some kind of initiative and outgoing character, and so the choice was made to put a "U" in the Directional Code.

Second, the observer asked about the same act: *"Does it seem noticeably Positive (friendly), or noticeably Negative (unfriendly), or not noticeably either?"* There seemed to be no doubt that the remark reflected a friendly intent, and the response of the observer was a friendly feeling, so a "P" was put down in the second position of the Directional Code.

Third, the observer asked about the same act: *"Does it seem noticeably Forward (work-oriented or value-controlled), or Backward (expressive) or not noticeably either?"* In this case the observer probably felt some elements both of desire for free feeling and desire that events be controlled, about evenly balanced, but since neither predominated noticeably, both F and B were omitted in the Directional Code. As explained above, omission of the mention of either direction of a given dimension may mean that the two directions are about evenly balanced, as well as that neither is noticeable.

The question arises as to how far out from zero a given act needs to be in order to receive a directional component name. At the level of the description of the single act the judgment is a ''yes'' or ''no'' discrimination as to whether the act contains a noticeable predominance of the direction in question. The eventual test of the validity of such a discrimination is whether, in feedback to the actor in the context of the group discussion about the act, it is the consensus of the group members and the observers that the component was indeed present and predominant.

There are twenty-six Directional Codes in the present system, plus one designating the center location itself, which is called AVE, thus making twenty-seven. The logical reason for the number twenty-seven may be clarified by recalling that there are three dimensions, upon each of which there are three logically defined classes of locations: (one ''toward one terminus,'' another ''around the center point,'' and another ''toward the opposite terminus.'' The total number of combinations of such classes is thus: 3 locations for U–D, $\times$ 3 locations for P–N, $\times$ 3 locations for F–B = 27. The combinations are illustrated in the logical cube shown in Figure 32. The class AVE is the one where the location on all three named dimensions is around the center point. Since the class AVE gives little information, it is often omitted in the listing, and it is often said there are twenty-six directions. The language of SYMLOG assumes that each dimension is independent of the other (the dimensions are ''orthogonal''), and hence any position on a given dimension may be combined with any position on each of the other two dimensions. Note also that the two opposite directions of a given dimension (e.g., U and D) are never combined in the description of a given act. A decision is always made to characterize the act as moving in one direction, *or* the opposite, *or* neither.

In making up the name of a Directional Code from the three judgments of the component directions, one always names *first* the position on the U–D dimension (one specifies either U or D, or omits both letters); then, *second,* one names the position on the P–N dimension (specifies either P or N or omits both); and *finally* one names the position on the F–B dimension (specifies either F or B or omits both).

Wherever a listing of all Directional Codes is given, as in Appendix A, the list is always in the following standard order: U, UP, UPF, UF, UNF, UN, UNB, UB, UPB, P, PF, F, NF, N, NB, B, PB, DP, DPF, DF, DNF, DN, DNB, DB, DPB, and D. AVE is finally added. This order may be remembered easily by tracing it on the three-dimensional diagram in Figure 32. The enumeration starts at U, continues with the adjacent UP, and then continues counterclockwise around the upper tier. Upon completion of the upper tier it falls to the P direction and goes around the middle tier. It then falls to the DP position and goes around the downward tier. It concludes with D, then AVE. In learning to use the space one should learn to name off the directions or directional codes and to visualize their location in this order as one learns to box the compass. The content in terms of behavioral meaning is much easier to handle if one does not have to struggle to remember the purely formal aspects of the spatial model. The spatial names of the directions (rather than the behavioral names) are used for the formal aspects of the model in order to obtain the benefit they give of easy visualization in relation to each other and easy memory.

The system for naming directions and relating them to each other in a formal way is the same for all levels, but the meanings differ somewhat for the various levels. The meanings assigned to the terms at different levels are based on research findings so far as possible, but much remains to be done to determine how closely they represent the intuitive frame of reference of observers and whether they are maximally useful.

For purposes of easy reference the definitions of each of the twenty-six directions on each level of behavior and image content are presented in Appendix A. We shall refer to these extensively in the following discussion. The definitions should be read and studied carefully, as they constitute the bridge between the abstract formal concepts of the directions and the concrete forms in which the observer will perceive various aspects of the behavior. It is intended that the observer should have this manual at hand at the time of observation, for reference, but it is not expected that it will be necessary (or possible) to look up each detailed definition at the time of writing the message. The observer will depend mostly upon the general conception of the dimensions at each level formed by preliminary study and will make the judgments intuitively on that base. Definitions should be reconsidered and reviewed at frequent intervals as the observer builds up experience in scoring.

Chapter 16

The Nature of Interpretations

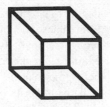

The observer is not trying to record every event that takes place in the group. That is impossible. The goal of the individual observer is to record events that seem to have important impact on the group process and that the observer thinks deserve notice in feedback. This judgment of significance constitutes a unique aspect of SYMLOG as an observational procedure. SYMLOG does not try to eliminate the particular selectivity and bias of the individual human observer in order to increase inter-observer reliability or agreement. Instead, it attempts to codify and refine the individual perceptions of observers and to reveal their differing sensibilities to interaction events.

An event may be significant for various reasons. It may be significant because it is characteristic of the actor and throws light on the actor's personality. Or an event may be significant because it is a missing piece in understanding some group mood or conflict. But whatever the nature of the significance in a given act, the judgment of the individual observer as to the salience and importance of an event is called upon by SYMLOG observation.

The message is an observer's interpretation, intended to be read by the actor whose behavior is being interpreted. Thus, it is important whether the group member can understand the message and remember the behavior, so as to compare his or her own interpretations with those of the observer. Of course, there are some things the observer may consider significant that the actor will not remember. The actor will also be motivated to interpret some things about his or her own behavior in ways that other group members do not. For these and like reasons, then, whether or not the actor will remember or understand the message cannot be the final consideration for the observer in deciding whether to write a given message or what the message should be.

The interpretations will also be read by other group members. But other group members also may be selective in their memory and perhaps motivated in their perceptions. It may seem likely that a majority judgment of the group would be a more dependable criterion of the validity of an interpretation than the judgment of the individual actor. For some aspects of behavior this may be true—for example, it is probably true that individual actors frequently do not recognize the degree to which they are dominant or submissive as clearly as other members do. Sometimes most of the members of a group see themselves as Positive and do not recognize anybody's Negative behavior to the degree that observers may, for example. In this case, the majority opinion of the group may be biased, and hence the majority agreement of the group cannot be the final consideration.

Is the majority opinion of the observers then the final criterion? Not necessarily. The observers discuss what goes on in the group and may arrive at views that are motivated misrepresentations even though consensual. Motivations of observers are likely to be different in certain ways from those of self-analytic group members. For example, it may be true that observers more often identify with the analytical task of the self-analytic group. Observers may thus tend to note departures from Forward movement with more anxiety and to perceive the Backward phases of group movement more anxiously than the self-analytic group members. In such a case, the majority opinion of the observer group about the value of some activities and content may be biased.

The individual observer at a particular time may realize or perceive something that nobody else does. It does not seem appropriate that the observer should always just try to conform to the view other observers will have. The observer must strive for an independent judgment. Are we then to say that the final criterion is the judgment of the individual observer? That will not quite do either. Individual observers often have biases that they perceive only when their observations are compared to those of other observers or when the interpretation is discussed by the self-analytic group. In the long run, the test of other people's perceptions should be applied to the judgment of the individual observer.

The average perception or judgment of all the persons involved, in the self-analytic group and the observer group, over the longest run, that is, until the completion of the series of observations, is about as close as one can come to specifying the ultimate criterion as to what is the best or most significant observation. At the time of writing each message the observer must simply do the best he or she can.

But "the best the observer can do" improves as time goes on. In the very beginning, the observer has no choice but to follow his or her own perceptions pretty much as they come intuitively. But as time goes on, one sees what the other observers do. It is possible to see and understand how one departs from the average. Some interpretations seem to help the self-analytic group while others do not. The observer should try to discover and overcome particular biases and to write more helpful (that is, *ultimately* acceptable) interpretations for individual group members in the self-analytic group.

What is it more exactly that the observer does in making the judgment necessary to describe the act in directional terms—the description that forms the interpretive content of the message? Is it possible for the observer to decide what directional code to put down without trying to "read the mind" of the actor in some actually impossible way? The answer to this is a qualified "yes." What the observer does in making the judgments of "Upward" or "Downward," "Positive" or "Negative," or "Forward" or "Backward" is to give his or her own reaction to the act of the actor. The dimensional description classifies the behavior not according to its "causes" but according to its "consequences," that is, the effect it has upon the receivers and observers. The observer's reactions are part of the consequences. Ultimately, the consequences include the reactions of all other observers and group members, and so the judgment of an act is also a prediction of what those other consequences will be.

The observer takes into account how the act may affect other observers, and perhaps sees signs of its effects upon other group members, so that the first intuitive reaction may be moderated to some degree. But when the observer makes a judgment of an act as "ascendant" or "dominant," for example, the observer is saying: "What the actor just did or said would make me feel I were being forced into a submissive position, if I were a group member." This is different from saying, "The act was caused by a motivation to be ascendant or dominant."

It is true that when the observer tries to put himself or herself in the place of other group members and tries to sense how they are reacting to the actor the observer is trying to read the minds of those other group members. So it is not the case that the observer can entirely escape the paradox of trying to read the minds of others when trying to judge the direction of an act. But this is the normal kind of attempt made in all natural interaction to try to understand in a commonsense way what the other is trying to do. It is at this concrete level of the consequences of a given act on the ongoing interaction among persons in a small group that the dimensions of the spatial model and the directions have their meaning.

The theory of the directions, or the three dimensions in the spatial model, is thus not primarily a theory of types of motivating forces in the personality. It does not posit, for example, anything like the following: "The infant is born with three basic motives, one toward Upward behavior, one toward Positive behavior, and one toward Forward behavior." The spatial model is compatible with a vareity of assumptions about original inborn motivating forces, but it is not a theory of original motivating forces at all. It is rather a theory about the kinds of evaluative reactions members of small groups tend to have about each other's acts when they interact over a long period. The dimensions are the main dimensions of social evaluation. They are the result of a cognitive classing together on the part of individuals, as *receivers* of acts, of attitudes of actors and properties of objects that seem similar. The receiver classifies acts together not because they have the same cause in the actor, but because they have similar consequences for the receivers. (The receiver's evaluation in turn, of course, affects the actor. The actor, for example, may come to evaluate his own acts in the way important others evaluate them, and this presumably affects or molds to an important extent the motivations of the actor, so the theory is not irrelevant to motivation of the actor. But it is not a theory of *original* motives.)

The evaluative reactions of *each individual as a receiver* become an important part of the rewards and punishments of *each other as an actor* in any small group situation. Rewards come not only from the outside environment or an outside group but from other group members and from their evaluations. It is thus appropriate to speak of "motives toward Upward behavior," "motives toward Positive or Negative behavior," and "motives toward Forward or Backward behavior,'' even though one regards these motives as complex and learned, and conditional on the stability of the small group, the larger group, and the situation to a considerable degree.

The observer using SYMLOG already knows very well how to make the distinctions and give most of the evaluative reactions to the behavior of others common in his culture. If the theory is correct about the essential nature of the dimensions, they are dimensions of evaluation that have their genesis in small group interaction. The assumption is that whenever small group interaction takes place, the evaluative dimensions tend to be constituted. The observers as well as the group members have learned to react in terms of these dimensions in all of the different groups in which they have participated and in which they have acquired their social nature, including the language they speak. The observer makes all or most of the important distinctions on an intuitive level; there are many words in the language to describe them verbally, for people make such distinctions constantly. What the observer is being asked to do in the method of observation is to locate the correspondences between this intuitive frame of reference and the three dimensions as named and described in the model. The observer is asked to write messages that express his or her already existing intuitive reactions in terms of that language.

From the actor's point of view, the message of the individual observer is only a sample of the kind of evaluative reaction the actor can expect to get. It is only the reaction of one person, and a person who is not a member of the participating group at that. So that actor may not have a very good idea of how still other persons may react. But many messages from many observers will give a larger and more representative sample. The group member will also gain information from direct discussion in the participating group.

Chapter 17

The Frequency of Messages

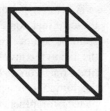

Since the observer is obliged to omit much behavior and write messages only about selected incidents, how does the observer tell what to drop and what to select? There is no getting around the fact that the observer must *select* the behavior for a particular message from a much larger field of behavior. One cannot hope to write a message on everything that is perceived. One must sample in some fashion. The observer should work steadily at the process of formulating messages, selecting according to significance and opportunity, *attempting to get a sample representing all persons observed, all levels, and all directions*. Most observers produce at least one message per minute after some experience. Some are faster. Very slow observers are not usually the best observers.

A message is justified when one observes something sufficiently salient or distinct that the group members are likely to recognize and remember what the observer is talking about in the message. If they do not, the message fails in its most essential purpose. The observer, then, should select instances for description that are sufficiently salient to be recognized.

The concept of the salience of the event and the potential for communicating it to the group members has one important qualification. Occasionally it may happen that the observer notes behavior that seems very salient, but which group members seem not to notice. An example of this might be a note passed between two members, or a semi-audible remark in the midst of laughter. Much nonverbal behavior may fall in this category—salient but either ignored or not recognized at the time by group members. In these cases the test should be whether the group members are likely to recognize the behavior and its significance once it is pointed out by the observer's SYMLOG.

Single acts are often salient enough to satisfy the definition and may be scored. In such a case, if similar acts follow in a repetitive fashion for the same actor, it is not necessary or desirable, to write more than one message for the episode. If a similar thing happens again in another episode, then it may justify another message. It is desirable that frequency of messages of the same level and direction concerning a given individual should reflect actual frequencies to some extent, but the number of messages that could be written is much greater than the number any single observer can actually produce. Each observer depends to some extent on other observers to pick up what he or she cannot find the time to formulate.

A reading of the definitions of the different directions in Appendix A will indicate that sometimes an "incident" or an "episode" taking place over some short period of time seems the more natural unit for the SYMLOG message than the behavior involved in a single sentence or the single word (although sometimes one word is enough). The definition for ACT U, for example, reads "takes the initiative in speaking, or speaks loudly, or firmly, or rapidly, or with few pauses for others to reply," etc. The observer would have had to be paying attention over a period of time to everybody's interaction in order to make this judgment. Hence, a single message reporting the occurrence of ACT U may actually be a report of a considerable stretch of interaction. This is also true of ACT D, "participates only when asked direct questions, then speaks only to the person who asks questions, or gives only minimal information or does not address the group as a whole."

The judgments required for most SYMLOG messages require the observer to pay attention in a general way and to aggregate impressions and perceptions over time. This process of paying attention, putting together and remembering, goes on intuitively in the mind of the observer, and ordinarily, after a short period of observing some behavior or content that is a little unusual, the observer will have a sudden feeling of "realization" or "recognition" that a certain aspect of behavior is salient or significant. This is the occasion the observer should seize to write a message. This kind of "realization" or "recognition" is especially likely to occur, we may suppose, at the end of some period in which the interaction has become intense, repetitive, perhaps stalled in some way, in an "encounter," a "confrontation," an "incident," an "episode," an "interchange," or whatever may be an appropriate term for the short-term pattern. When the pattern comes to some completion or interruption, and the group pauses for a retrospective look or suddenly changes the pattern of interchange, the observer has an appropriate reminder and opportunity to write down a number of messages that describe the outstanding patterns of behavior of *each* of the salient participants, if possible. Nevertheless, one should not deliberately postpone recording events, since the messages of different observers are coordinated by time and are used, among other things, to make "time tracks," that is, a record of the ups and downs minute by minute of the different types of behavior and content in the group (see Appendix S).

A salient event may occur which the observer finds it difficult to characterize. The observer should not omit such an event from his record or else he trivializes SYMLOG so that it includes only easily scored events. The observer should include as much information as he or she can and return to complete the message at a later point, perhaps after the meeting, or even with the help of the tape recording, if one exists.

It is important to realize that SYMLOG is designed to pick up *expressions of attitude about persons, images, and issues*. Frequency of occurrence of an expression of attitude is important, but it is qualitatively less important than the information that the attitude has been expressed at least one. Accuracy of representing actual frequency of a given attitudinal expression is sacrificed to some extent in order to improve the coverage of persons, levels, and directions. On important issues, for example, it is more important to represent what value judgment (PRO or CON) each person expressed about the IMAGE than to represent how *much* each person talked. Hence an important issue will require the observer to write a PRO or CON message about each group member who has expressed an attitude.

In the tabulation of results one often depends on the aggregation of the results of different observers in order to detect a certain tendency. In practice we are often in the position of wanting to know about a type or aspect of behavior that is ordinarily low in frequency. When the normal frequency is very low, it is hard to pick up an increase or a decrease in rate, especially from the SYMLOG record of a single observer, who regularly tries to get good qualitative coverage rather than accurate reflections of actual frequency. One can often obtain the indicator he needs by aggregating the observations of all observers. This procedure gives up the question, "How frequently did the behavior occur?" and substitutes for it the question, "How frequently did all observers taken together write down messages of a given kind?"

In most observation methods observers are trained very hard to achieve identical records, and the observation method is simplified as far as necessary in order to get to the point where observers more or less dependably put down the same thing at the same time. This is an appropriate procedure when one has a specific hypothesis and wants to put it to a crucial test. But this procedure may involve a sacrifice of usefulness of the method as an instrument of general education for the participants. An instrument appropriate to a crucial test may be too specialized to have general intellectual interest over any period of time for participants; it may fail to give information on most of the things in which they are interested and is likely to be qualitatively too coarse. The present method takes the alternative route; it is designed in the first instance for feedback and training and permits great qualitative richness. It sacrifices to a considerable extent the dependable duplication between observers, which is the customary kind of test of reliability.

It is our experience that on particularly salient events, however, duplications do occur, with two, three, four. or five observers out of ten putting down the same messages. Emotional intensity of the event probably tends to make it more salient to observers and increases the probability that they will duplicate messages. An index formed by aggregating the messages of a given kind over all observers thus probably reflects the emotional intensity of the original behavior as well as its actual frequency, but for feedback purposes this is not a disadvantage. It should also be noted that, although the qualitative distinctions permitted for the original observations are many, the directions and levels may easily be aggregated into a few very comprehensive indices, if this seems appropriate to the purpose. In other words, with SYMLOG similar messages are easily recognized as similar (UP is similar to P in that both contain P).

In spite of proceeding by a rationale opposite to that which is customary in designing observational measures, it is our impression that in context the measures are quite good for both feedback and research. Part III of this book will present results of a study of reliability that are quite encouraging. But perhaps one should not be too much surprised. The measures in a given case result from the efforts of a large number of observers, as against the two who are usually depended upon for special purpose observation. And the efforts of a large number enable one to experience the gain in accuracy usually associated with the use of a mean of many observations around which random errors in perception and judgment tend to cancel out (see Appendix T).

Chapter 18

Identifying the Receiver
of Acts

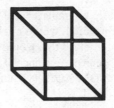

Verbal interaction is ordinarily addressed either to a particular person or to some subgroup, or else in a more general sense to "the group as whole." The way the head and eyes are directed and whether the movements are broad or focused usually give cues as to who is being addressed. In verbal interactions (perhaps to a greater extent than in nonverbal behavior, for example), conscious intentions to communicate and to elicit a response are ordinarily present. The person to whom the actor is talking is thus usually identifiable, and the standard abbreviation for his name, e.g. JIM, is entered in the TOWARD WHOM position in the format.

However, if more than one person is addressed, the problem arises as to whether more than one message is to be written. The SYMLOG system provides a standard abbreviation for the "group-as-a-whole" as an addressee: the term GRP. (The term GRP may also be used in the ACTOR position of the format, if it appears to be appropriate to describe some kind of behavior occurring simultaneously among all or most members of the group. In general, however, this creates problems in later tabulation; it is better to be specific about the ACTOR than vague.) There is no designation for a *subgroup* as an ACTOR or RECEIVER. There are too many different subgroups possible. The observer must resolve the dilemma in such cases by deciding either to write several messages for the several persons involved or to use the general vague term GRP.

The observer should keep in mind that the information about WHO ACTS TOWARD WHOM will generally be used to throw light upon the attitude of the particular ACTOR toward the particular RECEIVER. Thus it is better to be specific than vague as to who is addressed, and it is desirable to obtain some record of each person in relation to each other one.

When the piece of behavior recorded in a message is a single "act" (rather than a series of acts in an interaction pattern of some duration), then the term RECEIVER may be taken to refer literally to the person addressed. But where a message is written to sum up an outstanding feature of a series of acts in an interchange, several different persons may have been addressed, and yet the term GRP may give the wrong impression. If RICH had been attacking TOM and JIM, for example, but it was not clear whether RICH was also attacking the whole group, it would not be a good description to write a message: RICH to GRP ACT N, since this would imply that RICH stood opposed to the group *as a whole*. In such an instance it would be better to write several messages, e.g., RICH to TOM ACT N: RICH to JIM ACT N: TOM to RICH ACT N, and JIM to RICH ACT N.

Chapter 19

The Concept of Multiple Levels of Behavior and Content

One purpose of the concept of levels is to allow us, within the context of the observer's language—indeed, to force us—to be more exact and specific about just what it is we are paying attention to in the behavior we are observing. Often we base our impressions and evaluations of a person on something that could be specified, but we fail to note, or remember, just what it was.

More important than the general sensitizing purpose, however, is the purpose of dealing more realistically with the complexities of behavior as one believes them really to be. A fundamental assumption is that important motivational pressures within the individual personality tend to affect the direction of the person's behavior. We assume that if a motivational pressure is present and persistent in the personality it is likely that the directionality of the motivation will tend to be shown *on some level*. For example, we may suppose that aggressive feelings as a motivational pressure will tend to increase the probability of behavior on some level in the Upward Negative direction, UN. If the UN behavior does not show on the ACT level, then perhaps it may show more covertly at the level of nonverbal behavior, NON. Or perhaps it will not appear on either of these levels but will appear in the form of aggressive fantasy images and be expressed verbally at the FAN level. Or perhaps it may show on still some other level. If it does not appear on *any* level, we have no evidence of the existence of the motivational pressure.

A primary purpose of the level distinction is to make it possible to pick up presumed effects of pervasive motivational pressures according to some of the main alternate ways in which they may be manifested. We make the assumption that an individual may become fixated in his general striving in any of the directions we distinguish in the system, and this may be seen in a higher frequency index for this direction than other individuals show on the average, on some level or combination of levels. Of course, we do not have direct access to the postulated "motivational pressures," but we are able to compare frequency indexes in various ways and for various levels, and from these comparisons we can make some inferences about the underlying dynamic processes. The knowledge of the different levels makes possible some "surface" to "depth" understanding of behavior.

The levels formulate alternative ways in which motivations show themselves and thus call attention to determinants of behavior characteristic of the individual. But they also formulate the various ways in which the individual may *see* the determinants operating upon his or her own and others' behavior. It is important to become sensitized to this, since within limits whatever the individual *thinks* is important in explaining his or her behavior tends to *become* more important. Finally, we need to recognize that the "observers" are not any different from the "actors" in this respect. Observers may be "stuck" in their emphasis on one level of determinant and may neglect other levels that would greatly increase their insight if they learned to pay attention to them.

The first two levels, the *Behavioral Levels,* ACT (Overt and Verbal Communication) and NON (Nonverbal Behavior Signs), are similar in that they deal with the *form* of the behavior itself. The other person in the interaction pays attention to what the behavior of the actor conveys about the attitudes of the actor toward him. "The Medium is the Message." If the actor gives negative nonverbal signs and acts negatively *in the way* he acts or talks, the other tends to think that the actor has a negative attitude toward him, regardless of what the actor may be saying.

In contrast, the levels of *Images Presented* deal with the *content* of what the actor is saying rather than with the *form* of his communicative behavior. The IMAGE levels are typically formulated in *language* at the time of communication. The underlying mental processes are thus more complex (and multiple-leveled in themselves) than at the level of nonverbal behavior and overt interaction.

Among animals there is no great distinction between what we call nonverbal behavior signs and overt behavior, nor is there among prelanguage children. The overt behavior is simply the completion, at the level of gross muscular movement, of the tendencies that show at the beginning of the act in facial expression and posture. Even after the development of language there tends to remain a close relationship, on the average, between nonverbal behavior signs of facial expression, posture, and so forth and the qualities of verbal interaction shown in tone of voice, timing, loudness, and the like.

We know that human beings become able to control certain aspects of their behavior if they can become aware of them, and it sometimes happens that a person will conceal an attitude toward the other at the ACT level but betray it on the nonverbal level. For humans it is helpful to make a distinction between the two levels and to realize that sometimes the actor conveys the same message on both levels, sometimes conflicting messages. When the complications of language are added, with the many kinds of objects that may be talked about, the possibilities of representing and at the same time concealing attitudinal conflicts are greatly multiplied.

In judging the meaning of behavior at the nonverbal level the observer surmises that the actor is having certain feelings and preparing to do certain things on the basis of the expressions on the face or movements of the body. The observer presumes that there is a process of "imagery" going on in the actor's mind, but the behavior is preliminary or tentative in character, it is not expressed in words, and presumably it may be quite minimal in conceptual complication as it exists in the mind of the actor. The observer, looking at the behavior of the actor, may in fact go much farther in conceptualization than the actor himself. In SYMLOG, the observer's conceptualization of the way in which the nonverbal behavior makes the actor appear is used, even though it may go beyond what is in the awareness of the actor.

At the level of overt and verbal interaction the behavior of the actor is no longer preliminary but actually carried through. The observer has more evidence on which to base the classification of direction than in the case of nonverbal behavior. The rapid adjustment and readjustment of actor and other in the course of the act can be witnessed visually. The observer may see many things about the manner of the interaction that give an impression about the attitude of the actor. As in the case of nonverbal behavior, the observer uses these signs and the reaction of the OTHER as the basis of scoring, even though it may not be very clear how conscious the ACTOR is of the attitude expressed toward the OTHER.

Many animals give nonverbal signs of the way they are about to behave overtly and react to each other on the basis of nonverbal signs, which give them cues as to how the other is about to behave. However, the interaction that takes place at the animal level seems not to be a very good representation of what is involved at the human level when human beings make reference verbally to objects and events in their environment. Language—the words and concepts upon which language is based and the intellectual combinations it permits—introduces a large degree of complication into the mental processes.

At the human level we find we need to speak of "cognition"—a process of knowing or getting to know in an *idea* context—rather than simply "perception," which is the sensory part of the process. At the human level it is quite difficult, even by careful experiment, to study the "purely sensory" part as if it were isolated from the more broadly cognitive parts of the process. The past experiences, expectations, and knowledge of the individual, as well as his desires, hopes, and fears, seem to invade the sensory process of representation and to affect perceptions even at a very basic level. One of the components that can often be distinguished is the effect of prior, or accompanying, fantasy processes. Often we think in partly imaginal terms, in terms of complex IMAGES.

In human interaction individuals often exert pressures upon each other to tone down the individually unique elements in the IMAGES they present in their content. Perhaps they are more likely to do so when they need to be "realistic" and can tell whether they are being realistic by rapid feedback from the situation. But the very use of language seems to involve the pressure of individuals on each other to preserve the constancy of meaning of words. A word, with its connotation along with its denotative meaning, is a kind of IMAGE when one focuses attention on it.

The meaning of the term "instrumental" (as the description of the meaning of the Forward direction in the SYMLOG language) is that the total stream of behavior of the individual at the time of action seems to be strongly influenced by intellectual processes of control over emotion and feeling. Intellectual control of behavior is made possible in part by the ability to think and speak in terms of language; and language, in turn, is made possible in part by the social control of the meaning of words. This control of meaning, in turn, is a part of the socially interactive control of all aspects of behavior. Language is socially or interactively controlled in its meaning, but the language processes within the individual are also "controlling" over some aspects of behavior. Intellectual control of the individual over his own behavior is dependent in part upon his acquisition of language, and in this learning he is taught and controlled by others. The concept of "value-control" as used in SYMLOG should be understood to mean (for all levels above the nonverbal and the overt wordless act level) "control of behavior through the use of language, and the reference to objects made possible by language."

There are types of nonverbal behavior that may be called "controlled," such as paying close attention with the eyes or, among animals, the stalking of prey, which depend strongly upon sensory processes and do not require language-mediated processes. But at the human level most of the behavior we call "controlled or value-controlled" is mediated by language-based concepts and mental processes, which make value judgments possible. Recognition of the use of language-based concepts as a means of controlling and being controlled makes it possible to distinguish between what is called the "Forward" direction in SYM-LOG from the direction of "dominance" (called "Upward"). Among animals one does see dominance and submission, but not language-based conceptual control of behavior. Language-based control of behavior may apply to both self and other. Through the use of this level of control one may be both controlled and controlling, as in a "government of laws, not of men." At a level above this, one may also be controlled by value judgments of one's own making.

When it becomes important in a family to teach the child language, a new viewpoint is set up that competes with the existing levels of control of behavior of the child. The new viewpoint is one in which the content of the words used is the thing to which the parents want the child to pay primary attention. The Receiver (the child), by the intention of the Actor (the parent), is supposed to pay attention to the content of what the Actor is saying. The Other is not supposed to pay attention to the *behavior* of the Actor. The emotions and attitudes the Actor expresses are supposed to refer to the objects the Actor is talking *about*, that is, to focus attention on the IMAGES presented, not to indicate what the Actor is like as a person, what kind of position the Actor wants in the group, or how the Actor wants the Other to treat the Actor.

This attempt of the Actor to control the direction of attention of the Receiver to the IMAGE seems to be inherent in language. The use of language in a group presumes that the members have the ability to understand overt social interaction (the ACT level) as well as nonverbal emotional signs (the NON level); but the use of language requires them to distinguish between these two levels and the higher levels, where objects and attitudes are represented as IMAGES by *words* and sentences rather than by acts or nonverbal behavior. The direction of attention necessary, and the inhibition required, most be embodied in group norms of some sort before the higher levels of language can be developed.

If one is looking for the root phenomenon in human personality, group interaction, or culture that makes it likely that a dimension we can call F–B will appear along with U–D and P–N, it is surely in the set of norms, values, and complications that surround the use of *language,* which in turn is necessary to effective *instrumental cooperation in meeting the demands of problem-solving and work.*

In the development of a child, the evolution of the human species, and the development of a given group, it is easy to see that external demands that would make an increase in value-control advantageous may exist, and such demands may be responded to by effort, but without success. Efforts may or may not be sustained; efforts may or may not be rational; they may or may not be cooperative; they may not be controlled by a special language, a special set of rules, a value on rationality, a value on stability of situation and group sturcture, a value on authority, a value on values themselves. All of these characteristics appear to depend on common roots, the necessity of work and the possibility of value-controls on behavior, but the more highly developed forms do not necessarily go together.

The associations among the various elements of the direction F are *learned associations* and, perhaps even more important, are associations taught in a developmental process—*intentionally,* for the most part. It is quite otherwise, for example, with nonverbal behavior. The child learns (or knows how) to read its significance very early; it is not intentionally taught. Probably many aspects of expressive movement and the means of interpreting it are inborn. The nonhuman primates show many traits of nonverbal expressive behavior similar to humans', and, of course, they read such behavior very well, without a verbal language and without teaching. They show minor elements of nonverbal behavior in the F direction—fixation of attention, for example—and even perform some mildly astonishing acts of finding objects in nature they can use as tools (as Jane Goodall's motion pictures have shown us), but animals generally do not communicate with each other in advance about cooperative instrumental behavior. It is not altogether clear whether there may be important exceptions. At any rate, it seems safe to say that the dimension F–B in the interaction of nonhuman primate troops is minimally developed, whereas the dimension U–D is highly developed and the dimension P–N is also quite clear.

It is a repeated finding in the factor-analytic study of behavior in human groups that the dimension F–B is less clear, with lower correlations among its elements, than the other two dimensions. Most such studies show the dimension U–D to be the clearest, followed by the dimension P–N, with lower intercorrelations among the elements, followed by the dimension F–B, which sometimes is not found as a separate dimension or is found with some elements missing or fractionated. Sometimes the dimension P–N is the clearest. In other words, groups differ in the clearness and independence with which the dimensions appear.

Persons are very much concerned with the stereotypes that are applied to them and the ones they apply to themselves. Stereotyped images of the SELF, OTHER, GROUP, and SOCIETY are "loaded"—they have social and emotional consequences. They bear directly on the self-picture that the individual tries to maintain, even though individuals differ widely in the kind of self-picture they try to maintain. Many or most individuals try energetically to get rid of anything about themeselves that does not fit with their desired self-picture and social image. Perhaps the commonest defense of the self-picture is to "project" the undesired aspects of the self or social image onto other persons involved in the interaction, to some outside group, to the society, or to some situational or fantasy object.

The self-description may be sharply held apart from the description of the other in the mind of the actor, and the two may in some respects be opposite to each other. This is true for social status and role traits also—the social traits one attributes to oneself may be the opposite of those one attributes to the other. It is always necessary to distinguish the self and other descriptions and to compare the directions.

The images concerning the actor that exist in the minds of others are not under the actor's immediate definitional control, and yet they affect the actor crucially. Such images may be changed, but usually only rather slowly and in limited respects. The reality of these images is an "interpersonal" and a "social" reality, existing as an interacting set or system of concepts in the minds simultaneously of a number of others. In the case of one's image in the larger society, the people are so numerous and so dispersed in space and time that it is impossible for the individual to visualize clearly the nature of the reality. Social and interpersonal images are so loaded with anxiety in some cases that they may become the focus of attempts to conform (or resist conformity) almost superstitious in quality.

Sometimes the images of the GROUP and of SOCIETY are not clearly visualized in anybody's mind. In a value judgment or a suggestion in a group that certain elements of the GROUP or SOCIETY should be changed, it often is not clear whose behavior is to be controlled—that of some individual, of a subgroup, or of the group or society as a whole. It usually is not clear who is to exert the control, whether one, some, or all; or by what signs anybody may determine whether they have agreed to exert such control; or by what means they are to exert it, to what degree, to what end or ends; and when, if ever, they are to slacken or modify control. Sometimes neither individual actors nor all of the individuals in a group trying to cooperate are able to determine just what they are up against in the confusion of concepts they have created or to find a way to change the norms and values that control them. They are controlled, in part, by defects in their conceptual controlling mechanisms, whether they individually will it so or not.

One should not be surprised, then, that resistance to evaluative control regularly appears in systems of social interaction. In the norms and values of a given group, and in the personality of individuals, a dimension of "controlled" (and controlling) *versus* "counter-to-control" is regularly found. One must expect changes and reversals in direction from level to level, and certainly in behavior directed to different objects and at different times. In some groups individuals at the ACT level are controlled and rationalistic in their behavior as individuals but at the level of proposals for group norms, PRO or CON some particular important issues, they cannot agree except to give up and go home.

In the process of development of the individual one will see reversals in the strength and priority of various levels of process and in the predominant directionality of behavior and content. An important instance is the development of attitudes toward authority in our society. The child at first has no idea of authority, but with the impact of language and teaching, around the age of five or six, he or she begins a period of relative acceptance of authority. In our culture, this pattern is usually disturbed with the onset of adolescence, when there is a process of individual revolt against some of the previous acceptance of authority. With adulthood the degree of revolt tends to moderate, and some less literal conceptions of authority are usually developed and accepted. With increasing age, there is a general tendency toward conservatism and perhaps a more general acceptance of the necessity of authority, at least in some form. In this process of developmental change the individual tends to go through at least one full cycle in his general attitudes toward authority after he first becomes aware of it and begins to accept it: first Forward (PRO F), then Backward (CON F, PRO B), then toward Forward (PRO F) again, and perhaps to a balance.

With regard to observations taken using the SYMLOG system of levels one may expect to find that the direction of behavior at the value judgment level is not very predictably related to the ACT level of the same individual. A given person may be going through developmental changes in which the direction of behavior at two different levels is more or less opposite. He or she may not have started these developmental changes or may be on the rebound from them. Or else it is quite possible for the person to realize that his or her behavior at the ACT level is not satisfactory and to set up value judgments to counteract the lower-level behavior, perhaps without success.

There are more than developmental reasons for expecting to find differences and reversals of direction in the different levels of behavior of the same person. The various levels reflect the different sorts of determinants operating at a given time in the group, in the situation, and in the personality.

And yet there *is* an expectation of some kind that most of us have, as participants in social interaction, that other people and we ourselves will *somehow* be consistent—over time, over situations, and over levels. Is this wishful thinking? Perhaps one hypothesis may be ventured: "Consistency" is probably more a characteristic of our high-order cognitive processes in *thinking about* behavior than it is of our concrete behavior at lower levels. A number of research studies, for example, have shown that, as time passes after an actual period of observation of behavior, observers tend retrospectively to transform and distort their descriptions of what happened toward a simpler pattern that is cognitively easier to grasp and remember.

It is an important hypothesis underlying SYMLOG that the three *dimensions* and the *directions* of the system do indeed approximate quite closely a simplified cognitive structure that exists more or less similarly in the minds of many people. Indeed, there is theoretical reason to suppose that the structure is basically similar across many cultures, though surely there are important differences.

In the theory of SYMLOG, the implication is that the cognitive structure, is a reflection of the fact that in human behavior every object of cognition—every element of every IMAGE—is *evaluated* and that the mind tends to put together "in the same box," as it were, elements and images that are sufficiently similar in their evaluative connotations. To continue the simile, one may suppose that the mind is willing to set up "a new box" (another dimension of evaluation) only when it is persistently confronted with elements that it cannot put in one of the existing boxes. It thus exercises a kind of economy in the number of dimensions recognized. Each box (a dimension) is itself subdivided into two opposite polarities, and this too is a kind of economy or simplification.

The directional space in SYMLOG is thus a graphic representation of the kind of simplifying economies the mind is hypothesized to make in its evaluations as to the polarities and as to the most common dimensions. The fact that in naming the directions the U or the D, if there is one, is named first is a representation of the hypothesis that the characterization of "dominant or submissive" is the most universal or predictable dimension of evaluation. The distinction of "value-controlled versus counteractive to value-control" is thought to be more complicated, less universal and predictable, than the other two. It is thought to become important only at the human level, when it becomes necessary to distinguish control that takes place through language-based concepts from raw dominance, and this dimension ordinarily fractionates further in the process of development of the individual.

Some kind of weighing up of all evaluative reactions to the element of the image is a process we suppose may often take place as one of the last and highest-order processes of abstraction prior to decision and the guidance of processes of action. If so, economy in the number of dimensions—and polarization of the directions—of evaluation would surely have advantages of speed and decisiveness as well as integration and consistency of the cognitive processes.

The highest-order processes of value judgement, we suppose, *finally connect* the weighing up of the significance of the elements of images with a set of executive processes that guide the actor's reaction on lower levels. We would suppose that there is not only a problem of economy with regard to reducing the number of directions of evaluation, hence of action, but also a problem of reducing the number of levels one takes account of in the behavior of the other person. Somehow the unique qualities and multiple-level inconsistencies of the other person as well as of the self need to be reduced to a simpler concept for purposes of action.

It is a working hypothesis of SYMLOG that, in the perception of persons with whom the actor is in social interaction, there is typically a *tendency toward a reduction in the number of levels with which the actor deals conceptually toward a single level, the level of the ACT*. That is, the actor, in a manner of speaking, tends to translate everything the other says and does, at no matter what level, into a conception of the way the other is likely to ACT toward him.

Thus, behavior of the other at the nonverbal level tends to be read by the actor as a sign of how the other is likely to ACT; the actor understands the nonverbal behavior because it is similar to some ACT in complete form. If the signs predict (sometimes they do not), they telegraph what the other is going to do at the ACT level in the next few minutes, seconds, or fractions of a second. Nonverbal signs are probably mostly used for short-time predictions, and, of course, as predictions they may be quite wrong. We are interested in the concept that the nonverbal signs may be "read" and "understood" as to their direction by "translating" them into the overt behavior to which they would tend if carried out at the ACT level. The ACT level is perhaps the level of least ambiguous reference and conceptually the final common path to simplification.

Similarly, we suppose, the Actor is usually able to understand something about the fantasy images presented by the Other (at the level FAN) by translating them into images at the ACT level. This translation tells the Actor what kind of *images of action* the Other is preoccupied with. These images do not give good predictions as to how the Other will behave at the ACT level, because fantasy processes often reflect motivational tendencies that are for one reason or another blocked. But at the same time translation of an image to the ACT with which it is most closely associated mentally gives a partial means of understanding what the blocked tendency is. In the final simplification of the concept of the Other the Actor may tend to drop the fantasies of the other out of his evaluation, but not if he believes they may result in ACTs.

When the Other makes reference to situational objects or events (SIT), it is usually more or less apparent to the Actor that what the Other selects reflects as much about the Other as about the situation; that the Other is calling to attention things that will tend to justify or explain his or her behavior or desired or planned behavior. The Actor can, and we suppose more or less regularly does, translate the Other's remarks about situational objects into what they may imply or predict about the behavior of the Other at the ACT level.

The images the Actor has of SELF, OTHER, and GROUP are presumably closely related to the way they ACT. It is as if those three levels of images were generalizations from the ACT level perception. If one wants to remember the act of the Other, or the quality of a number of acts, one translates them into a conception of the *personality trait or image* of the Other. On the other hand, if one wants to visualize the significance of some kind of personality *trait* of the Other, one translates the trait conception into an inference as to what the behavior of the Other will be, at the ACT level, in the given situation. Acts are often attributed to personality traits, and personality traits are defined by the kind of acts to which they are supposed to translate. The image of SELF or OTHER that may come from position in society (the image at the SOC level) also translates to the kind of ACT that may be expected from such a kind of person.

A value judgment that is at the same time a suggestion for a group norm is intended to introduce or establish expectations that will encourage a given type of ACT or a kind of behavior on some other level that may be translated to the ACT level. The content of a norm is roughly delineated by the type of act it is intended to regulate.

Abstract, general value statements specifying how things should be done in the larger society are sometimes almost metaphoric and have the same qualities as fantasy images. They are subject to the complications that pertain in the case of reference to social traits. The Actor may have to compute a while before he can figure out just what the enunciation of an abstract, general value statement by the Other implies for the way the Other may ACT toward the Actor, but probably most people intuitively discount value statements by others that they think will not be realized in the Other's actual behavior.

Because all levels seem to be translatable to the ACT level, conceptually a single set of descriptive adjectives for the directions (Dominant, Submissive, Friendly, Unfriendly, value-Controlled, counteractive to value-control) seems to work more or less well over all the levels. We assume that translation of all the other levels to the ACT level is characteristic of the way most people tend to think, and we utilize this assumption in defining the directions for observers on each level. The observer is encouraged, in trying to decide what direction to attribute to the element of images on other levels, to make mentally the best translation he can to the ACT level.

We may comment briefly on several somewhat overlapping distinctions that may be helpful in understanding some aspects of images on the various levels especially pertinent to interaction in self-analytic groups. The first such concept is the distinction made in psychoanalytic theory between "ego-syntonic" and "ego-alien" aspects of one's own behavior. The distinction deals with the extent to which the Actor perceives an aspect of his behavior as an acceptable expression of the self-concept or self-image. The second distinction is that between voluntary and involuntary behavior: To what extent is the behavior a result of some conscious choice, a choice made in full awareness of consequences? The third distinction concerns responsibility: To what extent does the image reflect behavior for which the Actor takes responsibility or is assigned personal responsibility? The concept of responsibility becomes especially important if the individual himself or others have some desire to change behavior.

Of all levels of interactive behavior, the PRO or CON value judgments of the individual are perhaps perceived by the Actor as the elements most closely associated with the self-image and under voluntary control. They are also the level of behavior for which actors are perhaps most willing to be held responsible. Others, however, often take the overt behavior of the individual more seriously than his or her value judgments.

Behavior at the ACT level is usually seen by others as the expression of the actor's true character, whether or not it fits with the Other's self-image. Overt behavior is the subject of most legal conceptions of responsibility. This legal focus on overt behavior is based partly on its being observable, on its directly affecting the object, and on its being the supposed end product of all the causes of behavior, whether situational, status-related, or internal-drive-related. Only the presentation of images of others can so directly affect others as overt behavior, and the things one says about the Other, too, are defined in legal understanding as something for which one can be held responsible. The Actor may occasionally, in the process of communication, feel that the ACT emerged involuntarily, that he or she was "out of control" (a term we use because of the usual expectation of control of ACT). However, the other group member may still hold the person responsible for the ACT regardless of the intentions and motives expressed. Some group members will attribute "good" ACT behavior to the voluntary control of the actor and explain undeniable "bad" ACT behavior as involuntary and due to factors at some other level. Of course, some members may do the reverse.

Nonverbal behavior, NON, when perceived by others, is usually accepted as emanating from the true characteristics of the Actor, not necessarily from the Actor's self-image. The Actor does not wish to be held responsible for his or her own nonverbal behavior, since it is not voluntary, and may wish to dissociate it from the self-image. The other members, however, may hold the Actor responsible for the attitude expressed, especially because the nonverbal behavior is seen as not subject to voluntary control and therefore even more surely the expression of the Actor's character.

Some images of the SELF are presented voluntarily. The Actor accepts the personality traits he or she presents as truly descriptive of himself or herself. Yet such statements may also have the function of presenting a fixed image of the self such that the person cannot be held accountable. By describing his or her personality in trait terms, the Actor may be absolving the self as Actor of present responsibility for voluntary action. Behavior is explained as emanating from more fixed elements in the personality over which the Actor has no control. The respondent to such fixed personality images in a self-analytic group might want to answer, "Yes, that is the way you usually are, but why were you not different this time? Do you want to be like that or do you want to try to change?" Presentation of fixed images of the self may be signals for raising questions as to whether the person has the will to change and the extent to which actors may identify positively with aspects of their "personality" that others regard negatively. Not infrequently traits that are seen negatively by others are ego-syntonic, or seen positively by the Actor.

When the Actor describes the Other, the Actor sees the Other as the person responsible for the description the Actor makes. To the Actor it is the Other's behavior that is the manifest explanation for the image. Not infrequently, however, the Other sees the Actor as "projecting"; the Actor is regarded as responsible for misperceptions.

Images of the OTHER, the GROUP, and SOCIETY may be quite ego-alien when the SELF is not in some way identified with them. They are then elements for which the ACTOR takes no responsibility and regards as certainly not what they are by any voluntary action of the SELF.

Images of the location of the *SELF in SOCIETY* (one's social background) are perhaps the parts of the self-picture most often portrayed as fixed and determined prior to the present. The general social status of the person is often (not always) accepted as part of the self-image, but the Actor may take less responsibility for the behavioral implications of this part of the self because it has been decided, as it were, in the past, not in the present. References to social characteristics help to explain, or explain away, present behavior and interaction. The elements are at least partially determined by others, especially parents and other authority figures, and partly by events and circumstances that were no responsibility of the Actor. The Actor may be held responsible by other group members, however, for presenting certain images at a particular time for the enhancement of the self-image.

Images of the SITUATION deal with elements the Actor feels to be external to the self, or *ego-alien*. The situation is also something that the Actor does not voluntarily create; rather, the Actor feels that the situation already exists. The Actor's statement claims to be nothing more than the acknowledgement or calling to awareness of an already existing reality. Furthermore, the Actor does not expect to be held responsible for the situation, although persons are sometimes blamed for bringing undesirable facts to awareness and thus increasing the psychological hazards to others. Of course, the Other may detect a bias and silently hold the Actor responsible, but it is hard, usually, to make a strong case.

Fantasy images are quite variable and ambiguous on the voluntary–involuntary dimension. Dreams are seen by the ACTOR as the most involuntary of behavior, yet the writing of fiction or other productions of the imagination have at least an important element of voluntarism. Fantasies are sometimes paradoxically seen as very much the expression of the Actor, and yet some persons represented in the fantasy are seen by the Actor as "others," not associated with the self-image. The behavior of images of others as presented in fantasy may be strongly ego-alien. The Actor may reject in a double way the responsibility for his or her fantasy. It may be seen as having "come upon" one, not as willed. And one may see much of the behavior in the fantasy as carried out by quite alien others. The levels FAN, SIT, and SOC are often similar in their ego-alien quality. The self-image is often seen in sharp conflict with elements of the situation, society, and images of fantasy.

The relations between the levels, how they differ by individuals, in different groups and interaction situations, and how they change over time are very complex and constitute major problems of research. The theory of levels and directions in SYMLOG only opens up these problems to a new method of observation. No doubt, as research proceeds, one will want to modify concepts of levels and also, perhaps, those of the directions.

Chapter 20

Recording Incongruence of Direction between Levels

In human behavior all levels are potentially active and important in every act. Our separations between levels are to some degree arbitrary and selective, for purposes of communication and learning. For example, verbal behavior is normally accompanied by a flow of nonverbal signs of attitude and feeling. The observer ordinarily uses the impression conveyed at one level to amplify the meaning at other levels. Often the different levels, for example, verbal and nonverbal, will give the observer the impression they should be described as having the same direction. In our stock example, TOM's verbal interaction was described as UP (ACT UP); he gave the group a kind of compliment. We would ordinarily expect in such a case that he would also give nonverbal signs of positive feelings—perhaps smiling or in other ways that are suggested by the definition of the direction UP at the nonverbal level (see Appendix A). If so, his nonverbal interaction (NON UP) would seem congruent with his verbal interaction (ACT UP).

In many cases, then, the observer depends on nonverbal signs to help him read the meaning of verbal interaction at the ACT level. This is not necessarily a problem in scoring—the observer could describe the act at either level or both, according to how salient the various aspects seemed. On the other hand, a dilemma is created if the direction of the behavior on one level does not seem congruent with the direction on another level. Suppose that, while saying he liked the members of the group, TOM had shown some of the kinds of nonverbal behavior described in NON NF (Appendix A): tightens jaw muscles, or tends to press lips together, or keeps face set grimly, or keeps minor signs of rejection patiently in check, or shows occasional breakthroughs of negative expression in tics or grimaces, etc. Certainly these kinds of nonverbal behavior seem incongruent with the verbal professions of liking and would suggest, if one really observed them, considerable internal conflict in the personality. In this case, the observer would write separate messages for the ACT and the NON level, keeping the minute the same. This double message would highlight the incongruity and raise the probability that the incongruity would be discussed.

This example illustrates one of the prime advantages of the multiple level approach to the description of behavior. It makes possible a fine qualitative description of behavior in a way especially useful in analyzing the motivational complexity or depth of behavior. The theory does not assume consistency of direction of various aspects of behavior and content over all levels, nor, on the other hand, is the perception of some single aspect of behavior on some particular occasion given too strong an emphasis. Various kinds of theory in psychology and sociology differ markedly in their approach to this problem. So-called statistical approaches to personality, for example, usually depend upon the measurement of one or a few traits of the individual studied over a broad population of individuals. In contrast, the "clinical" approach usually involves a multiple level approach applied to one or a few individuals, and often there is no explicit measurement or quantitative treatment of data. The present approach gives scope to either a statistical or a clinical emphasis and, to a certain extent, suggests a resolution of the dilemma.

The important thing to note, for purposes of improving observation, is that the observer should be on the lookout for instances of incongruity in the direction of behavior of the same individual at different levels. One should give priority to the writing of double and triple messages that point up the incongruity and should take care that comments make the incongruity clear.

The same kind of priority should be given to the writing of double and triple messages that point up the similarities and differences between individuals. If the PRO or CON attitude of one individual about a given image has been recorded, the observer should take care to pick up and record the expressions of attitudes by other individuals about the same image. This is basically similar to what the secretary of a group may do in recording who votes for and who votes against, a given motion.

Chapter 21

Overt and Verbal Communication, the ACT Level

The level ACT is defined for our purposes as consisting of acts of *Overt and Verbal Communication,* which communicate *by their form* the attitude shown by the actor toward the other.

The ACT level is the level of *the overt action or behavioral process of communicating* in social interaction rather than the substance intended in the words of the communication. The ACT level is the level of the most direct expression of attitude. It is the level we mean when we say that "actions speak louder than words." It is the level of interaction at which the actor expects an immediate communicative reaction from the other. It is not the content of the words as such, but the manner of behavior to which the other must respond in communication: for example, whether the actor treats the other as someone who is not allowed to interrupt, whether the actor asks the other questions, whether the actor expects the other to conceal his disagreement, whether the actor seems really interested in what the other has to say. The ACT is the way one really "treats" the other, not what one says to him literally.

Behavior at the ACT level is at least potentially under voluntary control—the actor can presumably change it to some extent, according to intention, and for short periods by paying close attention—but the actor is not always keenly aware of the form of his or her own interaction and what its *manner* conveys to the other. Frequently, the actor is more aware of the *content* and wants the listener to pay attention to "what I say" rather than to "what I do." The ACT is not necessarily the content of what the actor says, however, but what the other feels that the actor is *doing.* Sometimes the actor's words may present the same picture of the actor's attitude as the form of the actor's overt verbal interaction, sometimes not. If there is a discrepancy, sometimes the actor is aware of it, sometimes not.

The overt behavior of the ACT level, especially the frequency of various types of acts, is not usually at the level of highest conscious voluntary control, although it may be brought to the center of attention and controlled to a considera-

207

ble extent by conscious attention. Usually the manner and frequency of verbal interaction are less highly conscious and less in the center of attention than the content of the intended message of the communication. Probably the manner of interaction of the *actor* is usually closer to the center of attention of the *other* and more consciously examined by the other in the communication than by the *actor*. The other visually *sees* more of the behavior of the actor, and also *hears* more, than the actor does. The actor is not able to see his or her own facial expressions, for example. One has a poor view of one's own posture. One does not hear one's own voice as others hear it. These aspects of behavior are classified in the present system as nonverbal behavior (NON). One would be expected to have some difficulty in paying attention to these manifestations of the self, of which one has poor sensory awareness, and to be less "conscious" of them, as a rule. Overt behavior at the ACT level is probably easier for the actor to perceive, to bring to the center of attention, and to control by voluntary effort than behavior at the NON level. But it is still somewhat more difficult than paying attention to the *content*. To bring the ACT level into high consciousness, the actor would have to perceive, "Now I am agreeing," "Now I am failing to ask questions," "Now I am disagreeing too frequently," and the like.

An important part of what we mean by the "level" of the behavior must be described from the point of view of the *other*. From the point of view of the other the ACT level of the actor is the one with the most pressing implications. The other must try to cope with *what is being done to him and what is being demanded;* the other must try to decide whether to try to make a given remark, whether to agree or disagree, whether to increase or decrease physical distance from the actor, and so on. The only aspect of behavior of the actor that would be more pressing to the other would be direct physical action. Acts of communication generally take the place of direct physical action. In the present system, then, we do not make a distinction between "act" in the sense of an act of communication and "act" in the sense of direct physical action. These two are designated by the same category, ACT, in our system. This is true even though direct physical action is sometimes unaccompanied by verbal communication and in this sense is "nonverbal." Direct intentional physical action is not classified under the level "nonverbal." In our system the term "nonverbal" really applies in a more restricted way to the nonverbal *signs* (facial expression, bodily position, etc.) of the direction overt communication or direct physical action would probably take if the covert attitudes were to be expressed more directly.

With regard to each level of behavior it is important to consider what kind of perceptual access the actor and the other have to the behavior at the time of the behavior. We can think of the behavior as being under some degree of conscious control, whether of a high degree or of very low degree—"unconscious," as we might say. This is also called the degree of "intention," and in interpersonal interaction, just as in criminal legal proceedings, the degree of "intention" is very important. The basic rule in social interaction is simple: If at the time of an ACT there was little or no intention to commit the act, then the actor is not to the same degree "responsible", and this means that the other is *not* free to the same extent to "punish" the actor. The act may be talked about and defined more carefully, and some steps may be taken to bring it under more conscious control of the actor, but the kinds of steps that may be taken are usually defined by the degree of intentionality. One cannot assume that punishment will always follow intentional deviant acts in all kinds of relationships—this varies greatly. But it is probably generally true that the degree of intentionality of the actor in committing the act defines to some extent the steps that the other can or will take in anticipation of possible future instances.

Behavior at the ACT level is somewhat ambiguous as to intentionality, and perception of it is far from dependably good. The fact that the behavior took place in the presence of both actor and the other, or the group, does not guarantee that it can be recalled and discussed without disagreement as to what actually took place. On the other hand, attempts to recall and define it are not unreasonable.

Behavior in the ACT category is precontractual, or constantly emerging prior to the contractual evaluation of it. If the actor, for example, is acting in a dominant and unfriendly way (ACT UN), it is immediately pressing for the other to react to it as dominant and unfriendly, no matter whether there is some prior norm as to whether the actor shall have a right to behave in that way or not. He *is* behaving that way in fact, and it is this incontrovertable factual or "actual" feature that is central to the level. Of course, the other may protest that the actor has no "right" to act in that way, especially if there is some kind of social contract to this effect, but the behavior is "actual" whether it conforms to a social contract or controverts one, or is simply undefined. In this sense, to "act" is always to exert direct influence, no matter what the direction of the act or the content of the words, if any.

The urgency to the OTHER of satisfactory control of the ACTOR's behavior on the ACT level is sometimes considerable, and if so, the stage is set for strongly motivated attempts by the OTHER or others to change the behavior of the ACTOR at the ACT level. The outcome of such attempts is usually quite problematic, especially since the ACT in recall is inherently somewhat vague and subject to differences. Paradoxically, it is usually easier to come to agreement as to what the actor "said" in literal words. Since the levels above the behavioral levels ACT and NON are usually based upon the literal words used by the actor, the objects of perception and later memory in the recall of these words are perhaps usually clearer than the memory of the ACT.

Chapter 22

Nonverbal Behavior, the
NON Level

In the present system, the term "nonverbal behavior" applies primarily to nonverbal signs of emotion and attitude given in facial expression, bodily position, and bodily movement. This level does not include direct overt physical action, which is an intentional act directed toward another and expected to produce a reaction. The term "nonverbal behavior" is less broad than it seems since it does not include all behavior that is literally nonverbal. But the term is well established and seems to be generally understood in approximately the more narrow sense we desire, hence we adopt it.

To repeat: Direct physical action, intentionally directed, is excluded from our category NON, although literally it is "nonverbal." It is classified under ACT. Another kind of behavior is excluded also: symbolic "acting out" in order to arouse fantasy images. "Acting out" is literally nonverbal, but it is not classified under NON. Symbolic acting out is classified under FAN. The following list summarizes these points:

Direct intentional physical action } Verbal interaction process acts }	= ACT
Nonverbal signs of emotion or } attitudinal states, unintentional }	= NON
Symbolic (nonverbal) acting out } Report of fantasy content }	= FAN

Nonverbal behavior, as we define it, is for the most part unintentional or out of the focus of attention of the actor, but in the spotlight of attention for the other. When nonverbal behavior becomes intentional it approaches the much more sophisticated kind of nonverbal behavior that we call symbolic acting out and is classified as a variety of fantasy, FAN. Our category nonverbal, NON, implies the lack of intention. The nonhuman primates certainly "give off" signs of their emotional and attitudinal states that in many ways appear very human, and these signs are apparently understood very well by other observing primates, though the signs are not very clearly or certainly "intentional." The "signs" given out by a non-human primate in the process of excitation and muscular preparation for direct physical action are regularly observed and reacted to by other non-human primates in appropriate ways, prior to the onset of the direct physical action they portend. This "conversation of gestures" as it was called by George Herbert Mead, is a nonverbal precursor to communication by language as we know it.

Whether or to what extent the ability to "read the signs" of nonverbal behavior is inborn in nonhuman primates or humans is not known. But it is reasonable to suppose that, whether a specific ability is built in or not, the situation created by social interaction is such that intelligent beings could be expected to learn a good deal about the meaning of nonverbal signs by the ordinary learning processes of classical and operant conditioning.

Learning to "make" signs *intentionally in order to "communicate"* is a considerably more complicated thing. On the other hand, neither humans nor nonhuman primates have to *learn* to "give off" signs that are read by the other in nonverbal behavioral interaction. This is because the part or aspect of the behavior taken by the other as the "sign" is simply the natural *early part* of the behavior as it proceeds toward direct gross muscular action. According to Darwin and others, the snarl, for example, is a muscular action baring the teeth, ordinarily preparatory to an attack in which the teeth are used. A smile requires a relaxation of the facial muscles usually activated in an attack, and a replacement of the snarl pattern by activation of the complementary set of muscles. (In Appendix A, compare NON UN with NON DP—opposite directions.) Nonhuman primates snarl and relax the snarl, but they do not smile—or do they? Human beings smile, but not when they are first born. Perhaps they are partly taught to smile by parents who want to be reassured by signs on the baby's face that are contrary to those it must show if it is about to cry. The ingredients of a human smile are still not known.

There are many unsolved problems about the nature of nonverbal behavior and its relations to more developed forms of verbal interaction. But perhaps enough has been said to make it plausible to suppose that the ordinary well-socialized human being is able to read the signs of nonverbal behavior of others very well indeed for all practical purposes. It may be that many individuals have poor awareness of the nonverbal behavior signs they themselves are giving off to others. Our vocabulary and language-based concepts do not give us a good way of talking or thinking about nonverbal behavior. It is also probably true that, even if we saw ourselves as others see us, we would still have trouble changing our behavior to what we would like it to be. But these probable facts do not make it implausible that on the average most individuals can probably read with a good deal of accuracy and effectiveness the nonverbal behavior signs that others give off. It is probably true, however, that people differ in the nonverbal channels they read most effectively, and we do not read the signs of persons from another culture as well as we do those of persons from our own culture. These are probably indications that the performing and reading of nonverbal behavior are at least partly learned.

The hypothesis that nonverbal behavior functions in interaction in much the same way as verbal interaction, often as a precursor to it and as more or less continuous with it, makes it plausible that our three-dimensional space should provide an appropriate descriptive framework for its meaning. The descriptions of specific forms of nonverbal behavior one will find in the Appendix are coordinated to the directions largely on the basis of hypothesis. This hypothetical map was constructed from a knowledge of artistic anatomy, particularly the facial muscles and postures that artists of the past have associated with the expression of various emotions, supplemented by experience from observation. These elements were coordinated by the general theory of the space. The SYMLOG scorer is not expected to memorize the verbal descriptions but is expected to use them to raise questions and sharpen perceptions of the meaning of the variety of cues that members give in the nonverbal expressions of their attitudes.

Chapter 23

Images of the SELF, OTHER, and GROUP

Our natural language is full of words and images describing persons or, more exactly, traits of persons, such as "dominant," "submissive," "friendly," "unfriendly," "hard-working," "dreamy." The levels SEL and OTH consist of references to such IMAGES, and the level GROUP consists of such trait characterizations when they are applied in a loose collective sense to the group as a whole.

It is fortunate that our system of observation and the setting in which it is used make it clear that when we speak of "traits" we are talking about *attribution* of personality characteristics to the actor by others participating in the interaction, or by the actor. That is, we use the term "trait" without making any strong assumption as to whether the attribution is accurate, whether such an attributed characteristic describes anything very lasting in the personality, or even whether there is any organization in the personality that corresponds to the trait name being applied. There have been various attacks lately by behavioristic psychologists upon personality tests that have been developed by another school in psychology sometimes called the "trait psychologists." The critics do not usually deny that personality tests give evidence of some organization in the personality, but they contend that the situational and other influences on behavior are typically so powerful that personality tests given ahead of time do not help much to predict or understand what actually happens later, nor do they help much in figuring out how to try to change behavior or personality, if that is an aim.

The trait approach was not invented by psychologists, however, nor will they be able to do away with it even if they wish to. The trait approach was invented by people in interaction with each other, and it represents a level of abstraction or conceptualization that they cannot do without. A trait description of a person in natural interaction is a means of storing memories of what he or she has said or done and of indicating something about the probability that he or she will do similar things in the future. This is important to the people with whom the actor is in interaction, and they will attribute "traits" to the actor in some form, no matter what the actor says or does. Furthermore, the generalization of perceptions of individual behavior into trait descriptions allows the group member to make use of previous learning and interaction experience in dealing with new individuals. Early in the group's history, people may represent themselves in trait terms and then only later begin to present images about others. The actor often demonstrates first the links he wants others to make to past experience in thinking about him and later shows the learning categories he is using in understanding others. Trait descriptions help limit the bombardment of novel stimuli. Sometimes the trait conceptions are distorted and prejudicial, but not always, and they make the cognitive task of interacting with many people and with new people more manageable. The actor cannot help "building a reputation" of some kind in the group, and others cannot help their tendencies to encapsulate their expectations in the words, gestures, and basic evaluative concepts that they have learned as a part of their language and culture. The trait descriptions that exist in the language are "categorizations" and "stereotypes," just as are the categorizations of social background factors in the case of race and social class. The trait conceptions of a person in a given small group are simply more "microscopic," "specialized," "individualized," "temporary" stereotypes than broad social categorizations such as social class, race, age, and sex, but they have the common characteristics of being culturally formed and sometimes prejudicial, but to some degree unavoidable and to some degree difficult to change once they have become set.

We do not attempt to give any exhaustive listing of the trait names in the English language or to describe all the ways in which given social background factors may affect the images of SELF, OTHER, and GROUP. The simplifying assumptions of the present method are that a very great number of the evaluative and qualitative *implications* of trait names *for interaction of persons together in small groups* can be usefully represented by the three dimensions and the conceptual space of the present system. The same simplifying assumption is made for each of the levels. The existence of the three dimensions as major factors within each of the levels has been demonstrated independently to various degrees. The level ACT has the best evidence for the three-dimensional model in terms of independent factor analytic studies, and the attitudinal and value levels, PRO and CON, perhaps next best. Evidence is accumulating for SEL and OTHER. Evidence probably exists now for NON but has not yet been identified and pulled together. The levels SIT, SOC, and FAN have not been viewed before in terms of whether or not their major evaluative implications can be represented in the three-dimensional model.

We make a further assumption that observers do not have to be walking "*Appendixes*" in order to translate and categorize the qualitative implications of the trait names used by group members. It is our hypothesis that observers, taken as a team, will be able to make the necessary judgments satisfactorily by using the conceptualized three dimensions and directions in the space as their frame of reference (rather than the multitude of trait descriptors in natural language). The observers are expected to study carefully the detailed literal descriptions of examples at each level in order to form their conceptions of the dimensions and the space, but it is believed that the conceptual space of SYMLOG is so closely matched to the conceptions that already exist in the minds of most observers that they will be able to do the actual scoring with only supplementary use of the Appendix.

The level OTHER refers to other *group members present*. The term OTH is not written in the message; instead, the name of the member is used. In addition to the list of names of group members and the instructor, the term GRP may be used where the personality trait description seems to describe the average behavior or character of the group.

Many if not most of the images presented of SELF, OTHER, or GROUP will not literally contain personality *trait names*. Some will be remarks about particular acts of the other or a single act. In the present method all references made to the behavior of the other person are recorded at the OTH level. Similarly, acts of the actor, when viewed retrospectively by the actor, are translated to the SELF level.

In the present method it is understood that there may be a great deal of error and mistaken attribution in the minds of observers as well as in the minds of persons in the social interaction. Thus statistical methods are brought to bear. When we look at the tabulated results we notice how many people make similar attributions about a particular person and how often. We also notice whether some actors make similar attributions about many people, thus raising the possible interpretation that they are "projecting."

Other persons are likely objects upon which to "project" one's own unacceptable impulses or to "displace" one's preexisting feelings. Often, other persons are unconsciously associated with the images of earlier known people who are emotionally important to us. When the patient in psychoanalysis begins to give evidence that he unconsciously associates the analyst with his father, mother, or other important person in his emotional development, such misattribution is called "transference." When the analyst begins to misattribute in some reactive way, this is called "counter-transference." Psychoanalysis probably provides conditions for triggering and perhaps aggravating transference, since, for example, once the analysis is really started the analyst sits out of view of the patient and says very little or provides very infrequent feedback and thus increases the probability that the patient's imagination or fantasy will begin to interfere with rationality. This effect is intended. The patient knows about it to some degree and accepts it as a part of the original contract. The patient agrees to what is called in psychoanalytic language "regression in the service of the ego." The transference is an expected part of the imaginal material produced by the patient in "free association." The principal business of the psychoanalysis, once this condition appears, is the "analysis of the transference." In the process the analyst tries to take care that "counter-transference" does not interfere with his or her own rationality. The principle therapeutic tool of psychoanalysis is the "analysis of the transference." The dependability with which the transference in fact appears under the conditions of psychoanalysis is one of its most solid empirical findings.

Transference and counter-transference also appear in our conditions (the academic self-analytic group), involving not only the instructor but also the observers and the group members vis-à-vis each other. These phenomena are probably provoked to some degree by the slow feedback from instructor to group members that is built into the standard expected pattern for each meeting and by the still slower feedback from observers to group members. The free-form group discussion has some resemblance to "free association," and the agreed upon intention to analyze what is produced is quite similar to the "therapeutic contract" in psychoanalysis. The goal of using the material so produced as a means of learning for group members is similar to the goal described in psychoanalysis as "regression in the service of the ego."

On the other hand, there are many important differences between the self-analytic group situation and that which pertains in psychoanalysis. In the group psychology course we intentionally reduce the prominence of the transference to the instructor by more active and more friendly leadership. We attempt to reduce the effects of counter-transference by the addition of many observers, who also observe the leader and discuss with the leader and group members together. We intentionally substitute the free-form discussion of situational objects, social background factors, personality traits, the present group, general values, nonverbal behavior, and current interaction for the great emphasis on earlier life in the family that one typically expects in psychoanalysis. The self-analytic group situation differs from the psychoanalytic situation in that we have a group interaction situation instead of a pair, our time is short, we live in an academic institution, and so on. Our purpose is learning, not therapy. Nevertheless, much of the psychoanalytic point of view is apparent in SYMLOG and in the organization of the self-analytic group with observer feedback.

It is expected that there will be many differences in the way group members see each other, themselves, and other persons. We are interested in the analysis of these differences and in differences among observers, and between group members and observers. The levels of SELF, OTHER, and GROUP are used more frequently when group members really get down to the business of analyzing their behavior and personalities, and it is probably not a bad formulation of a desirable goal in our groups to endeavor to bring analyses of these images to a high frequency at least periodically and to increase their frequency over a long time trend. In our tabulations of data so far, it seems to be the case that content at these levels becomes more frequent from the beginning to the end of the period of the single meeting, while content on the levels SIT and FAN occurs frequently in the beginning and then diminishes. These latter two levels are important to the "warm-up" of the group as domains in which material can be presented at a greater "distance" or with a feeling of "nonreality," but, of course, unless that material is analyzed, it is essentially useless for learning. If it is analyzed in the communications of the group—and to the degree that it is so analyzed—the number of messages at the levels of GROUP, OTHER, and SELF will increase. The ups and downs of the number of references to the SELF, in particular, give us our best index, perhaps, of analytic efforts of members in the self-analytic group.

Chapter 24

Images of Situational Objects, the SIT Level

The level SIT refers to remarks about or descriptions of the immediately present environment or general *situation* external to the SELF of the actor, the OTHER, and the GROUP. We may think of each individual as making certain distinctions between the self and specific *other persons*. We may also distinguish between particular other persons, with whom he interacts one at a.time, and the *group as a whole,* a lumping together of particular others. The group as a whole, in turn, can be distinguished from the immediate nongroup environment of the group. The latter is the domain of images called the SITUATION.

These categories of perception and conceptualization (the levels) are not very clear cut or very stable. Sometimes the actor may extend the concept and feeling of *self* to include specific *other* persons, or perhaps to the *group as a whole,* in which case we say that the self is "identified with" those other persons or with the group as a whole. At other times, the individual may contract the concept and feeling of the self so that he or she does not feel identified with other persons or with the group as a whole.

The term "situation" is often understood to mean "that which is psychologically external to the self." In this usage, "the situation" includes the OTHER and the GROUP (as well as SOC and FAN). The self alone confronts the situation and acts in it and on it. In SYMLOG we make a finer breakdown than simply "self" and "situation." The term SITUATION in SYMLOG *excludes* OTHER, GROUP, SOCIETY, and FANTASY. This leaves only the residual immediate environment of the group as a whole as the meaning of SITUATION in SYMLOG language.

In any group many remarks purport to be about things in the situation external to the speaker, and also external to the other. "The weather" is an example. The weather can be praised, blamed, or made the object of practically any feeling without implying (in ordinary polite conversation) that the praise or blame or the feeling have anything in particular to do with the self or the other. This "externality" is one of the things that give images of the SITUATION their particular character.

Objects in "the situation" of the actor and other, or of the group as a whole (the weather, the time, the clock, the room, the table, the rug, the course, the syllabus, the observer, the elevator, the people in the halls, can be talked about *as if* they were completely external, hence nonrevealing about the self. In fact, of course, a great many of the things said about objects perceived to be "out there" in the situation can be read as giving clues about the concerns and feelings of the speakers. Talk about objects in "the situation" is not infrequently consciously used by participants as an indirect way of talking about themselves. The great advantage is that one does not usually have to admit that one has chosen a particular thing to talk about because of very special things about the self. In ordinary social interaction, the other is obliged by polite social norms to avoid a direct personal interpretation to this effect. Not only may the norms of such an interchange tend to prevent direct personal interpreation, but the personality defenses of the participants may also tend to make them repress or suppress awareness of the direct personal significance and to attribute the "causation" of the things they are saying and the feelings or opinions they are revealing to the nature of the object "out there" in the situation, rather than to themselves.

If objects are perceived to be "out there" in the situation, they may be examined, made the object of information gathering, argued about, and agreed about. They may be acted upon, if accessible. The group may decide what they are, how they are to be regarded, and how they are to be treated or reacted to, but the objects themselves are thought of as independent entities. The objects are "out there" and not a part of the group or the other or the self; the participants agree to regard situational objects as really "out there." Situational objects are "out-group" objects, referred to as "it," "them," "those," or "they."

Situational objects may include other human individuals when they are treated as "objects" rather than as "persons." An *"object"* is something that does not have consciousness of you, the actor. You may act in ways that affect an object, and it may simply exist in ways that affect you, an actor. But you are never in conscious interactive communication with an object. If you treat another human individual as an object, you *pretend* that you are not conscious of the other as a person, that the other is not conscious of you, and that you are not in interactive communication. On the other hand, when you treat another individual "as a *person*" you do engage in conscious interactive communication. It is a fairly well-tested generalization in social psychology that, when persons regard others as persons, their behavior is, on the average, more positive and less dominant than when they, for any reason, define others as more distant "objects." In fact, the dehumanization or "depresonalization of the victim" is a common prelude to, and perhaps a precondition to, the most negative forms of behavior.

When non–group members are referred to as objects they are classified as elements of the SITUATION. Conversely, when the other human individual is regarded as a person with whom the actor is in *conscious, two-way, interactive communication,* then the level chosen for the description should be OTHER. If the name of the other is not on the list of persons, the observer supplies the name (very rare). A similar problem arises with regard to the level on which descriptions of the group should be recorded. The rule is similar. If an actor really seems to regard the group as a kind of object or collection of objects, completely external to any identification with the self, which affects the actor in a one-way manner, then the level chosen for the description should be SIT (also very rare).

In the usual case the group is regarded as a kind of extention of the self, or at least as a group of others with whom the actor is in two-way interactive communication. In this case, the level chosen for the description should be OTHER or GROUP.

An easy way to determine whether an image should be classified as SIT or GROUP or OTHER is simply to read the definitions under the given direction. Pick the one that seems to give the most precise meaning. In general, the SIT level descriptions describe a one-way effect; the SELF, OTHER and GROUP descriptions describe the personality traits of a human individual with whom the ACTOR is assumed to be in interaction or potential interaction. One can *communicate* with an OTHER or with the GROUP, but one cannot "communicate" with a SITUATIONAL object. One can only "react" to it or act upon it. Any human individual can, in principle, be viewed either from the interactive person perspective or, more distantly, in terms of one-way effects upon the group or the actor. Nonhuman objects are never described at the levels of SELF, OTHER, or GROUP.

The level SIT or, rather, things described at this level, are kept apart from the self-picture and often energetically "disowned." They are "ego-alien." Freud's term, the "id," was chosen to imply that part of the motivated behavior of an individual may be attributed by the actor to the outside—to somebody or something other than the voluntarily acting self, the ego. Such an outside agent may be called "it," as in the phrase: "It made me do it," or "It was not my fault," or "It was not me." The German word "Es" is derived from the Latin word "id," "it." The term "id" was adopted in English translation for Freud's concept, rather than the term "it," but the implication was originally meant to be the same. The id is the "it" that makes us do things we cannot consciously admit to ourselves that we want to do. The id, for the ACTOR, is part of the SITUATION.

The id in psychoanalytic theory is further associated with "the unconscious," which in turn is associated with important biologically based drives in the personality. A distinction is made between the drive ("trieb," usually translated as "instinct") and the *object* of the drive. The object of a drive is said to be "cathected." This means that a "motivational charge" or an emotionalized meaning is placed upon an object. We consciously know about some drives only because the *objects* of the drive appeal to us, that is, because of the cathexis. There are objects which appeal to drives we cannot accept as a part of ourselves. The objects that are cathected unconsciously are dissociated from the conscious self-picture. These objects are relegated to the situation—out there—or situational objects are found that can be associated with the unconscious motivational combination already formed. An unconscious drive is said to be "projected" to the outside when the drive is attributed to some other person or to some situational object. An unconscious drive or a feeling is said to be "displaced" when another person or situational object is cathected as a substitute for the unconscious (repressed) cathected object. The "unconscious" includes the original biological "id" and its objects, but it also includes the whole structure of derived *drives and their cathected objects* that have been "repressed" in the course of personality development and the struggle for ego control.

In the present system we are concerned with the descriptions that the actor gives of situational objects and of other persons, as well as those he gives of the self, since we are interested in the dynamic processes described above as "displacement," "projection," and "repression." In psychoanalytic therapy the patient's attribution of various traits to the self, other persons, and situational objects are seldom taken at face value. The analyst, at least, and eventually the patient too, generally supposes that these attributions *may* be a part of the ego's "mechanisms of defense." Much analytic effort is spent in trying to discover and to reconstruct the operation of the ego defenses.

This regular understanding between the psychoanalyst and the analytic patient not to take as final the attribution of some trait or motivation to an outside "it" is a norm that does not fit in well with normal everyday conversation or academic discussion. The "analytic tendency" that the enthusiastic analytic patient or new student of Freud may bring into everyday situations goes against the common conventions of polite normal conversation, namely that one should take the other at face value when the other purports to be talking about some outside "it," some situational object or condition. Taking the other at face value, or at least pretending to, is a part of maintaining the other's "face," and openly to challenge it is to attack the other. In such a challenge the other is told in effect, "the thing you are trying to dissociate from your self is really a part of your self." This is sometimes called an *ad hominem* attack.

In the "attack ad hominem" one accuses the other of trying to maintain a false self-image or being motivated actually by some form of self-interest. In ordinary situations it is usually about as easy for one person as for another to bring such charges, and they are almost never accepted. The usual result is a quarrel of some sort. Hence, there is often a kind of mutual pact not to raise issues of this kind if they can be suppressed, so that a cool rational approach can at least be *imitated,* if not realized in fact. The result is a norm of "impersonality" where each is permitted, indeed required, to deal with everything talked about as if it were "out there" and not affected by one's own particular personality. "Let's keep personalities out of this" is a common expression of the norm.

The psychoanalytic approach potentially threatens this polite norm in that it regularly says (in the analytic situation at least), "Let's get personalities into this." The psychoanalyst in a social gathering is intuitively viewed by the normal conversationalist as an outlaw who cannot be trusted to abide by the norms to preserve the other person's face. Any kind of psychologist, in fact, is likely to be viewed in this way by nonpsychologists. Some persons (not often, it is to be hoped, psychologists or psychoanalysts) are not willing to keep their thoughts tentatively to themselves but insist on speaking them straight out in a defiant attack on normal sophisticated and tolerant discourse. This is sometimes called "being honest" and "frank" and is regarded by those who do it as a virtue. It should be possible, however, to improve the quality of human understanding and discourse through self-analysis without becoming an obtrusive pest or a psychological outlaw—but it is a subtle matter. In the self-analytic group the norm is to proceed gently, but nevertheless to proceed, with the analysis of how personalities and relationships between persons do affect images presented as elements of the SITUATION.

In multiple level observation, we make the assumption that the different levels do indeed have different perceptual qualities as viewed by the actor, and hence have different implications for the self-picture. For example, we assume that behavior at the level of verbal interaction—at the ACT level—is more likely to be perceived by the actor as produced by the SELF, by voluntary choices, as something for which the SELF is "responsible," than is behavior on the level of fantasy, FAN. In our normal, noninterpretative frame of mind we do not regularly accept our fantasies as the result of our own motivational tendencies. We may dream about bad things, but we ordinarily think that our dream is simply truly reflecting the bad tendencies of other persons we have to deal with in waking life or bad elements of the situation.

The method represented in SYMLOG does not try to render a judgment as to how much of "it" is internal to the ACTOR, versus how much of "it" is external. The method rather provides a way of describing behavior at a number of different levels in such terms that the levels may be compared—that is, in terms of how often each "direction" is portrayed at each level. Congruence or incongruence of preponderant direction between levels then gives information. After a time lag sufficient to aggregate some amount of such factual information, the feedback to the actor gives the actor an opportunity to make these comparisons. If the implications are strong that something the actor thought was "outside" is actually a projection or displacement of some kind of persistent "inside" motivation, then that potential attack on the self-picture is one which the actor can choose to make or not. Others take care not to push an attack. The norms of the self-analytic group legitimize some degree of "ad hominem" analysis of the other, but considerable delicacy is usually maintained, because all the members are vulnerable.

In assuming the possibility that discrepancies between levels may reveal motivation, we are making the assumption, at least in part, represented by the concept of "unconscious motivation." This concept in itself is often resisted vigorously in polite conventional society, and when "unconscious motivation" is attributed on little or no evidence, vigorous resistance is probably a virtue. The present method provides feedback of the profile of directions at each level over a substantial period of time and may give some more respectable food for thought. In some cases, probably, individuals will recognize and be able to explain discrepancies or incongruities within and between levels and, in this sense, may be conscious of the motivation. In other cases the discrepancies will not be clearly recognized or known about prior to feedback, or even after feedback. The evidence of "unconscious motivation" in such cases is simply that a number of different observers, working to a considerable degree independently, converge on directional descriptions of behavior that show the direction of the actor's behavior at one level to be incongruous with his or her behavior at another. The hypothesis of "unconscious motivation" in such a case has some evidential basis—it is not simply an ad hoc surmise that a specific unconscious content may exist about which neither the actor nor the observer has any evidence.

SYMLOG does not assume that some of the levels are more important or revealing of the "reality" of the person than other levels. A psychoanalytically oriented theorist might posit the primacy of biological drives revealed by images of the level FAN. Image content on this level reveals the less well-controlled parts of the self; the imagination and fantasy are least directly controlled by environmental and other external stimuli. On the other hand, a sociologically oriented explanation of behavior might focus more on levels of SITUATIONAL and SOCIETAL images as revealing; in the one case the situational determinants of behavior and in the other the demographic and other status-relevent characteristics are taken to be important predictors of behavior. A social psychologist who focuses on the attitude–behavior nexus might be especially interested in the relationship between the levels of value judgments, PRO and CON, on the one hand, and overt behavior, ACT, on the other.

SYMLOG does not make a prior judgment about the priority of levels in explanation, in causal sequence, or in importance. It focuses interest instead on the complicated pattern of consistencies and divergencies across levels, and its user is motivated to search for explanations for characteristic and unique discrepancies among levels.

With regard to the *attitude–behavior* relationship, SYMLOG clarifies each of these terms. It distinguishes among a number of sets of *attitudes* (attitudes toward external environment; attitudes toward social images; attitudes about self or other or group; PRO and CON attitudes arising out of group norms; and so on). It also suggests a number of different kinds of *behaviors* to look at, including nonverbal behavior, fantasy, and imaginative construction. What is usually considered *behavior*, ACT (as well as FAN and NON), can be understood as the expression of *attitudes* toward objects, and conversely *attitudes* toward objects are known only through some form of behavior. "Behavior" and "attitude" are two abstractions from the same event, and in SYMLOG both aspects are included in the same message.

Since psychoanalytic theory has been mentioned so prominently above, it is important to recognize that SYMLOG stands at the juncture of a number of bodies of psychological theory. Reinforcement theory is another body of theory with which SYMLOG intersects. The three-dimensional frame of reference at the level of situational objects, SIT, is essentially that of "operant conditioning" or "reinforcement theory." The directions of the spatial model at the level of SITUATION are associated with the main variables of reinforcement learning theory as follows: "Reward" is associated with the positive direction—a situational object from which reward is expected is evaluated as positive (PRO P in SIT). "Punishment" is associated with the negative direction—a situational object from which punishment is expected is evaluated as negative (CON N in SIT). An object or change in the situation that impels action is called in reinforcement theory a "stimulus," and in the present theory it is evaluated as upward—it is recorded as SIT U (whether PRO or CON). A stimulus demands or elicits a response of some kind. (The sheer quantity of action or response of the individual in the present system is also characterized as upward at the act level, ACT U). A lack of stimulation and lack of response are characterized in the present system as downward—a situation that elicits no action or very minimal action is described as SIT D. Thus U is associated with high frequency or intensity of stimulus, while D is associated with low frequency or intensity. Finally, the forward direction in the present system is associated with what is called the "schedule of reinforcement" or the timing of the reward or punishment in reaction to the action of the individual. This timing—whether or not *any* reaction comes back from the situational environment; whether it comes back sometimes but unpredictably; whether it comes back in a rewarding way or in a punishing way; whether it is dependent on whether the actor has responded in the prescribed way or not; and other such factors—all these characteristics yield "information" of some sort to the individual about his situation. The flow of this information is called "feedback" in our language. A situation that returns immediate and ample feedback and yields reward or punishment dependably for behavior that fills specifications that can be learned and understood by the actor is designated SIT F or Forward. On the contrary, a situational object or condition about which the actor can get no dependable information, one that gives no feedback or very uncertain feedback and does not respond consistently with either reward or punishment for any specifiable behavior is designated SIT B, or Backward.

The idea of an act that "fills specifications" (as mentioned above) suggests conformity to a social norm of some kind, and one does not have normative relations to situational objects, of course. But *physical objects* react or provide information in predictable ways to action performed upon them, provided the action indeed meets certain physical requirements. The physical object does metaphorically "react" predictably when sufficiently knowledgeable human beings formulate the specification for effective action and act accordingly. In this sense physical objects, as well as human situational objects, can be said metaphorically to "impose a standard" or "make requirements" if as objects they can be known, predicted, and to some extent controlled by human efforts. These kinds of efforts and the various formulations in terms of rules, social norms, and so on that are closely associated with them require "information" and "rationality." But not all kinds of situational objects are like that—some yield little (or even no) information and cannot be predicted. Attempts at "rationality" do little good in such instances, except perhaps to satisfy a general value placed on rationality. For such kinds of situational objects, including all kinds of imaginary objects supposed to be in the situation, fantasy and dramatization are quite as effective as "rationalistic effort" and are often more satisfying. We assume that, in cases where the object can be characterized as SIT B, there is a tendency for fantasy and dramatization to be utilized. Thus the dimension from F to B can be said to pass from "rationalistic instrumental action" to some other way of guiding action resembling fantasy.

In this context, one can understand why it seems to be a good idea to think of the third dimension of the system, F–B, as in principle independent of the other two, U–D, and P–N. Simply stated, the assumption is that the demands of rationality or effective control of behavior across a broad range of "external" situations cannot be depended upon always to require either positive behavior or negative behavior on the part of the group members, nor can it be counted upon to require either upward behavior or downward behavior.

The demands of the situation and, more concetely, the task, so far as rationality is concerned, are independent of the preferences of the group members regarding their internal relationships of power and affection. This is easy enough to see where the omnipresent situational object is an "employer" or "boss," but it also seems plausible across a range of situations where the group is in contact with the demands of the physical environment. It is also easy to see that, in teaching by operant conditioning, the experimenter is the manager of the important variables—the stimulus, the rewards, the punishments, the reinforcement schedule, and his or her own definitions of the standards of performance that are demanded. Reinforcement theory is a theory of the effects of SITUATIONAL variables, defined in one-way terms.

For groups, it is important whether or not the situation is set up or exists in such a way that the rewards, punishments, etc., come to each individual separately, or whether the rewards and punishments come to the group as a whole (and are then parceled out to individual members by decisions about distribution made by the group members themselves). This is an important variable and is treated as contributing to the direction. Situations that do not divide the members for individual treatment but allow the members to maintain a strong over-all solidarity are associated with the positive direction. Situations that do divide the group into separate individuals and hence interfere with a strong over-all solidarity are associated with the negative direction.

Chapter 25

Images of Society, the SOC Level

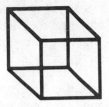

The level of SOCIETAL images is concerned not just with images of the complete society in a global sense but with images of various parts of society, elements in it, public persons, institutions, and particular organizations. It also includes references to social entities and relationships larger than the complete society, such as international relations, the world community, and human life in other times. The definitions in Appendix A will give some idea of the variety.

Most images of elements in society have some factual base, but it is often difficult to tell just what the factual base is—our knowledge of things in society outside our immediate experience is obtained very selectively through the news, literature, or secondhand and thirdhand reports, often from persons and sources that may be expected to be biased or prejudiced. There is sometimes not much difference between an image of some element in society and a fantasy image. Such images are commonly vehicles for the projection of characteristics of the self not acceptable to the actor. Thus, persistent and predominant concern of the individual with images of the same or similar direction, even though the images purportedly deal with elements "out there in society," may in some cases suggest that the individual is selecting and concentrating on particular images because of their motivational significance in relation to the self.

The social origin and social position of the actor constitute a special section of the societal images that may have a particular significance. In presenting one's social background, one usually discloses, emphasizes, or withholds facts selectively, according to their relevance for the present group. The facts presented are apt to have a marked effect upon one's status and role in the present group, and hence people are often careful about the images they present, with a view to the effect they sense the presentation may have. In cases where the individual presents an image of his social origin or experience that seems to be an acceptable or valued part of the SELF-image, the image may be classified at the level SELF rather than the level SOCIETY.

In cases where the individual presents an image of social origin or background as associated with the SELF even though the individual feels it to be not desirable, the image may be classified at the level of SELF rather than the level of

SOCIETY. If the individual accepts the social fact as something that will inevitably affect the SELF-image, the image is classified at the SELF level. Social images that are actively dissociated from the self are classified at the SOCIETAL level.

The following kinds of facts (and no doubt many others of a social character, as well) are likely to have a bearing on the status and role of the individual in the group, and are thus potentially relevant to the SELF image of the actor, or to the actor's image of the OTHER: age, sex, place of origin, residence, race, religion, social class, economic class, family roles, health, physical energy, personal appearance, disease, disability, education, occupation, special interests, abilities, experience, intelligence, sophistication, wealth, formal rank in government, the military, finance, large industry or organization, social status of family or friends, social connections, citizenship, criminal record, escapes, notoriety, reputation, community services.

These kinds of facts are often the basis of social categorizations made by members of the society. In terms of social stereotypes (prejudices if you will), certain characteristics are *attributed* to the individual on the basis of the social categories into which he is placed. These social categorizations influence the role and status the individual is expected to assume in the society. They influence the way other people treat the individual, sometimes to his advantage, more often, perhaps, to his disadvantage. But stereotypes work in both directions. Attributed characteristics include both desirable and undesirable elements, from the point of view of the actor.

Reference to SOCIETAL images that are associated with the SELF are similar to items from the individual's curriculum vitae. Such a document provides information about successes in schools and other contexts. It provides basic "demographic" data such as age, sex, and so on. If a form asks about marriage and children, it begins to show that even the history of one's relationships and sexual experience can be a fact in influencing one's present status. The curriculum vitae and the letter of recommendation give information about experiences of leadership and other interests, abilities, and talents. They suggest, by reference, how well or poorly connected the actor is. SOCIETAL images relevent to the SELF may, however, also include status-lowering items of information, a kind of upside-down curriculum vitae, including failures and criminal record, for example, which may be revealed in a group as part of the individual's self-presentation.

There is some tendency, on the average, for individuals to mention social background facts that they think will favorably influence their status and role in the present group and to omit mention of facts they think will have an undesirable influence. Different individuals want different kinds of roles, however, and this influences greatly the kinds of facts they mention. A position in the group that is desirable to one individual may be very undesirable to another. The kind of position or role desired depends upon the individual personality and upon the person's reaction to elements in the larger society. It is common, for example, for individuals who want a high social status position in the immediate group to mention wealth, high social status of the family, important people known, and the like, but it is also common for individuals to suppress this kind of information because they are not sure how they would come out in the competition or because they fear they will be placed too far upward in the group, which might result in feelings of envy directed at them. Some individuals feel impelled to mention things that have an adverse effect upon their status, and mention damaging facts for reasons they do not understand. Nevertheless, the mention or nonmention of social background facts is one of the means by which individuals attempt to manage their status and role in the present group and constitutes a set of choices they can hardly escape making to some extent.

"Social background facts" include facts that pertain to events in the life of the individual outside of the present group. Many such facts refer to *past events* in the life of the individual but may also refer to *present conditions* such as age, sex, color, religion, and outside friends and acquaintances. The individual comes with an extensive set of such facts, which are revealed only selectively and over time in the present group. Mentions of identity outside the present group tend to cause members to attribute characteristics to the individual that are not based on performance or behavior in the group itself. This may be either an advantage or a disadvantage from the actor's point of view. Mentions of general social events outside and in the past that are not background facts pertaining to the social image of a particular individual are recorded under SOC or, if appropriate, under FAN. Mention of events that took place in the history of the present group are *not* recorded under SOC but as images of the GROUP, the OTHER, or the SELF. Information about general social events (SOC) and their socially current meanings are more or less equally accessible to all present participants, but this is not always the case with social and personal background facts about the individual. The reporting individual is the expert in the social background facts about himself; the actor can select from the facts and even distort them to fit the desired social image or self-image more closely. Although some of the social background facts presented by a particular individual may be challenged or later subjected to check, still the particular individual has a kind of "ownership" of these facts and a leeway in their selection and interpretation, which give that individual a special degee of power and control when the conversation is centered on the social background of the self. Other group members have no actual experience of the actor's particular family members, friends, and unique background or present life. Thus when the actor presents images of these unique persons and events, the other group members have to "fill out" the image from their own imagery. The image presented thus acts upon others almost as if it were an image from fantasy. Such images are thus classified as FANTASY images rather than as SOCIETAL images (see Appendix A, Fantasy or FAN).

Even though the images presented are drawn directly from the past experience of the individual, the image as presented may be so emotionally colored and image-provoking it should be classified as a fantasy image, under FAN. In general, classification at the fantasy level is given priority over that in SOC. The level FAN also takes priority over the level SELF. In fact, it takes priority over any other level because of its peculiar motivational relevance and interest.

There may be mentions of SOCIETAL images so ambiguous that it cannot be determined how the actor feels about the image. For example, in the case of race, and also to some extent in the case of sex categorizations, opinions are so divided in the society and the reactions of individuals in the present group may be so divided that mention of the background fact cannot be classified as to the direction of the element. In these cases the mention of the background fact should be given the designation AVE, which also means undetermined, unclear, fractionated, and so on. However, the fact that this kind of classification may be given should not be taken as a directive for automatically avoiding a directional classification in the case of conflict, if one can be discerned.

Chapter 26

Images from Fantasy, the FAN Level

Fantasy operates on all the reference objects or images provided by the other levels of behavior. The prior content or picture of an object around which the feeling may gather in a fantasy may be that of a situational object of some kind, a social fact, a person or personality, a value statement, a group norm, an act or nonverbal behavior of a person. Pictures of these kinds are formed and stored in the memory and remain there a while. Night dreams are usually built, in part, around objects and events perceived during the day. Visual memories are probably favored, although words, names, and other characteristics may also be used. In the present system our conception of "fantasy" is very broad—it includes reports of night dreams, but also daydreams, jokes, anecdotes, slips of the tongue, activities of imagination and entertainment of others, and poetic or metaphoric modes of thought and expression.

An individual in social interaction with others may *report* a fantasy, in the form of a dream, for example, or may *speak in a way that reflects the present activity of imagination*. In SYMLOG both are grouped under the concept of the level of fantasy images, FAN. Other members often call up fantasy images of their own that are similar in some vague way. When members respond or react to a fantasy image, they usually know, in some sense, that the objects portrayed are not to be taken literally; the fantasy images stand for something else that is not known or not clear. Behavior at the level of fantasy images is behavior at some level of "unreality." The significance of the image in terms of everyday reality is hidden or disguised. But there typically *is* a "real" object and a motivational tendency hidden under the disguise, which may be uncovered if one really tries, particularly by "free association." The real object is typically one that arouses a good deal of feeling. The object is sometimes disguised from the conscious self as part of a defensive effort to conceal the feeling or emotion associated with the original or real object. This emotion in turn may arise from real interaction with that object, or the emotional cathexis may be the "transference" or "displacement" of an old emotional state to a new object. The transformations of reality for emotional purposes that can take place in terms of fantasy images are astonishing and complex.

The observer does not try to untangle all the transformations of motivation that may be present in a fantasy image. The observer first notes that the individual is presenting material that seems to be on the fantasy level, FAN. The next step of the observer is to divide the anecdote, dream, or other fantasy material into separate images. These may be fantasy images of separate persons, objects, acts, or any other kinds of elements. A given dream or anecdote may present several describable images or objects, perhaps one for the self and one standing for some important object or person with whom the self is in interaction. Since a fantasy may present a little drama, with different kinds of actors and events, a number of very different and conflicting images may be included. A separate message is then written for each separate image, giving the actor's PRO or CON attitude toward the relevant ELEMENT in the IMAGE.

From the later tabulations of the number of fantasy images presented by a given individual in each direction, we will know that the individual tends to have fantasy images located in certain directions more than others, and that certain of these directions may conflict. It may be that certain of these directions will match with the direction of the self-image while others will match the direction of the person's most disliked situational objects, for example. Or other hypotheses may be suggested by the directions most frequently mentioned.

Because an object of perception or conceptualization at any level may be represented in a fantasy image, it may be that *some degree of fantasy is an aspect of all perception*. Behavior at any other level in fact may be suffused by the activity of the imagination or the operation of fantasy. Distortions may be introduced into the "reality" level and into the "rational" processes by fantasy. But it is also probably true that the actor's representation of images in fantasy often precedes the actor's rational recognition and insight. For these reasons, a general priority rule is set up in SYMLOG that wherever the probable operation of fantasy can be detected the incident should be described at the fantasy level, FAN. The level FAN, if the fantasy component can be detected, takes priority over all other levels.

Chapter 27

Value Judgments, the PRO and CON Levels

Any remark or statement of an individual may contain clues as to the attitude or feeling the individual may have about the IMAGE presented. The attitude for or against some element of the image is the level of value judgment present in the act. In cases where the observer cannot tell whether the direction of a value judgment is PRO or CON, a question mark may be entered on the observation form in the column PRO or CON.

The remark or statement of the individual may merely contain *clues* as to the PRO or CON attitude, or the individual may make an *explicit statement* intended to communicate the attitude. Explicit statements of attitude are often equivalent to a *suggestion* that the other should *agree*. The PRO or CON component, however, whether it is minimal or very prominent, is recorded with regard to each image presented. The value judgment level of the behavior is regarded as its "highest" level. This means that we treat it as the "highest" "higher-order control"—the level of self-control that operates upon all of the other levels. The value judgment level does not always in fact exert the decisive control over all other levels, but we assume that it consists of the mental processes by which the ACTOR "tries," as it were, to exert the final decisive control. The feeling PRO or CON is the feeling the ACTOR experiences as a *decision*, after consideration of all factors, as an intention to ACT in a certain way. In cases of conflict among the various levels of control, the PRO or CON decision may be experienced as an act of "will." In cases of little conflict the individual may not even be conscious of making a decision or of weighing competing values. These less well-considered expressions of attitude, however, are also considered to be value judgments and are scored PRO or CON.

The levels of behavior as formulated in the present system must be understood partly in terms of their relationships to the processes of *social* control in social interaction. Parts of the control of behavior are established in the individual mental processes of the actor and are felt by the actor as "consciousness," "attention," "intention," "feeling of responsibility," and so on. But the processes of control do not stop with the individual mental processes that operate at the time of emergence of a given act.

As a given act of a given actor emerges into overt form and is perceived and interpreted by the *other,* reactions are set up in the mental processes of the other that may lead the other to try to bring the behavior of the actor under control, especially if the behavior is objectionable. It may be that attempts of the other to control the behavior of the actor are effective only so long as the other is actively continuing efforts to control the actor by reward or punishment or the like. But there may also be a process of teaching and learning and/or a process of negotiating a "social contract" of some kind, and by these means a "normative" control may be established between the two, which consists in part of new attitudes in the personality of the actor so that the new attitudes may be counted upon by the other to exert control over the behavior or the actor without constant further attention and effort.

Such an arrangement is usually called a "group norm," if it applies to the behavior of all the persons in the group and all stand ready to exert the control. The term "group norm" without further specification, however, is very vague in common usage, since it does not specify whether all members are actually involved or only some subset, whether all members of the group are bound to the same behavior or to complementary behavior of some kind, who exerts the control, and so on.

The setting up of any kind of group norm, however, if successful, affects the dynamic character of the behavior controlled by it. Behavior regulated by a group norm is more complicated to change, once the norm is established, than it was before the establishment of the norm. Cooperative efforts, more or less explicit decisions, are sometimes necessary to set up such control initially and to change it once it is established.

The beginning of the formation of a group norm may be some kind of suggestion by some individual that members should decide to encourage or discourage some kind of behavior (for example, PRO P in GRP, or CON N in GRP). The next step is an agreement of some kind to that proposal, and the norm is established more completely as more and more members accept the suggested attitudes PRO or CON toward the kind of behavior. Sometimes the suggestion is implicit, not verbalized, and not even intended; sometimes members assume that others agree when in fact they do not; and so on, through many complications. A group norm may be a very "shaggy" image but still a real one.

In writing messages the observer tries to catch the *suggestion* in the form of a PRO or CON value judgment about some element of some image (see Appendix A). The observer then writes a *separate message for each act of agreement or disagreement by each other group member,* just as if one were taking the minutes of a parliamentary procedure and recording the motions and votes. The acts of agreement or disagreement are recorded as PF or N acts at the ACT level, but as PRO or CON the element of the image at the value judgment level. In other words, each message contains the information as to what *content* the actor agrees or disagrees with.

An agreement to a statement of attitude (a value judgment) about a kind of behavior is a kind of primitive "contract" and is the nub of a "social norm." Where a bid for agreement on a given content is actually followed by agreement on the part of the other, an important transition takes place in the attitudes of the members toward the image. The attitude of each of the contracting individuals, when acknowledged as part of an agreement and witnessed by all the group, *becomes a part of the image of the social and cultural entity—the pair, sub-group, or group as a whole*—that acknowledges the social norm. The norm is now a property of the image of the *group* of individuals and their interaction history, taken together. An attitude or value judgment of an individual prior to an agreement exerts some controlling influence on the individual's behavior. The new social norm *thereafter* exerts an *additional* controlling influence. The social norm is a more complex structure of images, more culturally embodied and embedded and often more durable, than an attitude or value of the individual. None of the controlling influences over behavior is ordinarily absolute, but each tends to exert some influence. As controls are built up to higher levels of cultural embodiment, more powerful control over the behavior of the individuals in the group is exercised.

The overpowering qualities of social norms, the society, culture, and civilization, are well recognized and, of course, often become the objects of strong individual and subgroup efforts counter-to-control.

Sometimes the element of value judgment in the statement of an individual is very explicit. The term "value statement" may be used in these cases. Individuals make verbal generalizations about their beliefs or their values as to how things should be in the outside society, in general, or in life. The most familiar ones, perhaps, are those of the UNF authoritarian variety: "Spare the rod and spoil the child!" (PRO UNF in SOC). But value statements occur in all directions of the space: "There is no such thing as a bad boy!" (PRO UPB in SOC), "When the going gets tough, the tough get going!" (PRO UN in SOC), and so on. Sometimes value statements seem like beliefs, at other times like admonitions, arguments, or cryptic suggestions. Very often they deal with the way social relationships should be. They include statements of social, economic, and political attitudes. They also include religious, philosophical, aesthetic, and psychological beliefs and attitudes. They are abstract and general verbalized encapsulations of experience or viewpoints. They provide advice on, or orientation to, potentially all kinds of unsolved and unsolvable problems, conflicts within the individual, and conflicts between individuals. They are stereotyped solutions of decision dilemmas and value conflicts.

As stereotypes, general value statements often gain currency because they are particularly pithy and are expressed with some play on words that makes them easy to remember. For example, the saying, "Children should be seen and not heard" owes some of its impact to the fact that it opposes two sense modalities, seeing and hearing. The reference to "bad boys" above catches the ear because of the alliteration. The third example uses the word "tough" in two opposed senses. Although there is often some such feature in value statements that become popular, this is not so characteristic when the individual spontaneously puts into words his existing values. Verbal cleverness is not of the essence. The thing that is of the essence is the communication of an attitude in a general form, in a way that makes a bid for agreement, sometimes as an explicit suggestion for a social norm, but usually in a somewhat more vague way. Value statements may contain several images (as fantasies often do), and if so, the observer may choose which one to record or may write several messages, one for each main image. For example, the statement ''Children should be seen and not heard'' suggests that the speaker is in the position of a disapproving parent and wants to justify his or her own expression of disapproval (PRO UNF in SELF). It also tends to suggest, perhaps, that the listener is in the position of the disapproved child if he should fail to agree (CON UNB in OTHER).

In view of the rather vague and cryptic nature of many general value statements and, indeed, the inescapable vagueness of generalizations that purport to deal with the larger society and life at large, it is not implausible to suppose that value statements often function in much the same way for some individuals as do their fantasy images. That is, they provide a screen upon which the individual may project various unwanted elements of the self and represent various anxieties and other motivations.

The abstract general value statement may be presented to the actor in verbal form, ready-made. The statement, indeed, may be a part of a more or less complete ideology, religion, or body of beliefs and attitudes, with a history, a literature, and a body of adherents. Not infrequently a particular ideology, philosophy, or religious tradition has currency among persons of particular social statuses or roles in the larger society and expresses a world view and values motivationally connected with those positions. Individuals in those positions may have acquired the ideology along with other aspects of their subculture and not for any particular or unique motivational reasons.

In order to avoid the pitfalls of ''overpsychologizing'' we must recognize the behavioral reality of ''culture,'' the cultural transmission of ideas and attitudes, the differentiation of culture by subgroups in the society, and the slow change of culture over time. Bodies of cultural tradition consist in the behaviors, at high levels of abstraction, of multitudes of individuals; they have a long extension over time and a high degree of cognitive organization. All of these characteristics make it impossible for any one individual to do very much to change a body of culture, and put all of the individuals who participate in the culture more in the position of a ''carrier'' of the culture than in the position of an ''author'' of changes in it.

For these and similar reasons, the attitudes an individual expresses at the level of general value statements should not be expected to bear a very close relation, on the average, to the kinds of behavior one sees expressed at the level of overt interpersonal behavior of that individual, ACT. The directions approved in value statements may predict ACTs of the individual or they may not. By the time the general value level of abstraction is reached, reversal on reversal of the individual's motivational direction may have taken place. The most common reversal, perhaps, is along the dimension F–B.

The situation for a self-analytic group with observer feedback is paradoxical with regard to the F–B dimension. The analytical task makes strong demands for ACT F behavior, at least periodically, but since the task is a self-analytic one it requires ACT B behavior, to an important degree, in order to have fantasy material to analyze and to avoid smothering the individuals whose natural behavior inclines toward B. Thus the group needs to establish values and group norms that encourage analytical behavior part of the time (PRO F in GROUP), and encourage fantasy behavior at other times (PRO B in GROUP). This is difficult, because the two norms seem to clash with each other. The solution is to develop a still higher-order control for combining the two in some kind of optimum timing or alternation.

Another built-in paradox in our self-analytic groups is that the course probably attracts an unusual *variety* of students, including *some* who tend to reject certain conventional modes of teaching (CON F in SOC), and *some* who seem implicitly to formulate the goal of the course as that of "forming a group" in the sense of PRO P in GROUP. Neither kind of value fits with the suggestions for group norms built into the syllabus of the course, which call for cycling flexibly back and forth between the ACT F and the ACT B directions.

All of these paradoxical features tend to make the F–B direction less clear in its development, more confused in conception, and more franctionated into uncorrelated components in our particular groups than they would be in, say, an adult, conservative, middle-class, nonacademic work group strongly focused on an externally imposed task, dealing with clear situational objects, and led in an active businesslike way. In such a kind of group, we would expect to find a more clear-cut F–B dimension.

Small groups of a nonspecialized and communal nature such as families, living organizations, or communes, may define ACT F behavior and ACT B behavior in very different ways from a special-purpose work group. We suppose that the F–B dimension tends to fractionate into more various components and reversals as one goes up the scale of levels toward the level of values and group norms and also as one compares groups of many different kinds.

In any case, one does not need to assume a high degree of consistency of directions for the individual or the group, either between levels or within a given level, in order to use SYMLOG observations to advantage. The method permits a very atomistic concentration on particular aspects of behavior if this is helpful, as well as a means of adding many similar aspects together.

Chapter 28

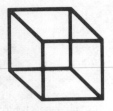

The Integration of
Theoretical Perspectives

We have now completed the detailed description of SYMLOG Interaction Scoring. In brief summary, it is a procedure in which the observer records his observation of some event of interactive social behavior in the form of a message to the participants. The message is made up of a number of elements describing features of the event—when it occured, who performed the behavior, toward whom, and the direction of the meaning communicated at each of three levels: the behavioral level, the image content level, and the value judgment level.

The discussion of the elements of the message has enabled us to develop the multiple level field theory underlying the SYMLOG System more fully than was possible in discussing the Rating procedure in Part I. We are now in a better position to sense, perhaps, the possible relevance of multiple level field theory and the SYMLOG system of measurement to the integration of the major theoretical perspectives in social psychology. It may be useful to mention these briefly again, as related to elements in the SYMLOG message.

The recording of who performs the act and to whom it is directed enables one to determine the kinds of behavior, rewarding or punishing, that a given individual receives for the performance of a given kind of behavior, and to note, over longer time spans, modifications in the behavior. Hence, with SYMLOG Interaction Scoring (particularly the exhaustive scoring of every discernable act, using videotapes) one can produce time-ordered data of the kind studied in operant conditioning, and the theory of operant conditioning becomes relevant to understanding our results.

Since each individual acts both as a performer of acts, and as a source of reward and punishment for each other in a social interaction situation, the quality and quantity of the behavior each actor directs to each other can be analyzed according to the assumptions of social exchange theory. Actually, at the time the observer scores an act, he scores it from the point of view of its probable significance to the other and thus employs an assumption as to the social exchange value, or social exchange significance, of the act at the time the initial recording is made.

The ACT level of analysis in SYMLOG is closely related to the tradition in the study of small groups that has concentrated on the observational study of social interaction (interaction process analysis), and this tradition in turn is rooted fundamentally in the social behaviorism of George Herbert Mead and the pragmatic tradition in philosophy and social psychology.

The NON-verbal level of analysis of SYMLOG is related to the same tradition of early social behaviorism, as represented by Mead, to the currently very active observational study of behavior of animals in natural settings (ethology) and to the experimental study of nonverbal behavior in humans.

The theory of images and image levels in SYMLOG draws heavily on psychoanalytic theory, especially with regard to the assumption of an ACTOR (essentially the same as the ego-functions in psychoanalytic theory) as a set of underlying processes by which the field of images is constructed and maintained. The concept of the image *field,* however, and its dynamic qualities as a configuration, is a concept which is closely related to Lewinian theory of the life space as well as to the psychoanalytic theory of the topological areas of the personality: ego, id, superego, the unconscious, preconscious, and the conscious.

The theory of the SELF image in SYMLOG combines elements of psychoanalytic theory concerning the ego and the ego ideal, and the theory of the ego mechanisms of defense, which in our language consists of things the ACTOR can do to protect the SELF-image and alter the dynamic character of other images in the field. The theory of the SELF and OTHER images combines elements of symbolic interaction theory in social psychology and object relations theory in neopsychoanalysis. The range of levels from the SELF to the FANTASY level corresponds to what Lewin called "levels of reality" and provides a whole range of images that may be used as targets and sources of "attributed causes" of behavior, to and from which the ACTOR can displace affects, project traits, transfer feelings, and so on, as hypothesized in the theory of the ego mechanisms of defense. This same range of images provides the sources or the "causal cores" (whether the SELF, the OTHER, the SITUATION, etc.) to which the person (the ACTOR) attributes "causality," as treated in the branch of cognitive social psychology known as attribution theory.

The level of value judgment in SYMLOG Interaction Scoring is an observational measure of "attitudes," as studied by social psychology. The ways in which attitudes PRO and CON the image of a given issue and the attitudes PRO and CON the images of the SELF and the OTHER may combine in an actual dynamic episode are very complex. Such a combination in the mind of an individual may be "dissonant" or "congruent," and the dynamic tendencies toward change of given kinds of constellations may be identified as the field of "attitude change" in social psychology, which in turn features a number of subtheories, such as "balance theory," "dissonance theory," "congruity theory," theories of "contrast and assimilation," theories of change according to "reward and punishment" and according to "functional needs." Although there has been much interest in the study of attitude change and in the relationships between attitudes and behavior, there has been little study of the observational kind made possible by SYMLOG Interaction Scoring, where one can compare the kinds of PRO and CON value judgments made with the kinds of ACT and NON-verbal level behavior shown in the same dynamic episode of polarization or unification.

For the theories we have so briefly touched upon above, SYMLOG Interaction Scoring gives a *microscopic operational definition* of many of the principal variables as they are found embedded in the same process. The variables can be measured by observation and can be brought into direct relationship to each other in the same set of observations. In addition, the perceptual–evaluative perspectives of the individual actors regarding the same set of events, measured in terms of the same conceptual dimensions, are accessible, at least retrospectively at only a short time lag, through the SYMLOG Adjective Rating procedures discussed in Part I. New possibilities for research of a kind that integrates the principal varieties of theory in social psychology thus seem to be opened up by the SYMLOG System and appear to be extraordinarily rich.

For real hope of theoretical progress, however, our measures must be reliable and valid, as well as theoretically central and capable of being brought into empirical conjunction with each other. In Part III of the book, which follows, the questions of reliability and validity of the two major types of SYMLOG System measures (Rating and Scoring) are approached through a special study conducted in the laboratory with full methodological rigor.

Part III

A Study of SYMLOG Adjective Ratings and SYMLOG Interaction Scoring

Stephen P. Cohen

Chapter 29

The SYMLOG "American Family" Study

The two methodological pillars on which SYMLOG stands are SYMLOG Interaction Scoring and SYMLOG Adjective Ratings. The Scoring method tries to record behavior as soon as possible after the observer perceives it. The Adjective Rating method proceeds from the evaluations that persons make of each other's behavior after a period of interaction or interaction observed. Such post-hoc ratings may be subject to retrospective reconstruction, causing them to differ substantially from the results of Scoring interaction events (D'Andrade, 1974). On the other hand, they may reflect better the balancing of the meaning and weight given to events by those who experience them or observe them.

What, then, is the relationship between these two forms of analysis of group process, one derived from interpersonal evaluative perception (Ratings), the other from systematically observed social interaction (Scoring)? This question is not only important to the understanding of SYMLOG itself, but of significance to the more general problem of the relationship between patterns of interpersonal behavior and the post-hoc judgments or attitudes one derives from such behavior upon reflection, through memory and selective retention. In the past, these two approaches to studying interpersonal behavior have remained relatively separate, and a strength of SYMLOG for the researcher is the ability to compare directly the results of these two approaches.

The basic issue of the interrelations between Interaction Scoring and Adjective Rating was a central concern to the SYMLOG project at the time Myron Wish of Bell Laboratories approached us about a comparative study of interpersonal communication being carried out at Bell Laboratories. Wish had determined that it would be a valuable supplement to his own work to see a SYMLOG Interaction Scoring analysis of his extensively studied stimulus materials. The results could be compared with results of other forms of analysis in which he was engaged (Wish, 1975; Wish and Kaplan, 1977).

The stimulus materials were a series of short interaction sequences (one to two minutes each) carefully selected from the "American Family" television series, depicting vivid, unrehearsed interactions in an American family. The Loud family had consented to extensive, long-term filming of their interaction, so the scenes had a richness and emotional vitality rare for laboratory interaction study. The full Wish study will be described by Wish elsewhere. I am deeply grateful for the opportunity provided to collaborate on aspects of the study. Peter Bricker of Bell Laboratories, who located all the usable dyadic scenes from the series, was also very helpful in the enterprise.

The fusion of Wish's proposal of a SYMLOG Interaction Scoring of the "American Family" scenes with the primary goal of the study for this book (a comparison of the results of SYMLOG Interaction Scoring with SYMLOG Adjective Rating) produced a study much larger than either of us had originally envisaged. Not all the elements of the study will be reported here. In a joint publication by this author and Wish those aspects comparing SYMLOG with the Wish scales measuring interpersonal communication will be given in detail. Furthermore, comparisons of the results of this SYMLOG American Family study with other studies in the remarkably intensive Bell Laboratories project on interpersonal communication using these and other American Family sequences will be reported in publications on this study by Wish and by Wish and D'Andrade.

Purposes of the Study

As the study became more clearly defined, it was possible to incorporate several valuable purposes in its design and analysis:

1. The relationship between SYMLOG Interaction Scoring and SYMLOG Adjective Rating was examined.

2. A study was made of the reliability of the items used in SYMLOG Adjective Rating (which had not hertofore been formally studied).

3. The factor structure of the Adjective Ratings when used with this new kind of data was re-examined.

4. A systematic look at the reliability of SYMLOG Interaction Scoring was afforded.

5. The effects, if any, of training people in the use of SYMLOG Scoring on their use of the Rating method were examined. By including a sample of trained Scorers along with our Raters but asking them to Rate instead of Score, we could estimate what was learned from the Scoring training; and conversely, we could ascertain how similar to the Ratings of trained people are the Ratings made by persons without any acquaintance with SYMLOG Scoring. This is, of course, very important for both field and laboratory research use of SYMLOG, and also important to practitioners who might wish to gather SYMLOG Ratings without entering into detailed explanation of the system as a whole.

6. Other researchers have used adjective lists or bipolar scales to assess persons or interaction situations. How does SYMLOG relate to such scales as those of Wish (1976) or those of Osgood (Osgood, Suci, and Tannenbaum, 1957) (the semantic differential)? Detailed comparisons with Wish scales properly belong elsewhere, but some remarks on this question, especially as related to Osgood's semantic differential, will be in order.

7. The particular context in which SYMLOG Ratings and Scoring are typically done is a very specialized atmosphere. It is valuable to know how SYM-

LOG is used in a more standard laboratory situation with materials and situational control typical to a laboratory setting. The study provides some validation of the usefulness of SYMLOG in the usual systematic research environment. Also, there is a particular way in which SYMLOG adjectives are ordered on the rating form that may arouse some concern; for example, items are not scrambled but are arranged in a careful theoretically relevant order. What happens when SYMLOG Rating is administered in a random order?

8. Most of the examples of SYMLOG reported in this volume are drawn from self-analytic groups. Yet there is some experience now with the use of SYMLOG in families, teams of workers, schoolrooms, and other settings. The American Family study provides a carefully researched example of the use of SYMLOG to produce a picture of a family, even if a unique one, and even if not observed extensively. Would a SYMLOG analysis of the Loud family of the "American Family" series reveal anything interesting about the family? In the last section of the report on this study a brief analysis of the family will be presented to demonstrate the diagnostic usefulness of the Field Diagrams and Summary Ratings.

Method

The study was divided into four parts with four separate groups of subjects as indicated in Figure 33.

Subjects

Groups 1 and 2 were recruited through advertisements in the *Harvard Crimson,* the student newspaper. The subjects performed the task in groups of eight to twelve. All recruited subjects were undergraduate or graduate students at Harvard. Only one of the recruited students had any familiarity with SYMLOG, and his ratings were not included in the analysis. In Group 3, the subjects had a beginner's knowledge of SYMLOG, having used it in a group psychology course for a period of about one month to six weeks at the time of administration. Group 4 subjects included persons familiar with SYMLOG Scoring for a period of at least four months and some for as long as three or four years. Separate analysis was carried out for the *most* experienced SYMLOG scorers among the nineteen subjects and will be reported below when the results indicate differences.

Stimulus materials

Twenty interaction sequences were included in the study. Seventeen sequences came from the "American Family" television series and constituted all the usable dyadic scenes from the series. Each sequence contained from one to two minutes of dyadic communication between members of the Loud family (father, mother, sisters, brothers) or between the family members and their friends or acquaintances. In two cases, a third person entered the scene very briefly, but these people were not rated, although some of the Interaction Scorers did score

FIGURE 33 Groups of Subjects Used in the SYMLOG "American Family" Study

Group 1	Naive Raters N = 64
	Interspersed 26 SYMLOG Adjective Ratings
	                       Wish Scales
	                       Semantic Differential Adjectives

Group 2	Naive Raters N = 24 Consecutive 26 SYMLOG Adjective Ratings
Group 3	Trained Raters N = 11 Consecutive 26 SYMLOG Adjective Ratings
Group 4	Trained Scorers or Coders N = 19 SYMLOG Interaction Scoring

their interventions. These "minor characters" were not included in the analysis. The videotaped segments took place in various natural settings (restaurant, home kitchen, living room, warehouse, etc.) and captured some of the complex and vivid quality of live, unrehearsed interaction. Some of the family members appeared in several scenes; in particular, the mother (Pat) appeared in eight of the scenes and the father (Bill) in seven. In most analyses, each person in each scene was treated as a separate unit. In the illustrative case analysis, the family members will be examined as individuals by summing over the scenes in which they appear.

Three of the scenes, presented as the last three scenes in a sequence of ten in most administrations, were scenes of dyadic debates on current events drawn from a sample of such scenes prepared in a study at Bell Laboratories by Peter Bricker. They were introduced as comparison material, with much less physical movement, more direct confrontation, and with interacting pairs who did not know each other before the "debates" were videotaped.

Procedure

The procedure for Groups 1, 2, and 3 was identical. Subjects were shown the scenes in various orders. (No order-of-scene effects were found.) After each scene, the Raters would rate the persons in the scene on forms provided for that purpose. Half of the subjects in each administration would rate one person in the dyad first and half would rate the other person first. In Group 1, subjects rated one person on a particular adjective item, then the other person on the same adjective item. This was called the *Interspersed* condition. Also in Group 1, the SYMLOG adjective items were intermingled with adjective items developed by Wish to tap the dimensions of his and other studies (Wish, 1976; Osgood, Suci,

Your Name_____   Group _____

Name of person described _____   Circle the best choice for each item:

		(0)	(1)	(2)	(3)	(4)
U	active, extroverted, self-confident	never	rarely	sometimes	often	always
UP	outgoing, open, sociable	never	rarely	sometimes	often	always
UPF	shows friendly, democratic leadership	never	rarely	sometimes	often	always
UF	businesslike, impersonal, managerial	never	rarely	sometimes	often	always
UNF	bossy, disapproving, authoritarian	never	rarely	sometimes	often	always
UN	dominating, competitive, tough	never	rarely	sometimes	often	always
UNB	showing off, self-centered, impulsive	never	rarely	sometimes	often	always
UB	humorous, entertaining, dramatic	never	rarely	sometimes	often	always
UPB	warm, helpful, supportive, nurturant	never	rarely	sometimes	often	always
P	friendly, informal, equalitarian	never	rarely	sometimes	often	always
PF	attentive, agreeable, cooperative	never	rarely	sometimes	often	always
F	analytical, task-oriented, problem-solving	never	rarely	sometimes	often	always
NF	conscientious, controlled, persistent	never	rarely	sometimes	often	always
N	unfriendly, negativistic, individualistic	never	rarely	sometimes	often	always
NB	contrary, noncompliant, disrespectful	never	rarely	sometimes	often	always
B	emotional, expressive, changeable	never	rarely	sometimes	often	always
PB	affectionate, likable, fun to be with	never	rarely	sometimes	often	always
DP	trusting, calm, appreciative	never	rarely	sometimes	often	always
DPF	gentle, respectful, responsible	never	rarely	sometimes	often	always
DF	cautious, submissive, hard-working	never	rarely	sometimes	often	always
DNF	self-sacrificing, complaining, martyred	never	rarely	sometimes	often	always
DN	resentful, depressed, rejecting	never	rarely	sometimes	often	always
DNB	frustrated, discouraged, withdrawing	never	rarely	sometimes	often	always
DB	anxious, tense, fearful, holding back	never	rarely	sometimes	often	always
DPB	grinning, pleased, happy, smiling	never	rarely	sometimes	often	always
D	passive, introverted, inhibited	never	rarely	sometimes	often	always

NOTE: A revised form based on changes introduced as a result of this
study and additional data and examination is reproduced in Appendix C.

and Tannenbaum, 1957). In order to equalize the number of adjective items administered to Group 1 subjects with the number in Group 2 and Group 3, half of the scales were administered to one half of the subjects and the other half of the scales to the other half of the subjects. The SYMLOG Adjective Rating list was dispersed in several orders randomly chosen, not corresponding to their position in the SYMLOG Adjective Rating Form.

Group 2 and Group 3 each rated all of the scenes only on the SYMLOG Adjective Ratings in the order usually used and indicated in Figure 34. Both Group 2 and Group 3 rated each person in each scene on all twenty-six adjective sets and then the other person on all twenty-six adjective sets. This is the usual method of SYMLOG administration and is the *Consecutive* condition. However, Group 2 did not have the directional indicators (U, UP, UPF, etc.) listed with the adjective sets. More significantly, Group 3 had a three-point scale for each item, while Group 2 and Group 1 had five-point scales.

For Group 4, the Interaction Scorers were given SYMLOG Interaction Scoring Forms plus typewritten transcripts of the scenes they were about to score. They were instructed to mark on the transcript a number indicating which interaction event (ACT or NON) they were scoring for later comparison of acts chosen by the Scorers. Each Interaction Scorer was instructed to produce at least ten scores per scene, but no instructions were given about the distribution of those acts between the pair of interacting persons in the scene.

Administration

Subjects were shown the scenes on a regular video console, with scene order prepared in advance. The administration took place in the same facilities usually utilized for the self-analytic groups described elsewhere (Bales, 1970).

It was clear that the Interaction Scorers would require more time to code the scenes than it would take the Adjective Raters to complete their work. Furthermore, it seemed that for the Scorers more than one exposure to each scene was necessary to code the scenes. The solution was to allow five minutes after each scene for all groups in the study, and to show the segments twice in all cases. Furthermore, the Interaction Scorers were assisted by a transcript. Thus time of exposure to the scenes was equalized, but Scorers differed in having a written transcript.

Chapter 30

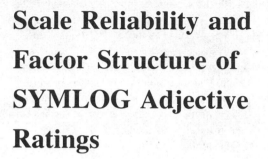

Scale Reliability and Factor Structure of SYMLOG Adjective Ratings

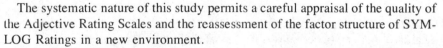

The systematic nature of this study permits a careful appraisal of the quality of the Adjective Rating Scales and the reassessment of the factor structure of SYMLOG Ratings in a new environment.

The typical SYMLOG environment had been relatively large groups of twelve to fifteen persons with group members rating each other. After completion of the Interpersonal Rating Forms in the Bales 1970 volume *Personality and Interpersonal Behavior,* I conducted a series of studies of item reliability and item-to-scale correlation to produce the best possible single set of questions for the Rating Form. When the decision was made to move to Adjective Rating, it was this form and the definitions of the directions as described in Appendix A that served as the basis for the first version of the Adjective List.

However, revisions followed, as described in Appendix C, and a systematic study of item quality was needed. The present context allowed such an assessment. One general indication of the reliability of the items themselves is provided by the split-half correlations method. Using Group 1 subjects, the aggregate score of half of the subjects on each item for each of the scenes was correlated with the aggregate scores for the other half of the subjects. Because not all subjects answered all items, this involved the comparison of the scores of sixteen subjects with the scores of the other sixteen subjects who used the same items for each of the twenty-six SYMLOG items as well as the twenty-two other items included. The correlations are best at indicating clarity of the items, and should not be taken as indicating inter-Rater agreement. The range of correlations is from .74 for the DF item to .93 for several items. The mean for all twenty-six items is .88 with only two items below .80. These correlations are comparable to those obtained for other scales used. (The mean for the other twenty-two items is .86.)

More important for present purposes is the extent to which the items measure what they are intended to measure. To determine this, particular items can be correlated with the six summary scales, U, D, P, N, F, and B. For example, the item UNF should correlate positively with the scale U comprising the nine items that have a U component (U, UP, UPF, etc.). The item-to-scale correlations for Group 1 are given in Table 1. They are very similar to those of Groups 2 and 3, which are not shown.

The item-to-scale correlations, together with the standard deviations (and variances) of the items, can produce a reliability coefficient as indicated in Gulliksen's Formula (Tryon, 1957). The special usefulness of this Part–Whole form of the reliability coefficient is that it allows comparative assessment of the usefulness of each item in contributing to the reliability of the scale in question.

In analyzing the validity of SYMLOG items, it is important to state that the goal is not only to achieve highly reliable scales of the specific directions U, D, P, N, F, B. The goal is also to achieve a sense of the characteristics of *each* of the twenty-six directions in order to have a more accurate diagnostic sense of the behaviors and traits characteristic of different parts of the space. There are other, perhaps simpler, ways of achieving an accurate measure of a person's position on each of the three dimensions. A more standard scaling technique is to use items measuring only the "pure" dimensions themselves, i.e., the U item, the D item, the P item, etc., or, alternatively, one might ask people to rate others on some definition of each of the directions. Or one could construct bipolar scales with U at one end (a definition of U, or an Adjective Rating set for "pure" Upward) with D at the other end (a definition of D, or an Adjective Rating set for "pure" D).

These methods, as illustrated in Figures 35 and 36 respectively, may be deisrable for speed of administration and simplicity but they are simplifications with theoretical and diagnostic costs. The bipolar method assumes that one can measure the two ends of a dimension simultaneously. Data in this study and elsewhere suggest that this changes the meaning of the adjectives at each end of the scale. More important, both of these methods make assumptions about the stability of the factor structure and the relation among items from sample to sample and from group to group that seem unwarranted by experience so far. Finally, the item combinations help to provide a concrete meaning to the complexities of interpersonal behavior when it is to be thought of in all three dimensions simultaneously. A person who is high on U, high on F and neither P nor N is given concrete descriptions through the Adjective Lists, through the type descriptions in *Personality and Interpersonal Behavior* (Bales, 1970) and through directional and level descriptions in Appendix A of the present book. For diagnostic and intervention purposes this is especially important. For example, a person may be seen as neither P nor N because he or she exhibits much behavior that is P and much that is N, or because of showing flat affect such that he or she is high on neither N nor P items. It is always useful for diagnostic or intervention purposes to check to see which items contributed most to a person's location in the three-dimensional space. This method also helps to concretize the meaning of multidimensional scaling to both researcher and subject.

TABLE 1　Item-to-Scale Correlations for Twenty-six SYMLOG Adjective Items

		U	D	P	N	F	B	U-D	P-N	F-B
1.	U	Active, extroverted, self-confident	.939	-.736	.305	-.068	.372	.110	.945	.205	.166
2.	UP	Outgoing, open, sociable	.550	-.140	.840	-.564	-.101	.630	.406	.741	-.387
3.	UPF	Shows friendly, democratic leadership	.405	-.214	.729	-.685	.612	-.111	.356	.734	.426
4.	UF	Businesslike, impersonal, managerial	.212	-.332	-.373	.254	.759	-.754	.297	-.331	.846
5.	UNF	Bossy, disapproving, authoritarian	.435	-.356	-.615	.773	.347	-.268	.446	-.711	.347
6.	UN	Dominating, competitive, tough	.559	-.490	-.506	.661	.484	-.324	.589	-.597	.459
7.	UNB	Showing off, self-centered, impulsive	.334	-.239	-.281	.520	-.577	.601	.330	-.403	-.658
8.	UB	Humorous, entertaining, dramatic	.616	-.190	.604	-.277	-.294	.815	.472	.472	-.599
9.	UPB	Warm, supportive, nurturant	.211	.121	.938	-.817	.078	.382	.067	.914	-.151
10.	P	Friendly, informal, equalitarian	.325	.057	.930	-.718	-.082	.577	.169	.864	-.348
11.	PF	Attentive, agreeable, cooperative	.211	.015	.917	-.901	.325	.080	.121	.942	.155
12.	F	Analytical, task orientec, problem-solving	.354	-.329	-.102	.089	.922	-.674	.383	-.099	.903
13.	NF	Conscientious, controlled, persistent	.495	-.487	-.048	.066	.894	-.635	.548	-.058	.866
14.	N	Unfriendly, negativistic, individualistic	-.149	.026	-.897	.925	-.235	-.077	-.104	-.942	-.102
15.	NB	Contrary, noncompliant, disrespectful	-.165	-.055	-.796	.829	-.456	.107	-.073	-.840	-.329
16.	B	Emotional, expressive changeable	.498	-.021	.256	.115	-.138	.648	.314	.091	-.418
17.	PB	Affectionate, likeable, fun to be with	.325	-.003	.947	-.787	-.062	.559	.199	.906	-.326
18.	DP	Trusting, calm, appreciative	.104	.158	.918	-.877	.192	.192	-.017	.931	.016
19.	DPF	Gentle, respectful, responsible	.065	.156	.846	-.860	.392	-.006	-.040	.883	.238
20.	DF	Cautious, submissive, hardworking	-.149	.252	.167	-.307	.732	-.595	-.218	.238	.748
21.	DNF	Self-sacrificing, complaining, martyred	-.215	.475	-.621	.797	-.153	.107	-.372	-.775	-.148
22.	DN	Resentful, depressed, rejecting	-.457	.518	-.785	.830	-.260	-.018	-.541	-.834	-.148
23.	DNB	Frustrated, discouraged, withdrawing	-.613	.698	-.650	.649	-.333	.062	-.727	-.673	-.232
24.	DB	Anxious, fearful, withholding	-.665	.831	-.391	.361	-.348	.168	-.826	-.391	.296
25.	DPB	Grinning, pleased, happy	.444	-.162	.802	-.616	-.230	.657	.353	.744	-.479
26.	D	Passive, introverted, inhibited	-.863	.730	-.242	.001	-.408	-.026	-.896	-.138	-.232

FIGURE 35   SYMLOG Six-Directional Adjective Rating Form (For
Demonstration Only)

U   active, dominant, talks a lot

0   1   2   3   4   5   6   7   8   9   10   12   13   14   15   16   17   18
never   sometimes   always

D   passive, introverted, talks little

0   1   2   3   4   5   6   7   8   9   10   11   12   13   14   15   16   17   18
never   sometimes   always

P   friendly, equalitarian

0   1   2   3   4   5   6   7   8   9   10   11   12   13   14   15   16   17   18
never   sometimes   always

N   unfriendly, negativistic

0   1   2   3   4   5   6   7   8   9   10   11   12   13   14   15   16   17   18
never   sometimes   always

F   analytical, task-oriented, problem-solving

0   1   2   3   4   5   6   7   8   9   10   11   12   13   14   15   16   17   18
never   sometimes   always

B   shows feelings and emotions

0   1   2   3   4   5   6   7   8   9   10   11   12   13   14   15   16   17   18
never   sometimes   always

Item Analysis

All of this having been said, the criteria for the value of specific items must still include their contribution to the overall scales, as well as their face validity and their clarity.

All three samples (Group 1, Group 2, and Group 3) yielded similar results for the specific items.

A survey of the results of these item analyses indicates that the items that were supposed to measure particular directional combinations did so with a few exceptions (see Table 1.) The DPB item (grinning, pleased, happy) actually measured UPB. DNF measured slightly B instead of F. However, a number of items did not correlate as highly with particular dimensions as one would like, and this led to changes in items as indicated in Appendix C, the SYMLOG Adjective Rating Form.

For most purposes, users of SYMLOG will want to be sure that the overall

FIGURE 36   Hypothetical Bipolar SYMLOG Adjective Rating Form (For
Demonstration Only)

```
U                                                                      D
9   8   7   6   5   4   3   2   1   0   1   2   3   4   5   6   7   8   9
active,                          neither                        passive,
dominant,                                                       introverted,
talks a lot                                                     says little
```

```
P                                                                      N
9   8   7   6   5   4   3   2   1   0   1   2   3   4   5   6   7   8   9
friendly,                        neither                        unfriendly,
equalitarian                                                    negativistic
```

```
F                                                                      B
9   8   7   6   5   4   3   2   1   0   1   2   3   4   5   6   7   8   9
analytical,                      neither                        shows
task-oriented,                                                  feelings
problem-solving                                                 and emotions
```

scales are accurate and reliable. Either they will be thinking of the U, D, P, N, F,
B overall nine-item scales or, for many purposes, the further simplification of
U–D, P–N, F–B eighteen-item scales. These three scales are the ones to be used,
for example, in constructing the Field Diagram. In the cases of U, D, P, N, F,
B, we have nine items constituting each scale, while in the latter case (U–D;
P–N; F–B) we have eighteen items. Table 2 gives the uncorrected reliability co-
efficients for the nine-item and eighteen-item scales for each of the three samples.

Table 2 indicates that the eighteen item scales in the form used in the present
study have reliability coefficients varying greatly across dimensions. The P–N
scale is clearly the most reliable, while the U–D dimension is the most problematic. However, even the minor change of removing the DPB item from this scale
produces a significant positive increment in the coefficient, which brings it close
to the desirable coefficient range of .80 for the eighteen-item scale.

The problem for the U–D dimension can be seen more clearly as a problem of
the D scale itself. With the DPB item included the scale cannot be used at all.
The nature of the difficulty and the direction for solution of the problem emerge
from an examination of a matrix of the intercorrelations of these nine Downward
items. It would be cumbersome to reproduce the correlation matrices for all three
sample groups. Table 3 provides an example of a rearranged correlation matrix
using Group 1 data. That the other sample groups are similar is indicated by the
mean correlations of the item clusters given in Table 4 for all three groups.

If we separate out the five items D, DB, DNB, DN, DNF, we find items all

TABLE 2   SYMLOG Adjective Rating Scale Reliability Coefficients (Based on Gulliksen's Formula)

		GROUP 1 NAIVE RATERS INTERSPERSED 5-PT. SCALE (N = 64)	GROUP 2 NAIVE RATERS CONSECUTIVE 5-PT. SCALE (N = 24)	GROUP 3 TRAINED RATERS CONSECUTIVE 3-PT. SCALE (N = 11)
9-item scale	U	.55	.65	.57
	D	.01(.26)[a]	.12(.32)[a]	.03(.10)[a]
	P	.98	.93	.95
	N	.87	.87	.84
	F	.65	.65	.68
	B	.46(.60)[b]	.54(.62)[b]	.60(.72)[b]
18-item scale	U–D	.64(.75)[a]	.62(.78)[a]	.66(.79)[a]
	P–N	.96	.97	.95
	F–B	.72(.76)[c]	.75(.77)[c]	.81(.87)[c]

[a]Reliability coefficient deleting DPB item.
[b]Reliability coefficient corrected by deleting worst item.
[c]Reliability coefficient corrected by deleting worse two items.

intercorrelated with each other, the mean positive intercorrelation ranging from .62 in the Trained sample, Group 3, to .72 in the Interspersed Naive sample, Group 2. Furthermore, the three items DF, DP, DPF are intercorrelated. However, the intercorrelations between these two sets of items are uniformly negative in Group 2 and Group 3 and negative in fourteen of fifteen cases for Group 1. The rearranged correlation matrix demonstrates this most clearly.

The set of five items (D, DB, DNB, DN, DNF) all seem to capture the element of Downward, which indicates alienation from the group or self-exclusion from ongoing group activity. However, quite another aspect of D behavior is seen in the relatively silent, unobtrusive member who accepts the group leadership and direction gladly and does his share of working toward the goal. As we look at the factor analysis of these data, and also compare this finding with some additional results, it will be possible to clarify this distinction. For the moment, it is important to indicate that these items (DF, DPF, DP) have been substantially altered in the revision seen in Appendix C to reflect the Downward component more clearly and to try to differentiate this kind of group involvement from that of more U members of the group.

If a scale were created of these five items alone, it would be possible to achieve a high reliability coefficient. However, this would skew the meaning of the Downward dimension and would weaken our ability to differentiate among the various silent or inactive group members. Since these are the members of a group about whom least is known, it is essential for the usefulness of a systematic technique of group study to be able to throw light precisely on this part of the group field. As we learn more about the ways in which D members differ from each other, it may be possible to design interventions specific to the problem of a particular Downward group member.

TABLE 3   Adjective Rating Downward Items: Intercorrelations among Items for Group I

	D	DB	DNB	DN	DNF	DF	DPF	DP
D								
DB	.78							
DNB	.65	.86						
DN	.44	.74	.83					
DNF	.18	.58	.77	.88				
DF	.17	−.04	−.10	−.19	−.21			
DPF	−.03	−.24	−.50	−.68	−.62	.55		
DP	−.07	−.25	−.54	−.70	−.56	.34	.88	
DPB	−.29	−.41	−.61	−.68	−.53	−.24	.44	.59

NOTE: $\bar{x}_r$ for whole matrix = .07.

To a lesser extent, the B items cluster into two sets with positive intercorrelations within each set and negative correlations between them. One cluster includes DPB, PB, B, UPB, UB, while the other cluster includes DB, DNB, NB. UNB correlates positively with most items in both clusters. The first set of items suggests a happy, extroverted, expressive set of behaviors. The second suggests a more negative orientation toward the group and its work. The items have been carefully reworked in the hope that the different aspects of B will be reflected more clearly. (See Appendix C.)

The principle of maintaining hetereogeneity of the item sets for each dimension can be illustrated further by designing, from the present data, the most internally consistent set of items for each summary scale. This has already been illustrated for the Downward scale. It is possible to reduce the set of items in such a way that the intercorrelations among all items are consistently high, and thus the internal consistencies of the scales are very high.

The U–D and U,D scales can be improved in internal consistency by dropping the UF and UNF items and by treating the DPB item as a UPB item. The r_{kk} (reliability coefficient) for the eight-item scale measuring U is .84. When the UN item is also dropped, the reliability becomes .89. A scale constructed of only the five items U, UP, UPF, UB, UPB has r_{kk} = .90. This example is drawn from Group 2 data. For Group 3 a scale adding DPB (an item which actually measured UPB) and deleting UN, UNF, UF, would have r_{kk} = .85, considerably higher than the uncorrected measure. Following the same procedures for maximizing internal consistency, one can construct a ten-item U–D scale with r_{kk} = .95 for Group 2 and r_{kk} = .92 for Group 3. Such scales would use only the following items: U, UP, UPF, UPB, UB, and D, DB, DNB, DN, and DNF.

The F–B dimensional scales can also be reconstructed in this way to increase internal consistency. Using Group 2 data for illustration, we can see stepwise increases in the measure of reliability as we gradually eliminate items with low intercorrelations with other scale items. The r_{kk} for the nine-item Forward scale is .64. Dropping DNF increases r_{kk} to .74; also dropping DPF, r_{kk} = .80; also dropping the PF item, r_{kk} = .86; finally dropping the UPF item, r_{kk} = .92. Our resulting scale has five items, UF, UNF, F, NF, DF. For the Backward scale,

TABLE 4 Adjective Rating Downward Items: Mean Correlations among Item Clusters for Each Group of Subjects

	AVERAGE CORRELATION WITHIN 3-ITEM CLUSTER (DF, DPF, DP)	CORRELATIONS BETWEEN CLUSTERS	AVERAGE CORRELATION WITHIN 5-ITEM CLUSTER (D, DB, DNB, DN, DNF)
Group 1	$\bar{x}_r = .69$	$\bar{x}_r = -.30$	$\bar{x}_r = .59$
Group 2	$\bar{x}_r = .72$	$\bar{x}_r = -.38$	$\bar{x}_r = .61$
Group 3	$\bar{x}_r = .62$	$\bar{x}_r = -.38$	$\bar{x}_r = .64$

beginning with the nine-item scale $r_{kk} = .48$. Stepwise deletions increase r_{kk} as follows: $-DNB$, $r_{kk} = .64$; $-DB$, $r_{kk} = .77$; $-NB$, $r_{kk} = .89$; $-UNB$, $r_{kk} = .94$. We remain with the five-item scale that is highly internally consistent: UB, UPB, B, PB, and DPB. A ten-item F–B scale can be constructed with $r_{kk} = .93$ by adding together these two sets of items and exchanging UNB for UPB.

For Group 3, the results of this procedure differ, reflecting the differences for trained observers on the F–B dimension. Here the only two Forward items whose deletion markedly improves internal consistency are DNF and UNF (r_{kk} goes from .67 to .78 to .82; deleting the next worst item does not change r_{kk}). For B, deleting DNB increases r_{kk} from .63 to .71, then deleting DB, to .80, and NB, to .87, leaving six of nine items, UNB, UB, UPB, B, PB, DPB. The F–B scale already meets the .80 criterion, but deleting DNF ($r_{kk} = .83$), DNB ($r_{kk} = .85$), and PF ($r_{kk} = .87$) can raise the internal consistency measure. Trained observers have higher reliability on this dimension only.

What has happened in the process of deletion is the dilution of the theoretical unity of the dimensions in such a way that they are now skewed in one way or another. In other words, the possibility of orthogonality of the three dimensions is surrendered. The U scale has become mostly UP and the D scale mostly DN. The F scale (in Groups 1 and 2) is now NF versus PB.

It should be recognized that in many cases a particular data set will not have these three dimensions orthogonal to each other. Still, we would not want to construct the scale so that it was the normative expectation that U and P would be positively related simply by the item construction. It would require many separate studies to be certain that it was simply not possible to construct successful UN, UNF, UNB items or DP and DPB items. The preferable way of proceeding is to try to reconstruct the poorly working items in the hope that, by successive approximations, they might be made to conform to the desired meaning.

What is important about this approach is its choice of clarity of item and scale meaning (face validity) rather than the usual emphasis on first maximizing reliability. Given the present set of items, it is clearly possible to construct highly internally consistent scales using the limited sets of items indicated for measuring the dimensions. Indeed, some users might wish to utilize the present data to construct just such highly internally consistent scales and ignore the attempt to reconstruct the twenty-six-item scale in such a way that each item measures the appropriate combination of dimensions.

Reliability Measurement and Weighted Scales

This emphasis on item clarity has an impact on reliability measurement as well. As pointed out in Appendix D, the construction of scale based on all combinations of three hypothetically orthogonal factors results in some unusual psychometric properties. The most important result for present purposes is that the hypothetical maximum reliability of scales produced this way is not 1.00. For nine-item scales the reliability of an ideally constructed twenty-six item set would be $r_{kk} = .86$, and for an ideally constructed eighteen-item scale, $r_{kk} = .93$. Second, the expected item-to-scale correlations for different items should be systematically different according to whether they are singly named items (U, D, P, N, F, B), doubly named items (UF, UP, UB, UN, etc.), or triply named items (UPF, UNF, UNB, UPB, etc.). Therefore, we should be able to evaluate the entire set of scales constructed here, as well as the specific items used, by a more appropriate criterion of goodness of fit to a hypothetical ideal scale in which all items measure exactly as expected. A perfectly constructed scale would maximize not only every item's reliability but also the goodness of fit between the observed item-to-scale correlations and the hypothetical correlations.

In Appendix D it is demonstrated that one can calculate the expected item-to-scale correlations for a perfectly constructed set of items and the actual reliability of scales so constructed. This calculation is based on assumptions of orthogonality of the three dimensions and equal weight of each in accounting for the variance in the items. The third assumption is that in the ideal scale all the variance is accounted for. Departures from this ideal model can be explained in terms of (1) poor item selection; (2) the predominance of one factor over the others in a particular sample; (3) correlations between factors, or nonorthogonality. Since this last is least central to the use of SYMLOG and to the desired fit of the scale, the calculation of the fit between observed and ideal item-to-scale correlation minimizes that element.

An ideal scale is constructed of twenty-six items, with each item measuring the assigned combination of the three dimensions. It is clear that items measuring only one dimension should have all of their variance accounted for by that dimension; those measuring two dimensions (doubly named items, like UP, FB, etc.) should have half of their variance accounted for by each dimension; and items measuring on all three dimensions should have one-third of their variance accounted for by each of the three dimensions. This provides a theoretical approach to the weighting of items in summing the scales whereby items are given their appropriate weight in calculating the summary scale. Simply stated, the singly named items should have a weight of 6; the doubly named items a weight of 3; and the triply named items a weight of 2 (see Appendix E).

We would expect that weighting the items in scale sums would increase the overall reliability of each dimensional scale precisely because items *should not* contribute equally to the making of particular scales. This *"should not"* is a matter not of measurement error but of the particular properties of a scale constructed by the means here described. Nunnally (1967) strongly discourages weighting as a waste of time compared to simply adding more items. However, he indicates the conditions under which weighting would make a difference. Those conditions are (1) when the number of items is relatively small (less than twenty) and (2) when item-to-total correlations vary markedly.

In the present situation adding new items would be possible only at the expense of the clarity and economy of the method of measurement. The best way of adding items would be to have an additional full set of twenty-six items. However, for most purposes, that would make administration cumbersome, because judgments are usually required of many individuals, sometimes repeated a number of times at spaced intervals. On the other hand, the two conditions of Nunnally for weighting are fulfilled: There are eighteen items per scale (nine if one thinks of the poles of the dimensions), and the item-to-scale correlations are *expected* to vary widely and, in the present study, do so. This wide variation will be especially prominent when one factor predominates in a particular interaction study, so that doubly and triply named items are measuring mostly that one factor. For example, the DP and DPF items are mostly measuring P in this study, an outcome that is partly a flaw in item construction but also reflects the overriding significance of the P–N dimension in this study. Indeed, it is very difficult to separate out the two explanations.

To summarize, the existence of an ideal pattern of item-to-scale correlations or factor loadings provides us with (1) an opportunity to measure the goodness of fit of the present scales with an appropriate criterion, and (2) a theoretical basis for weighting items in scale construction and in measuring the reliability of scales.

We have already discussed the problematic reliability of the U–D scale and to a lesser extent the F–B scale. Generally, as we shall see below, the weighted scale reliabilities are substantially higher than those of the unweighted scales. This reflects the fact that the singly named items that are most heavily weighted have, as expected, the largest item-to-scale correlations overall. Also the doubly named items on the whole have higher correlations than the triply named items.

For Group 2, the weighted U scale reliability is .76 compared to .65 for the unweighted scale. For D, the weighted scale has $r_{kk} = .46$, compared to .12 for unweighted. The weighted eighteen-item U–D scale, even with the obviously poor DPB item, has $r_{kk} = .81$—above the usual level of acceptability. This compares to .62 unweighted. Omitting the DPB item ($r_{kk} = .86$ without DPB) is all that is needed to reach an acceptable level of reliability, if we use a weighted version of the earlier draft of the SYMLOG Adjective Form, as given in Figure 34.

Weighting has its most dramatic effect when items vary most widely in quality. Thus, it is hoped that item improvement will reduce the importance of weighting. Still it does have an effect on the F–B scale in the present sample, where the item-to-scale correlations are more even, and will have some effect even with a much improved scale.

The nine-item Forward scale reliability increases from .65 to .79 as a result of weighting (Group 2) and the B scale from .54 to .63. The whole F–B scale reaches the criterion of .80, with r_{kk} (weighted) = .83 (up from .75). Improvement as a result of weighting is also marked for the other samples. For example, for Group 3, the U scale r_{kk} increases from .57 to .67 and the D scale from .03

to .46 (dropping the mistaken DPB item, $r_{kk} = .58$). For the whole scale $r_{kk} = .79$, and .82 without DPB.

Item Quality Index

It has been stated that even a perfectly constructed scale for a given dimension would not have $r_{kk} = 1$. (Of course, one would never get such a reliability coefficient in reality.) However, if the internal consistency desired is less than one, a measure of the fit of the observed scale to the ideal scale is in order. Moreover, the item-to-scale correlations of particular items should be different, so a comparison with the criterion of 1.0 would not be appropriate. For doubly named items, item-to-scale correlations should be $\sqrt{.5}$, and for triply named items, $\sqrt{1/3}$. These values are .7071 and .577. Only the singly named items should have item-to-scale correlations approaching 1.0.

One possible appropriate measure is the correlation between observed reliability coefficients and hypothetical factor loadings or item-to-scale correlations. However, we need some benchmark of how high a correlation is satisfactory. One criterion is derived from the reliability coefficient acceptability standard of $r_{kk} = .80$. Given a weighted scale $r_{kk} = .80$, and each scale item as good as any other item, an exact determination of the needed item-to-scale correlation for each separate item is obtainable (Appendixes D and E).

Another criterion can be derived from the examination of item quality. Any item may be given a measure of its quality by dividing its actual item-to-scale correlation by the hypothetical or ideal item-to-scale correlation (for either a nine-item or an eighteen-item scale). Let us say that any item must be improved if its item quality index is less than .50 (that is, if its item-to-scale correlation is less than one-half as large as desired). For a singly named item a correlation of at least .5 is required, for a doubly named item a correlation of at least .35, and for a triply named item a correlation of at least .29 is required. If all items were only this good, however, the scale would have an unweighted $r_{kk} = .68$ and a weighted $r_{kk} = .72$. Some items need to be better than this to reach the criterion of .80.

By a statistical coincidence, a more stringent criterion of item quality of .6 actually meets that conventional reliability criterion. If all items have an item-to-scale correlation .6 as large as the hypothetical loadings, then the unweighted r_{kk} would be .77, and the weighted $r_{kk} = .80$. This would require, for singly named items, a .6 correlation; for doubly named, .424; and for triply named, just less than .35. (Another way of expressing this is to say that each item should explain 36 percent of the variance accounted for by ideal items.)

Overall, one would like to approximate the more stringent criterion, but since items will vary in quality, so long as some deviate in the high direction it is possible to use the less stringent criterion for low-end deviations. Table 5 provides measures of the quality of items for the poorest items for Group 2 and Group 3. An item with an index less than zero is correlating negatively with the scale, however slightly, and clearly requires revision, but any item with an index

TABLE 5 Item Quality Index: List of Poor Quality Items[a] with Index
(see Appendixes D and E for Ideal Correlations)

	GROUP 2		GROUP 3	
SCALE	Item	Index	Item	Index
U–D	DPB	<0	DPB	<0
	DP	<0	DP	<0
	DPF	.02	DPF	<0
	DF	.08	DF	.09
	UF	.44	UF	.41
	(UNF	.67)	UNF	.44
	UPB	.45	UPB	.50
P–N	UNB	.43	UNB	.24
	NF	.31	NF	.44
F–B	PF	<0	PF	.20
	DPF	.10	DPF	.44
	DNF	.11	DNF	<0
	DNB	.19	DNB	.27
	DB	.23	DB	.30
	NB	.25	(NB	.66)
	UPB	.28	UPB	.25
	UF	.29	UF	.36

[a]Poor Item = $\dfrac{\text{Actual item-to-scale correlation}}{\text{Ideal item-to-scale correlation}} < .50$

less than .50 should also be revised. (Many additional items were improved based on these data, and the result is seen in Appendix 6, the revised Rating form.)

The item quality index shows that the problem of the U–D dimension is most directly a problem of four poor items, as has been indicated before. A number of U items are just on the borderline of acceptability and need improvement. The P–N dimension has only two problematic items, both of which are N items. The F–B dimension has a longer list of somewhat unsatisfactory items. Also, there is more difference between the trained and untrained Raters on the items that are problematic.

If all items met the criterion of item quality (.50) exactly, the overall correlation between the observed and hypothetical scales would be .89. If all items met the more stringent .60 criterion, the correlation with the ideal weight would be .97. Thus, we would want the observed correlation for the scales to be about .90 as a criterion (unweighted).

The high correlations actually obtained (shown in Table 6) are a result of the ten or so excellent items in the U–D, F–B dimensions and the sixteen excellent items for the P–N dimension. The high correlations indicate that the scales are corresponding to the desired structure of correlations, but these correlations must be very high to assure a high enough reliability coefficient as a measure of internal consistency.

TABLE 6   Fit of (Unrevised) SYMLOG Adjective Rating Form with Perfect Scale Correlations

	GROUP 2		GROUP 3	
	Unweighted	Weighted	Unweighted	Weighted
U–D	.88	.95	.83	.93
P–N	.99	.99	.97	.99
F–B	.86	.93	.89	.95

The weighting procedure places special emphasis on the quality of the singly named items. Only in Group 1 for the B item is there any difficulty about these particular items. Given this fact, one direction of scale construction would be to build scales from these particular forms of items. To achieve $r_{kk} = .889$ (the weighted scale reliability of a perfect scale constructed as in the SYMLOG scale) would required five items intercorrelated with each other at $\bar{x}^r = .61$. For the one-pole (nine-item) scales. For the two-pole (eighteen-item) scales (U–D) it would require ten items intercorrelated at the level of $\bar{x}^r = .68$. However, this is not an easy task for scale construction. To reach the level of reliability of the weighted scales obtained in this study of about .80 for the two-pole scales (F–B, U–D) would require ten items intercorrelated at $\bar{x}_r = .29$. This feasible alternative is by no means an easy one because of the limits on the adjective terms appropriate to each of the uncombined directions (U, D, P, N, F, B). Soon one would start to use concepts or terms that include elements from the other dimensions. Furthermore, the benefit of clarifying the conceptual structure and of identifying characteristics associated with dimensional combinations would be lost. Probably the best alternative is provided in Figures 35 or 36 or by the Wish scales (Wish, Deutsch, and Kaplan, 1976).

Inter-Rater Reliability

In addition to the internal consistency of the scales, another form of reliability is essential: the agreement among Raters. Two separate analyses of inter-Rater agreement were undertaken. The first was a split-half reliability check for the items treated separately and for the scales taken as a whole, using Group 1 data. The group of Raters was split in half, and the ratings for Raters within each half were summed. The second analyses treated Group 1 and Group 2 as alternative forms of the same test, since the subjects were randomly assigned to one of these groups, and the results were compared.

The split-half correlations for each of the twenty-six items range from .74 to .94, with only two items below .80 (DF, B). (These reliability coefficients are based on two groups of sixteen subjects randomly assigned.) The low inter-Rater agreement in Group 1 on the B item recalls previous mention of the peculiarity of the meaning of the B item in Group 1. It may well be that one set of random ordering so placed the B item as to change its contextual meaning. The reason for the low DF coefficient is harder to ascertain, especially as the correlation between Group 1 and Group 2 for DF (r = .91) is so much higher.

Table 7 gives the pertinent information as to inter-Rater reliabilities on the scales as a whole. Clearly they are quite high, whether derived from the split-half method or from the comparison of the two groups of naive subjects. The high correlations between Group 1 and Group 2 also show why for many analyses it is unnecessary to report separate data for these two groups.

Table 7 also shows the number of Raters necessary to attain a minimum standard of inter-Rater reliability. These are lower limits, to be sure, as one would like to be able to attribute as little variance as possible to error due to Rater disagreement. Still, it is clear that a small Rater team can achieve a reasonable and usable level of agreement. As a rule of thumb, it seems best to suggest that for a group of five Raters only the eighteen-item scale measures be separately interpreted and the nine-item scales should be used most cautiously. For many applied purposes a group of four or five Raters would be adequate, but for many research purposes a minimum of twelve Raters ($r_{kk} = .90+$) would be desirable. These estimates are based on the least reliable scales, which are D and B for the nine-item scales.

Summary

Thus far we have demonstrated that in two of the senses of reliability—internal consistency and inter-Rater agreement item-by-item—the SYMLOG Adjective Rating Scale is reliable. Raters do agree with each other on the meaning of items, and they rate using individual items similarly. However, the items require some revision (Appendix C) to measure what they are intended to measure in the three-dimensional scheme. A weighting procedure derived from the SYMLOG scale three-dimensional structure (Appendix D) increases the internal consistency of the scales substantially, and from this weighting procedure a more reliable measure may be derived (Appendix E). In addition, a measure of goodness of fit of individual items to the ideal structure is provided. This measure is appropriate to scales constructed using adjectives representing all combinations of the three dimensions, or other scales constructed on similar principles. The goodness-of-fit measure should be used by researchers applying the Adjective Rating Form to different settings and populations from the ones described here.

The complexity of this structure derives from the three-dimensional conception developed by Bales (1970). The entire model was based on a series of studies of personality tests and other measures in which these three dimensions emerged. Does the three-dimensional model best explain the data from the SYMLOG Rating Form? To revalidate the three-dimensional conception, factor analytic techniques were applied to the data, and we turn now to these results.

Factor Analysis: The Dimensional Structure of the Adjective Rating Form

An important part of the explanation of the findings about the relatively greater reliability of the P and N scales and the problem of the D scale emerges from factor analysis of these data.

TABLE 7   Inter-Rater Reliability on Summary Scales from SYMLOG Adjective Ratings (r_{kk} = Reliability Coefficient)

	GROUP 1 (r_{kk} FROM SPLIT-HALF CORRELATIONS)	GROUP 2 (r_{kk} FROM CORRELATIONS OF GROUP 1 WITH GROUP 2)
U	.96	.97
D	.95	.97
P	.99	.99
N	.99	.98
F	.97	.97
B	.96	.98
U–D	.98	.98
P–N	.99	.99
F–B	.98	.98

NOTE: Estimates of the number of Raters required to reach r_{kk} = .80 for summary scales are as follows:

	Split-Half Estimate	Group 1–Group 2 Estimate
9-item scales	6 Raters	7 Raters
18-item scales	3 Raters	5 Raters

A question basic to all of SYMLOG is whether the Adjective Rating Form captures the three-dimensional structure that Bales (1970) found to underlie so many analyses of personality and interpersonal behavior. A separate factor analysis was done for each of the three groups of Raters. In Group 1, subjects answered other non-SYMLOG items as well, in some cases items explicitly designed to tap factors additional to or different from those underlying Bales's three-dimensional formulation. Table 8 shows Group 1, analyzed both for all forty-eight items in the study and for the twenty-six items of SYMLOG Adjective Ratings taken separately.

The overall results are a strong confirmation of the posited three-dimensional factor structure. In all three samples, three factors emerge which very much resemble the expected factor structure. The P–N dimension factor loads on precisely those items intended. The second largest factor is the F–B factor, and the third largest resembles U–D.

One of the problems discussed above was the relative difficulty in measuring the U and D directions. Part of the explanation lies in the large part of the overall variance accounted for by the P–N dimension. Any item having a P component (or, to the lesser extent, an N component) becomes, at least for this study, heavily weighted so that the P or N component is the psychologically most salient element in the item. For example, the factor loadings for DP and DPF on the first factor P–N are .92 and .86, leaving only 20 to 25 percent of the variance of the items to be accounted for by the other factors. One guideline for the construction of multidimensional items of the SYMLOG sort must be to prevent the overwhelming of an item by one if its directional components (see Appendix D).

TABLE 8   SYMLOG Adjective Ratings Factor Analysis: Variance Accounted for by First Four Factors

	GROUP 1 (ALL 48 ITEMS)	GROUP 1 ONLY SYMLOG ITEMS)	GROUP 2	GROUP 3
Factor 1 (P-N)	39.3	45.1	50.4	44.1
Factor 2 (F-B)	24.8	21.9	21.8	24.8
Factor 3 (U-D)	17.8	18.1	16.0	16.4
Factor 4 (Intensity)	6.4	5.4	4.0	2.6
Three factors	81.9	85.1	88.2	85.3
Four factors	88.2	90.5	92.2	87.9

The factor loadings indicate that for untrained subjects in both Group 1 and Group 2 the U–D factor is somewhat skewed, so that it is almost UB versus DF. However, for both the second factor and the third factor, the trained SYMLOG users show factor loadings much more similar to those expected from the item construction. This is illustrated in a simplified manner in Table 9, which gives the mean factor loadings on (a) the second factor for those items designed to measure F, designed to measure B, and designed to be neutral on the F–B dimension; and (b) the third factor for those items designed to measure U, designed to measure D, and designed to be neutral on the U–D dimension. Table 9 compares these mean factor loadings for the trained subjects, Group 3, with those for the untrained subjects, Group 2, who used the most similar form, the consecutive condition.

Training Effects

Table 9 demonstrates that the effect of training with SYMLOG is to reinforce the dimensional structure. The trained Raters learn to see the items, and the relations among them, in the way that the three-dimensional conception proposes that they should see the items. The training seems to involve, in particular, the clarification of the meaning of the F–B dimension and of the U–D dimension in a way that corresponds to the theoretical expectation. Table 9 demonstrates this by reference to the factor loadings on the different dimensions. If we look at the factor loadings of particular items we can see this picture in more detail. For trained raters (Group 3) the items loading highest for the U–D dimension are the singly named U and D items. The U item loads .88 on the U–D dimension, while the D item loads −.91. For Group 2 untrained observers, these two items still load high on the U–D dimension, but not as high as some other items in the scale. Furthermore, these two items load on other dimensions as well, which is not true for the trained Raters of Group 3. (The table of factor loadings is available upon request. It is not included here for reasons of length.)

Since these two groups used the same Rating Form, the position of the items cannot account for this discrepancy. Nor is it only that trained Raters are using

TABLE 9   SYMLOG Adjective Ratings Factor Analysis: Mean Factor Loadings for Predicted Items

| | (a) FACTOR 2 (FORWARD-BACKWARD) | |
	Group 2 (Untrained)	Group 3 (Trained)
9 F items x̄ =	.52	.59
9 B items x̄ =	−.30	−.52
8 other items		
x̄ =	.33	.23

| | (b) FACTOR 3 (UPWARD-DOWNWARD) | |
	Group 2 (Untrained)	Group 3 (Trained)
9 U items x̄ =	.38	.44
9 D items x̄ =	−.32	−.40
0 other items		
x̄ =	.25	.19

the known directional identifications to generate item meaning. If that were so, then the DPB item should load negatively on the U–D dimension for the trained Raters. In fact, DPB is rated as U even by the trained Raters. Rather it seems that the training involves superimposing the hypothetical three-dimensional structure upon the "natural" structuring of the subjects, so that the space becomes better structured and more correspondent to the SYMLOG conception.

The most salient effect of training is in the interpretation of the B dimension. Table 9 indicates that for untrained Raters B items load much less highly on Factor 2 than for trained Raters. For trained Raters, B has come to be the opposite of F more clearly than it is for the untrained. This can be illustrated by correlating the scales at the opposite poles of each dimension across all Raters, as indicated in Table 10.

In all three dimensions, trained Raters tend to see the scale items as opposites more than untrained Raters do. However, the finding is most striking for the F–B dimension. The B dimensional pole, as discussed in Part II of this book, is the least intuitively obvious, as it has two components of oppositeness to its F opposite pole. One opposite to task orientation is the emotional expressiveness that is highlighted in the DPB, PB, UPB, UB items as constructed for this study. The other opposite is the refusal to engage in the group task or the passive neglect of it or downgrading of it. This is captured more clearly in the DB, DNB, and NB items. The trained observers have been taught to "see" the relationship between these two elements of B and to see them both as opposites to F. A good indication of this is the item measuring B itself ("emotional, expressive, changeable"), which loads −.94 on Factor 2 for Group 3 and only −.64 for Group 2. (For Group 1, the B item is mostly assimilated into Factor 4, which will be briefly discussed below.)

The emotionally expressive B is not treated by the untrained Rater as opposite to the F direction but instead as somewhat distinct from it. In Group 2 the items most highly loaded on Factor 3 (U–D) were UB (.98) and DF (−.74) whereas

TABLE 10   SYMLOG Adjective Rating Scales: Correlations of Nine-Item Scale
Polarities

	GROUP 1 TRAINED INTERSPERSED	GROUP 2 UNTRAINED CONSECUTIVE	GROUP 3 TRAINED CONSECUTIVE
U with D	−.60	−.68	−.72
P with N	−.86	−.87	−.91
F with B	−.60	−.62	−.82

these two items are much less salient for the trained observers, where the highest
loadings are for U and F. Factor 2 in Group 2 has very high positive loadings for
the F items and much less high negative loadings for the B items, as reflected in
Table 9.

The Fourth Factor

In all of the factor analyses undertaken in this study, a fourth factor emerges,
explaining, as indicated in Table 5, some 2.6 to 6.4 percent of the variance. The
trained observers have minimized the significance of this factor, a further indication of the effects of training on restructuring the meaning of the items.

Among trained observers no item on this factor loads higher than .35, and from
these loadings it would be very difficult to interpret the factor. However, Group 2
factor analysis has two higher loadings: one of .47 for B ("emotional, expressive, changeable"), and one of .53 for DNB ("frustrated, discouraged, withdrawing"). Furthermore, in the factor analysis for both Groups 2 and 3, there are
moderate positive loadings (around .30) for DNF ("self-sacrificing, complaining, martyred"), DN ("resentful, depressed, rejecting"), DNB ("frustrated,
discouraged, withdrawing"), and DB ("anxious, tense, fearful, holding back").
But the nature of this intriguing fourth factor is indicated most clearly in the
forty-eight-item factor analysis of Group 1. Here the Wish scale items "intense,
emotional, engrossed" and "superficial, unemotional, uninvolved" both have
high loadings, as do the SYMLOG items for B ("emotional, expressive, changeable") and DNF ("self-sacrificing, complaining, martyred"). The items for DN
("resentful, depressed, rejecting"), DNB ("frustrated, discouraged, withdrawing"), and DB ("anxious, tense, fearful, holding back") have loadings of between .3 and .4

A full account of this factor has been given by Wish elsewhere (Wish, Deutsch
and Kaplan, 1976; Wish and Kaplan, 1977; Wish, 1978a and 1978b). In the
present circumstances, this factor further complicates the meaning of some of the
D items, such as the cluster DNF, DN, DNB, DB, which tap into Factor 4 as well
as into the three-dimensional system. In the Wish studies this factor is named
"Intensity" and emerges more strongly. It presumably would have emerged
more strongly in the present study if more adjectives designed to tap it had been
included. The exact implication of this fourth factor for the SYMLOG three-

dimensional space is not yet clear and remains an important problem for future study. In Part II of this book (p. 178), we point out that the B direction has two disparate components, logically, and it may be that the fourth factor is related to one of these (the emotional aspect of "counteraction of control").

Orthogonality

It is not a necessary assumption for the use of SYMLOG that the three a priori factors be orthogonal to each other in a given population. In previous small studies U, P, F have been correlated with each other, or P and F have been correlated with each other. The factors extracted in the present study are orthogonal, but since they do not precisely represent the a priori factors we should not assume that the dimensions are uncorrelated. Table 11 shows the intercorrelations among the a priori eighteen-item scales for each of the three samples.

If a study were made in the self-analytic group context, the negative correlation between P-N and F-B might well be reversed so that Positive and Forward would be positively correlated. It is probably a characteristic of the set of interactions in the Loud family that there are very few opportunities for cooperation around task accomplishment, and any Positive affect is more of the joking and "fooling around" kind, associated with PB, UPB behavior. The correlation among the dimensions in a particular group is likely to be a diagnostically useful indicator of the group's atmosphere and interaction pattern. (See the discussion of the Loud family below.)

Summary

Most of the items chosen to represent the twenty-six combinations of the three dimensions of interpersonal behavior and interpersonal perception are confirmed in this carefully controlled laboratory study. The Positive-Negative is the strongest and clearest dimension, but the other two dimensions are found relatively clearly as well. P-N is also the most reliable dimension.

The structure of the Adjective Rating Form allows the user to benefit from a large number of items measuring each dimension without thereby multiplying the necessary size of the instrument. The benefit of such a procedure is to give meaning to a hypothetical space where combinations of dimensions provide location. A rating that is high on two dimensions and low on the other can be pictured as representing specific characteristics and modes of behavior rather than an abstract addition of dimensions. Furthermore, the contradictions in a person's behavior, including the violation of strong preexistent biases about what behaviors and traits fit together, can be detected more successfully by having independent Ratings of the separate combinations of dimensions. The present data show that it is difficult to construct adequate items for behavioral characteristics that are not frequent, but it also demonstrates that it is necessary to do so to avoid the constriction of the meaning of behavior such as silence or nonparticipation, which can have multiple meanings.

TABLE 11   Intercorrelations of SYMLOG Adjective
Rating Summary Eighteen-Item Scales

		U–D	P–N	F–B
Group 1	U–D			
	P–N	.125		
	F–B	.183	−.070	
Group 2	U–D			
	P–N	.188		
	F–B	.208	−.203	
Group 3	U–D			
	P–N	.285		
	F–B	.144	−.110	

The training of persons in SYMLOG tends to strengthen an already present tendency to simplify experience into a small number of dimensions, usually three. The predominance of P–N declines for trained observers, who give more relative weight to the F–B and U–D dimensions. Trained observers regularize their conception of the three-dimensional space, seeing Backward more clearly as opposite to Forward rather than as an additional dimension.

In an unpublished study using SYMLOG Ratings of dramatic actors by members of the audience (data from Richard Polley), the Forward and Backward dimensions are even more clearly split off, so that they emerge as separate factors. In such a population, task-orientation and emotional expression may indeed seem not opposites but dimensions orthogonal to each other. It is hoped that the rewriting of some of the items used to measure the B part of the space will show the intended relationship between expressiveness and non–task-orientation. It is clear, however, that in some group situations, the element of B, which represents an expansive, imaginative quality, is not seen as diverting the group from the task-orientation and hard-working style. This issue is one that was anticipated theoretically, as indicated in Part II of this book, and emerges clearly in the data.

At this juncture, it seems not to be necessary to reassess the three-versus four-factor question for general SYMLOG use. Although the fourth factor of Intensity of Involvement emerges, it does not invalidate the use of the first three stronger factors as the basis of the SYMLOG Scoring and Rating System. The three factors are not exhaustive, but they account for the major part of the variance and have the great advantage that they can be kept in mind easily using the three-dimensional spatial analogue. Some researchers, however, may wish to assign factor scores rather than use the a priori scales. Such researchers should bear in mind the fourth dimension.

Chapter 31

SYMLOG Interaction Scoring Rates and Reliability

Nineteen trained observers participated as Scorers in the part of the American Family study involving SYMLOG Interaction Scoring. These nineteen Scorers had different levels of experience as SYMLOG Scorers, but all had a minimum of three months' experience scoring a self-analytic group, live and in real time. These groups met twice or three times a week for an hour. None of the observers had any but very limited experience scoring videotape, however.

This study, with its unusually large observer team, provided an excellent opportunity to examine observer scoring patterns and rates and to test for inter-Scorer agreement. Because this aspect of reliability is especially difficult to achieve for behavioral coding, and the present method allows the observer much leeway to unitize the communication as he sees fit, it is important to see in detail what level of inter-Scorer agreement is achievable. SYMLOG places a strong emphasis on the validity and psychological meaningfulness of scoring, with an attendant cost in precision of unit definition and observer-to-observer reproducibility. From the present data we can determine just how costly in reliability these emphases on psychological salience and observer choice are.

Each Scorer was given minimal instructions. Each of the twenty videotape segments was to be scored with at least ten acts but not more than fifteen. No particular distribution between the two participants in each scene was required, though observers were urged to balance their scoring. There were no instructions at all about the use of ACT versus NON, or about Image level scoring and the use of PRO and CON. The rates of use of NON, PRO, and CON, therefore, provide useful guidelines for SYMLOG Scorers as to the behavior of a large team of trained SYMLOG users.

Scoring Rates

Over all observers and all scenes, the mean number of scores was 13.2, approximating the instructions given. This means that for each person in each scene there is an average of 6.6 judgments per observer. This compares with twenty-six judgments made in the SYMLOG Ratings, of which eighteen are relevant to each of the three dimensions. For time periods as short as these, there can be little question that it is easier to gather a large number of Rating judgments using fixed scales than to acquire a comparable number of behavioral judgments. The ratings, in this context, have the advantage of being fixed as to the number of judgments made (the number of scoring units requires observer judgment), of being more frequent (the scoring units in the present study do not yield as many as eighteen separate acts per person/scene), and of being equated for each actor in each scene (in scoring, one actor may receive the lion's share of the scores and the others very few, while in Rating, regardless of the amount of behavior we see of each actor, the same number of judgments is made.)

In a situation of live scoring of a group over one hour, the data-base—the number of judgments made—for scoring will be higher than eighteen for central actors and may be substantially smaller for quiet members. The scoring rate per minute is much higher in the present study than would be the case for live scoring. Producing more than thirteen scores for two minutes of interaction is a rate of 6.5 scores per minute. In live scoring observers produce not more than one to two scores per minute. It is a question of some interest whether the correlations between Scoring and Rating are different for actors of varying levels of dominance. This is part of the more general question as to whether the multiple Rating judgments made about actors who appear very infrequently or who interact very little are valid indicators of the person being rated or are simply observer stereotypes. These questions will be examined in additional studies.

ACT and NON Scoring Rates

Eighty-two (81.8) percent of all scores were at the ACT level, and 18.2 percent were at the NON level. We may compare the variability in the use of NON among observers with the variability among person/scene units in yielding NON scores.

For each observer, we may compute the total number of scores and the total number of NON scores. We can then compute the percentage of NON for each observer, and thus derive the mean observer percentage of NON and the standard deviation. For observers, the mean percentage of NON is 17.7 percent, and the standard deviation is 10.6 percent. For person/scene units, the mean is 18.5 percent, but the standard deviation is only 6.9 percent. This indicates that the use of NON is more variable among observers than from scene to scene, an impression strengthened by plotting the percentages in each case. For observers, there is almost a bimodal distribution: The largest group of observers (twelve of nineteen) cluster between 5 percent and 19 percent, but a smaller group of four of the nineteen are between 25 percent and 35 percent, with one additional observer scoring over 40 percent of his acts as NON. The person/scene units are much more concentrated, with thirty-one of forty between 10 percent and 25 percent and with no gaps in the distribution.

It is important to note that this variability in observer use of NON is not simply a reflection of observer scoring frequency. There is a slight negative correlation (r = -.27) between number of ACTs and number of NON scores among observers. That is, to a limited extent the number of NON scores comes at the expense of ACT scores. However, the variability in NON scores is mostly an observer characteristic, only slightly related to overall rate of scoring. (There is also almost no correlation, r = -.07, between number of ACT scores per person/ scene unit and number of NON scores.) The rate of NON scoring can be affected by training as will be discussed in Part IV of this book. In the present study, the use of NON is not as standardized as would be desirable.

Even though overall nearly one-fifth of the scores were at the NON level, this still translates into only 1.3 NON scores, on the average, per observer per person in a scene. This compares to 5.4 ACT scores. This low frequency cannot but have consequences for inter-Scorer agreement. On the average, for split-half reliability we are comparing summary three-dimensional positions based on about eleven scores per person/scene, only a fraction of the discrete judgments in the Rating procedure tests of reliability. Given this small number of judgments it is striking that the location of persons in the three-dimensional space computed from NON alone correlates highly with location from ACT alone (ACT U-D with NON U-D: r = .59; ACT P-N with NON P-N: r = .77; ACT F-B with NON F-B: r = .81).

PRO and CON Scoring Rates

At a maximum, each ACT score and each NON score can be accompanied by one Image level score, either PRO or CON. (Indeed, the scorer may have two Image scores for the same ACT, but this would be infrequent.) Yet, it is not to be expected, in practice, that all ACT and NON scores will be accompanied by Image Level scoring.

Observers vary greatly in their frequency of Image level scoring. One observer recorded 223 ACT and NON scores and of these was able to score 222 PRO or CON image statements. Other observers also surpassed a 90 percent rate of Image level scoring. On the other hand, one observer scored only 34 percent, and five other observers ranged between 39 and 54 percent. The mean over the nineteen observers was 67.7 percent, and the standard deviation 19.8 percent. a high variability indeed (for person/scene units the s.d. = 12.4 percent). Rather than showing a normal distribution, the distribution of observer rates is flat over a wide range.

For contrast, the person/scene units are less variable than observers in the frequency of PRO and CON scoring. Twenty-eight of the forty person/scenes have a rate of between 55 and 75 percent.

It is not the case that the rate of PRO and CON use is predictable from the rate of NON. One might surmise that it is harder to find Image level scores for NON. There is a small negative correlation (r = -.13) between percentage of NON scores and percentage of PRO and CON scores over scenes. Over observers there is a positive correlation (r = .28), indicating that observers who are good scorers, in the sense of their more frequent use of NON, are also good at picking up Image level scores.

PRO and CON are relatively equally divided. The mean percent of PRO among the nineteen observers is 52.1 percent, and the standard deviation is 15.3 percent. (These figures slightly exaggerate the rate of CON and the variability because of one outlier. This observer scored only one PRO statement and seventy-four CON statements. Without the outlier, mean PRO = 54.9 percent, s.d. = 9.3 percent.)

The rate of PRO bears no relation to the rate of CON of the same observer (r = .10; deleting outlier, r = .07). As indicated above, even the variation among observers in relative use of PRO and CON is not large, if the outlier is excluded from the analysis. However, the variation from person/scene to person/scene is much higher. The mean PRO percentage is 54.5 percent, but the standard deviation is 23.8 percent. The distribution itself is very flat with weak peaks in the 85, 65, and 35 percent range. The correlation between number of PRO statements for a person/scene and number of CON statements is highly negative (r = −.57). The flat distribution and the high standard deviation, together with the negative correlation between PRO rate and CON rate, suggest that individuals may differ widely in their PRO/CON ratio as a characteristic of personality. It is also suggested that the pattern of polarization–unification of a given scene may be important.

The significance of context is emphasized by combining the PRO and CON statements of the two interactors in each scene. The correlation between PRO and CON sums across scenes (summing the PRO scores of both interactors, and then summing both on CON) is r = −.83. Scenes have a characteristic interaction style, such that both interactors tend either to advocate certain positions (PRO) or to attack rejected positions (CON), giving conversations either a nay-saying or yea-saying tone.

Intercoder Agreement: General Considerations

SYMLOG scoring procedures emphasize the individual observer as a filter of interaction events, who selects those events deemed to be the most psychologically salient to the interaction. The procedure does not aim to treat all utterances or nonverbal communications equally. Units of communication are units of meaningful interaction as understood by the observer. This emphasis on validity of scores and on the meaningfulness of the observer's "log" of scores to group members threatens the possibility of achieving high levels of intercoder agreement.

Disagreements among observers may stem from a number of sources:

1. Coders may choose different acts to score.
2. Coders may score different numbers of acts.
3. Coders may differ in the location of acts in the three-dimensional space. (That is, they may score the same act differently on any or all of the three dimensions on which each scored act is evaluated.)

The main concern of the SYMLOG user is that the overall location (in the three dimensions) of each observed individual be a reliable location. The summary scores of each individual in each dimension for a given set of observers should reach a criterion level of agreement among these scorers. A more stringent demand might be made that observers agree on the particular events to be coded and that these events be scored the same way. The present report of the SYMLOG results derived from the American Family study does not attempt to calculate agreement on choice of events to be coded or on the three-dimensional scoring of those acts chosen. These are important questions in themselves, particularly to ascertain the extent to which the same aspects of behavior are perceived as salient by different observers. For present purposes, the question is whether the summary scores of individuals (person/scene units) in each of the three dimensions are consistent across observers. In a subsequent study, other aspects of the SYMLOG scoring method will be scrutinized. First, observer agreement on the events chosen as significant and worthy of being scored will be analyzed. Second, the three-dimensional placement of the events chosen will be compared to the three-dimensional placement of events that were not chosen as important to score. This could be part of the general comparison between Interaction Scoring based on the attempt to be exhaustive in including all acts (such as in Interaction Process Analysis) and those scoring methods that, like SYMLOG Interaction Scoring, use some selection principle for sorting out events.

The present study examines intercoder agreement with brief videotaped segments of dyadic communication (with some minor third roles in a few scenes). Often only one of the two interactors is on camera. The coders, just like the SYMLOG Adjective Raters discussed previously, see each segment twice and have a discrete and limited time in which to score it. The scenes are brief, and the conversations tend to be about one issue, thus giving each scene a homogeneous emotional tone.

These elements of the present stimulus materials stand in contrast to the complexity of SYMLOG coding of live, multiperson groups in real time over an hour meeting or longer. Shorter segments leave less opportunity for selection, as there are fewer events from which to choose. In live scoring, the stimuli are more varied: There may be simultaneous speech of several persons, there are frequently nonverbal responses of persons not part of the conversation, and there is much "unfocused" communication, in the sense of communication not directed to the topic at hand. The video camera makes a preselection of the focus of attention of the coder, whereas the live coder faces a much more demanding task of selection and attention. Live scoring also requires immediate judgment, while videotape has the playback option (which does not have to be exercised, of course). All of these elements make live scoring more difficult and probably more idiosyncratic. On the other hand, the live group coder knows far more about the interacting group, and thus his judgment of the salience of events is much better founded. He also typically scores interaction over an hour so that summary scores are computed on the basis of more information and more SYMLOG acts. This is especially true for high participators. Indeed, it is a worthwhile question in itself whether the validity and reliability of scoring, and also Adjective Rating, of low participators produce different results from those obtained for high participators.

Finally, the homogeneity of issue-orientation and emotional tone in a two-minute interaction segment is not matched in an hour-long interaction. In long, intensive interaction, the same individual may demonstrate a variety of attitudes and interaction styles. It is unlikely, for example, that the pattern of PRO–CON negative correlation would be striking over longer interaction periods.

All of these contrasts recommend caution in extrapolating the results here reported about coding reliability to self-analytic group use. Some preliminary evidence suggests, however, that the main features of the results to be cited are reproduced with live group data.

Intercoder Agreement: Methods of Calculation

The measures of intercoder agreement utilized here correspond closely to the uses to which the data are usually put as indicated in Part I and Part IV of this volume. The main interest is in agreement among observers, in each of the three dimensions, and in summary scores of each actor (person/scene) in the interacting group being observed.

The summing over observers of summary scores may be computed in two alternative ways, based on two different psychological assumptions. The first method, the Intensity method, gives greater weight to the most active scorers by simply adding raw scores of all observers. The score for an actor on a given dimension is the ratio of scores in a particular dimension summed over all observers to the sum of all scores made, summed over all observers.

Method 1: $$(U - D)_i = \frac{\Sigma_{1...n} U_i - \Sigma_{1...n} D_i}{\Sigma_{1...n} \text{ acts}_i}$$

$(U - D)_i$ = Summary score of Actor i on U–D dimension

$\Sigma_{1...n} U_i$ = Sum over all observers (1, 2 . . . n) of U scores of Actor i

$\Sigma_{1...n} D_i$ = Sum over all observers (1, 2 . . . n) of D scores of Actor i

$\Sigma_{1...n} \text{acts}_i$ = Sum over all observers (1, 2 . . . n) of all acts scored (whether ACT or NON) of Actor i

The alternative method gives equal weight to each observer's scores of a particular actor, regardless of the frequency of such scores. This is the *one-observer/one-vote* method. This method calculates percentages in each dimension *for each observer* and uses the mean of those percentages (or the sum of those percentages) as the summary score (in each dimension).

Method 2: $$(U - D)_i = \Sigma_{1...n} \frac{U_i - D_i}{\Sigma \text{ acts}_i}$$

$(U - D)_i$ = Sumary score of Actor i on dimension U–D

$\Sigma_{1...n} \dfrac{U_i - D_i}{\Sigma \text{ acts}_i}$ = Each observer's separate ratio of U scores minus D scores for Actor *i* to that observer's number of acts for *i* is added together for all observers (1 . . . n)

The former method, Intensity, is most commonly used as it simplifies calculations. It also takes advantage of especially competent observers who are likely to produce more scores. However, it can be more erratic, because a single observer can skew the whole summary score of an individual. This is especially problematic when an observer records many scores but has not fully grasped the assignment of acts to the appropriate dimensions. (Part IV of this book contains some practical steps to avoid this pitfall.)

In the present study, both methods of calculation were used and compared. Generally speaking, the more tedious *one-observer/one-vote* computation produced slightly higher reliability estimates, especially for computations involving NON. (The method of calculation used in the study of correlations between SYMLOG Interaction Scoring and SYMLOG Adjective Rating is the one-observer/one-vote computation with its higher interscorer reliability.)

Split-half reliability was calculated for ACT, NON, PRO, and CON separately. Two separate calculations were made, one utilizing an odd–even splitting procedure, the other a randomized assignment distribution. The results were very similar, and the lower results will be reported here as a conservative estimate of reliability (see Table 12).

The ACT level results are especially encouraging for P–N and F–B. In both cases only a small number of observers (three for P–N; five for F–B) are required to reach an acceptable level of inter-coder reliability. For U–D, the requisite number is ten observers, more than would usually be available. The reliability for U–D is slightly higher for different calculations but not enough to lower the number of observers required to fewer than eight.

On the other hand, the number of acts as an alternative measure of dominance is more highly reliable. The split-half correlation is .87, which means that one could reach the criterion level of reliability with only five observers. It may be that until ways are found to increase the reliability of judgments on the U–D dimension, the best measure of dominance would be this frequency of ACTs measure. (Other evidence indicates that frequency in itself is also a highly valid measure of dominance, correlating very highly with Ratings, for example.)

The reliability of the U–D dimension when combining NON and ACT scores on the U–D dimension does not differ much from the reliability of ACT itself. The correlation of .78 shows no improvement over ACT alone. Combining *frequencies* of ACT and NON also does not improve the reliability for the U–D dimension.

The NON level results are less encouraging, as might be expected from the lower frequency of NON scores and the greater variability among observers in the use of NON scores. Both U–D and F–B produce shaky results, such that the criterion level is just barely reached even in this study with its many observers. Judgments on the P–N dimension are more reliable.

For the NON level, the reliability is greater for those scenes which have greater numbers of scores. When there are very few scores the results are erratic and lower the reliability. It is also the case that observers who use NON infrequently are stereotyped in their use of NON so that NON is not diagnostic of individual differences for these persons. This combination of results indicates the

TABLE 12   Reliability of SYMLOG Interaction Scoring: Intercoder Agreement Using Split-Half Method

DIMENSION	SPLIT-HALF CORRELATION	SCORING RELIABILITY ESTIMATE[b]
i) ACT level		
U–D	r = .79	.88
P–N	r = .93	.96
F–B	r = .88	.94
ii) NON[a] level		
U–D	.67	.80
P–N	.81	.90
F–B	.68	.81
iii) PRO[a] level		
U–D	.47	.64
P–N	.67	.80
F–B	.87	.93
iv) CON[a] level		
U–D	.69	.82
P–N	.72	.84
F–B	.80	.89

[a] Based on person-scenes with at least five scores for each half of the data.
[b] Reliability estimates are slightly lower than actual relability of scoring in this study as split-half estimates are based on only eighteen of nineteen observers.

need for greater attention to training in nonverbal observation and clarification of the use of NON in relation to ACT.

The results for PRO and CON reveal quite a different pattern. Only the F–B dimension is highly reliable, while the PRO U–D scoring in particular is not at an acceptable level of agreement. The PRO and CON distinction is intended to be a measure of value preferences. The F–B dimension is especially relevant to these preferences, as it indicates the orientation of the individual to the surrounding normative and cultural system, whether by approval or disapproval. Indications are that scorers will need better training in the scoring of images, as well as in scoring nonverbal behavior. It is also the case, however, that summing all levels together by PRO or CON introduces certain inaccuracies and that further analysis by specific image levels is needed.

Chapter 32

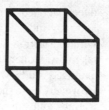

SYMLOG Interaction Scoring and SYMLOG Adjective Ratings: A Comparison

The validity of SYMLOG as a method of studying interpersonal interaction and interpersonal communication is not easily demonstrated in the usual research environment in which it has been developed. The interaction laboratory uses SYMLOG feedback to the groups as a fundamental element in group development, and the meaningfulness of the feedback process has been a basic test for us in SYMLOG development.

However, the face validity of an instrument such as the Adjective Rating Form in developing a Field Diagram of the group is not sufficient to establish the instrument as scientifically valid. For one thing, retrospective ratings have come under serious question as to their validity through research showing systematic rater bias toward reproduction of the already present cognitive-evaluative space (D'Andrade, 1974). For present purposes, this would indicate that retrospectively the rater tends to reconstruct the picture of the behavior observed so that it corresponds with the expected patterning of traits and characteristics, thus losing the unique pattern of a particular behavior sequence or the overall complexity of a single person.

This reconstruction of memory would be especially likely to occur over longer periods of time. Thus, in the usual application of SYMLOG ratings in groups meeting over extended periods of time such reconstruction of events may occur quite easily. In the present American Family SYMLOG study the elapsed time from observation to rating is very small: Ratings are done immediately after each scene. Furthermore, the interaction sequences are short, and this may minimize retrospective distortion. Finally, the scenes are dyadic, and the memory of such an interaction is less complex than that of a group of many persons.

To indicate the relationship between SYMLOG Adjective Ratings and act-by-act Interaction Scoring over long periods of time requires study of many groups over extended periods. Such studies in specific groups have been undertaken, and they indicate correlations of +.60 or more in SYMLOG summary Ratings with Interaction Scoring summaries over periods of a month to six weeks (undertaken by Cohen and also by Williamson, 1977; Solomon, 1977, 1978). An extended study with many groups is still in the process of being carried out. However, any such attempt must be based on the knowledge of whether the Ratings and Interaction Scoring are highly correlated even in the research environment employing (1) short interaction sequences; (2) short response time after observation to Rating; (3) dyadic rather than multiperson communication. It is essential to the use of SYMLOG in research to establish the relationship between behavior coded in an act-by-act form, as in SYMLOG Interaction Scoring, and that encoded in retrospective Ratings. It is to this purpose that the comparisons below are addressed.

In a subsequent chapter, another kind of validity check is provided: the more clinical or applied test of seeing whether the results of SYMLOG analysis "make sense" of the stimulus materials, in this instance the American Family study. (The clinical analysis of validity is not intended to meet research criteria of validity but is designed to demonstrate the process of using SYMLOG in group analysis and the comparison of Adjective Rating and Interaction Scoring.)

A most important test of the validity of SYMLOG is related to the use of SYMLOG to generate a conception of the relations among people in the group. We would like to know how persons close to each other in the three-dimensional space actually relate to each other and whether they seem to have significant relationships with each other. A large study of fifteen self-analytic groups (together comprising more than 200 persons), examining the predictive validity of SYMLOG-like ratings for relationships in the group, is planned for later publication to investigate this additional aspect of the validity of SYMLOG. (Earlier steps in this direction may be seen in Cohen, 1972)

The data of the Interaction Scorers were analyzed for the two primary interaction levels ACT and NON and, subsequently, for all PRO images taken together and all CON images taken together. Separate analyses for each level of images will be reported elsewhere, but the frequency of each level in each scene was too small for useful inclusion here. For each of the nineteen scorers a mean of about sixteen acts were scored for each scene. The analysis was carried out in percentages of total acts scored per person per scene to control for frequency differences among scorers. For normative purposes it is useful to supply the mean percentages of acts scored in each of the levels ACT, NON, PRO, and CON by each direction. These data are given in Table 13. This summary table indicates much similarity to the comparable tables reported for two self-analytic groups recently studied by this author over a three-month period for each group. That is, the stimulus materials do not indicate a radically different overall usage of the levels in each directional set. For example, in these data and in those self-analytic groups, PRO images are primarily found in the U, P quadrants and CON images in the U, N quadrants. In both sets of data Forward PRO and CON scores are somewhat more frequent than Backward, but not markedly so. Finally, in both sets of data, the F–B dimension is the one most frequently included in scores of PRO and CON images. In other words, scorers more often judge an image to be

TABLE 13   Percentages of Each Interaction Scoring Category in Each of the Six Summary Directions

		ACT	NON	PRO	CON
	U	46.2	29.5	35.2	41.6
		(31.9)	(31.4)	(53.9)	(37.3)
	D	21.9	39.1	10.9	21.1
Mean %	P	41.4	32.9	45.8	12.3
of all acts		(21.8)	(24.7)	(40.3)	(34.8)
in category	N	36.8	42.4	13.9	52.9
	F	53.0	21.5	49.0	42.1
		(10.1)	(26.7)	(16.3)	(18.3)
	B	36.9	51.8	34.7	39.6

NOTE: Numbers in parentheses indicate percentage of acts in the categories not scored in that dimension, i.e. (31.9) means that 31.9 percent of acts scored were not scored for U–D dimension.

either F or B (in combination with other dimensions or alone) than either P, N or U, D.

Comparisons of Rating and Scoring

Table 14 provides the first set of comparisons between the results of Rating and the results of Interaction Scoring. For all three groups of Adjective Raters the correlations between ACT Level scores and Adjective Ratings are very high for both the Positive–Negative dimension and for the Forward–Backward dimension. These very high correlations are impressive especially when one keeps in mind the imperfections in the Forward–Backward scale utilized in this study.

ACT and NON for these two dimensions are also highly correlated with each other. ACT P–N and NON P–N correlate .77, and ACT F–B and NON F–B correlate .81. However, Ratings are better predicted by the ACT level scoring than by the NON level scoring, these differences being both consistent across groups and statistically significant.

The complications are greatest for the U–D dimension. ACT U–D and NON U–D correlate with each other only .59. They also both correlate in the range of .70 with summary U–D Adjective Ratings of these same American Family scenes. If a new measure is created combining ACT and NON, with equal weight given to each, the correlations for the P–N dimension and F–B dimension with ratings do not increase and some even decline slightly, though not significantly. However, U–D correlations increase substantially.

The same point can be made rather precisely through multiple correlations of the two behavior levels, ACT and NON, with rating summaries of each of the three groups (see Table 15). The multiple correlations are the greatest improvements over the ACT level correlations for the U–D dimension. Only for the U–D

TABLE 14   Correlations between SYMLOG Adjective Ratings and SYMLOG Interaction Scoring for Summary Eighteen-Item Scales

			Group 1 Naive, Interspersed			Group 2 Naive, Consecutive			Group 3 Trained, Consecutive		
			U–D	P–N	F–B	U–D	P–N	F–B	U–D	P–N	F–B
	ACT level	U–D	.72			.71			.68		
		P–N		.89			.89			.91	
		F–B			.85			.87			.86
CODERS	NON level	U–D	.71			.68			.67		
		P–N		.80			.77			.75	
		F–B			.71			.76			.77
	ACT + NON	U–D	.80			.78			.76		
		P–N		.90			.88			.88	
		F–B			.82			.86			.86

dimension are the Beta weights for the NON level comparable to those of the ACT level.

The significance of this finding about the U–D dimension should not be overlooked. It is the dominance dimension that is most affected by the inconsistencies between ACT level and NON level communication. Judgments of friendliness and of task-orientation by inexperienced raters do not reflect any very noticeable contribution of the nonverbal level. One qualification to this overall conclusion is necessary. The trained observers are noticeably helped in their ratings, it seems, by NON level observations. The multiple correlation of Group 3 reaches the .95 level for F–B when the NON level is appropriately weighted. The difference between .95 and .86 is significant even though the β^2 for NON is less than one quarter that of ACT. We recall that the trained observers differ from the untrained especially on this dimension and especially with reference to the B part of the three-dimensional space. It may well be that the difference comes from greater attention to nonverbal cues of emotional excitement and disorientation from the group task. Such nonverbal sensitivity is one of the first effects of observing from behind a one-way mirror, a form of observation that is a typical part of what is meant here by training observers.

Why is NON level scoring particularly important in assessing the dominance rating of an individual? It is most likely that the answer should be sought (see Table 13) in the infrequency of D ACT coding and the consequent importance of nonverbal cues for the assessment of less assertive and less talkative persons. Attention to the nonverbal level of behavior may be the critical road to gaining knowledge about the less assertive group member.

Both trained and untrained raters seem to utilize nonverbal cues for the assessment of dominance in these dyadic sequences from the "American Family." What training seems to enchance is the use of the nonverbal channel for gathering information relevant to the F–B dimension.

TABLE 15   Multiple Correlation Coefficients for Adjective Ratings Predicting from ACT and NON Levels

	Multiple r	BETA WEIGHTS (β^2)	
		ACT	NON
Group 1			
U–D	.80	.21	.19
P–N	.91	.45	.08
F–B	.86	.62	.005
Group 2			
U–D	.78	.22	.16
P–N	.90	.56	.04
F–B	.92	.54	.08
Group 3			
U–D	.76	.19	.17
P–N	.91	.66	.07
F–B	.95	.55	.12

Nonetheless, even the adding of nonverbal cues does not allow the prediction of Ratings from Scoring on the U–D dimensions to reach the same level of certainty as is the case for the other two dimensions. If Rating and Scoring remain more different on the dimension of dominance, it may again reflect the problems experienced with some of the items in the Adjective Rating Form, and therefore a close look at those items most strongly related to U–D Interaction Scores is valuable.

Item Analysis

Table 16 demonstrates that the items with the highest correlations with ACT U–D are reflective of a dominating UN quality rather than the more Positive outgoing forms of leadership and prominence. Some previous research has indicated that overtalking produces a negative effect on liking while moderate to large amounts produce positive results (Bales, 1956). Too dominant a dyadic relationship in terms of ACT level behavior may be perceived as an authoritarian trait which is not only U but UN, UNF, etc. Both for ACT and NON, the DB item (anxious, fearful, withholding) seems a very good opposite pole predictor. The best items from the other scales are included in the table. It is interesting to note that both Osgood's strong–weak and active–passive dimensions are relatively good correlates of the ACT U–D scores.

The Semantic Differential

A thorough comparison of the Wish scales with SYMLOG and of both of these with the items derived from the semantic differential will be provided in a

TABLE 16   Best Items for Predicting Scoring from Rating: Correlations of ACT and NON Level Summary Scores with Adjective Ratings of SYMLOG and Other Scales used in Group 1 (Interspersed Condition, Untrained Raters)

(a) ACT U–D

SYMLOG Rating Items		Other Items		
UN	.68	Wish	dominant, talkative	.69
U	.65		submissive, quiet, shy	−.70
UNF	.61			
D	−.60	Osgood	strong, forceful, hard	.65
DB	−.52		weak, timid, soft	−.68
NF	.48		lively, active, fast-moving	.52
			sluggish, passive, slow-moving	−.49

(b) ACT P–N

SYMLOG Rating Items		Other Items		
PF	.87	Wish	cooperative	.86
UPB	.84		competitive	−.86
DP	.84		cheerful	.73
N	−.83		gloomy	−.75
DPF	.76			
PB	.75	Osgood	sincere	.77
P	.75		insincere	−.64
DNF	−.65			

(c) ACT F–B

SYMLOG Rating Items		Other Items		
UF	.82	Wish	task-oriented	.79
F	.82		person-oriented	−.78
NF	.81		informal	−.57
UN	.57		formal	.63
UB	−.50 (−.63)			
B	−.43 (−.75)	Other	intelligent (Rosenberg and Sedlak, 1972)	.66
			neurotic	−.59

(d) NON U–D

SYMLOG Rating Items		Other Items		
U	.62	Wish	dominant	.42
DB	−.60		submissive	−.52
DNB	−.54			
D	−.52	Osgood	lively	.56
F	.47		sluggish	−.44
UN	.44			

(e) NON P–N

SYMLOG Rating Items		Other Items		
PF	.81	Wish	gloomy	−.74
DP	.79			
NF	−.76	Osgood	sincere	.75

continued

TABLE 16 (cont.)

N	−.73			
DPF	.75	*Other*	normal	.71
UPB	.71			
DN	−.71			
(f)	NON F–B			
	SYMLOG Rating Items		*Other Items*	
F	.75		*Wish* task-oriented	.78
NF	.77		person-oriented	−.71
UF	.71			
UN	.68		*Osgood* strong	.69
UNF	.54		sluggish	−.57
			Other intelligent	.55
			neurotic	− 45

NOTE: Correlations given are for Group 1. Groups 2 and 3 have comparable correlations and the same set of "best items" except when indicated by a number in parentheses after the Group 1 correlation is given. In such cases, the parenthetical correlation is from Group 3, the trained raters. In Groups 2 and 3 only SYMLOG items were used, so no comparison with other items is possible.

subsequent publication with Wish. For present purposes, it is important to note that some of the Wish items are particularly good correlates of the ACT and NON level scoring. Most striking in this regard is the Wish item for the B end of the F–B dimension. No SYMLOG item is as good a correlate of either ACT F–B or NON F–B as the Wish item "person-oriented, unproductive." This is true even though the Wish items have more typically been used as bipolar items rather than as unipolar items as in the present study. In the U–D dimension and the P–N dimension the Wish items are very comparable to the SYMLOG items. The similarity between the two scales derived from such different kinds of data tends to strengthen the sense of the validity of the dimensional schemes that the two approaches have developed independently.

The Wish scale items correlate highly with their cognate scales in the SYMLOG Rating procedure with the exception of the intense–superficial scale, which as we have pointed out seems to represent a characteristic distinct from those measured by the SYMLOG scales.

The removal of the scales from their usual bipolar environment does not seem to have a dramatic reorientation effect on the Wish scales. However, the Osgood scales are affected differently. Table 16 shows that both the items for strong–weak and the items from the active–passive dimensions correlated highly with ACT U–D. However, at the NON level differentiation does occur. "Active" is correlated with NON U–D, while "strong" is correlated highly with F–B. But the other ends of these scales behave differently. "Sluggish, passive, slow-moving" correlates with D and with B. But "weak, timid, soft" also correlates at a similar low level with both D and B. This lack of differentiation at one end of the two Osgood scales suggests that the "low" ends of his scales are differentiated only in the context provided by the opposite polar adjectives, and not in themselves.

Evidence for this nondifferentiation at the "low" end of the Osgood scales can be drawn from other parts of the study as well. For example, both "weak, timid, soft" and "sluggish, passive, slow-moving" are highly negatively correlated with the SYMLOG Rating scale for U–D. On the other hand, "Active" is highly positively correlated, while "strong" is not. All of this evidence could be faulted in that it involves comparisons with SYMLOG. However, the correlations among the Osgood items themselves demonstrate the problem in an even more striking way. It is clear that at the "high" end there is differentiation: "Strong" is only moderately correlated with "active." On the other hand, the adjective set "weak, timid, soft" correlates with "sluggish, passive, slow-moving" very highly ($r = .80$).

For reasons like this much attention is given in SYMLOG construction to the identification of individual adjective sets for each of the twenty-six combinations of the three dimensions. It is important to define the meaning of the dimensions at both the "high" end and the "low" ends and not simply to assume that the concepts of the opposite will emerge by themselves, by intuition, or by dictionary opposites. The Osgood adjectives are ordinarily paired in a bipolar fashion, so that this problem is sidestepped, but in order to achieve conceptual clarity at both ends of the scale we need to find adjectives that are differentiated when presented separately and not simply in the context of polar opposites.

Evaluative Tendencies of Raters and Scorers: A Suggestive Finding

The array of correlations heretofore presented provides a representation of the overall relationship between the three-dimensional locations of stimulus persons based on rating as compared to scoring methods. There is a relatively strong correlation between the two, especially for the P–N dimension but also for the other two dimensions when the appropriate NON scoring is factored in. However, there is one other intriguing question in the comparison of the two methods: Are there any systematic differences between raters and scorers in the way they locate the persons overall in the three-dimensional space?

Raters are asked to make global judgments about the stimulus persons after observing some selection of their interaction. They are not asked to dwell on the details, but to weigh global impressions, even in those cases where they have little behavior on which to base their judgments. Coders or scorers, on the other hand, are supposed to stick closely to the individual interaction event, not allowing themselves to be overly influenced by global impressions of the individuals they are observing. They are supposed to "stick to the facts" and allow the later summing of these scores to constitute the summary impression of the individual.

From a methodological point of view, it is not very easy to compare directly the locations of individuals derived from the two methods of observation—they have such different properties from so many points of view. However, making such a comparison, with all its pitfalls, is too interesting to be overlooked, so long as the results of the comparison are seen as generating hypotheses rather than attempting to prove or disprove them.

Table 17 represents an initial attempt to compare the overall evaluative tendencies of SYMLOG scorers and raters. The comparison numbers were generated by taking the grand means of each method of observation within each group of observers for each summary dimension and dividing that grand mean by the standard deviation of the means for all observing individuals in the sample. This seemed like the best approach, because the rating scales differ as to the number of points on the scale (a five-point scale for Groups 1 and 2; a three-point scale for Group 3), and they differ still further from the calculations that produce Scoring summary locations for the individually rated stimulus persons. (The main differences discussed emerge from other comparison methods as well.)

The most striking finding from this table is the tendency of the Raters to see the behavior as more Positive than do the Scorers. The global ratings in all three groups are quite substantially positive (almost half a standard deviation) while the Scorers see the behavior overall as neither Positive nor Negative at the ACT level and somewhat Negative at the NON level. This suggestive finding could be explained in a number of ways.

One possibility is that the retrospective raters are subject to some halo effect. They could be under the influence of a norm that obligates them to give Positive evaluations of other persons, in the absence of strong evidence to the contrary, or strong reason for criticism. Such an explanation stresses by implication the "objectivity" of an act-by-act approach that sticks closer to the actual behavior and involves fewer steps of inference from the actual interaction perceived.

An alternative possibility is to begin the analysis from precisely the reverse assumption: that the scorers do not have an adequate perspective on the interacting persons and cannot be said to give appropriate weights to individual acts in reaching a global impression of the individual. A simple procedure that weights all acts similarly may not capture cues as to the basic aspects of the relationship. Such an explanation treats the Ratings as the standard of evaluation, and prepares one to look for the determinants of bias in the Scoring methods.

Among *Scoring* methods including Interaction Process Analysis (Bales, 1950), the present SYMLOG method constitutes an intermediate point between these two extremes, as it does not involve recording every act as an equally weighted event but actually involves some process of selection on the part of the observers. It is possible that selecting significant events in the interaction is a process of selecting the more dramatic hostile events, to the exclusion of the more expected humdrum niceties of normal polite social interaction. The humdrum base-level interaction may give the essential key to the normal state of the relations between the interacting individuals, which is missed by concentrating on the more dramatic and attention-getting acts.

Some preliminary data reported orally by Wish suggest that in fact the act-by-act method, as represented, for example, by Interaction Process Analysis (Bales, 1950), produces a still more Positive bias than even the Rating data show. If this proves to be true, then the hypothesis would be strengthened that selecting events is a process that encourages emphasis on the nonnormative aspects of social communication, especially the expression of hostility.

TABLE 17 Evaluative Tendencies of Adjective Raters and Interaction Scorers: Mean Scores on Summary Directions Divided by Standard Deviations of the Mean Scores for Each Dimension

| | SYMLOG ADJECTIVE RATING | | | SYMLOG INTERACTION SCORING | |
	Group 1 Untrained Interspersed	Group 2 Untrained Consecutive	Group 3 Trained	ACT	NON
U–D	.292	.516	.356	.749	−.254
P–N	.412	.444	.424	.085	−.173
F–B	.333	.343	.338	.387	−.862

Nevertheless, the two forms of explanation remain intact without any immediate way of choosing between them. Persons who prefer to think of reality as a compilation of the micro-behavior of the actors will tend toward explanations that see the Raters as having some retrospective cognitive selection process or reinterpretation process whereby the world is made to seem more pleasant than it might actually be. Others might prefer to treat the Raters as having the more balanced approach, the long view, as it were. In this perspective, the Scorers are seen as prone to losing sight of the overall tenor of the relationship by concentration on the minutiae of the behavior.

This difference in perspective reflects methodological and value differences. However, the findings shown in Table 17, subject as they are to differences of interpretation, are important enough and ambiguous enough to warrant much fuller examination. For example, one characteristic of the stimulus material of this study (the Loud Family) is a predominance of Negative over Positive cooperative interaction. Perhaps the Raters are influenced by an assumption as to what family interaction should be like. Perhaps the Scorers are overinfluenced by the shock of some of the more open confrontations between family members. One would like to see whether the positivity–negativity bias holds up in other studies with other stimulus persons or groups.

It should be noted that the present finding fits our more impressionistic sense of differences between the perceptions of group members and those of SYMLOG Interaction Scorers. We have the impression that the Ratings group members make of each other tend to crowd people into the Positive side of the Field Diagram, while the SYMLOG Interaction Scoring seems to yield a wider distribution. Second, group members overall tend to see the group mean as farther on the Positive side than do their non–group-member observers. These impressions suggest that group members may be making their judgments under a norm of a Positive Rating bias, which may not operate to the same extent at the behavioral scoring level.

To summarize then, we have several different, and possibly competing, hypotheses. One suggests that Raters tend retroactively to make their world more

Positive than direct experience would suggest. Another suggests that group-member Raters generally accept a norm of not seeing others in too Negative a light. These explanations may compete, in turn, with the idea that Scorers are "biased." Either they are selecting (in SYMLOG Scoring) the more hostile interaction from a pool of events that contains overall the same ratio of P to N that is present for the Raters in their global assessment, or the Scorers are unable to grasp the context in which the behavior they are rating takes place. The context, of which the Raters are more aware, tends to alter the meaning of the interaction (in the present instance, in the direction of softening of the impact of the specific events). The context is not recorded in the act-by-act record or in the SYMLOG Scoring record of the events.

To evaluate these various hypotheses would require some careful comparison of Scoring methods involving different degrees of selectivity on the part of observers. In addition, we would need variation in the kinds of stimulus material that is Scored and Rated.

The differences in the U–D dimension do not seem to require so many hypotheses as those in the P–N dimension. The Scorer is emphasizing what he or she sees in the interaction. Dominant acts seem a priori more likely to be attended to, and also likely to crowd out the acts of more submissive persons, so that "talking a lot" and "doing a lot" are characteristics of the Upward part of the space. On the other hand, the Raters have to make the same number of judgments about the more silent and less active people as about the active ones. For this reason their attention is more evenly divided between U and D. An important aspect of the training of SYMLOG Scorers is learning to direct their attention away from the most frequent talkers to focus on the less active members, so as to score their nonverbal responses to group events and to group members who are more active. It is clear from Table 17 that the nonverbal behavior scores are especially likely to emphasize the B direction more than the ACT scores and, to a lesser extent, the D direction and the N direction.

Finally, it should be stressed again that these differences between rating and scoring occur despite the fact that, overall, there is a high correlation between rating and scoring, especially in the P–N dimension. Thus, we must look for the explanation either in some aspect of the overall processes involved in the two forms of observation or look for a methodological explanation that will make the differences irrelevant.

What is intriguing is that the findings reviewed here seem to reflect larger issues about the appropriate units for studying communication and interpersonal interaction. The results suggest that data must be gathered at different points on the spectrum of time spans involved, from the perception of micro-units of behavior, recorded and evaluated almost simultaneously with the behavior itself, to the emotion recollected in tranquility some time later when both present perspective and retrospective reconstruction have had a chance to operate.

Chapter 33

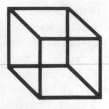

An Illustration of
SYMLOG Case Analysis:
The Loud Family

Throughout this part of the book, the focus has been on the formal aspects of SYMLOG reliability and validity. The basic properties of SYMLOG Rating and Interaction Scoring have been examined and compared with one another. In the development of SYMLOG and in the progressive refinement of it, another form of validation played a paramount role. SYMLOG is designed to provide concrete assistance to group members and group leaders, as well as the outside observer and researcher, in elucidating phenomena in a particular group or family. The SYMLOG generated data should provide valuable clues as to patterns of interaction in the group and ideas on how to induce change in directions desired by leaders and members. Such validation is not easily demonstrable except through case illustrations and case study models such as that developed in Part I.

As indicated, the primary purpose of this part of the study undertaken with M. Wish and Bell Laboratories was the testing of the reliability of SYMLOG and elucidation of the relation between Scoring and Rating. However, the data are derived from a particular group, the Loud family, and this group is amenable to case analysis so far as our data reflect it faithfully. Here we have an example drawn from a context other than that of a self-analytic group and studied in a laboratory-like situation, rather than through live observation. Furthermore. many SYMLOG users may wish to examine the use of the method for family studies and this possibility is illustrated here. Bonny Parke is engaged in an extensive study using SYMLOG with children in family and classroom interaction. The study uses field settings and a special Adjective Rating Form suitable for use by children.) The present study uses observers rather than participants and employs both Rating and Scoring data.

The scenes so carefully edited and chosen for the study at Bell Laboratories are not a random sample of the scenes in the hundreds of hours of film originally made of this family interaction. Nor can it be said with certainty that even the original large sample fully represented the family interaction. The scenes were chosen with a keen eye to interaction liveliness and emotional variety, and this may emphasize conflict over calmer cooperation. Furthermore, all scenes used in the study are dyadic, excluding any subgroup interactions or full family interactions. Some family members are underrepresented in the scenes.

Since we are interested only in using the data for illustrative purposes, it might seem unnecessary to enumerate the problems of sampling in drawing conclusions about the Loud family as such. However, most studies of ongoing group interaction will also proceed from limited data, and with still more limited observation of those instances of interaction studied. The results deduced from a systematic method of group analysis cannot be more valid than the quality of the data input that the method must process. The practical test of a systematic observation method may be as much in its ability to generate ideas about the group from limited and imperfect data as in its ability to produce a completely representative picture.

In addition to its function as an illustration, the present analysis also helps to put in perspective the more formal results on reliability and the relation between scoring and rating. These results are, after all, based on a particular set of data, and the peculiarities of those data may affect the conclusions about SYMLOG described above.

Figure 37 provides a standard two-dimensional (P–N by F–B) Field Diagram of all the individuals in the twenty scenes in the study. Standard scores are plotted so that the diagram for Rating from the five-point scale can be compared to the diagrams produced from Interaction Scoring. The numbers next to the names indicate scene number, so that positions of two persons in the same scene may be compared, e.g. Bill (13) and Pat (13) represent the rated position of the husband and wife in the scene in which she ejects him from their house. Some scenes represent interaction between a family member and a non–family member. In addition there are three scenes of interaction from another Bell Laboratories study, which are included here for comparison purposes.

The range of positions that each person occupies is wide enough to suggest caution in interpretation (of these or other data). The estimate of the interactive "personality" of the individual should always be carefully hedged, with indication given of the range of interaction situations which form the basis of the generalization. SYMLOG ratings of individuals at different points in time offer an opportunity for studying the consistency of personality across time and different interaction settings.

The Field Diagram also suggests a possibility of analysis of individuals and group interaction through the calculation of distance in the space. For example, it may be important to know whether a particular person is characteristically close to or far from the person with whom he or she is interacting. Pat (the mother) is always distant from her sons (Lance, Grant, and Kevin) in the F–B dimension, and from Bill (her husband) in the P–N dimension. The use of distance matrices as an approach to group structure is a branch of SYMLOG analysis that will be reported elsewhere. Suffice it to indicate for present purposes that such an approach could provide mathematical representation of such concepts as cohesion of a group, isolation of members and the like. Distance analyses are probably best carried out separately for the U–D dimension, while the P–N and F–B dimensions may need to be combined for most meaningful analysis. Coalitions

FIGURE 37   Locations of Persons in Each Scene, American Family Study:
Data Derived from Group 1 Ratings (Standard Scores:
1 S.D. = Scale 9)

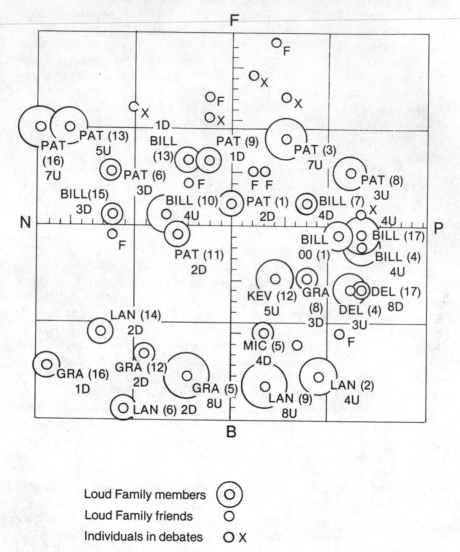

Loud Family members	⊙	
Loud Family friends	○	
Individuals in debates	○ X	

can involve persons of different levels of dominance. On the other hand, it is important to know whether persons in coalitions in similar locations in the F–B and P–N plane tend to be equal on the U–D dimension in some parts of the field and unequal in other parts.

Figure 37 has a number of striking features. Most prominent is the underpopulated of the PF quadrant by family members. In self-analytic groups this has typically been the most densely populated quadrant. In this case, only three of the twenty-seven points representing family members lie in the PF quadrant. Of the thirteen points representing non-family members, six are in this quadrant. These comparisons suggest that the finding is not likely to be an artifact of the form of Rating (videotape) or of this large sample of raters. Casual observation of the Field Diagrams in other parts of this volume will confirm how unusual this low density is.

The underpopulated quadrant represents the cooperative work of the group toward shared goals. It is such solidarity in the pursuit of common tasks under agreed leadership that is most conspicuously lacking in the scenes included of the Loud family. The lack of a clear pole of legitimate authority may account for the low consensus on the meaning of U–D in these data.

The second striking feature in the diagram is that all points representing the parents (Pat and Bill) are farther F than each and every point representing the children (Grant, Kevin, Delilah, Michelle, Lance). This nonoverlapping distribution is strong evidence of a family "characteristic." The evidence is strengthened by pointing out that prior to standardizing the data, each parent point was in the F half of the space and each child in the B half. This may indicate a schism between the values propounded by the parents and the children's value preferences, at least so far as their values are expressed in their behavior. Third, the main concentrations of points are in the NF and PB quadrants, indicating that these two form the focal points for the main polarization of family conflict. The conflict seems to be between authoritarian demands of the mother and their rejection by the children in the pursuit of individual pleasure. Whatever P behavior is exhibited by the children is more in the form of joking or playing around than through camaraderie in common goals. There is much outright avoidance of the conflict-filled area of group cohesion around performance of family tasks.

Fourth, the overall distribution shows no UPF leadership and no examples of P behavior very far out in the F side of the space. The range of N is wider, including even some extreme cases.

Fifth, the most F points in the Diagram are those of nonfamily actors. Again we are dealing with a family characteristic (at least as represented in these scenes) and not an artifact or observer bias.

In summary, the Loud family as it appears in these scenes, with its density of behavior in N and B and paucity of PF, stands in stark contrast to the norm in self-analytic groups. Occasionally there have been groups with strong PF–NF conflicts with both of these quadrants well populated, or PF–NB polarizations, but the present distribution is rare for groups with a self-analytic emphasis, though it may not be so rare in conflict-laden families.

The individual scenes also provide valuable information. Bill (the father) is closest to the other participant when it is his daughter Delilah. With her, his behavior is at its most P and is more than usually B for him. Pat has only one P rating with family members. In that single case she is consoling her son Grant after an accident, and that also is the single instance in which he emerges as P. It is with the same son Grant that she has the most N scene of the entire set. Her only other P scene is with a friend outside the family. Bill, on the other hand, expresses his anger in two scenes with non-family members. Even in the scene of being ejected from the house he is N but still D. He is most often U in the

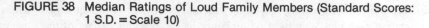

FIGURE 38   Median Ratings of Loud Family Members (Standard Scores: 1 S.D. = Scale 10)

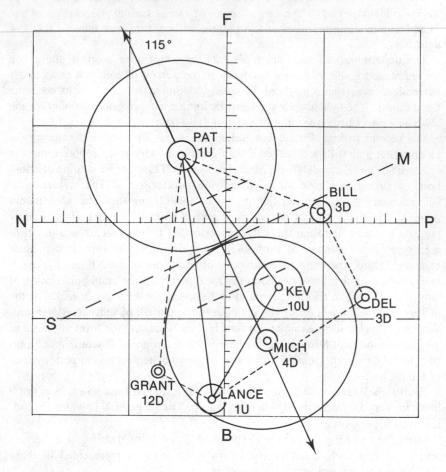

fatherly scenes with his daughter Delilah. From these limited data, it would seem that Pat is able to express her more P side outside the family, while Bill can express his upset and anger only outside its confines.

The analysis so far has been on the basis of plotting individual scene ratings. The standard Field Diagram uses summary ratings for each person and applies the general hypotheses of polarization and unification at the level of family infrastructure. We can construct a standard diagram for the Loud family, based on the median of the mean ratings of each family member over all the scenes in which that member appears. Figure 38 presents such a diagram. It stresses again the points made above about the F direction of parents and the B of children, and about the absence of UPF leadership.

The polarization shows Pat, the mother, standing against the children. The polarization is NF versus PB, or F versus B. In this polarization Bill emerges as the possible mediator of the family conflict, although the fact that he was ejected from the house by Pat indicates that for her at least he may have been the

FIGURE 39 Median Ratings of Loud Family Members: First Alternate
Polarization (Standard Scores: 1 S.D. = Scale 10)

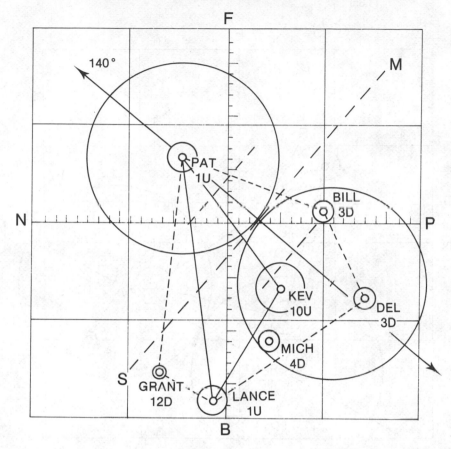

scapegoat. Grant and Delilah remain slightly outside the polarization circles. These imperfections of fit suggest an alternative polarization shown as Figure 39. This analysis of the polarization leaves Pat again in isolation in one circle but would oppose her to Bill, Delilah, and Kevin, leaving Michelle close to the latter group, with Lance and Grant near the scapegoat-mediator line. Such a rotation is slightly less convincing technically and also seems less incisive as an interpretation of the major family dynamics as they appear in these scenes.

A third possibility emerges more clearly from the Field Diagram based on Scoring summaries rather than on ratings. This diagram is shown as Figure 40. Michelle is located quite differently in this diagram (data on Michelle come from only one scene). The result of this location of the overlay is to place Bill, Delilah and Kevin as a subgroup in one circle and Michelle, Grant, and Lance as an opposed subgroup on the Negative side. This leaves Pat near the scapegoat-mediator line. This suggestion about group interaction is especially interesting, because there is no scene in which father and sons interact. In one very Positive scene, Bill, the father, and his daughter Delilah interact. In another scene, Bill is

FIGURE 40   Median Scores at ACT Level of Loud Family Members: Second
Alternate Polarization (Standardized Percentages: 1 S.D. = Scale
11.35)

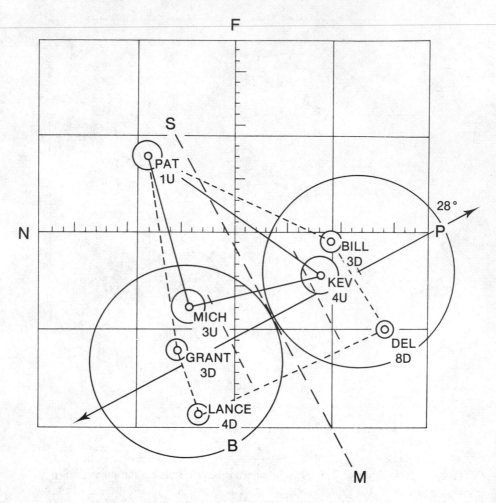

shown in a very Negative conflict with his wife Pat. In still another Negative
scene, Pat, the mother, confronts all the children. One would very much like to
know whether the father and sons Lance and Grant also conflict (as the diagram
suggests) and whether they interact infrequently. In the group of scenes selected
the evidence suggests two subsystems of Pat versus children and Pat versus Bill
and Delilah.

Each polarization presents a hypothesis about the pattern of family interaction. The best-fit polarization should not be the only one examined. Others may
also provide some insights into less dominant themes in the interactive network.
Communication sampling may have affected the prominence of different
"themes" in group history. Alternative polarizations may also provide ideas
about changes that a group may experience, or changes that, through directed

FIGURE 41   Adjective Ratings Received by PAT and BILL in Different
                    Scenes: Naive Subjects Rating (Standard Scores: 1 S.D. = Scale

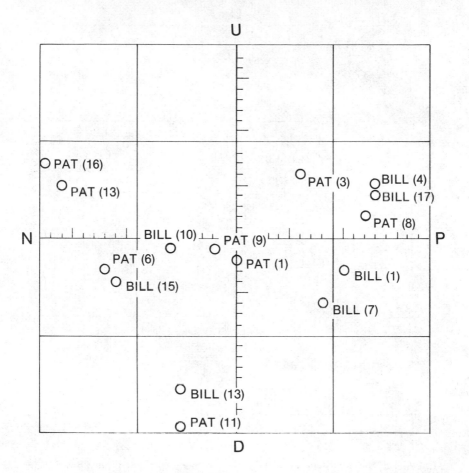

intervention, they might be led to experience. In a long-run complex group, different sets of issues and different situations may bring to the fore alternative polarization possibilities. And in a group with persons and subgroups so nearly triadically located, as in this one, unstable fluctuation from one polarization to another may indeed be characteristic, in the manner described by Simmel for groups of three persons.

For some purposes it may also be useful to plot separately the positions of persons at each of the different Levels of Scoring. Figures 41 and 42 present plotted Ratings and ACT and NON level Scores for the parents (in standard score form). For demonstration purposes the diagrams use the U–D, P–N dimensions rather than the standard Field Diagram dimensions (P–N by F–B). Scenes that produce marked discrepancies across levels can be picked out for special analysis. (In other applications, individuals with strongly contradictory level locations could be singled out for attention.)

FIGURE 42 ACT Level Codings Received by PAT and BILL in Different
Scenes: Trained Scorers (Standard Scorers: 1 S.D. = Scale 9)

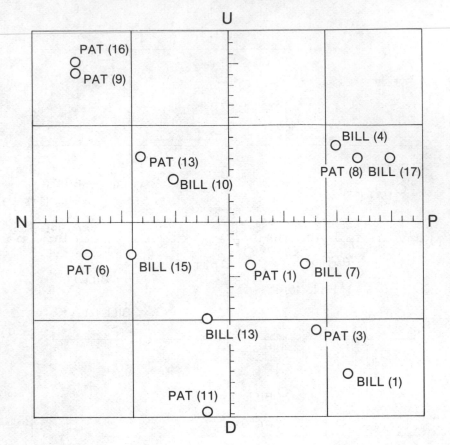

In general, the locations produced by Ratings are similar to those produced by ACT level Scoring, but with occasional marked discrepancies. For example, the ACT level Scoring of Pat in Scene 9 is in an extreme UN location, whereas the Rating is close to the origin. In this case, the NON Scoring is quite close to the Ratings at the origin. Another marked discrepancy between Rating and ACT level and NON level Scoring can be found in the point Pat (3), a scene in which Pat was interacting with one of her nonfamily friends. In Figure 41, the Ratings, Pat (3) emerges as moderately U, while in Figure 42, representing the ACT level, she is quite far D. This contradiction between Rating and Scoring is put in a different light by reference to Figure 43, representing the NON level. Here Pat (3) is far U, more U in fact than any other point plotted in this NON level diagram. It appears that the Rating has compromised the discrepancy between the ACT level dominance and the NON-verbal level dominance.

We are reminded of the more general finding that the U–D dimension is the one dimension most affected by the combination of the NON and ACT levels for predicting Rating outcome. On this dimension, raters seem to be utilizing infor-

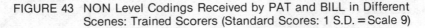

FIGURE 43 NON Level Codings Received by PAT and BILL in Different
Scenes: Trained Scorers (Standard Scores: 1 S.D. = Scale 9)

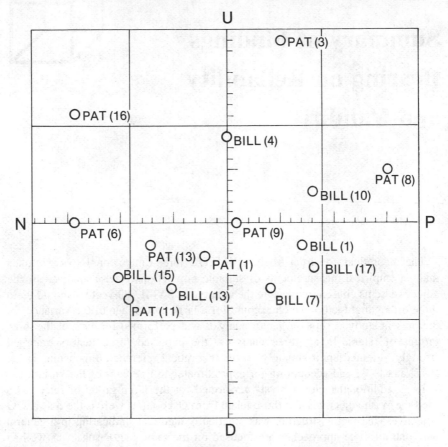

mation from both nonverbal and verbal cues. It may be that particular settings or interaction styles require both the ACT level and the nonverbal cues for successful understanding of the communication.

In the absence of a detailed description of the actual family, it is difficult to evaluate the hypotheses gained from the SYMLOG analyses. From these few scenes it is possible, as we have seen, to derive a far-reaching set of hypotheses about the family and its issues. However, it is not possible, nor is it in the present context desirable, to do more than use this as illustration of the idea-generating character of SYMLOG.

The systematic findings presented some problems with the clarity of the U–D dimension in this study. The peculiarities of this family interaction, as indicated here, are such that no UPF leadership exists. It may be that without such leadership to anchor the meaning of the U rating and scoring, the clarity of this dimension recedes. On the other hand, the F–B conflict in this family is very marked, and that may have produced more clarity and hence reliability of this dimension than is usually the case.

Chapter 34

Summary of Findings
Bearing on Reliability
and Validity

The theoretical construct of the SYMLOG three-dimensional space implies that, in empirical measurements of suitable populations, factor analyses of the adjective items chosen to measure the twenty-six SYMLOG vectors should yield three orthogonal factors which account for a large percentage of the variance. In the present study, a separate factor analysis was performed for each of the three groups of raters. In all three analyses, the expected three factors emerged strongly, oriented approximately on the theoretical reference dimensions U–D, P–N, and F–B, and accounting for approximately 85 percent of the variance.

In an additional factor analysis performed for the large group of raters who used the Wish adjectives and those taken from Osgood, as well as the SYMLOG adjectives, the factor structure was practically identical, indicating in a general way that all three approaches are focused on the same factor space, as we had supposed.

The expected factor structure was clearer and stronger among the trained raters than among the naive, indicating that training makes a difference in the way the raters understand or use the adjective items.

An additional factor appeared, as predicted from Wish's previous work—a factor that seems to be tapped by the adjective "intense." This "intensity" factor appears to be weaker than the other three, in Wish's previous studies as well as in the SYMLOG twenty-six-item space. Whether this fourth factor is an element of "quantitative intensity" that operates within each of the qualitative directions of the SYMLOG space (U, D, P, N, F, B) or whether it is an additional qualitative dimension is not yet clear. In either case, it does not call into question the appropriateness of placing a major descriptive emphasis on the first three factors, which correspond empirically to the three theoretical SYMLOG dimensions, U–D, P–N, and F–B.

The theoretical construct of the SYMLOG space assumes that the three dimensions are logically independent of each other (theoretically orthogonal). However, it is assumed that they may be correlated to some degree in particular ways that are diagnostic of particular populations of persons rated or particular populations of raters. In the present study, the eighteen-item dimensional scales are nearly orthogonal to each other. The U–D dimension is correlated positively with the P–N dimension with an average correlation of .20 over the three groups of raters. The U–D dimension is also correlated with the F–B dimension with an average correlation of about .18. The P–N dimension is slightly negatively correlated with the F–B dimension, with an average correlation of −.13.

The theoretical construct of the SYMLOG space of three orthogonal dimensions implies that empirical measures of the opposite poles of each of the dimensions in a given population will be highly negatively correlated with each other. Scales made by adding together the nine items that are supposed to measure each of the directions U, D, P, N, F, B show the polar ends of each of the three dimensions to be highly negatively correlated with each other. The P and N poles show the highest negative correlation, an average correlation over the three groups of raters, of −.88. The F and B poles show an average negative correlation of −.68, while the U and D poles show a negative correlation of −.67. Both of the latter two polarities are less marked than one might expect, and improvement of the adjective items as shown in Appendix C is expected to increase the negative correlations between poles.

Not all of the six directions were measured equally well by the twenty-six items actually used. The P direction was measured best, with an average reliability coefficient (based on Gulliksen's formula) of .95. The N direction was next most reliably measured, with a coefficient of .86. The F direction was next with a coefficient of .66, followed by the B direction with a coefficient of .65. The U direction followed with a coefficient of .59, and the D direction was completely unsatisfactory with a coefficient of only .14. It was obvious that certain items needed reformulation or replacement, and this has been done with much careful thought, but as yet without retest for the Adjective Rating Form that appears in Appendix C. It is not clear whether the directional scales for F, B, U, and D can be made sufficiently reliable for independent use. In practical use, we typically do not try to measure the two poles of a given dimension separately but combine them into one dimensional measure, based on eighteen items. Combined into the eighteen-item scales for the three dimensions, but omitting the three worst items, the reliability coefficient for the P–N dimension was .95, for the F–B dimension, .80, and for the U–D dimension, .77. These improvements by omission of the worst items imply that one should be able to reach the desired levels of reliability by item improvement for the three dimensional scales U–D, P–N, and F–B, though not perhaps for all six directional scales.

Although some individual items were not near enough to the vector in the space they were meant to measure (and have been replaced in Appendix C), it is clear that the individual items (and not simply the summary scales) were highly similar in meaning from one group of raters to another. Naive raters using the twenty-six adjective sets designed for the study were split into two groups of sixteen raters each, and the ratings produced by each group of raters on each item were summed for each person/scene. The correlations for given adjective items between the two groups of raters over the N of forth person/scenes ranged from .74 to .93, with a mean of .88 across all twenty-six adjective items. When the items are added into the six summary scales, U, D, P, N, F, B, the reliability coefficients expressing agreement between groups of raters in the present study are very high, ranging from .95 to .99. And when the six scales are added together into the three dimensional scales actually used for most measurement, U-D, P-N, and F-B, the coefficients are all .98 or .99.

An important finding for practical use is the estimate derived from the data that one can reach satisfactory levels of reliability using the results of comparatively small groups of raters. For the nine-item scales, U, D, P, N, F, B, a group of six or seven raters added together will probably reach a reliability of .80. And for the eighteen-item scales, U-D, P-N, and F-B, one is likely to reach this criterion by summing the results of a group of three to five raters.

The hypothesis that the three-dimensional SYMLOG space derives from relative similarities in the way individuals perceive and react evaluatively to the acts of others implies that there should be similarities between the global retrospective ratings one group of raters may make of group members and the act-by-act scorings that other raters may assign, using the concepts of the three SYMLOG dimensions applied directly to each act scored. The results of the two methods, Ratings and Scoring, do indeed tend to converge, and thus each tends to give increased confidence in the validity of the other. The indices obtained from ACT level Scores of the group of observers were found to be substantially correlated with the global Ratings made by three separate groups of Raters, over the forty person/scenes of the present study. The average correlation for the U-D dimension was .70. The comparable correlation for the P-N dimension was .90, and for the F-B dimension, .86. The indices obtained from the NON-verbal level Scores are a little less highly related to the global ratings than are the ACT level scores, but they are still substantially, and perhaps surprisingly, high. The comparable correlations are, for the U-D dimension, .69, for the P-N dimension, .77, and for the F-B dimension, .75.

In general, the SYMLOG Interaction Scoring indices tend to be less reliable in the present study than those obtained from the global Ratings, as one must expect, since the Scoring procedure makes many fine distinctions and produces many more indices as to behavioral level, image content, and pro and con value judgments. The fine qualitative distinctions in the Scoring require more time for the observer to make and record. The observer must decide which acts to score and which to omit. Such selection introduces unreliability, as observers will inevitably select somewhat differently. In short, with SYMLOG Scoring, some reliability of measurement is sacrificed in order to obtain a greater number of fine-grained qualitative distinctions in what is measured. The rationale for this sacrifice is that one obtains compensating gains in the richness and relevance of the data for use in feedback to group members, training in observation, development of theory, and integration of theory with observational measures and with practice.

In spite of the sacrifice of some reliability for some of the SYMLOG Scoring variables, the ACT level is very satisfactory. Correlations of the summary scores of one group of eight observers with another group of eight over the forty person/scenes show reliability coefficients of .88 to .96 for the dimensions U-D, P-N, and F-B at the ACT level. The NON-verbal level is less reliable, with coefficients ranging from .80 to .90. The CON level of imagery is about the same, with coefficients from .82 to .89, while the PRO level has a low coefficient of .64 for the U–D scale, but coefficients of .80 and .93 for the P–N and F–B scales, respectively.

The ACT level scores are the most reliable, and the number of observers required to reach a satisfactory level of reliability (.80) for that level is practical for a rotating observer team. For the P–N dimension, a group of three observers will probably be large enough, and for the F–B dimension, a group of five. Although the U–D dimension is not satisfactorily measured with the index used in the present study, indications are that when total amount of participation is used as a part of the U–D index, as it is in practical use (see Appendixes J and S), a group of about five observers will give sufficiently reliable results.

Our comparative study of the Rating method and the Interaction Scoring method has thus, on the whole, produced very reassuring results. The theoretical construct of the three-dimensional SYMLOG space is strongly supported by the findings from both methods, and the two methods tend to converge, implying that each method produces valid measures, although each produces some independent information. The interobserver reliabilities are high enough for each of the two methods to reassure us that groups of a practical size for rotating observer teams can give results of satisfactory reliability.

In Part IV, uses of the two methods in feedback to group members and in the training of observers will be discussed in detail. Some of the ways in which information produced by each of them, and by comparisons between them, may be used to generate higher-order inferences concerning the personalities of individuals and their relationships as group members.

Part IV

The Use of SYMLOG for Training in Observation and Feedback to Group Members

Robert F. Bales, Stephen P. Cohen,
and Stephen A. Williamson

Chapter 35

Feedback of the Results
of Intermember Ratings

In this chapter we shall devote particular attention to the feedback of results of intermember ratings, but by way of introduction it will be helpful to consider briefly what we mean by feedback and why it is considered important in the development and change of individual personalities and groups.

There is a natural order of events in a feedback cycle, which may be elaborated in many ways, according to the specific purposes of the group and the kind of observations made. A feedback process as applied to the guidance of interpersonal behavior in a group is a sequence of events in which: (1) Characteristics of the interpersonal behavior during one period of time are observed, and (2) the observations, arranged and interpreted by some kind of theory, are evaluated and used to modify or guide certain aspects of the behavior during a subsequent period of time. These two steps may be called a single "cycle" of feedback.

When members rate each other on the SYMLOG Adjective Rating Form and the data are summarized, given back to the members, and discussed, this sequence of events may be considered to constitute a single cycle of feedback. When SYMLOG Scoring is used by a team of observers in the format of a group psychology course, the cycle of feedback is repeated each week for about ten to twelve weeks. When members learn to switch their attention and discussion content, within a single given meeting, from the production of material to be analyzed (which may be content at the levels of FAN, SOC, and SIT) in the first part of the meeting to analysis and interpretation of that material in terms of its interpersonal relevance (content at the levels of SELF, OTHER, and GROUP), they may be said to be going through a cycle of feedback within the course of the single meeting.

But the cycle may take place over still smaller time spans. When individual members learn to use their observations and knowledge in the natural course of their participation and to modify their emerging behavior accordingly, they may be said to have *internalized* the feedback process and to have made it continuously cyclical, rather than intermittently cyclical, within their own mental processes. The aim of externally induced episodes of feedback, generally speaking, is to help the individuals in a group to develop internal continuously cyclical feedback. To the extent that this is realized, individuals may be said to have learned about group process and about their own behavior. Internalization of the feedback process in which we learn with others takes place naturally in all social interaction to some extent and is the means by which we are all socialized and develop a sense of self, other, the group, society, and social norms, as George Herbert Mead so well describes (Mead, 1934).

We suppose that individual learning, individual behavior change, and change in group roles and group dynamics take place more or less concurrently within interacting groups and are dependent upon each other—various aspects of the total interaction process limit or facilitate other aspects. The maintenance of change in desired directions, once started, will presumably require continuation of the feedback guidance within individual personalities and in the content of interpersonal communications. It may require periodic reinforcement and further articulation by more explicit and formal procedures, by planned group events and ritual enactments in the natural social case, or by observational, evaluative, and rational reassessment of some kind.

We should not assume that a single experience of learning, either of the single individual or of all the individuals in the group in interaction with each other, will automatically generalize to other times and situations in which the group will find itself. The degree of generalization is problematic, and repetition of the learning events across a range of situations and times is typically necessary to develop and establish new norms in a group. In learning theory, of course, the importance of repetition and generalization is well recognized. And in the theory of psychotherapy the importance of "working through" is also well recognized. Perhaps repetition and generalization have not been so clearly recognized as important for the establishment of new group roles and group norms, but surely they are important here also. Mead's work on games and rituals also represents this repetition and generalization process in the development of the self and the concept of the "generalized other."

One should not assume that individuals will automatically carry over learning or behavior change from one group to another. The learning or behavior change is presumably at first specific to the given group and the individual's role in it, and its generalization to other groups is problematic. It may be that, when learning and behavior changes are consistent with the general preexisting dynamics of the individual personality, they are more likely to be retained and generalized spontaneously, but when they go counter to preexisting dynamics, they may tend to be extinguished unless reinforced in other settings. Generalization to other situations and retention of new patterns may be called "personality change." Learning and behavior change in a given group do not necessarily amount to personality change, but sometimes, presumably, they begin a process of personality change.

We should not expect too much of a single cycle of feedback as represented by an application of the SYMLOG Adjective Rating procedure with group discussion of the results. But our experience indicates that it is nearly always an eye-opening procedure in some respects, and it may be expected to raise into salience many aspects of individual personalities, of the group, and the particular interpersonal relationships within it. These newly salient aspects may then be subject to further analysis, evaluation, and attempts to change, if members are willing and able to do so.

The degree to which various kinds of problems may be brought to light or glossed over can be controlled to some extent in advance. One can exercise some degree of control by choice of the kind of summaries and detailed breakdowns that are returned to members, by making some data concerning individuals available only to them as individuals, by planning and controlling the way in which the feedbak session is conducted, and perhaps in other ways. The same kinds of considerations that apply to the optimum conduct of leadership, teaching, and psychotherapy generally apply to the gathering and feedback of interpersonal ratings. One should take care and should apply all that one knows about the psychology of these processes, and not assume that because a standard method is employed some standard degree of protection against the risks of the process is guaranteed.

When using the Adjective Rating Form, judgments of the frequency with which a given person shows a particular kind of behavior are usually not very hard for the rater to make. They are not nearly so hard to make, for example, as a judgment of whether one "likes" the person or not. But the individual items gain in the force of information they carry as they are aggregated into dimensional scores for each of the three dimensions, instead of the twenty-six discrete items. The information gains in force again as the dimensional scores are aggregated down the columns of the interpersonal rating matrix to obtain a representation of the way in which the person rated is seen on the average by all others. There is another gain in the force of the information conveyed as the dimensional scores representing one individual's perceptions of others are aggregated along the row of the interpersonal rating matrix to obtain a representation of each rater's average perceptual biases or rating sets. (An interpersonal matrix in which this may be visualized is shown as Figure 55, Appendix I. It will also be helpful to read Polley's description of his computer program for the analysis of interpersonal matrices in Appendix T.)

By the aggregation of information as just described, one obtains numbers representing both the rater's rating bias (the average at the end of the matrix row), and the average way in which the person rated is seen (the average at the bottom of the matrix column). Both factors can now be taken into account in extracting more exact information from the ratings contained in a particular cell of the matrix. That is, one can compute the way in which the particular rater, JOHN, would be *expected* to see the particular person rated, MARY, if the only determinants were JOHN's general rating bias and MARY's average rating received. But we also known how JOHN *actually* rated MARY—that is, the numbers actually in the cell. We can, then, determine the *difference* between the way we *expect* JOHN to rate MARY, given all the aggregated information of the matrix, and the way JOHN *actually* rated MARY. This difference represents what we may call JOHN's *unique* perception of MARY. If the difference is great (compared to the other differences found in the same matrix), we can say that JOHN has an *unusual perception* of MARY.

In order to compute JOHN's *unique perception* of MARY, the following procedure may be followed for each of the three dimensions. We start with a separate matrix for each of the three dimensions, with numbers in the cells that represent U minus D, P minus N, or F minus B. The steps for a given matrix on one dimension now follow: (1) Find JOHN's average rating of all members, including his own EXPECTED rating of himself, by adding all the cell contents along the horizontal row and then dividing by the number of cells. (2) Find MARY's average rating received, including her own EXPECTED, by adding the cell contents down the vertical column for MARY as a receiver of ratings, and then dividing by the number of cells. (3) Find the grand average of ratings given and received in the whole matrix by adding all the row averages together and dividing by the number of rows, and check this grand average by adding all the column averages together and dividing by the number of columns. (4) From the contents of the cell reporting the raw rating that JOHN gives MARY, subtract JOHN's average rating of all members; then *from* this residual, (5) subtract MARY's average rating received, and then, *to* this residual, (6) add in the grand mean. The resulting number will represent JOHN's *unique* perception of MARY, with his rating tendency and her receiving tendency taken out. If the number is very high, either in the plus or the minus direction, as compared to the other unique perceptions in the matrix, then one may say that JOHN has an *unusual* perception of MARY. We do not as yet have an accepted standard as to what should be considered "very high," but an arbitrary cutoff point that seems appropriate for the particular feedback session may be adopted.

By the time we have computed the *unusual perceptions,* the processing of the information we have received from the ratings is quite far advanced. In our experience, this level of information is psychologically quite powerful. It typically goes beyond what group members in general have recognized and often goes beyond what the rater has consciously recognized about his or her perception of the particular other person. When a member of a self-analytic group is asked in a feedback session to try to account for the *unusual perception* he or she appears to have of a particular other member, the reply is often something like this: "I don't know what it is. It's something about her. Maybe it's because she reminds me of my sister. My sister was always trying to get better grades in school than I did, and I didn't like it." Or, "I realize now that when Mary told about leaving her husband, I thought, 'She's just like my mother.' My mother left my father, you know, and I always held it against her.'" Or, "He reminds me of my father. I am afraid he will disapprove of me." In other words, the *unusual perceptions* quite frequently turn out to be "transferences" in the psychological sense, familiar in group therapy as in individual psychotherapy. In our experience, it is possible to surface more instances of transference in one application of the rating procedure, carried to this depth of analysis, than will spontaneously surface in a whole term of less focused self-analytic group interaction.

Not all cases of unusual perceptions turn out to be apparent cases of transference. Sometimes the unusual perception turns out to be the result of some unusual outside contact or observation, which has given the rater a kind of information not available to other group members. Or the unusual perception may be traced by the rater back to something the particular person has said or done in the group that had special significance to the rater but was unnoticed or barely remembered by others. But these instances are also generally emotionally loaded for the person who has retained the unusual perception and appear to be particularly good entry points for deeper analysis of the individual personality, if this is desired.

If one desires to intensify the process of analysis in the group by making the data on unusual perceptions available, it is a great help to have a computer analysis of the matrix, as provided by Richard Polley's program (Appendix T). The unusual perceptions may be located by noting the most extreme cases of difference between the expected and the actual ratings that appear in the matrix, or in the ratings of each group member, and obtaining the agreement of group members to discuss each one in turn. This is our usual procedure after both the first and the second ratings in a course on group psychology. A less intensive procedure is to concentrate attention on the general rating biases of particular members, as shown by their row totals on the matrix. This procedure gives useful results but seems to be less likely to turn up usable insights than concentration on the unusual perceptions the rater has of particular other persons. It seems that the rater is more likely to be able to pinpoint the reason for a particular unusual perception than for a general rating tendency, since the cues in the behavior, appearance, or content presented by the particular other person are more specific and more likely to lead into historically or developmentally important memories for the rater.

An alternative procedure to the matrix analysis, which accomplishes basically the same thing but in graphic rather than numerical form, is to make a properly expanded field diagram of the way in which each individual member sees the field, as well as a properly expanded group average field diagram, and to compare each individual diagram with every other and with the group average diagram. Discrepancies in the way particular members see particular other members are easily spotted by this procedure and can be made the subject of specific discussion in the feedback session, as described above. The individual diagrams given in Chapter 12, Part I, will provide illustrations; see, for example, SARA's rating of SUE, and SUE's rating of SARA. This example is also useful in pointing up the fact that unusual perceptions may be mutual, and may reflect a polarized or unified relationship between two persons in the group that may have gone unnoticed. In some cases, such a relationship may be critical in the operation of the group, and analysis of such relationships in feedback may provide a strategic focus for change.

The group average field diagram is made from the average ratings received by each of the group members, and these ratings, of course, are always a matter of importance to group members. The group average field diagram, obtained from the bottom row of cells in the matrix, represents a still higher degree of processing of the information contained in the matrix, and this additional processing in turn results in additional analytic power. The plotting of the images on the group average field diagram tends to reveal the overall, most nearly consensual patterning of the total constellation, and the application of the polarization–unification overlay enables one to make additional inferences about the role of each person in terms of its probable causes and effects in the overall dynamics of the group. The fact that certain individuals may be in strategic positions to precipitate or reinforce changes in the total pattern (as a potential subgroup leader, a mediator, or a scapegoat, for example, or as a person in the swing area) may constitute genuine new insights and useful information for group members.

In our experience, the group average field diagram of the ratings received is perhaps the most generally useful summary of information for feedback to the group. It can hardly fail to make salient some of the most important things about the group and the constellation of relationships in it. The facts revealed are likely to compel attention, and often a large degree of consensus as to their truth, since they represent, after all, the average of the perceptions of all the members. The recognitions by some persons of the positions they have in the group are not always welcome, but the diagram makes it very likely that at least the most salient positions will be discussed. Sometimes it is the case that even glaringly evident role characteristics of some persons have not been publicly recognized or discussed in the group. There are some cases, no doubt, where the group members, or some of them, would prefer not to discuss particular problems, and this should be taken into account, of course, if it can be foreseen, before embarking upon the intermember rating procedure.

In addition to providing the most nearly consensual picture of the constellation of relationships in the group, the group average field diagram provides a strategic base line for examining the field diagram of each individual in turn. The position of the polarization–unification overlay on the individual diagram, as compared to its position on the group average diagram, contains a very large amount of information, aggregated and arranged in a very economical and powerful way for interpretation and further exploration. It is often possible to form a conception of the major interpersonal modes of defense of the personality through this procedure.

It is hard to realize, as one plods through the adjective rating form item by item and person by person, that quite unexpected insights and inferences may arise as the perceptions of one's self and others are aggregated to higher and higher levels and subjected to intensive comparison. It is the broad scope of the underlying theory, of course, and the thoroughgoing implementation of the theory in the modes of measurement and analysis that make new insights and inferences a probable outcome of the procedure. Even so, it should be recognized that the theory is still in a primitive state and that new theoretical insights and hypotheses may arise from the particular group engaged in the process of analysis. It is helpful and satisfying for group members to realize that they are not going through an occult process of divining some absolute hidden truth, but that all inferences made from the data are only heuristic hypotheses, and in the end only the individuals concerned can provide the validation for inferences that the procedure may suggest. Proceeding in this tentative and inquiring spirit, they can participate in a process of creative discovery. What they learn about themselves and their own group may be of great interest in strengthening or reformulating basic theory, as well as helpful in a practical way to themselves and persons in other groups.

Chapter 36

Training Observers to Do SYMLOG Interaction Scoring

Both SYMLOG Retrospective Ratings, when analyzed in feedback to group members, and SYMLOG Interaction Scoring give opportunities for the training of observers. The Interaction Scoring, however, presents better opportunities for the improvement of observation and the learning of theory, since the processes involved in scoring require specific attention to the behavior and content presented by each group member. In order to make the distinctions required in scoring, the observer has to learn a good deal about the theory. The observation method is a vehicle for the teaching of theory.

In the context of the group psychology course in which SYMLOG was developed an observer team is drawn from the membership of the self-analytic group. The team is composed of different members each week. On Monday of a typical week the scoring is done primarily for the training of the observers and may consist of a series of exercises followed by discussion of observer problems; on Wednesday, the scoring is done primarily for the feedback of results to the group on Friday. During the period between the Wednesday observation and the Friday feedback session, the observation team prepares the feedback report.

Stephen Cohen's study of reliability described in Part III of this book has indicated that one needs a team of five or six observers to reach a satisfactorily high level of reliability. Richard Polley's results with actual observer teams in the course (see Appendix T) indicate that, by using the average obtained from a team of four or more, one may reasonably hope to obtain scores for the individual group members observed that will reflect their behavior with less than 20 percent of the variance due to observer bias and error. Satisfactory levels of reliability are thus compatible with a reasonable size for a course group, and all members may have satisfactory opportunities to receive training, prepare reports, and receive feedback on their own behavior in the group. For example, with a total class membership of sixteen, meeting for the usual twelve weeks, with the use of observer teams of four each member of the group would have an opportunity to observe and prepare feedback three different weeks. With a group of twenty the teams could be made up of five persons, and with a group of twenty-four the teams could be made up of six persons.

The observer team schedules should be drawn up in advance and the persons chosen for each team by a random process. At some point the group members are likely to wonder whether there has been some manipulative intention in the withdrawing of certain members from the participation group at a given time, and it is better to have it clearly evident what the selection process has been. It is not out of the question that the teams should be composed with some specific intention, but if so the group members should know that this is the case. If it is desirable to use the withdrawal of specific members from the group as an experimental variable, members may be told that this is desired and asked whether they will agree to wait until results are ready for feedback before knowing the design.

Learning the Names of the Members

As the observers begin their training, the observation task may be approached one piece at a time. Learning the names of the members is a prerequisite to any effective recording of observations. In the first or second session, when the group meets with all members present, prior to the beginning of observation, the instructor should help the members determine a three- or four-letter code word to be used for their names in observation, and also the names by which they wish to be addressed in the group. The code name may be the same as the name used for the member in the group, but it need not be. The code name must be short—the SYMLOG computer programs and print-outs use three-letter abbreviations—but it is helpful if the short code name resembles the name used in the group so that the two may be easily associated and remembered together.

At the beginning of the first observation session, each observer should have a list of the names. The first thing the observers may be asked to do is to draw a diagram of the table on the back of the first SYMLOG observation sheet and to put the code names of participants around it in the proper place. For the first meeting or two, probably not all observers will be able to recognize all group members, but between them they will usually be able to determine the name of each member. The leader of the self-analytic group can be most helpful both to observers and to the members of the group by calling the list of names slowly at the beginning of the session, and allowing time for both group members and observers to make a memorizing effort for each name and code name. The roll may be called in this fashion for several meetings until it seems clear that most people are able to remember most of the names. The first element of observation, then, is to learn to attach the name used in the group and the code name to the person. The diagram of the physical locations of persons is a great help in this. Learning the names of all participants in a group of twenty or so is not a trivial accomplishment. Many groups in ordinary social life continue to operate under a handicap for considerable periods simply because not all of the participants know each other's names and are embarrassed to ask.

Observing the Time

The first element of the message format is the time. A digital clock should be visible to all observers for the best results. We have discovered that observers using a regular clock (especially if the clock is at some distance) do not agree on the minute and tend to round to the nearest five-minute mark. The teacher of the observation team should explain which digits on the clock are to be recorded. The observers may then begin their observation. The observer looks at the group and, when a new person speaks, tries to recall the person's name, checking with the diagram on the back of the sheet if necessary. The observer then looks at the clock and writes the time on the message form followed by the code name of the person speaking. This exercise should be continued, obtaining observations for as many participants as possible, including those who only nod in agreement or make some other nonverbal sign, until the observer finds that the names come automatically and that the time is easily noted and recorded.

Attending to Each Member

At this point it may be well for the observers to take another approach, namely to stop writing and canvass around the group some number of times, silently looking at each individual and recalling the name. In many sessions of interaction some participants say little or nothing, and unless a special effort is made the observer may learn to ignore the silent members, just as the more active participants in the group frequently do. It may be helpful in this exercise to shift attention to the nonverbal level and to note just what each member is doing at the nonverbal level. One may note that Bill is saying nothing but slumping a little listless to the left and stirring the ashes in the ashtray at his side with the stump of a cigarette. The observer should silently formulate what he observes into a few words. Having formulated BILL's nonverbal behavior, the observer shifts attention to the next person beside BILL. The name, MARY, is recalled, and it is noticed that MARY is staring at JOHN with one hand over her mouth. PHIL, who sits next in the circle, is noticed to be drawn somewhat back, staring at JOHN with a disbelieving frown. And so the observer continues shifting attention from one person to the next in the circle, recalling the name and formulating the nonverbal behavior.

Observing Who Addresses Whom

Once the names are easy to remember and the nonverbal behavior of every member can be brought into attentional focus, a logical next exercise is to begin writing again, but this time writing not only the name of the person speaking but also the name of the person to whom the action is addressed. One may take into account both the nonverbal acts and the verbal acts. Nonverbal acts are often addressed to the person speaking, but they may also seem to have no particular person as the target; in such a case the abbreviation GRP may be entered in the TO WHOM position. By this time the observer should be able to write steadily, never at a loss for some act, verbal or nonverbal, to record, and the names should be recalled almost automatically.

It should not be surprising if one experiences persistent difficulty in recalling the names of some particular persons. The observer may or may not be able to determine just why the names of certain persons in the group seem persistently hard to recall, but we are all familiar with this annoying experience. The remedy is simple. The observer should look at this person and recall the name repeatedly until the memory sticks, in spite of the tendency to forget. Later, as a member of the self-analytic group, the observer will have a chance to learn, perhaps, why the names of certain members seem elusive. It seems to be the case that, when there is something to be repressed about one's reaction to the person, the name tends to disappear also. As an observer in training, one's attention should be drawn to this tendency to neglect or repress, and specific efforts should be made to overcome it.

Classifying the Direction of the Behavior

The next elements in the message format are concerned with the direction of the behavior of the actor and with its level, whether ACT or NON. The element ACT or NON is placed immediately after the names, since it functions as the *verb* in a simple sentence-like statement: JOHN to MARY ACT(s) P. The term ACT or NON functions as a *verb,* and the direction, e.g., P, acts as an adverb describing the manner of the act. The term NON may be thought of as standing for a verblike phrase: "shows nonverbal behavior," whereas the term ACT translates directly into the ordinary verb "acts." The simple sentences the observer now writes in code may be paraphrased in the following way: "At time 15 JOHN to MARY acts P (in a friendly manner)." "At time 16 MARY to JOHN shows nonverbal behavior PB." Since the reader of the message usually wants to know just what the nonverbal behavior was, the observer always takes care to supply an ordinary language description of it, e.g., "smiles." There is no IMAGE presented in language by the actor in nonverbal acts, so the observer puts a short description of the piece of nonverbal behavior in the message location labeled ORDINARY DESCRIPTION OF BEHAVIOR OR IMAGE.

Concentration on Nonverbal Behavior

A certain enthusiasm seems to develop for the scoring of nonverbal behavior once one gets into it and finds that the SYMLOG language is apt for recording it. Our tabulations of the general volume of nonverbal behavior recorded over a long series of sessions for a number of groups seem to indicate that the NON level is at first neglected, then the rate rises, probably because attention is drawn to it by discussion in the self-analytic group and by tabulations of observer performance which reveal that it has been neglected. During this period the proposal is often made that one or two observers should be designated to record only nonverbal behavior. It is our inclination as teachers of observation to resist these suggestions on the ground that one of the important things observers need to learn is to balance attention between the ACT level and the nonverbal behavioral level. As an exercise, however, it is valuable to concentrate specifically on the nonverbal behavior. In observations of a long series of sessions, after an initial rise to a rate of about one-quarter that of the rate of ACT level behavior, the rate of recording nonverbal behavior begins to drop off, perhaps to a point where only about one-tenth as many NON level scores are given as ACT level scores (see Williamson, 1977). This is probably too low. In any case, the balance struck between the two levels seems to be greatly affected by the emphasis given in training and by the interest of the observers.

There is, however, some reason to expect that nonverbal behavior will be more salient to observers when the group is in an emotional state or when particular members begin to withdraw. There is clearly a difference between the directions of behavior that observers tend to score at the ACT level and those they tend to score at the NON level. When behavior is scored at the ACT level, the directions U, P, and F tend to predominate. On the contrary, when behavior is scored at the NON level, the directions D, N, and B tend to predominate (see Williamson, 1977). The tendency of observers to notice nonverbal behavior mostly when it indicates D, N, or B directions is probably consistent with the tendencies of participants to avoid overt expression of these kinds of behavior and to show them nonverbally instead.

In many groups, if not most, the directions U, P, and F are felt by the majority to be more desirable than their opposites. There is some tendency indeed, for these value judgments to become crystallized in group norms that are too literal, and too monolithic, for optimum group operation. Part of the function of group leadership in such groups is to encourage group members to be more tolerant of D, N, and B behavior and to recognize that behavior of these kinds may be optimum at certain times and in certain amounts, for the needs of particular individuals and for the reformulation of relationships, goals, and values in the group. When group members are in their role as observers, they are not, for the time being, bound by the same group norms as participants, and hence they pick up the nonverbal signs of the D, N, and B behavior that participants tend to suppress. But observers nevertheless tend to go along with group norms to the effect that when the overt behavior is U, P, or F in direction, if the nonverbal components are also U, P, or F, there is no need for special comment. The nonverbal components tend to be separated out from the ACT level behavior for special attention only when they are incongruent with the overt verbal components or when they betray feelings that are disapproved and hence tend to be suppressed. Indeed, the scoring rules follow the same lines. However, the scoring rules also encourage the recording of nonverbal behavior in the U, P, and F directions that would otherwise pass unnoticed, as well as D, N, and B behavior. Observers should be encouraged and trained, then, to scan the group frequently and to record the U, P, and F nonverbal behaviors when they see them. One should try not to fall into the habit of looking for D, N, or B behavior at the nonverbal level only.

Avoiding Overdependence on the Ordinary Language Description

After concentration of attention on the nonverbal level of behavior one may next focus attention on the element of the message called the ORDINARY LANGUAGE DESCRIPTION. One of the problems of beginning scorers is that they may come to depend too much on the ordinary language description. One may fall into a set of avoiding the coding of the behavior or image and instead try to follow the interaction by taking down a near-verbatim account of what is said. Two exercises may be suggested as a corrective to this. The first is to adopt a temporary rule that one should write no messages except those in which *all* the elements in the format are filled out. This will tend to force attention to the coding of the images, since in general the image coding is probably the most difficult part of composing the message.

A second exercise may follow this, namely the attempt to write messages with all elements complete *except* the natural language description. This will tend to force attention still more strongly to the coding process as such, at levels of abstraction above the natural language level. The goal in this exercise should be to select and write the messages so well that they seem almost self-explanatory without the natural language description. It is important in the long run that this should be the set, since it is only the coded elements of the interaction that are tabulated and treated quantitatively.

Coding PRO and CON

Most images first come to attention as some set of key words in the natural language of the conversation, and this set of words gives the cues for the coding of the image. The first element of the image coding is the PRO or CON attitude of the actor toward the focal element in the image. The attitude is often inferred from the tone of voice or the value-laden connotations of the descriptive words used, for example, "I am persistent, you are obstinate." Sometimes the actor explicitly states that the attitude is PRO or CON, e.g., "I like . . . ," "I don't think we should . . . ," "I wish . . . ," etc. The problem for the beginning scorer is usually not to determine whether the attitude is PRO or CON but rather which one to write down where both seem to be involved, toward separate objects. For example the statement "I think we ought to be friendly with each other" may present a dilemma as to whether it should be scored "PRO P in GRP" or "CON N in GRP." The scorer should stick as closely as possible to what the actor literally says, in this case "PRO P in GRP." The problem with trying to turn a literally PRO statement into a seemingly equivalent CON statement, or vice versa, is that there are nine other directions that are negatively correlated to any given direction, and the scorer may be quite mistaken about which one the actor really has in mind. For example, there are nine vectors negatively correlated to P (N, UN, UNF, NF, DNF, DN, DNB, NB, and UNB). When the actor makes a PRO P statement, the observer often does not know which one of these (or perhaps even some other) is the CON direction the actor has in mind.

It may be helpful as an exercise to concentrate specifically on coding the PRO and CON direction of the image for a period and to practice putting down only the coding that most literally translates what the actor says, but meanwhile to consider all the directions that might be in any way the opposite. The aim should be to reinforce the most literal coding and to consciously reject all the seeming converse codings that may be mistaken. Incidentally, this may be useful in bringing to mind some possible meanings that the observer has not thought of because they are different from the ones that seem obvious to him.

No doubt there is a lot of mistaken inference in reasoning about the affective meanings of others, because a PRO or CON value statement is only a one-directional specification of the speaker's desired movement in a three-dimensional (or twenty-six-vector directional) space. The lesson one may learn from this in the context of observation is equally applicable, of course, to real-life interaction. Much disagreement might be avoided if we habitually tried to elicit more information from others when they express an attitude, so that we are more sure we know what they really mean in more concrete terms: what they are really for or against, rather than what we mistakenly infer they are for or against.

Another reason for taking care to record as literally as possible what is expressed is that individuals differ significantly in their habitual modes of expression, whether PRO or CON. Some persons, for example, will be found to give a very large proportion of CON images. They may be surprised and perplexed to find that they are viewed negatively as persons when they thought they were standing up for some good PRO causes. Other persons who do not identify with them may simply associate them with the CON images they persistently present and feel that the actor is unpleasant, as well as the images. It is important in observation, then, not to lose the information about the proportion of PRO to CON images by making inferential transformations of PRO into CON or vice versa. One of the things to check for, of course, in the observer feedback is whether any particular observers seem to be selectively picking up attitudes in either the PRO or the CON direction.

Coding the Direction of the Image

The next element in the message is the DIRECTION of the IMAGE about which the PRO or CON attitude is being expressed. On the average, most CON attitudes expressed will be about images of behavior on the Negative side of the space, and most PRO attitudes will be about images on the Positive side of the space. But this should certainly not automatically be assumed in any given case. Some individuals are threatened by images of P behavior and express attitudes CON P in OTHER, PRO N in SELF. And many individuals in circumstances where they feel great threat from images of N behavior in OTHERS, the

SITUATION, or SOCIETY will feel justified in returning Negative behavior for Negative behavior received. Thus they may express their attitudes in the following way: CON N in OTHER, PRO N in SELF.

There is a tendency for individual observers to identify with one side or the other in polarizations that occur in the group just as they would if they were participating members. In such cases they may tend also to transform the attitudinal statements in a way that makes the best argument for the side with which they identify. For example, if the member who is their hero for the time being makes the argument CON UNF in SOCIETY, PRO UNB in SELF, the identifying observer may take the argument one step farther and translate the PRO UNB in SELF to PRO UPB in GRP. (Robin Hood UNB robs the Sheriff of Nottingham UNF, and is seen as good old Robin Hood UPB who helps the poor.) Careful study of the observer tabulations (see Polley's program, Appendix T) will indicate when systematic deviations of an individual observer are occurring, and these should be made the subject of observer discussion sessions in which the observers carefully compare their messages to note their differences and work out more detailed guidelines.

Avoiding Too Much Inference in Image Coding

After one has learned how to code images, the SYMLOG language may come to seem a natural mode of expression to the coder, and there may be a tendency to fill in an image for every act, including nonverbal acts, even though no explicit image is presented by the speaker. The observer, in other words, tends to use the SYMLOG language to express what he thinks the speaker meant by the act, and so to extend by inference what the speaker literally expressed. For example, if the observer sees MARY pick up her knitting and withdraw attention from the overt interaction in the group while they are working analytically, the observer may write down MARY to GRP NON DNB (knits) CON F in GROUP. The image code given is inferential in such a case. It may add to our knowledge of what the observer thought MARY was trying to express to the group, but the observer may be wrong. It may be, for example, that MARY is trying to control rising anger, and in her own interpretation of what she is doing she is expressing CON UN in SELF. The observer's interpolation of an image code in this case is also redundant—the sense of the nonverbal behavior from an interaction process point of view as the opposite of F behavior has already been given in the characterization MARY to GRP NON DNB. The image code, with only a few exceptions (where it is clear that the meaning is *intentionally conveyed* by a symbolic act) should be omitted from messages describing nonverbal acts.

Learning to Code All Levels of Images

Observers differ in their tendencies to score images at one level rather than others. As a training exercise for proper level classification it is a good plan for the observer to put down a list of the six levels SELF, OTHER, GROUP, SITUATION, SOCIETY, and FANTASY where it may be seen while scoring, and to scan this list each time a message is written. There is sometimes a tendency to get ''stuck'' on one level and to repeat scores on that level only rather than to be watchful for changes in level. Some levels may be avoided because they seem difficult to apply. The FANTASY level classification is perhaps the most difficult at first, since it includes many images that the speaker does not identify as fantasy at all. The speaker in giving information about his life outside the group certainly does not usually consider that he is offering ''fantasy images'' to the group—he is reporting facts. But to those who have no access to the private life of the speaker, there is no reality check on what the speaker is saying. The images the speaker offers function to stir their imagination, and this is the rationale for classifying such reports at the fantasy level. Perhaps if the level were called ''private life'' it would seem more natural. An exercise that may be helpful occasionally in learning to score is to try deliberately to switch one's identification back and forth from speaker to listener, and so to sense the way in which the reports that seem like undoubted facts to the speaker may seem like an imaginative story or a movie to the listener.

Increasing the Rate of Scoring

The successive elements of the SYMLOG message format thus give a kind of progressive outline for a series of training exercises. The exercises described above will help to focus attention on all parts of the observational message. When the elements of all parts of the message are well understood, one may begin to focus attention on the total number of messages written per period of time. Our tabulations for one-minute periods within a given session of an hour or longer indicate that not all observers start scoring at the same time, so that there is a rising volume of scores for the first five minutes or so of a session. There may also be a kind of ''warm up'' period for the individual observer, during which one gets into the set of the task and increases the number of messages written. The rate of writing messages tends to reach a plateau and then to start a slow fall-off perhaps halfway or two-thirds of the way through the meeting. Probably there is a physical fatigue factor, but it is also likely that there is a rising resistance of a psychological nature to writing down scores as the content of the interaction becomes more emotional or intimate. Observers, naturally enough, tend to react emotionally to what is going on in the group. When the content is serious and emotionally loaded, a group member who does not feel the same emotion may be regarded as deviant. The coding operation behind a one-way mirror may also seem deviant or sacrilegious, and as an observer one may slow down or quit coding altogether. The same slowing down effect may occur during the latter part of a series of sessions as members' relationships become more significant. No doubt these effects tend to impair the quality of the scoring: if it is desired to avoid them, probably the best approach is to make sure the scores are used for a purpose that the members of the group consider legitimate and important. This in turn will tend to alleviate conflict on the part of the coder and to maintain motivation. If the feedback is not expected to be regarded as helpful, the coder will surely be put in conflict and slowed down.

In our tabulations of the rate of writing messages it is clear that there are considerable differences between observers. Some observers write fewer than one message per minute, and some write more than two or three per minute. It is our impression, though we have not yet made explicit studies of this, that there is a positive correlation between the rate of writing messages and the qualitative goodness of the scoring, although some scorers may adopt some mechanical set that increases their speed but lowers the quality of their scoring. Perhaps it is self-evident that very slow scoring is likely to indicate poor scoring on the part of some scorers in the early part of training, where lack of preparation and practice on the part of some scorers positively interferes with the ability to code what is going on, and the number of messages the observer can produce is a more or less direct measure of exposure to and familiarity with the language.

We have no evidence as to whether various abilities of a psychological kind (concentration, attention span, freedom from hampering personality defenses, etc.) also play a large part in both the speed and the quality of scoring. Presumably they do. In any case, repeated reading of the SYMLOG Interaction Scoring manual (Part II of this book) and of the Directional Definitions (Appendix A) are surely necessary in order to produce the best scoring. This part of the training task may be approached in the usual academic way, by reading, review, and testing, in order to achieve the necessary intellectual understanding of the langauge.

Detecting Motivated Peculiarities in Scoring

Even though the intellectual understanding of the language may reach a high level and the other abilities required for good scoring may be present, it is still necessary to detect and give some attention in training to the individual peculiarities of scoring that may be produced by motivational tendencies in the personality of the scorer. It is usually the case, for example, that different observers pay attention to different group members because of motivated interest.

One might infer from the general theory of polarization and unification that the individual scorer would tend to give special attention both to those group members with whom he identifies and those whose attitudes or behavior he particularly rejects, providing they are prominent in a polarization. In general, we may suppose that the same personality characteristics that affect an individual's perception, evaluation, and behavior when he or she is a group member also affect scoring performance when the individual acts as an observer. The study of scoring performance is thus a fine-grained way of throwing light upon the individual's characteristic subjective processes as a group member in reacting differentially to other group members and the images they present.

One of the procedures we have found most useful in spotting the differences between observers is for the teacher in the observation room to pick certain salient acts as they occur and to call out for all observers to score that particular act for later discussion. Comparison of the way observers have scored these key acts can then be used as a basis for identifying scoring problems for discussion at the end of the observation session. Both motivated differences and differences due to imperfect theoretical understanding can be detected with this procedure. It is especially useful early in the training process in providing concrete examples for teaching the concepts of the method.

One of the most promising features of the SYMLOG System, either in the Rating of all group members by all group members or in the Scoring performed by a team of five or six members temporarily in the role of observers, is that one may obtain reliable measures of the individual's rating and scoring characteristics, which may then be related to the individual's behavior and imagery as a group participant. "Unusual perceptions" as they appear in the ratings of group members of each other have been discussed in the previous chapter. Unusual perceptions in the scoring behavior of individual group observers may be used as part of the data about the personality of the observer.

The approach to the study of unusual perceptions of observers may be the same as that used for the study of unusual perceptions of member ratings, using the matrix approach as described in Chapter 35 (see also Appendix T). The only essential difference is that the matrix is not a square matrix showing the same members along both margins, but a matrix showing the observers along one margin and the group members along the other. The matrix may contain any of the many measures that can be obtained by tabulation from the observer's messages—for example, the total number of acts recorded as initiated by each group member; the total number received by each; the total of U minus D, P minus N, or F minus B; the total number of PRO value statements or CON value statements; or the like.

Observers differ not only with regard to the group members to which they pay selective attention and with regard to the directions of behavior and PRO and CON images, but also with regard to the IMAGE levels: SELF, OTHER, GROUP, SITUATION, SOCIETY, and FANTASY. To study observer peculiarities in the recording of levels, it is useful to construct a matrix showing the observers along one margin and the levels along the other. An observer's unusual selectivity or neglect with regard to particular levels may be detected, then, by taking out the effect of the observer's general recording level and the effect of the average salience of the particular level in the particular meeting or episode of interaction observed. Whether JOHN records an unusual number of FANTASY images, for example, can be determined by summing JOHN's image scores over all levels and dividing by the number of levels (JOHN's average recording level), then summing the number of FANTASY images recorded over all observers and dividing by the number of observers (the average salience of FANTASY images for the episode observed), and then taking these two effects out and obtaining the residual, exactly as described in Chapter 35 for ratings. If the residual is very large, far above the expected or far below the expected, then one may say the number originally recorded in the cell is "unusual" and may well be worth further analysis. Further analysis may indicate simply that the scorer has not yet mastered the conceptual distinctions necessary to score the given level, or it may seem to be linked to motivated preferences or perceptual defenses stemming from the personality or the group role of the individual when in the interacting group. The analysis of unusual recording tendencies of individual observers may be undertaken in sessions of the observer team or, just as appropriately, within the context of the feedback session of the group as a whole.

It is clear that a considerable amount of computation may be required if one goes far in the analysis of unusual scoring tendencies of observers and machine computations of the kind made possible by Richard Polley's programs may be required to make it practical (see Appendixes T and U). It is also true, however, that the volume of data produced by machine computation tends to be large, and observers need to be taught how to pick out the things most likely to be useful for comment and further analysis. A feedback session may become deadly dull and unprofitable if an observer launches into an unselective, and more or less complete, readout of all the numbers the computer has produced.

As far as possible, the raw tabulations should be converted into field diagrams and matrices, which give a more global view of all facts taken into account at once and enable one to locate salient features that are of particular interest and are likely to repay efforts at further analysis. It has been our experience, both with groups in the group psychology course and with work groups in field settings, that the presentation of feedback data in a visual format greatly aids understanding and interpretation. The visual diagrams seem to allow members to "externalize" their observations of group process and group relationships in a concrete and observable manner and to speak about them much more easily and directly than they generally can about numerical data.

Chapter 37

Some Empirical Results of SYMLOG Observation

In developing SYMLOG we have observed a number of self-analytic groups with course formats that have been modified year by year. The observation system has also evolved through a series of changes. The course format as it existed in 1970 will be found in Bales's book *Personality and Interpersonal Behavior*. The course format as of Spring 1978 is shown in Appendix X.

Although the course format has evolved and the method has been different enough from group to group so that the results can hardly serve as empirical norms for the system, it is useful nevertheless to look at some of the main findings and to try to assess some of their implications for our general theoretical point of view, for the training of observers, and for the feedback of data to group members. The usefulness of the system does not depend upon general empirical norms. The next chapter will describe ways of analyzing the data from a team of observers in such a way as to assess their reliability and at the same time to throw light on the dynamics of the group without the use of general norms.

Directional Profiles

Table 18 from Williamson (1977) shows the directional profile obtained by tabulating the scores of all observers of all sessions of five different self-analytic groups, aggregated across all levels. The first group included in Williamson's study was the course group of spring 1973. Two additional groups were observed that fall, and two more groups in the spring of 1974. During that period, not all acts were scored at the levels ACT and NON (in contrast to the procedure in the present method). An act was classified into *one* and only one of the following categories, according to the observer's judgment of salience: ACT, NON, SELF, OTHER, SITUATION, SOCIETY, FANTASY, VALUE STATEMENT. (Note that the level GROUP was omitted and that value statements were treated as a separate category.) It is not clear that, if the present set of levels had been used, there would have been any significant difference in the frequencies with which different directions were observed, but the different method of coding needs to

TABLE 18 Percentage of Total Acts Scored in Each of 27 Directions, Aggregated across All Levels and All Observers, for Five Self-Analytic Groups

DIRECTION	N	%	RANK ORDER	DIRECTION	N	%	RANK ORDER
U	855	2.2	20[b]	NB	1496	3.9	10[a]
UP	1273	3.3	13	B	956	2.5	16[c]
UPF	3782	9.8	1	PB	972	2.5	16[c]
UF	3628	9.4	2	DP	759	2.0	24
UNF	2296	5.9	3	DPF	863	2.2	20[b]
UN	1847	4.8	8	DF	979	2.5	16[c]
UNB	1580	4.1	9	DNF	679	1.8	25
UB	841	2.2	20[b]	DN	1053	2.7	15
UPB	980	2.5	16[c]	DNB	1508	3.9	10[a]
P	2136	5.5	5	DB	1320	3.4	12
PF	2067	5.3	6	DPB	473	1.2	26
F	2258	5.8	4	D	810	2.1	23
NF	1224	3.2	14	AVE	143	0.4	27
N	1890	4.9	7				
				Total	38678	100.00	

[a]Two-way tie in rank order.   [c]Four-way tie in rank order.
[b]Three-way tie in rank order.   Source: Data from Williamson (1977).

be mentioned in order to avoid confusion in looking at the various data involving levels, to be presented later.

The summary directional profile shown in Table 18 has some interesting properties, which probably reflect general scoring tendencies of group observers as well as general behavior and content tendencies of group members. It is not possible to make a clean separation between features of the data that may trace to observer tendencies and features that may trace to group member behavior tendencies. We need to consider both sources of influence in looking at each of the bodies of data to be presented in this chapter.

If one assumed that each direction had an equal chance of being used, the expected percentage frequency for each direction would be 100/27, or 3.7 percent. Eleven of the directions exceed this figure, two by a very large margin—UPF (9.8 percent) and UF (9.4 percent); four by more than one and a half percent—UNF (5.9 percent), F (5.8 percent), P (5.5 percent), and PF (5.3 percent); two by more than a percentage point—N (4.9 percent) and UN (4.8 percent); and three by less than half a percentage point—UNB (4.1 percent), NB (3.9 percent), and DNB (3.9 percent). One of the things of interest, however, is that with one conspicuous exception (the gap between UP and UPF) the frequencies grade more or less smoothly from a given directional vector to the adjacent vectors. This is an indication of the "continuity" of the space, which is due, probably, both to the behavioral tendencies of individuals and to the perceptual tendencies of observers.

At one time the authors thought that some of the differential scoring of different directions might be due to conceptual difficulties in making the abstractions required to visualize the directions according to whether they were described by one directional component (e.g., U), or by a two-directional combination of components (e.g., UP), or by a three-directional combination (e.g., UPF). We had some impression that the singly named directions were hardest to visualize, while the triply named directions were easier. The direction U in the present data is indeed lower in frequency than any of its surrounding directions.

In general, however, the data disconfirm this hypothesis, since for each type of directional combination the actual frequencies are nearly equivalent to the expected frequencies. (The expected frequencies were obtained by multiplying the number of directions in each type of directional combination by 3.7 percent). The only variance, really, is the underutilization of AVE (scoring in none of the directions), and this score was actively discouraged by the teachers during training.

A more interesting hypothesis emerges from inspection of the data. Five of the six most frequently utilized directions tend to define the boundaries of the UPF sector of the space (UPF, UF, P, F, and PF, the exception being UNF). The next five most frequently used directions tend to cluster in and around the NB sector of the space (N, UN, UNB, NB, and DNB). Omitting AVE, the five least frequently used directions all contain a D element, and to a certain extent define the boundaries of the D part of the space (DPB, DNF, DP, D, DPF).

These data suggest the existence of a chronic and overriding polarization either in observer perceptions or in group behavior, or both, between two particular opposite quadrants of the space, that is, active, task-oriented, and friendly leadership behavior (UPF) versus active, emotionally expressive, and individualistic negative behavior (UNB). The behavior of more submissive members in the marginal area between these two poles (D) and in locations at the *ends of the Line of Balance and orthogonal to the line of polarization* (DPB and DNF) tends either to be rare or to be unnoticed. It may be that DPB and DNF forms of behavior tend to be infrequent because of the dynamics of the most usual direction of polarization in these groups.

Most likely it is the case that observers in making their scores, as well as members in their ratings of each other, tend to polarize their perceptions, and that the variables in adjacent directions which tend to become more highly correlated during a process of unification or polarization also tend to *move together in a correlated way* in the perception of the observer under various distortions or displacements of the line of polarization. For example, if it is the case that an observer who sees the group polarized along the line UPF to UNB tends to cluster the adjacent behavior toward UPF and UNB and to neglect the behavior that might be seen in the orthogonal locations DNF and DPB (as mentioned above), our present hypothesis would predict that another observer of the same group who saw it polarized along the line UNF to UPB would tend to cluster other variables around the UNF and UPB poles and would tend to neglect the behavior that might be seen in the orthogonal locations DPF and DNB.

On the average, we suppose, both the polarization of observers' perceptions and the patterning of members' behavior due to polarization of members' perceptions are reflected in the differential use of the twenty-seven directions. We suppose that in the case of group members their perceptions are interdependent with their overt behavior, and that their behavior and their perception of their behavior tend to influence each other in a circular fashion. That is, when an actor perceives the overt behavior of the other, the actor also evaluates the behavior. The evaluative significance tends to distort (polarize or unify) the perception and to influence the behavior which the actor returns to the other. The other, in turn, perceives, evaluates, and distorts his perception according to his tendency to unify or polarize and modifies his overt behavior toward the previous actor. When the polarizing or unifying vectors of the two fall along the same or adjacent or opposite directions, a circular reaction tends to be set in motion and to amplify. An observer witnessing this interaction may well be drawn into the polarizing or unifying tendency and perceive it in his own characteristic polarizing or unifying way.

The particular groups of Williamson's study were not observed by group member teams (as they are at present), but we know from the informal report of many group observers that observers tend to identify to a certain extent with the interacting group and with particular group members, even though they never interact with them. When the interaction of group members for the particular day is observed by a temporary team of observers drawn from the regular group, it seems probable that in many respects the individual members continue to feel much as they do as participating group members, except that they are now substituting their scoring performance for the interaction they would otherwise seek to deliver in the group. The group may function differently because of the absence of certain key members, but those key members may still be perceiving and wishing to interact in their accustomed way and may show their motivation in their scoring peculiarities.

Directional Locations of Images at Each Level

The different SYMLOG levels appear to reflect motivational pressures differentially, as we expected in designing the system of levels. Table 19 shows the distribution of scores falling at each end, or neither, of each dimension for each level in the five groups of Williamson's study.

A number of interesting points may be made about this table. First, one may note that the ACT level tends to reflect the U, P, and F components of motivation, while the NON level tends to reflect the D, N, and B components.

Descriptions of the SELF in these groups tend to emphasize, perhaps surprisingly, the D, N, and F components. Perhaps this is related to the fact that the individuals in these groups were engaged in self-analysis, and the most serious moments of self-analysis tend to come in the examination of aspects of the self that one may regard as somewhat negative. One can imagine other groups in which most of the characterizations of the self would be status-seeking or status-enhancing descriptions in the U and P directions. It is not clear why the F direction should predominate over the B in the descriptions of the self, but it may be a reflection of effort to change, the expression of the intention to behave differently, and the like. When the emotional, or B, components of self-feeling are predominant, it is more likely that the individual will show this at the nonverbal level or, as we shall see, by fantasy content.

TABLE 19 Distribution of Scores at Each Level Falling at Each End, or Neither End, of Each Dimension, Aggregated across All Observers, All Sessions, All Groups[a]

LEVEL	U/D		P/N		F/B	
ACT	U	47.3	P	39.9	F	59.6
	—	38.8	—	32.3	—	25.5
	D	13.9	N	27.8	B	14.9
	Total	100.0	Total	100.0	Total	100.0
NON	U	24.7	P	25.5	F	22.0
	—	31.4	—	33.5	—	29.4
	D	43.9	N	41.0	B	48.6
	Total	100.0	Total	100.0	Total	100.0
SELF	U	34.0	P	27.6	F	37.1
	—	23.8	—	37.0	—	31.1
	D	42.2	N	35.4	B	31.8
	Total	100.0	Total	100.0	Total	100.0
OTHER	U	43.5	P	32.3	F	38.6
	—	35.3	—	28.3	—	35.1
	D	21.2	N	39.4	B	26.3
	Total	100.0	Total	100.0	Total	100.0
SIT	U	46.4	P	25.6	F	46.7
	—	33.7	—	31.1	—	28.4
	D	19.9	N	43.3	B	24.9
	Total	100.0	Total	100.0	Total	100.0
SOC	U	48.8	P	29.1	F	36.9
	—	30.1	—	48.4	—	35.4
	D	21.1	N	22.5	B	27.7
	Total	100.0	Total	100.0	Total	100.0
FAN	U	46.6	P	28.9	F	31.9
	—	26.2	—	25.6	—	28.7
	D	27.2	N	45.5	B	39.4
	Total	100.0	Total	100.0	Total	100.0

[a]The same five self-analytic groups as shown in Figure 44.
Source: Data from Williamson (1977).

Descriptions of the OTHER in these groups tend to be specialized in the attribution of dominance (U), negativity (N), and disapproving control (F). As in the case of the descriptions of the SELF, there may be some reason to suppose that this kind of attribution is related to the self-analytic task of the group, which also means analysis of the other. In many kinds of groups, it may be that the most frequent context in which the OTHER may be directly characterized is in a context of praise, encouragement, ingratiation—in other words, on the P side. But a self-analytic group, like a therapy group, may more often specialize, as time goes on, in the examination of negative aspects of one's perception of both the self and the other, and perhaps the most common inner core of felt complaint is that the other is UNF—authoritarian, controlling, disapproving. The various components, U, N, and F of the OTHER descriptions and D, N, and F of the SELF descriptions, need not occur together in the neat way suggested by the combination of CON UNF in OTHER, CON DN in SELF, PRO F in SELF. Unfortunately, in the earlier stages of the development of SYMLOG the message format did not call for the recording of the distinction between PRO or CON attitudes toward the images. With the inclusion of these distinctions, a more discriminating kind of clinical analysis becomes possible.

At the time these data were gathered, the level GROUP was not included in the format, and so it does not appear on the table. Its inclusion in the message format as it now exists makes it possible not only to pick up descriptions of the way in which individuals view the group, but also to record explicit efforts to establish norms for the group as a whole. In the earlier format these efforts were recorded under one general rubric VAL (Value Statements, without the distinction as to PRO or CON). Although data for these are not shown on the table, the distribution was strongly on the U, P, and F side, and it is likely that with the present distinctions one would pick up these statements as PRO U, P, and F (or various combinations of these three components) in GROUP.

The SITUATION is most frequently characterized as U, N, and F—a more exaggerated expression of the same components as those most frequently used to characterize the OTHER. Most frequently the specific images were those of the self-analytic group task, the observation situation or the observers, the pressure of time, and the like. In many instances the value judgment was probably CON UNF in SIT. It appears not unlikely to us, on the basis of much experience in context, that some, perhaps many, remarks CON UNF in SIT may be regarded as a displacement of the feelings members have about disapproval they anticipate and fear they may receive from others in the group—the more direct statement would be CON UNF in GROUP or in OTHER, or perhaps even CON UNF in SELF.

Images at the SOCIETAL level in this set of groups tend to be found in the U, P, and F directions. The reasons for this are not altogether clear, but, as we shall see later in this chapter, SOCIETAL images tend to be at a peak in the first few sessions in the beginning of the group, at the time just before leaving for the midterm vacation as well as just after return from vacation, and at the very end of the group when members are considering what they will do during vacation between terms or after graduation. Many of the images in the beginning, concerned with home towns, high schools or prep schools, honors and former glories, seem to function as part of establishing the individual's identity by references to his or her place in the larger society, and in this context UPF images are understandable as part of establishing a desirable identity. From many discussions in the groups, as well as from the fact shown earlier in Table 18 that UPF is the direction of behavior most frequently attributed by observers, it seems clear that there is a general cultural bias among these students in favor of U over D, P over N, and F over B. Although some students express dread at going home and encountering parents again at vacation time, by and large the familial imagery is Positive, and the imagery of occupational futures at the end tends to the UPF direction.

FANTASY images were the primary conveyers of UNB directions of motivation in these groups. They seem to be the counterparts of SITUATIONAL images in these groups. Aversive feelings of obligation, threat, fear of disapproval, and the like seem to be projected to the SITUATIONAL focus (UNF), while repressed or suppressed feelings of hostility, rebelliousness, unconventionality, exhibitionism, and the like seem to be projected into FANTASY images (UNB).

The tendencies for different levels of imagery to reflect different directions of motivational tendencies are only average tendencies, of course, and one should not overemphasize their diagnostic usefulness. But the differences are marked enough to suggest that the different levels do have different dynamic loadings, and different degrees of closeness or distance from the preferred location of the self image. It is reasonable to suppose that different individuals have preferences for imagery on different dynamic levels, according to their personality defenses. And we would expect this to be true whether the individual is participating as a group member or is observing and writing down SYMLOG scores. We have not yet begun specific studies of differential preference of individuals for particular levels of imagery or directions within levels, but the SYMLOG System of levels was set up to make this possible. Even in the absence of specific studies, however, the aggregate data are enough to suggest that the training of observers may need to recognize that observers have preferences for specific levels, and they may need to be taught to recognize other levels and to read them diagnostically. This appears to be one of the ways in which specific training as an observer may help improve the individual's understanding of psychological dynamics in individuals and groups.

Correlations of Variables Within Sessions

Given the general theory of polarization and unification, we expect that under conditions of heightened emotion individuals in the group will tend to cluster the images in their perceptual fields into a simpler pattern. It is assumed that they will tend to search for salient images on various levels that may serve as symbolic targets of displaced, projected, or transferred feelings. If images on one level, for example, a FANTASY level, may serve as substitutes for images on another level, say at the level of characteristics of the SELF, or the OTHER, or the GROUP, then we would expect that the individual would tend to select substitute images that have the same evaluative quality or *direction* as the original image. We would suppose that it would often be the *similarity of directional location* that makes the substitute image an appropriate target, plus the fact in some cases that the choice of a different and more distant level makes the substitute image a safer target than the original—less likely to arouse anxiety or to involve a negative evaluation of the self or an image associated with the self.

If these various conjectures have some truth, then we would expect to find that over a large population of dynamic episodes of polarization–unification, we should find clusters of images having the same direction but different levels. Or to state it slightly differently, we should expect to find images of different levels clustered together according to similar directions.

Table 20 shows the results of a large factor analysis carried out by Williamson over the population of 150 sessions of our five self-analytic groups (thirty sessions each). Sixty-two SYMLOG variables were included, each consisting of a percentage of the total scores for the session. Rates were computed for each of six directions, U, D, P, N, F, B, aggregated over all levels; each level ACT, NON, SELF, OTHER, SIT, SOC, FAN, and VAL, aggregated over all directions; and then separate rates for each of the six directions within each of the eight levels. A factor analysis of the sixty-two variables using the SPSS principal components program suggested a four-factor structure; six factors were distinguishable, but the eigenvalues for factors five and six dropped considerably, and these two factors could be interpreted as variants of factor four. The first four were therefore retained as the "best" solution and were rotated using orthogonal varimax criteria. The items loaded most heavily on each of the four factors in this final orthogonal rotation are shown in Table 20. The four factors combined explain 34.5 percent of the total variance in the data, a moderate level considering the random variation, yet larger than previous factor analyses of this sort (see, e.g., Mann, Gibbard, and Hartman, 1967; Dunphy, 1968).

The communality estimates for most of the variables are acceptably high, but at least twenty-one of the variables did not load significantly on any of the factors (fourteen of these were associated with the SOC, NON, and SIT levels). These variables are omitted in the list shown in Table 20, which contains only the variables that have loadings of .35 or above on any of the four factors. We thus have four sublists of variables almost, though not quite, mutually exclusive of each other. The variables in a given sublist are all loaded on the same factor, which means that they also tend to be correlated with each other and in this sense tend to form a cluster of variables that tend to move together, moving up or down together from session to session, and each cluster moving independently of each other cluster.

A given session is not necessarily made up of just one dynamic episode of polarization–unification—it may or may not contain one, or it may contain several in succession, different from each other. Hence it is not the perfect unit for testing our hypothesis that variables from different levels should tend to cluster according to similarity of their direction over a population of dynamic episodes. A session is only a rough approximation of a single dynamic episode, but it will serve for a first look.

The first cluster, making up Factor 1, combines most of the variables measuring the U and F directions, as if they were combined in the observer's perception of task-oriented leadership of the several varieties, UPF, UF, and UNF. But this factor is essentially uncorrelated with the second factor, which inspection indicates is the observer's perception of a P cluster versus an N cluster. The third factor, uncorrelated with the other two, indicates an observer's perception of a cluster of B variables. And finally, the fourth factor, essentially uncorrelated with any of the preceding three, indicates an observer's perception of a cluster of D variables, with a sprinkling of N and B.

One's first reaction may be dismay that the factor analysis does not simply show the three postulated dimensions of the SYMLOG space. Are not the SYMLOG dimensions based upon previous factor analyses, in which the items

TABLE 20 Orthogonal Factors in the Intercorrelations of Sixty-two SYMLOG Variables over a Population of 150 Sessions[a]

VARIABLE	FACTOR 1	FACTOR 2	FACTOR 3	FACTOR 4	COMMUNALITY
U % (All Levels)	.91	−.06	.08	.00	.98
ACT U%	.83	−.07	.29	.08	.96
VAL U%	.73	−.01	−.01	−.03	.79
F % (All Levels)	.72	.14	−.44	−.01	.97
OTHER U%	.69	.10	−.03	−.14	.81
OTHER F%	.64	.15	−.16	.00	.79
SIT U%	.63	.01	.08	−.04	.78
VAL F%	.59	.05	−.14	−.01	.80
SELF F%	.59	.18	−.28	−.03	.78
FAN F%	.50	.10	−.19	−.02	.80
VAL %	.49	−.08	.24	−.22	.99
ACT F%	.48	.04	−.30	.26	.93
SIT F%	.48	.07	−.16	.06	.73
SELF P%	.43	.19	−.17	−.21	.67
FAN U%	.42	−.03	.01	.02	.97
SOC F%	.39	.02	−.06	−.05	.59
SELF U%	.36	.09	−.36	−.14	.98
ACT %	−.53	.07	−.37	−.31	.99
SIT N%	−.36	−.17	.11	.07	.72
P % (All Levels)	.28	.84	.14	−.20	.96
ACT P%	.17	.64	.18	.02	.91
OTHER P%	.40	.48	.00	.03	.74
FAN P%	.11	.46	.04	−.14	.73
VAL N%	.05	−.40	.19	−.01	.73
OTHER N%	.00	−.59	.17	−.24	.82
ACT N%	.00	−.62	.20	−.31	.89
N % (All Levels)	−.02	−.85	.32	.00	.95
B % (All Levels)	−.18	−.14	.81	.16	.95
NON %	−.01	.09	.58	−.08	.99
ACT B%	−.12	−.07	.57	−.31	.87
SOC B%	−.16	.08	.43	.04	.59
OTHER B%	−.19	−.09	.38	−.04	.69
FAN B%	.12	−.09	.37	.10	.76
D % (All Levels)	−.10	.12	.13	.81	.91
SELF D%	.08	.04	.04	.51	.78
FAN %	.00	−.01	−.21	.50	.99
FAN D%	−.02	.00	.20	.47	.99
SIT D%	.03	−.04	−.04	.41	.68
SELF N%	.10	−.30	.05	.39	.64
SELF B%	−.11	−.22	.12	.35	.71
VAL D%	−.08	−.02	−.01	.35	.62
SELF %	.29	−.04	−.29	.35	.99
EIGENVALUE	9.00	4.73	3.89	3.77	
% of VARIANCE	14.5%	7.6%	6.3%	6.1%	34.5%

[a]In the earlier version of SYMLOG used here, there was no level GROUP, and the distinction between PRO and CON was not made. "VAL" includes both PRO and CON value statements. Five groups, 30 sessions each = 150 sessions.
Source: Data from Williamson (1977).

seemed, by their intercorrelations, to define three orthogonal bipolar factors? The answer to this is yes, but two important qualifications need to be recognized. The first is that the populations in the previous factor analyses have been populations of *individual persons,* not populations of sessions, as in the present case. It is obviously possible, with the meeting or session as the unit, to have a subgroup of persons acting and presenting content in a UF direction and another subgroup of persons acting and presenting content in a B direction. In fact, this would seem to be the expected pattern in a session polarized between a subgroup somewhere on the F side and another somewhere on the B side. And in addition it is possible to have a subgroup of "dropouts," showing in the field diagram as scattered around in the marginal area between the two poles, but far downward in the space. And finally, it is consistent with our observations in such a case that there may be a sprinkling of persons near the P vector, acting as mediators, or near the N vector, acting as scapegoats, but whether or not there are such individuals or small subgroups, it is usually the case that as the polarization becomes more acute the average of the whole constellation tends to become more Negative. When the group as a whole is far on the Positive side, the pattern tends to be unified or the polarization is mild and not very disruptive, but when the polarization becomes severe and disruptive, the whole constellation tends to move to the negative side. In summary, then, there is nothing necessarily inconsistent between findings that tend to show three orthogonal dimensions when the population is of individuals, but show the four orthogonal factors discovered when the population is one of sessions, in which there may be various subgroups and patterns related to polarization and unification.

A second qualification needs to be stated in moving from empirical factor-analytic results to a conception of the three orthogonal dimensions of the SYMLOG theoretical space: The factor structure discovered over a particular population is *a measure of that population.* Other populations, or larger populations of the same kind, or smaller, may show a different factor structure—one set of groups, for example, may show U, P, and F, all intercorrelated when the factor analysis is done over individuals—that is, for those groups, the individuals who are high on U also tend to be high on P and on F. Another set of groups, however, may show that U, *N,* and F are all intercorrelated. Still another set of groups may show the dimensions U–D, P–N, and F–B to be essentially uncorrelated—or when many sets of groups of individuals are thrown into the same population for the factor analysis, the three SYMLOG dimensions may then come out uncorrelated. And for some populations, such as our population of *sessions,* directions which are ordinarily highly negatively correlated with each other (in this case UF and B) may be uncorrelated with each other.

We are thus led to the conclusion that, although the empirical results of factor analyses have gradually led to a refinement of the conception of the three dimensions of SYMLOG as "orthogonal" and have helped in the definition of descriptions of behavior and rating adjectives with which to make the measurements, in the end we need to emphasize that the "orthogonality" at base is a *conceptual* or *logically defined* orthogonality. Or perhaps we may say that the orthogonality refers to an independence of the general *semantic meaning* of the words used to define the orthogonal directions. We define the measuring instrument in terms of *conceptually independent* dimensions and then use it to determine how the dimensions (or factors) are *actually* related or intercorrelated in a *particular* population or ultimately in a single field of images. The pattern of polarization or unification in a single group or a single field of images in the perception of an individual can be *defined* as a particular *pattern of departure* from the orthogonality of the dimensions. Or to put it in a slightly different way, the hypothesis that under certain conditions a dynamic process of polarization–unification tends to set in is precisely the hypothesis that under those conditions there will be a patterned departure from orthogonality of the SYMLOG dimensions in a factor analysis of the population of images involved in the polarization–unification process. "Polarization" means that the empirical factors in the given case are *not* orthogonal but are correlated in some way.

The factor analysis of the sixty-two SYMLOG variables over the population of all 150 meetings of the five self-analytic groups may then be said to give us measures of the way in which the processes of polarization–unification tend to produce departures from the theoretical orthogonality of the three SYMLOG dimensions used by observers writing messages to describe the single act and the single image in these sessions. The results give strong evidence in favor of the reality of the kinds of processes postulated by the general theory of polarization–unification. Moreover, they tell us something about the most frequent patterns of polarization–unification. They do not resolve for us the question as to the degree to which the observed patterns may be attributed to observers' perceptual and evaluative tendencies or to the members' perceptual-evaluative and behavioral tendencies. The most plausible guess is that both observers and group members contribute to the effects, but perhaps in different degrees and in different ways.

But what about the hypothesis with which we started this examination of the factor analytic results—namely, that, given the hypotheses about the nature of personality defenses such as transference, projection, displacement, and rationalization, we should expect to find images of *different levels* clustered together according to *similar directions?*

The results for Factor 1 seem strongly in line with the hypothesis. All of the variables measuring the F direction, of whatever level, except for NON F%, are significantly loaded on the factor. And similarly, all of the variables measuring the U direction, of whatever level, except for NON U% and SOC U%, are included, with significant loadings. It would appear that motivations to move in the UF direction may be indicated by images on any of the different levels or, conversely, that UF images on all of the different levels may tend to appear in a concerted movement in the UF direction.

But why should the directions U and F be so highly intercorrelated or fused into one factor for this series of sessions? Is it because they are not distinguished from each other in perception and evaluation, or because there is some felt dynamic need to have them go together? Our conceptual distinction between the two directions (see Part II of this book) relates the direction U to power exercised through sheer dominance, and the direction F to legitimate normative control of behavior in the instrumental direction. From the viewpoint of many or most individuals trying to make the group operate in a satisfactory way for the majority, whether these individuals are task leaders or others, it may seem desirable that the exercise of power in the group, through sheer dominance as well as by other means, should be in the service of the legitimate normative control of behavior—more simply, that the most dominant members in the group should be working in the direction of the group goals. Unless the balance of power is on the side of more or less consensual group goals, the goals will not be achieved, and frustration will result.

Legitimate leaders of a group, whether appointed, elected, or emergent, typically have power conferred upon them if they are first legitimate or have legitimacy conferred upon them if they are first powerful and lead in the direction of group goals. This fused complex of acts, images, and expectations is often called simply "authority," and if all the component elements are not in fact fused together, we say that there is a "problem of authority." It is not surprising that in the early stages of a group's formation the members will have to deal with "problems of authority" since legitimate group norms may not yet exist, and no settled order of dominance may yet have appeared. It typically takes time and interaction to fuse these elements together into a satisfactory settlement of the problem(s) of authority. In some groups this may not be possible, and in many groups, if not most, there are occasional or periodic crises of authority.

The images of the UF fusion, then, to a considerable extent may be consciously and rationally brought together to reinforce one another because of a felt need for the fusion. That is, PRO F values in SELF, OTHER, SITUATION, and SOCIETY may be brought in to reinforce F behavior in SELF and OTHER by suitable rationalization. Values PRO F in FAN may help in the same way. For what image, then, may these images from various levels be a substitute? If the fusion in fact exists, none of them needs to be presented as a substitute for others. But if the fusion does not exist, and there are problems of authority, then images from other levels may substitute for the fusion at the ACT level which does not exist. Or in instances where individuals are in conflict about elements of their own personality or in conflict with the existing solution of the authority problems in the group, they may make substitutions, displacements, or transferences. Feelings CON F in SELF may be displaced by statements CON F in OTHER. Or feelings CON F in previous figures of authority may be transferred by statements CON UNF in OTHER, to a person in the present group. And so on. There seem to be many complex possibilities, but the similarity of direction of the images seems to be necessary to make them psychologically useful.

For the second factor, the P–N factor, the clustering of images of similar direction seems to be much less marked, though present. On the Positive end the cluster includes the total of all images without regard to level, the ACT level images, images of the OTHER as Positive, and Positive FANTASIES. It is not clear why the P images at other levels are not significantly high, although they may in fact make some contribution, since the P% of all levels added together has a very high loading. On the Negative end of the factor, the cluster of image levels includes the aggregate of all levels of direction N, with a high loading, ACTs of the N direction, references to N elements in the OTHER, and PRO N VALUE statements. Part of the answer as to why more levels are not included in defining the P–N factor may be that references to the SELF as P are more heavily loaded on the UF fusion factor than on the P–N factor (interesting, in view of the fact that the average polarization of the group makes UPF the most highly valued reference direction). It is also interesting that references to the SITUATION as N tend to be more highly loaded on the Negative end of the UF factor than on the Negative end of the P–N factor. The implication is that, given the average polarization of sessions of these self-analytic groups, when the SELF is viewed in a positive light, the image tends to be associated with the UPF direction and possibly when it is viewed in a Negative light, the Negative feeling tends to be displaced into a SITUATIONAL image and associated with the DNB direction.

The B factor shows that all B images added together produce a variable that has a high loading. ACTs in the B direction are included in the cluster of significant items, along with references to B elements in the OTHER, in SOCIETY, and in FANTASY. One might also expect to find VAL B also in the cluster, but it is possible that it is harder to make value arguments in favor of B behavior in the group than it is to express PRO B feelings by reference to B elements in SOCIETY and FANTASY. It is also interesting in this respect that the total of all directions of NON-verbal behavior recorded by observers tends to be highly loaded in the B direction. It appears that B elements of motivation tend to be expressed nonverbally rather than in value statements, while UF elements of motivation tend to be expressed in VALUE statements rather than nonverbally. The total of all directions of VAL is loaded on the UF factor significantly, although it does show some loading below the level of significance on the B factor.

Finally, the D factor shows a considerable cluster. The D% rate of all levels added together is the most highly loaded. It is also clear that references to the SELF as D, as N, and as B are all found together in this factor, as well as the sum of all references to the SELF added together without regard to direction. It may be that individuals are likely to make reference to elements in the SELF when they are questioned about their lack of participation by others, and that these references tend either to be unfavorable or to reveal motivational elements that go counter to the prevailing UPF goal direction. References to the SITUATION as responsible for D behavior (SIT D) are also loaded on this factor, as well as fantasies of D behavior (FAN D). Indeed, the total of all FANTASY images added together, without reference to direction, is highly loaded on this factor, and this tends to suggest that among persons who are silent, as part of the "dropout" subgroup, there are at least some who are substituting fantasy for overt behavior that they might wish to perform. It is our impression that for persons who are persistently silent in a self-analytic group it is very important to obtain some idea of their fantasies as a first step to increasing their participation, and that they are more accessible to questions or guesses about their fantasies than to other kinds of attempts to provoke their participation.

Developmental Trends

There are a great many articles in the literature that postulate an average developmental sequence which is believed to characterize groups of many kinds, though most of the studies have been made of self-analytic groups of one kind or another. These theories are reviewed by Williamson (1977) in his dissertation devoted to the attempt to find such a general developmental sequence in groups we have observed in the Social Interaction Laboratory at Harvard, using SYM-LOG Interaction Scoring. Williamson finds some support for a revised and more articulate theory of a general average developmental sequence for our groups resembling some of those described in the literature, and his study clarifies many of the issues that have so far been too ambiguous even to permit a test. But the average tendencies one may discern are quite weak and are so dependent upon particular conditions in particular groups that it seems to us better for the purposes of a self-analytic group to recognize the variability from group to group according to conditions and to formulate, instead, a value-based concept of the way one might wish the process to go in order to realize specified values, and then to devise ways to measure and monitor progress toward the goals so defined. The directions and levels of behavior recognized by SYMLOG permit one to do this, at least for a very broad range of values and goals.

It may be of interest to present briefly the developmental trends in one group of the five studied by Williamson, which illustrates the use of SYMLOG indices as they may be used to monitor the general progress of a group. This particular group, PSR 1330r, Spring 1974, comes closer than any of the other four, to the kind of progress one might hope for, given the goals of a self-analytic group as described above.

Figure 44 shows five time plots for each of the kinds of images included in the SYMLOG format at the time this group was observed: FANTASY, SOCIETY, SITUATION, OTHER, and SELF, (the level GROUP was not distinguished at that time). Each time plot is based on the standard scores for the particular kind of imagery for the particular group, over thirty sessions. (The score for a given session is obtained by finding what percentage the particular kind of image, e.g. FAN, is, of all imagery for that session. The thirty such scores for the thirty sessions constituting the life of the group are then converted to standard scores.)

As Figure 44 shows, the level of FANTASY starts out very high in the first session, and then precipitously declines. There is a large amount of fluctuation from meeting to meeting at first, but the fluctuation tends to become less marked, and the general level tends to fall, over the course of the 30 meetings of the group. It appears that FANTASY is utilized in this group more or less as intended—as a way into analysis of the here-and-now—and the need for this indirect approach seems to decline as the group learns how to analyze its own processes and the members are better able to tolerate analysis.

The level of SOCIETAL images appears to be very high at first, with another marked peak somewhere close to the middle and a final peak at the end. The first peak is associated with getting acquainted, with many references to home towns, general background, and other kinds of information about social identity. The peak in the middle may seem mysterious, but the reason for it is really very simple—it is associated with the spring vacation, talk of home and family before departure and upon returning. The final peak is associated with the ending of the group and looking ahead to what will happen to the members, with some graduating, some looking forward to a summer's activities, and so on. SOCIETAL images in this group seem to be associated with the points in time when members make a transition from the "outside" to the "inside" of the group and vice versa as a consequence of outside events in calendar time.

The trend for SITUATIONAL images in this group is gratifyingly downward, given the instructor's goals for the group. The level is high at the beginning as the group gets used to its unusual setting, the nature of the course, the observation, the mirrors, the cameras, and so on, but attention to these elements of the immediate environment decreases in a more or less regular trend. There are fluctuations, to be sure, but the indications are that the group does not persist for long periods in a substitution of concern with SITUATIONAL images for analysis of the present interaction of the group and the emotional reactions of its members.

The trend of references to OTHER members in the group by the acting member in general goes up, but with wide fluctuations and, one may guess, with considerable effort, in view of the several marked lapses. It is low in the beginning, as expected, if one supposes that it is hard at first for members to address interpretative and evaluative remarks about others to them in their presence. But it seems clear that in time the members are able to achieve it for limited periods. It is high at the very end, even though the peak of SOCIETAL images indicates preparation for departure.

Finally, the trend of references to the SELF is generally upward, though with considerable fluctuation, as in the case of references to the OTHER. The fact that the trends of references to SELF and OTHER are upward while the trend of references to FAN and SIT are generally downward is in line with the evaluative aims of the course.

Taken together with the aims of the course and the efforts of the instructor to bring the interaction around to the analysis of the SELF, OTHER, and GROUP, these results suggest an average record of success in the development of group norms and in learning about the nature of personality defenses—such as displacement and projection—which gradually permitted or enabled group members to turn their attention from images of things external to the group to images of self and other. It is important to recognize, however, that these trends do not occur automatically in all self-analytic groups and that they are markedly variable from session to session. They appear to us to be the result of persistent efforts to turn the process in an analytic direction on the part of the instructor and other members of the group. The trends are probably dependent on the initial composition of the group, particularly its tendencies to polarize, and also upon success in analysis of the polarizations and in the building of group norms that tend to contain or overcome the polarizing tendencies.

To illustrate the variability from group to group, we may compare the other four groups (not shown) to the one shown. None of the other four showed a downward trend in the use of FAN, and at least two of them show an upward trend. All of the groups show references to SOC to be high in the beginning, and at least three of the four show the peak in the middle, but two of the four others fail to show the peak at the end. Three of the other four groups show a downward trend in the use of SIT, though one of them shows a markedly high period in the third quarter; however, one of the other four groups shows a steady upward trend

FIGURE 44   Time Plots over Thirty Sessions of the Rates of the Levels FAN, SOC, SIT, OTH, and SELF (In Standard Scores, One Self-Analytic Group, PSR 1330r, Spring 1974)

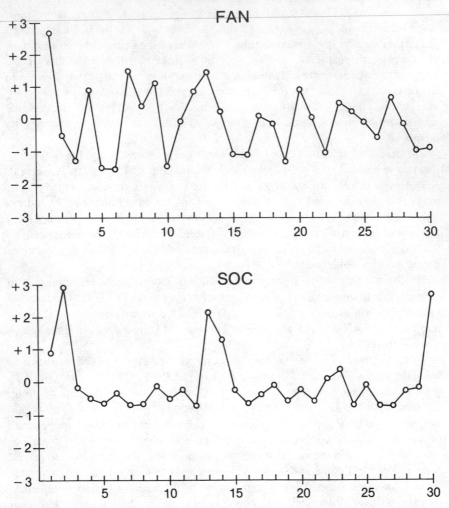

in the use of SIT. Only two of the other four groups show a rising trend in the use of OTHER, and one of these falls off in the final quarter. Only one of the other groups shows a rising trend of references to the SELF, while the other two seem to show a peak in the middle, after which they fall off. Thus we may conclude that there is nothing automatic about success in turning a group effectively in the desired analytic direction.

It is important to state, however, that none of the five groups we have been discussing had the benefit of current feedback from week to week. During this period we were struggling to input the data to the computer and to iron out various problems in the scoring system. The best we were usually able to do was to return a large summary feedback toward the end of the term, and this without

FIGURE 44 (cont.)

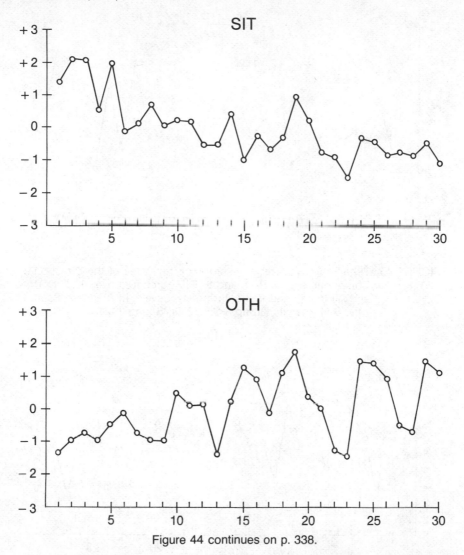

Figure 44 continues on p. 338.

the benefit of the modes of analysis and compression represented by the field diagrams and matrices developed more recently. It is our impression that the mode of rotating team observation and feedback we now employ is markedly effective—the SYMLOG language rapidly becomes a part of the group culture, all members study the data with considerable care, and the analysis is more specific, more focused on particular members and particular behaviors. It seems very probable to us that members learn more, change more, and approximate more closely the ideal pattern in their trends over time. Eventually we shall have the data to test this.

Finally, we may find it helpful in thinking of problems of group development to look briefly at the way in which the general atmosphere of the group may

FIGURE 44 (cont.)

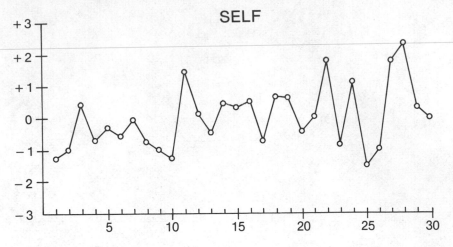

SELF

FIGURE 45 Time Plots over Thirty Sessions of the Rates of the Directional Components U–D, P–N, and F–B, Aggregated over ACT, NON, and All Image and Value Judgment Levels, in Standard Scores (One Self-Analytic Group, PSR 1330r, Spring 1974)

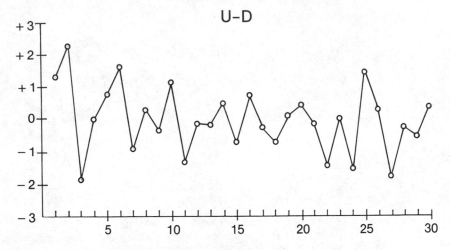

U–D

change, as reflected in the average direction of the components U, D, P, N, F, and B aggregated over all levels, ACT, NON, SELF, OTHER, SIT, SOC, FAN, and VAL—that is, over the multiple levels of behavior, images, and value judgments about images. It seems to be the case that most of the existing theories about group development (see Williamson, 1977) presuppose such an aggregation of all levels of images, though they generally do not make clear distinctions as to levels and sometimes seem to refer to one level and then another, or more usually simply do not recognize the problem of specifying levels at all.

Figure 45 shows time plots for our illustrative group of the rates of the directional components U–D, P–N, and F–B, aggregated over all levels. The logic of

FIGURE 45 (cont.)

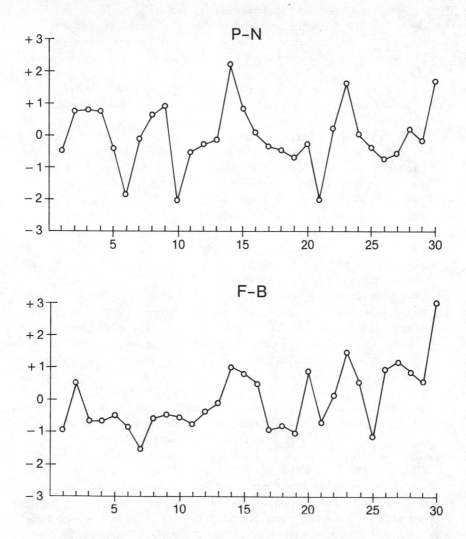

aggregating all levels is given by the assumption that, if there are important general emotional conditions among group members or motives toward given directions of behavior, they may be shown on any of the levels—most directly at the ACT level, but more indirectly at the NON level if the ACT level is inhibited, and at the image levels at increasing levels of distance from the SELF-image. The hypothesis is that, if the motivation is present, we may not be able to predict on what level it will be shown, but we will be able to discover it on one level or another, and hence will be most likely to discover it if we aggregate all levels.

In our illustrative group, the U–D time plot indicates that dominant behavior and imagery are very prominent in the first two sessions but collapse into a deep trough of submissive behavior and imagery in the third. The U–D index fluctuates markedly over the course of the thirty meetings, but there is a general trend downward toward less dominant behavior and imagery. The early occurrence of the high peaks of dominant behavior and imagery tend to fit our heuristic hypothesis that "dominant members may clash right away." Two of our other four groups show a similar pattern, but the other two, though they start with some emphasis on dominant behavior and imagery, show the most marked peaks in the final third of the thirty meetings.

By way of contrast, the P–N time plot for our illustrative group shows its highest peak in the center, more or less coincident with the time just before the group disbands for vacation, but also shows moderately high peaks alternating with low valleys over all thirty sessions, with a peak at the end. There is some tendency among all four of the other groups to show peaks toward the center, and they also show some tendency to have peaks at or near the beginning and at or near the end. One may have the impression that the pressure of impending separation, as well as the pressure of forming the group in the first place, tends to result in motivation to show friendly behavior but that it is very difficult to hold onto a constant state of friendliness, and the group tends to lose it and regain it with some faltering and interrupted periodicity.

Finally, the time plot of F–B for our illustrative group shows a general upward trend, climbing and falling with something approaching a faltering periodicity, to a triumphant high peak at the end. This may be considered an achievement resulting from persistent effort to focus analysis and is consistent with the gradual switch from more distant images to those dealing with the self and others shown in Figure 44. This particular group seems to have realized the self-analytic goal described in the syllabus for the course. Three of the other four groups show a similar pattern of gradual rise in the F–B index. Two of them show a high peak in the first two or three sessions, which gives the impression of a "false start"—it appears that they tried hard to be analytical, but other conditions in the group, apparently rising negativity or perhaps struggles for dominance, brought their brave "false start" to an end. The remaining group of the four showed an apparent false start at the beginning but recovered and showed a substantial peak in the second quarter, as well as another in the third and one at the end.

There is some resemblance of the pattern of our illustrative group to the pattern of phases described by Bennis and Shepard (1956), as well as others reviewed by Williamson (1977), and this group also illustrates well the more articulate model developed by Williamson on the basis of his study of our five groups. However, as we have seen, there is much variation from group to group, and any expectation of a set pattern of phases must be very general. With the aid of SYMLOG observation and feedback, the leader and members of a group do not need to depend upon a theory of phases that hardly ever fits the facts of their particular group. They are encouraged to clarify their values, to define their goals as individuals and for the group in terms of variables that the observation method provides, and to monitor their progress. With this value-based approach, one does not just wait to see if some phase mysteriously happens—one decides what developments are desired and then tries to bring them about.

Chapter 38

Feedback of the Results of Observers' Interaction Scoring

The information provided by observers' SYMLOG Interaction Scoring is extensive and very rich in possibilities of feedback and analysis. A self-analytic group in an academic setting, where many of the members have lively intellectual interests and abilities, is likely to create new ways of selecting and aggregating the data for feedback. It is apparent to us from our experience so far that we have only begun to tap the possibilities of preparing and analyzing the data in feedback. But we have begun to develop some conceptions as to what makes for a good feedback session and what are some of the pitfalls.

The Qualitative Review

One of the pitfalls in giving feedback reports is the failure to tie the tabulations of data from SYMLOG observations back to the concrete memories of the actual events as the participating members experienced them. A qualitative review of what happened during the period selected for analysis, in advance of the numerical analysis, is very helpful in refreshing memories of the session. The sound recording of the session, if there is one, should be listened to by one of the observation team who undertakes to give the qualitative review. The qualitative reporter should have a copy of the SYMLOG Interaction Scoring sheets of all the team members at hand while listening to the tape. Each message is identified as to time, and hence the messages from different observers may be coordinated into an approximate time order as one listens to the tape. The ordinary language description portion of the message will usually allow the listener to locate what the observer has written the message about. The listener will be able to form some useful impressions about the selectivity and seeming biases of given observers, which will later illuminate the numerical data about observer differences. And also the listener will be able to fill in gaps that still remain even after the messages of all observers are taken into account and to add notes of things that seem critical to a better understanding of what happened. From the study of the sound tape and the messages of all the observers, the qualitative reporter prepares a connected concrete story of the session, with events in the proper time order, supported by actual quotations of what persons said at the most salient points and divided into topical episodes of unification or polarization, if these are apparent.

Because it is so important that group members be able to recall their own experience of what happened in connection with the feedback data presented in the form of numbers or diagrams, it is wise not to try to review more material than can be recalled. A potentially useful rule of thumb is to expect a detailed feedback and analysis to take about as much time as the original interaction took (if not more). In our own experience with the group psychology course, we find that we do better in the Friday feedback session if we focus our attention only on the previous Wednesday meeting and do not try to analyze both the Monday and the Wednesday sessions. For recall to be effective, it is important to minimize the time gap between the original interaction and the feedback session.

A further refinement may be worthwhile for some purposes. This is to focus attention on one episode of unification or polarization at a time, if there is more than one major episode in a given session. The diagrams and tabulations naturally make more qualitative sense if they deal with only one dynamic episode or connected chain of events in time than if several different episodes are collapsed into one. The disadvantage of this clarifying refinement, of course, is that more tabulations and diagrams are required, and more time and effort are required to prepare them and to analyze them in the group. Our general practice is to make one set of tabulations and diagrams for the complete session, but sometimes this is not very satisfactory, and one loses the exact connection between the concrete recall of what went on and the abstract relationships shown by the feedback data.

The exact connection between the abstract data and the concrete memories is important for analysis, but of course aggregation of data over long time spans has the compensating advantage of allowing one better to assess the strength of various tendencies, either within the personality or in the group dynamics. One compromise is to use large aggregations to assess the strength of general tendencies and to use fine-grained qualitative analysis of particular episodes that seem to be representative of the general tendencies. To assess the general tendencies, one may wish to aggregate all sessions studied to date or to make plots of the movement of selected variables from session to session over the complete life of the group.

The ACT + NON Field Diagram

Following the qualitative review of the events of the session or episode to be analyzed, one may well want to look at the ACT + NON Field Diagram. For some purposes it is useful to examine the nonverbal behavior separately, but our global impression of the behavior of persons apparently tends to include both the ACT level behavior and the NON-verbal level (see Part III). Our general practice is to add these two levels together over all observers to produce a field diagram representing the behavior of individuals in the group toward each other—the ACT + NON Field Diagram (for the computation procedure, see Appendixes J and S). This diagram usually approximates fairly closely the perception that group members had of each individual.

Thomas Bixby (1978) has made a study of one recent self-analytic group that indicates that the observers' SYMLOG Interaction Scores may give quite a close approximation of the group members' own perceptions of the meeting. Bixby used the short-short form shown in Appendix S, Figure 60, to obtain group members' ratings of each other after each Wednesday session (nine in all) of the group. The correlations obtained between the observers' ACT + NON scores and the members' short form ratings of each other are shown in Table 21. They are quite high.

The same study by Bixby also indicates that the group members' ratings are more closely approximated by the observers' ACT + NON scores than by the observers' scores for the PRO level value judgments presented by group members. In other words, the indications are that the ACT + NON Field Diagram is probably closer to the group members' perceptions of each other than any of the other measures from SYMLOG Scoring, and it is a fairly good predictor, on the average.

Individuals are usually greatly interested in their location on the Observers' Average ACT + NON Field Diagram. Polley's computer programs or hand tabulations may be used to examine the observer's reliability for each of the dimensions. It seems a good plan to introduce a short assessment of observer reliability at the time the Diagram is shown. The Diagram should be complete with all inscriptions, as shown in Figures 9 and 10, Part I. For presentation to the group a normal sized diagram may be shown with an opaque projector, or a large display sized diagram may be prepared on newsprint. The latter method is preferable in our experience, since the opaque projector produces considerable fan noise and must be used in a darkened room, and both of these factors tend to interfere with the discussion.

It is desirable to have all of the inscriptions on the diagram, since these highlight the dynamic characteristics of the constellation of group member locations and serve as a reminder of the heuristic hypotheses that are associated with the inscriptions. The outline of the discussion of the diagram may well follow the order of the discussion of the heuristic hypotheses in Part I of this book. The logic of the analysis of the observers' average field diagram is essentially the same as for a field diagram of the group average ratings of group members. One difference is that for the group member ratings we can examine the unique way in which each *group member* sees the field, whereas for the observer scores we can examine the unique way in which each *observer* sees the field. The unique way in which each individual member views the field is demonstrated in Chapter 12 of this book, and from this demonstration one can see how the motivational and perceptual tendencies of each member may be inferred in part from the unique way in which the individual sees the field. Chapter 35 discusses further the way in which the unusual perceptions of members may be related to the motivational dynamics of the personality, particularly to the tendencies to make certain kinds of transferences.

TABLE 21   Correlations Obtained between Observers' ACT + NON Scores and Members' Short Form Ratings of the Same Meeting, Nine Meetings of One Group, PSR 1330r, Spring 1978

DIMENSION	AVERAGE CORRELATION	RANGE OF CORRELATIONS
U–D	.716	.606 to .863
P–N	.739	.516 to .857
F–B	.673	.355 to .854

From the observers' scores, the data exist for an exactly parallel examination of the way in which particular observers see the field, the biases they show, and the unusual perceptions they have. Ideally, one would like to have a field diagram produced from the scores of each observer separately, and these diagrams could then be compared with each other and with the observers' average field diagram as a part of the discussion of the reliability of observers. In the context of the concrete events of the episode analyzed and the dynamics of the particular constellation of the field, the examination of the unique way in which each observer sees the field could be as enlightening as the analysis of the behavior of the participants toward each other. Practically speaking, however, the production of a separate diagram for each observer and the analysis of it require time and effort that can otherwise be given to the participants, and so something short of this degree of detail may be chosen. At least the group members should know the overall level of confidence that they can place in the observations for the particular diagram discussed, that is, what percentage of the variance for each dimension (U–D, P–N, and F–B) over all group members is due to group members rather than scorers (see Appendix T, Figure 72, the measure called "T").

The discussion of the Observers' Average ACT + NON Field Diagram should include information from the qualitative reporter (the author of the qualitative report at the beginning) and from the maker of the diagram, as to just what kind of concrete things each group members said and did that resulted in the particular location the member has on the diagram. The feedback is not very helpful to the member for purposes of understanding or change, unless the concrete form of the behavior is recognized. One of the persistent faults of feedback reporters is that they do not carry through their analysis of the diagram to the point of making sure they know what the concrete forms of the behavior were for inclusion in their report. In training observers to make feedback reports, it is necessary to stress this point repeatedly. This last bit of effort can make a critical difference in the quality of the feedback. Without it, all of the foregoing effort may be virtually wasted so far as learning is concerned.

The discussion of the dynamics of the field shown in the ACT + NON diagram may well deal with the role of each individual group member in turn, especially those who have played a prominent role in creating the constellation and those who may have been in a strategic location to neutralize the polarization or otherwise change the pattern, though they may not have done so. Once it has been recognized what happened, and why, the individual may ask, "Is this the way I want it to be, or to remain?" And if not, "How can I change?" "What can others do to help me to change?'' ''What can I do to help others change?'' This is the context in which new patterns for the individual and new norms for the group can be articulated, if there is sufficient consensual desire to do so. Even in the absence of consensual desire individuals may be able to recognize that they are in strategic positions and, by taking action in a critical direction, may be able to change the pattern of operation of the group.

The PRO & CON Field Diagram

It is very useful to follow the analysis of the ACT + NON Field Diagram with the presentation and analysis of the Observers' Average PRO & CON Field Diagram, since the IMAGES presented by individuals in their verbal discussion are part and parcel of the dynamic constellation of an episode. A model of the PRO & CON Field Diagram we have found most useful is shown in Appendix S, Figure 61. (The location of the two types of images may be computed by hand, if computer programs are not available, by using the methods described in Appendix J). The average location of each individual's PRO images is shown, with the proper sized circle for the U–D location. And in addition, the average location of the individual's CON images is shown, using only a tiny location circle. The CON image location is connected with the individual's PRO image location by a line. The effect is something like that of particles passing through a cloud chamber and leaving a trail. These two locations, the CON and the PRO, and the direction of the vector connecting the two, give a great deal of information about the individual, his values, his perceptual and evaluative defenses, a clue as to what he is defending against, and the probable location of the self-image, among other things. The ACT + NON location, and the CON-to-PRO image vector summarize perhaps the most important aspects of the individual's personality relevant to the dynamic role the individual has played in the episode.

Important aspects of the relationship of each pair of individuals may be inferred from the CON-to-PRO directional vectors of the two individuals compared with each other. Two individuals may agree more or less closely in the location of their PRO imagery, but if they differ considerably in the location of their CON imagery, one may infer that the things they will try hardest to avoid are quite different, and hence they may react quite differently in another polarization; they may even be on the two poles vis-à-vis each other. Or two individuals may seem to be trying to avoid the same thing, more or less, but disagree on the direction in which they wish to go, as indicated by their PRO imagery. Hence, they may unite only when both are in opposition to the same CON image. One would expect the greatest probability of agreement between two individuals when they agree in the location of both their PRO and their CON imagery. One would expect the greatest probability of disagreement when the PRO image location of each one is the same as the CON image location of the other. An individual whose CON-to-PRO directional vector is nearly at right angles to those of some set of parallel vectors may be singled out as tending to act as a neutralizer, a mediator, or a scapegoat. The CON-to-PRO image directional vector diagram gives information about the dynamics of the episode that may not appear or be so evident in the ACT + NON behavioral diagram since it shows directions of movement as well as present locations. It is desirable to have the inscription of the polarization–unification overlay on the diagram and to compare the constellation with that of the ACT + NON Field Diagram.

It is critical that the member of the feedback team presenting the PRO & CON Field Diagram, in collaboration with the team qualitative reporter, should be able to supply the exact concrete images that resulted in the diagram locations of the PRO and CON images. We make the heuristic assumption that the particular imagery the individual may have presented or focused upon in the particular episode may well be due to a displacement, transference, or projection of feelings generated by unconscious needs and imagery. We assume that the present object or image may be chosen as a substitute because it has the same or a similar *evaluative significance*—that is, for the individual in question it is located close in the field to the previously significant object. The location of the PRO and CON images of the individual in the present episode, then, may well give important clues as to the location of the enduringly significant objects or images for the individual, and hence, through further analysis, guided by the location, one may hope to discover the identity of the developmental precursors of the present imagery.

We assume that images that are close to each other in the perceptual evaluative field of the individual may be connected with each other by associations, and that by following the associations (as in "free association") one may learn more about the reasons for the degree of feeling invested in the particular episode and hence about the important dynamics of the personality. These assumptions, of course, are the usual assumptions of the psychoanalytic point of view. What is new is the hypothesis that location of an image in the three-dimensional SYMLOG evaluative space may be an important clue to the possibly unconscious imagery. Objects or images located in the same place in the evaluative space are psychologically appropriate substitutes for each other, or so we suppose, for heuristic purposes. Others as well as the actor may thus be able to help discover the imagery that is unconscious for the actor.

Who-to-Whom Matrices

From an examination of the ACT + NON Field Diagram and the PRO & CON Field Diagram, one can derive certain predictions as to how members may be expected to relate to each other as pairs. Neither of the two diagrams actually presents this information, however, since they are made by summing the behavior or content presented by each particular individual over all pairs and to the group as a whole. It is of interest next, then, to look at the WHO-to-WHOM matrix information to see whether the persons we might expect to agree with each other or to disagree with each other, according to their location in the dynamic configuration of the polarization or unification of the episode, actually do so.

It is convenient to examine the WHO-to-WHOM matrix for one direction at a time, as described in Appendix U. The program, called TABULA, gives a tabulation of the raw scores in matrix form for each of the directions U, D, P, N,

F, B, as well as the total of all these. If one wishes to examine the degree to which the interaction directed from one individual to another is "unusual" (in the sense used earlier for "unusual perceptions" in the ratings), the program for matrix analysis may be used, with the option called "Round Robin ANOVA and Jackknife," a new development by Warner, Stoto, and Kenny (1977) for the analysis of matrices with the diagonal missing. (In interpersonal ratings, each individual member also rates the self, so that the diagonal is filled, but in ACT + NON level behavior directed from one individual to another, the diagonal is blank, since we omit the logical possibility that an individual might direct overt behavior toward the self.) Observer reliability may be examined at the same time, and "unusual observations" may be detected and analyzed from data provided by the program called BIAS, described by Polley in Appendixes T and U.

The difficulty with this more thorough approach to feedback of information concerning the kind of behavior each individual directs to every other is that it is so voluminous and complex, as well as atomistic. What one would like, for easier assimilation and discussion, perhaps, is a summary matrix reduced to summary letter types, similar to that shown in Appendix I, Figure 55, but based upon the ACT + NON level behavior instead of ratings. From such a matrix the cells containing unusual behavior of one individual toward another could be detected by simply searching with the eye along the rows and the columns. Such a matrix is not easy to come by, however, since it actually requires a large amount of computation and integration of the information. It would require the information provided by the Round Robin ANOVA and Jackknife program on the six different directional matrices all assembled into one matrix, and this is quite an order.

For most practical purposes, one is more interested in the Positive and Negative quality of the interaction directed from one individual to another than in the U–D and F–B dimensions, and for this, the P matrix and the N matrix will suffice. Nor is it necessary to useful feedback to have the fine-grained computation of the "unusual behavior" that is the residual that remains when the sending tendency of the actor and the receiving tendency of the receiver is taken out. Much of the useful information is contained in the raw frequencies, as delivered by the program TABULA. Alternatively, one may hand-tabulate easily by assigning one observation team member to read the WHO-to-WHOM cell of all the ACT + NON behavior with a P component directly from the SYMLOG message sheets, and the other to fill in the WHO-to-WHOM matrix with tally marks as directed by the reader. The same may be done for the ACT + NON behavior with an N component. These two matrices of raw frequencies can form the basis of a very useful piece of feedback. The team member who makes the report should make sure he or she knows, in terms of having read the messages, just what the concrete Positive and Negative acts were for those relationships that are salient by their frequency of either type of act.

One might proceed in exactly the same way to prepare a WHO-to-WHOM matrix that would show the persons to whom each of the members addresses PRO images and a similar matrix for the CON images. This would be of great interest in connection with the PRO & CON Field Diagram, with the heuristic hypothesis that an individual would tend to direct CON value judgments to the persons who are on the opposite side of a polarization from the self and, conversely, would tend to direct PRO value judgments to the persons within the same circle of reference as the self. Presumably this would hold only when the persons in the group were divided from each other in their PRO and CON value judgments and would not hold where all were united in opposition to some CON image. We have not yet had the opportunity to explore these ideas, but they illustrate very well the way in which the pursuit of analysis in a regular feedback session verges over into the pursuit of new general insights and heuristic hypotheses that may help to build the discipline of group psychology.

Feedback on the Relative Levels of Imagery

We have experimented with various indices that represent what we consider to be the "work" of a self-analytic group. A verbal and normative description of the work we hope for is described in the syllabus for the group psychology course. We are quite satisfied to start a given session with conversation devoted to images of more distant persons and scenes, at the levels of FANTASY, SOCIETY, or SITUATION, and by doing so we hope to allow group members to locate the feelings and attitudes that are their preoccupations at the time. As certain images begin to become focal, however, in a pattern of unification or polarization of attitudes among the group members, we hope that members will begin to note the general character of the images and to search their minds to find more general or chronic issues in the group or characteristics of individual personalities of members that may be providing the deeper levels of motivation for the directions and kinds of images that are being presented at the more surface levels of FANTASY, SOCIETY, or SITUATION. The analytic work of the group, properly speaking (as distinguished from this prework phase) consists in attempting to interpret, by rational, problem-solving processes, what the corresponding issues may be at the level of images of the GROUP, the OTHER, and the SELF.

The work is successful if the interpretation gives members some additional consensual insight into the underlying issues in the here-and-now interaction that may be talked about at the levels of SELF, OTHER, and GROUP. In such a case the image or images at the more distant or surface levels (FANTASY, SOCIETY, or SITUATION) may be treated in discussion as a set of metaphors used to further define and express the underlying issues at the levels of SELF, OTHER, and GROUP. This reinterpretation and use of earlier images to reveal present concerns of persons as individuals and group members constitutes a "feedback cycle," though not based on formal tabulations of data, but on immediate memory. A still further stage of success may be reached if this interpretive process enables the individuals most involved or the group as a whole to reach some new normative consensus as to the way behavior should go in the future, in order better to realize the values of the individuals or of the group as a whole.

Given this conception of the self-analytic "work" of the group and its desired outcome, a number of indices are suggested that may be used for monitoring the process within a given session or over a series of sessions. A relatively simple one may be formed by assigning weighted values to each of the levels as follows: FANTASY = 6, SOCIETY = 5, SITUATION = 4, GROUP = 3, OTHER = 2, and SELF = 1. The number of images presented in a given time period at each of the levels is multipled by its weight, and the total is divided by the total number of images. The index will thus be high when the images presented are relatively more "distant" from the self-image and low when they are closer or specifically about the self-image. This index is regularly computed by Swann's program for making time plots (see Appendix S). This index will ordinarily fluctuate from a high level to a low level within a given session as group members first search around for a topic or theme that gives rise to a unification or polarization at the image level within the group and then subject it to more rational analysis. It is interesting and useful in feedback sessions to see whether this turning from more distant imagery (represented by a high level of the index) to imagery focused on the relationships of self to other and to the group (represented by a low level of the index) has been accomplished, and if so by whom or what subgroup of persons acting together, and whether the cycle (a feedback cycle within the course of a single meeting) occurs only once or, as may be desired, a number of times within the session.

Although the time plot of fluctuations of image level within a given session may be especially helpful in pinpointing the events by which the level is changed, very useful characterizations of the kind of imagery of the session may be made simply by tabulating the total amount of imagery at each level over the whole session, or longer periods of interaction. Table 22 shows the percentage of total imagery falling at each level for two different groups over the total span of their existence. Several points of interest may be mentioned. First it may be seen that there are marked differences between the two groups. The spring group shows about 28 percent of its imagery at the relatively distant level of SOCIETAL images, as compared to about 6 percent of the fall group. (The spring group contained one member who considered herself quite unconventional, and the content she presented in the group sparked off many discussions of communes, changes in the family and sexual mores, parental responsibility for the care of children, and many other issues of life in the larger society.) Nevertheless, this group managed to give considerable attention to images of the SELF, with a percentage score of about 21 percent of the imagery at that level. Moreover, in this group the attention given to imagery of the SELF exceeded that given to imagery of the OTHER, which in turn exceeded that given to the GROUP.

The fall group, by way of contrast, shows relatively little concentration on SOCIETAL imagery, but, on the other hand, neither do the members manage to reach a high level of concentration on SELF imagery. Only 13 percent of the imagery in this group was at the level of SELF, only about half as much as was devoted to the level OTHER, which in turn was exceeded very considerably by imagery at the level of the GROUP as a whole. Although the fall group avoided concentration on the most distant imagery, at the levels of SIT, SOC, and FAN they fell short of a major concentration at the level of least distant imagery, that concerned with the SELF.

The most desirable level or levels of imagery will depend on the nature of the

TABLE 22   Percentage of Total Imagery at Each Level for Two Self-analytic
Groups over Their Total Time Span

	IMAGE LEVEL						
GROUP	Self	Other	Group	Sit	Soc	Fan	TOTAL
PSR 1330r, fall 1976	13.3	26.9	37.7	5.7	6.4	10.0	100.0
PSR 1330r, spring 1977	20.9	19.8	13.9	9.2	28.3	8.0	100.0
Average of the two	17.0	23.4	25.8	7.4	17.4	9.0	100.0

group, of course, and can be defined only by reference to values. Values, in turn, are always the values of some individual or individuals. In the definition of the goals of the academic self-analytic group, the instructor defines his goals in the syllabus and hopes to persuade members to adopt similar goals. In this particular case the instructor's goals for the group are stated in such a way that there is no general priority given to concentration on the SELF level, as distinguished from the level of analysis of the OTHER and of the GROUP. All three are encouraged, while images at the levels of SIT, SOC, and FAN are encouraged as beginning points for the formation of unifications and polarizations that may then be analyzed, but they are discouraged if they persist in a given session beyond the point where they provide enough material for analysis at the levels of SELF, OTHER, and GROUP. The latter three levels are thus given priority, and their predominance over the levels of SIT, SOC, and FAN may thus be taken as a measure of the efficiency of the process from the instructor's point of view.

In a therapy group the therapist might want to place first priority on content dealing with the SELF, with other levels of content given lower priority in accordance with the theoretical orientation of the therapist. A psychoanalytically oriented therapist might place a relatively high priority on content at the level of FANTASY as well as at the level of the SELF. In some kinds of training groups, such as those used in organization development, the trainer might place a high priority on content at the level of the GROUP, and perhaps on SIT and SOC, if these were the categories in which references to the organizational contexts usually fell. In a task-oriented team engaged in the performance of its task, the leader might place the highest priority on content at the level of the SITUATION that presents the task. In a classroom seminar on a sociological topic, the teacher might well place the highest priority on content at the level of SOCIETY. The priorities one might want to give to particular levels plainly vary according to the purposes for which the group is called together.

One must add to this a few qualifications, however, if one wishes to take the specific purpose of the group as the main point of reference for value judgments. Although the person or persons who convene the group or are the designated leaders of it may be able to establish a clear priority in their own minds as to level of content, there is no guarantee that group members will always have the same values, and hence the same priorities. It may or may not be easy to establish norms regulating the level of content, and such norms, like all social norms, require effort and learning in their development and will be subject to vagueness, difficulties and differences in interpretation, degrees of variation and deviation, fluctuation through time, and so on.

A second qualification regarding the norms one may hope to develop regulating content is that most groups, perhaps all, have necessities or needs given by the fact that they are groups, quite apart from the specific purposes or goals that may be identified as their primary reason for being. Most groups probably need to engage in some discussion of their nature as a group, the constellation of locations of members, their leadership and organization, the specific roles and functions of different members, the personalities and needs of particular members, the situation in which the group exists, and the larger society of which the group is a part. These needs or necessities will result in the devoting of some time and attention to content levels other than those given top priority. Those content levels of lower priority should nevertheless be recognized and given an appropriate value and enough time and attention. A too literal-minded deduction of the content priorities from the specific primary purposes of the group is likely to prove oppressive as well as unrealistic and to generate dissatisfaction over the long run.

In any event, the SYMLOG system provides the group leader and group members with theory and methods for maximizing desirable features in the development of the group in a systematic fashion, based openly upon explicitly stated values. The use of SYMLOG in continuous or intermittent cycles of feedback should improve the operation of the group and enable it more effectively to reach its stated goals. It is our hope that the SYMLOG system will make valuable contributions both to researchers and to practitioners in efforts of this kind.

Part V

Technical Appendixes

Robert F. Bales, with contributions by
Stephen P. Cohen, Howard Swann,
and Richard Polley

Appendix A

SYMLOG Directional
Definitions

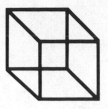

Direction U

Behavior

ACT U — Acts overtly toward others in a way that seems Dominant (Upward). Examples: takes the initiative in speaking; speaks loudly, firmly, rapidly, or with few pauses for the other to reply; holds the floor with "uh . . ."; or addresses communications to the group as a whole rather than to individuals.

NON U — Gives nonverbal signs that seem Dominant (Upward). Examples: moves strongly, rapidly, or expansively; sits or stands very straight; keeps very alert and active; keeps arms or legs in open posture; holds shoulders squarely back; holds chest high; holds elbows back with palms forward as if ready to grasp; holds wrists firm; or, in standing, holds the knees firmly back or grips the ground with the toes.

Content Image

U in SEL
U in OTH
U in GRP
— Mentions a content image of some U element in the SELF, in the OTHER, or in the GROUP. Examples: describes self, other, or group as active, talkative, strong, assertive, powerful, adventurous, thick-skinned, extroverted, superior, of high social status, rich, highly educated, experienced, successful, older, or self-confident.

U in SIT — Mentions a content image of some element in the external SITUATION immediately facing the group as if it were acting toward the self, other, or group in a U manner. Examples: Some outside stimulus is described as imposing powerful demands for response, or as overwhelming. "Time is running out." "There

355

is too much to do." "We are about to lose." "We are up against it." "It is a great challenge."

U in SOC   Mentions a content image of some U element in SOCIETY. Examples: a rich person; a powerful public figure; a person of high formal rank in government, the military, finance, large industry, or the arts; a person of distinctive achievement; or a high-status collectivity such as the upper classes, powerful corporate groups, management, owners.

U in FAN   Mentions a content image of some U element from some form of FANTASY, or with some fantasy-arousing quality. Examples: a giant in a dream, a general in a play, a literary reference to destiny, a myth of ascension, an expensive car, an anecdote of walking on water; or, from the past or current outside experience of the individual: "My father was huge." "My mother was more dominant than my father." "I just won the pole vault!"

Value Judgment

PRO U   Makes a value judgment in favor of or against some U image.
CON U   Examples: "I am not going to try that trick of walking on water again!" (CON U in FAN). "I think we should all feel free to speak up whenever we like" (PRO U in GRP).

Direction UP

Behavior

ACT UP   Acts overtly toward others in a way that seems Dominant (Upward) and Friendly (Positive). Examples: takes the initiative in asking others about themselves; talks about others in the group in a friendly way; or initiates new actions to symbolize friendly social interest, such as making introductions, beginning the use of nicknames, giving compliments, or making social small talk.

NON UP   Gives nonverbal signs that seem Dominant (Upward) and Friendly (Positive). Examples: takes the initiative in exchanges of smiles or waves, shakes hands warmly, approaches closer to the other, places hands on the shoulders of others, claps others on the back, links arms, or puts arms around the other; gives the other a seat, food, or drink; physically demonstrates affection or good will.

Content Image

UP in SEL   Mentions a content image of some UP element in the SELF, the
UP in OTH   OTHER, or in the GROUP. Examples: describes self, other, or

UP in GRP	group as outgoing, open, sociable, good-natured, happy, hale and hearty, cordial, genial, socially extroverted, or popular.
UP in SIT	Mentions a content image of some element in the external SITUATION facing the group as if it were acting toward the self, other, or group in a UP manner. Examples: defines some sponsor or condition outside the group that encourages the self and others to form a strong solidary group; some outside inducement that rewards the identification of the members with each other as a group; or some outside source of reward that induces the members ot identify themselves with it, e.g., "The money is out there just waiting for us!" "We are bound to win the pennant!" "This is our happy home!" "Our luck is holding!"
UP in SOC	Mentions a content image of some UP element in SOCIETY. Examples: one's own ethnic group, the good institutions, the generous foundations, our founding fathers, our sponsors, our totem group.
UP in FAN	Mentions a content image of some UP element from some form of FANTASY or with some fantasy-arousing quality. Examples: a dream of a big dish of ice cream, a play about the most popular person at the party, a book called *All-Time Greats,* the myth of the birth of a hero, the crowning of Miss America, an anecdote about Queen for a Day; or from the past or current outside experience of the individual: "My old man was a hockey star." "My older brother was always ready to back me up in fights."

Value Judgment

PRO UP	Makes a value judgment in favor of or against some UP image.
CON UP	Examples: "We are lucky to be Americans!" (PRO UP in SOC), "The higher they rise, the harder they fall!" (CON UP in FAN).

Direction UPF

Behavior

ACT UPF	Acts overtly toward others in a way that seems Dominant (Upward), Friendly (Positive), and Instrumentally Controlled (Forward). Examples: takes the initiative in persuading or offering to help the group on a task of confronting the group as a whole, offers democratic leadership, or tries to smooth out conflicts between group members by mediating, conciliating, or moderating so as to get ahead with the tasks of the group.
NON UPF	Gives nonverbal signs that seem Dominant (Upward), Friendly (Positive), and Instrumentally Controlled (Forward). Examples:

takes a position in front of the group in the direction of attention or physical movement necessary for a group task; places the self between the group and some threatening location; sits in a prominent place in order to communicate with as many group members as possible about the task; demonstrates some form of task-oriented behavior for others to perform; or tries to persuade others to perform work by work gestures.

Content Image

UPF in SEL UPF in OTH UPF in GRP	Mentions a content image of some UPF element in the SELF, in the OTHER, or in the GROUP. Examples: describes self, other, or the group as high in leadership; as interested in the group's success in the task; as taking the initiative in helping the group's task performance or in building group unity or morale in relation to group tasks; as a "natural leader"; or as an "inspirational leader."
UPF in SIT	Mentions a content image of some element in the external SITUATION immediately facing the group as if it were acting toward the self, other, or group, in a UPF manner. Examples: "The management of this business is showing good leadership." "The reward for our improved performance will be given to the group as a whole." "The incentive system here is arranged so that we will have to cooperate and maintain a high standard of performance in order to receive the highest rewards."
UPF in SOC	Mentions a content image of some UPF element in SOCIETY. Examples: a school where one can obtain needed teaching, a labor union that is regarded positively, a positively regarded action-oriented organization, one's own political party, or one's own candidate for election.
UPF in FAN	Mentions a content image of some UPF element from some form of FANTASY or with some fantasy-arousing quality. Examples: a dream of a ladder leading to heaven, a play about Abraham Lincoln, a myth about a messiah, or, from the past or current outside experience of the individual: "I was the leader of the team in high school." "My mother was the real head of the family." "Our team won today!"

Value Judgment

PRO UPF CON UPF	Makes a value judgment in favor of or against some UPF image. Examples: "John has what it takes, why not let him lead?" (PRO UPF in JOHN). "I've had enough of pie in the sky!" (CON UPF in FAN).

Direction UF

Behavior

ACT UF   Acts overtly toward others in a way that seems Dominant (Upward), and Instrumentally Controlled (Forward). Examples: acts as chairman or manager of the group, calls the meeting together, suggests an agenda, calls on individuals to participate, regulates communication between others, makes impersonal attempts to persuade or guide others, makes suggestions for group performance, gives routine signals regulating performance, closes the meeting, or dismisses the group.

NON UF   Gives nonverbal signs that seem Dominant (Upward), and Instrumentally Controlled (Forward). Examples: starts a new phase of activity prior to the others or goes first; maintains a facial appearance of confident dignity, impartiality, or self-control; or holds head well up, holds face composed, with wings of nose relaxed, mouth and brows relaxed.

Content Image

UF in SEL
UF in OTH
UF in GRP   Mentions a content image of some UF element in the SELF, in the OTHER, or in the GROUP. Examples: describes self, other, or group as firm, resolute, managerial, identified with impersonal ideals, identified with external task demands, determined, businesslike, controlling, concerned with receiving loyalty rather than love, or concerned with receiving effective performance in relation to the task.

UF in SIT   Mentions a content image of some element in the external SITUATION immediately facing the group as if it were acting toward the self, other, or group in a UF manner. Examples: the situation is described as providing a fast and dependable feedback on success or failure of efforts to perform according to a work standard or according to a value standard, or as providing reward or punishment according to individual performance: "Our job is cut out for us." "This is not an easy situation, but it is a fair one." "People will get what they deserve in this organization, no more, no less."

UF in SOC   Mentions a content image of some UF element in SOCIETY. Examples: a high-status business or occupational group, a judge, a manager, a certified public accountant, a priest, a customs inspector, an administrator, the courts, the law, an examining and certifying system.

UF in FAN   Mentions a content image of some UF element in some form of FANTASY or with some fantasy-arousing quality. Examples: a play about justice, a book on constitutional powers of the president, a myth about Solomon, a dream about blind justice holding the scales, an anecdote about red tape in the bureaucracy, or, from the past or current outside experience of the individual: "I've got to go take that test tomorrow."

Value Judgment

PRO UF CON UF	Makes a value judgment in favor of or against some UF image. Examples: "I found that being businesslike didn't pay off" (CON UF in SEL). "I wish you weren't so impersonal" (CON UF in OTH). "We've got to keep our eyes on the ball" (PRO UF in GRP).

Direction UNF

Behavior

ACT UNF	Acts overtly toward others in a way that seems Dominant (Upward), Unfriendly (Negative), and Instrumentally Controlled (Forward). Examples: tries to take control arbitrarily or moralistically, tries to control what should be considered right or wrong in the group, tries to restrict others, makes demands, gives commands, shows disapproval or moral indignation, or assumes a pose of moral superiority.
NON UNF	Gives nonverbal signs that seem Dominant (Upward), Unfriendly (Negative), and Instrumentally Controlled (Forward). Examples: raises brows in disapproval, closes eyes as if giving up in disgust, or indicates hauteur by facial expression, e.g., shows fullness of the throat below the jaw (suggesting a rising of the gorge), opens mouth slightly (as if about to gag), pushes the lower lip somewhat forward (as if in disdain), or constricts the nostrils (as if sampling an offensive odor).

Content Image

UNF in SEL UNF in OTH UNF in GRP	Mentions a content image of some UNF element in the SELF, in the OTHER, or in the GROUP. Examples: describes self, other, or group as authoritarian, moralistic, inflexible, inhibiting, demanding, punishing, prejudiced, dogmatic, insistent on discipline, self-righteous, arbitrary, pompous, or self-important.
UNF in SIT	Mentions a content image of some element in the external SITUATION immediately facing the group as if it were acting toward the self, other, or group in a UNF manner. Examples: "We're in a tough situation." "Some of us are not going to get out of this alive." "This situation will separate the men from the boys." "In this situation, individual failure to conform or meet

the standards will be punished.'' ''In this situation every man is expected to do his duty.''

UNF in SOC   Mentions a content image of some UNF element in SOCIETY. Examples: the Marine Corps, a drill sergeant, the boss of a chain gang, a restaurant inspector, a fire chief, the warden of a prison, a hell-fire-and-damnation preacher, a prosecuting attorney, a dictator, the draft, or, when negatively regarded, the police, the system, the establishment.

UNF in FAN   Mentions a content image of some UNF element from some form of FANTASY or with some fantasy-arousing quality. Examples: a dream about Hitler, a play about DeGaulle, a book on dictatorship, a myth about the Last Judgment, the recruiting poster ''Uncle Sam wants *you*!'' a negative anecdote about the Pope, or, from the past or current outside experience of the individual: ''Dad was very strict with all of us.'' ''I had to walk six miles to school every day when I was a kid, and got a dressing down if I was late on either end!''

Value Judgment

PRO UNF   Makes a value judgment in favor of or against some UNF image.
CON UNF   Examples: ''What this country needs most is law and order!'' (PRO UNF in SOC). ''I'm tired of being bossed around by you'' (CON UNF in OTH).

Direction UN

Behavior

ACT UN   Acts overtly toward others in a way that seems Dominant (Upward) and Unfriendly (Negative). Examples: overrides others in conversation, interrupts and outtalks others, refuses to give way in conversation, disregards others' feelings, attacks or deflates the status of others, asserts own status, or shows aggression or active hostility.

NON UN   Gives nonverbal signs that seem Dominant (Upward) and Unfriendly (Negative). Examples: frowns, scowls, knits and lowers the brows, glares with rigidly open eyes, dilates the nostrils (as in anger), pushes the lower lip and lower jaw forward (as if about to bite), puffs out the upper lip and the cheeks with mouth pressed closed (as if barely containing rage), or physically attacks, propels, or restrains others.

Content Image

UN in SEL   Mentions a content image of some UN element in the SELF, in
UN in OTH   the OTHER, or in the GROUP. Examples: describes self, other,

UN in GRP	or group as dominating, aggressive, or hostile, tough-minded, ambitious, contemptuous of others, insensitive, competitive, overbearing, or threatening.
UN in SIT	Mentions a content image of some element in the external SITUATION immediately facing the group as if it were acting toward the self, other, or group in a UN manner. Examples: says there is not enough of some necessary resource to go around or that the situation guarantees that some of all members of the group will fail: "It's every man for himself." "It's dog eat dog." "Let the buyer beware."
UN in SOC	Mentions a content image of some UN element in SOCIETY. Examples: gangsters, hired guns, crime in the streets, armaments of other nations, a prize fighter, a con man, a kidnapper, an assassin, the secret police, roller derby, violence on television, foreign agents, foreign intelligence.
UN in FAN	Mentions a content image of some UN element from some form of FANTASY or with some fantasy-arousing quality. Examples: a dream of murdering someone, a play about spies, a book about an execution, an ad for handguns, an anecdote about a mad dog, or, from the past or current outside experience of the individual: "I was afraid he was coming at me!" "My roommate was robbed last night." "My mother was a terror!"

Value Judgment

PRO UN	Makes a value judgment in favor of or against some UN image.
CON UN	Examples: "So far as other countries are concerned, you have to be prepared to meet force with force" (PRO UN in SOC). "Only the strong have a right to survive" (PRO UN in SEL). "I've tried to control my anger" (CON UN in SEL).

Direction UNB

Behavior

ACT UNB	Acts overtly toward others in a way that seems Dominant (Upward), Unfriendly (Negative), and Emotionally Expressive (Backward). Examples: attacks authority or conventionality, shows disrespect, attracts attention by extravagant mannerisms or dress, displays the self as fascinating, amazing, shocking, unrestrained, spectacular, mysterious, or incalculable.
NON UNB	Gives nonverbal signs that seem Dominant (Upward), Unfriendly (Negative), and Emotionally Expressive (Backward). Examples: preens the self; displays the self through mannerisms; laughs derisively (with lower lip down and retiring, corners drawn down); mimics for effect the facial expressions of sur-

prise, disgust, or vexation (e.g., depresses the inner brow as in aggression, raises the outer brows as in surprise, opens mouth in an angry position as if shouting, raises the wings of the nose as in anger, curls the upper lip as in anger, or depresses the corners of the mouth and pushes the lower lip forward as if "making a poor face" to ridicule submissive dependency).

Content Image

UNB in SEL UNB in OTH UNB in GRP	Mentions a content image of some UNB element in the SELF, in the OTHER, or in the GROUP. Examples: describes self, other, or group as rebellious, self-centered, deviant, exhibitionistic, narcissistic, ruggedly individualistic, selfish, self-gratifying, or conspicuous.
UNB in SIT	Mentions a content image of some element in the external SITUATION immediately facing the group as if it were acting toward the self, other, or group in a UNB manner. Examples: says there is something about the situation that interferes with the exercise of authority or with the maintenance of standards, or that tends to make authority weak, unpredictable, or negative in its effects: "Our rules don't mean anything any more." "Don't leave any doors unlocked." "The streets aren't safe anymore."
UNB in SOC	Mentions a content image of some UNB element in SOCIETY. Examples: Public enemy number one, smugglers, motorcycle gangs, guerrilla leaders, anarchists, outlaws, criminals, wealthy playboys, big-time gamblers, revolutionaries, capitalist bandits, robber barons, sexual and sex-role deviants, delinquents, freethinkers, drug peddlers, Watergate burglars, lobbyists, junketing Congressmen, wire-tappers, mail openers, highjackers, terrorists, income tax evaders.
UNB in FAN	Mentions a content image of some UNB element from some form of FANTASY or with some fantasy-arousing quality. Examples: a dream of taking off all one's clothes, a book about *Daredevils over Niagara Falls,* a book about witchcraft, an anecdote about Halloween tricks, or, from the past or current outside experience of the individual, "I used to rip off cameras and things like that." "I'm out for fun and profit."

Value Judgment

PRO UNB CON UNB	Makes a value judgment in favor of or against some UNB image. Examples: "This place is too square—let's get out of here" (PRO UNB in GRP). "All work and no play makes Jack a dull boy" (PRO UNB in SEL). "I rob banks because that's where the money is" (PRO UNB in SEL). "What an ego trip!" (CON UNB in OTH).

Direction UB

Behavior

ACT UB	Acts overtly toward others in a way that seems Dominant (Upward) and Emotionally Expressive (Backward). Examples: takes the initiative in entertainment, jokes, tells stories, dramatizes, or speaks in emotionally toned words designed to evoke feelings, fantasies, or moods; acts out an emotion; stimulates the imagination of others, exaggerates, amuses, or releases tension in self or others.
NON UB	Gives nonverbal signs that seem Dominant (Upward), and Emotionally Expressive (Backward). Examples: physically dramatizes to entertain, strikes poses, or takes roles; mimics humorously the expressions, emotions, voice, manner, or bodily movement or attitudes of persons or animals in anecdotes; or exercises indirect suggestion on others by physical movement that initiates a change in mood toward greater emotional expression.

Content Image

UB in SEL UB in OTH UB in SIT	Mentions a content image of some UB element in the SELF, in the OTHER, or in the GROUP. Examples: describes self, other, or group as expressive, dramatic, entertaining, joking, playful, full of novelty and creativity, whimsical, fanciful, changeable, or having a good sense of humor.
UB in SIT	Mentions a content image of some element in the external SITUATION immediately facing the group as if it were acting toward the self, other, or group in a UB manner. Examples: defines some aspect of the external situation as tending to relax standards, to relax enforcement of rules, or to suspend instrumental demands; or as tending to release tension or to arouse humorous or playful response, e.g., "This is a holiday." "Time for a coffee break." "It's after five." "This is my birthday." "It will all look different tomorrow—relax!" "End of the line—everybody out!"
UB in SOC	Mentions a content image of some UB element in SOCIETY. Examples: stand-up comedians, the creative arts, the theater, the ballet, the circus, Mardi Gras, fiestas, fairs, spectacles, parades, celebrations, dances, ethnic holidays, amusement parks.
UB in FAN	Mentions a content image of some UB element from some form of FANTASY or with some fantasy-arousing quality. Examples: a dream of going up in a balloon, a musical called *The Fantasticks,* a book about Bob Hope, a trip to Disneyland, or, from the past or current outside experiences of the individual, "I had a funny dream last night." "I thought everybody was clapping." "They loved me in Detroit."

Value Judgment

PRO UB	Makes a value judgment in favor of or against some UB image.
CON UB	Examples: "Don't you think we've goofed off long enough?" (CON UB in GRP). "Surprise! Happy Birthday!" (PRO UB in SIT).

Direction UPB

Behavior

ACT UPB	Acts overtly toward others in a way that seems Dominant (Upward), Friendly (Positive), and Emotionally Expressive (Backward). Examples: takes the initiative in protecting or nurturing the other(s), gives unconditional praise or reward, boosts the status of the other, gives approval and encouragement, gives warm acceptance without regard to the excellence or failure of performance of the other, or gives support, reassurance, comfort, or consolation.
NON UPB	Gives nonverbal signs that seem Dominant (Upward), Friendly (Positive), and Emotionally Expressive (Backward). Examples: gives emotional support by touching, feeding, protecting, or helping physically, or shows emotional warmth in facial expressions, e.g., smiles or laughs warmly and supportively (in a warm laugh, wrinkles are formed against and beneath the eyes as the lower eyelids are pushed up by the cheek muscles).

Content Image

UPB in SEL UPB in OTH UPB in GRP	Mentions a content image of some UPB element in the SELF, in the OTHER, or in the GROUP. Examples: describes self, other, or group as enthusiastic, emotionally supportive, helpful, warm, nurturant, or rewarding, or anxiety-reducing; as making one feel at home; or as protective of the underprivileged or helpless.
UPB in SIT	Mentions a content image of some element in the SITUATION immediately facing the group as if it were acting toward the self, other, or group in a UPB manner. Examples: defines some aspect of the external situation as providing easy rewards or resources for success. "There's no hurry here." "We're in free." "We'll be safe here." "We can hold out here indefinitely." "There's no place like home." "Home was never like this!"
UPB in SOC	Mentions a content image of some UPB element in SOCIETY. Examples: the home, the family, the foster home, the welfare system, the liberal political party, the land, the farm, the homestead, the community, the old-style political boss, the "old-fashioned mother," America as the "home of the homeless," a

pension system, an old people's home, medical insurance, the "old-fashioned doctor."

UPB in FAN   Mentions a content image of some UPB element from some form of FANTASY or with some fantasy-arousing quality. Examples: a dream of being safe in a castle, a myth of paradise, a book about the South Sea islands, the *Mona Lisa,* the symbol of America as the granary of the world, or, from the past or current outside experience of the individual, "There's nothing she wouldn't do for me!"

Value Judgment

PRO UPB   Makes a value judgment in favor of or against some UPB image.
CON UPB   Examples: "*My* mother was so good to me she was suffocating!" (CON UPB in FAN). "I'll bring some cookies next time" (PRO UPB in SEL). "My mother always used to try to console me when I'd lose a game, and I just couldn't stand that sickly sweet stuff!" (CON UPB in FAN).

Direction P

Behavior

ACT P   Acts overtly toward others in a way that seems Friendly (Positive). Examples: assumes equality between self and others, asks others for their opinions, balances talking with listening, or starts talking and stops talking flexibly and easily in response to the needs of the other.

NON P   Gives nonverbal signs that seem Friendly (Positive). Examples: pays attention to others with eyes, pays attention by turning to other, by approaching the other physically to a comfortable distance, or by listening carefully.

Content Image

P in SEL   Mentions a content image of some P element in the SELF, in the
P in OTH   OTHER, or in the GROUP. Examples: describes self, other, or
P in GRP   group as equalitarian, friendly or informal, interested in others, interested in each other, humanistic, uncompetitive, self-accepting, likeable, or liking each other.

P in SIT   Mentions a content image of some element in the SITUATION immediately facing the group as if it were acting toward the self, other, or group in a P manner. Examples: defines the rewards or resources of the situation as so distributed that they are equally available to all or as being provided for maintaining the internal solidarity of the group. "They don't grade on a curve in this class." "In this problem our success depends upon how well we cooperate with each other." "Our task here is simply to become a good group." "This is our turf." "We all seem to be about the same age."

P in SOC   Mentions a content image of some P element in SOCIETY. Examples: the vote of all elements in society, the ideal of equal opportunities for all, antidiscrimination organizations, the ideal of the women's movement, the ideal of the black movement, equal rights under the law, freedom of speech, freedom of the press, freedom of assembly, freedom from unreasonable search and seizure, jobs for all, the steeply graduated income tax, the negative income tax.

P in FAN   Mentions a content image of some P element from some form of FANTASY or with some fantasy-arousing quality. Examples: Martin Luther King's "dream," the myth of universal brotherhood, the Emancipation Proclamation, a poem about America as the melting pot, or, from the past or current outside experience of the individual, "All the guys in my entry are nice guys."

Value Judgment

PRO P   Makes a value judgment in favor of or against some P image.
CON P   Examples: "If we have too much emphasis on equality here, we'll never be able to agree on a leader" (CON P in GRP). "Let's go around and each tell what we think" (PRO P in GRP).

Direction PF

Behavior

ACT PF   Acts overtly toward others in a way that seems Friendly (Positive), and Instrumentally Controlled (Forward). Examples: shows agreement with other's task-oriented communication, saying "Yes," "I see," "M-hmn," "Sure," "Yeah," or "I agree that's what we should do."

NON PF   Gives nonverbal signs that seem Friendly (Positive), and Instrumentally Controlled (Forward). Examples: shows interest in the content of the other's task-oriented communication, shows receptiveness to task-oriented communication by looking at the speaker, gives the speaker signs of recognition, shows one expects the other to speak, sits erect in a position to hear better, or nods head in agreement.

Content Image

PF in SEL   Mentions a content image of some PF element in the SELF, in
PF in OTH   the OTHER, or in the GROUP. Examples: describes self, other,

PF in GRP	or group as cooperative, responsible, idealistic, optimistic, altruistic, dedicated, devoted, or concerned.
PF in SIT	Mentions a content image of some element in the SITUATION immediately facing the group as if it were acting toward the self, other, or group in a PF manner. Examples: describes rewards as available from the situation contingent upon the successful cooperation and performance of the group as a whole, that is, the reward is given to the group as a whole, and the members may distribute it equally among themselves. "We will have to cooperate closely, but I think we can win." "We can do it if we try hard together."
PF in SOC	Mentions a content image of some PF element in SOCIETY. Examples: the marriage contract, devotional services, the pledge of allegiance, the oath of office, the Hypocratic Oath for physicians, Thanksgiving Day, baptism, the granting of citizenship, the ideal of civic service, service clubs, institutionalized giving (the Community Chest).
PF in FAN	Mentions a content image of some PF element from some form of FANTASY or with some fantasy-arousing quality. Examples: a dream of a wedding ring, the myth of the good soldier, a poem called *Forever Faithful,* or, from the past or current outside experience of the individual, "He's trying to help this kid improve his reading." "He's always willing to do his part."

Value Judgment

PRO PF	Makes a value judgment in favor of or against some PF image.
CON PF	Examples: "I just don't want to be tied to anybody" (CON PF in SEL). "I think we ought to try to cooperate with each other as much as we can" (PRO PF in GRP).

Direction F

ACT F	Acts overtly toward others in a way that seems Instrumentally Controlled (Forward). Examples: works on the task of the group by serious efforts at problem solving; makes sincere statement of beliefs, values, or assumptions, but in a judicious and controlled way; or verbally explores hypotheses by conjecturing, interpreting, or inferring; or tries to understand, assess, or diagnose the problem by communicating opinions and attitudes.
NON F	Gives nonverbal signs that seem Instrumentally Controlled (Forward). Examples: keeps face alert, but impersonal in expression; keeps eyes active in instrumental observation (lids well open with jaws relaxed); performs work or keeps eyes on the work; or keeps attention focused on instrumental activity.

Content Image

F in SEL F in OTH F in GRP	Mentions a content image of some F element in the SELF, in the OTHER, or in the GROUP. Examples: describes self, other, or group as work-oriented, task-oriented, instrumentally oriented, tending to come directly to the point, or analytical; as serious about rules, values, norms, or beliefs; as impersonal or emotionally neutral; as searching, tentative, or faithful; or as observant, careful, watchful, straight, or straight-arrow.
F in SIT	Mentions a content image of some element in the SITUATION immediately facing the group as if it were acting toward the self, other, or group in an F manner. Examples: describes the situation as demanding a particular and specific kind of instrumental behavior, as providing clear immediate feedback or evidence of success or failure of action, or as imposing a clear standard of performance. "If you get this thing exactly right it will work every time."
F in SOC	Mentions a content image of some F element in SOCIETY. Examples: a technical school, the discipline of mathematics, the study of logic, the Protestant Ethic (hard work as the assurance of salvation), drivers' tests, automobile inspection, on-the-job training, savings banks, middle-class jobs, work schedules.
F in FAN	Mentions a content image of some F element from some form of FANTASY or with some fantasy-arousing quality. Examples: the story of the Sorcerer's Apprentice, Charlie Chaplin's movie *Modern Times,* the myth of the computer that never makes mistakes, a propaganda movie called *Socialist Workers,* or, from the past or current outside experience of the individual, "I'm trying to work out a budget." "I used to deliver papers as a kid."

Value Judgment

PRO F CON F	Makes a value judgment in favor of or against some F image. Examples: "Let's figure out what we each have to do" (PRO F in GRP). "Let's flip a coin to get the answer, and take a coffee break" (CON F in GRP).

Direction NF

ACT NF	Acts overtly toward others in a way that seems Unfriendly (Negative) and Instrumentally Controlled (Forward). Examples: works on the tasks of the group harder than anybody else, guards the working rules of the group, or persists in work efforts in a distant and impersonal way which implies that at least *one* per-

son in the group is conscientious and principled; apparently attempts to be very patient with others, but seems rigid and dogmatic; always assumes self to be right, never changing; or tends to provoke guilt in others.

NON NF   Gives nonverbal signs that seem Unfriendly (Negative) and Instrumentally Controlled (Forward). Examples: tightens jaw muscles, tends to press lips together, keeps face set grimly, keeps minor signs of rejection patiently in check, or shows occasional breakthroughs of negative expression in tics or grimaces, blinks persistently, or rubs eyes to keep concentration focused.

Content Image

NF in SEL   Mentions a content image of some NF element in the SELF, in
NF in OTH   the OTHER, or in the GROUP. Examples: describes self, other,
NF in GRP   or group as conscientious; ruled by principle; legalistic; very controlled; overaccepting of pain, unhappiness, or punishment; or guilt-inducing.

NF in SIT   Mentions a content image of some element in the SITUATION immediately facing the group as if it were acting toward the self, other, or group in an NF manner. Examples: defines some aspect of the situation as imposing a standard of performance so specific or so high as to make failure and punishment likely: "That clock just keeps ticking on." "We've got to keep working like hell or we won't make it." "One mistake and we're out of luck."

NF in SOC   Mentions a content image of some NF element in SOCIETY. Examples: cameras that take pictures of patrons in banks, floor detectives, public auditors, the income tax auditor, traffic officers, guards, customs officers, ticket collectors, time clocks, warning bells, inspection times, fire drills.

NF in FAN   Mentions a content image of some NF element from some form of FANTASY or with some fantasy-arousing quality. Examples: a dream of being caught in a public place naked, a movie about survival on the frozen tundra, the symbol of Father Time, or, from the past or current outside experience of the individual, "I just feel stretched to the breaking point most of the time." "My mother never took her eye off me." "There was no place where I could be alone and relax."

Value Judgment

PRO NF   Makes a value judgment in favor of or against some NF image.
CON NF   Examples: "What are you trying to do, show up the rest of us?" (CON NF in OTH). "We'd better not forget, this all has to be reported to the income tax people" (PRO NF in GRP).

Direction N

Behavior

ACT N   Acts overtly toward others in a way that seems Unfriendly (Negative). Examples: shows predictable disagreement with others in communication, e.g., frequently says "No," "I don't think so," "I disagree," "I can't accept that," "Well. . . . ," or "But. . . ."; seems unfriendly in response to the friendly approach of others; seems detached, isolated, indifferent, distant, unsocial, secluded, unapproachable, or not a member of the group.

NON N   Gives nonverbal signs that seem Unfriendly (Negative). Examples: looks away, takes off glasses, raises one brow skeptically, covers the mouth, or turns the face away; closes posture by placing arms or legs as if to block communication or approach of the other or as if to protect the self; observes surreptitiously from the sides of the eyes; turns the back; or avoids turning toward the other.

N in SEL   Mentions a content image of some N element in the SELF, in the
N in OTH   OTHER, or in the GROUP. Examples: describes self, other, or
N in GRP   group as unfriendly, disagreeable, isolated, unsocial, seclusive, negativistic, self-protective, reserved, retentive, retractive, doubtful, suspicious, or jealous.

N in SIT   Mentions a content image of some element in the SITUATION immediately facing the group as if it were acting toward the self, other, or group in an N manner. Examples: describes some aspect of the situation as exposing individuals in the group to frustration or punishment, as reducing their ability to protect or defend themselves, or as threatening their privacy or their property: "They can hear everything we say in here." "If we do turn out anything good, they will take the credit." "There isn't room enough in here to turn around." "There isn't any right answer."

N in SOC   Mentions a content image of some N element in SOCIETY. Examples: secret societies, people who don't care about their neighbors, high walls and fences around private property, individual competition, cultural dissimilarity, segregation, prejudice, social rejection, social indifference.

N in FAN   Mentions a content image of some N element from some form of FANTASY or with some fantasy-arousing quality. Examples: a dream about being locked out, a poem about "good fences make good neighbors," the symbol of the disinterested bystander, or, from the past or current outside experience of the individual, "These guys are always taking my stuff." "I have to go over to the library in order to get away from the noise of my roommates."

Value Judgment

PRO N
CON N

Makes a value judgment in favor of or against some N image. Examples: "Nobody has to agree to anything if he doesn't want to" (PRO N in GRP). "It makes me feel terrible when some people in the group say they don't care about others" (CON N in GRP).

Direction NB

Behavior

ACT NB

Acts overtly toward others in a way that seems Unfriendly (Negative) and Emotionally Expressive (Backward). Examples: gets into conflict with some person felt to represent authority or conventionality; shows autonomy with regard to any kind of control; shows noncompliance with any kind of rules or requests; rejects, refuses, or purposefully ignores any kind of direction, command, demand, or authoritative requirement; rejects convention; or disavows or disclaims failure or guilt.

NON NB

Gives nonverbal signs that seem Unfriendly (Negative) and Emotionally Expressive (Backward). Examples: jerks away or looks away when addressed; slouches, yawns, or closes eyes when addressed; shrugs shoulders; or ignores or shows contempt for the other, e.g., holds mouth closed and curled, holds corners of the lips pulled down, wrinkles the skin below the corner of the mouth, stretches the fold of the skin that comes from above the wing of the nose down around the mouth, appears as if preparing to spit something out, or lowers the mouth as if to disagree.

Content Image

NB in SEL
NB in OTH
NB in GRP

Mentions a content image of some NB element in the SELF, in the OTHER, or in the GROUP. Examples: describes self, other, or group as autonomous, resistant to authority, cynical, nonconforming, pessimistic, intolerant of control, antisocial, impervious to influence, refractory, contrary, noncompliant, sulky, or sullen.

NB in SIT

Mentions an image of some element in the SITUATION immediately facing the group as if it were acting toward the self, other, or group in an NB manner. Examples: defines some aspect of the situation as punishing conformity to standards, rewarding deviance, or undermining the standards of performance. "Anything we say will be held against us." "You don't get any credit for doing a good job." "You'd better look out for your own neck around here."

NB in SOC   Mentions an image of some NB element in SOCIETY. Examples: nonconventional people with regard to work roles (drifters, tramps, burglars, thieves, confidence men, gamblers), with regard to citizenship roles (traitors, nonvoters, outlaws, resisters of government), or with regard to conventional sex-typed roles or modes of dress, manner, display, speech, cosmetics, or place of residence (e.g., Bohemia).

NB in FAN   Mentions a content image of some NB element from some form of FANTASY or with some fantasy-arousing quality. Examples: a dream of a trapped animal showing its teeth, a poem entitled *The Song of the Road,* the legend of the waiter who took the customer's order and never came back, or, from the past or current outside experience of the individual, "Sometimes I feel like just taking off!" "My father left home when I was three."

Value Judgment

PRO NB   Makes a value judgment or statement in favor of or against some
CON NB   NB image. Examples: "If they push us too far, we'll bite back" (PRO NB in GRP). "I don't like for you to put your feet up on the table" (CON NB in OTH).

Direction B

Behavior

ACT B   Acts overtly toward others in a way that seems Emotionally Expressive (Backward). Examples: changes mood of interaction suddenly, indicates that the content or manner of what is going on is too controlled or constricting, or indicates a desire for a switch from work to play, from reasoning to acting out, or from self-control to expression.

NON B   Gives nonverbal signs that seem Emotionally Expressive (Backward). Examples: shows shifting and drifting of attention away from task, shows preoccupation with passing thoughts and feelings unconnected with the current communication of group members, shows occasional mixed expression—e.g., a smile tending to win over a frown of contempt, the raising of the brows in self-abnegation combined with the thrusting out of the lower lip and jaw as in aggression—or shows a blank look.

Content Image

B in SEL   Mentions a content image of some B element in the SELF, in the
B in OTH   OTHER, or in the GROUP. Examples: describes self, other, or
B in GRP   group as disbelieving, heretical, resistant to common beliefs,

unrealistic, scatter-brained, distractable, or uninterested in facts; distrustful of concepts, words, or rational arguments; or preferring fantasy, dramatization, acting out, change, or variety.

B in SIT   Mentions a content image of some element in the SITUATION immediately facing the group as if it were acting toward the self, other, or group in a B manner. Examples: defines some aspect of the external situation as crazy, unpredictable, uncontrollable, making it impossible to concentrate, or interfering with the feedback of information on success or failure of performance, or defines some condition that makes intellectual control of behavior impossible. "I can't hear myself think in here." "We don't seem to be getting through." "They don't seem to understand us." "It's like dropping a feather down a well." "Doesn't it seem too hot in here?" "Wow, this stuff is going to my head!"

B in SOC   Mentions a content image of some B element in SOCIETY. Examples: isolated parts of the population, illiterates, the deaf, the mute, the blind, persons who do not speak the language of the major part of the society, new immigrants, or cultural subgroups in poor touch with the rest of society; mountain people, desert people, migrant workers, isolated religious sects, ethnic or racial ghettos.

B in FAN   Mentions a content image of some B element from some form of FANTASY or with some fantasy-arousing quality. Examples: a dream of being in a completely strange place, a novel by Kafka, a movie of the Marx Brothers, or, from the past or current outside experience of the individual, "My father never told us what he did for a living." "I'm completely fed up with studying."

Value Judgments

PRO B   Makes a value judgment in favor of or against some B image.
CON B   Examples: "Just let your mind wander" (PRO B in OTH). "Stop dreaming and wise up" (CON B in OTH).

Direction PB

Behavior

ACT PB   Acts overtly towards others in a way that seems Friendly (Positive) and Emotionally Expressive (Backward). Examples: shows friendly good feeling for the group or a subgroup by acting as "one of the gang"; offers to share; increases special communication with particular individual members; makes offers of special friendship; or looks for entertainment or "a good time" with other group members.

NON PB   Gives nonverbal signs that seem Friendly (Positive) and Emotionally Expressive (Backward). Examples: listens attentively to some particular group member (but meanwhile ignores to some extent the whole group); shows a preference by posture, attention, or a stream of nonverbal communication for friendship with a particular person or subgroup, rather than solidarity with the group as a whole; reminds a particular other of private jokes or outside contact by winks, grins, or changes of seating.

Content Image

PB in SEL
PB in OTH
PB in GRP   Mentions a content image of some PB element in the SELF, in the OTHER, or in the GROUP. Examples: Describes self, other, or group as very friendly, likable, affectionate, ready to share and enjoy sociability, looking for entertainment, liberal, generous, or "fun to be with."

PB in SIT   Mentions a content image of some element in the SITUATION immediately facing the group as if it were acting toward the self, other, or group in a PB manner. Examples: defines some aspect of the external situation as making rewards freely available, not contingent upon performance or conformity to standards, or as not requiring performance: "No need to fuss, here." "There's plenty of everything for everybody." "All they want is for us to have a good time." "We've got all this food left, let's eat it."

PB in SOC   Mentions a content image of some PB element in SOCIETY. Examples: the liberal political parties, philosophies of creativity and self-realization, kindergartens, friendship groups, recreational clubs, leisure pastimes, ethnic centers, vacation times, vacation industries, playgrounds, pleasure cruises.

PB in FAN   Mentions a content image of some PB element from some form of FANTASY or with some fantasy-arousing quality. Examples: a dream of having a picnic with friends, beer ads featuring friends in a small boat, the symbol of the social drink, or, from past or current outside experience of the individual, "We had a great gang in high school." "I came from a large family and we had a lot of fun." "I have made a lot of new friends around here."

Value Judgment

PRO PB
CON PB   Makes a value judgment in favor of or against some PB image. Examples: "To me, friendship is more important than success" (PRO PB in SEL). "Cronyism is no good in politics" (CON PB in SOC).

Direction DP

Behavior

ACT DP	Acts overtly toward others in a way that seems Submissive (Downward) and Friendly (Positive). Examples: shows a trusting attitude; expresses gratitude or appreciation or shows admiration, esteem, respect, or awe for the other; defers positively to the other; or accepts domination without loss of positive feeling.
NON DP	Gives nonverbal signs that seem Submissive (Downward) and Friendly (Positive). Examples: imitates or mirrors the bodily attitudes or acts of one or more other members (apparently identifying the self with the other); smiles trustfully; shows open posture of arms, legs, and feet in relation to the other; or shows an open, rapt gaze.

Content Image

DP in SEL DP in OTH DP in GRP	Mentions a content image of some DP element in the SELF, in the OTHER, or in the GROUP. Examples: describes self, other, or group as calm, stable, appreciative, ready to admire others, trustful, tender-minded, ready to identify with others, thoughtful of others, docile, or willing to learn.
DP in SIT	Mentions a content image of some element in the SITUATION immediately facing the group as if it were acting toward the self, or other, or group, in a DP manner. Examples: "If we trust them, they will trust us." "I'm sure there is no danger there." "He looks like a nice dog to me!" "They are fans of ours!"
DP in SOC	Mentions a content image of some DP element in SOCIETY. Examples: "the people" seen as basically good, honest folks; the lower classes seen as "the salt of the earth"; the small business man, the young, the graduating class in high school, the good student, the apprentice.
DP in FAN	Mentions a content image of some DP element from some form of FANTASY or with some fantasy-arousing quality. Examples: a dream of being patted on the head, a book by Horatio Alger, Adam in Michelangelo's picture of God creating Adam, the fairy tale of the ugly duckling who became a swan, or, from the past or current outside experience of the individual, "Sometimes I wish I could read all the books in the library, or maybe just eat them."

Value Judgment

PRO DP CON DP	Makes a value judgment in favor of or against some DP image. Examples: "You've got to get out of school sometime" (CON

DP in OTH). "If we can't trust each other here in this group, who can we trust?" (PRO DP in GRP).

Direction DPF

Behavior

ACT DPF	Acts overtly toward others in a way that seems Submissive (Downward), Friendly (Positive), and Instrumentally Controlled (Forward). Examples: defers positively to authority or to task leadership, complies obediently, admits responsibility for whatever he or she may have done that might be disapproved, performs work cheerfully, or tries to improve.
NON DPF	Gives nonverbal signs that seem Submissive (Downward), Friendly (Positive), and Instrumentally Controlled (Forward). Examples: looks down, makes self small, minimizes bodily movement, moves carefully or gently, closes the posture but remains positive in orientation to the other, as if in petition, with knees bent, back bowed, head low, arms folded and held in front, or hands clasped or touching, as if to bow, pray to the other, or beg.

Content Image

DPF in SEL DPF in OTH DPF in GRP	Mentions a content image of some DPF element in the SELF, in the OTHER, or in the GROUP. Examples: describes self, other, or group as respectful, believing, gentle, good, practical, having high will control, having character stability, dedicated to service, modest, humble, retiring, meek, nice, or sensitive.
DPF in SIT	Mentions a content image of some element in the SITUATION immediately facing the group as if it were acting toward the self, other, or group in a DPF manner. Examples: defines some aspect of the external situation as responding in a dependable and gratifying way to performance demands: "We can absolutely count on them." "This thing always works." "I've driven it eighty thousand miles without a major repair."
DPF in SOC	Mentions a content image of some DPF element in SOCIETY. Examples: faithful religious congregations, the traditional role of servants, clerical workers, nurses, grade school teachers, the traditional company employee, the civil service, the mailman, the small grocer or butcher, the mom and pop store.
DPF in FAN	Mentions a content image of some DPF element from some form of FANTASY or with some fantasy-arousing quality. Examples: a dream of uncovering one's head, a certificate of community service, the legend of the Dutch boy who held his finger in the dike, or, from the past or current outside experience of the

individual, "He said he wanted to give part of his life to help other people."

Value Judgment

PRO DPF   Makes a value judgment in favor of or against some DPF image.
CON DPF   Examples: "No more of that Uncle Tom stuff for me" (CON DPF in SEL). "I'm ready to do my part, and I hope that all of us are" (PRO DPF in GRP).

Direction DF

Behavior

ACT DF   Acts overtly toward others in a way that seems Submissive (Downward) and Instrumentally Controlled (Forward). Examples: works very hard, asks for approval of a task-oriented leader, seems to be oversensitive about the good opinion of others, or seems to be submissively conforming, conscientious, conventional, or dutiful, apparently out of fear of breaking group norms or failing to meet the expectations of authority.

NON DF   Gives nonverbal signs that seem Submissive (Downward) and Instrumentally Controlled (Forward). Examples: turns to the leader to act first; sits in silent contemplation of the task or work, head bent down in thought, eyes looking forward or downward, or eyes held fixed, unfocused, or unseeing; or makes work gestures repeatedly and compulsively.

Content Image

DF in SEL
DF in OTH
DF in GRP   Mentions a content image of some DF element in the SELF, in the OTHER, or in the GROUP. Examples: describes self, other, or group as dutiful, conventional, cautious, persistent, hardworking, or fearful of disapproval; concerned with controlling inner feelings, thoughts, or impulses; or obsessional, slow to react, or slow to change.

DF in SIT   Mentions a content image of some element in the SITUATION immediately facing the group as if it were acting toward the self, the other, or the group, in a DF manner. Examples: defines some aspect of the external situation as persistent in its performance of hard, grinding work according to exact standards. "It doesn't lose one second in a year." "It cleans up the worst masses in a jiffy." "It's a real Mr. Clean." "Just feed the data into the computer and it does all the rest."

DF in SOC   Mentions a content image of some DF element in SOCIETY. Examples: coal miners, assembly line workers, oil drillers, proofreaders, draftsmen, researchers, bookkeepers, surveyers, watch repairmen, income tax accountants, mail sorters, ascetic religious groups, patients.

DF in FAN   Mentions a content image of some DF element from some form of FANTASY or with some fantasy-arousing quality. Examples: a dream of doing the same thing over and over, a book about migrant farm workers, a game of counting telephone poles, an anecdote about carrying water for an elephant, the symbol of "dishpan hands," or, from the past or current outside expeience of the individual, "I kept trying to get up, but he kept holding me down." "I thought I'd never finish that job." "Every day is the same to me, get up, go to work, go to bed."

Value Judgment

PRO DF   Makes a value judgment in favor of or against some DF image.
CON DF   Examples: "If I had to work that hard, I'd jump off a bridge" (CON DF in SEL). "There's nothing for it but to plow through" (PRO DF in SEL). "It's a back-breaking job, but we've got to do it" (PRO DF in GRP).

Direction DNF

Behavior

ACT DNF   Acts overtly towards others in a way that seems Submissive (Downward), Unfriendly (Negative), and Instrumentally Controlled (Forward). Examples: attempts to shame others by acting as if injured, hurt, imposed upon, or martyred by overwork or overconformity; or tries to provoke rejection or punishment in order to shame the other.

NON DNF   Gives nonverbal signs that seem Submissive (Downward), Unfriendly (Negative), and Instrumentally Controlled (Forward). Examples: shows a martyred expression, e.g., lower lip tending to protrude, lip perhaps quivering slightly as if about to cry, eyes tending to tears, brows elevated in self-abnegation, head turning from side to side as if in pain; or shows signs of anger toward the other, but in suppressed form, breaking out periodically.

Content Image

DNF in SEL   Mentions a content image of some DNF element in the SELF, in
DNF in OTH   the OTHER, or in the GROUP. Examples: describes self, or
DNF in GRP   other, or group as self-sacrificing, self-pitying, ready to play the martyr, passively accusing, self-punishing, injured, hurt by overwork or overcomformity, ashamed, or remorseful.

DNF in SIT   Mentions a content image of some element in the SITUATION immediately facing the group as if it were acting toward the self, other, or group in a DNF manner. Examples: defines some aspect of the external situation as arousing guilt because its demands are not met, "That thing is always out of whack!" "It requires constant attention and adjustment." "It's more trouble than it's worth." "It shows the slightest bit of dust." "It's a pain in the neck."

DNF in SOC   Mentions a content image of some DNF element in SOCIETY. Examples: religious cults that announce the end of the world; professional athletes who take drugs to keep down the pain as they get older; secular prophets who warn of the decline of the West or the nearness of nuclear war; forecasters of overpopulation and world starvation; despairing environmentalists.

DNF in FAN   Mentions a content image of some DNF element from some form of FANTASY or with some fantasy-arousing quality. Examples: the sufferings of Job, the myth of Purgatory, the symbol of hara kiri, or, from the past or current outside experience of the individual, "I propped my eyes open and kept driving all night." "After exams I'm going to fall in a heap." "My efforts were never appreciated."

Value Judgment

PRO DNF   Makes a value judgment in favor of or against some DNF image.
CON DNF   Examples: "Americans have no sense of tragedy" (PRO DNF in SOC). "No human being should have to stand that" (CON DNF in SIT). "It's our fate to suffer" (PRO DNF in GRP). "Here's the crying towel, have a good time" (CON DNF in OTH).

Direction DN

Behavior

ACT DN   Acts overtly toward others in a way that seems Submissive (Downward) and Unfriendly (Negative). Examples: shows resentful passive rejection of others; refuses to reciprocate friendly acts; remains responseless in the face of friendly approaches of the other; remains inexpressive, impassive, reticent, or self-conscious; or seems to attempt to avoid social notice.

NON DN   Gives nonverbal signs that seem Submissive (Downward) and Unfriendly (Negative). Examples: holds body rigid, restrained, or silently rejecting; holds head down with brow knitted, lower lip protruding, eyes closed or averted, as if to suppress jealousy, envy, anger, or to ward off extraneous ideas and interruptions; or turns away, holds stomach, or closes posture.

Content Image

DN in SEL
DN in OTH
DN in GRP   Mentions a content image of some DN element in the SELF, in the OTHER, or in the GROUP. Examples: describes self, other, or group, as resentful, passively rejecting, depressed, morose, inexpansive, unsmiling, unappreciative, unacknowledging, ungrateful, or hard to please.

DN in SIT   Mentions a content image of some element in the SITUATION immediately facing the group as if it were acting toward the self, other, or group in a DN manner. Examples: defines some aspect of the external situation as having suffered some irreparable injury, "It will never be the same again." "It's too late." "I feel so sorry about it." "It makes me want to go crawl in a hole."

DN in SOC   Mentions a content image of some DN element in SOCIETY. Examples: stigmatized persons; condemned, disfigured, handicapped, sick, chronically ill, or diseased persons; persons of low intelligence, poor education, inferior or uncertain citizenship status, or inferior social origin; the poor, the old, the unattractive, the hungry, the neglected, and the rejected; those who will never achieve popularity or success; the abandoned and ruined.

DN in FAN   Mentions a content image of some DN element from some form of FANTASY or with some fantasy-arousing quality. Examples: a dream of having lost an arm and a leg, the legend of Devil's Island, a play called *The Miserable of the Earth,* or, from the past or current outside experiences of the individual, "When I woke up, I couldn't see." "I was born with this defect." "Sometimes I feel that people are staring at me as if I were some kind of worm."

Value Judgment

PRO DN
CON DN   Makes a value judgment in favor of or against some DN image. Examples: "Sometimes I've felt just like you do" (PRO DN in OTH). "Look, while there's life there's hope—let's just pick up the pieces and move on" (CON DN in GRP).

Direction DNB

Behavior

ACT DNB   Acts overtly toward others in a way that seems Submissive (Downward), Unfriendly (Negative), and Emotionally Expressive (Backward). Examples: expresses a desire to withdraw and leave as a sign of rejection of both the group and the group norms; expresses feelings of unhappiness, dissatisfaction, discontent, frustration, deprivation, disappointment, discouragement, resignation, or despair.

NON DNB   Gives nonverbal signs that seem Submissive (Downward), Unfriendly (Negative), and Emotionally Expressive (Backward). Examples: sits down without removing hat or coat; takes a seat nearest the door; indicates submissive restlessness, boredom, or disinterest; jiggles the foot, doodles, or reads a newspaper rather than joining the conversation; holds head in hands, turns to leave, increases distance from others, looks repeatedly toward the door, looks repeatedly at the clock, gathers up things, puts on coat or hat before the end of the session, stands up, or leaves before the session is over.

Content Image

DNB in SEL   Mentions a content image of some DNB element in the SELF, in
DNB in OTH   the OTHER, or in the GROUP. Examples: describes self, other,
DNB in GRP   or group as alienated, discouraged, despairing, miserable, out of touch, autistic, apathetic, resigned, despondent, or suicidal.

DNB in SIT   Mentions a content image of some element in the SITUATION immediately facing the group as if it were acting toward the self, other, or group in a DNB manner. Examples: defines some aspect of the external situation as dwindling, disappearing, fading out, withdrawing support, or receding in significance, "It's completely impossible—we may as well go home." "There's no sense in staying here." "There's nothing to work with." "It's hopeless." "There's nothing left of it."

DNB in SOC   Mentions a content image of some DNB element in SOCIETY. Examples: suicides, skid row alcoholics, drug addicts, hospitalized mental patients, terminal patients who have given up hope, aborted fetuses, cadavers, abandoned infants, patients who can be kept alive only by machine, the hopelessly mentally deficient and deformed, the prisoners on death row.

DNB in FAN   Mentions a content image of some DNB element from some form of FANTASY or with some fantasy-arousing quality. Examples: a dream of becoming smaller and smaller, the symbol of a skull and crossbones, O'Neill's play *Long Day's Journey into Night,* or, from the past or current outside experience of the individual, "My mother committed suicide when I was four years old." "I have dreams that I'm going to die."

Value Judgment

PRO DNB   Makes a value judgment in favor of or against some DNB im-
CON DNB   age. Examples: "I like sad movies" (PRO DNB in FAN). "Come on, let's snap out of it" (CON DNB in GRP).

Direction DB

Behavior

ACT DB Acts overtly toward others in a way that seems Submissive (Downward) and Emotionally Expressive (Backward). Examples: hangs back fearfully and refuses to perform task; shows signs of tension or difficulty in speaking as a reaction to pressure by other for task performance; or shows confusion by stammering, blocking up, gulping, or swallowing; wets the lips persistently; laughs in a strained way apparently close to tears; cries; or moans.

NON DB Gives nonverbal signs that seem Submissive (Downward) and Emotionally Expressive (Backward). Examples: shows nervous movements or signs of anxious emotionality; shows grooming, blushing, trembling, or sweating; shows signs of fright (e.g., eyes open wide, corners of mouth depressed, lower area of the face pulled down); shows signs of sorrow or grief (e.g., inner brows raised, forehead wrinkled horizontally, inner or middle part of upper brow raised, corners of mouth depressed, cheeks depressed, nose constricted); or laughs hysterically (muscles around the corners of the mouth tending to lead downward in a struggle with those pulling upward.)

Content Image

DB in SEL Mentions a content image of some DB element in the SELF, in
DB in OTH the OTHER, or in the GROUP. Examples: describes self, other,
DB in GRP or group as tense, anxious, fearful, emotionally blocked, distressed, distractable, passively resistant to the demands of authority or leadership, uncooperative, withholding, or holding back.

DB in SIT Mentions a content image of some element in the SITUATION immediately facing the group as if it were acting toward the self, other, or group in a DB manner. Examples: defines some aspect of the external situation as failing in task performance, as not cooperating in the tasks of the group, or as holding back, "They aren't trying." "We'll never get any cooperation out of them." "They just won't move." "They can't do it." "They just don't get the idea." "They just resist all persuasion."

DB in SOC Mentions a content image of some DB element in SOCIETY. Examples: draft evaders, pacifists, nonviolent resisters, the silent majority, strikers, boycotters, nonvoters, defectors, deserters, protest marchers, "teach-ins," hunger strikes, peaceful demonstrations.

DB in FAN Mentions a content image of some DB element from some form of FANTASY or with some fantasy-arousing quality. Examples:

> the song "We Shall Overcome," the symbol of the clenched fist, the symbol of the bloody flag, the cartoon of the little taxpayer, or, from the past or current outside experience of the individual, "I was thinking of leaving the country, but maybe I'd better stay here and fight injustice."

Value Judgment

PRO DB
CON DB

Makes a value judgment in favor of or against some DB image. Examples: "I don't know how" (PRO DB in SEL). "I can't" (PRO DB in SEL). "Come on, shape up" (CON DB in OTH).

Direction DPB

Behavior

ACT DPB

Acts overtly toward others in a way that seems Submissive (Downward), Friendly (Positive), and Emotionally Expressive (Backward). Examples: asks for protection or special attention in a particular relationship with one or more others in a friendly subgroup, asks for special consideration.

NON DPB

Gives nonverbal signs that seem Submissive (Downward), Friendly (Positive), and Emotionally Expressive (Backward). Examples: shows special signs of pleasure and expectancy in relationship to another; smiles, giggles, or grins with pleasure; beams and appears charmed in response to a more ascendant other person's stimulation and care; shows pupillary dilation in relation to that other, moves closer, or sits together with particular other liked persons in the group apparently so as to increase the possibility of special communication with them; holds on to other; or appears to seek protection or love.

Content Image

DPB in SEL
DPB in OTH
DPB in GRP

Mentions a content image of some DPB element in the SELF, in the OTHER, or in the GROUP. Examples: describes self, other, or group as dependent on love; helpless but lovable; expectant of help or nurturance; hoping for stimulation; expectant of having needs met without achievement; as infantile or immature.

DPB in SIT

Mentions a content image of some element in the SITUATION immediately facing the group as if it were acting toward the self, other, or group in a DPB manner. Examples: defines some aspect of the external situation or persons not in the group as feeling they will be taken care of by easy rewards or provision of resources indefinitely, with low or no demands for performance,

"They're being spoiled." "They think there's no need to work around here." "They think money grows on trees." "He's so cute and helpless!"

DPB in SOC Mentions a content image of some DPB element in SOCIETY. Examples: infants and children, pets, children of the idle rich, persons illegitimately on welfare, "featherbedding" in union contracts, teachers' pets, chronic patients with no discernible disease, consumers of political patronage, favored and protected industries.

DPB in FAN Mentions a content image of some DPB element from some form of FANTASY or with some fantasy-arousing quality. Examples: a dream of lying in the sun, a dream of Christmas presents, the symbol of the baby chick, a children's book titled *Happiness Is a Warm Puppy,* a picture by Grandma Moses, or, from the past or current outside experience of the individual, "I really had an easy time of it when I was a kid." "I remember once getting my fist stuck in the cooky jar." "I seem to have a craving for sweets."

Value Judgment

PRO DPB Makes a value judgment in favor of or against some DPB image.
CON DPB Examples: "You're only young once" (PRO DPB in OTH). "G'wan, kid, beat it!" (CON DPB in OTH).

Direction D

Behavior

ACT D Acts overtly toward others in a way that seems Submissive (Downward). Examples: participates only when asked questions, then speaks only to the person who asked the direct question; gives only minimal information in response to a question; or does not address the group as a whole.

NON DB Gives nonverbal signs that seem Submissive (Downward). Examples: remains quiet and motionless or gives signs of utter resignation, e.g., brows raised, lower lip and jaw receding, eyes closed, nostrils constricted, or body bent upon itself in closed posture with tendency to curl up, shoulders forward, chest sunken, elbows coming forward, arms tending to fold inward across the body, wrists slack and closing inward, fingers tending to fold up or curl, knees bent and tending to come together, heels tending to turn outward and to separate, feet slack and closing inward.

Content Image

D in SEL D in OTH D in GRP	Mentions a content image of some D element in the SELF, in the OTHER, or in the GROUP. Examples: describes self, other, or group as introverted, self-effacing, self-abnegating, powerless, passive, without enthusiasm or desire, colorless, restrained, uncommunicative, inexpressive, impassive, reticent, quiet, inactive, inert, immobile, or inhibited.
D in SIT	Mentions a content image of some element in the SITUATION immediately facing the group as if it were acting toward the self, other, or group in a D manner. Examples: defines some aspect of the external situation or persons outside the group as failing to offer any stimulation or any opportunities for expressive or communicative activity, or as supressed, depressed, or inhibited. "We don't meet often enough to get to know each other." "This town is really Dullsville."
D in SOC	Mentions a content image of some D element in SOCIETY. Examples: religions, cults, or sects that teach the abnegation or devaluation of the self, the reduction or elimination of desire, the transformation of the self by giving up, the achievement of a new psychological or spiritual state of peace, or a state of nothingness.
D in FAN	Mentions a content image of some D element from some form of FANTASY or with some fantasy-arousing quality. Examples: a dream about being swept out to sea, the saying that "religion is the opiate of the masses," the belief that "death is like a sleep," or, from the past or current outside experience of the individual, "I was completely unconscious for three days." "I was limp as a dishrag." "I couldn't stand up."

Value Judgment

PRO D CON D	Makes a value judgment in favor of or against some D image. Examples: "You have to be ready to die in order to live" (PRO D in SEL). "Look, you can't count on dying" (CON D in OTH).

Appendix B

General Instructions for Making Ratings

1. The instructions given in general form here may be used to prepare specific instructions for group members in a particular study. In the case of the academic self-analytic group, the group members themselves may make the final summaries of their ratings. In other cases, the researcher will ask the group members only to fill out the simplified Adjective Rating Form (Appendix C). In order to make the ratings and analyze them, certain forms are needed, to be mentioned below.

2. It must be decided what person or persons are to be rated. In the self-analytic group each member, including the instructor, rates each other member, from one's own point of view as a rater, and also the self, as one EXPECTS to be rated, and finally as one WISHES others might rate the self. Each member needs a full list of the members in a standard order, so that the ratings made by all members may be collated and added together to obtain the Group Average Ratings.

3. It must be decided whether the ratings are to be made using the definitions in Appendix A or by using the simplified SYMLOG Adjective Rating Form. When it is desired to use the rating procedure mainly to teach the nature of the dimensions, the directions, and the various levels of behavior and content, ratings made by reading specific levels of the Appendix A descriptions may be preferable. When it is desired to make the rating procedure more economical of time and effort, the simplified Adjective Rating Form may be preferred.

4. If ratings are made from the Appendix A descriptions, the level or levels at which the ratings are to be made must be decided. Ratings at the ACT level are simplest and probably generally most useful, but ratings made by reading both the ACT level and the NON level descriptions and considering the two jointly give a more accurate picture of the global perception of the persons. If it is desired to focus attention on a particular level for learning or sensitizing purposes, such as learning to pay more attention to nonverbal behavior, ratings may be made using the single appropriate level. Interesting studies may be made by rating on various levels separately and comparing the ratings, such as a comparison between the ACT level and the PRO value statement level. Other interesting

comparisons are the ACT level with the NON level, the SELF description level with the description of OTHERS, the descriptions of the GROUP versus the descriptions of SOCIETY, the descriptions at the FANTASY level with the CON value statement level, and so on.

5. It must be decided whether the ratings are to be confined to interaction in the fully assembled group only or are to include behavior between members outside the regular meetings as well. In the rating procedure it is probably difficult to make such a distinction unless a quite limited recent (or prospective) time period can be isolated for special attention.

6. It must be decided for what time period the rating is to be made. In the Group Psychology Course there is ordinarily a First Rating, made about one-third of the way through the course, and a Second Rating, made quite close to the end, in order to trace changes. For the First Rating in this context, all behavior observed up to the time of the rating is included, from the beginning of the course, and including behavior both within and outside the regular sessions. For the Second Rating, all behavior from the time of the first rating until the time of the second rating is included. There is an effort to make the second rating reflect only the behavior of the specific time period since the previous rating, so that, if there have been changes, they will be picked up.

7. It must be decided whether to use the answer alternative with three choices or the one with five choices. These two scales are as follows:

The three-choice alternative
  0 = "Not often" (below average)
  1 = "Sometimes" (average, including "Don't know")
  2 = "Often" (above average)

The five-choice alternative
  0 = "Never"
  1 = "Rarely"
  2 = "Sometimes"
  3 = "Often"
  4 = "Always"

The three-choice alternative, designated (0, 1, 2), is to be preferred for simplicity in rating and processing of the data. The raw summary numbers are at the appropriate scale for plotting on the Field Diagram, which is constructed with a limit of 18. The five-choice alternative designated (0, 1, 2, 3, 4), is to be preferred for greater flexibility and accuracy but requires a little more work in processing, since the numbers to be added are larger and the added sum must be divided by 2 in order to put the summary rating into the proper scale for plotting on the Field Diagram with a scale limit of 18. Note: When the (0, 1, 2) scale is used, the highest rating a person may receive in a given direction is 18, since there are 9 items that will measure the direction, and each item may receive a rating of 2. When the (0, 1, 2, 3, 4) scale is used, the highest rating a person may receive in a given direction before the division by 2 is 36, since there are 9 items that will measure the direction, and each may receive a rating of 4.

8. However the choices described above are made, the *Directional Profile Form* is used to assemble the numbers and add them together in the proper way to

obtain the summary rating or scoring one individual gives another. The Directional Profile Form is shown in Appendix G. Each column is called a directional profile, made up of twenty-six directions, listed vertically, with space at the bottom for the summary ratings or scores. There are six directional profile columns per sheet, and from this one may determine the number of sheets that will be required to hold one individual's ratings or scorings of all the members of the group.

9. To prepare the forms, your name, or that of whoever prepares the forms (it may be the rater) is put at the top of each sheet. "What group," means the group of participants whose behavior is rated. "Present Date" means the date on which you prepare the form. "From what date . . . to what date" refers to the period during which the behavior occurred. Number the pages of the form and then enter on each page the total number of pages. After "What method" write either (0, 1, 2) or (0, 1, 2, 3, 4), or "Scoring." (Remember, the same form serves as a tally sheet in counting messages from SYMLOG Interaction Scoring.) After "Whose perceptions" write down the name of the rater or scorer. After the question "What level" write ACT, or ACT + NON, or whatever is appropriate. For the simplified SYMLOG Adjective Rating Form, the level is not specific and the term ADJ, standing for "Adjective," may be entered.

10. Next, take the standard list of members of the group, and list the names of the members in the standard order along the tops of the columns. These are the members as the receivers of the ratings or scorings. The standard abbreviations, if any, should be used. If you are a group member, and thus a receiver of ratings, include yourself in the regular place in the order, using your name. In the self-analytic group, the name of the leader or instructor may be either in the standard order or at the end of the list. At the very end of the list, add a column entitled WISH.

11. If you are a group member, thus a receiver of ratings, your rating of yourself is to be made as you EXPECT others in your group will rate you. Hence, the column headed with your name should be marked EXPECT, lettered in above your name. Your description of yourself in the final column at the end is to be made as you WISH others would rate you (this may or may not be different from what you EXPECT others to rate you).

12. The forms are now ready to receive the data already gathered using the simplified Adjective Rating Form or SYMLOG Interaction Scores. If you are rating using the descriptions of some level from Appendix A, the Directional Profile Form is used for the direct recording of your ratings. In this case, the procedure is to read first the Appendix A description of the chosen level for the first direction, U. Then think about the first member you have listed to see if any of the subitems of the description apply. It is not necessary for all of the subitems to apply in order for you to make a rating. The subitems are illustrative, not strictly definitive. They are meant to stimulate your memory and to help you to form, by examples, a concept of the quality of behavior that seems to have the meaning of the direction. In the end, the meaning of the Direction is the abstract conception you have of the *general type* of behavior or content, not the specific subitems.

13. After having brought the concept of the type of behavior and the memory

of the specific person rated into focus in your mind, put down the scale number (0, 1, 2) or (0, 1, 2, 3, 4), according to the scale decided upon beforehand, which you think best describes the *frequency* of that type of behavior or content for the person rated. Continue the ratings for the same direction, i.e., U, across the forms for all columns, that is, for all of the members of the group to be rated, ending with your WISH rating. The rating is done in this way to avoid having to repeat the reading of the directional definition for every member. In order to keep your memory active, however, and to form the general concept of the direction, it is well to keep checking back to the definition of the Direction.

14. Now make the ratings for the next direction, i.e., UP at the chosen level, and so on in turn, for all directions applied to all members (plus the column for your own WISHED-FOR rating). The Directions are listed in the standard order on both the Directional Profile Form and in the Appendix A descriptions. While you are rating, try to fix the definitions, the general concepts of the types, and the relations of the directions to each other more firmly in your mind.

15. Whatever method is used, once the numbers are entered on the form for all directions and all members, the next step is to obtain for each member a numerical summary at the bottom of the column for each of the component directions: U, D, P, N, F, and B. This is done with the aid of the directional names of each of the twenty-six directions at the left side of the form or by using the Key shown in Appendix H. The Key may be folded under, one component column at a time, and placed alongside the profile of numbers in order to help you pick out easily all the cells that contribute a given component, for example, U, as you go down the profile list of numbers. The object is to locate all of the numbers to be added together to obtain the total to be entered at the bottom of the column profile.

16. To illustrate, suppose we wish to find the number to place in the cell marked U at the bottom of the column for the first group member. One may look at the directional names at the left of the form and note that the first nine directions, and only those directions, contain the component U. These nine directions are more easily picked out by the use of the Key. Add together the numbers you have put down for these nine directions, and place the total in the cell marked U at the bottom of the column for that member. Then do the same for D (note that only the last nine directions in the vertical list contain the component D). Then continue for components P, N, F, and B. Note that the pattern of location is different for each of these components.

17. Obtain these totals (U, D, P, N, F, B) for each of the columns, i.e., for each of the members, including the EXPECTED rating of the rater and the WISHED-FOR rating.

18. The next step is to obtain a final summary of the data for the three square spaces at the bottom of the column. These squares are for the *dimensional balances:* U minus D, P minus N, and F minus B. The dimensional balances for each person (column) are obtained as follows: Subtract the D total from the U total if the U total is larger, and designate the remainder as U. Write both the number and the letter in the square, for example, 3U. If the D total is larger than the U total, subtract the U total from it, and designate the remainder as D. In this way you will obtain a single number and direction for the U–D Dimension, for

example, 3U, 4D, 11U, etc. In case the remainder is zero, use the indication 00. (If one is using the scale [0, 1, 2, 3, 4], the required division by 2 is postponed to a later stage but should be remembered as necessary.)

19. Do the same to find the single number and direction for the P-N dimension and the F-B dimension. Then do the same for all columns.

20. The forms now contain all the information necessary to make a Field Diagram of the way the rater perceives each other member in the group. If the ratings have been made using the scale (0, 1, 2, 3, 4) it is necessary to divide each of the final balance numbers by 2 before they are plotted, and it may be desirable to do the computation necessary to expand the constellation of points at the same time, as described in Appendix K. If the ratings have been made using the scale (0, 1, 2), it is possible to plot the locations of the members on the Field Diagram directly (without dividing by 2), but again, for proper analysis, it is desirable to expand the constellation of points, as described in Appendix K, prior to plotting.

21. The mechanics necessary to produce a standard Field Diagram are described in a series of appendixes: L, M, N, and O.

22. If the ratings of a number of members are to be added together to make a Group Average Field Diagram, the ratings of each member should be given to a single person or team for this purpose. A form called the *Interpersonal Matrix Form* (Appendix I) is used to facilitate the collation and addition of the ratings of all members necessary to produce a Group Average Field Diagram.

23. Once a Group Average Field Diagram has been produced, it may be returned to group members (along with the detailed Interpersonal Matrix), as they wish, and they may compare it to the Field Diagram they have made from their own ratings alone. In order to make the most advantageous comparison, both diagrams should show the properly expanded constellation of points, along with all standard inscriptions. For some purposes of feedback, however, when group members will not have a complete enough grasp of the theory and purposes of the expansion and the overlay inscriptions, it may be preferable to give the feedback in raw score form. The expansion of the constellation may create a sense of dismay in the rater who has carefully refrained from making extreme ratings and has tried to avoid making ratings that might be considered undesirable. These matters should be taken into consideration in making the original contract as to what kind of feedback, if any, group members wish to receive. In some cases group members may prefer to receive no specific feedback or only raw score averages, or they may prefer to receive feedback individually, or the like. If the group is properly prepared and supported, however, the receiving of complete detailed feedback is a prime opportunity for learning, both about the specific details of the perception of personalities and group relationships, and about the theory which may help group members to better understand how they may modify or change the way they relate to each other if they wish.

Appendix C

The SYMLOG Adjective Rating Form

Robert F. Bales and Stephen P. Cohen

For many purposes the experienced rater may need a more compact method of rating than the reading of the full descriptions of the various levels in Appendix A. In particular, where group members who have no knowledge of the method at all are being asked to make ratings, the simplified form is a necessity.

The Form shown as Figure 46 is the result of a long process of evolution, much of which is not documented by published studies. It began with three Forms, A, B, and C, consisting of twenty-six questions each, published in Bales's 1970 book, *Personality and Interpersonal Behavior* (pp. 6, 12, and 13), which were the result of the extensive studies on which that book was based. These were used in various forms in the self-analytic groups of the Group Psychology Course and were gradually improved by item analysis and by logical and theoretical criticism. A number of factor analytic studies were made by persons using selections of the items in special studies with different populations. In adapting the questions to different populations, a transition was made to a shorter adjective form, and the adjectives were examined in each factor analysis as to whether they had the proper place in the factor structure to assure us that they were measuring what we wished them to measure; new adjectives were substituted in each subsequent study, which we hoped would be more satisfactory over new populations. The studies of Lee Hamilton and Frederick Miller with a general mixed community population on jury duty, and of Bonny K. Parke with ratings made by grade school teachers of children in their classrooms and by parents and children of each other have been particularly helpful. (She made up a special list that may be closer to the child's vocabulary of behavior than the list provided in this Appendix, which is geared to an adult population of moderate to good education.)

The most important studies of factor structure and item-to-scale correlations, however, have been those made by Stephen P. Cohen, reported in Part III of this book. On the basis of his findings we have again carefully reworked the adjective list, attempting to make the individual directional adjectives more exact in

FIGURE 46 The SYMLOG Adjective Rating Form

Your Name_____ Group _____

Name of person described _____ Circle the best choice for each item

		(0)	(1)	(2)	(3)	(4)
U	. . . . active, dominant, talks a lot	never	. . rarely	. . sometimes	. . often	. . always
UP	. . . extroverted, outgoing, positive	never	. . rarely	. . sometimes	. . often	. . always
UPF	. . . a purposeful democratic task leader	never	. . rarely	. . sometimes	. . often	. . always
UF	. . . an assertive business-like manager	never	. . rarely	. . sometimes	. . often	. . always
UNF	. . authoritarian, controlling, disapproving	never	. . rarely	. . sometimes	. . often	. . always
UN	. . . domineering, tough-minded, powerful	never	. . rarely	. . sometimes	. . often	. . always
UNB	. . provocative, egocentric, shows off	never	. . rarely	. . sometimes	. . often	. . always
UB	. . . jokes around, expressive, dramatic	never	. . rarely	. . sometimes	. . often	. . always
UPB	. . entertaining, sociable, smiling, warm	never	. . rarely	. . sometimes	. . often	. . always
P	. . . . friendly, equalitarian	never	. . rarely	. . sometimes	. . often	. . always
PF	. . . . works cooperatively with others	never	. . rarely	. . sometimes	. . often	. . always
F	. . . . analytical, task-oriented, problem-solving	never	. . rarely	. . sometimes	. . often	. . always
NF	. . . legalistic, has to be right	never	. . rarely	. . sometimes	. . often	. . always
N	. . . . unfriendly, negativistic	never	. . rarely	. . sometimes	. . often	. . always
NB	. . . irritable, cynical, won't cooperate	never	. . rarely	. . sometimes	. . often	. . always
B	. . . . shows feelings and emotions	never	. . rarely	. . sometimes	. . often	. . always
PB	. . . affectionate, likeable, fun to be with	never	. . rarely	. . sometimes	. . often	. . always
DP	. . . looks up to others, appreciative, trustful	never	. . rarely	. . sometimes	. . often	. . always
DPF	. . . gentle, willing to accept responsibility.	never	. . rarely	. . sometimes	. . often	. . always
DF	. . . obedient, works submissively	never	. . rarely	. . sometimes	. . often	. . always
DNF	. . self-punishing, works too hard	never	. . rarely	. . sometimes	. . often	. . always
DN	. . . depressed, sad, resentful, ...	never	. . rarely	. . sometimes	. . often	. . always
DNB	. . alienated, quits, withdraws	never	. . rarely	. . sometimes	. . often	. . always
DB	. . . afraid to try, doubts own ability	never	. . rarely	. . sometimes	. . often	. . always
DPB	. . . quietly happy just to be with others	never	. . rarely	. . sometimes	. . often	. . always
D	. . . . passive, introverted, says little	never	. . rarely	. . sometimes	. . often	. . always

measuring the specific directions for which they are designed, of higher reliabilities over split halves of the rater population, of higher item-to-scale reliability, and more semantically unambiguous. Our best expectations as to how well the present version will do are given in Part III of the book.

One objection that may be raised to the approach is that several adjectives are usually given to measure each direction, and this introduces a certain ambiguity, since the two or three adjectives do not mean exactly the same thing. Persons making the ratings will sometimes make this objection. They may be told that, if any one of the adjectives applies but not the others, they should take this one as the meaning and disregard the others. The reason we are willing to retain the ambiguity of several adjectives is that we are concerned with obtaining the best measure of the precise direction in the space that we can, and in many cases this cannot well be done with a single adjective. A given direction is defined by its relation to each of three dimensions considered simultaneously, and this makes it harder to find a single adjective that does the job well over many populations. Consequently we have resolved to depend upon the meaning that emerges when the rater reads the several adjectives in direct conjunction with each other, with the knowledge that they are supposed to modify each other.

The version in this Appendix makes a change in the answer form from the earlier form, which used a scale reading "not often," "sometimes," and "often." Cohen's study indicates that slightly higher item-to-scale correlations and item reliabilities are obtained using the finer breakdown of alternative answers: "never," "rarely," "sometimes," "often," and "always." Consequently, we have adopted it for the short form, even though it makes the job of doing the ratings and processing the data a little harder. It also makes it probable that sometimes the rating a person receives will go beyond the extreme limit of the scale of 18, which was adopted originally because it was the limit that could be obtained using the three-alternative answer form. All of the ratings discussed in other parts of this book were made or are reported at the scale of the three-alternative answer form (0, 1, 2), and the procedure for Expansion of the Constellation of Points (Appendix K) depends on having the limit of the U–D scale at 18. The U–D circles need to be kept at that scale in order to keep them within the optimum limits of size for the Field Diagram. *Consequently, when ratings are made with the five-alternative form (0, 1, 2, 3, 4), they should always be divided by 2,* which will bring them to exactly the same scale as the three-alternative form (0, 1, 2). The five-alternative form will regularly be designated as Scale (0, 1, 2, 3, 4) ÷ 2. The result of this division should be rounded to the nearest whole number, with .5 being rounded to the next larger number, except where this would exceed the limit of 18.

It will be noted that the items are identified with the directional codes, which will be unintelligible to the uninitiated, although they may note similarities on the basis of the letters and content of the items. If the user wishes, the items may be scrambled into other orders.

Cohen's study indicated, however, that the order, whether scrambled or standard, as shown here, seems to make no difference. We prefer the standard order, because the ratings are often used for feedback to the raters, and it is a great advantage in explaining results to have the letter code and standard order which may be easily related to the cubic diagram of the three-dimensional space, shown in Part I, Figure 3, p. 23. Since the ratings are often made as an instructive exercise, the easy identification and standard order of the items is to be preferred, as the rater then learns the association between the directional name and the descriptive adjectives.

Appendix D

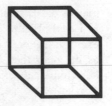

The Structure of SYMLOG Adjective Rating Scales

Stephen P. Cohen

The SYMLOG Simplified Adjective Rating Form utilizes an unusual form of scale construction. The twenty-six items attempt to represent each possible combination of three factors (Upward–Downward, Positive–Negative, Forward–Backward). Rather than constructing separate scales for each dimension, an overall rating form has been developed in such a way that six items measure only one dimension, twelve items ($2 \times 3 \times 2$) measure all combinations of dimensions taken two at a time, and eight items ($2 \times 2 \times 2$) measure all combinations of dimensions taken three at a time. The purpose is to clarify the behavior and trait descriptions referred to by each factoral combination and to attempt to construct a conception of the dimensions so that they are conceptually independent.

Such a form of scale construction has interesting psychometric properties. Some items are designed to measure more than one dimension simultaneously. Therefore, the internal consistency of a scale composed of all items including a particular dimensional component will be theoretically less than complete.

In fact, it is possible to determine the precise expected or ideal loading of each item on each factor. Assume first that the three factors explain all of the variance in this hypothetical perfect scale. Then the variance over the three factors for each item sums to 1.0. In other words, the squared factor loadings for each item sum to 1.0. Second, we know that the singly named items name the axes of the dimensions and are uncorrelated with each other, except for polar opposites, which have a correlation of -1.0 (U with D, P with N, F with B). Thus, the loading for each item naming an axis is 1.0 on that factor and 0.0 on the other factors. For the opposite end of the dimension, it would be -1.0 on that factor and 0.0 on both other factors. The doubly named items should weigh equally on both the factors that they measure and zero on the third factor. Since those two

TABLE 23 Hypothetical Factor Loadings for Each Item on Each Factor: Ideal Item-to-Scale Correlations

	FACTOR 1 U–D SCALE	FACTOR 2 P–N SCALE	FACTOR 3 F–B SCALE
1. U	1.0	0	0
2. UP	.707	.707	0
3. UPF	.577	.577	.577
4. UF	.707	0	.707
5. UNF	.577	−.577	.577
6. UN	.707	−.707	0
7. UNB	.577	−.577	−.577
8. UB	.707	0	−.707
9. UPB	.577	.577	−.577
10. P	0	1.0	0
11. PF	0	.707	.707
12. F	0	0	1.0
13. NF	0	−.707	.707
14. N	0	−1.0	0
15. NB	0	−.707	−.707
16. B	0	0	−1.0
17. PB	0	.707	−.707
18. DP	−.707	.707	0
19. DPF	−.577	.577	.577
20. DF	−.707	0	.707
21. DNF	−.577	−.577	.577
22. DN	−.707	−.707	0
23. DNB	−.577	−.577	−.577
24. DB	−.707	0	−.707
25. DPB	−.577	.577	−.577
26. D	−1.0	0	0

NOTE: .707 is an approximation to $1/\sqrt{2}$.
.577 is an approximation to $1/\sqrt{3}$.

factors account for all of the variance of the item, each factor accounts for one-half of the variance. Thus the factor loading for such an item would be $\sqrt{\frac{1}{2}}$ or $1/\sqrt{2}$, approximately .7071. Similarly, the variance explained by each factor on a triply named item should be equal for all three factors. Since the three factors account for all of the variance, this means that each factor accounts for one-third of the variance of the item. Thus the factor loading on each item of this kind would be $\sqrt{\frac{1}{3}}$ or $1/\sqrt{3}$, which is approximately .57735 or .577 or .58, rounding off.

The appropriate sign for the items is determined by convention so that U, P, F are the plus (+) ends of the dimensions and D, N, B are the negative (−) ends of the dimensions. The full table of hypothetical or ideal factor loadings is given in Table 23.

Note that the factor loadings in this case are identical with item-to-scale correlations, because these are perfect scales with all variance accounted for.

TABLE 24 Hypothetical Correlation Matrix

	U	UP	UPF	UF	UNF	UN	UNB	UB	UPB	P	PF	F	NF
U		.71	.58	.71	.58	.71	.58	.71	.58	0	0	0	0
UP			.82	.50	0	0	0	.50	.82	.71	.50	0	−.50
UPF				.82	.33	0	−.33	0	.33	.58	.82	.58	0
UF					.82	.50	0	0	0	−.58	.50	.71	.50
UNF						.82	.33	0	−.33	−.71	0	.58	.82
UN							.82	.50	0	−.58	−.50	0	.50
UNB								.82	.33	0	−.82	−.58	0
UB									.82	.58	−.50	−.71	−.50
UPB										.58	0	−.58	−.82
P											.71	0	−.71
PF												.71	0
F													.71
NF													
N													
NB													
B													
PB													
DP													
DPF													
DF													
DNF													
DN													
DNB													
DB													
DPB													
D													

Two Triangular Submatrices (8 + 7 + ... + 1)
   For each: $\bar{x}_r = .398$
Square Submatrix (9 × 9)
   $\bar{x}_r = -.465$
Two Rectangular Submatrices (9 × 8)
   For each: $\bar{x}_r = .000$
Middle Triangular Submatrix (7 + 6 + ... + 1)
   $\bar{x}_r = -.142$

	N	NB	B	PB	DP	DPF	DF	DNF	DN	DNB	DB	DPB	D
U	0	0	0	0	-.71	-.58	-.71	-.58	-.71	-.58	-.71	-.58	-1.0
UP	-.71	-.50	0	.50	0	0	-.50	-.82	-1.0	-.82	-.50	0	-.71
UPF	-.58	-.82	-.58	0	0	.33	0	-.33	-.82	-1.0	-.82	-.33	-.58
UF	0	-.50	-.71	-.50	-.50	0	0	0	-.50	-.82	-1.0	-.82	-.71
UNF	.58	0	-.58	-.82	-.82	-.33	0	.33	0	-.33	-.82	-1.0	-.58
UN	.71	.50	0	-.50	-1.0	-.82	-.50	0	0	0	-.50	-.82	-.71
UNB	.58	.82	.58	0	-.82	-1.0	-.82	-.33	0	.33	0	-.33	-.58
UB	0	.50	.71	.50	-.50	-.82	-1.0	-.82	-.50	0	0	0	-.71
UPB	-.58	0	.58	.82	0	-.33	-.82	-1.0	-.82	-.33	0	.33	-.58
P	-1.0	-.71	0	.71	.71	.58	0	-.58	-.71	-.58	0	.58	0
PF	-.71	-1.0	-.71	0	.50	.82	.50	0	-.50	-.82	-.50	0	0
F	0	-.71	-1.0	-.71	0	.58	.71	.58	0	-.58	-.71	-.58	0
NF	.71	0	-.71	-1.0	-.50	0	.50	.82	.50	0	-.50	-.82	0
N		.71	0	-.71	-.71	-.58	0	.58	.71	.58	0	-.58	0
NB			.71	0	-.50	-.82	-.50	0	.50	.82	.50	0	0
B				.71	0	-.58	-.71	-.58	0	.58	.71	.58	0
PB					.71	0	-.50	-.82	-.50	0	.50	.82	0
DP						.82	.50	0	0	0	.50	.82	.71
DPF							.82	.33	0	-.33	0	.33	.58
DF								.82	.50	0	0	0	.71
DNF									.82	.33	0	-.33	.58
DN										.82	.50	0	.71
DNB											.82	.82	.58
DB												.33	.58
DPB													.71
D													

NOTE: Values entered are approximations as follows:

.71 is $1/\sqrt{2}$ or .7071
.58 is $1/\sqrt{3}$ or .57735
.82 is $2/\sqrt{3}\sqrt{2}$ or .8165
.50 is $1/\sqrt{2}\sqrt{2}$ or 1/2 or .50
.33 is $1/\sqrt{3}\sqrt{3}$ or 1/3 or .33

The factor loadings can also be seen as the coordinates for the location of each of the twenty-six items as vectors in the three-dimensional space. Thus, we can calculate precisely the distance between these points or the angle between the vectors that they subtend at the origin of the coordinate system. These distances, or the cosines of these angles, actually define the correlation between the vectors. Thus we can generate the precise correlation between any pair of vectors (any two theoretically perfect items). This hypothetical correlation matrix can be derived by calculating the distance between the coordinates by the usual formula. More simply, the dot product of two points finds the cosine of the angle between the points and that cosine is equal to the correlation coefficient r.

The dot product is the sum of the product of the coordinates on the first axis of each point, plus the product of the coordinates on the second axis of each point, plus the product of the coordinates on the third axis (see Harman, 1976). For example, the dot product of UPB (coordinates .58, .58, .58) and PB (coordinates 0, .707, .707) is $(0 \times .58) + (.707)(.58) + (.707)(.58)$ which sums to .8165, which is the cosine of the angle between the points, which is equal to their correlation, r.

A hypothetical correlation matrix, giving the r for any two vectors is given in Table 24. This correlation matrix has many interesting features, which may be brought out best by dividing it into six submatrices, as indicated in Figure 47. Triangular submatrices 1 and 2 are identical (except for the informal order of the cells.) They represent respectively the intercorrelations among the U items and the intercorrelations among the D items. Square submatrix 3 has the correlation between U items and D items. When using the full U–D scale, these interitem correlations are added in. Rectangular submatrices 4 and 5 are also identical. Submatrix 4 is the correlation of the U vectors with the vectors that are neither U nor D, while submatrix 5 contains the correlations between D items and those neither U nor D. Triangular submatrix 6 represents the intercorrelations among the items neither U nor D.

Structurally, matrix 3 is a combination of matrices 1 and 2 with signs reversed plus nine correlations of -1.0 representing nine of the thirteen polar opposite correlations, those of the nine U items with their opposite (angle of 180°) D items. Matrix 6 has exactly an equal number of positive .71 and negative .71 correlations plus the remaining four -1.0 correlations, representing four pairs of polar opposites.

Submatrices 4 and 5 have sums of correlations equal to zero as each column for 4 and each row for submatrix 5 has exactly three zero correlations, three positive correlations, and three equal and opposite negative correlations.

It should be clear that by simply reordering the names the same combination of submatrices could be derived from the perspective of P–N or F–B rather than U–D. For P–N, submatrix 1 would be intercorrelations of P vectors; submatrix 2 intercorrelations of N vectors; submatrix 3 intercorrelations between P and N vectors; submatrix 4 correlations between P vectors and vectors neither P nor N; submatrix 5 correlations between N vectors and vectors neither P nor N; submatrix 6 correlations among vectors neither P nor N. Furthermore, the matrix would be identical.

Notice as well the sum of correlations in the matrix. Since submatrix 1 and

FIGURE 47 Numbered Submatrices for Discussion of Correlation Matrix

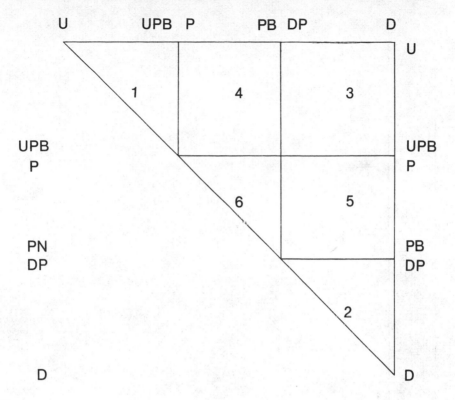

submatrix 2 are equal numerically but opposite in sign to submatrix 3 except for the -1.0 correlations, and submatrices 4 and 5 sum to zero, and submatrix 6 is zero minus the $4 -1.0$ correlations, the sum of all matrix entries is -13.0. It is important to see that the overall mean correlation $(\bar{x}_r)$ for the square submatrix 3 is higher than that for 1 and 2. Since reliability increases if $\bar{x}_r$ increases, it can be seen that using scales at both polar ends increases the chances for high reliability.

The zero sums for submatrices 4 and 5 indicate the orthogonality of the hypothetical dimensions, and thus we can move to a simplified matrix (Table 25), which deletes submatrices 4, 5, and 6.

Looking carefully at submatrix 1 we notice that there are very widely varying intercorrelations and that two are even less than zero. The hypothetical expectation is not of a totally internally consistent scale but rather of one made up of somewhat disparate elements.

Table 26 gives some summary data based on the hypothetical matrix. (We shall return to the idea of weighted scales below.) The eighteen-item scales benefit from the polar opposite items so that they are more reliable than the nine-item scales both from having more items and because of a higher mean intercorrelation of items. The reliability coefficients are less than 1.00, and thus we cannot expect as high reliabilities for a scale constructed in this way as would be expected from eighteen items all measuring only one dimension. We can see

TABLE 25 Hypothetical Correlation Matrix for Eighteen-Item Scale and Nine-Item Scales (Using U–D as Example, with Perfectly Constructed Items)

($\bar{x}_r$ for 18 items by 18 items: .434)

	U	UP	UPF	UF	UNF	UN	UNB	UB	UPB	P	PF	F	NF
U		.71	.58	.71	.58	.71	.58	.71	.58				
UP			.82	.50	0	0	0	.50	.82				
UPF				.82	.33	0	-.33	0	.33				
UF					.82	.50	0	0	0				
UNF						.82	.33	0	-.33				
UN							.82	.50	0				
UNB								.82	.33				
UB									.82				
UPB													
P													
PF													
F													
NF													
N													
NB													
B													
PB													
DP													
DPF													
DF													
DNF													
DN													
DNB													
DB													
DPB													
D													

$\bar{x}_r = .398$

402

	N	NB	B	PB	DP	DPF	DF	DNF	DN	DNB	DB	DPB	D
U					-.71	-.58	-.71	-.58	-.71	-.58	-.71	-.58	-1.0
UP					0	0	-.50	-.82	-1.0	-.82	-.50	0	-.71
UPF					0	.33	0	-.33	-.82	-1.0	-.82	-.33	-.58
UF					-.50	0	0	0	-.50	-.82	-1.0	-.82	-.71
UNF					-.82	-.33	0	.33	0	-.33	-.82	-1.0	-.58
UN	$\bar{x}_r = .465$				-1.0	-.82	-.50	0	0	0	-.50	-.82	-.71
UNB					-.82	-1.0	-.82	-.33	0	.33	0	-.33	-.58
UB					-.50	-.82	-1.0	-.82	-.50	0	0	0	-.71
UPB					0	-.33	-.82	-1.0	-.82	-.33	0	.33	-.58
P													
PF													
F													
NF													
N													
NB													
B													
PB						.82	.50	0	0	0	.50	.82	.71
DP						.82	.50	0	0	0	.50	.82	.71
DPF							.82	.33	0	-.33	0	.33	.58
DF								.82	.50	0	0	0	.71
DNF									.82	.33	0	-.33	.58
DN										.82	.50	0	.71
DNB	$\bar{x}_r = .398$										.82	.33	.58
DB												.82	.71
DPB													.71
D													.58

TABLE 26 Hypothetical Scale Reliabilities for Scales Constructed by Three-dimensional Vector Combinations

---

(a) 9-item scales of one pole of one dimension
    e.g. all 9 U items; all 9 P items; all 9 D items; etc.

	$r_{kk} = .856$	$\bar{x}_r = .398$
Weighted:	$r_{kk} = .887$	$\bar{x}_r = .466$

(b) 18-item scales of two poles of one dimension
    e.g. all 9 U items minus all 9 D items, etc.

	$r_{kk} = .932$	$\bar{x}_r = .434$
Weighted:	$r_{kk} = .954$	$\bar{x}_r = .536$

(c) Mean item intercorrelations ($\bar{x}_r$) for item sets (with all items):

			Ratio
9-item scale	Triply named	.3179	$\simeq 1$
	Doubly named	.4175	$\simeq 1.5$
	Singly named	.6422	$\simeq 2$
18-item scale	Triply named	.3450	$\simeq 1$
	Doubly named	.4408	$\simeq 1.5$
	Singly named	.6565	$\simeq 2$

NOTE: r_{kk} = reliability coefficient
    $\bar{x}_r$ = average intercorrelation among items

as well that the mean correlations for each set of items is such that the singly named items have higher correlations than the others in a ratio of 6 to 3 (for doubly named items) to 2 (for singly named items).

This ratio corresponds to the ratio of the variance of each kind of item accounted for by a particular factor. For singly named items this is 1.00, for doubly named .50, and for triply named .333 or ⅓. The ratio is 6 to 3 to 2.

This ratio provides the theoretical basis for weighting SYMLOG items. Such a weighting procedure is not usually recommended. However, given the wide discrepancy among the theoretical intercorrelations and the small number of items, this becomes justified (see Nunnally, 1967). This choice is strengthened by the existence of an a priori basis for weighting. This contrasts with the usual post facto basis that would change from sample-to-sample based on obtained item-to-scale correlations. Appendix E gives a weighted version of the SYMLOG scale for easy use and a table for converting weighted scores to units appropriate for Field Diagrams. Part III discusses the empirical benefits of weighting in increasing scale reliability. Table 26 shows that weighting substantially increases the ceiling reliability of scales constructed by combinations of three dimensions like SYMLOG Rating scales. At these high levels of r the increased correlations are a valuable asset. Even if an unweighted version of the SYMLOG Adjective Rating Scale is used, it would be advisable to use the weighting procedure for the U-D and F-B dimensions, at least until data on the revised scale have been gathered and reported. Paradoxically, if the revisions work as designed, weighting may be equally desirable for the P-N dimension as well, since the reliabilities of the three dimensions should become more equal around the .80 level or higher.

TABLE 27   Angular Separation and Correlations between Combinations of
Three-dimensional Vectors

Singly named orthogonal axes with each other:
    U with F, B, P, N $< = 90°$
    P with F, B $r = \cos 90° = 0$
    etc.
Singly named axes with doubly named combinations:
    U with UP, UF, UN, UB $< = 45°$
    D with DP, DF, DN, DB $r = \cos 45° = .7071$
    P with UP, DP, PF, PB
    etc.
Singly named axes with triply named combinations:
    U with UPF, UNF, UNB, UPB $< = 54.3°$
    D with DPF, DNF, DNB, DPB $r = \cos 54.3° = .57735$
    etc.
Doubly named combinations with each other (same hemipshere);
    UP with UF, UB, PF, PB $< = 60°$
    UF with UP, UN, PF, NF $r = \cos 60° = .50$
    DP with DF, DB, PF, PB
    etc.
Doubly named combinations with triply named similar in *two* of three dimensions
    UP with UPF, UPB $< = 35.3°$
    UF with UPF, UNF $r = \cos 35.3° = .8165$
    PF with UPF, DPF
    etc.
Triply named combinations with other triply named similar in *two* of three dimensions
    UPF with UNF, UPB, DPF $< - 70.5°$
    UNF with DNF, UPF, UNB $r = \cos 70.5° = .333$
    etc.
Triply named combinations with other triply named similar in only *one* of three
    dimensions:
    UPF with UNB, DNF, DPB $< = 109.5°$
    UNF with UPB, DNB, DPF $r = \cos 109.5° = -.333$
    UPB with UNF, DPF, DNB
Singly named with doubly named on other dimensions:
    U with PF, PB, NF, NB $< = 90°$
    etc. $r = \cos 90° = 0$
Doubly named combinations with doubly *or* triply named similar in one dimension,
    opposite on the second dimension:
    UP with UN, DP, and with UNF, UNB, DPF, DPB $< = 90°$
    UF with UB, DF, and with UNB, UPB, DPF, DNF $r = \cos 90° = 0$
    PF with PB, NF, and with UPB, DPB, UNF, DNF
    etc.
Doubly named combinations with each other, opposite on *only* common dimension:
    UP with DF, NF, NB, DB $< = 120°$
    UF with DP, DN, PB, NB $r = \cos 120° = -.50$
    etc.
Singly named axes with triply named combinations in opposite hemisphere:
    U with DPF, etc. $< = 125.7°$
    F with UNB etc $r = \cos 125.7° = -.57735$

TABLE 27 (cont.)

Singly named axes with doubly named combinations in opposite hemisphere:
  U with DF, DP, etc. $< = 135°$
  F with NB, DB, etc. $r = \cos 135° = -.7071$
  etc.
Doubly named combinations with triply named opposite in *two* dimensions:
  UP with DNF, DNB $< = 144.7°$
  etc. $r = \cos 144.7° = -.8165$
  PF with UNB, DNB
  etc.
Polar Opposites
  U with D
  P with N $< = 180°$
  UP with DN $r = \cos 180° = -1.0$
  PB with NF
  UPF with DNB
  UNB with DPF
  etc.

NOTE: $<$ = angle
    cos = cosine
     r = correlation coefficient

To simplify the argument made here and the basis of the correlation matrices, Table 27 presents the generalizations in verbal form giving angular separation between vectors and showing how the matrix is structured.

Finally, the argument presented here and the tables and matrices provided can be used for other scales constructed from a multidimensional approach to interaction or other social science problems. The method of solution could be generalized to more than three factors or to N factors if so desired, though the number of combinations might become prohibitive beyond three.

Appendix E

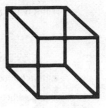

The Weighted SYMLOG Adjective Rating Form

Stephen P. Cohen

The weighted version of the SYMLOG Rating Scale is introduced to increase the reliability of the summary scales. Under most circumstances it will produce more reliable scale measures, but this will be especially so for scales that are being masked by one of the factors explaining a large proportion of the variance. In other words, when one dimension of interaction is being especially emphasized by raters, weighting will help obtain a better measure on the other factors as well.

If the usual form is used it is a simple procedure to transform the scores by the appropriate weight. The appropriate weight for all singly named items is 6. Multiply the obtained scores on U, for example, by 6. Thus, if a person is rated "always" (4) on the U item, multiply 4 by 6, and tabulate 24 for that item. The weighted form (Figure 48) makes this procedure clear for all items.

The sums obtained from a weighted scale are too large to fit into the scale used for the Field Diagram. The exact solution is provided by setting the maximum of 104 for the weighted scale equal to 18 on the Field Diagram, (the maximum for a scale of U or D, P or N, F or B.) For exact calculation of other weighted scores one would multiply the weighted sum by 18/104 and round upward at .5. This is too cumbersome for most practical purposes, so a simple table is provided (Table 28).

Example: The weighted score for a group member is 50U, 13N, 2B. The circle would be a 9U equivalent circle. The Field Diagram location would be at 2N, neither F nor B.

FIGURE 48 The Weighted SYMLOG Adjective Rating Scale

		never	rarely	sometimes	often	always
U	active, dominant, talks a lot	0	6	12	18	24
UP	extroverted, outgoing, positive	0	3	6	9	12
UPF	a purposeful democratic task leader	0	2	4	6	8
UF	an assertive business-like manager	0	3	6	9	12
UNF	authoritarian, controlling, disapproving	0	2	4	6	8
UN	domineering, tough-minded, powerful	0	3	6	9	12
UNB	provocative, egocentric, shows off	0	2	4	6	8
UB	jokes around, expressive, dramatic	0	3	6	9	12
UPB	entertaining, sociable, smiling, warm	0	2	4	6	8
P	friendly, equalitarian	0	6	12	18	24
PF	works cooperatively with others	0	3	6	9	12
F	analytical, task-oriented, problem-solving	0	6	12	18	24
NF	legalistic, has to be right	0	3	6	9	12
N	unfriendly, negativistic	0	6	12	18	24
NB	irritable, cynical, won't cooperate	0	3	6	9	12
B	shows feelings and emotions	0	6	12	18	24
PB	affectionate, likeable, fun to be with	0	3	6	9	12
DP	looks up to others, appreciative, trustful	0	3	6	9	12
DPF	gentle, willing to accept responsibility	0	2	4	6	8
DF	obedient, works submissively	0	3	6	9	12
DNF	self-punishing, works too hard	0	2	4	6	8
DN	depressed, sad, resentful	0	3	6	9	12
DNB	alienated, quits, withdraws	0	2	4	6	8
DB	afraid to try, doubts own ability	0	3	6	9	12
DPB	quietly happy just to be with others	0	2	4	6	8
D	passive, introverted, says little	0	6	12	18	24

TABLE 28   Plotting Scores in the Field Diagram Corresponding to Weighted
Scores by a Given Dimension

WEIGHTED SCORES		FIELD DIAGRAM UNITS
3–8	=	1 unit on the Field Diagram
9–14	=	2 units on the Field Diagram
15–20	=	3 units on the Field Diagram
21–25	=	4 units
26–31	=	5 units
32–37	=	6 units
38–43	=	7 units
44–49	=	8 units
50–54	=	9 units
55–60	=	10 units
61–66	=	11 units
67–72	=	12 units
73–77	=	13 units
78–83	=	14 units
84–89	=	15 units
90–95	=	16 units
96–101	=	17 units
102–104	=	18 units on the Field Diagram

Appendix F

The SYMLOG Interaction Scoring Form

Robert F. Bales and Stephen P. Cohen

The SYMLOG observer needs a supply of Scoring Forms, shown as Figure 49.

One sheet of the Scoring Form provides space for twenty messages. A moderately good scorer should produce at least one message per minute, hence one should expect to fill at least three sheets per hour. Very good scorers may produce two or even three times as many messages.

The messages recorded on the Scoring Form may be tabulated in various ways by hand, using the Directional Profile Form (see Appendix G) in preparation for the construction of Field Diagrams for various levels, or time plots for various directions of behavior and content over the time period covered by the observation. If the computer programs described in Appendixes S and T are obtained, the messages recorded on the Scoring Form are entered directly into the computer from the console, by literally typing in each message (with the exception of the words used in the ordinary description of the behavior or image). The number of useful tabulations that may be made quickly by this method, of course, is very great. Hand tabulation, by contrast, limits the number of tabulations that may be made but has the advantages of more complete learning of exactly what is done with the data and of greater availability and dependability.

FIGURE 49 The SYMLOG Interaction Scoring Form

Observer _____ Group_____ Date_____ Page_____

Draw a diagram of the physical location of group members on back of page 1

Time	Who Acts	Toward Whom	Act/ Non	Direc- tion	Ordinary Description of Behavior or Image	Pro/ Con	Direc- tion	Image Level

Appendix G

The Directional Profile Form

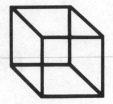

Figure 50 shows a form entitled *Directional Profiles*. Complete instructions for its use are given in Appendix B, General Instructions for Making Ratings.

The Directional Profile Form is used for three kinds of data: (1) Data obtained from Rating, with the aid of the descriptions in Appendix A, (2) data obtained from Rating using the simplified SYMLOG Adjective Rating Form, see Appendix C, and (3) data obtained from Scoring using the observation and recording procedures outlined in the SYMLOG Manual for Interaction Scoring, using the Scoring Form shown in Appendix F.

1. In the procedure where the ratings are made with the aid of the descriptions in Appendix A (or possibly just the descriptions on the simplified Adjective Rating Form), the rater, using memory alone or memory refreshed by listening to sound recordings or by reading any notes that may have been taken (which might include the SYMLOG Interaction Scoring sheets), rates the frequency of each type of behavior for each individual at the level decided upon, and puts the numbers down directly upon the Directional Profile Form, properly prepared, as described in detail in Appendix B.

2. In the procedure where raters have used the simplified SYMLOG Adjective Rating Form shown in Appendix C and have recorded their answers on that form, the researcher copies the ratings made to the Directional Profile Form in order to facilitate the addition of the scores.

3. In the procedure where observations have been made using the SYMLOG Interaction Scoring method, the researcher determines what tabulations are to be made (for example, how many ACT level instances of behavior are recorded for each person in the group), and puts the proper headings on the Directional Profile Form. If the record is not too long, the actual tally marks may be placed in the proper cells of the profile and then counted.

No matter which of these several kinds of data may be recorded on the Directional Profile Form, the tabulations are performed in the same way, as described in Appendix B, using the Key shown in Appendix H.

Figure 51 shows the rating data of RFB, properly processed to obtain the summary scores used in making the Field Diagram shown as Figure 1 in Part I.

FIGURE 50 The SYMLOG Directional Profile Form

Your Name_____

Of what Group: _____Present Date_____

From what date:_____ to what date:_____ Page_____ of _____

What Method: _____ Whose Perceptions: _____ What Level: _____

Who, or What Image→ Direction↓						
U						
UP						
IIPF						
UF						
UNF						
UN						
UNB						
UB						
UPB						
P						
PF						
F						
NF						
N						
NB						
B						
PB						
DP						
DPF						
DF						
DNF						
DN						
DNB						
DB						
DPB						
D						
TOTAL						
U						
D						
P						
N						
F						
B						

FIGURE 51 Illustrative Ratings on the Directional Profile Form

Your Name_____

Of what Group: _____ Present Date_____

From what date:_____ to what date: _____ Page_____ of _____

What Method: _____ Whose Perceptions: _____ What Level: _____

Who, or What Image→ Direction	CARL		BILL		SARA		SUE		LAIN		HIP	
U	1		O		1		O		O		2	
UP	O		1		O		O		O		2	
UPF	O		2		0		O		1		1	
UF	O		1		0		O		1		1	
UNF	1		O		0		O		1		1	
UN	2		O		1		O		O		1	
UNB	2		O		2		O		O		2	
UB	1		O		2		O		O		2	
UPB	O		2		1		1		O		2	
P	O		2		1		2		1		1	
PF	O		2		O		2		1		O	
F	1		2		O		2		2		1	
NF	1		O		O		O		O		1	
N	2		O		O		O		O		1	
NB	2		O		O		O		O		1	
B	2		O		2		O		O		1	
PB	1		O		2		O		O		2	
DP	O		2		O		2		2		O	
DPF	O		1		1		1		1		1	
DF	O		1		O		1		2		O	
DNF	1		O		O		O		O		O	
DN	2		O		2		O		O		O	
DNB	2		O		O		O		O		O	
DB	1		O		1		O		1		O	
DPB	O		O		1		1		O		O	
D	2		O		1		O		O		O	
TOTAL												
U	7	1D	6	2U	7	1U	1	4D	3	3D	14	13U
D	8		4		6		5		6		1	
P	1	14N	12	12P	6	1P	9	9P	6	5P	9	2P
N	15		0		5		O		1		7	
F	4	7B	9	7F	1	10B	6	4F	9	8F	6	4B
B	11		2		11		2		1		10	

FIGURE 51   (Continued)

Your Name_____

Of what Group _____ Present Date_____

From what date:_____ to what date:_____ Page_____ of _____

What Method: _____ Whose Perceptions: _____ What Level: _____

Who, or What Image→ Direction ↓	HUGH	PAL	ANN	TINA	TED	TOM
U	O	O	O	O	2	1
UP	2	O	O	O	1	O
UPF	1	O	O	O	1	O
UF	O	O	O	O	1	O
UNF	O	O	O	O	2	1
UN	O	O	O	O	1	1
UNB	O	O	O	O	O	O
UB	1	O	O	O	O	O
UPB	2	O	1	O	1	O
P	2	1	1	1	1	1
PF	2	O	O	O	2	O
F	O	O	1	O	2	1
NF	O	O	O	O	2	O
N	O	O	O	O	O	1
NB	O	O	O	O	O	1
B	O	O	1	O	O	1
PB	2	1	O	O	O	O
DP	2	2	2	2	O	O
DPF	1	2	O	2	2	O
DF	1	1	O	1	2	1
DNF	1	O	O	O	1	1
DN	O	O	O	O	O	2
DNB	O	O	1	O	1	2
DB	1	O	1	O	O	2
DPB	O	2	2	1	O	1
D	O	1	O	2	O	1

TOTAL	HUGH		PAL		ANN		TINA		TED		TOM	
U	6	00	0	8D	1	5D	0	8D	10	5U	3	7D
D	6		8		6		8		5		10	
P	14	13P	8	8P	6	5P	6	6P	8	1P	2	7N
N	1		0		1		0		7		9	
F	6	00	3	∞	1	5B	3	2F	15	13F	4	3B
B	6		3		6		1		2		7	

FIGURE 51 (Continued)

Your Name_____

Of what Group: _____ Present Date_____

From what date: _____ to what date: _____ Page_____ of _____

What Method: _____ Whose Perceptions: _____ What Level: _____

Who, or What Image→ Direction ↓	MOOS	ACE	RFB	(WISH)			
U	2	2	1				
UP	1	2	1				
UPF	O	O	1				
UF	1	O	2				
UNF	1	1	1				
UN	2	2	O				
UNB	1	2	O				
UB	1	2	1				
UPB	O	1	O				
P	1	O	2				
PF	1	1	2				
F	2	1	2				
NF	2	O	1				
N	1	2	O				
NB	1	2	O				
B	O	2	O				
PB	2	1	O				
DP	O	O	O				
DPF	1	1	1				
DF	1	O	O				
DNF	O	O	O				
DN	O	O	O				
DNB	O	1	O				
DB	O	O	O				
DPB	O	O	O				
D	O	O	O				
TOTAL							
U	9	7U	12	10U	7	6U	
D	2		2		1		
P	6	2N	6	4N	7	5P	
N	8		10		2		
F	9	4F	4	7B	10	9F	
B	5		11		1		

Note that these ratings were made using the scale (0, 1, 2). The scale (0, 1, 2, 3, 4) will give larger numbers, of course, and in this case the numbers are divided by 2 at the next step in processing.

In the case of tabulations of SYMLOG Interaction Scoring data, the numbers may be of any size, and they are transformed into the proper scale for plotting by use of one of the formulas described in Appendix S. If desired, this transformation may be accomplished by hand calculation using the Form in Appendix J. In the case of substantial amounts of data, however, it is a great convenience to use the computer programs that have been prepared by Howard Swann, with the help of Richard Polley. These programs may be entered either with data tabulations from the Directional Profile Form (tabulations made by hand) or by typing the original SYMLOG Interaction Scoring Messages in, one by one, at the computer console.

Appendix H

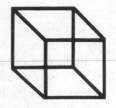

The Key for Tabulation of
Directional Profiles

Figure 52 shows the key which is used in conjunction with the data that has been entered on the Directional Profile Form. The Key is of the same size and format as the form. It may be constructed without much trouble by simply marking the location patterns shown on a regular Directional Profile Form.

In order to use the Key, the right edge is folded under, column by column, and placed up against the appropriate column on the Directional Profile Form. In order to obtain the total for the cell marked U at the bottom of the Directional Profile, for example, one uses the column marked U on the Key. The portion marked in black then indicates the location of all the directional cells on the directional profile for the individual that contain ratings with a U component. The first nine directions on the profile are U, UP, UPF, UF, UNF, UN, UNB, UB, and UPB. Each of these directions contains a U component. The numbers in the cells for these directions are all to be added together to obtain the summary number to be placed in the U cell at the bottom of the profile.

It will be noted that some cells contribute only to one dimension; for example, the cell U contributes only to the U–D dimension. Others, for example, UP, contribute to two dimensions, namely U–D, and P–N. Still others, for example, UPF, contribute to all three dimensions. For this reason, some directional ratings are more important than others in obtaining the summary scores (e.g., UP is more important than U, UPF is more important than UP), but this is true for all three dimensions, and the measurement of each is counterbalanced by the measurement of the others.

A more accurate method of measurement involves making a factor analysis of the twenty-six items for each particular use and weighting the items according to the factor loadings. However, the simplicity of the method represented by the use of the Key is a very important advantage in practical use, and a great deal of experience indicates that it produces very satisfactory results.

Another alternative, which will give more accurate measurement, is to utilize the differential weighting system worked out by Stephen P. Cohen, described in Appendix E. This method involves more work but it will result in higher reliability and may be worthwhile in research studies; perhaps even in practical use.

FIGURE 52 The SYMLOG Key for Tabulation of Directional Profiles

	B	F	N	P	D	U
U						■
UP				■		■
UPF		■		■		■
UF		■				■
UNF		■	■			■
UN			■			■
UNB	■		■			■
UB	■					■
UPB	■			■		■
P				■		
PF		■				
F		■				
NF		■	■			
N			■			
NB	■		■			
B	■					
PB	■			■		
DP				■	■	
DPF		■		■	■	
DF		■			■	
DNF		■	■		■	
DN			■		■	
DNB	■		■		■	
DB	■				■	
DPB	■			■	■	
D					■	
TOTAL						
U						
D						
P						
N						
F						
B						

FOLD THIS EDGE UNDER, THEN FOLD UNDER ONE KEY AT A TIME

Appendix I

The Interpersonal Matrix Form

Once the ratings each member of the group has *given* to each other member have been recorded on the Directional Profile forms and the summaries have been obtained, the ratings of all members must still be collected and added together in order to make the Group Average Field Diagram. One must determine how each individual as a *receiver* of ratings has been rated by each other individual as a *giver* of ratings. This is done with the aid of the Interpersonal Matrix Form, shown as Figure 53.

The Interpersonal Matrix is a systematic array of data blocks displaying the relationships between each person as a source of ratings (or in some cases as a source of ACTS), and each person as a receiver of ratings, or of ACTS. Let us speak of ratings only, for the time being, in order to simplify the discussion. The persons as raters are shown along the vertical margin of the square array under the title "WHO" (who is rating). The persons as receivers of ratings are shown along the top horizontal margin of the array under the title "TO WHOM" (to whom the rating is given).

Since the SYMLOG System provides for ratings in each of six directions (as a summary of the twenty-six), and for the reduction of the six directions to a location on each of three dimensions, and finally for a summary letter type that omits even the numbers, a person-to-person "cell" on the Interpersonal Matrix is actually a *block* of cells, as will be seen in Figure 53. Each block contains six separate cells for the ratings in the form U, D, P, N, F, B, followed by three square cells for the summary ratings in the form 5U, 2P, 3F, etc., and finally three more square cells for final letter types or for additional computations. A page of the matrix provides for the ratings of five persons rating five persons.

The first page of the matrix for the illustrative group studied in Part I of the book is shown as Figure 54. Only the first page is given, since the complete matrix requires sixteen pages, and the information is given graphically in the Field Diagrams in Part I, which were made from this matrix.

In order to determine how many sheets of the form will be needed to construct the full square matrix for the group, the following calculation may be used. First one needs to find the number of horizontal blocks one will need to record, add

FIGURE 53   The SYMLOG Interpersonal Matrix Form

Your Name_____

Of what Group _____ Present Date_____

From what date:_____ to what date:_____ Page_____ of _____

Content of the Matrix: (Describe in detail) _____

_____

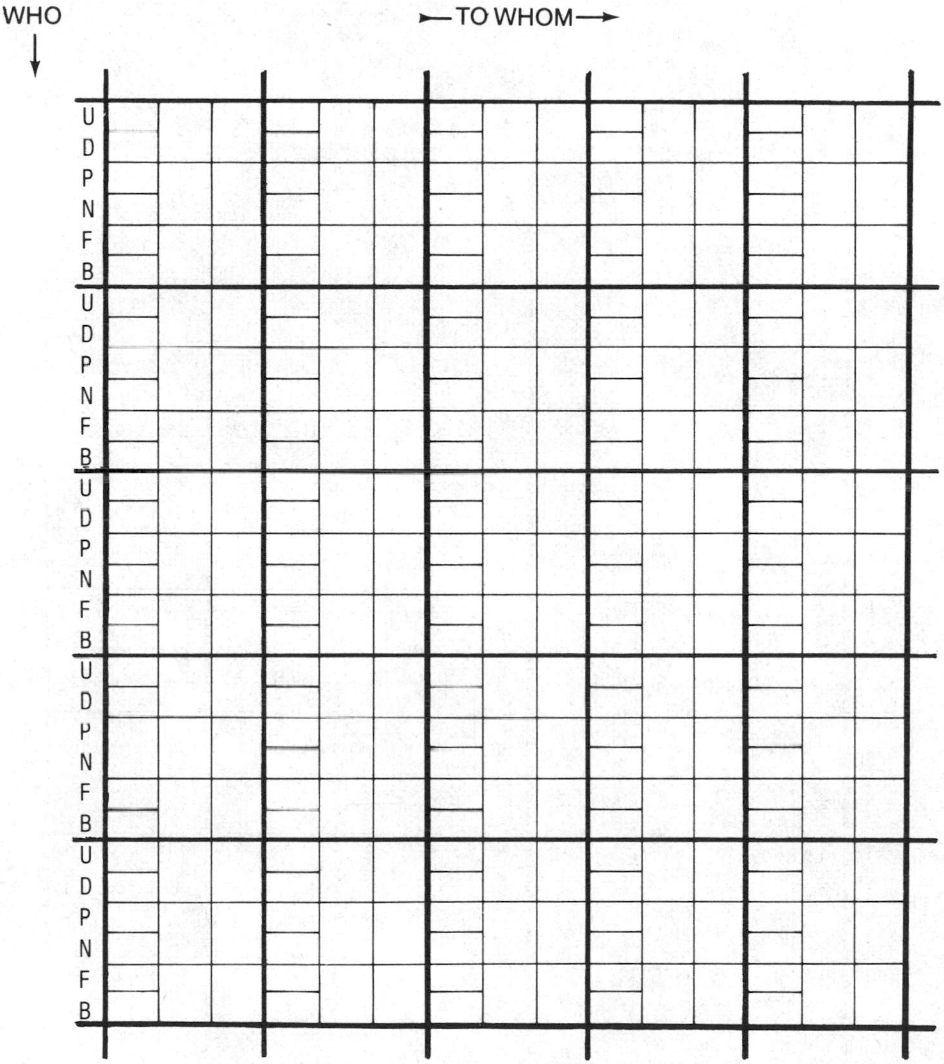

WHO   ►─TO WHOM─►
↓

	U
	D
	P
	N
	F
	B
	U
	D
	P
	N
	F
	B
	U
	D
	P
	N
	F
	B
	U
	D
	P
	N
	F
	B
	U
	D
	P
	N
	F
	B

FIGURE 54 Illustrative Members' Ratings on the Interpersonal Matrix Form

Your Name _____RFB_____

Of what Group: _____PSR 1330 R_____ Present Date_____

Of what date: _____2ND RATING_____ to what date: _____ Page _1_ of _16_

Content of the Matrix: (Describe in detail) _MEMBERS' SECOND RATINGS_

OF EACH OTHER ON ACT LEVEL DESCRIPTIONS, 0, 1, 2.

WHO ↓   ► TO WHOM →

WHO		CARL		BILL		SARA		SUE		LAIN	
CARL	U	8 / 3	5U U	9 / 1	8U U	5 / 6	1D D	8 / 7	1U	10 / 5	5U U
	D										
	P	7 / 10	3N N	8 / 4	4P	5 / 6	1N N	9 / 6	3P	8 / 9	1N N
	N										
	F	3 / 12	9B B	9 / 4	5F F	5 / 8	3B B	8 / 6	2F	13 / 4	9F F
	B										
BILL	U	8 / 10	2D D	12 / 7	5U U	13 / 10	3U	11 / 7	4U	12 / 9	3U
	D										
	P	4 / 16	12N N	14 / 5	9P P	12 / 10	2P	12 / 8	4P	14 / 8	6P P
	N										
	F	4 / 15	9B B	11 / 6	5F F	9 / 13	4B B	15 / 6	9F F	12 / 7	5F F
	B										
SARA	U	5 / 6	1D D	8 / 4	4U	8 / 3	5U U	3 / 6	3D D	9 / 4	5U U
	D										
	P	7 / 8	1N N	13 / 1	12P P	10 / 4	6P P	4 / 5	1N N	12 / 1	11P P
	N										
	F	2 / 11	9B B	8 / 3	5F F	4 / 6	2B B	5 / 4	1F	6 / 4	2F
	B										
SUE	U	6 / 1	5U U	8 / 2	6U U	7 / 5	2U	5 / 2	3U	7 / 1	6U U
	D										
	P	0 / 10	10N N	12 / 0	12P P	1 / 11	10N N	8 / 2	6P P	9 / 0	9P P
	N										
	F	3 / 6	3B B	9 / 2	7F F	2 / 10	8B B	6 / 2	4F	7 / 2	5F F
	B										
LAIN	U	10 / 4	6U U	9 / 2	7U U	9 / 2	7U U	5 / 7	2D D	5 / 3	2U
	D										
	P	4 / 11	7N N	12 / 0	12P P	11 / 3	8P P	12 / 0	12P P	10 / 0	10P P
	N										
	F	3 / 9	6B B	13 / 2	11F F	7 / 9	2B B	6 / 5	1F	8 / 2	2F
	B										

up, and average the ratings of a single rater. Each rater rates each member, including the self as EXPECTED, and also makes a WISHED-FOR rating. In addition, a block is needed to record the Total Given Out, and another to record the Average Given Out. For our illustrative group of fifteen persons this is, then, $15 + 1 + 1 + 1 = 18$. Eighteen horizontal blocks are needed for the single rater. Each page of the Interpersonal Matrix Form will display five horizontal blocks. Three pages, then, will display fifteen blocks; however, in this case eighteen are needed. Hence, one will require four horizontal pages, since a complete final page will be needed, even though it will not be full. Since the matrix is square, the same number of pages will be needed to hold the vertical blocks. The number of pages is thus $4 \times 4 = 16$.

For a five-person group the number of horizontal blocks needed would be $5 + 1 + 1 + 1 = 8$, which is three more than the five blocks given on a single page; hence, two horizontal pages will be required. The square matrix will thus require $2 \times 2 = 4$ pages. The number of pages required goes up rapidly with the number of persons in the group. The pages are orindarily arranged consecutively so that they display one complete horizontal row of pages, then another horizontal row, and so on.

The square Interpersonal Matrix puts the information originally separated on the Directional Profiles of ratings *made* by each member, into one place where the totals *received* by a given member from all the others may be obtained by adding together the numbers in a column. The original numbers for each direction (U, D, P, N, F, B) may be entered, and the form then provides a place to record the result of the U minus D, P minus N, and F minus B subtractions, which result in the summary location. If the summary locations have already been recorded in the Directional Profile Form, of course, they may be entered directly, without repeating the detailed numbers for U, D, P, N, F, and B. The form also provides three additional spaces in each person-to-person cell, which may be used if one wishes to reduce the numerical locations to still simpler letter types by the use of cutting points that allow one to drop small numbers and retain only the letter designation of the larger ones. The use of this procedure to obtain a more compact summary matrix is discussed below.

The square Interpersonal Matrix allows one to obtain totals of rows and columns easily and also to compare the two cells concerned with the same relationship, e.g., to compare how CARL rates BILL with the way BILL rates CARL. The Matrix may thus be a more convenient arrangement of data than the Field Diagrams when one is concerned with the two-way nature of the relationship. The Individual Field Diagram keeps the emphasis on the perceptions of a single individual rater of all the other members of the group.

The Individual Field Diagram displays the data of a single horizontal row of the Matrix. The Group Average Field Diagram displays the totals *received* by each individual from all others and is obtained by the addition of each column of the Matrix. The square matrix is completed by places to record the totals given out and received, as well as the averages computed at the end by dividing the total by the number of members in the group. When these computations are completed, the data are ready for the additional steps needed to put the locations into the proper scale for plotting on the Field Diagrams (see Appendix J).

The Matrix permits many statistical and mathematical operations that are not detailed here. One useful operation is to sum the cells in a horizontal row in order to obtain measures of the individual's rating tendencies. For example, one can find if an individual is high or low in the tendency to rate others positively. The approach of making a Field Diagram for each individual is a more detailed approach, however, since with the Field Diagram one can also detect polarization and unification, and many other relationships which a single average number conceals.

The same square matrix form may also be used for the collection and display of SYMLOG Interaction Scores, in which case the "WHO-ACTS-TOWARD-WHOM" information in the message may be the basis for the tabulation of the given message in a given cell of the matrix. A matrix of this kind, of course, can be made for any level of behavior or content.

The matrix should also be visualized as potentially containing cells for each Image that one wants to keep track of. Of course, Images do not talk back, so they appear on the matrix only on the horizontal headings. Also, in place of the six directions recorded for acts toward other interacting persons, in the case of Images, only two directions, PRO and CON, are recorded for attitudes expressed toward the Image. One may want to collect all individual Images referred to according to the PRO or CON attitude and the Direction, so there would be twenty-six types of PRO images and twenty-six types of CON images. Thus, if one wanted to make a *complete* tabulation one would place not only the names of each member of the group and the WISH rating along the top row of the Matrix, but also the twenty-six directions of PRO images and the twenty-six directions of CON images. This would be a most unwieldly matrix, of course, and in practice one takes a more piecemeal approach.

However, in understanding the detailed dynamics of a group in real time, one is very much concerned with the appearance of salient images in the group (images other than the images of the group members, as well as of the group members), and it is important to recognize that such images are, for many practical purposes, very much like an additional "actor" in the dynamic scene; they affect the pattern of polarization and unification. Reactions to images are parallel to those toward human actors in some important respects. This is recognized by giving types of PRO and CON images a potential place in the matrix of relationships.

Figure 55 shows a reduced form of the matrix that is worth the special attention of the lone investigator working without member ratings. It provides a model for a simpler approach, if one wishes to try to take the role of each individual in turn and to consider how that individual is likely to rate each other individual.

To fill out the complete Adjective Rating Form as each individual might hypothetically rate each other for a group as large as fifteen is probably more of a job than even the most enthusiastic and tireless investigator is likely to undertake. It is practical, however, even for a group as large as fifteen to make a square matrix for the individuals in the group, as shown in Figure 55, and then consider the final letter type (e.g., U, UPF, P, N, etc.) that best describes how one predicts each individual is likely to view every other. The numbers for the estimated Group Average Field Diagram can be obtained from such an estimating

FIGURE 55 An Interpersonal Matrix of Ratings Reduced to Summary Letter Types

FROM   TO →

	CARL	BILL	SARA	SUE	LAIN	HIP	HUGH	PAL	ANN	TINA	TED	TOM	MOOS	ACE	RFB	WISH
CARL	UNB	UPF	DNB	F	UNF	UNB	UP	N	U	DF	UNF	NF	UNB	UNB	UPF	UPB
BILL	DNB	UPF	PB	PF	PF	UNB	PB	DB	PF	DPF	UPF	DNB	NF	UNB	UPF	UPF
SARA	DNB	PF	UPB	DNF	UPF	UNB	PF	DP	DPB	DPB	PF	DP	B	UB	F	UPB
SUE	UNB	UPF	NB	PF	UPF	UB	UPF	DPB	DP	DPF	N	AVE	UPB	UNB	UPF	UPF
LAIN	UNB	UPF	UPB	DP	PF	UNB	UPB	PB	P	DP	UNF	D	UP	UNB	UNF	UP
HIP	NB	F	DPB	DP	DF	NB	DNB	DPB	DPF	DB	NF	DNB	DN	DNB	UPF	UPF
HUGH	NB	PF	DB	D	DF	NF	PB	DPB	DPB	DPB	NF	AVE	UN	B	DPF	PB
PAL	NB	UPF	PB	PF	UPF	UB	P	PB	P	DPF	UPF	PB	UF	UB	PF	PB
ANN	UNB	UPF	UPB	F	UF	UB	UPF	DNB	PB	PB	U	PB	UNF	UN	UNF	UPB
TINA	NB	UPF	PB	PF	UPF	UN	UPF	DPB	UP	PF	UNF	DNF	UN	UNB	UPF	PF
TED	NB	UPF	DNB	UPF	UPF	UNF	UPF	P	P	DP	UF	DB	UF	UNB	UF	UF
TOM	NF	UPF	UB	PF	PF	UN	UP	UNB	PB	DPF	·F	DB	UNB	UNB	UF	UPB
MOOS	UNB	PF	UB	P	PF	UNB	UPF	DNB	PB	DPF	UNF	NB	UN	UNB	UPF	UN
ACE	DNB	UNF	UNB	DNB	UNF	UNB	UPB	DNB	PB	DNB	UNF	DB	UNB	UNB	UF	UB
RFB	DNB	PF	B	DPF	DPF	UB	P	DP	DB	DP	UF	DNB	UNF	UNB	UF	
U-D	1D	10U	2U	5D	5U	13U	8U	9D	3D	13D	10U	9D	11U	12U	11U	11U
P-N	15N	12P	3P	8P	8P	11N	13P	4P	13P	11P	5N	3N	8N	12N	6P	10P
F-B	13B	15F	15B	9F	15F	9B	1F	11B	5B	2F	13F	7B	00	14B	15F	2B

NOTE: This matrix was constructed from the expanded field diagrams of each member, using the following cutting points:
5U or more = U   6P or more = P   3F or more = F
1D or more = D   1N or more = N   1B or more = B

approach by simply counting how many times a given letter component (e.g., U) appears and subtracting from it how many times its opposite (e.g., D) appears (see Figure 55). The estimated Group Average Field Diagram can then be compared with the field diagram the investigator has obtained by the regular rating procedure. I have found the results of this procedure to be most enlightening. It appears that using the "role-taking" procedure some individuals in the group come out with more Negative locations than I had assigned them when rating from my own point of view; some come out with more Positive locations, and some more balanced. And so on for the other dimensions. The "role-taking" procedure seems to force one to make discriminations that are suppressed when one takes the rating set of trying to weigh all factors and come out with a rating that represents one's *own* best judgment.

Summary letter types are much easier to grasp and think about intuitively than the numerical locations. Although the simple letter type omits important information, it is often quite satisfactory, and for verbal discussion, unless one is looking at actual diagrams or the numbers in a printed matrix, it is practically impossible to retain the numbers. In self-analytic groups, the use of letter types in discussion is common and effective, since the members are also using SYMLOG Interaction Scoring and recording their original observations in terms of letter types. It is also the case that feedback in terms of simple summary letter types is easier to grasp and use than the full numerical matrix and in some cases may be the preferred form. It may be noted, however, that the cutoff points shown in Figure 55 are quite stringent and may produce a stronger emphasis on the directions D, N, and B than is desirable for feedback. The cutting points shown in Figure 55 are more or less arbitrary and may be changed according to experience and judgment.

The next steps in computation required to prepare the numbers recorded in the Interaction matrix for the construction of Individual and Group Average Field Diagrams are described in Appendix J.

Appendix J

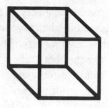

Computations on Raw Ratings or Raw Interaction Scores Required for Making Field Diagrams

The Interpersonal Matrix may contain information of various kinds, depending on the method of rating or observation used. It contains the information required for plotting Individual Field Diagrams and the Group Average Field Diagram. The information must go through some intervening computation, however, in order to put it into the proper scale for the Field Diagram, and the computation required differs according to the method of rating or observation used. The sources of information and the computation steps required for each are detailed below.

1. *Rating, using the (0, 1, 2) scale.* Ratings may be made by reading the Appendix A descriptions of a given level, by reading the adjectives on the simplified Adjective Rating Form, or by circling on the Adjective Rating Form. When the (0, 1, 2) scale has been used, the final numbers representing the way a given individual has rated a given other individual on a given dimension are already scaled so that they must fall within the scale of 18. In this one case, then, the raw dimensional balance numbers may be plotted without further computation, if the researcher so desires. The method of plotting the points is described in Appendix O. However, it is usually desirable to expand the constellation of points before plotting for the optimum application of the Polarization–Unification Overlay. This is done by the method described in Appendix K.

The Group Average Field Diagram is made from the average ratings received by each individual, which are found along the bottom row of the Interpersonal Matrix. Because the cancellation effect tends to make the average points regress toward the zero point of the Field Diagram, it is nearly always desirable to expand the constellation of group average points, according to the method in Appendix K. After the expansion, the points are plotted as described in Appendix I.

2. *Rating, using the (0, 1, 2, 3, 4) scale.* When the five-alternative scale is

used, it is very probable that the scale limit of 18 will be exceeded by some points, whether one is concerned with one individual's ratings or with the group average ratings. The regular procedure, then, in each of these cases is to reduce the numbers taken from the matrix by dividing by 2. After this the expansion is made in the usual manner, as described in Appendix K. In this case, the Expansion Multiplier is determined *after* the division by 2, so that its meaning will be directly comparable to the meaning it has when the (0, 1, 2) scale has been used. Once the Expansion Multiplier has been determined, it is relatively easy to combine the reduction of the number by one-half and the expansion multiplication in the same operation. After the expansion, the points are plotted as described in Appendix O.

3. *SYMLOG Interaction Scores.* The raw numbers in a matrix of SYMLOG Interaction Scores may be of any size, since the observations are made by some number of observers that may vary from meeting to meeting, the meetings may vary in length, and the number of persons present and interacting may vary. In order to put these raw numbers into a standard scaled form for display on a Field Diagram, a more complex computation is required than for ratings. Appropriate formulas for performing this set of operations have been worked out by Dr. Howard Swann, with the help of Richard Polley, and are described in Appendix S. However, the computations may be performed by hand, using a simplified formula.

Figure 56 shows a form that uses the formula for hand computation given by Swann and Polley in Appendix S to accomplish the conversion of raw SYMLOG Interaction Scores to Regular Plotting Scores. The form is labeled for the P-N dimension, but with appropriate substitutions it may be used for the other two dimensions as well. The appropriate substitutions are these:

For the dimension U–D, substitute: u_i for p_i

d_i for n_i

U for P

D for N

For the dimension F–B, substitute: f_i for p_i

b_i for n_i

F for P

B for N

As the form will make clear, the lowercase letters with the subscript "i" stand for the directional scores received by individuals from SYMLOG Interaction Scoring; the capital letters, e.g., P, N, stand for the group totals obtained by adding together the scores of all individuals in the group.

The names of individuals participating in the session observed, for whom scores have been recorded (or could have been recorded even though perhaps none were), are placed in the first column. The total number of these members is recorded in the box at the bottom of the column, designated "m."

A Field Diagram always represents behavior or content at some specified level or set of levels added together, thus it is determined in advance of tabulation from the SYMLOG Interaction Scoring sheets just what levels are to be tabulated. The ACT level alone may be chosen, but it is common to add together the two behavioral levels ACT plus NON. The Image levels PRO and CON may be taken

FIGURE 56 The SYMLOG Computation Form: Raw Interaction Scores to Expanded Plotting Points

Your Name _____ Group _____ Running time_____ Date_____

Observers' Names _____ Level(s)_____

Members' Names	DIMENSION:				QUAL. FACTOR	QUAN. FACTOR		REG. PLOT	EXPAN. PLOT
	Indiv. Raw Scores p_i	Indiv. Raw Scores n_i	Indiv. Dimen. Total $p_i + n_i$	Indiv. Direc. Surplus $p_i - n_i$	$\dfrac{p_i - n_i}{p_i + n_i}$	$\dfrac{p_i - n_i}{(A)}$	Indiv. Total Q QUAL. FAC. + QUAN. FAC.	Indiv. Total Q x 5 (Scale Factor)	REG. PLOT x EXPAN. MULT.:

$$\frac{P+N}{m} = (A)$$

m   P   N   P+N

in whatever combination is of interest. Once the level or combination of levels has been chosen, Directional Profile Forms are prepared with the names of members, as described in Appendix B. It is convenient for one person to read from the Scoring Sheets and another to make tally marks on the Directional Profile Form. When this is completed, the raw scores for each member are totaled and entered in the cells marked U, D, P, N, F, and B at the bottom of the Directional Profile Form.

The Computation Form, Figure 56, takes only one dimension at a time. Hence, three such sheets will be required, each properly identified, one for the U–D dimension, one for the P–N dimension, and one for the F–B dimension. For convenience, let us illustrate the computation in terms of the P–N dimension, since the labeling on the form is for that dimension.

The raw scores for each individual, p_i and n_i, are transferred from the Directional Profile Form to the Computation Form. The totals, P and N on the Computation Form, are obtained by addition of the columns and recorded at the bottom of the Computation Form. Let us suppose, for an illustration we shall call BILL's group, that there have been sixty P scores and eleven N scores in the session. These scores are entered in the boxes marked P and N. These two totals, P and N, are added together and the sum is placed in the box marked "P + N" at the bottom of the sheet. For BILL's group $P + N = 60 + 11 = 71$. This number may be called the Group Dimensional Total.

The next operation is to divide the Group Dimensional Total $(P + N)$ by the number of members, recorded in the box labeled "m," to find the Average Individual Dimensional Total. In BILL's group, with seven members, P + N divided by m = $71/7 = 10.14$. This number is best kept to at least two decimal places and is entered in the box marked (A) at the bottom of the form.

We are now ready to perform the computations to find the Regular Plotting Point for each individual. The rationale of the computation is best seen when one takes a single individual at a time and follows the instructions at the top of each column, using the information generated in the preceding columns. For this purpose a pocket calculator is a great convenience, if not a necessity.

Let us run through one line of computation as an illustration. Let us suppose that BILL is the first member listed for his group of seven members and that the number of P scores the observers have given him, designated P_i, is eight. His corresponding number of N scores, designated n_i, let us say, is two. The total number of scores he received in the P–N dimension is thus the sum of the two, $p_i + n_i$, that is, $8 + 2 = 10$. The number 10 is entered in the column labeled "Individual Dimensional Total."

The next column is called the "Individual Directional Surplus," and the number required is simply the p_i scores minus the n_i scores, which for BILL is $8 - 2 = 6$. (The Individual Directional Surplus may come out either on the P side or the N side. If it is on the N side, the operation $p_i - n_i$ will produce a negative number, and in this case, a minus sign is placed in front of the number entered in the column.)

The next operation produces what is called the "Individual Qualitative Factor," and it is obtained by dividing the Individual Directional Surplus number by the Individual Dimensional Total number; in BILL's case, $6 \div 10 = .60$. The number .60 is entered in the column headed "QUAL. FACTOR."

The next step is concerned with arriving at what is called the "Individual Quantitative Factor." This is a measure of the size of the Individual Directional Total as compared to the Average Individual Dimensional Total. The latter number has been obtained previously and is found in the box marked (A) at the bottom of the column. In our example it is 10.14. The Individual Directional Surplus $(p_i - n_i)$ is divided by (A), and this gives the number called the

"Individual Quantitative Factor." In BILL's case, the number is 6 divided by $10.14 = .59$. This number is recorded in the column marked "QUAN. FACTOR."

We want our final index on the P–N dimension to represent both the Individual Qualitative Factor, that is, the ratio of positive to negative behavior on the individual's own base total, and the Individual Quantitative Factor, that is, the relative prominence of the individual's contribution toward the total behavior in the group on the P–N dimension. Hence, our formula calls for adding these two factors together. The number under QUAN. FACTOR, in our example .59, is added to the number under QUAL. FACTOR, in our example .60, to obtain the number for the column labeled Individual Total Q: $.59 + .60 = 1.19$.

One more step is necessary to obtain what is called the Regular Plotting Point for the individual, to be put in our column labeled REG. PLOT. It is obtained by multiplying the Individual Total Q Score, in our case 1.19, by a scaling factor contained in the formula derived in Appendix S. It happens to be the number 5; hence, $1.19 \times 5 = 5.95$. The REG. PLOT score is thus 5.95.

The Regular Plotting Score will fall within our desired limit of 18 for the Field Diagram in many cases but unfortunately not in all, because of differences in the size of groups and the fact that in some groups the participation is very unequal. Hence, one more scaling operation is regularly performed for purposes of plotting the constellation of points on the Field Diagram. This step is the "expansion" of the regular plotting scores by the method described in Appendix K. What is conventionally called the "Expansion Multiplier" is actually a factor that will *expand* the constellation of points when they are too closely clustered to fill the Field Diagram, but will *contract* the constellation of points when any of them exceeds the scale limit of 18. In addition, it takes into account the size of the circles one will use in plotting the U–D position. For this reason, the Expansion Multiplier cannot be found until all three dimensions have been computed for all individuals.

One must stop short of the final column, then, until BILL's locations in all three dimensions, U–D, P–N, and F–B, and those of all the other individuals in the group have been determined in terms of Regular Plotting Points. When these points have been determined, one turns to Appendix K and follows the directions there to find the proper Expansion Multiplier. When it is found and checked to make sure it is right, it is entered in the box at the head of our final column, titled EXPAN. PLOT. The Expansion Multiplier will be larger than 1.00 if the constellation of points in fact needs to be expanded. If it needs to be contracted, the Expansion Multiplier will be smaller than 1.00. The sign of the Expansion Multiplier, however, is *always plus* (see Appendix K). Hence, when it is applied to a Regular Plotting Point that has a minus sign, the result will still carry the minus sign, which indicates that it should be plotted in the N direction from the zero point of the P–N dimension on the Field Diagram.

To finish our example, let us suppose that the Expansion Multiplier for BILL's group turns out to be 1.09. BILL's Regular Plotting point is 5.95, hence BILL's EXPANDED PLOTTING POINT, finally needed for the optimum Field Diagram, is $5.95 \times 1.09 = 6.49$

The Field Diagram we obtain from the SYMLOG Interaction Scores using this method should be optimum for comparison with the expanded Field Diagram we might obtain from an interpersonal rating of the members of each other, completed just after the meeting, giving their own description of their behavior during the meeting. A short-short form, which may be practical for this sort of test, is described in Appendix S.

Appendix K

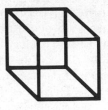

How to Expand a Constellation of Image Points for a Field Diagram

The Ratings of an individual rater or a SYMLOG scorer are affected not only by his or her perceptions and evaluations of the persons rated but also by tendencies to be expansive or cautious in the use of the rating scale, by general attentiveness, and so on. It is useful to know these tendencies, and for certain purposes, such as observer training, one wishes to put the spotlight on them, but for other purposes, those of trying to understand the particular way the individual polarizes or unifies the field and how particular images relate to that pattern, one wishes to expand very constricted patterns so that they can be more carefully analyzed by the use of the Polarization–Unification Overlay.

When one makes a Group Average Field Diagram, many differences in the way particular observers see the field cancel each other, and the average location of the image points tends to regress toward the zero point of the Diagram. Group Average Field Diagrams, in particular, need to be expanded before they can be compared optimally to Individual Field Diagrams. For careful analysis, then, one usually expands both the group average constellation of image points, and the constellation of image points as seen by each rater or observer.

The Interpersonal Matrix contains the raw numbers representing how each individual sees each other along the horizontal row for each individual rater. The numbers down the vertical column from each individual's name as a receiver of ratings are added (algebraically, e.g., 1D cancels 1U) to obtain the raw total received. The raw total is divided by the number of raters to obtain the average rating received. The adding and averaging operations are performed and kept to two decimal places prior to the computation for the expansion of the constellation.

The procedure for expansion may be explained most easily in terms of an example. Let us take as our problem the expansion of the Group Average Diagram shown as Figure 4 (p. 26). What we want to do is to expand the constellation of images by just the amount necessary to bring the most "far out" image to the edge of the diagram. This is done by multiplying each of the numbers indicating the location of the image point by a number somewhat greater than 1. But how do we find the multiplier? And particularly, how do we take into account that the outer edge of the U–D circle of the image will extend past the actual location of the point and that these circles are of various sizes?

We can see by inspection of Figure 4 that the image for ANN, *including the outer edge of the U–D circle,* is farther removed from the zero point of the diagram, the intersection of the two dimensions, than any other image. If the multiplier is chosen to bring the edge of this image just to the edge of the diagram, we know that all the others will then fit in, since they are all less far out. We can see by inspection that the center point of the image for ANN is at 9 P, and if we take into account the outer circle of the image, the image extends to something past 10 P. How far past? We know that by definition the outer edge will be found by adding the radius of the U–D circle to the location of the center point of the image on the dimension on which the point is most far out—in this case the P dimension. We need a table showing the size of the radius of each size of U–D circle in field diagram units. This information is given in Table 29.

Our diagram, Figure 4, shows that the U–D location of ANN's image is 1 U. Referring to Table 29, we find that the radius of the circle standing for 1 U is 1.41 of our field diagram units.

Now, remembering that the purpose of all this is to expand the constellation of images on the diagram so that the outer edge of the most far out image extends just to the edge of the diagram, we take the next step. The diagram extends 18 units in each direction. But since we want to add the radius of the circle after we have plotted the center point, we need to first subtract the radius of the circle from the maximum extent of the scale. Following our example, we subtract the radius, 1.41, from the maximum extent of the scale, 18. This leaves 16.59. We want to find out what multiplier will be required to expand our 9 units (the center point of the image) to 16.59, so we divide 16.59 by 9. This gives 1.84. This is the multiplier required for all the points on the diagram. Now we check back; the image center point for ANN is at 9 P. We multiply 9 P by 1.843, which gives 16.59. We plot the image center point for ANN at 16.59. Then when we inscribe the 1 U circle around it, with a radius of 1.41, it comes just to the end of the scale, 18. The formula, then, for finding the multiplier is

$$\frac{18 - \text{U–D Circle Radius}}{\text{Original Center Point Location}} = \text{Expansion Multiplier}$$

(change any − sign to +)   (sign is always +)

Once the proper Expansion Multiplier is found, it is applied to the location of all points in both the P–N and F–B dimensions. If we have made sure that we began in the first place with the image that is most far out in any direction (including the radius of its U–D Circle) it is guaranteed that all other points and their circles will fall within the diagram. Figure 5 (p. 27) shows the Group Average Diagram of Figure 4, now expanded by the multiplier of 1.843.

In working from the numbers along the row of an Interpersonal Matrix, it is a

TABLE 29   Size of the Radius of Each Size of U–D Circle in Field Diagram Units

18U = 4.50	9U = 2.16	1D = 1.22	10D = 0.70
17U = 4.13	8U = 2.06	2D = 1.13	11D = 0.66
16U = 3.75	7U = 1.97	3D = 1.03	12D = 0.61
15U = 3.38	6U = 1.88	4D = 0.98	13D = 0.56
14U = 3.00	5U = 1.78	5D = 0.94	14D = 0.52
13U = 2.81	4U = 1.69	6D = 0.89	15D = 0.47
12U = 2.63	3U = 1.59	7D = 0.84	16D = 0.42
11U = 2.44	2U = 1.50	8D = 0.80	17D = 0.38
10U = 2.25	1U = 1.41	9D = 0.75	18D = 0.33
	00 = 1.31		

little more trouble than working from an already plotted Diagram, as in our example, since it is a little harder to locate the most far out image *edge*. It is done by finding the largest number designating a location in either the P–N or the F–B dimension, then adding to it the radius of the U–D circle of the image, obtained from Table 29. Other images that might give a higher total because of a larger U–D circle are then checked, until one is sure he has the one with the highest total. Having found the proper image, one applies the formula to find the Expansion Multiplier and then applies the Multiplier to all point locations on the P–N and F–B dimensions.

In making an expansion, the multiplier is not applied to the U–D scale but only to the P–N, F–B scales. Using the multiplier with the U–D scale would result in circles of too large a size, and it serves no useful purpose. The expanded Diagram thus carries the same size circles and the same numbers designating the U–D location of the image as the unexpanded Diagram would carry.

When an expansion is made, the Multiplier is rounded to three decimal points and is recorded on the Diagram, so that the original size can be estimated.

In plotting the center points of the expanded locations, the scale location numbers are rounded to the nearest whole step on the scale, unless this would put the extreme edge of the image over the edge of the Diagram. Whole scale step locations are preferred for the final plotting, since they can be read more easily.

We may finally note, after having gone through all this, that after some experience one may be able to work sufficiently accurately with diagrams without expansion of the constellation of the images. The regular Overlay may be used for this, and it is certainly more simple just to plot the raw scores.

Appendix L

Instruments Required to Make the Field Diagram

It is a great convenience and advantage to be able to make the Field Diagrams for your group, and for each individual in it, so that they are directly and visually comparable to the ones in this book. In order to make the standard diagrams the following instruments are necessary.

1. An automatic pencil that will hold *thin* leads is necessary in order to get a thin, trim line of uniform character.

2. A package of *thin* leads, Black-2B (very soft), will produce a sufficiently dark line without too much pressure and thickness.

3. A package of extra erasers may be needed.

4. A drafting ruler with a scale of 60 divisions to the inch is necessary if the base lines of the diagram are to be constructed in the proper length with the proper number of divisions on the scales.

5. A plastic template with a long series of circles of graduated size is needed. The template recommended is made by Pickett and designated Circle Master, No. 1204 (See Appendix M for illustration.) The circle template permits the user to make the circles with sufficient ease and uniformity, and in the proper size. A compass is not a satisfactory substitute.

6. The plain white bond paper used should be sufficiently heavy to withstand erasures and have three-punch edges for easy attachment in a notebook.

7. A transparent plastic protractor is needed.

8. See Appendix P for additional materials and instruments necessary to make the Polarization–Unification Overlay.

Appendix M

Illustration of the U–D Scale of Circles

It is necessary, for the construction of the Field Diagram and for the construction of the Polarization-Unification Overlay, to have a circle template with a graduated series of circles. Figure 57 is an illustration drawn from a commercially available circle template that is exactly what is needed.

Given the module of the Field Diagram, a template with a three-inch circle is necessary. The exact scale of the U–D circle is not so critical, and if the proper template is not available, some approximation may be acceptable. It is required that the scale extend from a zero size down for 18 steps and up for 18 steps. Table 30 shows the diameters of the circles shown in Figure 57.

Technical Appendixes

TABLE 30   Diameters of Circles on the Circle Template, in Inches

Reference circle for the Overlay = 3		∞ Zero size circle = $^7/_{16}$	
$18U = 1\,^1/_2$	$9U = {}^{23}/_{32}$	$1D = {}^{13}/_{32}$	$10D = {}^{15}/_{64}$
$17U = 1\,^3/_8$	$8U = {}^{11}/_{16}$	$2D = {}^3/_8$	$11D = {}^7/_{32}$
$16U = 1\,^1/_4$	$7U = {}^{21}/_{32}$	$3D = {}^{11}/_{32}$	$12D = {}^{13}/_{64}$
$15U = 1\,^1/_8$	$6U = {}^5/_8$	$4D = {}^{21}/_{64}$	$13D = {}^3/_{16}$
$14U = 1$	$5U = {}^{19}/_{32}$	$5D = {}^5/_{16}$	$14D = {}^{11}/_{64}$
$13U\ {}^{15}/_{16}$	$4U = {}^9/_{16}$	$6D = {}^{19}/_{64}$	$15D = {}^5/_{32}$
$12U - {}^7/_8$	$3U = {}^{17}/_{32}$	$7D = {}^9/_{32}$	$16D = {}^9/_{64}$
$11U = {}^{13}/_{16}$	$2U = {}^1/_2$	$8D = {}^{17}/_{64}$	$17D = {}^1/_8$
$10U = {}^3/_4$	$1U = {}^{15}/_{32}$	$9D = {}^1/_4$	$18D = {}^7/_{64}$
Size of core circle $= {}^1/_8$[a]			

[a]The irregularity of the fact that the core circle falls at 17D instead of at 18D is accepted because the $^1/_8$ inch circle is visually more satisfactory.

FIGURE 57 Illustration of the U-D Scale of Circles

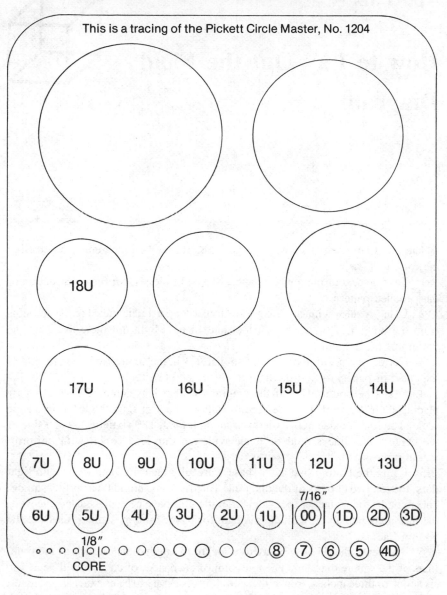

Appendix N

How to Lay Out the Field Diagram

The Field Diagram is shown as Figure 58. It may be prepared by hand using the following steps:

1. Take a sheet of plain white paper, 8½ × 11 inches, for the construction of the penciled pattern.

2. Using a ruler with a scale of 60 divisions per inch, measure 70 sixtieths from the bottom of the sheet of paper and place a light dot there to locate the bottom of the diagram.

3. Correct the position of this dot so that it is in the center from side to side of the sheet of paper, to find the bottom center point of the diagram.

4. Draw the bottom line of the diagram so that it is centered on the dot by placing the ruler so that the center dot falls at the 180 sixtieths location on the scale. The line is made 360 sixtieths of an inch long, 180 sixtieths to each side of the center. The line should be made with the thin-lead pencil with uniform, medium pressure.

5. Using the bottom line as the base, carefully measure, and mark with light dots, the top two corners of the diagram. The diagram should be a perfect square, 360 sixtieths, or six inches, per side. After the dots have been placed and checked, the lines may be laid in, with the same uniform, medium pressure as used for the bottom line.

6. The scale should now be used to locate the midpoints of each of the outer lines of the square diagram. The midpoint of each side, of course, will be at 180 sixtieths, or three inches, from either end. It is necessary to be as exact as you can.

7. After locating and checking the midpoints, they should be connected with the lines representing the two orthogonal dimensions, (P–N and F–B). These lines may be made with pressure a little lighter, or made a little thinner, than the outside lines of the diagram.

8. Now place the ruler on the P–N horizontal dimension, with the zero point of the 60 divisions per inch scale exactly at the line of intersection of the two dimensions. Lightly mark off the points of the scale, to the right, toward P; the first at 10 sixtieths, the second at 20, and so on out to 50 sixtieths. At that point make the line a little longer to make the 5-unit division easier to find (see the

FIGURE 58   The SYMLOG Field Diagram Form

Your Name_____

Diagram of what Group: _____ Present Date_____

Group met from what date _____ to what date _____ Page_____ of _____

Diagram based on whose perceptions _____ Playing whose role _____

Rating or Scoring _____ If Rating, scale (0,1,2) or (0,1,2,3,4 /2) _____

Expansion Multiplier_____ Comment_____

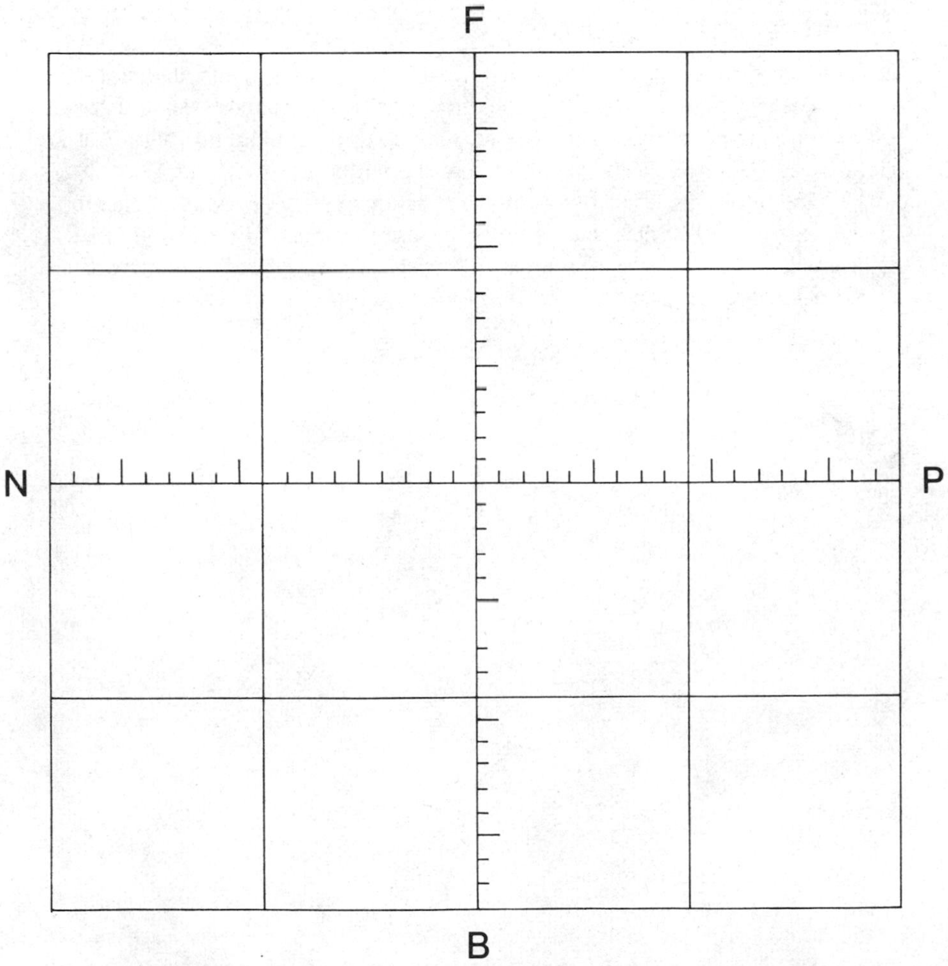

Diagram). Continue with single units in short lines, until you hit 10 (100 six-tieths). Make the 10-unit line a little longer, and more evident, as you did the 5. Continue to 15 in the same way, and at 18 you will hit the side of the diagram.

9. The diagram should show the scale marks out to 18 in exactly the same way for each of the directions. Proceed with the N direction, then turn the page so that F is at the left and mark off the divisions for B, then for F. The scale reads to 18 in each direction because 18 is the maximum number that an individual could receive from a single rater, using the scale: (0, 1, 2). The maximum of 18 would be received only if every directional combination in a given direction (there are nine of these in each direction) were marked 2. The diagram is thus constructed in such a way as to receive directly the raw scores that are obtained from the rating procedure using the answer form (0, 1, 2).

10. Marker lines halfway out in each direction should now be indicated with a line of light pressure, passing through the 9 point on each scale (note, 9 rather than 10, since the scale reads to 18). The halfway marker lines should be made exactly parallel to the outer lines of the diagram. The halfway marker lines complete the subdivision of the square diagram into sixteen subquadrants.

11. The designations of each of the directions, P, N, F, and B, should now be placed in their proper locations around the edge of the diagram, with P at the right, N at the left, F at the top, and B at the bottom.

12. The information heading for the diagram may now be added at the top, as shown in Figure 58. Since the diagrams are used for many different purposes, it is desirable to be very specific in describing the content of each diagram. Blank space is left for the specific description after the title "comment."

Appendix O

How to Plot a Set of Images on the Field Diagram

1. In plotting images a standard procedure is desirable, since one does not know in advance just where the points will be, how close they will be to each other, and whether there will be room to make the necessary notations. One starts with a set of numerical locations of images representing the behavior of individuals as determined by one of the observation or rating procedures.

2. In the ordinary case, the balances of Upward with Downward, Positive with Negative, and Forward with Backward will have been obtained, so that the position of the image of the individual in the field is represented by three numbers, one in each of three directions, e.g., 2U, 5P, 3B. (Note that a zero balance between two opposing directions is also regarded as a number and is designated by the symbol 00.)

3. The first step is to locate the position of each of the individuals in the group by a light dot in the proper location in the two dimensions of the Field Diagram, P–N and F–B. The scale marks on the Diagram may be adequate for measurement, but a better job will be done if a ruler with a scale of 60 divisions per inch is used in conjunction with the lines. The first time around, only the dots are placed in the proper locations, in order to see what adjustments one will have to make in the placement of the labeling in order to have room.

4. The second step is to go over the list of individual locations again, this time adding inscriptions and notations. For each point, a small circle, ⅛ inch in diameter as read from the circle template, is inscribed around the center dot, using the template and the thin-lead pencil with moderate pressure. Before the small circle is inscribed, the location of the point should be rechecked to make sure that it has not been misplotted, and to make sure that one has the right dot for the name one is about to put down. This small circle is called the "core circle." (See Appendix M, Illustration of the U–D Scale of Circles.)

5. After the ⅛-inch core circle has been inscribed around a given point, one checks the location of points nearby to see where there will be adequate room, and then choosing the spot of least interference with other notations to come, prints the abbreviation of the group member's name, e.g., BILL, JANE. Then, again checking for adequate room, the number and letter standing for the location

443

Upward or Downward, e.g., 11U, 12D, is placed below the name if possible. If there is no crowding, the name ordinarily will be placed to the immediate right of the small circle, slightly below it, and the U–D notation will be placed immediately below that.

6. After all points have been checked as to proper plotting and have been inscribed with the ⅛-inch core circle and identified as to name and location in the U–D dimension, one is ready to proceed with the inscription of the larger circles, which designate the location Upward or Downward. This is done with the aid of the circle template. The 7/16-inch circle is taken as the equivalent of the zero point on the scale. It is convenient to mark this circle as the zero point by putting a line between it and the 1U circle, and another between it and the 1D circle. It is now easy to start with zero and, by counting either upward or downward in the graded series, to locate the proper circle to represent the location of the individual Upward or Downward in the space. These inscriptions are now added one by one, locating the proper circle to correspond with the notation under the name, carefully centering it upon the core circle, using the sighting guide marks at the periphery of the circle, and making the inscription with the thin-lead pencil, evenly and moderately applied.

7. In drawing the U–D circle, the rule is followed that it is not allowed to pass through the *core* circle locating another member or through any inscription of name or location. It is interrupted at these points. On the other hand, it *is* continued through the outer circle inscriptions of any members it may intersect. The visual effect is thus one of the superimposition of transparent disks, each of which shows as much of its circumference as possible. It is desirable that the name label should be placed so as to interrupt the outer circle of its proper image, since that helps to tie the name to the proper core image.

8. In plotting a group member's ratings of other group members, the rating that the rater expects to receive from others (the EXPECTED location of the self image) is plotted in exactly the same way as the other points. One recognizes the special nature of that point by noticing whose ratings are being used as the basis of the field diagram. The point with the same name on the diagram as that of the rater will then, of course, be that person's EXPECTED rating.

9. Group members' ratings will also ordinarily include a WISHED-FOR location. The location of this rating is added last. The dot indicating the exact location is placed as usual, and the core circle is added. Instead of the usual circle inscription indicating the location Upward or Downward, however, a lightly dashed circle inscription is used, with the U–D numerical location inserted at some convenient point in the peripheral dashed line. The rule of not allowing the inscribed dashed circle to intersect any *core* circle or notation is followed, as in the case of the regular outer circle inscriptions. The member's name is omitted, since it is clear that the dashed circle always represents the WISHED-FOR location of the member who made the ratings.

10. In preparing the numerical description of the locations, including the U–D locations, the general practice is to round the numerical location to the nearest whole interval on the scale, so that the plotted point can be read unambiguously. Exceptions are sometimes made when a point is the most extreme point on the diagram and one wishes to keep its outer circle within the diagram.

Appendix P

How to Construct the Polarization–Unification Overlay

In order to provide a convenient way to analyze and describe the pattern of images represented in a field, a transparent overlay with a set of guidelines for measurement is used.

Sheets of clear plastic, 8½ × 11 inches, of the kind ordinarily used to prepare transparent diagrams for use with an overhead projector, can be obtained from a stationery or drafting supply store for about twenty cents each. In addition to a clear plastic sheet, you will need a pen with ink that will stick to the plastic surface. A special pen, called Vis-a-Vis, is made for use with acetate transparencies.

It may seem excessively mechanical to go to so much trouble in order to have a transparent overlay to use with the Field Diagram, when one can make the appropriate inscriptions directly on the Field Diagram with a pencil. This can be done, of course, but it assumes that you have already found the best location, and finding the best location is the purpose of the adjustable overlay. The adjustable overlay in combination with the Field Diagram is in fact a kind of computer, and it substitutes for a considerable amount of computation one would otherwise have to do with numbers. The present method has not yet been detailed in mathematical terms, but it appears amenable to exact treatment when the time comes. At present it is neither completely exact nor completely settled, but it seems good enough for developmental purposes.

The geometric configuration to be placed on the plastic sheet is shown in the accompanying Figure 59. It is constructed as follows:

1. It is easier to make a full-size pattern in pencil on a sheet of 8½ × 11 white paper, and then later to clip the plastic sheet over it and repeat the design in ink against the penciled guide.

2. It is easier to make the measurements using a ruler with a scale of sixtieths of an inch, as this is the module used for the Field Diagram. Measurements below will be stated in terms of this scale.

3. Locate the center of the sheet of white paper and put down a dot to serve as a marker.

FIGURE 59 The Inscription to be Made on the Polarization–Unification Overlay

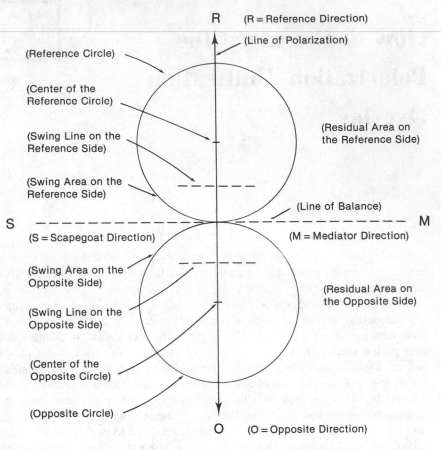

4. Lay down a vertical line 420 sixtieths of an inch long, centered at 210 sixtieths on the marker dot. This is the representation of the Line of Polarization, as labeled on Figure 59. Put an arrow sign at either end, as shown, to help symbolize the concept of forces pulling against each other in opposite directions. Inscribe the letter R at the top end of the line, as shown, and the letter O at the lower end, to represent the Reference Direction and the Opposite Direction.

5. Lay down a dashed horizontal line 420 sixtieths of an inch long, centered at 210 sixtieths on the marker dot, exactly at right angles to the Line of Polarization. The dashed horizontal line represents the line of Balance. Put the letter M at the right end of the line to represent the Mediator Direction, and the letter S at the left end to represent the Scapegoat Direction.

6. The circle template described in Appendix M has a three-inch-diameter circle, which is used for the next step. It will be noted that this circle, 180

sixtieths of an inch in diameter, fits exactly within one quadrant of the Field Diagram. Using the template, inscribe a circle on each side of the Line of Balance, as shown, each centered at 90 sixtieths of an inch from the center of the Line of Polarization. The top circle, in the Reference Direction, is called the Reference Circle. The bottom circle in the Opposite direction is called the Opposite Circle. Mark the center of each circle by a short dash on the Line of Polarization.

7. Next, locate each Swing Line, the short dashed line within each circle, 45 sixtieths of an inch out from the Line of Balance, toward the center of the circle—that is, just half the radius of the circle. Each Swing Line is 90 sixtieths of an inch long, centered at 45 sixtieths of its length on the Line of Polarization. Three short dashes are put on each side of its length. A Swing Line is inscribed on both the Reference Side and the Opposite Side.

8. The design for the overlay is now complete. Next, clip the plastic sheet securely over the pattern sheet, and repeat the pattern in ink on the plastic sheet, preferably using the ruler and making all measurements again to check for small errors. The names for the lines and areas are for reference only and are not inscribed on the overlay.

When the Overlay is located in a given way by placing it on the Field Diagram, the Field Diagram may be said to be divided into several areas. The areas within the two circles are called, respectively, the Area Within the Reference Circle and the Area Within the Opposite Circle. The total area outside the two circles, but still within the boundaries of the Field Diagram, is called the Residual Area of the Field. This area in turn is subdivided by the Line of Balance into the Residual Area on the Reference Side and the Residual Area on the Opposite Side. The area within the two Swing Lines may be thought of as extending to the edge of the Diagram in both the Mediator and Scapegoat Directions, and is called the Swing Area. It falls partly within the two circles, and partly in the two residual areas. The total Swing Area is bisected by the Line of Balance into the Swing Area on the Reference Side and the Swing area on the Opposite Side.

Appendix Q

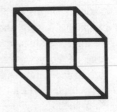

How to Use the Overlay with the Individual's Field Diagram

The Polarization–Unification Overlay represents a theory that postulates a tendency in the mind of the individual (under conditions of attention and emotional arousal) to group certain images together and make them more similar in evaluative location (that is, to "unify" them), if they are sufficiently similar to each other in evaluative location at some initial time; but on the other hand, if at the initial time other images are too dissimilar from those so unified, the tendency is to separate those other images in location from the unified cluster more completely (that is, to "polarize" them in relation to the unified cluster.) If there are two such groups of images, the first may be called the Reference group from the point of view of the rating individual and ordinarily contains the EXPECTED and/or WISHED-FOR self-image. The second may be called the Opposite group and ordinarily contains rejected images, sometimes rejected and dissociated aspects of the self-image. An Opposite group may be opposite in only one or in both of the P–N, F–B dimensions. There may be more than one Opposite group, in which case it is supposed that the polarizing tendency will ordinarily tend to center on one at a given time, but it may alternate from time to time.

The Polarization–Unification Overlay is applied to a Field Diagram containing a constellation of images, the locations of which have been ascertained by some kind of measurement—retrospective rating of the images by the individual or scoring by observers of the behavior and content of the individual's communication (SYMLOG Interaction Scoring). A preliminary step to the attempt to fit the Overlay is the expansion of the constellation of raw-score locations of the images to the proper scale to fill the diagram (See Appendix K).

The Overlay is placed upon the properly expanded Field Diagram and is moved about in a search for the best fit, that is, the best hypothesis as to what may have gone on psychologically in the mind of the individual that could result in the particular pattern of images that one sees portrayed by the ratings the individual has made. It is assumed that the individual has gone through some process of trying to simplify and organize the images he or she has of the persons in the group and their relations to each other. The moving about of the Overlay upon the Field Diagram is a kind of hypothetical simulation of the psychological organizing processes the individual may have gone through in arriving at the constellation of comparative evaluations.

For purposes of making the expansion and for fitting the Overlay, in the present book the location of the WISHED-FOR image has been excluded from consideration, though it is inscribed on the diagram in a lightly dashed line and later used for help in interpreting the pattern. An alternative procedure, which may be preferable, is to try to include the WISHED-FOR image in the Reference Circle. Further research is needed to determine which is the better of these two alternatives. There will be instances, however (for example, see HIP's diagram, Figure 19), where the location of the WISHED-FOR image will be so paradoxical that it can not be included in the Reference Circle.

The steps in the fitting of the Overlay are usually quite simple in practice. The basic principle is to *try to contain all images within one circle inscribed upon the Overlay, or, if that is not possible, within the two circles.* The underlying formal assumption is that each image acts upon each of the others during an initial stage as if it were a vector extending from the zero point of the diagram to the location of the image. In practice we take the outer edge of the image circle as the limit of extension of the vector. The underlying formal assumption is that we may treat the amount of dominance of the image, its location Upward in the U–D space, as a measure of intensification or added power in the direction of the vector, hence the vector in the given direction on the plane P–N, F–B is extended by an amount proportionate to the degree of added intensity or power. The three-dimensional space of vectors is by this means reduced to a two-dimensional plane of vectors. If one were constructing a mathematical model of this procedure, one would probably want to give more weight to the U–D measure than is given by the simple procedure of adding the radius of the U–D circle around the image to the endpoint of the vector. However, being concerned with maintaining simplicity of operation at this stage in the development of SYMLOG, we must leave the problem of a more exact mathematical model to a later stage.

In trying to contain all the image areas on the Diagram within the two circles of the Overlay (or within one, if possible) we are attempting to arrive at a resolution of the dynamic tendencies given by the various vector forces, a resolution which recognizes that, as the initial vector strains result in changes in the initial locations of the images, new and more local attractions and repulsions among images may become more important and hence modify the constellation of images and hence the field of forces. We posit that images close enough to each other initially tend to become more tightly clustered, up to some point, and images sufficiently far removed from each other tend to repel each other, and so result in polarized clusters. The pattern we see at the end of some period of interaction and change (by the time we make our measurements) is hypothesized to be the result of some kind of compromise between the initial vectors and the tendencies toward unification and polarization that may have set in as movement from the initial position resulted in different fields. We use the location of the images on the Field Diagram, as measured, to estimate the initial vector picture, and we use the procedure of fitting the Overlay pattern to estimate the way in which the mofidying tendencies toward unification and polarization may have operated.

We also hypothesize that at the time represented by our measurement there may be tendencies still in operation that have not come to their limit, or that may represent unstable conditions of strain for the individual, in view of the EXPECTED location of the self-image in the constellation, the WISHED-FOR location, and various other features. Once having fitted the Overlay, we inscribe the pattern of the Overlay upon the constellation of images on the Field Diagram and then continue the process of analysis with the help of other hypotheses.

A more detailed stepwise procedure for fitting the Overlay is described below.

1. *Try to contain all image areas* (that is, the point plus the outer U–D circle around the point) *within one Circle* of the Overlay, without any overhang (that is, without any projection of image areas over the boundary formed by the Reference Circle). If this cannot be done, go to Step 2 below. If it can be done, then continue with (a), then (b), then (c):

   (a) If all image areas are within the Reference Circle and there is some room for adjustment without producing any overhang, then try to balance the images around the center point of the Reference Circle. The images may be "balanced" around the center point approximately by considering each of the circles to represent a small ball, with a weight proportionate to its size. Remember that the weight of a small ball farther from a fulcrum point will balance the weight of a larger ball closer to the fulcrum point. Try to find the fulcrum point around which all the balls would balance— the center of gravity—and place the center point of the Reference Circle there. However, stop short of this balance if necessary to avoid overhang of any of the image areas.

   (b) Leaving the center point of the Reference Circle located as determined by (a) above, rotate the Line of Polarization around the center point of the Reference Circle so that the line passes through the intersection of the lines P–N and F–B on the Diagram. This operation locates the Opposite Circle.

   (c) Inscribe the Overlay pattern on the Diagram in the location so determined.

2. If Step 1 above has failed, *try to contain all image areas within the two circles of the Overlay,* the Reference Circle and the Opposite Circle, without any overhang or any overlap of an image area into both circles. If this cannot be done, go to Step 3, below. If it can be done, continue with (a), then (b):

   (a) If all image areas are within the two circles of the Overlay, and there is some room left for adjustment without producing any overhang or overlap, then try to balance the images within each of the two circles, each of the clusters, around the center point of its own circle. Compromise between the two circles as necessary to produce a a balance within each that is no worse than the balance within the other. Stop short of this compromise if necessary to avoid overhang of any of the image areas.

   (b) Inscribe the Overlay pattern on the Diagram in the location so determined.

3. If Step 2 above has failed, and there is no fit that avoids all overhang and overlap, *try to make each Overlay Circle at least intersect* all image circles on its side of the Line of Balance. If one or more images must be left isolated in the Residual Area, go to Step 4, below. If all image circles can at least be intersected, maintain the intersections and try to produce a balance of the overhangs

around the center of each Overlay Circle that is as good as possible, so long as it does not increase the overhangs around the center of the other. If both Overlay Circles still have overhangs, compromise between the two as necessary so that the amount of overhang around each is the same. Then go to (a):

(a) Inscribe the Overlay pattern on the Diagram in the location so determined.

4. If Step 3 above has failed, and one or more of the images must be left in the Residual Area, then *allow the smaller image area(s) to remain isolated, and include, if possible, or at least intersect, the larger of the image area(s)*. Now, disregarding any images that must be left isolated, try again to make each Overlay Circle at least intersect, if not include, all the remaining image circles on its side of the Line of Balance. Maintain the intersections or inclusions and try to produce a balance of the overhangs around the center of each Overlay Circle that is as good as possible, so long as it does not increase the overhangs around the center of the other. If both Overlay Circles still have overhangs, compromise between the two as necessary so that the amount of overhang around each is the same. Then go to (a):

(a) Inscribe the Overlay pattern on the Diagram in the location so determined.

The general logic of the procedure is quite simple. With regard to the images on a given side of the Line of Balance, one tries to get them all within the Overlay Circle and balanced around the center point. If there is too much spread for this, one accepts overhang of the images and tries to balance the overhang around the center point. If there is too much spread for this, one accepts isolation of one or more of the smaller images and tries to balance the overhang of the rest around the center point. One does the same with regard to the other Overlay Circle, and then, if both have overhangs, tries to balance the amount of overhang between the two Overlay Circles.

By this means one makes the pattern of the two Overlay Circles, representing a polarized dynamic field, cover as much image area as they will. The conception of the dynamics of the field does not favor polarization over unification—either is a possible resolution of the field forces, depending upon the original scatter of images—but the theory posits that if unification is not possible, then there will be a dynamic separation of the images that cannot be brought within the major unification, and the dynamics of polarization will set it. The final constellation of images, then, should resemble a polarization–unification pattern more than a random scatter, given an initial random scatter.

By the above steps one can arrive at an approximate graphic solution to the problem of locating the lines of polarization and of balance for a given field of images. Though crude (and perhaps wrong in some respects), the method has the virtue of implementing a major, apparently consistent, and testable hypothesis as to the dynamic forces that are believed to set in when an initial constellation of emotionally loaded images are brought within the field of attention of the individual. It also has the virtue of speed, in spite of its apparent complication. With a little practice, the operation of locating the best fit becomes a very fast intuitive operation. It should be said, however, that both the theory and the procedure are very tentative and require more research for sharper articulation.

Once the lines of polarization and balance have been located for a given Field Diagram, they may be inscribed upon it. Their location may also be described numerically. The numerical description may be made by specifying the location of the *zero point* of the Overlay upon the Diagram and the *angle* of the line of Polarization of the Overlay in relation to the line defining the dimension P–N on the Diagram. The zero point of the Overlay means the intersection of the Line of Polarization and the Line of Balance on the Overlay. How to determine the angle will be described presently.

The inscription may also include the R at one end of the Line of Polarization, indicating the Reference end, and the O at the other, indicating the Opposite end. To determine which end is the Reference end for the given individual is not always easy. The location of the WISHED-FOR self-image is taken ordinarily as the best indicator, but this is sometimes ambiguous. The same may be said for the location of the EXPECTED self-image. If either the WISHED-FOR or the EXPECTED location of the self is on or near the Line of Balance, in either the Mediator or Scapegoat direction, then the Reference direction on the Line of Polarization loses its ordinary meaning as the direction with which the individual tends to identify. Nevertheless, one still needs to be able to speak of the R direction in a formal sense in order to describe the angle of the Line of Polarization.

When the R end of the Line of Polarization lies on the Forward side of the dimension P–N, then the line is said to be so many degrees "off P toward F" (and this includes those directions on past F and toward N). The scale runs from 0 to 180 degrees. For better intuitive grasp, the same scale is repeated from P toward B, and on past B toward N again, at 180 degrees. Thus, when the Reference end of the Line of Polarization lies on the Backward side of the dimension P–N, the line is said to be so many degrees "off P toward B." The direction F lies 90 degrees off P toward F. The direction B lies 90 degrees off P toward B. The direction NF lies 135 degrees off P toward F. The direction NB lies 135 degrees off P toward B. The direction N lies 180 degrees off P.

The angle may be measured by placing a protractor with its point of origin on the point where the Line of Polarization intersects the P–N dimensional line on the Diagram, with the zero angle on the protractor pointing directly toward P, and then reading the angle intersected by the line indicating the R direction. The zero point of the Overlay is described by specifying its location on the Diagram in the same way one describes the location of an image center point on the Diagram, for example, 1P, 4B.

After some use of the Overlay in relation to the Diagram it will become apparent that the Overlay provides a pair of orthogonal dimensions in addition to the pair P–N, F–B, but in some formal sense similar. Dynamically, the direction R is similar to the direction F, O is similar to B, M is similar to P, and S is similar to N. The dimensions F–B and P–N are tied to the method of measurement, that is, the actual adjectives used to describe the behavior in rating or scoring, and the meaning that those adjectives tend to have, on the average, to a broad population of raters and scorers. The dimensions R–O and M–S on the Overlay are tied to a theory of dynamic tendencies of perception and evaluation of individuals rating other individuals in the same interacting group at a given time, and give a set of heuristic predictions as to who is likely to do what to whom in that specific group, given its particular constellation of members and images.

It is not clear at this time whether the locations of persons in relation to the dimensions of the Overlay gives tangibly more information, or better predictions, than one can get by knowing the locations on the original dimensions P–N, F–B. It is implicit in the theory of polarization and unification of images within social interaction fields that it does, but this remains to be seen.

It is clear, however, that the procedure of locating the (hypothetical) pattern of polarization–unification in a field of images gives a set of additional specifications concerning the *context* of each image (e.g., it is within the Reference Circle, near the Scapegoat direction, or in the Swing Area), and there is some chance that knowing the context will allow better understanding and predictions. At the level of application of the theory, the use of the Overlay in addition to the Diagram allows us to make what sociologists call a "contextual analysis" that will tell us more about what kind of context the interacting group forms for each particular individual (see Davis, 1961, 1971; Pettigrew and Riley, 1972).

Appendix R

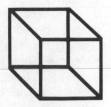

How to Use the Overlay with a Group Average Field Diagram

The identical *Overlay* is used for both Individual and Group Average fields. It is assumed that the constellation of images, whether those of an individual field or a group average field, has been expanded in such a way as to put the image farthest out from the zero point of the diagram just within the border of the diagram. (For the description of how to do this, see Appendix K).

The actual procedure of fitting the Overlay to the constellation of images is formally exactly the same for the Group Average Diagram as for the Individual Diagram, although the interpretation differs to some extent. In analyzing an individual diagram it is assumed that the location of the individual's EXPECTED or WISHED-FOR self-image will normally give the basis for calling the circle in or near which it is located the "Reference Circle." In a group average diagram, there is no such criterion, since there are a number of individuals involved, some identified with one reference group, perhaps, some with the other. If the group is unified, there is no problem, but if it is polarized, one can solve the problem by speaking of "the PF reference group," for example, or "the NB reference group," as appropriate, naming the group by its approximate location in the space. The designations "R" and "O" at the two ends of the Line of Polarization should be omitted on a Group Average Diagram.

We need to keep constantly in mind the differences between a social interaction field and an individual perceptual field whenever we are analyzing the potentialities of a field, even though the formal representation of the two is the same. The processes of polarization and unification in a social interaction field include the mental processes that constitute each individual perceptual field, but they include, in addition, the behavior and content images as expressed, act by act, in overt communication and interaction between individuals. The overt communication processes take longer to feed back upon each other than do the mental processes of the single individual. The overt communication processes are distributed among individuals and are affected by many features of the relations between individuals and the differences of individuals from each other. In brief, we may say that in social interaction fields the processes of polarization and unification are processes of subgroup formation and total group development. Of course, these processes are reflected in individual perception, but in order to understand them we have to take more into account than the psychology of individual perceptual gestalts.

In examining a Group Average Field Diagram, based on retrospective ratings, we are trying to use an aggregate picture of Individual Perceptual Fields of images (simply added together) in order to make an extension of those individual perceptions to a *hypothesis* as to what the full-bodied behavioral social interaction field was or may be. If we have the perceptions of other observers using retrospective ratings we also use them in helping us to build this picture. If we have SYMLOG sequential scoring of acts and image content, we also use this source of information. It is not yet completely clear just how we should add all of these different sources of information together, particularly how we might differentially weight the different sources of information. But it is clear that we use the partial information contained in the Group Average Field Diagram to try to infer what the actual social interaction field was like, especially in its dynamics.

When the Overlay is used with a Group Average Diagram, the circles now represent theoretically the boundaries of actual subgroups. The processes of unification include the overt interaction processes of forming a total group, or of forming a cooperative and solidary subgroup. Some of these processes may not even take place within the observation of all group members, as in a total group meeting. but may take place "outside." The processes of polarization include the actual overt social interaction by which the division of the total group into two or more conflicting subgroups develops. If an image representing an individual is included within a given circle, by a given placement of the overlay, the theory implies that the individual is likely to be seen as a real member of the subgroup. If the image is outside the circle, it is implied that the individual tends to be excluded to some extent from the subgroup within the circle because that individual is too different from the others. And so on. The theory is not fully developed for social interaction fields as yet, nor is it, for that matter, for individual perceptual fields. It is not clear how well the formal procedure may represent the real processes we want to capture.

In spite of these problems it seems clear enough that the best way to get ahead is to make definite assumptions on the formal level and then let experience and theoretical analysis improve upon that starting point. There is an opportunity in every case study to examine the assumptions anew, and the user should employ the procedures in this spirit.

Appendix S

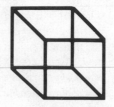

Methods for Aggregating SYMLOG Interaction Scores for the Construction of Field Diagrams and Time Plots

Howard Swann and Richard Polley

Once the raw SYMLOG Interaction Scores have been collected from a session of interaction, we are faced with the problem of aggregating the scores to transform them into a standardized summary description.

We are currently working with two kinds of summaries. One kind provides a series of Field Diagrams showing the way individuals differ from each other in both behavior and imagery, aggregating over a session or an episode within a session. The other provides a series of Time Plots that describe the rise and fall over three-minue subperiods of given directions and levels of both behavior and imagery aggregated over all individuals in the group.

There are many different ways in which the raw SYMLOG Interaction Scores could be aggregated, weighted, and standardized in order to put them into a form for the construction of Field Diagrams and Time Plots. How does one tell when one has a good method? It seems to us that a reasonable criterion is that the method chosen should substantially agree with the participants' retrospective appraisal of what happened during the session. It may be true, as Cohen's study (Part III of this book) suggests, that there are some dependable and perhaps identifiable psychological differences between a retrospective perception of an interaction process (even though the rating is done immediately after having observed the process) and the perception of it as reflected by a written record made of it while it is in process. But even if this is the case, in order to study the differences one needs measures that have been purified, so far as possible, of artifactual differences. The closer we can come to agreement between our summaries and the participants' retrospective appraisals, the better we will suppose our measurement to be in revealing differences between the two modes of perception, if they exist, and in reflecting the selective perception and individual biases of group members and observers, rather than artifactual differences in the methods of measurement.

If we accept the three dimensions and the levels defined in the system as the variables on which we are trying to maximize agreement, we first need to determine what is the most suitable questionnaire for participants to use for their retrospective ratings of a session. We assume that the behavior recorded by the SYMLOG scorers describes many of the incidents that form the basis for the participants' retrospective recall and appraisal of a session. Of course, there are aspects of interaction not covered by the SYMLOG categories that will influence the participants' retrospective ratings, just as, we suspect, there will prove to be subtleties of interaction that SYMLOG scorers detect that will not influence the retrospective appraisals of the participants. However, to establish a strong correspondence between SYMLOG summaries and the global retrospective impressions of participants, we would like our questionnaire to reflect ideally only those aspects of a session that are treated within the SYMLOG scoring framework.

One of the practical problems in finding the most suitable form of questionnaire for use in the self-analytic group setting is the amount of time required to make ratings. Even if the Simplified SYMLOG Adjective Rating Form is used, it is probably too much to ask fifteen or so participants to rate each other immediately after each of a series of sessions. We need a reduced form. One possibility is to use only the adjective items measuring the six directions, U, D, P, N, F, B. Cohen's study shows these items, as now represented in the Simplified Adjective Rating Form shown in Appendix C, to have high item-to-scale correlations, to be approximately orthogonal as to the dimensions U–D, P–N, and F–B, and for the pairs representing the opposite directions of the dimensions to be highly negatively correlated.

However, we are also directly concerned with the problem of an optimum match between the scaling of our measures derived from an aggregation of SYMLOG Interaction Scores and our retrospective rating measure. We want to get them both scaled so that they will coincide literally in location on the Field Diagram as nearly as possible. We think our chances for this are better if we put the adjectives for the two opposite ends of a given dimension at each end of a graphic scale, which runs from a zero point in the middle to 18 on each end with divisions just as they appear on the Field Diagram. The form we propose is shown in Figure 60.

It will be noted that the form proposed asks for ratings of all group members on one dimension at a time. The participants are listed one below another to assist in keeping the ratings within the group context. It is our assumption that one of the determinants of global retrospective perceptions of participants is some kind of comparison of themselves with each other. The perception is partly relative to group context. This assumption is represented directly in one of the components of our formula for processing the SYMLOG Interaction Scores (called the "quantitative" component), as we shall see. We hypothesize that we are likely to

FIGURE 60 Proposed Form for the Minimal Rating Questionnaire

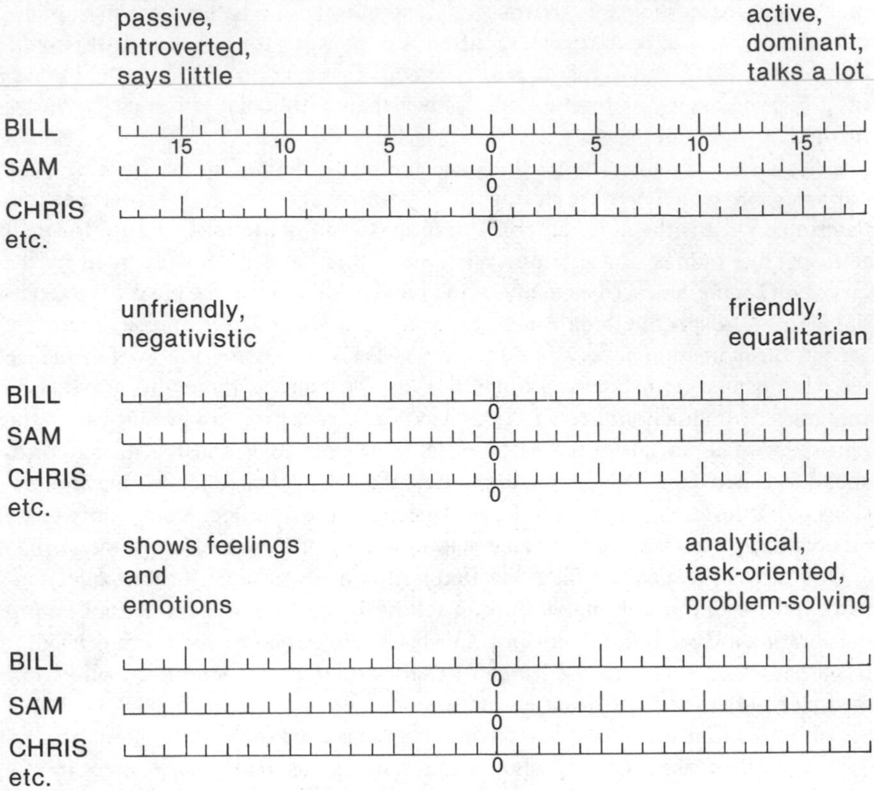

passive,
introverted,
says little

active,
dominant,
talks a lot

BILL

SAM

CHRIS
etc.

unfriendly,
negativistic

friendly,
equalitarian

BILL

SAM

CHRIS
etc.

shows feelings
and
emotions

analytical,
task-oriented,
problem-solving

BILL

SAM

CHRIS
etc.

obtain better agreement between our measures if we have the group relative contextual component built into both.

Once a retrospective rater has assigned a location to the first participant on the list, we assume that he will tend to locate the subsequent participants relative to the place he has located the preceding ones, as well as relative to his concepts of the dimensions, the scale, and the anchoring adjectives. As the final rating for an individual on each dimension, we simply take the average of his ratings received from the other participants. The averaging should help to cancel out (and reveal) differences in selective perception and bias among the participants. We expect the participants in this study to be members of a self-analytic group using SYM-LOG feedback. Thus they will know the dimensions and also will have regular feedback as to how observers perceive their behavior. Probably this will have effects on the rating process, tending in most cases to increase the agreement between the ratings and the SYMLOG scores. The correlations we obtain will possibly be higher than one may expect to find in other contexts, but we shall have to postpone to later studies the problem of generality of the findings.

Accepting this scaling for the retrospective ratings, our next task in preparation for the visualized criterion study is to find some way to transform the observers' SYMLOG data on participant behavior into an equivalent scale. The scaling procedure will be discussed in terms of the Friendly/Unfriendly (P–N) dimension, but it is designed to apply to the other two dimensions as well.

For any session, we can aggregate the SYMLOG messages for all observers for the entire session to obtain the following:

p_i = number of acts by the "$_i$th" participant scored P
n_i = number of acts by the "$_i$th" participant scored N
P = total number of acts scored P for the entire group
N = total number of acts scored N for the entire group
m = number of participants

By including all observer's records, bias in perception should be averaged out to some extent (see Appendix T), and particularly important events should be emphasized.

Somehow we need to find a formula for transforming this aggregated data to produce a Field Diagram that will be as nearly as possible the same as the Field Diagram constructed from the participants' retrospective ratings at the end of the session.

The procedure of simply using the raw score difference: $[p_i - n_i]$ to obtain an individual's location on the P–N dimension seems to us, intuitively, to be inadequate. Intuitively there seems to us to be considerable difference between the probable location of the following two persons:

INDIVIDUAL	p_i	n_i	$\{p_i - n_i\}$	$p_i + n_i$	$\dfrac{p_i - n_i}{p_i + n_i}$
1	18	3	15	21	.71
2	45	30	15	75	.20
Totals:	P – 63	N = 33		P + N = 96	

The raw score difference, $[p_i - n_i]$ is the same in both cases, 15. However, the "quality" of friendliness in the behavior of individual 1 seems to be convincingly greater; there is a greater preponderance of positive over negative behavior on his own base. The difference between individual 1's P total and his N total (15) accounts for 71 percent of his scores (21) on the P–N dimension, while individual 2's difference (15) only accounts for 20 percent of his scores (75) on this dimension. On the other hand, we do want to consider the quantity of interaction as well. If we think of each N act as canceling out a P act, the two individuals contributed equally to the total net P behavior in the group: 15 net P acts for each out of the 96 acts scored either P or N. We intuitively feel that these two considerations of "quantity" as well as the consideration of "quality" may count in the perceptions of the retrospective raters.

We develop our formula for composing final summary scores from the raw SYMLOG data in two steps. First we list a series of such properties as quality and quantity of participation that intuitively should be important in the process of retrospective appraisal by the participants. Then we derive a mathematical formula that possesses these properties. Many of these properties are concerned with the way an "ideal" objective participant would respond to the events scored by the observers, although in practice we shall have to get along with the retrospective rating received by an individual averaged over all the actual participants in the particular session.

Property 1. The formula should be insensitive to the number of scorers observing the session. If SYMLOG scorers all score a session identically, the formula should produce the same location for any particular individual no matter how many scorers' records are used.

Property 2. If, in the same session, two participants have the same number of messages scored "N," but the first participant has more messages scored "P" than the second, then the first participant should be located closer to the P pole than the second.

On the other hand, if, in the same session, two participants have the same number of messages scored "P," but the first participant has more messages scored "N" than the second, then the first participant should be located closer to the N pole than the second.

This property, which is concerned solely with the proportion of positive to negative acts within the behavior of the given individual, as compared with proportion of other individuals, seems to reflect what we might call the *quality* of the behavior of the individual.

The next two properties are concerned with *quantity* of interaction:

Property 3. Suppose, within the same session, three participants have the same *proportion* of scores on the positive side as compared to the negative side, but differ in total quantity of interaction, or participation, as in the following example:

	p_i	n_i	$\dfrac{p_i}{n_i}$	"QUANTITY" $p_i + n_i$
Bill	4	1	4	5
Sam	8	2	4	10
Chris	16	4	4	20

Because Sam has a higher quantity of interaction than Bill, but of the same qualitative proportion of positive to negative behavior, and Chris similarly has a higher quantity than both, we assume that Sam should be assigned a location between those of Bill and Chris on the P–N dimension.

Property 4. Suppose that, within the same session, two participants have the same proportional scores as in the above example. We would expect that if the participant with a lower quantity of interaction is given a positive location, then the other, with a higher quantity of participation, should also be assigned a positive location. Conversely, if the participant with a lower quantity of participation is assigned a negative location, we would expect the more active participant (with SYMLOG scores in the same proportion of p_i to n_i) also to be given a negative location.

Properties 3 and 4 can be called "quantitative" properties as compared to Property 2, which can be called a "qualitative" property, for our purposes. It can be shown by a mathematical formulation of the properties that the final formula that will satisfy them must consist of essentially two components, a "qualitative" and a "quantitative," that are added together. In order to make the present verbal exposition easier to follow, we have placed the mathematical formulation in a separate section under that title at the end of this Appendix. The Mathematical Formulation is organized in a way parallel to the present discussion of the Properties and may be consulted for a more exact presentation of the argument. To resume the argument here, what we call the "qualitative component" is constant for proportional p_i and n_i scores, while the "quantitative" component, having Properties 3, and 4, grows (or decreases) steadily with increasing p_i and n_i scores that are proportional. Property 5, which follows, is concerned with the tradeoff between these two components.

Property 5.   We conjecture that a retrospective rater will be sensitive to the tradeoff between the quantity and quality of participation and will sense that the critical amount of behavior where these two components can be weighted equally in his rating will be at the level of the amount of participation of an "average individual" in the group (with scores $p = P/m$, and $n = N/m$). If we use this hypothesis as one of the properties of interaction that our formula should reflect, then we surmise that the quantiative component should contribute more to the eventual location for a participant than the qualitative for individuals with higher than average participation, whereas the reverse will be true for individuals with lower than average participation. Intuitively it seems plausible that when an individual participates very little in the group, other participants are forced to pay more attention to the quality of what little behavior he does provide, and hence will weight the quality more heavily in their perception.

Property 6.   This property is concerned with the scaling of the final score and the choice of zero. For our SYMLOG Interaction Score based Field Diagram to have the same scale as that of the Retrospective Rating, we require our formula to produce numbers between -18 and 18, no matter how large or small the group is.

Determining where our formula should be zero is really an empirical question: What ratio of P-scored acts to N-scored acts would result in an individual being assigned a "neutral" location by a retrospective rater? We would suspect that it would take several convincing acts scored P to cancel out one act scored N for a participant to maintain a "neutral" position on the P–N scale, but we do not have sufficient data as yet to quantify this in any accurate way. Probably there should be different "zero points" for each of the three SYMLOG dimensions. Fortunately, the choice of where the formula should be zero does not affect correlations between retrospective ratings and interaction-based field diagrams, and the associated regression equations will eventually provide a good empirical basis for adjusting our formula appropriately. So, for the moment, we will arbitrarily adopt the 50:50 proportion as the zero point for our formula. Thus, if an individual has more acts scored P than N, he will be assigned a positive location on the P–N dimension, and conversely, if he has more acts scored N than P, the formula will assign him a negative location. (We suspect that this is actually roughly correct for the F–B (instrumentally controlled versus emotionally expressive) dimension, but probably not correct for the other two dimensions.)

Property 7. We suspect that the overall behavior of a group is likely to influence the retrospective recall of an individual participant's behavior. Suppose that the group interaction is fairly polarized during a session, with high quantities of friendly *and* unfriendly behavior on the part of different individuals, some striving to demonstrate friendly behavior, and some striving to demonstrate unfriendly behavior. We assume that a retrospective rater would then be strongly influenced by the quantity of interaction of the participants in such a battle of behavioral styles. The high participators would be strongly salient on both positive and negative sides of the polarization. On the other hand, if behavior is predominantly regarded as friendly (or unfriendly) without much difference between individuals on the P–N dimension, we assume that a retrospective rater would be more sensitive to the quality of participation in making distinctions amid such uniformity.

Thus, we propose that our formula reflect Property 7: When there is a good deal of contrast between participants on the P–N dimension, that is, when both total group P and total group N are large, the quantitative component of the formula should be emphasized. If behavior is mostly scored P (or mostly scored N), the qualitative component of the formula should be emphasized.

A number of mathematical results can be derived by assuming that our formula should have these seven Properties. The results suggest the following formula for computer use:

$$\text{Location for participant "i"} = C(m) \cdot \left(m\sqrt{\frac{p_i^2 + n_i^2}{P^2 + N^2}} + 1 \right) \begin{cases} \dfrac{p_i - n_i}{p_i + .4n_i} & \text{if } p_i \geq n_i \\[2ex] \dfrac{p_i - n_i}{n_i + .4p_i} & \text{if } n_i \geq p_i \end{cases}$$

$$\text{where} \quad C(m) = 18 / \left(1 + \frac{m}{\log_e (m + 5) + .58} \right).$$

The logarithmic term in the formula helps distribute the participants over the entire field diagram. Its use is suggested by results concerning the distribution of participation in small groups reported by Bales, Strodtbeck, Mills, and Roseborough (1951), using the scores produced by Interaction Process Analysis (Bales 1950). Observing groups of sizes 3 through 8, they found that the amounts of participation for individuals (ranked according to amount of participation) tend to approximate a "harmonic" distribution. Thus, for a group of size 5, amounts of participation lie in proportion $1 : \frac{1}{2} : \frac{1}{3} : \frac{1}{4} : \frac{1}{5}$. The harmonic distribution fitted size 5 best, and the authors concluded that there were significant departures from this distribution for their groups (the distribution tends to be somewhat flatter for groups under size 5, and somewhat steeper for groups over size 5). It is also true that SYMLOG Interaction Scoring differs from Interaction Process Analysis Scoring in that the latter records every act, while the SYMLOG methods picks up the more salient acts and misses many others. It is also the case that the groups we are working with tend to be around size 15. Thus, there are a number of reasons why the harmonic distribution may be a poor approximation for our data, but we adopt it until we are able to replace it with a better estimate.

A simpler formula that satisfies the first six properties listed above is:

$$\text{Location for participant ``}i\text{''} = 5 \cdot \left(\frac{m(p_i - n_i)}{P + N} + \frac{p_i - n_i}{p_i + n_i} \right).$$

The "5" in the formula is an approximation to the logarithmic term in the other formula. Although this formula does not adjust the scaling for different-sized groups and fails to have Property 7, the correlations with the retrospective ratings using this formula are nearly as good as those obtained using the previous more complicated formula. So we recommend this simple formula for making field diagrams by hand.

A computation form that uses this formula to convert raw SYMLOG Interaction Scores tabulated by hand to Expanded Plotting Scores (incorporating the procedure for expanding a constellation of points described in Appendix K) will be found in Appendix J. Since the simple formula does not take group size into account, and since the logarithmic approximation is not adequate for very extreme differences between members, it is possible that the plotting scores it produces will not be contained within the scale limit of 18. If the scores go higher than 18, the application of the procedure in Appendix J will result in an "Expansion Multipler" of less than 1.00, and hence the multiplier will produce a contraction of the constellation of points so that they fit exactly within the Field Diagram, as desired for the plotting procedure. The "Expansion Multipler" acts as an expander when the scores fall below 18, and a contractor when the scores fall above 18.

Correlations Between Behavior Recorded Using the SYMLOG Interaction Scoring Method and Retrospective Ratings

Interest in high correlations between transformed SYMLOG Interaction Scoring data and retrospective ratings springs from two sources. First, if high correlations can be obtained, it may help us to gain further insight both into the ways that people form their impressions of others' behavior and into the ways that people behave in the first place to make these impressions. Second, if SYMLOG Interaction Scores can be used to provide a reasonable profile of the behavior of participants in an entire session, we will feel justified in asserting that it also gives an accurate picture of shorter episodes within a session of interaction, where it is not possible to have immediate retrospective analysis without interrupting the flow of the session. Thus we will be in a position to study the processes postulated by balance theory, consistency theory, etc., which may operate most clearly within relatively short episodic periods of interaction when particular images or issues are the focus of attention in a process of polarization or unification.

A simple method was described earlier for use in obtaining retrospective ratings of a session. Only one pilot study, by Thomas Bixby (1978), has been made correlating the data obtained by this method and the field diagram scores produced by the formula described above.

For one session of a self-analytic group, eight observers made SYMLOG Interaction Scores and then immediately after the meeting made retrospective ratings, using a form very similar to that shown in Figure 60. The eleven group members also made retrospective ratings immediately after the session. The following average correlations were obtained:

> Observers' SYMLOG Scoring and
> Observers' Retrospective Ratings: .79
> Observers' SYMLOG Scoring and
> Participants' Retrospective Ratings: .76

The relatively high correlation between the observers' retrospective ratings and their SYMLOG Scores is perhaps not too surprising, since the observers had just finished making their SYMLOG Scores, and we would assume that they would recall how they had scored the individuals in the session. We are more interested in the correlation of .76 between the observers' SYMLOG Scores and the participants' retrospective ratings. The participants were not involved in the SYMLOG Scoring process during the session and so did not make the same sort of explicit SYMLOG-based judgments as the observers. A more extensive study is under way to test our methods more rigorously.

A more substantial study has been made by Manson Solomon (1977) based on data gathered by Stephen P. Cohen and Stephen A. Williamson (see Part IV). The data are from six self-analytic groups, which ran one full school term each. Retrospective ratings were obtained near the end of the term and were based on several earlier forms of the present SYMLOG Adjective Rating Form, the earliest of which consisted of fifty-two questions selected from Forms A, B, and C, from Bales (1970). The SYMLOG Social Interaction Scoring data are presented in full by Williamson (1977). In spite of some differences in both the Scoring and the Rating methods, the average correlation for individual groups between the SYMLOG Interacting Scoring, aggregated over all sessions by the methods described above, and the members' retrospective ratings was .64.

Summarizing Individual Imagery

In addition to the Field Diagrams based on the Behavioral levels ACT and NON (added together), we are currently using three types of Field Diagrams to describe individual imagery during a session or episode within a session. The diagrams are produced by computer and carry all essential numerical information in printed form, in addition to the graphic plot of the Field Diagram. Because of difficulties in reproduction of the large computer-produced diagram, our illustrations are shown here in the same format as other diagrams in this book. The behavioral-level diagram is the same as others shown in this book and need not be presented here. The other diagrams, however, have special features, which we illustrate.

Figure 61 is a Field Diagram that shows the location of both PRO and CON imagery for one group session (all levels aggregated). This diagram represents an effort to portray the impression conveyed by value-laden imagery presented by the participants during a session or episode. We reason that the same sort of considerations that produced the formula for converting SYMLOG Interaction Scores at the ACT plus NON level into plotting scores also hold for converting SYMLOG Image data into participants' PRO and CON image locations. We suppose that there should be the same concern with both the quality and the quantity of imagery and the tradeoff between the two. Thus, the formula that produces the plotting scores for the behavior Field Diagram is also used for the PRO and CON images in this diagram. (PRO images are represented in the computer-produced diagram by a plus sign before the participant's abbreviated name, and the appropriate U or D score is printed immediately below the name. Similarly, CON images are represented by a minus sign before a name. The computer program does not draw the U–D circles, but we have included them in our diagram for greater clarity.)

Figure 62 shows what we call the Qualitative Image Field Diagram. This diagram shows the quality of imagery of the participants during an episode. Individuals with the same proportional U–D, P–N, and F–B scores for PRO images or CON images will occupy the same position on the diagram independent of the quantity of imagery expressed. For example, two participants with the following summed SYMLOG scores for PRO imagery during an episode will be at the same location on this Field Diagram:

	U	D	P	N	F	B
First participant:	4	2	6	2	5	1
Second participant:	8	4	3	1	10	2

The plotting score for this Field Diagram is computed using the qualitative component of our previous formula. The same formula is used for all three dimensions. For example, if p_i is the number of PRO images for individual i scored P, and n_i is the number of PRO images scored N during an episode, the plotting score on the P–N dimension for the summary PRO image is:

$$18 \cdot \begin{cases} \dfrac{p_i - n_i}{p_i + .4n_i} & \text{if } p_i \geq n_i \\[2em] \dfrac{p_i - n_i}{n_i + .4p_i} & \text{if } n_i \geq p_i \end{cases}$$

We hope this Field Diagram can be used to investigate balance theory, consistency theory, coalition structure, and other aspects of group interaction that are

FIGURE 61   Illustration of an Image Field Diagram (Self-Analytic Group: 1
Session, 100 Minutes)

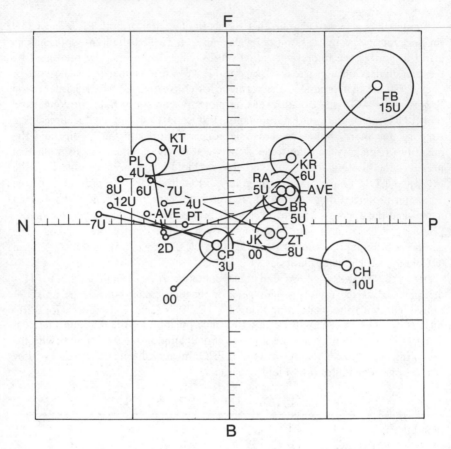

concerned with similarity and differences in individual attitudes rather than with
quantity of interaction.

Figure 63 shows what we call an Image Formation Diagram. This diagram
shows in detail the "dialogue of images" of participants during an episode. We
first describe its use informally with a simplified example.

Suppose that the subject of college professors is brought up during a session
and becomes the topic of an episode. Bill and Sam present the following sequence of images:

1. Bill says he likes professors who control the class well and keep on the
subject, but create a friendly atmosphere so that the class is encouraged to
participate (scored PRO UPF).

2. Sam says he likes well-organized classes, but doesn't care much for a
professor that is too "chummy" (scored PRO UF).

3. Bill remarks that real progress and learning are not achieved in the

FIGURE 62   Illustration of a Qualitative Image Field Diagram (Self-Analytic Group: 1 Session, 100 Minutes)

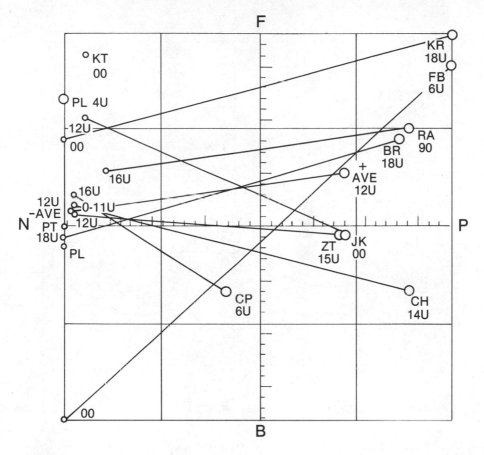

classroom unless the class is relaxed yet intellectually alive in the presence of a friendly and concerned professor (scored PRO PF).

4. Sam says, on the contrary, he likes professors who push students hard and provoke tough-minded intellectual debate (scored PRO UNF).

5. Bill concedes that a professor shouldn't be too friendly and says that the main goal is to get something done (scored PRO F).

6. Sam agrees that keeping attention focused on learning is really the most important aspect of teaching (scored PRO F).

In the course of portraying this episode, six separate Image Formation diagrams can be produced, one showing the state of affairs after each of the successive six remarks. These six diagrams can then be combined into a single diagram that portrays the development of each of the individuals' PRO Images and also the "jointly determined" PRO image.

Figure 64 reflects Bill's initial description of the kind of professor he favors

FIGURE 63 Illustration of an Image Formation Diagram (Self-Analytic Group: 37-Minute Episode)

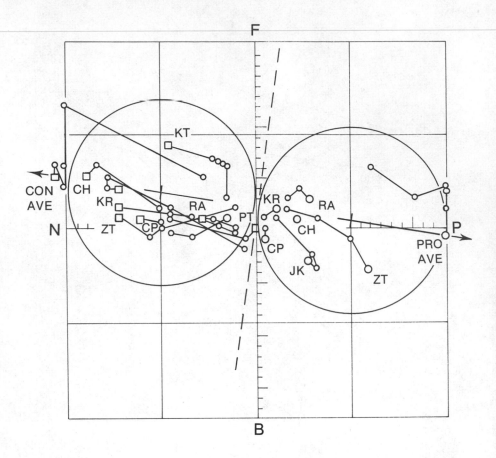

(PRO UPF). For this sample example, we ignore the U–D dimension and show the movement in the PF direction only. At this point, the "jointly determined PRO Image" (shown by the symbol +++) is at the same location as Bill's PRO Image, since there has been no agreement or disagreement, as yet, with Bill's value statement.

Figure 65 shows Sam's image as well as Bill's. The jointly determined PRO Image is now expressed as the vector sum of Bill's and Sam's PRO Images. Both Bill and Sam endorse the "PRO UF" aspect of professors but disagree on the amount of friendliness that is appropriate. The jointly determined PRO image reflects this by moving out in the F direction and "splitting the difference" on the friendliness issue. We draw a line to indicate the movement of the jointly determined PRO Image. The numbers below the names refer to the time stages of this dialogue of images. At Time 1, Bill is out one step in a PF direction, and Sam is still at the origin, that is, has not yet indicated a direction. At Time 2, Sam

FIGURE 64 Changes in PRO Image Location of BILL, SAM, and Jointly
Determined Image (Vector Sum) + + + at Time 1

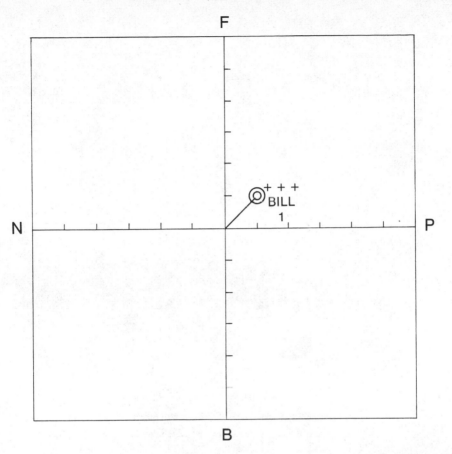

is out one step in an F direction, and Bill is still where he was at Time 1, so far as
we have information. At Time 2, the jointly determined image, however, which
we infer from the combination of the two individual images, is out two steps in a
direction between PF and F.

Figure 66 adds statement 3, moving Bill out farther in the PF direction as he
affirms his PRO PF stand in his second statement. The jointly determined PRO
image is moved out in the PF direction as well.

In Figure 67, Sam's second "statement vector" (PRO UNF) is combined as a
vector sum with his first location. We assume that he doesn't like the direction in
which Bill is "leading" the jointly determined PRO Image and, by his comment,
attempts to pull the location of the jointly determined image back in the PRO UF
direction.

In Figure 68, Times 5 and 6 are combined and a Polarization-Unification
inscription is added. Each diagram combines all the information in the previous
diagrams with the most recent development. Thus, one final Diagram shows the

FIGURE 65 Changes in PRO Image Location of BILL, SAM, and Jointly Determined Image (Vector Sum) + + + at Time 2

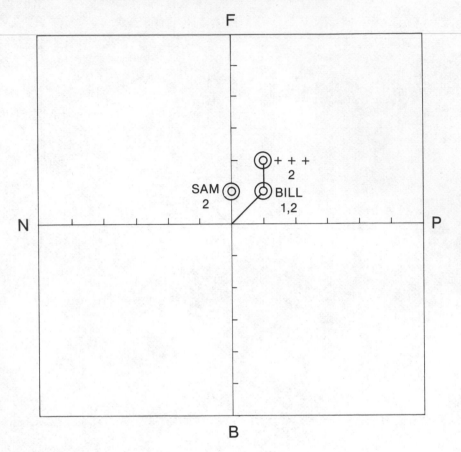

complete development of each individual's Pro Image as well as the formation of the jointly determined PRO Image.

Many episodes are characterized by such a comparison of impressions and values. Debate continues by affirmation of PRO Imagery (as in our simplified example) or in some other cooperative, competitive, or conflicting way. Since there are both PRO and CON Images, and individuals may agree or disagree by as many degrees as one may care to distinguish in terms of vector angles on either PRO or CON Images, or both, and with regard to six directions, it is no simple matter to determine the most useful classification of vector paths and patterns at their ending points. In our diagram showing the movement at times 5 and 6 there seems to be a consensus, since both Bill and Sam, along with the jointly determined image, are moving in the same direction, toward F.

The Diagram shown earlier in Figure 63 (p. 468) gives an actual example of such a dialogue of imagery. It differs from the simple example just described by

FIGURE 66   Changes in PRO Image Location of BILL, SAM, and Jointly
Determined Image (Vector Sum) + + + at Time 3

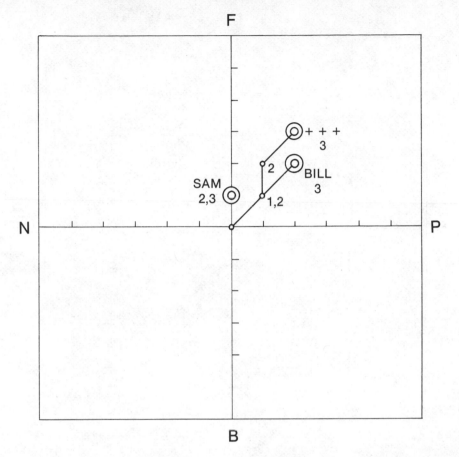

weighting the size of the vectors describing any individual participant's imagery
by the amount of dominance shown in the participant's ACT plus NON level
behavior. Thus, more dominant individuals at the behavioral level contribute
more to the eventual location of the jointly determined PRO and CON images
than less dominant individuals. Images have a location in the U–D image level
dimension, of course, but this dimension is not treated as a vector weight. It is
treated as a third dimension of image directions and is weighted by the U–D
behavioral level dominance, as are the other two image level dimensions, P–N
and F–B.

Figure 63 also differs from the simple diagrams in that each of the six steps
represents about five minutes of interaction. Showing the act-by-act formation of
images is generally much too detailed and time-consuming to be worthwhile.
Thus, the episode portrayed in Figure 63 represents about a half-hour during
which almost 200 PRO and CON images were scored for the nine participants.

FIGURE 67   Changes in PRO Image Location of BILL, SAM, and Jointly
Determined Image (Vector Sum) + + + at Time 4

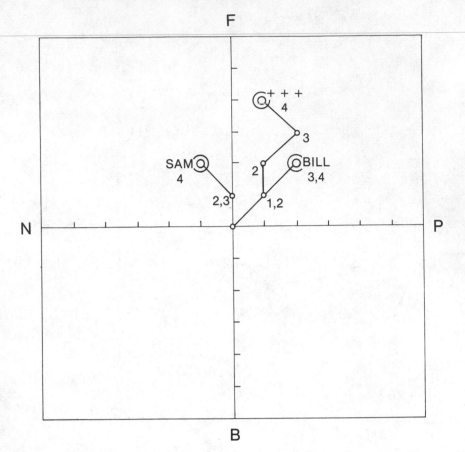

Methods for Producing Time Plots Summarizing Behavior and Imagery over a Session of Interaction

We describe here a method currently being used to summarize collective behavior and imagery of a group during each three-minute interval of a session of interaction. The observations for each three minutes provide the points for our time plots. For each three minutes, the behavior for the level under consideration is summed across all participants. A sample of these graphs for part of a session is given in Figure 69.

The computer program that produces these time plots allows a number of different options, since there are a number of different aspects of the collective behavior and imagery of a group that we would like to be able to study.

As an example, we describe various ways of representing U-scored behavior messages. For each three-minute time interval, we can obtain the number of

FIGURE 68 Changes in PRO Image Location of BILL, SAM, and Jointly
Determined Image (Vector Sum) + + + at Times 5 and 6

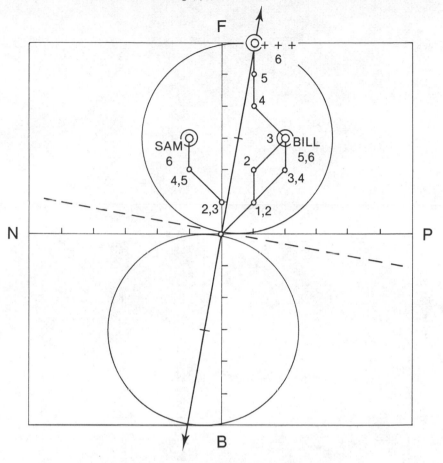

messages scored (U, D, or neither), denoted "NM," and we can also record the number of messages registering U behavior (denoted "NU"). The raw scores showing U-scored behavior would seem to be the basic statistic, and it is one of the options that the computer program will accommodate. However, the total number of messages scored during each three-minute interval is not constant, and this introduces some secondary considerations. Suppose we consider three three-minute periods producing the following data:

	PERIOD 1	PERIOD 2	PERIOD 3
Behavior messages scored U:	2	4	6
Behavior messages scored in any way:	3	6	9

Note that the fraction of messages scored "U" is the same (⅔) in each case. It

FIGURE 69 Sample of Computer-Produced Time Plots

```
     "U" SCORED BEHAVIOR TIME PLOT. AVERAGE SESSION U MESSAGES/3 MIN.
     -------------------------------------------------------------------
1.0                                                 1.0      +
 .9                                                  .9
 .8                              +               +    +         +          +
 .7                      *   +                       .7                *
 .6          *       +                       *       .6   *        *          *
 .5 -  -   -     * -   -   -   -   -     * -   -     .5 -  -  -  -   -   -   -  -
 .4                                                  .4
 .3                                  *               .3
 .2      *                                           .2
 .1                                                  .1
 .0   *                                              .0
    20 23  26  29  32  35  38  41  44  47  50  53  56   59  2  5  8   11  14  17  20
NO. OF MESSAGES:
      1  10  22  17  33  22  27  32  23  31  21  28  25   21 25 23 18  20  32 24  3

     "D" SCORED BEHAVIOR TIME PLOT. AVERAGE SESSION D MESSAGES/3 MIN.
     -------------------------------------------------------------------
1.0                                                 1.0
 .9                                                  .9
 .8                                                  .8
 .7                                                  .7
 .6                                                  .6
 .5 -  -   -   -   -   -   -   -   -   -   -   -     .5 -  -  -  -   -   -   -  -
 .4          +                                       .4
 .3                                                  .3
 .2              *   +           +   +               .2
 .1      *                   *           *   *        *      *  *      *      *
 .0   *                  *                       *   .0   *        *       *
    20 23  26  29  32  35  38  41  44  47  50  53  56   59  2  5  8   11  14  17  20
NO. OF MESSAGES:
      1  10  22  17  33  22  27  32  23  31  21  28  25   21 25 23 18  20  32 24  3
```

may be desirable to plot these fractions instead of the raw scores; again, the computer program can do this. But consider the following.

One use we see for such time plots is to help appraise and identify episodes within a session. From our experience with many feedback sessions, scorers seem to have no particular difficulty in identifying episodes using their SYMLOG Interaction records, and readily come to agreement as to the times such episodes begin and end. We assume that an episode is characterized by common themes, imagery, and behavior, and we would like to be able to have these time plots capture the impressions made upon the participants by the behavior and imagery of the episode. Neither the raw frequencies nor the fractions seem appropriate for this task.

If we use the raw frequencies, the U-scored behavior for the three periods shown above would stand in ratio 2 : 4 : 6, and this seems too strong a contrast. If we use the fractions, all three intervals will be given the same weight. This seems inappropriate also, since more behavior was scored in period 3 than in periods 1 and 2, and thus, presumably, the behavior during period 3 was considered more salient by the observers than the behavior during either of the other two periods. This argues that the U behavior in the third period should be rated higher on the time plot than the U behavior in the other two periods. We leave the resolution of this problem open by allowing the computer user to move between these two alternatives by setting a parameter equal to different values. For example, if we set the parameter equal to .3, the heights shown on thetime plots for the three periods will stand in ratio 1 : 1.23 : 1.39. In any case, the formula used to obtain the time plots has been the following property: If the number of messages scored is the same for each three-minute interval, the time plots produced by this program will appear the same for all values of the parameter.

The formula for producing the data for each three-minute interval, given for the Direction "U" alone, is:

$$(NU)^p (NU/NM)^{1-p} \qquad 0 \leqslant p \leqslant 1.$$

Exponent p is the parameter whose value is left up to the user. As can be seen from the formula, if p is set at 1.0, the raw score (NU) will be plotted. If p is set at 0.0, the ratio (NU/NM) will be plotted. A similar formula is used for the other directions.

In the time plots shown in Figure 69, the U and D time plots have the same scale, so that the tradeoff between behavior at the opposite poles of the U–D dimension can be portrayed. The other pairs of time plots also have this property.

Producing these Time Plots and the Field Diagrams described above can be a very time-consuming process if done by hand. A computer program has been written that accepts the messages directly from the SYMLOG Interaction Scoring sheets and produces not only the time plots but also the Field Diagrams for any session or episode within a session. Copies of this program are available from H. Swann, c/o Mathematics Department, San Jose State University, San Jose, California 95192.

Mathematical Formulation

In this section, we give a mathematical formulation of the first six properties listed in the previous section as desirable for transforming SYMLOG Interaction Scores during a session of interaction into summary scores for comparison with retrospective ratings. We show that the simple formula cited earlier satisfies these properties. More mathematical details, including the derivation of the more complicated formula are available from H. Swann at the address above.

For any session, we can aggregate the SYMLOG messages from all observers for the entire session to obtain the following:

p_i = number of acts by the "i^{th}" participant scored P
n_i = number of acts by the "i^{th}" participant scored N
P = total number of P-scored acts for the entire group
N = total number of N-scored acts for the entire group
m = number of participants

Our formula for transforming this aggregated data to Field Diagram plotting scores is abstractly represented by a function:

$$F(p_i, n_i, P, N, m) = \text{(Field Diagram score for ``}i^{th}\text{'' participant)}$$

We will convert the properties listed in the previous section into requirements that this formula F must satisfy. We will show that, if

$$F(p, n, P, N, m) = 5 \cdot \frac{m(p - n)}{P + N} + \frac{p - n}{p + n},$$

then F will satisfy these requirements.

Property 1. The formula should be insensitive to the number of scorers observing a session. If SYMLOG scorers all score a session identically, the formula should produce the same location for any particular individual no matter how many scorers' records are used.

Requirement for F: Scaling: For any positive integer k,

$$F(kp, kn, kP, kN, m) = F(p, n, P, N, m)$$

Verification that the formula satisfies this requirement:

$$5 \cdot \left(\frac{m(kp - kn)}{kP + kN} + \frac{kp - kn}{kp + kn} \right) = 5 \cdot \left(\frac{m(p - n)}{P + N} + \frac{p - n}{p + n} \right) \quad \text{(cancel ``k'')}$$

Property 2. (a) If, in the same session, two participants have the same number of messages scored N, but the first participant has more messages scored P than the second, then the first participant should be located closer to the P pole than the second.

(b) If, in the same session, two participants have the same number of messages scored P, but the first participant has more messages scored N than the second, then the first participant should be located closer to the N pole than the second. *Requirement for F:*

(a) If $p_i > p_2$, then $F(p_1, n, P, N, m) > F(p_2, n, P, N, m)$
(b) If $n_1 > n_2$, then $F(p, n_1, P, N, m) < F(p, n_2, P, N, m)$

Verification that the formula satisfies this requirement: We prove only (a). It suffices to show that the following is positive.

$$5 \cdot \left(\frac{m(p_1 - n)}{P + N} + \frac{p_1 - n}{p_1 + n} \right) - 5 \left(\frac{m(p_2 - n)}{P + N} + \frac{p_2 - n}{p_2 + n} \right) =$$

$$5 \cdot \left(\frac{m(p_1 - p_2)}{P + N} + \frac{2n \cdot (p_1 - p_2)}{(p_1 + n)(p_2 + n)} \right) > 0, \text{ since } p_1 - p_2 \text{ is positive.}$$

Property 3. Suppose, within the same session, three participants have the same proportion of scores on the positive side as compared to the negative side, but differ in total quantity of interaction, or participation, as in the following example:

	P	N
Bill	4	1
Sam	8	2
Chris	16	4

Then, because Sam has a higher quantity of interaction than Bill, with the same proportion of positive to negative behavior, and similarly Chris has a higher quantity than both, we assume that Sam should be assigned to a location between that of Bill and Chris on the P–N dimension.

Requirement for F: Radial monotonicity: Suppose, within the same session, three participants have the same proportional scores:

$p_1 = jp$
$p_2 = kp$
$p_3 = lp$
$n_1 = jn$
$n_2 = kn$
$n_3 = ln$

with $j < k < l$. Then the second participant should be located between the first and the third on the P–N dimension, i.e.,

$$F(jp, jn, P, N, m) < F(kp, kn, P, N, m) < F(lp, ln, P, N, m)$$
or $\quad F(jp, jn, P, N, m) > F(kp, kn, P, N, m) > F(lp, ln, P, N, m)$

Verification that the formula satisfies this requirement: First note that

$$5 \cdot \left(\frac{m(ip - in)}{P + N} + \frac{ip - in}{ip + in} \right) = 5 \cdot (p - n) \left(i \cdot \frac{m}{P + N} + \frac{1}{p + n} \right)$$

Thus, if $(p - n)$ is positive, the formula will increase as i increases, establishing the first set of three inequalities. If $(p - n)$ is negative, the formula will decrease as i increases, establishing the second set of inequalities.

Property 4. Suppose that, within the same session, two participants have the same proportional scores as in the example given for Property 3. We would expect that, if the participant with a lower quantity of interaction is given a positive location, then the other, with the higher quantity of participation, should also be assigned a positive location. Conversely, if the participant with lower quantity of participation is assigned a negative location, we would expect the higher participant (with SYMLOG scores in the same proportion) also to be given a negative location.

Requirement for F: If $k < l$, and $F(kp, kn, P, N, m) > 0$, then
$\qquad\qquad\qquad F(lp, ln, P, N, m) > 0$.
$\qquad\qquad$ If $k < l$, and $F(kp, kn, P, N, m) < 0$, then
$\qquad\qquad\qquad F(lp, ln, P, N, m) < 0$.

Verification that the formula satisfies this requirement: This follows easily from the properties of the formula described in the verification of Property 3.

Property 5. We conjecture that a retrospective rater will be sensitive to the tradeoff between quantity and quality of participation and will sense that the critical amount of behavior where the two components can be weighted equally in his rating will be at the level of the amount of participation of an "average individual" in the group (with scores $p = P/m$ and $n = N/m$).

The requirement for F is clumsy to state without proving some intermediate results concerning the form of F, and we omit it here.

Verification that the formula satisfies Property 5:

The quantitative component of our formula is
$5 \cdot [m(p - n)/P + N]$
and the qualitative component of the formula is
$5 \cdot [p - n/p + n]$.
Evaluating these both at $p = P/m$ and $n = N/m$, we see that they are equal:

$$5 \cdot \left(\frac{m(P/m - N/m)}{P + N} \right) = 5 \cdot \left(\frac{P - N}{P + N} \right);$$

$$5 \cdot \left(\frac{P/m - N/m}{P/m + N/m} \right) = 5 \cdot \left(\frac{P - N}{P + N} \right).$$

Property 6 is concerned with the scaling and choice of zero point. The formula is roughly scaled using an approximation to the results obtained using the empirical "harmonic" result cited in the previous section. Property 6 also postulated that the formula be zero when $p = n$. This is easily seen to be true.

Appendix T

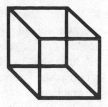

Investigating Individual Perceptual Biases of Group Members in Rating and of Observers in SYMLOG Interaction Scoring

Richard Polley

In the original version of Interaction Process Analysis (IPA), Bales (1950) proposed, for the purposes of training, a rather unorthodox means of monitoring interobserver reliability by using a Chi-square goodness of fit statistic as a descriptive index. The suggested procedure was confusing to most readers, because the statistical rationale behind Chi-square was not applicable in the case of interdependent categories. Consequently, most researchers using IPA and subsequent observational techniques simply calculated Pearson product-moment correlation coefficients between two observers over the N of the number of categories for a group member, a set of group members, or a set of meetings. The majority of the research reports present simply the mean and range across the various coder pairs of these correlations as the "interjudge reliabilities." It is unfortunate that Bales's early suggestion was ignored, as the logic behind it was sound. He observed that the correlation coefficient used in this way was generally very high and insensitive to important disagreements among coders; in essence, he was advocating descriptive reliabilities as an aid in examining inconsistencies in scoring.

Typically, IPA has been used to score behavior in very small groups. Coding is done by pairs of research assistants who have been trained together and taught to agree on the assessment of social behavior. In considering the variance among scores received by individuals in the group, there are really three factors involved: coder, subject (or group member), and category. Generally, in order to calculate the correlation coefficient for reliability, two rows of scores would be set up as shown in Figure 70. The reported r would be the value of the correlation between the two rows. One factor to which this measure is insensitive is the quantity of scoring done by the two coders. An r of 1.0 could be obtained even if coder 1 scored twice as much as coder 2. This is probably appropriate, though we might be interested in measuring this difference in quantity, as one scorer's observations will be weighted more heavily than the others', according to the size of the discrepancy.

Several factors could account for a high r using this method. First, r will be high if there is a great difference among subjects in the quantity of behavior scored. That is, if subject 1 receives twice as many scores as subject 2, r will be quite high. Similarly, if certain categories are used more often (for all subjects) than others, r will be high. This is invariably the case with the twelve categories of IPA. Some categories are regularly around 2 or 3 percent in rate, others are regularly around 20 or 30 percent. Of course, the correlation can be perfect only if the coders agree exactly on the distribution of scores among subject-by-category combinations. The point here is simply that it is very possible to obtain what appear to be very high reliabilities without really obtaining high interobserver agreement. What the researcher really wants to know is: How high is the reliability of the subject-by-category interaction across scorers? This question cannot be answered by calculating a single correlation coefficient; it requires some variant of a three-way analysis of variance.

When applied to IPA, all of this may seem a bit excessive. After all, if the reliability of the observations is actually much lower than we have estimated, then we are not likely to be able to support any of the interesting findings that we are looking for. That is, if the high reliability figures are due solely to main effects for subject and category, the only conclusions that we can draw from the results are of the forms: Subject 1 "acted more" than subject 2, or category 5 behavior (giving opinion) was more common for all subjects than category 1 behavior (showing solidarity). Clearly, these are not the compelling sorts of results that researchers in social psychology are looking for. The common types of results reported tend to be of the form: While subject 1 was unusually high in category 3 (agrees) and low in category 10 (disagrees), the reverse was true for subject 2. Without high subject-by-category reliabilities, the investigator very likely will have no significant differences in his means among subject-by-category cells and will not be able to make this sort of statement.

When we apply the same principles to SYMLOG interaction scores and to the retrospective rating system, our considerations take on an entirely new meaning. With SYMLOG, instead of having coders score every response on an arbitrary system and demanding high interjudge reliabilities as usual in observation methods (see Weick, 1968), Bales and Cohen emphasize the selection and coding of "salient acts" by a number of scorers. So far, SYMLOG has been used largely as heuristic feedback for the discussion of dynamics in particular self-analytic groups. The issue of reliability was shelved until Cohen's study (which

FIGURE 70   Tabulated Interaction Process Analysis (IPA) Record

Category	SUBJECT 1				SUBJECT 2				SUBJ . . .	
	1	2	3	4 . . . 12	1	2	3	4 . . . 12	1	2 . . .
Coder 1	5	6	13	7 . . . 2	3	2	15	4 . . . 4		
Coder 2	8	9	20	6 . . . 3	2	5	11	6 . . . 3		

appears as Part III of this book). From use in feedback, however, it seems clear that the global view of a session, as obtained from the SYMLOG Interaction Scores, has tremendous value for both the observers and the participants. Similarly, the group average field diagrams taken from the retrospective ratings seem to reflect quite accurately the chronic polarizations and alliances in the group.

In an attempt to tackle the issue of reliability in SYMLOG Interaction Scoring and the rating system, two computer programs have been devised. They are designed to provide as much information as possible about the ways in which multiple observers of a period of interaction agree and disagree on what they have seen. The plan for examining retrospective ratings will be considered first, because it is the simpler of the two.

The Retrospective Rating Method

Our plan calls for analyzing each of the three dimensions of the SYMLOG space separately. An individual's location on a given dimension is determined through the rating system by averaging his locations as seen by several raters. In obtaining this average score, several factors are of interest. The program accepts a symmetric matrix of interpersonal ratings. For our program, the rows represent group members and the columns represent raters. The matrix is symmetric when we are dealing with *participants'* ratings and each member of the group has rated himself (as he expects to be seen in the group) as well as each other member of the group. Although most of the analysis could apply even if the group were being rated by outside observers or by a small subset of the group, some of the most interesting findings will relate to this special case of a complete symmetric matrix.

Figure 71 is a typical computer print-out of the data for the SYMLOG Retrospective Rating system. This example is for the P–N dimension of a seventeen-member group in which all members rated each other, using the (0, 1, 2) scale. The names of the group members and the raters are omitted on this print-out.

The *grand mean* (A) is the average across all ratings given. In this case it indicates that the population was greatly skewed in the P direction. The average rating given was almost 7P. In a unified group this might indicate the approximate location of the consensus on acceptable behavior in the group setting.

The *member means* (B) are the average ratings received, that is, the raw plotting scores for the participants. In this case, everyone was, on balance, in the positive half of the space. Their locations varied from about 4P to about 10P.

FIGURE 71 Reliability Print-Out for Retrospective Ratings

A GRAND MEAN
   6.744

B MEMBER MEANS
   6.412   7.471   5.059   4.176   9.471   4.765   4.412 10.294   0.765

C RATER MEANS
   8.765   8.059   7.294   4.235   4.529   3.647   9.765   3.882   4.588

D MEMBER EFFECTS
   −0.332   0.727 −1.685 −2.567   2.727 −1.979 −2.332   3.550 −5.979

E RATER EFFECTS
   2.021   1.315   0.550 −2.509 −2.215 −3.097   3.021 −2.862 −2.156

F MEMBER BY RATER EFFECTS, ROWS=MEMBERS, COLUMNS=RATERS
   −4.433   1.273 −0.962   3.097 −1.197 −0.315   3.567 −5.550 −4.256
   −1.491   4.215   4.979   1.038 −1.256   2.626   1.509   2.391   3.685
    0.920   6.626   2.391 −0.550 −4.844   0.038 −1.080 −3.197   2.097
    3.803 −2.491 −1.727   5.332   4.038 −0.080 −3.197 −5.315 −4.021
   −2.491 −2.785 −1.021 −7.962   1.744   1.626   0.509   5.391   7.685
   −1.785   0.920 −1.315 −0.256   6.450 −0.668   4.215   4.097 −7.609
   −1.433 −0.727 −4.962   3.097   0.803 −0.315 −2.433   3.450 −6.256
   −4.315   0.391   4.156   1.215   3.920 −4.197   0.685   2.567   4.862
    7.215   0.920   1.685   1.744 −1.550   1.332   1.215 −4.903 −4.609
    1.038 −4.256 −2.491 −1.433 −0.727 −0.844 −1.962 −4.080 −1.785
    4.215 −0.080 −3.315   1.744 −1.550 −1.668   2.215 −6.903 −1.609
    0.567 −1.727 −6.962   2.097 −1.197   3.685 −0.433   1.450 −2.256
    0.920 −1.374   1.391 −0.550 −0.844   0.038 −2.080 −0.197   2.097
    0.803   0.509   0.273 −3.668 −4.962 −2.080 −0.197   0.685   1.979
   −0.609 −2.903   0.862 −2.080   6.626   3.509 −1.609   8.273   4.567
   −1.021   3.685   5.450 −1.491 −4.785 −0.903 −0.021   2.862   2.156
   −1.903 −2.197   1.567 −1.374 −0.668 −1.785 −0.903 −1.021   3.273

G   MMS   RMS   MRMS
     112.617233   90.315742   11.016109

H   MVAR   RVAR   MRVAR
      5.976537   4.664684   11.016109

   I   PERCENT VAR IN MEMBER MEANS DUE TO MEMBER
       90.21809

   J   PERCENT VAR IN IND MEMBER SCORE DUE TO MEMBER
       35.17131

   K   PERCENT VAR IN RATER MEAN DUE TO RATER
       87.80267

   L   PERCENT VAR IN IND RATER SCORE DUE TO RATER
       29.74776

FIGURE 71 (cont.)

B	6.941	5.765	7.412	6.059	6.176	9.588	10.000	9.882
C	5.412	6.765	10.765	5.824	6.647	5.529	8.765	10.176
D	0.197	−0.979	0.668	−0.685	−0.567	2.844	3.256	3.138
E	−1.332	0.021	4.021	−0.920	−0.097	−1.215	2.021	3.433
F	−4.080	0.567	0.567	−3.491	3.685	0.803	4.567	6.156
	−0.138	−2.491	−4.491	2.450	−7.374	−1.256	0.509	−4.903
	0.273	3.920	−2.080	−1.138	−3.962	−2.844	4.920	−1.491
	−2.844	3.803	4.803	0.744	6.920	−3.962	−3.197	−2.609
	0.862	−0.491	1.509	−0.550	−3.374	0.744	−1.491	0.097
	−2.433	3.215	−1.785	−5.844	6.332	1.450	−4.785	−0.197
	0.920	0.567	4.567	0.491	1.685	−0.197	1.567	0.156
	4.038	−5.315	−1.315	−4.374	2.803	−0.080	−6.315	1.273
	−2.433	−0.785	0.215	2.156	1.332	0.450	3.215	−7.197
	1.391	4.038	−1.962	7.979	−0.844	0.273	0.038	5.626
	4.567	−0.785	0.215	0.156	3.332	5.450	−2.785	−3.197
	−1.080	2.567	1.567	2.509	−2.315	−0.197	−1.433	3.156
	−0.727	−0.080	3.920	−0.138	−4.962	1.156	1.920	−0.491
	−2.844	0.803	−0.197	1.744	−1.080	4.038	0.803	3.391
	−1.256	−2.609	−2.609	−5.668	−2.491	−1.374	0.391	−1.021
	4.332	−6.021	−4.021	−0.080	0.097	−2.785	−0.021	2.567
	1.450	−0.903	1.097	4.038	0.215	−1.668	2.097	−1.315

The *rater means* (C) are average ratings given out and are thus measures of rater bias. Again in this case, everyone was rating almost everyone else as P, so all of the rater means are positive. They vary from about 4P to about 11P.

Member effects (D) are obtained by subtracting the grand mean from the member means, that is, from the average rating received by each individual. In some sense, the member effects can be thought of as relativized scores. In this group, a person who received 4P was almost 3N relative to the rest of the group, while a person who received 10P was only about 4P relative to the group average. These scores could be used for plotting instead of the member means in order to emphasize individual differences in a relatively homogeneous group.

Similarly, *rater effects* (E) relativize the average ratings given out by each rater and show us that the rater with an average given out of around 11P was biasing his perceptions strongly in the P direction, while the rater with an average given out of around 8P was actually very close in his perceptions to the group average. The relationships between subject and rater effects in a symmetric matrix can be used to test hypotheses about identification and projection. If we have a symmetric matrix, then we have information about each person both as a rater and as a group member. If the individuals' member effects are correlated highly with their rater effects, then we can make a strong argument for projection. In our example, the fourth person in the group has about the same member and rater effects (-2.6 and -2.5). We might want to suggest that he is projecting his own lack of friendliness onto the other group members. He is seen as less friendly and he sees other people as less friendly. Similarly, the last person in this group has a member effect of 3.1 and a rater effect of 3.4. He may be projecting his own friendliness onto others. Of course no inferences can be made as to cause and effect in this and similar cases. It could just as well be that people are seen as friendly because they see others as friendly as because they are friendly themselves. In any event, if this "projection effect" holds across an entire group or across particular types of individuals in several groups, it could provide some very interesting information on the nature of bias in person perception.

The *member by rater effects* (F) have generally not been dealt with in any systematic way but hold great potential interest. On a casual level, we can scan for large effects, which might point up important relationships. For example, the effect for the fourth rater rating the fifth member is -8. This means that, taking the grand mean and both main effects into account, the fourth person is rating the fifth person as unusually negative. We might want to see if this is a reflection of negative feelings between the two. Looking at the fifth person's rating of the fourth person, we see that the interaction effect is $+4$. So, if there are negative feelings, either they are not reciprocal or the fifth person is denying them. Similarly, the effects for the ratings exchanged between the eighth and the fifteenth persons indicate an unreciprocated positive feeling from the eighth person to the fifteenth person. This might turn out to be hero worship or identification with a strong leader.

We might also want to look for high interaction effects on the main diagonal. This diagonal represents self-ratings (members' ratings of themselves as they EXPECT to be rated by the other members of the group). High interaction effects here would indicate unrealistic expectations. For example, an individual in one of the self-analytic groups was rated as 14P by the group as a whole. He, however, remembering one particularly violent outburst on his part and unable to forgive himself for it, rated himself as 2N. Since he did not rate anyone else as particularly negative, this showed up as a huge interaction effect.

On a more formal level, network analysis can be applied to the member-by-rater interaction effects. With this particular matrix, a CONCOR (see Breiger, Boorman, and Arabie, 1975; White, Boorman, and Breiger, 1976) solution was tried. CONCOR is a hierarchical cluster analysis program that accepts a matrix and splits the population into two subgroups on the basis of similarities of relationships *within* and *between* the two groups. It can then be run on the two subgroups to further subdivide the population. In this case the routine was run only once. It reordered the group members in the matrix in such a way that the people who received high P scores were in one subgroup and the people who received low P scores were in the other. It should be remembered that there is nothing inherent in the form of the data that would automatically lead to this sort of split. Had we been running the program on the raw data, it would be obvious that the split would be based on the dimension for which the data were fed in. We were, however, dealing with *residuals,* which are assumed to be random, as we have already removed both main effects (subject and rater) and the grand mean.

When a single split is obtained, four *blocks* of residuals are formed. One represents the residuals for subgroup 1 member ratings of subgroup 1 members, one is for subgroup 1 member ratings of subgroup 2 members, and so forth. For our example, the average values in the reflexive blocks were positive while the average values in the other two blocks were negative. That is, the people in the high P part of the space rated themselves and their fellow high P members as even more P than would have been predicted from the subject means and the rater means, and at the same time, rated the low P members as even farther toward N than would have been predicted.

The other subgroup also appeared to have some internal solidarity. The low P members rated themselves and their fellow low P members as higher in P than normal and rated the high P members as lower in P than normal. The net effect of this is that high P members see greater individual difference in the friendliness of the group members, they see friendly people as *very* friendly and less friendly people as *much less* friendly. The low P members, on the other hand, tend to deemphasize individual difference on this dimension. They see themselves as quite friendly and the other subgroup as not so very much friendlier. While there have not been enough analyses of this sort to draw strong conclusions, this pattern has emerged for most of the groups analyzed and may be a general pattern in self-analytic groups. It may be the most characteristic form of the pattern of polarization and subgroup unification as we see it in self-analytic groups.

The same sort of analysis has been performed on the U–D dimension, with equally interesting preliminary results. The opposite pattern has emerged on this dimension. The more dominant members in the group tend to rate themselves and their fellow dominant members as lower in dominance than would be predicted while rating the less dominant people as more dominant than would be predicted. The less dominant people rate themselves and other less dominant members as even lower than would be expected while rating the dominant people as even more dominant. This would indicate that the low-dominance people are acutely aware of the status differential in the group, while the more dominant people tend to blur the distinctions. Work is under way to examine these complex patterns of interaction for all three dimensions.

MMS, RMS, and *MRMS* (G) are the mean squares for member, rater, and member-by-rater effects, respectively. They are provided so that F ratios (in an analysis of variance model) can easily be estimated. While significance of the F ratios cannot easily be ascertained because of problems of interdependence of measurements, it can be seen that, for example, the member main effect would have an F ratio of about 10 while the rater main effect would have an F ratio of about 8.

Measures of Variance (H) are also included for both main effects and for the interaction effect in order that types of analyses not included here can be performed on the data. For example, if we want to determine how the variance is partitioned among the effects, we can calculate ratios by dividing the effect variance by the total of the variance components. In this case, roughly 50 percent of the total variance is due to idiosyncratic variation (that is, particular raters' ratings of particular members), 30 percent is due to the member means (that is, differences among the people rated), and 20 percent is due to the rater means (that is, differences among raters).

Reliability. There are four separate reliability figures that are of interest here. (All of the formulas for reliability are adapted from Winer, 1971, ch. 4.) When we think of reliability we are usually asking: How well does the method allow us to discriminate among individual group members on the basis of ratings received? Our first two reliability estimates are attempts at an answer to this question. The other two represent the opposite approach. They are an attempt to determine the reliability with which we can estimate rater bias.

By *percent variance in an individual member score due to member* (J) we mean: How well can we estimate a member's "true" location if we have only one rater's ratings to go on? When we are considering the reliability of the rating he gives to an individual member on a dimension, we can ignore to some extent the elevation effects for the rater. That is, what is really important in this case is the member's location relative to the other members. We can consider a score to be quite reliable if all of the raters agree on the rank ordering of the members and also on the relative distances between the members. Given this perspective, the reliability of an individual score received by a member can be calculated as:

$$\text{Percent variance in an individual score received by a member due to member effect} = \frac{\text{Variance due to member effect}}{\left(\begin{array}{c} \text{Variance due to member effects } + \\ \text{Variance due to member-by-rater} \\ \text{interaction effect} \end{array} \right)}$$

We are considering as error only the idiosyncratic variation in ratings given by particular individual raters to particular individual members. In our example, this figure is about 35 percent. In other words, if we randomly selected a single rater and used only his ratings, about 35 percent of the variance among members would be due to actual differences among members while about 65 percent would be due to the rater's idiosyncratic evaluations. All of the figures suggested here have been calculated for each of the three dimensions on four complete sets of matrices of interpersonal ratings (group size ranged from sixteen to twenty-two members). The range for reliability of an individual score across these twelve matrices (three dimensions for each of the groups) was about 25 percent to about 70 percent.

As we add more and more raters, our confidence in a subject's average score received increases. Averaging across raters tends to cancel out idiosyncratic error and leave only the strong effects. Our formula for reliability of a subject mean (I) is as follows:

$$\text{Percent variance in a member's } \textit{mean score received} \text{ due to member} = \frac{\text{Variance due to member effect}}{\left(\begin{array}{c} \text{Variance due to member effect } + \\ \text{Variance due to member-by-rater} \\ \text{interaction}/n \end{array} \right)}$$

n = number of raters

In our example, about 90 percent of the variance in member means is due to consistent differences among members as opposed to idiosyncratic error. In the twelve cases mentioned above, this figure varied from about 84 percent to about 98 percent. Thus, the location of members on a Group Average Field Diagram for a group of fifteen members or so is quite well measured.

If our concern is for the reliability of measures of rater bias we can calculate analogous figures by substituting "variance due to rater effects" for "variance due to member effects" in the above two formulas. When we do this for our illustrative group, we find that 29 percent (L) of the variance in an individual rater's rating given out is due to the rater effect. That is, if we are trying to estimate rater bias by having a set of raters each rate the same single individual, then only 29 percent of the variance in the differences among the scores given by the various raters would be due to consistent differences among the raters. In the above twelve cases, this figure ranged from 7 percent to 30 percent.

Again, if we can average across several cases (K), we can obtain a better estimate of rater bias. An average score given out by a rater across fifteen or twenty members actually tends to be a quite reliable estimate of his or her rating bias. In the example, 87 percent of the variance in a rater average was due to a consistent rater bias effect. In the larger sample, from 40 percent to 90 percent of the variance in rater averages could be attributed to consistent rater bias effects.

SYMLOG Interaction Scoring

The issue of sources of variation and reliability becomes somewhat more complicated when dealing with SYMLOG Interaction Scoring. The plotting scores for an individual member's behavior cannot be obtained by averaging across the plotting scores assigned to him by several scorers. The formula for standardizing Interaction scores (given in Appendix S) requires the raw scores to be aggregated across scorers in order to obtain the individual's plotting score.

The program that has been devised for examining various aspects of perceptual bias and reliability in the SYMLOG Interaction Scoring data, like the plotting programs described in Appendix S, is designed to take the information directly from the recorded SYMLOG messages. Since this is the case, the first thing we shall want such a program to produce is a tally. Figure 72 is a typical print-out for reliabilities in SYMLOG Interaction Scoring. This particular case involved four coders and twelve group members and is for the *behavioral level* (that is, ACT + NON) on the P–N dimension. The *cell values* are displayed in columns representing coder (or rater), rows representing members, and in layers representing the two opposite directions of the dimension, here called "poles." So the underlined 19 means that rater 4 gave BRT a total of 19 "P" scores. This tabulation should be particularly useful to the coders in examining their biases. For example, it is clear that the fourth coder is paying an inordinate amount of attention to BRT and RFB. Further, he is giving them almost exclusively "P" scorings.

For the most part, the print-out through (O) should be self-explanatory after the discussion of the Retrospective Rating print-out. Essentially, every possible combination of means and effects has been calculated for examination. (F), for

FIGURE 72 Reliability Print-Out for SYMLOG Interaction Scoring

A   PN CELL VALUES, COLUMNS=CODERS, LAYERS=POLES

```
--------------------------------------------
    BIL    3    3    2    6
    BRT    6    1    6   19
    CAJ    3    0    2    2
    CAP    2    1    6    7
    JCK    1    0    2    5
    KAT    1    2    0    0
    KRS    0    2    1    3
    PTE    0    0    0    0
    RFB    2    3    7   13
    ROB    8    6   15   17
    UJI    0    0    0    0
    ZIT    3    3    2    7
--------------------------------------------
    BIL    0    1    0    0
    BRT    1    2    1    1
    CAJ    0    1    0    0
    CAP    0    0    0    0
    JCK    0    5    1    4
    KAT    0    0    0    0
    KRS    2    3    0    1
    PTE    0    0    0    0
    RFB    1    0    0    1
    ROB    0    0    0    0
    UJI    0    0    0    0
    ZIT    0    0    0    1
```

B   PN GRAND MEAN
       2.06250

C   PN MEMBER BY CODER MEANS, LAST COLUMN IS MEMBER MEANS

BIL	1.50000	2.00000	1.00000	3.00000	1.87500
BRT	3.50000	1.50000	3.50000	10.00000	4.62500
CAJ	1.50000	0.50000	1.00000	1.00000	1.00000
CAP	1.00000	0.50000	3.00000	3.50000	2.00000
JCK	0.50000	2.50000	1.50000	4.50000	2.25000
KAT	0.50000	1.00000	0.00000	0.00000	0.37500
KRS	1.00000	2.50000	0.50000	2.00000	1.50000
PTE	0.00000	0.00000	0.00000	0.00000	0.00000
RFB	1.50000	1.50000	3.50000	7.00000	3.37500
ROB	4.00000	3.00000	7.50000	8.50000	5.75000
UJI	0.00000	0.00000	0.00000	0.00000	0.00000
ZIT	1.50000	1.50000	1.00000	4.00000	2.00000

D   PN CODER MEANS
       1.375   1.375   1.875   3.625

E   PN POLE MEANS
       3.58333   0.54167

F
PN MEMBER BY POLE MEANS

BIL	3.50000	0.25000
BRT	8.00000	1.25000
CAJ	1.75000	0.25000
CAP	4.00000	0.00000
JCK	2.00000	2.50000
KAT	0.75000	0.00000
KRS	1.50000	1.50000
PTE	0.00000	0.00000
RFB	6.25000	0.50000
ROB	11.50000	0.00000
UJI	0.00000	0.00000
ZIT	3.75000	0.25000

G
PN CODER BY POLE MEANS

2.41667	1.75000	3.58333	6.58333
0.33333	1.00000	0.16667	0.66667

H
PN POLE EFFECTS

1.52083   −1.52083

I
PN MEMBER BY RATER EFFECTS, LAST COLUMN IS MEMBER EFFECTS

BIL	0.31250	0.81250	−0.68750	−0.43750	−0.18750
BRT	−0.43750	−2.43750	−0.93750	3.81250	2.56250
CAJ	1.18750	0.18750	0.18750	−1.56250	−1.06250
CAP	−0.31250	−0.81250	1.18750	−0.06250	−0.06250
JCK	−1.06250	0.93750	−0.56250	0.68750	0.18750
KAT	0.81250	1.31250	−0.18750	−1.93750	−1.68750
KRS	0.18750	1.68750	−0.81250	−1.06250	−0.56250
PTE	0.68750	0.68750	0.18750	−1.56250	−2.06250
RFB	−1.18750	−1.18750	0.31250	2.06250	1.31250
ROB	−1.06250	−2.06250	1.93750	1.18750	3.00750
UJI	0.68750	0.68750	0.18750	−1.56250	−2.06250
ZIT	0.18750	0.18750	−0.81250	0.43750	−0.06250

J
PN CODER EFFECTS

−0.687   −0.687   −0.187   1.562

K
PN MEMBER BY POLE EFFECTS

BIL	0.10417	−0.10417
BRT	1.85417	−1.85417
CAJ	−0.77083	0.77083
CAP	0.47917	−0.47917
JCK	−1.77083	1.77083
KAT	−1.14583	1.14583
KRS	−1.52083	1.52083
PTE	−1.52083	1.52083
RFB	1.35417	−1.35417
ROB	4.22917	−4.22917
UJI	−1.52083	1.52083
ZIT	0.22917	−0.22917

L
PN CODER BY POLE EFFECTS

−0.47917	−1.14583	0.18750	1.43750
0.47917	1.14583	−0.18750	−1.43750

FIGURE 72 (cont.)

M	PN MEMBER BY CODER BY POLE EFFECTS			
BIL	0.35417	0.52083	−0.81250	−0.06250
BRT	−0.39583	−2.72917	−1.06250	4.18750
CAJ	1.22917	−0.10417	0.06250	−1.18750
CAP	−0.52083	−0.35417	0.81250	0.06250
JCK	1.22917	−1.10417	0.56250	−0.68750
KAT	0.60417	1.77083	−0.56250	−1.81250
KRS	−0.52083	0.64583	0.31250	−0.43750
PTE	0.47917	1.14583	−0.18750	−1.43750
RFB	−1.89583	−0.22917	0.43750	1.68750
ROB	−1.27083	−1.60417	1.56250	1.31250
UJI	0.47917	1.14583	−0.18750	−1.43750
ZIT	0.22917	0.89583	−0.93750	−0.18750
BIL	−0.35417	−0.52083	0.81250	0.06250
BRT	0.39583	2.72917	1.06250	−4.18750
CAJ	−1.22917	0.10417	−0.06250	1.18750
CAP	0.52083	0.35417	−0.81250	−0.06250
JCK	−1.22917	1.10417	−0.56250	0.68750
KAT	−0.60417	−1.77083	0.56250	1.81250
KRS	0.52083	−0.64583	−0.31250	0.43750
PTE	−0.47917	−1.14583	0.18750	1.43750
RFB	1.89583	0.22917	−0.43750	−1.68750
ROB	1.27083	1.60417	−1.56250	−1.31250
UJI	−0.47917	−1.14583	0.18750	1.43750
ZIT	−0.22917	−0.89583	0.93750	0.18750

N	PN	MMS	CMS	PMS
		25.28409	27.37500	222.04167
	PN	MCMS	MPMS	CPMS
		4.13258	25.76894	29.15278
	PN	MCPMS		
		4.06187		

O	PN	MVAR	CVAR	PVAR
		2.64394	0.96843	3.56629
	PN	MCVAR	MPVAR	CPVAR
		2.06629	5.42677	2.09091
	PN	MCPVAR		
		4.06187		

P	PN	QUANT: PERC VAR IN MEMBER MEAN DUE TO MEMBER
		0.83655

Q	PN	QUANT: PERC VAR IN IND MEMBER SCORE DUE TO MEMBER
		0.56132

R	PN	QUANT: PERC VAR IN CODER MEAN DUE TO CODER
		0.84904

S	PN	QUANT: PERC VAR IND CODER SCORE DUE TO CODER 0.31912
T	PN	QUAL: PERC VAR IN MEMBER MEAN DUE TO MEMBER 0.84237
U	PN	QUAL: PERC VAR IND MEMBER SCORE DUE TO MEMBER 0.57192
V	PN	QUAL: PERC VAR IN CODER MEAN DUE TO CODER 0.86067
W	PN	QUAL: PERC VAR IND CODER SCORE DUE TO CODER 0.33983

example, is the list of *Member by Pole* means. The entries in the columns are averages across all coders. On the average, BIL received 3.5 P scores and .25 N scores.

The reliability figures parallel those for the retrospective rating system but are somewhat more complex. Essentially, for each type of reliability we need to know two things. First, is the quantity (number of scores produced by a coder, regardless of direction) reliable? Second, is the quality (the balance of P versus N regardless of number of scores received) reliable?

The first four figures, (P) through (S), are measures of quantitative reliability. The first two answer the question of whether or not the coders are paying attention to the same people while the second two answer the question of whether or not the coders are scoring vastly different amounts of interaction (across all members). (Q), in our example, indicates that 56 percent of the variance among members in total amount of interaction initiated is actually attributable to members' differences in quantity of interaction as recorded consistently by all coders. If we have only one coder, he will idiosyncratically spread his attention around among the participants in such a way that 44 percent of the variance in quantity attributed to the specific members will be error. (P) indicates that if we have four scorers, the figure improves significantly. The coders' lack of consistency in attention will average out, and 84 percent of the quantitative score will be due to differences among the amounts of participation for individual members.

Similarly, to the extent that (R) and (S) are high, then the coders are varying greatly in the amount of coding that they are doing (regardless of the member being coded). Again, if we are trying to estimate the *amount* of coding done by a scorer, we can do much better if we have him score a large number of people rather than just one person. (S) is 32 percent, and (R) is 85 percent.

The last four figures, (T) through (W), are much more closely analogous to the four reliability figures presented for the retrospective ratings. Essentially, the first two are answering the question: Regardless of the differential amount of attention that the coders are paying to the different members, how reliable are the ratios of P to $(P + N)$ and N to $(P + N)$? Specifically, this means: How much of the variance in the qualitative scores (ratios of P to $[P + N]$ and N to $[P + N]$) is due to consistent ratios for members across all coders and how much is due to the idiosyncratic ratios for particular coders scoring particular members? In the example, if we have only one coder's scores to go on, 57 percent of the variance in quality is due to differences among the members. If we can use the scores of all four coders, 84 percent of the variance in the resulting scores will be due to differences among members. Similarly, the last two scores are used as measures of the reliability of measures of rater bias. (W) shows that 34 percent of the variance in an individual score is due to a consistent rater bias, while (V) shows that 86 percent of the variance in the average given across all members is due to real differences among raters.

Separate programs exist for calculating all of these figures for the PRO images and for the CON images. In addition to the values printed out for the behavioral level, these programs tabulate *coder-by-level* frequencies. While they do not actually calculate any reliability figure for levels, they allow the rater to see if he is coding images on the same *levels* (SELF, OTHER, GROUP, SITUATION, SOCIETY, and FANTASY) as the other coders. Each of the three programs may be run either on an entire observed session or on any period of time within the session.

While these reliabilities so far have been calculated for only about twenty sessions of self-analytic groups, they have proved quite helpful. When a coder spots a low reliability, he has all of the information before him so that he can go back over the record and discover exactly where his biases are. There have been several cases where, over the whole observer team, reliability was quite high, but the tabulations showed that two of the coders completely disagreed on their assessments of a particular individual. This is particularly important information for discussion in the self-analytic group. It indicates that there are probably not great misunderstandings in the use of the system but rather real differences in the perceptions of particular people. It is hoped that this approach to reliabilities can serve two purposes simultaneously: to ensure that we are consistently recording what goes on in groups, and to highlight the individual differences in perception that are inherent in the social perception process, whether in the perceptions of group members or in the perceptions of "outside observers." The two are of equal interest to social psychologists.

Appendix U

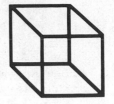

A Brief Catalogue of Computer Programs Available for Handling SYMLOG Data, as of November 1977

Richard Polley

The body of computer programs designed for users of SYMLOG is rapidly growing. It therefore seems desirable to provide a catalogue for potential users. While the list seems to have stabilized somewhat, there will no doubt be numerous changes and additions in the future. The catalogue will be updated as required. A current version of the listing may be obtained by writing Richard Polley, c/o R. F. Bales, William James Hall, Harvard University, Cambridge, Massachusetts 02138.

All of the programs have been designed for, and implemented on, a PDP 9 computer. They are written in Fortran IV and the maximum required core is 20K. For readers unfamiliar with this convention in specifying computer size, the standard packages used for statistical analysis in the social sciences (SPSS, for example) require a minimum core size of 270K. The programs are thus amenable to use on very small computers, which should be available at any university. If larger computers are available, the programs could easily be modified to handle a larger number of data files simultaneously, longer data files, or both. All of the input–output devices may be changed, of course, when implementing the program. At our facility, it has proved to be most convenient to control the programs and input data on a teletype, store it in files on DEC (Digital Equipment Corporation) tapes, and output the results of the programs on a line printer. As the programs stand, matrices are generally stored on and read from DEC Tape #6, and SYMLOG Interaction data is stored on and read from DEC Tape #7. The following is a listing of current programs with brief descriptions of their sizes, functions, and options.

I. FILDAT
   A. Core Required: 12K
   B. Program created by: H. Swann
   C. Most recent version: June 1977/H.S.
   D. FILDAT accepts SYMLOG Interaction Scoring data, line by line, from a teletype. Each line is checked for errors in syntax and person names and a hard copy is produced on the line printer. The program then asks the user if he/she wishes to edit the data or insert additional data. If so, the program recycles to the editor. If not, the data are transferred to DEC Tape #7 and given the file name previously specified by the user.
   E. Options: The program asks the user whether he/she wishes to enter a new person list. If so, it accepts up to thirty three-letter names and thirty two-letter names. The resulting list is stored on DEC Tape #7 as STPER SRC and will be used by the editor to check names as they are entered in the SYMLOG messages. If not, the program will use the file previously stored as STPER SRC for reference.

II. RATING
   A. Core required: 20K
   B. Created by: R. Polley
   C. Most recent version: November 1977/R.P.
   D. RATING accepts Interpersonal Ratings from a teletype. After all three matrices have been entered (one for each of the three SYMLOG dimensions) the program prints a hard copy of the matrices on the line printer and asks the user whether he/she wishes to edit. If so, the program recycles to an edit mode and asks for the location and new values for the desired changes. If not, the matrices are stored on DEC Tape #6 under the file name previously specified by the user.
   E. Options: none

III. TABULA
   A. Core required: 20K
   B. Created by: R. P.
   C. Most recent version: October 1977/R.P.
   D. TABULA reads and translates SYMLOG Interaction Scoring data from DEC Tape #7. It then tabulates "who-to-whom" matrices of (a) total number of acts, (b) U acts, (c) D acts, (d) P acts, (e) N acts, (f) F acts, (g) B acts. It sums rows and columns and prints a hard copy on the line printer.
   E. Options: The program asks the user whether he/she wishes to store the matrices on DEC Tape. If yes, it creates a file, as previously named by the user, on DEC Tape #6.

IV. MATAN
   A. Core required: 20K
   B. Created by: R.P.

C. Most recent version: November 1977/R.P.

D. MATAN is designed to analyze matrices. It will operate on either three matrices representing a set of retrospective ratings on the three SYMLOG dimensions, or seven "who-to-whom" matrices as provided by the TABULA program.

E. Options:

1. Reliability estimates: This program is for the interpersonal rating matrices only. It is an analysis of variance program which yields information on descriptive reliabilities and calculates the values of a variety of variance components and reliability estimates. It uses the EXPECT self-rating for the main diagonal.

2. Intraclass correlations: This routine works on either rating or scoring data and calculates a cell by cell correlation coefficient. When run on the interpersonal rating data, the purpose is to test for reciprocity in rating. If run on the Interaction Scoring data, the purpose is to test the hypothesis that individuals match their behavior to that of the other group member to whom they are speaking.

3. Round Robin ANOVA and Jackknife: This is a modification of a program developed by Becky Warner (Warner, 1978; Warner, Stoto, and Kenny, 1977) for the analysis of matrices which have missing main diagonals. It works on both types of data, always treating the main diagonal as missing. It yields mean square and variance component estimates for both of the main effects as well as for the interaction (or error) term. The jackknife part of the routine is designed to check for the possibility that a large variance estimate is due almost exclusively to one or two outlying members. It performs the ANOVA once for each group member, successively leaving people out. Thus, the fifth pass of the program calculates all of the estimates while treating the fifth row and column as missing data. Once "N" (number of persons) different estimates have been calcualted for each of the variance components, jackknife performs "t" tests to determine which of the estimates are significantly larger than zero.

V. BIAS

A. Core required: 20K

B. Created by: R.P.

C. Most recent version: October 1977/R.P.

D. The BIAS program calculates descriptive reliabilities for the ACT/NON (Behavioral) level of the SYMLOG Interaction scores. It is designed to serve two functions. First, it can be used as a tool in training observers. It thoroughly describes any differences in perception among up to ten observers. Second, it has proved to be a valuable aid in the feedback sessions of small groups. Once the observers have been adequately trained, any differences in perception can be attributed to real, psychologically significant differences in perception and can be as valuable to group members as actual descriptions of their behavior.

E. Options: none

VI. PBIAS

    A. Core required: 20K

    B. Created by: R.P.

    C. Most recent version: October 1977/R.P.

    D. PBIAS calculates the same information as BIAS, but for PRO images. In addition, it tabulates, for each scorer, the total number of images scored on each of the six levels (SELF, OTHER, GROUP, SITUATION, SOCIETY, and FANTASY).

VIII. CBIAS

    A. Core required: 20K

    B. Created by: R.P.

    C. Most recent version: October 1977/R.P.

    D. CBIAS calculates the same information as PBIAS, but for CON images.

VIII. TBIXBY

    A. Core required: 20K

    B. Created by: R.P.

    C. Most recent version: October 1977/R.P.

    D. TBIXBY was created for T. Bixby's senior honors thesis. It calculates correlations between Interpersonal Ratings and Interaction Scoring data, and also derives the regression equation for predicting scores from ratings. The Interaction Scoring data are taken from DEC Tape #7 and the Interpersonal Ratings are typed in on the teletype. After operating on the untransformed data, the program operates on ratings that have undergone one of the following transformations: (a) square, (b) square root, and (c) negative reciprocal. The primary purpose of the program is to demonstrate the close correlation between ratings and scorings and to calibrate further the formula we use to transform the raw act-by-act scores into locations on the field diagram.

    E. Options: The scoring location is based on a weighted average of ACT/ NON level and IMAGE level locations. The relative weightings for these two components can be varied. Within a single run of the program, several different weights may be used. The program can thus be used to search for the relative weightings that may best be used in determining a person's global location on the Field diagram.

IX. SIMGRP

    A. Core required: 20K

    B. Created by: H.S.

    C. Most recent version: October 1977/R.P.

    D. SIMGRP translates files of Interaction Scoring data from DEC Tape #7 into Field Diagrams.

    E. Options:

        1. AN produces a Field Diagram based on the addition of the ACT and NON level scores.

        2. EXAN produces an expanded AN diagram. It looks for the person who is closest to the edge of the field diagram and calculates a scaling constant such that the person will have the circle of his U–D dimension just touching the edge of the diagram. All scores on the P–N and F–B

dimensions are then multiplied by this constant. This prevents the diagram from being too constricted.

    3. IM produces a standard IMAGE level Field diagram. Each person is represented by two locations: one for his/her PRO image and one for his/her CON image.

    4. EXIM produces the expanded diagram for the IMAGE level.

    5. AIM plots each person's CON image and then takes a weighted average (weightings to be specified by the user) of the PRO image and behavioral level location and plots the resulting location as the global location of the person.

    6. VIM produces an image formation diagram. It is run cumulatively on small time periods within a given session. The result, which is made up of tracings from several such diagrams, allows the user to trace the changing location of PRO and CON images over time.

X. AGFD

  A. Core required: 20K

  B. Created by: R.P.

  C. Most recent version: October 1977/R.P.

  D. The AGFD program produces the AN, EXAN, IM, EXIM, and AIM diagrams from aggregated data as read in on the teletype. The user first reads in a list of names and then types in, in order, the U, D, P, N, F, and B totals scored for each of the group members on the ACT and NON levels and then on the PRO and CON image levels.

  E. Options: The user may specify the maximum width of the data he/she wishes to read in. Thus, if the user specifies a maximum width of 2, the program will ask her/him to type in the data under the following headings:

        UUDDPPNNFFBBUUDDPPNNFFBBUUDDPPNNFFBB

The first set of headings (U through B) is for the Behavioral level, the second is for the PRO image level, and the third is for the CON image level.

XI. TIMPLT

  A. Core required: 20K

  B. Created by: H.S.

  C. Most recent version: June 1977/H.S.

  D. TIMPLT plots collective behavior over time. It produces time plots for total number of scores, scores received on each of the six directions for Behavior, PRO image, and CON image. For the image levels, it also plots the average level (SELF, OTHER, etc.) for each segment. All time plots divide the session into three-minute subperiods.

  E. Options:

    1. The *Smoothing* option uses previous points to create a smooth plotting of trends. If this is not used, each point is based purely on behavior and images from the subperiod under consideration.

    2. An *Exponent* must be specified. The points are based on both raw frequency and frequency relative to the average frequency of the category. The exponent adjusts the relative weightings of these two components.

Appendix V

The Significant Relationships Form

Stephen P. Cohen

The Significant Relationships Form provides a detailed descriptive account of the pattern of relationships in the group under study from the perspective of the group members themselves. Each group member describes those relationships that he considers most important in his group experience, and also those he or she considers to have been most central in the group as a whole. The data can be treated in a quantitative way, with forms of analysis comparable to those available for any sociometric-like data, or it can be used in its raw descriptive form as a source of enriching information about the group under study.

On the one hand, the Relationships Form provides the user with concrete summary information in everyday language about the most important relationships and interaction networks as seen by the group members themselves. On the other hand, the Relationships Form can yield quantitative data for the construction of a sociometric matrix or a sociogram-like picture of the group structure. These may be used in conjunction with the more abstract SYMLOG analyses and the Field Diagrams. The structural representation derived from ratings and scoring can be compared to that derived from interpersonal choices of significant relationships. The descriptions provided by group members can help to flesh out the hypotheses of coalitions and subgroup formations that emerge in Field Diagrams.

The descriptions themselves can serve as valuable feedback on the common understandings in the group about the central events and relationships in the group experience. In particular, it is possible to see whether the central relationships indicate cooperation or conflict and whether they are indicative of an authoritarian or an equalitarian group pattern.

Since the data involve interpersonal preferences, they lend themselves to analyses appropriate to sociometric choice data. By choosing, for example, the first positive relationship mentioned by each member, a simple sociogram can be constructed.

Nonetheless, the Significant Relationships Form differs from the traditional form of sociometric questionnaire in a number of important ways:

1. The sociometric questionnaire almost always requires dyadic preferences. In the present Form, an individual member may see as the most significant relationship a triad or other close-knit clique rather than a particular single person. This is especially important in larger groups (such as youth groups, self-analytic groups, classrooms) where the locus of intense feeling and interaction may be a clique as well as an individual person.

2. The sociometric questionnaire defines for the group member the emotional relationship of interest to the researcher or at least the social situation that the researcher feels is most important to examine. Thus, the usual procedure would be to ask the group member to choose a person he likes, or would like to be with in a particular context that the questioner defines (e.g., working on a project, going on a trip). In the Significant Relationships Form, the questioner does not assume that he already knows what emotional area is most significant to the group he is studying or what social situation is most telling in terms of group structure. Instead, the Form allows the group member to define the most salient contexts of relationship and the most important feelings associated with those contexts and relationships.

A group member using the present Form may choose as the most significant of his or her relationships—for example, four hostile or conflictful relationships—and not include any that are positive and mutually satisfactory. In such a case, the liking relationships, if they exist at all, emerge as secondary in importance to the group member and should not be treated by the sociometric analyst as the determining factor in the "sociometric" location of that particular member. This member defines himself or herself not by positive preferences but rather by conflict.

In summary, the present Form treats the feeling and context associated with interpersonal preference as a variable rather than as part of the research instructions.

3. The common sociometric format treats interpersonal dyadic preference as the building block of social structure. However, individuals in groups may develop in addition to a sense of their own dyadic interaction pattern an image of the group structure as a whole. Members may see two or more persons as part of a clique and relate to them in a similar way, or they may see a particular member as having an essential group function even though they would not choose that person in a sociometric preference test. Such an image of group structure is especially important in complex groups where no member can hold in mind all the dyadic preferences that are relevant to the group interaction and where the existence of some simplified pattern of group structure is a necessity for behaving appropriately within the group. For example, having a conception of a certain set of people as having a similar status may be a simplification useful in predicting responses and appropriate targets for interaction.

If a person has both a picture of his own dyadic preferences (and even those may be not exclusively dyadic as indicated above) and a picture of group structure, it is important to elicit such pictures as another source of representation of group structure. The quasi-sociogram derived from these individual repre-

FIGURE 73   The SYMLOG Significant Relationships Form

Group: _____

Name: _____

Members of groups such as the one in which you are involved at present often feel that certain relationships in the group develop a special significance. These relationships may involve two, three, or more people; they may include the group leader or instructor. Some may include you.

PART ONE: Relationships Most Significant to You

You may share the results of this part of the Form with others in your group at your own discretion. The information you give here will *not* automatically be presented to the group as feedback. If the group agrees to feedback of this Part, only summary data may be given, rather than your specific preferences, unless so desired by the group.

a) Think of the relationships in the present group in which *your own feelings* have been most involved. Some of these relationships may have been developed in group interaction or related to group events, others may involve relations outside the group context, still others may exist in fantasy and/or dreams alone. Some may have involved cooperation, others conflict. Some may have aroused strong feelings of love or hate, admiration or contempt, fear or trust, shame or guilt, and some, great curiosity or intellectual interest. Some may have been mutual and some one-sided. Some relationships may have been known to the group. Others may have developed in your own imagination, and may still remain unrevealed even to the other members of the relationship.

b) Write a couple of sentences, not more, about each of the relationships listed, indicating the most salient characteristics. Specify the nature of the relationship (friendly, hostile, ambivalent) developed in the group and/or outside the group, and its importance to you (e.g. it was talked about in the group, it was referred to in private conversation, you wrote about it, the people in the relationship dominated group interaction, it aroused dreams, laughter, anger, etc.)

1.   Names: _____

     Comments: _____

     _____

     _____

continued

2. Names: _____

    Comments: _____

    _____

    _____

3. Names: _____

    Comments: _____

    _____

    _____

4. Names: _____

    Comments: _____

    _____

    _____

PART TWO: Relationships Most Significant to the Group

The group as a whole will receive a summary of this part of the Form in feedback.

a) For this part, think of the relatlonships most significant to the *group as a whole.* (These relationships may or may not include those you mentioned above.) Choose the four most significant and rank them in order of their *significance to the group as a whole.*

b) Write a couple of sentences about each of the relationships you have listed, with the guidelines mentioned above in mind, indicating the nature of the relationship and the evidence for its importance to the group as a whole. Remember that the relationship may be between two people or more and that it may involve a variety of feelings and forms of interaction. Remember to specify the nature of the relationship.

1. Names: _____

    Comments: _____

    _____

    _____

2. Names: _____

   Comments: _____

   _____

   _____

3. Names: _____

   Comments: _____

   _____

   _____

4. Names: _____

   Comments: _____

   _____

   _____

sentations of group structure can be compared with the standard sociogram results and with the results of the Field Diagram emerging from SYMLOG Ratings or Interaction Scoring.

Research (Cohen, 1972) has indicated that this second method of treating sociometric results can produce important corrections in the image of group structure. For example, some group members are important to the group as a whole and yet do not appear in any particular person's list of individual preferences. In the usual sociogram, they would emerge as isolates. In the sociogram constructed from relationships significant to the group as a whole, such persons are shown to have an important role either as deviants or as linking persons in group attempts at unification. For example, the deviant who is seen to be a primary object of group concern and attention in Part Two of the Significant Relationships Form is quite a different kind of isolate from the one who is ignored in both Parts of the Form and who is the silent, uninvolved, and uninvolving member.

A detailed exposition of the Interpersonal Relationships Form, its design, and its uses in research is beyond the scope of this appendix and will be presented elsewhere. The Form itself, Figure 73, is presented as a most useful qualitative (and quantifiable) companion to the Ratings and to the SYMLOG Interaction Scoring.

Appendix W

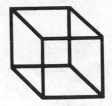

The SYMLOG Value Statement Rating Form

Figure 74 shows a form that may be used for the rating of value statements in a manner parallel to the rating of ACT level behavior using the adjective rating form shown in Appendix C. In some situations of application it may be easier or more appropriate to center a group self-study around value statements (and value positions) of the participants than around ACT level interpersonal behavior. In other situations, both kinds of ratings may be used.

Of course, we do not suppose that ratings of the two different levels will give identical results. Nevertheless, the two levels are cognate in the sense that a value statement that may be identified with a given vector often seems to give a more generalized evaluative rationale for the more specific forms of ACT level behavior identified with that vector. Perhaps it is the case that a value statement is often a generalized extension, to a larger class of images, of an evaluation that was originally placed on the more specific ACT level form of behavior. The relationships between the value statement level and ACT level behavior as determinants of the perceptions that others have of the actor are of great interest but as yet are almost unexplored.

The Value Statement Rating Form has been used only in a few case studies in exploratory form. It has been revised a few times, but as yet there have been no factor analytic studies on these particular short-form items that could help in their correction and refinement. However, the sources of the conceptions embodied in the items are the factor analytic studies of value statement items in complete sentence form administered with a Likert answer format, as reported in Bales's 1970 book, *Personality and Interpersonal Behavior*. These factor studies were done with Arthur S. Couch and were a major source of the three-dimensional spatial formulation first given full articulation in the book mentioned and, since then, further consolidated and extended in the SYMLOG System.

FIGURE 74 The SYMLOG Value Statement Rating Form

Your Name_____Group _____

Name of person described _____Circle the best choice for each item:

What kinds of values does the person seem to favor?   (0)   (1)   (2)   (3)   (4)

1 U . . . . material success and power . . . . never . . rarely . . sometimes . . often . . always

2 UP . . . popularity and social success . . . . never . . rarely . . sometimes . . often . . always

3 UPF . . social solidarity and progress . . . . never . . rarely . . sometimes . . often . . always

4 UF . . . efficiency, strong effective management . . . never . . rarely . . sometimes . . often . . always

5 UNF . . a powerful authority, law and order . . . . . . never . . rarely . . sometimes . . often . . always

6 UN . . . tough-minded assertiveness. . . . . never . . rarely . . sometimes . . often . . always

7 UNB . . rugged individualism, self-gratification . . . . never . . rarely . . sometimes . . often . . always

8 UB . . . having a good time, self-expression . . . . . . never . . rarely . . sometimes . . often . . always

9 UPB . . making others feel happy. . . . . never . . rarely . . sometimes . . often . . always

10 P . . . . equalitarianism, democratic participation . . . never . . rarely . . sometimes . . often . . always

11 PF. . . . altruism, idealism, cooperation . . . . never . . rarely . . sometimes . . often . . always

12 F . . . . established social beliefs and values. . . . . . never . . rarely . . sometimes . . often . . always

13 NF . . . value-determined restraint of desires . . . . . never . . rarely . . sometimes . . often . . always

14 N . . . . individual dissent, self-sufficiency . . . . never . . rarely . . sometimes . . often . . always

15 NB . . . social nonconformity. . . . . never . . rarely . . sometimes . . often . . always

16 B . . . . unconventional beliefs and values . . . . never . . rarely . . sometimes . . often . . always

17 PB . . . friendship, liberalism, sharing . . . . never . . rarely . . sometimes . . often . . always

18 DP . . . trust in the goodness of others . . . . never . . rarely . . sometimes . . often . . always

19 DPF. . . love, faithfulness, loyalty . . . . never . . rarely . . sometimes . . often . . always

20 DF . . . hard work, self-knowledge, subjectivity . . . never . . rarely . . sometimes . . often . . always

21 DNF . . suffering . . . . never . . rarely . . sometimes . . often . . always

22 DN . . . rejection of popularity . . . . never . . rarely . . sometimes . . often . . always

23 DNB . . admission of failure, withdrawal . . . . never . . rarely . . sometimes . . often . . always

24 DB . . . noncooperation with authority . . . . never . . rarely . . sometimes . . often . . always

25 DPB. . . quiet contentment, taking it easy. . . . . never . . rarely . . sometimes . . often . . always

26 D . . . . giving up all selfish desires . . . . never . . rarely . . sometimes . . often . . always

Appendix X

Sample Syllabus of a Group Psychology Course Designed around SYMLOG Observation and Feedback

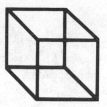

Syllabus
Psychology and Social Relations 1330r, *Group Psychology*
Professor Robert F. Bales
Half-course (fall term; repeated spring term). MWF 1–3:00 p.m.

Studies everyday interaction of individuals in groups. Introduction to practical problems of participation, leadership, teaching, and therapy. Each student becomes a participant in a self-analytic study group. In certain sessions he or she observes the group, and receives instruction in observation, interpretation of motivation, conceptualization of individual personalities, and group dynamics.

Application for Admission

If you wish to apply for the course, please make out an application after completing the reading of this Syllabus. Leave the application with the instructor and come to the next meeting.

In applying, remember that a meeting in this course requires two hours, and that we meet three times per week. Attendance at each meeting is important. You should not apply for the course during a term in which you anticipate the need for absences.

The course must be limited to one section, that is, one group, of about twenty members, due to its special nature.

Reading

The course is an introduction through actual experience to research and training in the areas of personality, interpersonal behavior, and the psychological understanding of groups for various kinds of task performance, education, therapy, behavior, and attitude change. It is relevant to practical work with many kinds of groups. Students are expected to build up their background by reading in the areas that particularly interest them. Relevant items in the literature of social psychology and related fields are offered in the reading.

The books in the Bibliography at the end of this Syllabus will be on reserve at the library. The books marked with an asterisk in front of the author's name have been put on the list sent to the university bookstore. Some of these, at least, will be available there for purchase if the student so desires.

Bales' book, *Personality and Interpersonal Behavior,* is required reading, although you are not required to purchase it. This book should be read early in the course, particularly the chapter on Group Fantasies, since the analysis of group fantasies plays an important part in the self-analytic efforts of the group. Slater's book is helpful with illustrative material, and is an exciting introduction. Both of these books are based on earlier groups of this same course, which goes back many years. The methods used in the present course are the product of research with earlier groups in the course. As a member of the course, you will help in developing still better methods.

Manuals and Materials, Required Participation in Research

Although the course is humanistic and broadly educational in its orientation, and provides a great many personal satisfactions for members in their participation with others, it is also a laboratory and field methods research course, devoted to the learning of practical methods that may be applied in other real groups of which the student may be a member. A sophisticated method of observation is taught, observations are made of the self-analytic sessions of the group, and reports of observation are prepared for feedback to the group members observed. The student is expected to put some of the methods learned to use in the case study of an outside group.

Various methods of studying behavior, personality, and group processes are explored in the group, and studies of these methods are usually in progress by students who have taken the course previously. The methods are evaluated and improved by actual use in the group, and by application in the study of natural groups on the outside. Students in the course are expected, at the ends of self-analytic sessions, to participate in current methodological studies which may result in honors theses or research papers by students who are repeating the course for research purposes. The two-hour meetings three times per week include the time necessary for participation in such current studies as well as the time necessary for training in observation and preparation of feedback reports.

An observation manual and a kit of materials are required for purchase. The manual is being prepared for publication, but is presently available only in multilith, and is not on library reserve. The kit of materials is used for the case study of an outside group. The manual is: *SYMLOG, A System for the Multiple Level Observation of Groups,* by Robert F. Bales and Stephen P. Cohen. The kit of materials is called *The SYMLOG Case Study Kit.* The manual and the kit are available from the secretary of the course, Room 1304, and should be purchased when you apply for the course. *The Observation Manual* should be read immediately, as the first team of observers from the group will begin observation at the beginning of the second week of the course. An additional manual, not required for purchase, called the *Case Study Manual* is available for reading on the premises, from the course secretary. This manual should be read during the second week of the course, since the theories, diagrams, and analytic methods described there are used for the feedback of observations to the group at the end of the week.

Organization of the Sessions

There is a typical pattern of organization of the sessions which repeats from week to week, with minor exceptions for holidays. On Monday and Wednesday of a typical week, the group will meet in "self-analytic sessions" as explained below. A small team of five or six observers drawn from the regular membership of the group for that given week will observe the Monday and Wednesday self-analytic sessions of the group, from the group observation room. They will take written observations in the systematic format of the SYMLOG scoring procedure. A teaching fellow attached to the course will head the observation team, and will help the members learn the observation system and prepare the "Feedback Report."

For the meeting on Friday of the given week, the observation team will prepare a report of their observations, along with interpretations, which they will present to the group. This is called a "feedback session."

The following week the pattern repeats, with a new observation team. The observation teams are made up by a rotating selection of regular group members. If the total group is of twenty members, the observation teams will be of five members each, and each student will observe and report three times in the course of the term. The regular size of the participating group during the self-analytic sessions will thus be about fifteen.

Procedure in the Self-Analytic Sessions

The "self-analytic" sessions are so called for two reasons, first because each individual is concerned with the analysis of his or her self-picture as it develops in the group, and second, because the group as a whole takes as its primary task the exploration and analysis of the interaction of the members, and the development of their relationships with each other.

In a typical self-analytic session, after any general announcements or arrangements are made, the instructor will considerably reduce his participation for the main period of the session, during which the responsibility for the interaction, its content, and the analysis of it, is left mainly to the group members. On occasion, however, the instructor may make an interpretation, or ask specific members to do so, particularly if they have not participated up to that point. Relatively equal participation by all members is the preferred pattern.

Topics for discussion grow out of spontaneous contributions, interests, concerns, experiences, or observations presented by members. There is no formal agenda or outline of topics. The content may deal with matters either inside or outside the session. The discussion may be general, or it may pertain to specific individuals or relationships, as members prefer. The group often proceeds by a free discussion similar to what is called "free association" in psychoanalysis, and also similar to what is commonly called a "bull session." Experience with many groups in the past makes it evident that apparently aimless social conversation among group members is not really aimless so far as individual motivations are concerned, and provides excellent material for analysis. The conversation may be casual, serious, humorous, or anecdotal, and may switch or change at will, with the aim of letting the situation or mood develop spontaneously until the optimum time for analysis. Any kind of material, behavior or content, so produced is likely to be useful, *provided it is actually later subjected to analysis*. The purpose of the "aimless freedom" is to provide material for analysis.

The group tries to swing back and forth effectively between spontaneous expression and analysis. This swing typically takes place over the period of the single session, or perhaps several times, as the group gains skill in self-analysis. The ideal is to balance and intermingle, so far as possible, the processes of spontaneous expression and rational analysis. The willingness and ability of members to engage in more or less self-revealing play, and subsequently in the analytic work, depends on the development of trust among group members, and a shared commitment to the group work of analysis. The development of trust and commitment takes time, and is not artificially hurried, but cultivated with patience and good will.

The self-analytic procedure of the course is thus marked by an interest in natural social interaction, reliance upon natural observation, voluntary verbal disclosure of fantasies and feelings, and periodic analysis. There is no high pressure of any kind, and no requirement or desire on the part of the instructor that you disclose more than you wish, or interact in any way you do not wish. The normal privacy of each individual is respected by all members of the group. On the other hand, there is no wish to discourage the discussion of any topic, or to inhibit the development of whatever degree of emotional intensity individual members may feel is appropriate for them, and for the goals of the course.

The self-analytic session is expected to run from 1 to 2:30 of the given day, and time is left at the end for current research studies.

Procedure in the Observation Team

During the observation the members of the observer group are seated in the observation room, and each keeps an individual written record of the behavior of individuals and events of group interaction in the self-analytic session. A systematic method of observation is used: SYMLOG. The manual describing the method is available in multilith, and should be obtained as soon as possible in preparation for the observation. The manual should be read carefully and repeatedly and kept at hand for reference.

It is important to keep a quiet and non-distracting atmosphere in the observation room during the actual observation. Each observer should work independently. The observers should not communicate with each other more than necessary while observing and should not display their reactions or attitudes to each other in non-verbal behavior. They should compare notes on problems of scoring afterwards, and during the preparation of their feedback report.

The observers prepare a team report in several parts, given during the Friday feedback session of the team. Detailed instructions and suggestions for this will be available. The report usually deals with *one* of the two sessions, the Wednesday session or a part of it, in some detail. Team work on a given session is done in the period following the regular sessions (2:30–3:00, Monday and Wednesday), and further as necessary and arranged by the team members. Often the labor is divided in some way by the team members, who may do part of the work of preparation individually.

Procedure in the Feedback Session

The group in its feedback session operates primarily as an academic seminar, led by various members of the observation team, who give their prepared reports briefly, and conduct discussion growing out of the report. References to the reading and discussion of more technical academic and applied problems are particularly appropriate in the feedback sessions.

After the feedback report on Friday, all data sheets, diagrams, etc., are given to the teaching fellow for the course who puts them in the LOG book, which will be kept in the Workshop, Room 1322. The LOG may be read at any time during regular hours during the work week. Each student should attempt to improve his or her observations by comparing them with those of other observers, both in discussion during the subsequent hour, and by careful study of the LOG book. The audio tapes regularly taken are also very useful for this study.

Interpersonal Ratings

Group members are asked to make descriptions of each others' behavior called SYMLOG Ratings according to the method described in the SYMLOG manual. The first ratings are made about a third of the way through the series of meetings, and constitute a kind of baseline description. The second ratings are made close to the end of the term, and may be used to note stability or changes in the way one's behavior is perceived over the course of the group. The rating material is summarized and returned as feedback to the group.

Significant Relationships Questionnaire

Near the end of the term each group member is asked to fill out a short questionnaire which asks for a few comments on the particular relationships in the group which have been most significant, or meaningful, to him or her, or to the group as a whole. Feedback on these comments will be returned to the group during the final three evaluation meetings.

Term Paper

A term paper is required for the course. The paper will ordinarily consist of a case study of an outside group, and will constitute an exercise in the application of what you have learned to a new group. The outside group should be on in which you have had extensive participation, such as a friendship group, your family, a group of roommates or entrymates, an academic course section or discussion group, a group in which you work on an outside job, an athletic team or recreational group, a group in which you function as a leader, teacher, advisor, helper, or the like. The case study of the outside group will depend primarily upon your own ratings based upon memory, but may be supplemented in other ways.

The *Case Study Manual* is specifically designed as an aid in making your study. It contains many suggestions, both practical and theoretical. The *Observation Manual,* the background book, *Personality and Interpersonal Behavior,* and other material in the readings, may also be helpful.

A case study based on literary materials, or on published observations of a sociological or anthropological character is not ruled out, although a real outside group known to you through your own experience is preferable. It is also possible to base the case study upon your self-analytic group if there are special problems in finding a suitable outside group, or if you wish to study some particular characteristic of the group that has not been already extensively treated in group discussion.

A statement of your plan for the case study is due by the eighteenth class meeting. Preparing this preliminary plan will give you a special occasion for reading the *Case Study Manual* more carefully, and considering any special problems there may be in the study you want to make.

The Basic Agreement

It is important that participation, observation, and feedback in the course group be conducted in a way that provides psychological comfort and security for each member. Everybody who becomes a part of the course enters into the following basic agreement:

> "We agree to treat each other with consideration, and not to transmit any identifiable personal information about any member to anybody outside the

course. We agree that each member has the right to control whatever information he or she may provide about the self."

Most members probably feel some mild anxiety occasionally, in participating, or observing, or making, or receiving feedback reports, but in the experience of the instructor, there has almost never been any real problem. However, you may meet with the instructor at any time if you do feel a problem, and other ways can be found for meeting the requirements of the course, if you wish.

Final Examination

There is a regular three-hour written examination in the course. Both graduates and undergraduates enrolled in the course take the examination. (Note: graduate students from professional schools of the University should check to make sure there are no schedule conflicts.) Questions on the examination will require a detailed knowledge of the two Manuals, and of Bales' book, *Personality and Interpersonal Behavior*. One question will require a substantial essay on a portion of the reading of the Bibliography, of the student's own choice, and this essay should be thought about ahead of time. In addition, one question will require some analysis of the data of a hypothetical case.

The final examination will count for approximately one-third of the final grade. The case study paper will count approximately one-third. The remaining third will be based upon the quality of your SYMLOG observations during the course, your feedback reports, and the quality of your contributions to the analyses made during the self-analytic sessions.

Bibliography

Argyle, Michael. *Social interaction.* Chicago: Aldine Publishing Company, 1969.

Argyle, Michael. *Social encounters: readings in social interaction.* Chicago: Aldine Publishing Company, 1973.

* Bales, Robert F. *Personality and interpersonal behavior.* New York: Holt, Rinehart and Winston, Inc., 1970.

* Freud, Sigmund. *On dreams.* (J. Strachey, trans.). New York: W. W. Norton & Co., 1952.

*Gibbard, Graham S., Hartman, John J., and Mann, Richard D. (Eds.). *Analysis of groups.* San Francisco: Jossey-Bass Publishers, 1974.

Hare, A. Paul, Borgatta, Edgar F., and Bales, Robert F. *Small groups, studies in social interaction.* New York: Alfred A. Knopf, 1965.

Homans, George C. *The human group.* New York: Harcourt, Brace, and Company, 1950.

Mann, Richard D., et al. *The college classroom: conflict, change, and learning.* New York: John Wiley & Sons, Inc., 1970.

McLeish, John, Matheson, Wayne, and Park, James. *The psychology of the learning group.* London: Hutchinson & Co., 1973.

Mehrabian, Albert. *Nonverbal communication*. Chicago: Aldine, Atherton, Inc., 1972.

Riley, Matilda White & Nelson, Edward E. *Sociological observation, a strategy for new social knowledge*. New York: Basic Books, Inc., 1974.

Shaw, Marvin E. *Group dynamics: the psychology of small group behavior*. New York: McGraw Hill, 1976. (2nd Ed.)

Slater, Philip E. *Microcosm, structural, psychological and religious evolution in groups*. New York: John Wiley & Sons, Inc., 1966.

Swenson, Clifford H., Jr. *Introduction to interpersonal relations*. Glenview, Ill.: Foresman and Company, 1973.

* Yalom, Irvin D. *The theory and practice of group psychotherapy*. Second Edition. New York: Basic Books, Inc., 1975.

Course Schedule

FIRST MEETING	Introductory meeting. Review of the Syllabus. Applications received. Those who apply should obtain the observation manual and the case study kit. The observation manual should be read and studied immediately.
SECOND MEETING	Group will meet as a whole. Preliminary list of group members will be available. Discussion of observation manual. Members will decide on their name abbreviations for use in observation and feedback.
THIRD MEETING	Group will meet as a whole. Preliminary list of observer teams will be available.
FOURTH MEETING	First regular self-analytic session, observed by first observer team. Reading of the observation manual should be completed prior to this meeting. Reading of the case study manual should begin immediately.
FIFTH MEETING	Short Quiz on the observation manual. First feedback session with reports by first observer team to group as a whole.
EIGHTH MEETING	Short Quiz on the case study manual. Second feedback session with reports by second observer team to group as a whole. Reading and study of *Personality and Interpersonal Behavior* should begin immediately.
ELEVENTH MEETING	Short Quiz on *Personality and Interpersonal Behavior*, followed by regular feedback session.
FOURTEENTH MEETING	Forms for Interpersonal Ratings to be passed out.
FIFTEENTH MEETING	First *Interpersonal Ratings* due. Begin reading in the *Bibliography*. Begin planning for *Case Study*.
EIGHTEENTH MEETING	Statement of plan for *Case Study* due. Review Case Study Manual.
TWENTY-FIRST MEETING	Case Study should begin.
TWENTY-NINTH MEETING	Forms for second Interpersonal Ratings will be passed out. Reading in *Bibliography* should be completed, with topic for examination essay of one hour decided upon.

THIRTIETH MEETING	Second *Interpersonal Ratings* due. Forms for Significant Relationships will be passed out.
THIRTY-FIRST MEETING	*Significant Relationships* Questionnaire due.
THIRTY-THIRD MEETING	Observation discontinued. Series of three final evaluation and feedback meetings of the group as a whole begins.
THIRTY-FIFTH MEETING	Last meeting of course, *Case Study* due. Final Examination. Examination at the time specified by the Registrar.

Bibliography and References

Abelson, R. P., E. Aronson, W. J. McGuire, T. M. Newcomb, M. J. Rosenberg, and P. H. Tannenbaum, eds. (1968). *Theories of Cognitive Consistency: A Sourcebook.* Chicago: Rand McNally.

Adorno, T. W., E. Frenkel-Brunswik, D. J. Levinson, and R. N. Sanford (1950). *The Authoritarian Personality.* New York: Harper.

Allport, Floyd H. (1924). Social stimulation in the group and in the crowd. In Floyd H. Allport, *Social Psychology.* Boston: Houghton-Mifflin.

Allport, Gordon W. (1955). *Becoming.* New Haven: Yale University Press.

Allport, Gordon W., and Leo J. Postman (1947). *The Psychology of Rumor.* New York: Henry Holt.

Argyle, Michael (1969). *Social Interaction.* Chicago: Aldine.

Argyle, Michael (1973). *Social Encounters: Readings in Social Interaction.* Chicago: Aldine.

Bales, Robert F. (1950). *Interaction Process Analysis.* Chicago: University of Chicago Press, 1976.

Bales, Robert F. (1956). Task status and likeability as a function of talking and listening in decision-making groups. In Leonard D. White, *The State of the Social Sciences.* Chicago: University of Chicago Press, pp. 148–161.

Bales, Robert F. (1958). Task roles and social roles in problem-solving groups. In Eleanor E. Maccoby, Theodore M. Newcomb, and Eugene L. Hartley (eds.), *Readings in Social Psychology.* New York: Holt, Rinehart & Winston, pp. 437–447.

Bales, Robert F. (1970). *Personality and Interpersonal Behavior.* New York: Holt, Rinehart & Winston.

Bales, Robert F., and Fred L. Strodtbeck (1951). Phases in group problem solving. *Journal of Abnormal and Social Psychology* 46: 485–495.

Bales, Robert F., Fred L. Strodtbeck, Theodore M. Mills, and Mary E. Roseborough (1951). Channels of communication in small groups. *American Sociological Reivew* 16, no. 4: 461–468.

Bandura, Albert, and R. H. Walters (1963). *Social Learning and Personality Development.* New York: Holt, Rinehart & Winston.

Bennis, W. G., and H. A. Shepard (1956). A theory of group development. *Human Relations* 9: 415–437.

Berger, Peter L., and Thomas Luckmann (1966). *The Social Construction of Reality: A Treatise in the Sociology of Knowledge*. New York: Doubleday.

Bixby, Thomas David (1978). Action and Speech Content: Perception in Small Group Interaction. Honors thesis, Department of Psychology and Social Relations, Harvard University.

Blau, Peter M. (1964). *Exchange and Power in Social Life*. New York: Wiley.

Blau, Peter M. (1968). Social exchange. In D. L. Sills (ed.), *International Encyclopedia of the Social Sciences*. New York: Macmillan, Free Press, 7: 452–458.

Blumer, Herbert (1969). *Symbolic Interactionism: Perspective and Method*. Englewood Cliffs, N.J.: Prentice-Hall.

Borgatta, Edgar F., and Robert F. Bales (1953). Interaction of individuals in reconstituted groups. *Sociometry* (November), pp. 302–320.

Bowen, Murray (1971). Family therapy and family group therapy. In Harold Kaplan and Benjamin Sadock (eds.), *Comprehensive Group Psychiatry*. Baltimore: Williams & Wilkins.

Breiger, R. L., S. A. Boorman, and P. Arabie (1975). An algorithm for clustering relational data with applications to social network analysis and comparison with multidimensional scaling. *Journal of Mathematical Psychology 12:* 328–383.

Breiger, Ronald L., and James G. Ennis (1978). *Persona* and Social Role: The Network Structure of Personality Types in Small Groups. Unpublished paper, Department of Sociology, Harvard University.

Burrows, Phyllis (1978). Early Recollections as an Indicator of Transference in a Self-Analytic Group. Unpublished paper, Department of Psychology and Social Relations, Harvard University.

Campbell, D. T. (1958). Common fate, similarity, and other indices of aggregates of persons as social entities. *Behavioral Science* 3: 14–25.

Cartwright, Dorwin (1959). A field theoretical conception of power. In Dorwin Cartwright (ed.), *Studies in Social Power*, Ann Arbor, Mich.: Institute for Social Research, pp. 183–220.

Cartwright, Dorwin, and Alvin Zander (1968). *Group Dynamics, Research and Theory*, 3rd ed. New York: Harper & Row.

Cohen, Stephen P. (1972). Varieties of Interpersonal Relationships in Small Groups. Unpublished doctoral dissertation, Harvard University.

Cooley, C. H. (1926). The roots of social knowledge. *American Journal of Sociology* 32: 59–65.

Dahrendorf, Ralf (1959). *Class and Class Conflict in Industrial Society*. Stanford, Calif.: Stanford University Press.

D'Andrade, R. G. (1974). Memory and the assessment of behavior. In H. M. Blalock, Jr. (ed.), *Measurement in the Social Sciences*. Chicago: Aldine, pp. 159–187.

Darwin, Charles (1872). *The Expression of the Emotions in Man and Animals*. New York: D. Appleton, 1896.

Davis, James A. (1961). *Great Books and Small Groups*. New York: Free Press.

Davis, James A. (1971). *Elementary Survey Analysis*. Englewood Cliffs, N.J.: Prentice-Hall.

Deutsch, M. (1949). A theory of cooperation and competition. *Human Relations* 2: 129–152.

Deutsch, Morton, and Robert M. Krauss (1965). *Theories in Social Psychology*. New York: Basic Books.

Dittes, James E. (1959). Attractiveness of group as a function of self-esteem and acceptance by group. *Journal of Abnormal and Social Psychology* 59: 77-82.

Dunphy, D. C. (1967). Planned environments for learning in the social sciences: Two innovative courses at Harvard. *American Sociologist* 2 (November): 202-206.

Dunphy, D. C. (1968). Phases, roles, and myths in self-analytic groups. *Journal of Applied Behavioral Science* 4: 195-226.

Ellis, A. (1962). *Reason and Emotion in Psychotherapy*. New York: Lyle Stuart.

Ezriel, H. (1957). The role of transferences in psychoanalytical and other approaches to group treatment. *Acta Psychotherapeutica* 7: 101-116.

Fairbairn, W. R. D. (1954). *An Object-Relations Theory of Personality*. New York: Basic Books.

Festinger, Leon (1942). Wish, expectation, and group standards as factors influencing level of aspiration. *Journal of Abnormal and Social Psychology* 37: 184-200.

Festinger, Leon (1957). *A Theory of Cognitive Dissonance*. Evanston, Ill.: Row, Peterson.

Fiedler, Fred E. (1964). A contingency model of leadership effectiveness. In Leonard Berkowitz (ed.), *Advances in Experimental Social Psychology*. New York: Academic Press, 1: 149-190.

Fine, Gary Alan (1976). A Group Space Analysis of Interpersonal Dynamics. Unpublished doctoral dissertation. Harvard University.

Foulkes, S. H., and E. J. Anthony (1957). *Group Psychotherapy*. London: Penguin Books.

Frank, Harold H., and Aaron Honori Katcher (1977). The qualities of leadership: How male medical students evaluate their female peers. *Human Relations* 30: 403-416.

French, John R. P. (1956). A formal theory of social power. *The Psychological Review* 63: 181-194.

Freud, Anna (1936). *The Ego and the Mechanisms of Defense*. New York: International Universities Press, 1946.

Freud, Sigmund (1900). *The Interpretation of Dreams*. In James Strachey (ed.), *The Standard Edition of the Complete Psychological Works of Sigmund Freud* (24 vols.), vols, 4, 5. London: Hogarth, 1953.

Freud, Sigmund (1901). *On Dreams*. Trans. James Strachey. New York: W. W. Norton.

Freud, Sigmund (1928). *Group Psychology and the Analysis of the Ego*. London: Hogarth Press, 1949.

Freud, Sigmund (1933). *New Introductory Lectures in Psychoanalysis*. In James Strachey (ed.), *The Standard Edition of the Complete Psychological Works of Sigmund Freud* (24 vols.). London: Hogarth Press, 1953.

Friedman, L. J., and N. E. Zinberg (1964). Application of group methods in college teaching. *International Journal of Group Psychotherapy* 14: 344-359.

Gamson, William A. (1964). Experimental studies of coalition formation. In Leonard Berkowitz (ed.), *Advances in Experimental Psychology*. New York: Academic Press, 1: 81-110.

Gerard, Harold B. (1953). The effect of different dimensions of disagreement on the communication process in small groups. *Human Relations* 6: 249-271.

Gibbard, Graham S. (1969). The Study of Relationship Patterns in Self-analytic Groups. Unpublished doctoral dissertation, University of Michigan.

Gibbard, Graham S., John J. Hartman, and Richard D. Mann, eds. (1974). *Analysis of Groups*. San Francisco: Jossey-Bass.

Glaser, Barney G., and Anselm L. Strauss (1967). *The Discovery of Grounded Theory: Strategies for Qualitative Research.* Chicago: Aldine.

Godard, Martine (1978). Some Reflections on the Use of Observation: R. F. Bales' Approach. Unpublished paper, Centre de Socianalyse, 21, Rue de Javel, 75015 Paris.

Goffman, Erving (1959). *The Presentation of Self in Everyday Life.* Garden City, N.Y.: Doubleday Anchor Books.

Grosser, Daniel, Norman Polansky, and Ronald Lippitt (1951). A laboratory study of behavioral contagion. *Human Relations* 4: 115–142.

Gulliksen, H. (1950). *Theory of Mental Tests.* New York: Wiley.

Hare, A. Paul (1976). *Handbook of Small Group Research,* 2nd ed. New York: Free Press.

Hare, A. Paul, Edgar F. Borgatta, and Robert F. Bales, eds. (1965). *Small Groups, Studies in Social Interaction,* rev. ed. New York: Knopf.

Harman, H. H. (1976). *Modern Factor Analysis,* 3d ed., rev. Chicago: University of Chicago Press.

Hartman, John J. (1969). The Role of Ego State Distress in the Development of Self-analytic Groups. Unpublished doctoral dissertation, University of Michigan.

Heider, Fritz (1958). *The Psychology of Interpersonal Relations.* New York: Wiley.

Holt, Robert R. (1964). Imagery: The return of the ostracized. *American Psychologist* 19: 254–264.

Homans, George C. (1950). *The Human Group.* New York: Harcourt Brace.

Homans, George C. (1961). *Social Behavior: Its Elementary Forms.* New York: Harcourt, Brace & World.

Kelley, Harold H. (1964). Interaction process and the attainment of maximum joint profit. In Samuel Messick and A. H. Brayfield (eds.), *Decision and Choice: Contributions of Sidney Siegel.* New York: McGraw-Hill, pp. 240–250.

Kelley, Harold H. (1971). *Attribution in Social Interaction.* Morristown, N.J.: General Learning Press.

Kelley, Harold H. (1972). *Causal Schemata and the Attribution Process.* New York: General Learning Press.

Klein, Melanie (1957). *Envy and Gratitude.* New York: Basic Books.

Leary, Timothy (1957). *Interpersonal Diagnosis of Personality.* New York: Ronald Press.

Lewin, Kurt (1938). *The Conceptual Representation and the Measurement of Psychological Forces.* Durham, N.C.: Duke University Press.

Lewin, Kurt (1939). Field theory and experiment in social psychology. *American Journal of Sociology* 44: 868–897.

Lewin, Kurt (1947). Frontiers in group dynamics. *Human Relations* 1: 2–38, 143–153.

Lewin, Kurt (1951). *Field Theory in Social Science.* New York: Harper & Brothers.

Lewin, Kurt, Tamara Dembo, Leon Festinger, and Pauline S. Sears (1944). Level of aspiration. In J. McV. Hunt (ed.), *Personality and the Behavior Disorders.* New York: Ronald Press, pp. 333–378.

McGregor, Douglas (1960). *The Human Side of Enterprise.* New York: McGraw-Hill.

McLeish, John, Wayne Matheson, and James Park (1973). *The Psychology of the Learning Group.* London: Hutchinson.

Mann, Richard D. (1966). The development of the member-trainer relationship in self-analytic groups. *Human Relations* 19: 85–115.

Mann, Richard D., et al. (1970). *The College Classroom: Conflict, Change, and Learning.* New York: Wiley.

Mann, Richard D., with Graham S. Gibbard and John J. Hartman (1967). *Interpersonal Styles and Group Development.* New York: Wiley.

Mead, George Herbert (1934). *Mind, Self, and Society.* Chicago: University of Chicago Press.

Meehl, Paul E. (1954). *Clinical Versus Statistical Prediction.* Minneapolis: University of Minnesota Press.

Mehrabian, Albert (1972). *Nonverbal Communication.* Chicago: Aldine, Atherton.

Merton, Robert K., and Alice S. Kitt (1950). Contributions to the theory of reference group behavior. In Robert K. Merton and Paul F. Lazarsfeld (eds.), *Continuities in Social Research: Studies in the Scope and Method of "The American Soldier."* New York: Free Press, pp. 40–105.

Miller, Neal E. (1944). Experimental studies of conflict. In J. McV. Hunt (ed.), *Personality and the Behavior Disorders.* New York: Ronald Press, 1: 431–465.

Mills, Theodore M. (1953). Power relations in three-person groups. *American Sociological Review* 18: 351–357.

Mills, Theodore M. (1954). The coalition pattern in three-person groups. *American Sociological Review* 19: 657–667.

Mills, Theodore M. (1964). *Group Transformation: An Analysis of a Learning Group.* Englewood Cliffs, N.J.: Prentice-Hall.

Minuchin, Salvador (1974). *Families and Family Therapy.* Cambridge, Mass.: Harvard University Press.

Newcomb, Theodore M. (1948). Attitude development as a function of reference groups: The Bennington study. In Muzafer Sherif (ed.), *An Outline of Social Psychology.* New York: Harper & Brothers, pp. 139–155.

Newcomb, Theodore M. (1953). An approach to the study of communicative acts. *Psychological Review* 60: 393–404.

Nunnally, J. C. (1967). *Psychometric Theory.* New York: McGraw-Hill.

Osgood, Charles E., and Percy H. Tannenbaum (1955). The principle of congruity in the prediction of attitude change. *Psychological Review* 62: 42–55.

Osgood, C. E., G. J. Suci, and P. H. Tannenbaum (1957). *The Measurement of Meaning.* Urbana: University of Illinois Press.

Parke, Bonny K. (1977). Balesian Space: A New Approach to the Study of Social Behavior in Natural Settings. Unpublished paper, Harvard University.

Parsons, Talcott (1951). *The Social System.* New York: Free Press.

Perls, F. (1969). *Gestalt Therapy Verbatim.* Lafayette, Calif.: Real People Press.

Pettigrew, Thomas F. (1967). Social evaluation theory: Convergences and applications. In *Nebraska Symposium on Motivation.* Lincoln: University of Nebraska Press, pp. 241–311.

Pettigrew, Thomas F., and Robert T. Riley (1972). Contextual models of school desegregation. In *Attitudes, Conflict, and Social Change.* New York: Academic Press, pp. 155–185.

Polley, Richard B. (1979). Both Sides of the Mirror: Small Groups and Subjectivity. Unpublished doctoral dissertation, Harvard University.

Riley, Matilda White, and Edward E. Nelson (1974). *Sociological Observation: A Strategy for New Social Knowledge*. New York: Basic Books.

Rogers, C. R. (1970). *Carl Rogers on Encounter Groups*. New York: Harper & Row.

Rosenberg, S., and A. Sedlack (1972). Structural representations of implicit personality theory. In *Advances in Experimental Social Psychology*. Vol. 6. New York: Academic Press.

Schachter, Stanley (1951). Deviation, rejection, and communication. *Journal of Abnormal and Social Psychology* 46: 190–207.

Schein, E. H. (1957). Reaction patterns to severe chronic stress in American army prisoners of war of the Chinese. *Journal of Social Issues*, 13, no. 3: 21–30.

Schneider, Johann (1977). Behind and in Front of the One-Way Mirror. *Arbeiten der Fachrichtung Psychologie*, no. 46. Universität des Saarlands, Saarbrücken.

Schutz, Alfred (1962). *The Problem of Social Reality*. Ed. Maurice Natanson. New York: Humanities Press.

Shaffer, John B. P., and M. David Galinsky (1974). *Models of Group Therapy and Sensitivity Training*. Englewood Cliffs, N.J.: Prentice-Hall

Shaw, Marvin E. (1971). *Group Dynamics: The Psychology of Small Group Behavior*. New York: McGraw-Hill.

Sherif, Muzafer (1936). *The Psychology of Social Norms*. New York: Harper.

Sherif, Muzafer (1953). The concept of reference groups in human relations. In M. Sherif and M. O. Wilson (eds.), *Group Relations at the Crossroads*. New York: Harper, pp. 203–231.

Sherif, Muzafer (1958). Superordinate goals in the reduction of intergroup conflict. *American Journal of Sociology*, 63, 349–58.

Sherif, Muzafer, O. J. Harvey, B. Jack White, William R. Hood, and Carolyn W. Sherif (1961). *Intergroup Conflict and Cooperation: The Robbers Cave Experiment*. Norman, Okla.: University Book Exchange.

Shibutani, Tamotsu (1961). *Society and Personality*. Englewood Cliffs, N.J.: Prentice-Hall.

Shils, Edward A. (1954). Authoritarianism: "Right" and "left." In R. Christie and M. Jahoda (eds.), *Studies in the Scope and Method of "The Authoritarian Personality."* New York: Free Press, pp. 24–29.

Skinner, B. F. (1953). *Science and Human Behavior*. New York: Macmillan.

Skinner, B. F. (1957). *Verbal Behavior*. New York: Appleton-Century-Crofts.

Slater, Philip E. (1966). *Microcosm, Structural, Psychological and Religious Evolution in Groups*. New York: Wiley.

Solomon, Manson (1977). An Impressive Validation of Systematic Multiple Level Observation of Groups. Unpublished paper, Harvard University.

Solomon, Manson J. (1978). The Bales Space and the Jackson Personality Research Form: A Cross-Validation within a Cognitive Interactionist Framework of Situation-Perception. Unpublished paper, Department of Psychology and Social Relations, Harvard University.

Sorokin, Pitirim (1957). *Social and Cultural Dynamics: Revised and Abridged in One Volume*. Boston: Porter Sargent.

Stone, Philip J., Dexter C. Dunphy, Marshall S. Smith, and Danile M. Ogilvie (1966). *The General Inquirer: A Computer Approach to Content Analysis*. Cambridge, Mass.: MIT Press.

Strodtbeck, Fred L. (1973). Bales 20 years later: A review essay. *The American Journal of Sociology,* vol. 79, no. 2.

Swenson, Clifford H., Jr. (1973). *Introduction to Interpersonal Relations.* Glenview, Ill.: Scott, Foresman.

Thibaut, John W., and Harold H. Kelley (1959). *The Social Psychology of Groups.* New York: Wiley.

Tryon, Robert (1957). Reliability and behavior domain validity. *Psychology Bulletin* 54: 229-249.

Tuckman, B. W. (1965). Developmental sequence in small groups. *Psychology Bulletin* 63: 384-399.

Varghese, Raju (1978). Ego-Identity and Interpersonal Behavior. Unpublished paper, School of Social Work and Community Planning, University of Maryland.

Warner, Rebecca (1978). Temporal Patterns in Dialogue. Unpublished doctoral dissertation, Harvard University.

Warner, Rebecca, Michael Stoto, and David Kenny (1977). A New Round Robin Analysis of Variance for Social Interaction Data. Unpublished working paper, Harvard University.

Weick, K. E. (1968). Systematic observational methods. In G. Lindzey and E. Aronson (eds.), *Handbook of Social Psychology.* Rev. ed. Reading, Mass.: Addison-Wesley, 2: 357-451.

White, Harrison C. (1974). Models for interrelated roles from multiple networks in small populations. In P. J. Knopp and G. H. Meyer (eds.,) *Proceedings of the Conference on the Application of Undergraduate Mathematics in the Engineering, Life, Managerial and Social Sciences.* Atlanta: Georgia Institute of Technology.

White, Harrison C., Scott A. Boorman, and Ronald L. Breiger (1976). Social structure from multiple networks: I. Blockmodels of roles and positions. *American Journal of Sociology* 81: 740-780.

Whitman, R. M., M. A. Lieberman, and D. Stock (1960). Individual and group focal conflict. *International Journal of Group Psychotherapy* 10: 259-286.

Williamson, Stephen A. (1977). Developmental Patterns in Self-analytic Groups. Unpublished doctoral dissertation, Harvard University.

Winer, B. J. (1971). *Statistical Principles in Experimental Design.* New York: McGraw-Hill.

Wilson, Stephen R. (1973). A course in small group sociology. The American Sociologist 8, no. 2 (May): 71-76.

Wish, Myron (1975). Subjects' expectations about their own interpersonal communication: A multidimensional approach. *Personality and Social Psychology Bulletin* 1: 501-504.

Wish, Myron (1975). The structure of interpersonal communication. *Industrial Research,* November.

Wish, Myron (1976). Comparisons among multi-dimensional structures of interpersonal relations. *Multivariate Behavioral Research* 11 (July): 297-394.

Wish, Myron (1978a). Measuring the Dimensions of Interpersonal Communication. Unpublished paper, Bell Laboratories, Murray Hill, New Jersey 07974.

Wish, Myron (1978b). Dimensions of diadic communication. In S. Weitz (ed.), *Nonverbal Communication.* 2d ed. New York: Oxford University Press.

Wish, Myron, and Susan J. Kaplan (1977). Toward an implicit theory of interpersonal communication, *Sociometry* 40, no. 3 (September): 234-246.

Wish, Myron, Morton Deutsch, and Susan J. Kaplan (1976). Perceived dimensions of interpersonal relations. *Journal of Personality and Social Psychology* 33: 409–420.

Yablonsky, L. (1965). *The Tunnel Back: Synanon*. New York: Macmillan.

Yalom, Irvin D. (1970). *The Theory and Practice of Group Psychotherapy*. New York: Basic Books.

Zeeman, E. C. (1976). Catastrophe theory. *Scientific American*, April, pp. 65–83.

Indexes

Author Index

Subject Index

Academic self-analytic group, *see* Self-analytic group
ACE, case study group member, 113–117
ACT Level behavior, 200–202, 207–209
ACT and NON, Field Diagram, 342; scoring rates, 268
Act-by-act scoring, single act, 16, 64, 462; *see also* Interaction Process Analysis
ACT or NON, message format, 172
ACTOR, 82, 83, 84, 87, 89, 168, 237
Adjective Rating data, computer analysis of, 481–487; correlations with Scoring data, 276–278, 280, 298, 456–457, 463–464; representativeness of own Ratings, 38; representativeness of Ratings, 41; computations required for Field Diagram, 427
Adjective Rating Form, source, xvi, 20, 392; unrevised form, 245, 247; revised form, 21, 393; standard order of items, 243–244, 246, 394; alternative arrangements of items, 248, 250–51, 457–458; alternative answer forms, 388, 394, 427–428, 457–458; weighted form, 401, 407–409; children's form, xvi, 392
Adjective Rating items, item-to-scale correlations, 248–249; inter-rater reliability, 259; factor analysis of, 260–266, 392; intercorrelations of, 252–254; ideal factor loadings of, 397; hypothetical ideal correlation matrix of, 398–399, 400–401, 402–403; item quality index of, 257–258; clarity of meaning of, 247–297, 394; revision of, 297
Adjective Rating procedure, compared with Scoring procedure, 4, 5, 9, 10, 241–242, 246, 268, 275, 282–285, 343, 463–464; general instructions for, 24, 387; number of raters needed, 260–261, 298; using Directional Definitions for Rating, 387–388

Adjective Rating scales, inter-rater reliability, 247, 259–261, 297, 479, 486–487; psychometric structure of, 396; reliability coefficients of, 252, 297–298; reliability, computer print-out of, 482–483; hypothetical maximum reliability of, 255, 404, hypothetical ideal scale, 255; weighting of items, 255–256; reliability of weighted scales, 256; effect of weighting, 259; correlations of polarities, 264
Administrative groups, 8
AGFD, computer program, 497
Aggregation of Interaction Scores, mathematical formula for, 462, 476–478
Aggregation of observations, 174, 189, 305, 308, 342, 455, 456–478
Alliances, 45, 97, 98, 101, 123, 136; *see also* Coalitions
Ambivalence, 47, 50, 51, 105
American Family Study, 241, 243, 244, 286–287
Amplification of a polarization-unification pattern, 34, 36, 45, 50, 70, 92, 324
Angle of polarization, 452
Angular scatter of points, 26
Angular separation between vectors, 44, 97, 405–406, 470
ANN, case study group member, 136–138
Applied social psychology, 6, 7
Approach-avoidance conflict, 105
Approach tendency, 86–88
Areas, on the Field Diagram, 41
Arousal, emotional, 82, 448
Assimilation, of an image to a cluster, 43, 237
Athletic team, 510
Atonement, 104
Attention, 32, 33, 34, 35, 61, 81, 83, 84, 87, 88, 89, 90, 92, 196, 231, 311, 448, 491

PAL, case study group member, 151–154
Parent, 106, 392
Parenthood, conceptions of, 106
Participant observer, xiv
Participation, characteristic rate of individual, 61; establishing participation, 77; Ratings of, versus raw IPA rates of, 64
Participation gradients, 60–64
Past experience, 33, 69–72; *see also* Developmental history of individual
PB, directional definition of, 374
PBIAS, computer program, 496
Perception, 195, 230; unique perception, 305; unusual perception, 305
Perceptual bias, 41, 305, 479
Perimeter Inscription, 54–56, 65, 68
Person, 218
Personality, 12, 35, 287, 304, 345–346, 505
Person perception, 484
Persuasion, 48
PF, directional definition of, 367
Phase movement, of behavior and imagery, 107
Phenomenology, 15
Phenotypical variables, 15
Physical space model, 22–23
Polarization-Unification Overlay, xv, 24–25, 38, 45–46, 433, 445–455; *see also* Overlay
Polarization-Unification processes, 11, 32, 34, 48, 50, 55, 62, 71, 90, 95, 102, 142, 154, 270, 290–292, 323, 331, 448–450, 452–453
Poles, of a dimension, 297, 487
Position in the group, 226
Positive bias, 283, 284, 285
Positive direction, 176
Positive members, 98
Power, 55, 179, 331–332
Power politics, 61
Preconscious, 237
Prediction, of order of dominance of members, 59; short term, within a pattern, 36
Prejudice, 214, 226
Present field, 14
Privacy, 508
PRO and CON, Field Diagram, 345–346, 465–466; scoring rates, 269
Problem solving, 197
PRO image, 80, 87, 88, 90, 95
Projection, 89, 90, 92, 198, 215, 219, 221, 327, 335, 483–484
PRO or CON, message format, 167, 172, 231, 314–315

Psychoanalysis, 216, 220, 508
Psychoanalytic theory, 13, 42, 70–71, 89, 92, 170, 215, 219, 222, 237, 346, 350
Psychological processes, 448–449
Psychotherapy, 12, 72, 304, 350
Punishment, 12, 84, 185, 208, 222–224, 232, 236–237

Quadrant, of the Field Diagram, 59, 73
QUAL. FACTOR, 430
Qualitative component of individual's interaction, 459–461, 479
Qualitative Image Field Diagram, 465–467
Qualitative review, in feedback, 341, 344
QUAN. FACTOR, 431
Quantitative component of individual's interaction, 459–461

Rater bias, 29, 307, 483, 487; *see also* Adjective Ratings
Rater effects, rating matrix, 483
Rating, *see* Adjective Rating
RATING, computer program, 494
Rationality, 215, 220, 223–224, 230, 508
Rationalistic calculation, 83–84, 86–87, 93
Rationalization, 83, 332
Reality, interpersonal and social, 198
Reality levels, 237, 349
RECEIVED Location, 91
Receiver of acts, 191
Recreational groups, 510
Recruiting, 97
Re-educative groups, 8
Reference Circle, 39, 42–44, 446, 450, 454
Reference Direction, 39, 41, 55, 452, 454
Reference group theory, 12, 454
Reference population, 41
Reference Side, 446
Reference Subgroup, 47
REG. PLOT, 431
Regression, in the service of the ego, 215–216; statistical regression of points toward zero, 25
Regular Plotting Point, 431
Reinforcement theory, 222, 224
Rejection, of group by observers and of observers by group, 79; of images, 47; *see also* Scapegoat, Scapegoat Direction
Reliability, sacrifice of, 189; *see also* Adjective Rating, Interaction Scoring
Repression, 42, 89–90, 92, 219–220
Rescue fantasy, 101
Research observer group, 79
Residential groups, 8
Residual Area, of Field Diagram, 40, 446